EUROPEAN ECONOMIC LAW

TEMPUS Textbook Series
on
European Law and European Legal Cultures

General Editors: Volkmar Gessner and Armin Hoeland

Titles in the Series:

Volume 1
European Legal Cultures
Volkmar Gessner, Armin Hoeland, Csaba Varga

Volume 2
European Economic Law
Hans-W. Micklitz, Steve Weatherill

Volume 3
European Environmental Law
Edited by
Gerd Winter

European Economic Law

HANS-W. MICKLITZ
STEPHEN WEATHERILL

Ashgate

DARTMOUTH

Aldershot • Brookfield USA • Singapore • Sydney

© Hans-W. Micklitz, Stephen Weatherill 1997

Published by
Dartmouth Publishing Company Limited
Ashgate Publishing Limited
Gower House
Croft Road
Aldershot
Hants GU11 3HR
England

Ashgate Publishing Company
Old Post Road
Brookfield
Vermont 05036
USA

British Library Cataloguing in Publication Data
Micklitz, Hans-W.
  European economic law. - (Tempus)
  1.European Economic Community 2.Commercial law - European
  Economic Community countries 3.European Economic Community
  countries - Economic policy
  I.Title II.Weatherill, Stephen, 1961-
  341.7'50614

Library of Congress Cataloging-in-Publication Data
European economic law / Hans-W. Micklitz, Stephen Weatherill.
      p.   cm. – (Tempus textbook series on European law and
  European legal cultures)
    ISBN 1-85521-557-8 (hb) – ISBN 1-85521-562-4 (pb)
    1. European Union countries–Economic policy. 2. Trade regulation-
  -European Union countries. 3. Europe–Economic integration.
  I. Micklitz, Hans-W. II. Weatherill, Stephen, 1963-   . III. Series.
  KJE6415.E86   1997
  341.7'5'0614–dc21
                                      97-18967
                                        CIP

ISBN 1 85521 557 8 (hb)
ISBN 1 85521 562 4 (pb)
Printed and bound by Athenaeum Press, Ltd.,
Gateshead, Tyne & Wear.

Contents

v

Abbreviations

a.M.	am Main
AcP	Archiv für civilistische Praxis
ADBHU	Association de défense brûleurs d'huiles usagées
AC	Appeal Cases (Law Reports, UK)
AE	Anonimi Etairia
AETR	European Agreement concerning the Work of Crews of Vehicles engaged in International Road Transport
AFG	Arbeitsförderungsgesetz
AG	Aktiengesellschaft
AJCL	American Journal of Comparative Law
AJIL	American Journal of International Law
ALL ER	All England Law Report
Antitrust LJ	Antitrust Law Journal
AöR	Archiv des öffentlichen Rechts
ATR	Avion de Transport Régional
BASF	Badische Anilin- und Sodafabriken
BBC	British Broadcasting Corporation
BEUC	Bureau Européen des Unions Consommateurs
BNA	Bond van Nederlandse Architecten
BullBReg	Bulletin der Bundesregierung
Bull.EC	Bulletin of the European Community
BV	besloten vennootschap
BVerfGE	Entscheidungen des Bundesverfassungsgerichts
CBEM	Centre belge d'études de marché – Télémarketing SA
CCL	Confédération du Commerce, Luxembourgeois
CEE	Commission de l'équipment électrique
CEE	Communauté économique européenne
cf.	compare
CFDT	Confédéderation française démocratique du travail
CFK	Christliche Friedenskonferenz
CMC	Common Market Group of Ceramical Tile Producers
CMLRev	Common Market Law Review
CMLR	Common Market Law Report

CMEA	Council for Mutual Economic Assistance
Co.	Company
COM	Common Organization of the Market
COMECON	Council for mutual economic assistance
Cornell Int'l L.J.	Cornell International Law Journal
DASA	Deutsche Aerospace
DEP	Dimotiki Etairia Pliroforissis and Sotirios Kouvelas
DG	Direction Générale
DVBl.	Deutsches Verwaltungsblatt
e.V.	eingetragener Verein
EAEC	European Atomic Energy Community
EC	European Community
ECHR	European Convention on Human Rights
ECJ	European Court of Justice
ECJ	The Economic Journal
ECJC	European Civil Jurisdiction Convention
ECLR	European Competition Law Review
ECR	European Court Report
ECSC	European Coal and Steel Community
ECU	European Currency Union
ed.	Editor / Edition
EEA	European Economic Area
EEC	European Economic Community
EFTA	European Free Trade Association
EG	Europäische Gemeinschaft
EHRR	European Human Rights Report
ELRev.	EUR.L.REV. = European Law Review
EMI	Emi Electrola GmbH
ENEL	Ente Nationale Energia Elektrica (National Electricity Board)
ERT	Elliniki Radiophonia Tileorassi AE
ERTA	European Road Transport Agreement
ESPRIT	European Programme for Research in Information Tech nology
ETA	European Technical Approval
EU	European Union
EUA	European Affairs
EuGH	Europäischer Gerichtshof (European Court of Justice)
EuZW	Europäische Zeitschrift für Wirtschaftsrecht

EWG	Europäische Wirtschaftsgemeinschaft
FAO	Food and Agriculture Organization
FDI	Foreign Direct Investment
ff.	pp.
FIM	Industrial Modernization Fund
FIW	Forschungsinstitut für Wirtschaftsverfassung und Wettbewerb
GATT	General Agreement on Tariffs and Trade
GDP	Gross Domestic Product
GEMA	Gesellschaft für Musikalische Aufführungs- und Mechanische Vervielfältigungsrechte
GIE	Groupement d'Intérêt Économique
GmbH	Gesellschaft mit beschränkter Haftung
GRUR int	Gewerblicher Rechtsschutz und Urheberrecht, Internationaler Teil
HARV L REV	HARV L R = Harvard Law Review
HFL	Holländische Gulden (Dutch currency)
IBP	Information publicité Benelux SA
ICI	Informations catholiques internationales
ICLQ	The International and Comparative Law Quarterly
ILO	International Labour Organization
INRA	National Institute for Agriculture Research
ITP	Independent Television Publications Ltd
KG	Kommanditgesellschaft
LDC	Less Developed Countries
LQR	Law Quarterly Review
MBB	Messerschmitt-Bölkow-Blohm
mbH	mit beschränkter Haftung
MEP	Member of the European Parliament
MLR	Modern Law Review
NJW	Neue Juristische Wochenschrift
NV	Naamloze Vermootschap
nyr	not yet reported
OJ	Official Journal
PIC	Inter-University Cooperation Programmes
PLC	Public limited-liability company
R&D	Research and Development
R&TD	Research and Technological Development

RabelsZ	Rabels Zeitschrift für ausländisches und internationales Privatrecht
REV MC	Revue du Marché Commun
REWE	Rewe Zentral AG
Rs	Rechtssache (Case)
RTDE	International Wafer Level Reliability Workshop
RTE	Radio Telefis Eireann
RTT	Telegraph and Telephone Corporation
SA	Société anonyme
SABENA	Société Anonyme Belge de Navigation Aérienne Sabena
SCIENCE	Plan to stimulate the international corporation and interchange needed by European research scientists
SEA	Single European Act
SMEs	Small and medium-sized enterprises
SPUC	Society for the Protection of Unborn Children
Srl	Società a responsabilità limitada
TEZI	Tezi Textil BV
TRIP	Trade-related aspects of Intellectual Property Rights
UK	United Kingdom
UNEP	United Nations Environment Programme
UNTS	United Nations Treaty Series
US	United States
USSR	Union of Soviet Socialist Republics
VerBAV	Veröffentlichungen des Bundesaufsichtsamtes für das Versicherungswesen
WTO	World Trade Organisation
WuW	Wirtschaft und Wettbewerb
Yale J.Intl.	Yale Journal of International Law
Yale LJ	The Yale Law Journal
YEL	Yearbook of European Law
ZaöRV	Zeitschrift für ausländisches öffentliches Recht und Völkerrecht
ZLR	Zeitschrift für das gesamte Lebensmittelrecht

Series Foreword

TEMPUS TEXTBOOK SERIES ON EUROPEAN LAW AND EUROPEAN LEGAL CULTURES

The Trans-European Mobility Scheme for University Studies (TEMPUS) is part of a broader programme of the European Communities for economic reform in Central and Eastern Europe (PHARE) and supports 'Joint European Projects' between academic institutions in order to improve university education in Central and Eastern Europe. Within this programme two academic institutions of the Community (International Institute for the Sociology of Law, Oñati/Spain, and Zentrum für Europäische Rechtspolitik, Bremen/Germany) and the Law Faculty of the Eötvös-Loránd University, Budapest/Hungary, collaborated during a period of three years for the publication of a textbook series on European Law and European Legal Cultures.

The series consists of collections of (original or reprinted) texts on European Legal Cultures, Economic Law, Environmental Law, Agrarian Law and Labour Law and will be eventually complemented by other volumes. They have been elaborated and discussed by multinational teams from different Western and Central European universities which have put together a large quantity of material in order to represent most legal systems and legal cultures of the area.

The conception of the series is based on three *Leitmotives:*
First, legal education in a period of rapid globalization must enable future practitioners to deal with foreign legal systems, to understand different regulatory structures in their own right and to defend their own positions in cross-cultural negotiations. Legal knowledge and familiarity with legal cultural differences together with a sufficient mastery of the English language are necessary elements.

Second, modern legal education is an interdisciplinary exercise where theoretical and empirical knowledge play an equal part and where neighbour disciplines like Economics, Sociology, Political Science and Psychology are not excluded. Students together with their intellectual training in legal reasoning must understand the law in action, its effects and the problems of its implementation. This knowledge enables them to criticize law and push for reform and legal change.

Third, legal education in the second half of the 1990s must account for the fact that the Berlin wall and all other political, economic and social barriers between East and West have fallen and that a legal community is going to be created which goes far beyond the EU, the EFTA and the EES. Whereas law reform in the beginning was and still is directed predominantly from West to East, scientific discourse takes place in a climate of equality and openness to learn. Consequently also students all over Europe (in its largest geographical definition) should be socialized as early as possible within this climate of mutual curiosity and recreate something that centuries ago was a reality: a common European Legal Culture.

Volkmar Gessner   Armin Hoeland

Foreword

EUROPEANIZATION

Our major interest in writing this book lies in the opportunity to explore the development of the 'Europeanization' of law. This process, however, is not presented in simplistic terms as the dissolution of national cultures in the European melting-pot. Nor is it presented as a plea for some mythical single European identity. We insist that Europeanization is a complex and nuanced phenomenon and one which operates on a number of levels. It is a notion which has many limitations; but it is a notion which has many possibilities too.

Does law make or characterize states? Even if only in part and even if subject to qualification, the answer must contain affirmative elements. In the light of this, an exploration of European law provides – at least in part – a glimpse of the developing structure of a European state. The construction of a European state, like the construction of European Law, is a complex and nuanced phenomenon. It too operates on a number of levels.

What is interesting and simultaneously challenging is the absence of any comprehensive blueprint for a European state or a European Law. Yet the reshaping of Member States' relations with each other and with European institutions is bringing about a new geographical and political pattern for the map of Europe. Law acts as an element in that restructuring. The process remains open-ended. It has no single constitutional packaging. The interest of this book is to explore the effect of European integration on law and the effect of law on European integration.

The EC and the EU

Our starting point is European Community law. This is the European system which is most overtly concerned with the creation of European structures at the expense of national sovereignty. The Treaty of Rome of 1957 contains reference in its Preamble to a determination 'to lay the foundations of an ever closer union among the peoples of Europe'. The European Court has long insisted that the attainment of the objectives of the Treaty dictates that EC law shall prevail over national law in the event of conflict. In Case 6/64 *Costa* v. *ENEL* [1964] ECR 585 it chose phrases which drew direct attention to shifting sovereignty:

The transfer by the States from their domestic legal system to the Community legal system of the rights and obligations arising under the Treaty carries with it a permanent limitation of their sovereign rights, against which a subsequent unilateral act incompatible with the concept of the Community cannot prevail.

It is well known that the process of market integration in the European Community, supported by the EC's constitutional legal order, has led to the need for a reassessment of the role of the state in the economy. The application of the Community rules governing the free movement of goods, persons and services confines the competence of states to regulate their economies in a manner which impedes intra-Community trade. The competition rules of the Treaty too, previously focused primarily on private economic activity, have increasingly been used to challenge state intervention in the market. The national state has been reshaped in the wake of the development of the European market.

Yet, for all the increasingly frequent claims of the European Court that it presides over a constitution based on the rule of law, there remain severe and quite proper limitations to the validity of viewing the EC as a European state in the making. The process of integration has made much more headway than the process of regulation. It is emblematic of this thrust that the focus of recent activity has been the 'open borders' policy of the 1992 project. The EC does not create any clear European state structure, for all its success in creating a European market.

Awareness of the limitations of the EC as a constitutional framework for Europe is accentuated by the Treaty on European Union. It purports to mark 'a new stage in the process of creating an ever closer union among the peoples of Europe'. Yet it envisages a novel structure. The EC remains in place, its competence extended, albeit to a limited extent. The subsidiarity debate tells us of the sharp sensitivity about what should be Europeanized and what should not. Social Policy too is a fierce battleground for competing conceptions of the appropriateness of Europeanization. Beyond the EC, there are now two additional pillars to the Union, covering Justice and Home Affairs and Foreign and Security Policy. The Treaty declares in Article A that 'the Union shall be founded on the European Communities', yet the two new pillars are carefully constructed outside the traditional EC structure, apparently beyond the scrutiny of the European Court and Parliament. These seem to be areas where the Member States will cooperate at the European level without committing themselves to pooling powers on the EC model. The 'European State' takes an odd shape, a rather inconsistent shape. The Union has been accordingly described as 'half-built ... suddenly abandoned by its builders ... a kind of Gaudi structure' ((1992) 29 CMLRev 199, 202). La Sagrada Familia in Barcelona, the church left unfinished by Gaudi on his death, is spectacularly beautiful, but it is also rather alarming, especially when one stands at the top. In addition, some would dismiss it as lacking practical value. The European state is unfinished and its constructors have the opportunity and perhaps the responsibility to undertake much refinement.

THE IMPLICATIONS OF EUROPEAN ECONOMIC LAW

The dynamism of EC economic law has taken it beyond the economic sphere into the realms of social regulation. Such an extension deepens the impact of EC law on national state structures. European Community law has within it a potential to have an impact on a range of social relations, public and private. Therefore, 'economic' in the title of this book must be interpreted broadly.

It is not only 'Economic' that is to be taken broadly. 'European' too is wide in its scope. The basic concept of market integration implies the creation of an economic space in which some kind of common law will run. EC law is that law. National law will continue to apply too, in so far as it is not blocked by the supremacy of EC law in the areas in which the EC is competent. So EC law affects public and private parties at national level. However, this book is necessarily concerned with European law beyond the EC. Account is also taken of the law deriving from the European Convention on Human Rights. As economic spreads into social, so too EC law and ECHR law have to coexist. They do not occupy defined separate territories. There are real problems of demarcation. Such issues are constitutionally very relevant to the construction of a wider European law. This is certainly an area where law in Europe is progressing rather erratically and without a firm blueprint. It should be appreciated that what emerges will determine the respective roles of the Member States, the EC institutions and the Human Rights institutions in European state-building.

European law does not stop at the EC and ECHR. From the start of 1994, the European Economic Area covered the EC's twelve Member States plus Austria, Sweden, Norway, Finland and Iceland. This amounted to an effective extension of the EC's free trade rules. That EEA pattern was of short duration, as Austria, Finland and Sweden joined the European Union 'proper' as early as the start of 1995.

This geographical spread must also take account of the Association Agreements which the EC has concluded with other European states. These Agreements too have led to a widening network of the free trade rules on which the EC is based. Domestic law systems in non-EC European states are increasingly influenced by the EC model. For example, several states in Eastern Europe have adopted competition law systems modelled on Articles 85 and 86. In contrast to the EC/ ECHR interface, there is here no clash of norms, but rather a spread of the EC norm. This provides a justification for the challenge of the terminology of 'European law' in this book's title rather than simply 'EC law'. Wider still, the rules of the GATT/ WTO play a part in the construction of the European system.

THEMES AND PRINCIPLES IN EUROPEAN ECONOMIC LAW

This is our background: more Economic law, more European law. Shifting state forms, shifting legal cultures. In this book, we want to initiate a search for underlying principles and, where these cannot be found, for the sources whence they might spring. At the very least we want to identify where and why underlying principles would help to guide us towards a European law which would help to make sense of the multi-layered, fragmented hints of a European state.

The purpose of this book is to draw out these problems in different areas affected by the integrative process and to provide a variety of national and international sources. These are designed to provide the basis for further thought and discussion. We do not pretend that this book is comprehensive. In the light of the ever-widening scope of European Economic Law outlined above, that would certainly be an impossible task. Nor do we consider ourselves capable in this book of resolving the many problems that confront the new legal order of Europe. We aim to shed light on areas of law and policy which are susceptible to Europeanization. We aim to provide a coherently structured package of materials that will draw out some of the issues that we identify as relevant to the shaping of 'European Economic Law'. We provide commentary, we have chosen the materials and we have developed the organizational structure of the book, so inevitably our own assumptions play a part in painting the picture of 'European Economic Law'. However, we have endeavoured not to pre-judge the issues. The reader must make his or her own choices about whether the Europeanization which is the subject of this book is a desirable or feasible process.

We hope our ideas can be developed into further areas. We have tried to write the book so that extension can easily be achieved. We do not directly engage in, for example, Company law, Social Policy, Environmental Protection law or Product Safety law. However such topics could readily be accommodated within the theoretical framework of the book. We invite those who use it to make their own preferred additions. Even within the topics which we have chosen to write about there is no attempt to supply exhaustive coverage. Again, this is unachievable. We are not here writing a book which will provide the last word on the detailed practical developments in the law. We are seeking to explain how and why European law is developing.

ACKNOWLEDGEMENTS

Stephen Weatherill wishes to acknowledge the financial support provided by the Academic Purposes Fund of the Society of Public Teachers of Law through the Butterworths Fund for European Exchanges; and by the British Academy through its Small Personal Research Grant scheme. He is also grateful for support and assistance provided by Toby Hamnett, Caroline Hudson, Karen Baxter, Rob Moulton and Damien Meadows. Hans-W. Micklitz would like to thank the Fachhochschule für Wirtschaft in Berlin for hosting us during our working sessions. He is also grateful for support and assistance provided by Fabian Amtenbrink, Maike Lerch and Franziska Rabl.

List of Cases

EUROPEAN COURT OF JUSTICE

Numerical List

Case			ECR	no.	Chapters
26/62	Van Gend en Loos		[1963]	1	1,11
6/64	Costa	v. ENEL	[1964]	585	Preface,1
56 & 58/64	Consten and Grundig	v. Commission	[1966]	299	4
47/69	France	v. EC Commission	[1970]	487	3
11/70	Internationale Handels-gesellschaft mbH	v. Einfuhr und Vor-ratsstelle für Getrei-de und Futtermittel	[1970]	1125	1,12
22/70	Commission	v. Council	[1971]	263 (ERTA)	9
21-24/72	International Fruit Company NV and other	v. Produktschap voor groenten en fruit	[1972]	1219	10
4/73	Nold	v. Commission	[1974]	491	12
120/73	Lorenz	v. Germany	[1979]	1471	3
155/73	Sacchi		[1974]	409	5
173/73	Italian Republic	v. Commission	[1974]	709	3
15/74	Centrafarm BV	v. Sterling Drug Inc	[1974]	1147	7
Opinion 1/75	Understanding on Local Costs Standards		[1975]	1355	9
43/75	Defrenne	v. SABENA	[1976]	455	12
119/75	Terrapin	v. Terranova	[1976]	1039	7
Opinion 1/76	Draft Agreement establishing a European lay-ing-up fund for inland waterway vessels		[1977]	741	9
3,4 & 6/76	Kramer		[1976]	1279	9
41/76	Donckerwolke		[1976]	1921	9
45/76	Comet	v. Produktschap	[1976]	2043	11

Case			ECR no.		Chapters
102/77	Hoffman La Roche and Co AG	v. Centrafarm	[1978]	1139	7
Opinion 1/78	International Agreement on Natural Rubber		[1979]	2871	9
120/78	Rewe Zentrale	v. Bundesmonopolver- waltung für Brannt- wein	[1979]	649	6
258/78	Nungesser	v. Commission	[1982]	2015	4
730/79	Philip Morris Holland BV	v. EC Commission	[1980]	2671	3
55 & 57/80	Musik-Vertrieb Mem- bran	v. GEMA	[1981]	147	7
270/80	Polydor	v. H.Record Shops	[1982]	329	10
104/81	Hauptzollamt Mainz	v. C.A.Kupferberg	[1982]	3641	10
286/81	Oosthoek's Uitgevers- maatschappij		[1982]	4575	6
296 & 318/82	Kingdom of Nether- lands and Leeuwarder Papierwarenfabriek BV	v. EC Commission	[1985]	809	3
240/83	ADBHU		[1985]	531	1
19/84	Pharmon BV	v. Hoechst AG	[1985]	2281	7
59 & 242/84	TEZI		[1986]	887	9
152/84	Marshall	v. Southampton Area Health Authority	[1986]	723	1
161/84	Pronuptia de Paris GmbH	v. Pronuptia de Paris Irmgard Schillgalis	[1986]	353	4
222/84	Johnston	v. Chief Constable of the Royal Ulster Constabulary	[1986]	1651	12
311/85	Vereniging van Vlaamse Reisbureaus	v. Sociale Dienst	[1987]	3801	5
66/86	Ahmed Saeed Flug- reisen and Silver Line Reisebüro GmbH	v. Zentrale zur Bekäm- pfung unlauteren Wettbewerbs e.V	[1989]	803	5

Case			ECR no.	Chapters
222/86	Union nationale des entraîneurs et Cadres techniques profession-nels du football (UNECTEF)	v. George Heylens	[1987] 4097	11
22/87	Commission	v. Italy	[1989] 143	11
70/87	Fediol	v. Commission	[1989] 1781	10
186/87	Cowan	v. Le Trésor Public	[1989] 195	12
247/87	Star Fruit Co.	v. Commission	[1989] 291	11
301/87	France	v. Commission	[1990] I-307	3
341/87	EMI Electrola	v. Patricia Import	[1989] 79	7
382/87	Buet	v. Ministère public	[1989] 1235	6
C-18/88	RTT	v. GB INNO	[1991] I-5941	5
C-143/88 & C-92/89	Zuckerfabrik Süder-dithmarschen and Zuckerfabrik Soest		[1991] I-415	11
C-202/88	France	v. Commission	[1991] I-1223	1
C-362/88	GB-INNO	v. CCL	[1990] I-667	1,6,8,12
C-10/89	SA CNL-SUCAL	v. HAG	[1990] I-3711	7
C-106/89	Marleasing	v. La Comercial Inter-nacional de Ali-mentacion	[1990] I-4135	1,10
C-213/89	The Queen	v. Secretary of State for Transport, ex parte Factortame Ltd and others	[1990] I-2433	11
C-221/89	Commission	v. UK	[1991] I-3905	11
C-246/89	Commission	v. UK	[1991] I-4585	11
C-260/89	Elliniki Radiophonia Tileorassi AE (ERT)	v. Dimotiki Etairia Pliroforissis and Sotirios Kouvelas	[1991] I-2925	5,6,12
C-261/89	Italy	v. Commission	[1991] I-4437	3
C-339/89	Alsthom Atlantique	v. Compagnie de con-struction mécanique Sulzer S.A.	[1991] I-107	8

Alphabetical List

	Case	ECR no.	Chapters
ADBHU	240/83 [1985]	531	1
Ahmed Saeed Flug-reisen and Silver Line Reisebüro GmbH v. Zentrale zur Bekämpfung unlauteren Wettbewerbs e.V	66/86 [1989]	803	5
Alsthom Atlantique v. Compagnie de construction mécanique Sulzer S.A.	C-339/89 [1991]	107	8
Andrea Francovich and others v. Italian State	C-6, C-9/90 [1991]	I-5357	1,11
British Aerospace plc & Rover Group Holdings v. Commission	C-294/90 [1992]	I-493	3
Buet v. Ministère public	382/87 [1989]	1235	6
Centrafarm BV v. Sterling Drug Inc	15/74 [1974]	1147	7
CMC Motorradcenter GmbH v. Pelin Baskiciogullari	C-93/92 [1993]	I-5009	8
Comet v. Produktschap	45/76 [1976]	2043	11
Commission v. Council	22/70 [1971]	263 (ERTA)	9
Commission v. Council	C-155/91 [1993]	I-939	9
Commission v. Italy	22/87 [1989]	143	11
Commission v. UK	C-221/89 [1991]	I-3905	11
Commission v. UK	C-246/89 [1991]	I-4585	11
Consten and Grundig v. Commission	56 & 58/64 [1966]	299	4
Costa v. ENEL	6/64 [1964]	585	Preface,1
Cowan v. Le Trésor Public	186/87 [1989]	195	12
Defrenne v. SABENA	43/75 [1976]	455	12
Deutsche Renault AG v. Audi AG	C-317/92 [1993]	I-2039	7
Donckerwolke	41/76 [1976]	1921	9
Elliniki Radiophonia Tileorassi AE (ERT) v. Dimotiki Etairia Pliroforissis and Sotirios Kouvelas	C-260/89 [1991]	I-2925	5,6,12

		Case		ECR no.	Chapters
TEZI		59 & 242/84	[1986]	887	9
Union nationale des entraîneurs et Cadres techniques profes-sionnels du football (UNECTEF)	v. George Heylens	222/86	[1987]	4097	11
Van Gend en Loos		26/62	[1963]	1	1,11
Vereniging van Vlaamse Reisbureaus	v. Sociale Dienst	311/85	[1987]	3801	5
W W Meng		C-2/91	[1993]	I-5751	5,6,8
Zuckerfabrik Süder-dithmarschen and Zuckerfabrik Soest		C-143/88 & C-92/89	[1991]	I-415	11

COURT OF FIRST INSTANCE

Case T-69/89 Radio Telefis Eireann v. Commission [1991] ECR II-485   (7)
Case T-37/92 BEUC v. Commission [1994] ECR II-285   (11)

DECISION OF THE COMMISSION

Case No. IV/M. 053 of 2 October 1991 – Aerospatiale-Alenia/de Havilland   (2)
(91/619/EEC), OJ L 334, 42

EUROPEAN COURT OF HUMAN RIGHTS

Marckx v. Belgium Series A vol. 31 (judgment of 13 June 1979)   (12)
Markt Intern and Beerman v. Germany (judgment of 20 November 1989)   (6)
12 EHRR 161; ECHR Series A No.165
Case No. 64/1991/316/387-388 Open Door and Dublin Well Woman v. (6,12)
Ireland
Case No. 24/1992/369/443 Sigurjonsson v. Iceland (judgment of 30 June   (1,5)
1993)
Case No. 36/1992/381/455-459 Informationsverein Lentia v. Austria   (6)

CASES BEFORE NATIONAL COURTS

Germany

United Kingdom

United States

Treaties and Legislation

THE TREATY ON EUROPEAN UNION

Article	Chapter
A	1
F(2)	12
G(2)	12

THE EC TREATY

Article	Chapter	Article	Chapter
3	5	100	1
3(g)	5	100(a)	1,8,9
5	1,5,8,11	109	9
30	4,5,6,7,8,10,12	113	9
34	8	115	9
36	5,7,8,10	118(a)	9
43	9	119	1,12
55	5	129	6
59	4,5,8,12	129(a)	6,8
66	5	130	2
85	1,4,7,8,11	130(n)	9
85(1)	3,4,8	130(q)	9
85(2)	4	130(r)	9
85(3)	3,4	130(s)	9
86	4,5,7,11	130(u)	10
90	1,4,5	130(x)	10
90(1)	5	130(y)	9,10
90(2)	5	145	9
90(3)	1,5	169	3,11
92	3,9	171(2)	11
93	3	173	10
94	3	177	1,3,11

THE EC TREATY CONT.

Article	Chapter
189	1,6
189(c)	6
220	8
222	7

Article	Chapter
224	9
228	9,10,12
235	1,9
238	9,10

THE EEC TREATY

Article	Chapter
3(f)	(5)

REGULATIONS

17/62	4,11
2603/69	9
288/82	9
1934/82	9
1983/83 Art.1,2,3	4
2349/84	7
2641/84	9,10
1734/88	9

4087/88	4
556/89	7
4064/89	2,4
2455/92	9
151/93 Art.1,2,3,4,5	7
404/93	10
40/94	7
518/94	9

DIRECTIVES

80/987	(11)
84/450 Art.2(2), 3, 4(1), 7	(6,11)
85/374	(8)
85/577	(6)
89/552 Art.10-22	(6)
89/662	(6)

89/665	(11)
91/156	(9)
92/13	(11)
92/41	(6)
92/59	(1)
93/13	(11)

EUROPEAN CONVENTION ON HUMAN RIGHTS

GERMAN LEGISLATION

US LEGISLATION

1 The Economic Constitution of the European Community

What is meant by 'Economic Constitution' of the European Community? And what are the possible functions of a European Economic Constitution?

The Treaty of Rome refers to the creation of a Common Market, the Single European Act focused instead on the Internal Market, the Maastricht Treaty will establish a Monetary and, albeit in somewhat misleading language, a Political Union. The language is misleading, because even after Maastricht there will be no developed Political Union, at least not in the sense of a 'European State'. The driving force of the European Community has always been and still is market integration. In realizing the four freedoms of the Treaty and in enforcing the competition rules, finally and definitely with the 1992 project on the completion of the Internal Market, however, it became clear that *market integration* entails perhaps not automatically, but has entailed within recent years, *market regulation*. Market integration is *negative integration*. The four freedoms and the competition rules are used to remove obstacles to cross-border trade resulting from either statutory rules or private restrictions. Market regulation is *positive integration*. Regulation is used to develop policies beyond negative integration, policies which embrace a broad range of subjects, from industrial policies to consumer policy. Negative integration is legitimized by the idea of open markets, or, in the Treaty language, of the creation of a common market/internal market. Positive integration needs legitimation beyond market integration. Positive market regulation is bound to a twofold condition: that there is a European regulator and that there is a concept of what should be regulated and why and how.

However, amid the process of market integration, less explicit attention is paid to the idea of a *'European State'*. It is true that there is no necessary logical need for a European Market to be accompanied by a fully formed 'European State'. However, it is equally true that one cannot construct a European Market without significant implications for existing State structures. The shorthand 'European State' may be taken to refer to the shifting patterns of legislative and administrative structures at national and European level which follow in the wake of market integration.

Perhaps the deepest tension in the Community today arises precisely from the need to identify what is meant by state-building at European level. For some states, the process of negative law which deregulates national markets is entirely desirable and sufficient. It creates a European Market and there is no need to think in terms

1

of a 'European State'. Indeed there *should* not be a 'European State' from this perspective, because a 'European State' would reregulate and overregulate the market. Better to have a deregulated, integrated market founded on a competition between regulators. Such a perspective, most commonly associated with the government of the UK, identifies the EC as essentially motivated by economic considerations at the expense of political ambition. A distinct point of view holds that deregulation at national level is only part of the process; that reregulation at Community level is not an optional extra, but instead fundamental to the process of 'creating an ever closer union among the peoples of Europe', as declared by Article A of the Treaty on European Union. This places a more political interpretation on European integration. It does not necessarily point towards a fully-fledged 'European State', but it does suggest a need to define and develop the constitutional framework within which Community action is taken.

This tension is reflected, but by no means resolved, in the European Union's constitutional documents. The several Treaties, culminating in the Treaty on European Union, leave unanswered many questions about the scope of *Community competence* and, as a corollary, the scope of the *Member States' competence*. As Lenaerts memorably expressed the Treaty's core ambiguity; 'there is no constitutionally protected nucleus of national sovereignty.'

The Community is not omnicompetent and must rely on the Treaty for conferral of its specific competences. However, those competences are not rigidly defined. Most of all, Articles 100, 100a and 235 offer broad scope for Community legislative activity, which has historically been developed with great flexibility. The Community is not built on a clear-cut federal division of powers. Paradoxically, those states such as the UK, which have governments most fiercely opposed to the word federal, might find their competences better protected if there *were* a rigid competence division in the Community's constitution. However, the progress of the European Community has been one of gradual extension in Community competence at the expense of the Member States, partly fostered by the European Court of Justice, partly resulting from legislation which has enhanced Community competence.

None of this means that there is a 'European State'. But it means that important regulatory functions are capable of being discharged at Community level – and, in some cases, that they may not be discharged at national level because of the influence of EC negative law. At the very least, this suggests a need for a theory of what may and may not be done by Member States and by Community institutions in developing regulatory activity in these and other areas – and how this affects individuals, Citizens of the European Union. That investigation is the heart of this volume.

In terms of legal matters: European Economic Law seems to be clearly distinguishable from European Constitutional Law. European Economic Law covers market integration (negative law) whereas European Constitutional Law encompasses the European institutions, their emergence as a 'European State' and market regulation (positive law). The idea of a *European Economic Constitution* starts from the idea that the European Treaties formulate 'constitutional principles' which could and shall determine market integration and market regulation. The constitutional principles of the Treaties define the reach of the four freedoms and the philosophy behind the competition rules – market integration, and they guide the European regulator, that is, the European institutions in setting the frame for the European 'economy', in formulating or limiting positive regulation. Do the Treaties provide for a specific coherent concept of the European economy, which legally binds the Member States and the Community organs and which contains an answer on the reach of the market freedoms and the intensity of market regulation? Or, is there no such 'economic constitution', are the Member States and the European organs free in the development of an economic order?

There is likewise a conflict between law and politics. The European Community has been created by law, but can law alone decide on the conflict between different concepts of the European economic order, on the extent to which state intervention needs to be restricted and market forces released? Does integration through law suffice? Or is integration through politics necessary – and, if so, where and how? Here the theoretical concept of European Economic Law is linked to integration theories. The *subsidiarity principle*, Art. 3b, has been designed to fill the gap between law and politics. The principle suggests clear-cut solutions: market integration for the Community, market regulation for the Member States, or even more simple: the market for the Community and the state for the Member States.

A. THE TRIPLE DILEMMA OF THE EC – A MARKET WITHOUT A STATE – THE BUILDING OF A QUASI-STATE VIA A MARKET – THROUGH LAW?

The key questions can be addressed by starting from a triple dilemma, from the EC being a market without a state, from the EC being a Quasi-State and from the EC being based on law (and less on politics).

1. First dilemma – the European Community, a market without a state

Christian Joerges' contribution, '*European Economic Law, the Nation State and the Treaty of Maastricht*' is meant to introduce the reader to the general problem of the EC: There is market integration on the one hand which is realized by the four freedoms and the competition rules, but there is at the same time market regulation undermining national sovereignty, although there is no 'European State' with a Constitution, no 'European State' which sets an institutional framework which defines tasks and competences.

EUROPEAN ECONOMIC LAW, THE NATION-STATE AND THE MAASTRICHT TREATY*

Christian Joerges

I. INTRODUCTION: A FRAMEWORK OF ANALYSIS

It might seem misplaced or, at best, evasive that this paper concentrates on the Europeanization of economic *law* in the context of an analysis of the Maastricht Treaty for at least two reasons. First, although the text of the new Treaty certainly contains important new economic law provisions,[1] its explosive core in terms of integration policy undoubtedly lies in the perspective of a Monetary Union;[2] second, the provisions on the Economic Union[3] are primarily concerned with a 'soft' coordination and supervision of economic *policy* rather than the completion of the Community's economic *law*. Yet, paradoxically, the difficulties, embarrassments and uncertainties provoked by the Danish vote of 2nd June 1992, the close outcome of the French referendum and the rejection of the Single European Space in Switzerland on 6th December 1992 justify a so-to-speak conservative approach to Maastricht for quite different reasons.

As a closer look will reveal, the integration strategy of the Maastricht Treaty does not break with, but instead rests upon, the politics pursued so far. The disillusionment of the proponents of a further deepening of European integration with the behavior of a substantive part of the European electorate on the one hand, and the mistrust of European voters of their pro-community minded political leaders on the other, does not just concern the agreements reached in Maastricht; it also affects the *acquis communautaire* and the future course of European legal policy.[4] The

---

*   Previously published in R. Dehousse (ed.), Europe After Maastricht – An Ever Closer Union, Munich, 1994, pp.95–100.

[1]   Such as Articles 73a–73h on capital and payments.

[2]   Articles 3a, 105–109m together with the two Protocols on the Statute on the European System of Central Banks and of the European Central Bank and the Statute of the European Monetary Institute.

[3]   Articles 102a–104c and the Protocol on Excessive Deficit Procedure.

[4]   Among the many documents indicating a search for new directives, see the speech of Delors, 'Die Europäische Union verständlich machen' *EG-Informationen* (V/1992, p.1); Delors, 'Le principe de subsidiarité: contribution au débat', in *Institut Européen d'Administration Publique, Subsidiarité: défi du changement* (1991, p.7) and the Report to the EEC Commission by the High Level Group on the Operation of Internal Market, 'The Internal Market After 1992. Meeting the Challenge' (1992).

Maastricht crisis has revealed integral problems of the integration process which are likely to remain on the Community's agenda regardless of the final outcome of ratification procedures.

It is almost impossible to overestimate the complexities of the integration process. We simply do not know of any grand theory that would enable us to fully understand the present course of European integration and provide us with a coherent and normatively attractive model of the future shape of a European republic. But such uncertainties do not exclude analytical and theoretical efforts. What we can do is identify problems that need to be taken into account when analysing the impact of European integration, and examine the ability of various integration strategies to cope with the problems we have identified.

This introductory section provides a theoretical framework for the analysis of what may provisionally be called the ongoing process of the Europeanization of economic law. The following section examines various legal theories of integration that attempt to explain and guide that process. The problems and perspectives thereby identified will then serve as a guide through the pertinent provisions of the Maastricht Treaty. Do the new provisions answer, or at least address, our queries with regard to the transformation of economic law in Europe?

A. Starting Point: Notions of Economic Law

The first difficulty which any enquiry into the Europeanization of economic law must take into account stems from this term itself. 'Economic law' (*Wirtschaftsrecht*) is a concept embedded within historical contexts and political and theoretical controversies. It is neither possible nor advisable to dissociate oneself from such intricacies. On the contrary, we should be aware that the process of integration concerns historically specific legal arrangements, that it is perceived and evaluated on the basis of different traditions of legal thought and also that historical contingencies affect our understanding of European economic law.

It is nevertheless possible to agree upon a range of legal fields which the term 'economic law' comprises: framework regulations providing for the administrative supervision of entire sectors of the economy; the organizational law of public, corporative and private actors; the protection of competitive structures and the control of anti-competitive practices; the legal institutions and instruments of macroeconomic control of economic processes. Any more substantial statement going beyond that taxonomy becomes more risky. What exactly are the objectives of the legislative activities just mentioned? If regulatory objectives are decisive, can mandatory contract law or product liability law be excluded from our concept? Does it make sense to include within this field modern regulatory techniques as they are practised by institutions and agencies operating in the fields of industrial policy, social regulation and the control of risks?

There is both a European and an international debate on all of these issues.[5] It seems safe to summarize the state of this debate as follows: there is no agreement as to the normative content and functions of economic law. But we do at least know why there is no consensus: the core problem of economic law always has been and continues to be to respect and to guarantee 'justified' demands through economic juridification processes. The theoretical contexts within which this juridification problem is addressed have changed and continue to evolve. Today, theoretical guidance is provided by neo-liberal legal theories (in Germany: *Ordnungstheorie*)[6] and economic analyses of law, system sociologies and their followers in legal theory,[7] interventionist approaches to regulation (in Germany: *Sozialstaatstheorien*) and, last but not least, 'proceduralized' versions of critical theories.[8]

The economic law of the European Community results from political processes, their transformation into law and further implementation. The legal, even the academic, discourse on European economic law has quite successfully avoided any theoretical and methodological pitfalls. It has been characterized as non-ideological, formalistic, purely doctrinal, strictly pragmatic and so forth.[9] However, neither is European economic law and its impact on national legal systems simply theoretically neutral, nor should we assume that abstract debates on the social functions and normative commitments of economic law do not relate to any practical problem. It therefore seems more adequate to interpret the formalism of European law as reflecting a specific way of coping with integration problems.[10] Be that as it may, there are many reasons to expect that it will no longer be possible to avoid a more overt debate on those fundamental problems and potential conflicts which have to date been kept hidden.

---

5   See, for example, G. Rinck (ed), 'Begriff und Prinzipien des Wirtschaftsrechts', 17, *Landesberichte zu einem internationalen Symposion* (1971); T. Daintith (ed.), *Law as an Instrument of Economic Policy: Comparative and Critical Approaches* (1987): G. Teubner, *Recht als autopoietisches System* (1989).

6   For a recent restatement, cf. Mestmäcker, 'Wirtschaftsrecht', 54, *RabelsZ* (1990) p.409.

7   See Teubner, 'Steuerung durch plurales Recht. Oder: Wie die Politik den normativen Mehrwert der Geldzirkulation abschöpft', in W. Zapf (ed.), *Die Modernisierung moderner Gesellschaften. Verhandlungen des 25. Deutschen Soziologentages in Frankfurt am Main 1990* (1991) p.528.

8   For an abstract recent summary, cf. J. Habermas, *Faktizität und Geltung*, Frankfurt a.M. (1992) pp.516–537.

9   Cf. the protests of Bengoetxea 'Institutions. Legal Theory and EC Law', 77 Archiv für Rechts- und Sozialphilosophie (1989) p.195; but see also infra part II A.

10 Cf. F. Snyder, New Directions in European Law (1990), pp.30.

B. First Concern: the Selectivity of EC Economic Law and its Disintegrative Effects

The framers of the Treaty did not seek to design a comprehensive institutional framework for economic policy. Rather, they agreed upon competences ('albeit in limited fields'),[11] rules and principles, which can at best be interpreted as elements of a legal order. At the core of this legal order are the Four Freedoms and the rules on competition. Only a few policy sectors – with agriculture, however, among them – were assigned to the Community. 'Economic policy' responsibilities continued to rest with the Member States. And yet, 'economic law' powers of legislation were established more or less accidentally wherever existing laws conflicted with the freedoms guaranteed by the EEC Treaty, wherever they resulted in trade restrictions (Article 30), where national regulations seemed irreconcilable with rules of competition and the resulting duties of the Member States (Articles 85 ff. and 5 paragraph 2), where the differences between legal orders affected the establishment or the functioning of the Common Market (Article 100) and where Community action appeared to be required in order to achieve one of its objectives (Article 235).

So far, all Community law measures based on these provisions have affected the economic laws of the Member States and their political responsibility only partially and selectively. Despite the rapid growth of European law during the last decade, its provisions merely concern fragments of national legal systems and do not totally transform national legal orders. Inevitable incoherences and coordination problems result from this selective expansion; an adoption of rules on competition may affect mandatory rules of contract law;[12] the harmonization of certain mandatory rules of contract law needs to be coordinated with existing bodies of legislation and case law.[13]

This dynamic expansion of European economic law had begun even prior to the adoption of the SEA in 1987. The European Court of Justice used Article 30 of the EC Treaty to increase Community control over national legislation. European competition law has been consolidated and used as an additional control standard for national regulations. We have witnessed an ever more extensive interpretation of the freedom to provide services. Articles 100 and 235 of the EC Treaty have served to open up one new policy sector after the other.

---

[11] Case 6/64, *Costa* v. *ENEL*, 585.

[12] For a more detailed analysis cf. Joerges, 'Contract and Status in Franchising Law', in C. Joerges (ed.), *Franchising and the Law. Theoretical and Comparative Approaches in Europe and the United States* (1991) p.11 and especially pp.60.

[13] Cf. Müller-Graff, 'Europäisches Gemeinschaftsrecht und Privatrecht', 46, *NJW* (1993), pp.13: Brüggemeier and Joerges, 'Europäisierung des Vertrags- und Haftungsrechts', in P.-C. Müller-Graff (ed.), *Gemeineuropäisches Privatrecht* (1993).

This gradual intrusion of the Community into areas of national competence has been both criticized and praised.[14] Harmonization policy in particular, which originally appeared to have a clear functional meaning and found its legitimacy and its limits within the definitions contained in Article 100 of the Treaty, has virtually transcended all conceivable boundaries. It is important to realize that each step towards harmonization does not only remove differences between legal orders, but similarly has to be understood as an act of 'positive' legislative policy. It would be unreasonable to expect the Community simply to follow pre-existing national models even should they seem outdated. Even if the Community were 'only' entitled to ensure equal competitive conditions, its powers of action in economic law would potentially be comprehensive since it could thus concern itself with all provisions affecting economic conditions.

Following the adoption of the SEA, the sphere, intensity and speed of the Community's legislative activities again increased dramatically.[15] To be sure, the Community was to promote a specific objective, i.e. bring about the Internal Market, while the political competences granted to the Community were to remain limited. But the Internal Market programme has proved so successful that attention is now drawn to the follow-up problems resulting from this success story.

Despite the ingenious jurisprudence of the European Court of Justice, which has redirected and intensified integration policy, important issues of primary law remain unsettled. For one thing, the application of Article 30 of the EC Treaty shows ever more clearly that the assignment and limitation of rights of market access need some more general guidance which can only be gained from a comprehensive understanding of the integration process and its objectives. It is apparent that the jurisprudence of the European Court of Justice which is based upon economic freedoms at times touches upon fundamental questions of legislative policy which have not been pre-decided by Community law.[16]

The Community's competition law has systematically been expanded into a comprehensive regulatory scheme through the adoption of the Merger Control Regulation. It is applied to control anti-competitive regimes within the Member

---

14   For a particularly thoughtful recent evaluation, cf. Steindorff, 'Quo vadis Europa? Freiheiten, Regulierung und soziale Grundrechte nach den erweiterten Zielen der EG-Verfassung', in Forschungsinstitut für Wirtschaftsverfassung und Wettbewerb e.V.(ed.), *Weiterentwicklung der Europäischen Gemeinschaften und der Marktwirtschaft* (1992) p.11.

15   For an informative and systematic survey see Falke, 'Föderalismus und rechtliche Regulierung der Wirtschaft in der Europäischen Gemeinschaft', in G. Stuby (ed.), *Föderalismus und Demokratie* (1992) p. 195; Steindorff, ibid., pp.19.

16   See, for example, Case C-362/88, Judgment of 7 March 1990, *GB-Inno*, [1990] ECR I–667.

States through Article 5.[17] However, the systematic expansion of competition law is no guarantee that there is agreement on the objectives of competition policy. The debate on industrial policy and other 'noncompetitive' considerations in appraising mergers and in exempting restrictive practices continues. The commitments of the Member States to the 'Economic Constitution' of the EC remain as disputed as the legal content of this constitution itself.

Article 100a of the Treaty has been designed and interpreted as a booster to the new Internal Market policy and as a means of protecting advanced legislative standards. By now, however, two unforeseen effects of this provision have become apparent: first, the Community now obtains access to more and more policy fields because of their connections with the Internal Market objective. Second, Article 100a, paragraph 4 grants protection against 'deregulation' but not against more stringent regulation. Debates on the reasonableness and legitimacy of regulatory objectives are settled by majority vote. It was inevitable that this should rekindle the discussion on the 'Limits of EC Competences'[18] which had long seemed a rather dry academic debate. It was equally inevitable that ways and means were sought to ensure that national constitutional law not be superseded by secondary Community law.[19]

More examples could be added to these. But it already seems safe to conclude that it is the very success and the new dynamism of integration policy, together with the widening and deepening of the Community's involvement in regulatory tasks, which now provokes new criticism as to the quality and legitimacy of Community law. When the Commission launched its Internal Market programme, these effects were not foreseeable. This strategy seemed to be solidly backed by the whole history of European integration. The Europeanization of economic law had been brought about gradually through the step-by-step adoption of legal frameworks aiming at the integration of markets. The vision of a single European market put new emphasis on this 'traditional' objective and it brought consensus. But once the machinery implementing that objective was set in motion, its 'interventionist' implications became apparent.

Such implications are twofold. Where the logic of market-building requires a common European legal framework, national regulatory traditions must be re-

---

[17] For a comprehensive recent analysis cf. A. Bach, *Wettbewerbliche Schranken für staatliche Maßnahmen nach europäischem Gemeinschaftsrecht* (1992).

[18] This is the title of E. Steindorff's monograph, *Grenzen der EG-Kompetenzen* (1991); cf. also Huber, 'Bundesverfassungsgericht und Europäischer Gerichtshof als Hüter der Gemeinschaftsrechtlichen Kompetenzordnung' 116, *AöR* (1991) p.210.

[19] Cf. among the many voices enunciating such concerns K.H. Friauf and R. Scholz, *Europarecht und Grundgesetz* (1990) (pleading, inter alia, for a commitment from the German Government to defend rights guaranteed by the Basic Law when voting at European level).

placed; this type of interventionism is usually perceived as a move towards deregulation. However, market building may also require or be supplemented by new regulatory activities at the European level. This type of interventionism has proven to be much stronger than was anticipated. Such consequences will be examined somewhat more closely in the next section. [...] It is, however, already possible to relate the two sides of market-building interventionism to the current debates on European economic law. These controversies are always about both the contents of EC economic law *and* the tension between market integration and national regulatory concerns; they tend to question both the competences of the Community *and* the legitimacy of interference by Community law. To put it slightly differently: the new debate is no longer confined to the gradual substitution of national by European law. It has instead revealed the interventionist implications of legal integration. It has highlighted the disintegrationist consequences of legal integration within national legal systems in their entirely.

C. Second Concern: the Nation-State and Democracy

It seems tempting to invoke the nation-state as a guardian against Community interventionism. Legal integration not only undermines the coherence and regulatory functions of national legal systems. It equally concerns the autonomy of national policy-making. It threatens the capability of national communities to pursue their own objectives. The tension between legal integration and national legal systems implies tension not only between European and national law but between supranational regimes and national democracies as well.

And yet, one should be cautious in playing the legitimacy of the nation-state off against the democratic deficiencies of European institutions. The nation-state is not inherently democratic or legitimate. European history has witnessed fundamentally different modes of nation-building. Nowhere has the merging of national identities with the principles of democracy been an easy task.[20] In Germany, to take a particularly worrying example, it was the defeat and the division of the nation-state that initiated the postwar move towards the *Staatsbürgernation*, i.e. the building up of a 'national' identity based upon constitutional rights and democratic political practices rather than on ethnic criteria and cultural heritage.[21]

---

[20] For a historically rich comparative assessment, cf. N. Elias, *Studien über die Deutschen. Machtkämpfe und Habitusentwicklung im 19. und 20. Jahrhundert* (1990) pp.159–222; see also the analyses of K.H.F. Dyson, *The State Tradition in Western Europe* (1980) especially pp.33–58 and P. Wagner, *Sozialwissenschaften und Staat. Frankreich. Italian, Deutschland 1870–1980* (1990).

[21] Cf. Lepsius, 'Ethnos und Demos', in R.M. Lepsius, *Interessen, Ideen und Institution* (1990) p.247; P. Glotz, *Der Irrweg des Nationalstaats* (1990); Habermas,

The history of economic law is inextricably linked with the history of the modern nation-state. From its beginnings, economic law has been conceived as a response to economic instability and the social problems of market economies. But this response has always had its parochial ingredients. In his famous inaugural lecture of 1895. Max Weber[22] named these elements with all his merciless analytical clarity. The economic policy of the nation-state, Weber explained in his critique of German idealism and the Historical School, must neither be mystified as representing some common higher morality nor be conceptualized as a nation-specific response to historically determined conditions. And yet, economic policy is bound to define national priorities and objectives. Economic law shares this in-built parochialism. It reacts to economic and social problems of capitalist market societies; but its reactions will tend to be one-sided definitions of the 'common good'. To be sure, the taming of the nation-state through democratic constitutions has the potential of ensuring that the common good will be defined in a legitimate way and will respect basic rights and freedoms. But the legitimacy which the economic law of the democratic nation-state can claim, rests upon processes in which only the members of the national community can participate. This holds true for statutory as well as for judge-made law. There is no built-in protection against one-sided definitions of economic objectives and the common good.

On the other hand, the logic of European integration cannot claim *a priori* superior legitimacy where it dismantles national concerns in the name of market integration. It is one thing to ensure free trade and to thereby overcome the 'state of nature' in international economic relations. It is quite another project to restructure national societies according to the logic of market integration.

(End of excerpt)

2. Second dilemma – the emergence of a Quasi-State

The spillover effects from market integration into market regulation do not only extend Community powers to the detriment of Member States' powers, the shift in competences entails *institutional consequences* thereby laying ground rules for a 'European State'. A Quasi-State is developing along the lines of market integration

---

'Staatsbürgerschaft und nationale Identität', in J. Habermas, *Faktizität und Geltung* (1992) p.632, and the remarks by Touraine, 'Existe-t-il encore une société française?', in D. Schapper and H. Mendras (eds.), *Six manières d'être Européen* (1990) pp.143, 152.

22 Weber, 'Der Nationalstaat und die Volkswirtschaftspolitik (1895)', in M. Weber, *Gesammelte Politische Schriften*, 3rd ed, (1971) p.1.

and market regulation rules without there being any explicit provisions in the Treaty that define the 'European State', not even after Maastricht.

A major player in the drift of gradual extension in Community competence at the expense of the Member States has been the European Court. It has confirmed competences in areas not covered by the Treaty of Rome. This is true for Case 240/83 *ADBHU*, [1985] ECR 531 at 31, where the Court declared in 1985, that is, before the adoption of the Single European Act, environmental protection to be 'one of the Community's essential objectives'. It was only in 1990 Case C-362/88 *GB-INNO* [1990] ECR I-667 that the Court went so far as to declare that 'under Community law concerning consumer protection the provision of information to the consumer is considered one of the principal requirements'. Consumer protection, however, was integrated into the Treaty only with the Maastricht Treaty. Case 240/83 and Case C-362/88 stand for the integration of new policies into the Treaty at a time where these policies have not yet gained an explicit legal status in the Treaty. The examples demonstrate the openness of the Treaty towards policies pursuing social objectives, towards regulating markets to the benefit of environmental and consumer protection.

In Case 11/70, *Internationale Handelsgesellschaft mbH* v. *Einfuhr- und Vorratsstelle für Getreide und Futtermittel* [1970] ECR 1125 the Court had built fundamental rights into the Treaty, by extending Community power, but also by extending Community responsibility. The ECHR has to compensate for the lack of fundamental rights in the Community legal order. It is somewhat ironic that the Court of Justice has been pushed into that direction by the Member States and the Member States Constitutional Courts (*Bundesverfassungsgericht, Solange I – 2 BvL 52/71* – Judgment of 29 May 1974, BVerfGE 37, 271 *et seq.*). A Community which is bound in one way or another to the European Convention on Human Rights is more than a common market or internal market alone. It is on its way to becoming a state, because only states can be bound to observe human rights.

It is not the Court of Justice alone which is extending the Community powers. Legislation too has enhanced Community competence. In 1992 the Council adopted Directive 92/59 on product safety (OJ L 228, 29.6.1992, 24 *et seq.*). Germany has challenged the legality of Article 9 which confers on the Commission the competence to take preliminary action for the safety of consumers. The Court, Case C-359/92, *Germany* v. *Council*, Judgment of 9 August 1994, (1994), I-3711 *et seq.* at 37) declared for the first time that Article 100a may serve as an appropriate basis for laying down rules on the enforcement of Community measures, that is, on the institutional patterns of cooperation and power sharing between the authorities of the Member States and the Commission:

Such action is not contrary to Article 100a(1) of the Treaty. The measures which the Council is empowered to take under that provision are aimed at 'the establishment and functioning of the internal market'. In certain fields, and particularly in that of product safety, the approximation of general laws alone may not be sufficient to ensure the unity of the market. Consequently, the concept of 'measures for the approximation' of legislation must be interpreted as encompassing the Council's power to lay down measures relating to a specific product or class of products and, if necessary, individual measures concerning those products.

3. Third dilemma – The European Community as a product of law

The European Community has been built on law and the European Court of Justice has been and still is the driving force of the integration process. Without the European Court of Justice, the European Community would have remained a supranational body just like dozens of others working more or less successfully at the international level. The first step was the establishment of Community law as being a 'Community legal order', deduced by the Court of Justice from the Treaty of Rome. That order provided for direct effect of the Treaty to the benefit of private individuals, Case 26/62, *Van Gend en Loos*, [1963] ECR, 1 at 10:

> The objective of the EEC Treaty, which is to establish a common market, the functioning of which is of direct concern to interested parties in the Community, implies that this Treaty is more than an agreement which merely creates mutual obligations between the contracting states... the Community constitutes a new legal order of international law for the benefit of which the states have limited their sovereign rights, albeit within limited fields, and the subjects of which comprise not only Member States but also their nationals. Independently of the legislation of the Member States, Community law therefore not only imposes obligations on individuals but is also intended to confer on them rights which become part of their legal heritage.

The second step followed in *Opinion 1/1991*, [1991] ECR-I, 6099 at 21 which represents the broadest and most vigorous statement that the Court has 'constitutionalized' the Treaty:

> In contrast, the EEC Treaty, albeit concluded in the form of an international agreement, none the less constitutes the constitutional charter of a Community based on the rule of law. As the Court of Justice has consistently held, the Community treaties established a new legal order for the benefit of which the States have limited their sovereign rights, in ever wider fields, and the subjects of which comprise not only Member States but also their nationals (see, in particular, the judgment in Case 26/62 *Van Gend en Loos* [1963] ECR 1). The essential characteristics of the Community legal order which has thus been established are in particular its primacy over the law of the Member States and

the direct effect of a whole series of provisions which are applicable to their nationals and to the Member States themselves.

Neither the Single European Act nor the Maastricht Treaty has inserted provisions on the legal character of Community law. The Community legal order, or now the Community law as a Constitutional Charter, remained a product of the European Court of Justice alone. There is, however, no legitimation for the existence of the European Community and its transformation from a Common Market to a 'Constitutional Charter' other than the 'law', more precisely, the law of the European Community as interpreted by the European Court of Justice. The democratic deficit of the EC has been outweighed by the Member States' insistence on national political sovereignty. Integration through (European) law and disintegration through (national) politics have balanced each other and have resulted all in all in the remarkable rise of the European Community even as a model for other economic regions. The question is in the aftermath of Maastricht whether the balance can be maintained and, if not, whether European law or national politics will come out on top. The decisions of the French *Cour de Cassation* and the German *Bundesverfassungsgericht* on the constitutionality of the Treaty of Maastricht offer a different perspective on what the European Community is – and perhaps more importantly on what it should or will become. The German *Bundesverfassungsgericht* concludes after the analysis of the Treaty of Maastricht with a view to the principle of enumerated powers:

Headnotes
to the ruling of the Federal Constitutional Court, Second Division
dated 12 October 1993
– 2 BvR 2134/92 –
– 2 BvR 2159/92 –

[...]

b) In other respects as well, the functions and powers of the European Union and the Communities belonging to it, as already discussed, are defined in terms of restricted factual circumstances, so that the wide-ranging statement of objectives in the Preamble and in Art. 8 of the Union Treaty do not justify the exercise of sovereign powers, but merely strengthen the intention to create an ever closer union of the peoples of Europe. The Union Treaty therefore satisfies the requirement accompanying the increasing closeness of integration, that possibilities for action by the European institutions not only should be defined in relation to their objectives but that the means be framed in factual terms so as to set concrete limits to their functions and powers.

The Union Treaty, and especially the EC Treaty, follow the principle of limited individual powers (see 2a. above). Although under that principle a specific provision conferring duties or powers can be interpreted in the light of Treaty goals, a Treaty goal is not by itself enough to create or extend duties or powers (H.P. Ipsen, *Europäisches Gemeinschaftsrecht*, 1972, p.559). Moreover, by express references to amendment (Art. N Union Treaty,) or extension (Art. K.9) the Union Treaty clearly delineates a legal development within the terms of the Treaties (see 75 BVerfGE 223 at p.240 *et seq.*) and the making of legal rules which overstep its boundaries and is not covered by applicable Treaty law. Article 23 para. 1 of the Basic Law adopts that criterion when it requires an assenting law for amendments to the treaty bases of the European Union and similar rules.

In as much as the Treaties establishing the European Communities on the one hand in limited circumstances confer sovereign rights, and on the other hand regulate Treaty amendments – through a normal and also in a simplified procedure – does this distinction take on meaning for the future treatment of the individual powers. Whereas a dynamic extension of the existing Treaties has been supported so far on the basis of a broad treatment of Art. 235 of the EEC Treaty in the sense of a 'lacuna-filling competence' (*Vertragsabrundungs-kompetenz*) and on the basis of considerations relating to the implied powers of the Communities and of Treaty interpretation as allowing maximum exploitation of Community powers or 'effet utile' (see Zuleeg in: von der Groeben / Thiesing / Ehlermann, *EWG-Vertrag*, 4th ed. 1991, Art. 2, note 3), in future the interpretation of enabling provisions by institutions and agencies of the Community will have to consider that the Union Treaty basically distinguishes between the exercise of a conferred limited sovereign power and the amendment of the Treaty, thus the interpretation will not result in an extension of the Treaty: such an interpretation of enabling provisions would not have a binding effect for Germany.

c) The treatment of this principle of limited individual powers is through the subsidiarity principle clarified and further restricted. For the European Community the subsidiarity principle is anchored in Art. 3b para. 2 of the EC Treaty; by reference in Art. B para. 2 of the Union Treaty it is extended to the Union's policies and forms of cooperation outside of the EC Treaty, and is again taken up in Art. K.3 para. 2b of the Union Treaty. In addition, individual powers, such as those conferred by Arts. 126 to 129b, 130 and 130g of the EC Treaty, restrict Community activity to an extension of the Member States' policies, which principally take precedence.

The subsidiarity principle therefore does not establish any powers of the European Community, but sets limits on powers already conferred elsewhere (see European Council in Edinburgh, *Conclusions of presidency*, Teil A Abschnitt 7 und Anlage 3, *BullBREG*, No. 140, 28.12.1992, 1278). Under Art. B para. 2 of the Union Treaty the objectives of the Union can only be achieved in accordance with the measures set out in the Treaty and in accordance with the conditions and the timetable set out in it; at the same time regard is to be given to the subsidiarity principle. Accordingly as a precondition for action by the

Community Art. 3b para. 1 specifies primarily that a power has been conferred on it by the Treaty, and its exercise is then by virtue of Art. 3b para. 2 subject to the subsidiarity principle.

This means: if there is a power under the Treaty to take action, whether and how the Community may act is determined by the subsidiarity principle. If the Community lawmaker wishes to exercise a power conferred on it to legislate, it must first make sure – and in accordance with Art 190 of the EC Treaty, show plausibly – that the objectives of the measure in question could not be adequately achieved by the Member States at the national level. This finding must then justify the further conclusion that in view of the scale and effects of the measure the objectives can be better achieved at Community level.

Through this principle of subsidiarity, adherence to which is a matter for the European Court to monitor, the national identities of the Member States are to be preserved and their powers retained (see European Council in Edinburgh, *loc. cit.*, p. 1280 *et seq.*). To what extent the subsidiarity principle will counteract an erosion of the jurisdictions of the Member States and thus of the functions and powers of the *Bundestag* depends – apart from the case law of the European Court relating to the subsidiarity principle – on the practice of the Council as the Community's actual legislative body. It is here that the Federal Government must exert its influence in favour of a strict treatment of Art. 3b para. 2 of the EC Treaty and so fulfill the constitutional obligation imposed on it by Art. 23 para. 1 of the Basic Law. For its part the *Bundestag* has the opportunity, through its right of cooperation established by Art. 23 para. 3 of the Basic Law, to effect the Council's practices and to exercise an influence on them within the meaning of the subsidiarity principle. The *Bundestag* as well will then be performing a constitutional duty incumbent on it under Art. 23 para. 1 of the Basic Law. Additionally, it is to be expected that the *Bundesrat*, too, will pay particular attention to the subsidiarity principle (see Goppel, *Die Bedeutung des Subsidiaritätsprinzips*, 1193, EuZW 367).

d) As the third fundamental principle of the Community constitution Art. 3b para. 3 of the EC Treaty incorporates the rule of proportionality. In the first place this principle contains a basic right prohibiting excessive measures, however, in the context of a confederation of allied states, which is not an entity organized as a state, it can restrict the intensity of Community action in the service of the obligation of Art. F para. 1 of the Union Treaty, and thus protect the national identities of the Member States and thereby the functions and powers of their parliaments against excessive European regulation. The principle of proportionality embodied in Art. 3b para. 3 – in contrast to the subsidiarity principle in the narrower sense of Art. 3b para. 2 – is applicable to all Community measures, whether based on 'exclusive' or on some other Community competence.

4. As a result, the Union Treaty regulates limited powers of action by the agencies and institutions of the three Communities, the exercise of which is graduated with regard to the means of implementation and the intensity of

regulation. The Treaty confers certain sovereign rights; the parliament could be held answerable for this conferment so that it has been democratically legitimized. The integration process set up in the Union Treaty and in the Treaties on the European Communities is not derived from the imposition of general objectives but from specific tasks and powers of action.

D.

The Maastricht Treaty – especially by the extension of EC competences and the inclusion of monetary policy – confers further essential functions and powers on European organs – which at Treaty level are not yet supported by a corresponding strengthening and extension of the democratic bases. It sets up a new stage of European unification, which according to the stated intentions of the Contracting Parties is to enhance further the democratic and efficient functioning of the institutions (fifth *considérant* of the Preamble). Democracy and efficiency are here not to be separated; it is also expected that the strengthening of the democratic principle will improve work at the Community level in all its organs. At the same time, in accordance with Art. F para. 1 of the Union Treaty, the Union will respect the national identities of its Member States, the governmental systems of which are based on democratic principles. To that extent the Union preserves the democratic bases already existing in the Member States and builds on them.

Any further development of the European Union cannot evade the conceptual framework set out above. The constitution-amending legislature had in connection with this Treaty taken that into account when they inserted Art. 23 into the Basic Law, as there the development of the European Union is expressly mentioned, subject to the principles of democracy and the rule of law, social and federal principles, and the subsidiarity principle. It is decisive, therefore, from the point of view of both the Treaties and of constitutional law, that the democratic bases of the Union will be built in step with integration, and also as integration progresses a living democracy will be maintained in the Member States.

The German court is challenging the supremacy of the community legal order, the second pillar of Community law beside direct effect. There is a very considerable literature on how the decision must and should be read. A pessimistic view would underline the rejection of an emerging 'European State'. Sovereignty lies and must lie, this is the message, with the Member States. A more optimistic view would interpret the German court's position as resulting from the pertaining democratic deficit of the European Community. One might be tempted to recall the interplay between the German Constitutional Court and the European Court of Justice on basic rights (cf. under (2) Second dilemma). Following that experience it would remain on the European Court of Justice, to find ways and means to compensate for the democratic deficiency in developing a 'European State' model, outside the

Treaty, based on the national legal orders. Such a legally created or, more correctly, judicially developed state, would again have to derive its legitimacy from law alone. The question after Maastricht must be more than ever before, whether the law can balance out the counter-rotating/counter-intuitive developments of integrative national and European law and disintegrative reluctant national politics? Or whether European law is on the decline, as recent decisions of the Court of Justice seem to indicate? Will national law prevail over European law, politics over law? Is the legal-political framework of the European Community too weak to unite the Member States under a 'European State'? The relationship and the tension between European law and Member States politics forms the focus of J.H.H. Weiler's contribution.

TRANSFORMATION OF EUROPE*

Joseph H. H. Weiler

IV. BEYOND 1992: TWO VISIONS OF THE PROMISED LAND – THE IDEOLOGY, ETHOS, AND POLITICAL CULTURE OF EUROPEAN INTEGRATION

[...] By way of conclusion I would like to examine, far more tentatively, another facet of the transformation of Europe: the ideology, ethos, and political culture of European integration, particularly in relation to *1992*.[1]

Ideological discourse within the Community, especially in the pre-*1992* period, had two peculiar features. On the one hand, despite the growing focus of Community activity on important issues of social choice, a near absence of overt debate on the left-right spectrum existed. *1992* (as a code for the overall set of changes) represents a break from this pattern.

On the other hand, there was abundant discourse on the politics and choices of the integration model itself. But this discourse was fragmented. In specialized political constituencies, especially those concerned with Community governance, public discourse was typically a dichotomy between those favoring the Community (and further European integration) and those defending "national sovereignty" and the prerogatives of the Member State.

The outcome of the debate was curious. In the visible realm of political power from the 1960's onwards, it seemed that the "national interest" was ascending.[2]

---

* First published in *The Yale Law Journal*, **100**, 1991, pp.2474, reprinted with permission of *The Yale Law Journal* and Fred B. Rothman & Company, New Haven, Connecticut.

1 In turning to ethos, ideology, and political culture, the screening process of the "self" (my "self") plays an even bigger role in the narrative. To try to "document" my assertions and conclusions here would be to employ the semblance of a scholarly apparatus where it is patently not merited. I do not, and cannot, claim to root this part of the Article on the kind of painstaking research and complex tools that characterize the work of the social historian or the historical sociologist. *Caveat Lector*! Nonethless, my brief narrative will, I hope, serve a function. Compared to the plethora of systemic and substantive theories and analyses of the processes of European integration, a real dearth of ideological and cultural scrutiny exists. Two recent extremely illuminating reflections on these issues are F. Snyder, supra note 7, and J. Ørstrøm Møller, *Technology and Culture in a European Context* (1991). By offering my perspective on ·these issues. I hope the reader is drawn to reflect, and thereby, challenged to take position.

2 The constitutional revolution was not immediately apparent even to relatively informed audiences. See Weiler, 'Attitudes of MEPs Towards the European Court', 9 *Eur. L. Rev.*

The "high moral ground" by contrast, seemed to be occupied fairly safely by the "integrationists."

So far as the general public was concerned, the characterizing feature of public discourse was a relatively high level of indifference, disturbed only on rare occasions when Community issues caught the public imagination. Although opinion polls always showed a broad support for the Community, as I argued earlier, it was still possible to gain political points by defending the national interest against the threat of the faceless "Brussels Eurocracy."

Here, the importance of *1992* has not been only in a modification of the political process of the Community, but also in a fascinating mobilization of wide sections of general public opinion behind the "new" Europe. The significance of this mobilization cannot be overstated. It fuelled the momentum generated by the White Paper and the Single European Act, and laid the ground auspiciously for creating Community initiatives to push beyond *1992*. These Community initiatives included the opening in December 1990 of two new Intergovernmental Conferences designed to fix the timetable and modalities of Economic and Monetary Union, as well as the much more elusive task of Political Union. Although no one has a clear picture of "political union,"[3] with open talk about Community government, federalist solutions, and other such codes,[4] even if the actual changes to the existing structure will be disappointing, in the ideological "battle" between state and Community, the old nationalist rhetoric has become increasingly marginalized and the integrationist ethos has fully ascended. The demise of Prime Minister Thatcher symbolizes this change.

(1984) p.169. One of the interesting conclusions of this survey of attitudes is that even those Members of the European Parliament strongly opposed to the dynamics of European integration and the increase in power of the Commission and Parliament regarded the Court with relevant equanimity.

[3] The term has no fixed meaning and is used to cannote a wide variety of models from federalist to intergovernmentalist. See generally. R. Mayne & J. Pinder, *Federal Union: the Pioneers* (1990); R. Pryce (ed.), *The Dynamics of European Union* (1987) (usefully tracing evolution of concept of political union over history of European integration up to Single European Act); J. Lodge (ed.), *European Union: the European Community in Search of a Future*, (1986).

[4] See, for example, President Delors' speech to the European Parliament of 17 January 1990: "Cet exécutif [of the future Community on which Delors was speculating – the Commission according to the logic of the Founders] devra être responsable, bien entendu. devant les institutions démocratique de la future féderation..." Jacques Delors Presente De Programmeme de la Commission et Dessine Un Profit de L'Europe de Demain, *Europe Doc.* (No.1592) 7 (24 Jan 1990) (emphasis added). Likewise, when speaking approvingly of Mitterrand's idea of an "all European Confederation," Delors adds: "Mais ma conviction est qu'une telle confédération ne pourra voir le jour qu'une fois réalisé l'Union politique de la Communauté!" ibid. p.4.

The impact of *1992*, however, goes well beyond these obvious facts of mobilization and "European ascendancy." Just below the surface lurk some questions, perhaps even forces, which touch the very ethos of European integration, its underlying ideology, and the emergent political culture associated with this new mobilization. Moreover, in some respects the very success of *1992* highlights some inherent (or at least potential) contradictions in the very objectives of European integration.

I shall deal first with the break from the Community's supposed ideological neutrality, and then turn to the question of the ethos of European integration in public discourse.

A. 1992 and the "Ideological Neutrality" of the Community

The idea of the single market was presented in the White Paper as an ideologically neutral programme around which the entire European polity could coalesce in order to achieve the goals of European integration. This idea reflected an interesting feature of the pre-*1992* Community: the relative absence of ideological discourse and debate on the right-left spectrum. The chill on right-left ideological debate derived from the governance structure of the Community.[5]

Since in the Council there usually would be representatives of national governments from both right and left, the desired consensus had to be one acceptable to all major political forces in Europe. Thus, policies verged towards centrist pragmatic choices, and issues involving sharp right-left division were either shelved[6] or mediated to conceal or mitigate the choice involved. The tendency towards the lowest common denominator applied also to ideology.

Likewise, on the surface, the political structure of the European Parliament replicates the major political parties in Europe. National Party lists join in Parliament to sit in European political groups. However, for a long time the politics of integration itself, especially on the issues of the European Parliament's power and the future destiny of the Community, were far more important than differences between left and right within the chamber. The clearest example was the coalescing of Parliament with a large majority behind the Independent-Communist Spinelli and his Draft Treaty for European Union.[7]

---

[5] Of course I do not suggest that choices with ideological implications were not made. But they were rarely perceived as such.
[6] Thus, the proposed European company statute was shelved for many years because of the inability to agree, especially on the role of labor in the governance structure of the company.
[7] Typically, right and left have differed sharply in Parliament on issues of foreign affairs and extra-Community policies.

Most interesting in this perspective is the perception of the Commission. It is an article of faith for European integration that the Commission is not meant to be a mere secretariat, but an autonomous political force shaping the agenda and brokering the decision-making of the Community. And yet at the same time, the Commission, as broker, must be ideologically neutral, not favoring Christian Democrats, Social Democrats, or others.

This neutralization of ideology has fostered the belief that an agenda could be set for the Community, and the Community could be led towards an ever closer union among its peoples, without having to face the normal political cleavages present in the Member States. In conclusion, the Community political culture which developed in the 1960s and 1970s led both the principal political actors and the political classes in Europe to an habituation of all political forces to thinking of European integration as ideologically neutral in, or ideologically transcendent over, the normal debates on the left-right spectrum. It is easy to understand how this will have served the process of integration, allowing a nonpartisan coalition to emerge around its overall objectives.

1992 changes this in two ways. The first is a direct derivation from the turn to majority voting. Policies can be adopted now within the Council that run counter not simply to the perceived interests of a Member State, but more specifically to the ideology of a government in power. The debates about the European Social Charter and the shrill cries of "Socialism through the backdoor," as well as the emerging debate about Community adherence to the European Convention on Human Rights and abortion rights are harbingers of things to come. In many respects this is a healthy development, since the real change from the past is evidenced by the ability to make difficult social choices and particularly by the increased transparency of the implications of the choice. At the same time, it represents a transformation from earlier patterns with obvious dysfunctional tensions.

The second impact of *1992* on ideological neutrality is subtler. The entire programme rests on two pivots: the single market plan encapsulated in the White Paper, and its operation through the new instrumentalities of the Single European Act. Endorsing the former and adopting the latter by the Community and its Member States – and more generally by the political class in Europe – was a remarkable expression of the process of habituation alluded to above. People were successfully called to rally behind and identify with a bold new step toward a higher degree of integration. A "*single European* market" is a concept which still has the power to stir. But it is also a "single European *market*." It is not simply a technocratic programme to remove the remaining obstacles to the free movement of all factors of production. It is at the same time a highly politicized choice of ethos, ideology, and political culture: the culture of "the market." It is also a philosophy, at least one version of which – the predominant version – seeks to remove barriers to the free movement of factors of production, and to remove distortion to competition as a means to maximize utility. The above is premised on the assumption of formal equality of individuals.[8] It is an ideology the contours of which have been the subject of intense debate within the Member States in terms of their own political choices. This is not the place to explicate these. Elsewhere, two slogans, "The One Dimensional Market" and "Big Market as Big Brother," have been used to emphasize the fallacy of ideological neutrality.[9] Thus, for example, open access, the cornerstone of the single market and the condition for effective nonprotectionist competition, will also put pressure on local consumer products in local markets to the extent these are viewed as an expression of cultural diversity. Even more dramatic will be the case in explicit "cultural products," such as television and cinema. The advent of Euro-brands has implications, for better or for worse, which extend beyond the bottom line of national and Community economies. A successful single market requires widespread harmonization of standards of consumer protection and environmental protection, as well as the social package of employees. This need for a successful market not only accentuates the pressure for uniformity, but also manifests a social (and hence ideological) choice which prizes market efficiency and European-wide neutrality of competition above other competing values.

It is possible that consensus may be found on these issues, and indeed that this choice enjoys broad legitimacy. From my perspective, it is important to highlight that the consensus exudes a powerful pressure in shaping the political culture of the Community. As such, it is an important element of the transformation of Europe.

B. The Ethos of European Integration: Europe as Unity and Europe as Community

As indicated above, *1992* also brings to the fore questions, choices, and contradictions in the very ethos of European integration. I shall explore these questions, choices, and contradictions by construing two competing visions of the Promised Land to which the Community is being led in *1992* and beyond. The two visions are synthetic constructs, distilled from the discourse and praxis of European integration.

Unitarian and communitarian visions share a similar departure point. If we go back in time to the 1950 Schuman Declaration and the consequent 1951 Treaty of Paris establishing the European Coal and Steel Community, these events, despite

---

8   There is an alternative construction of the Community political ideology also present in the European debate, one which recognizes "inequalities but deploring their inequities, considers the market to be just one of several basic means of governing society." F. Snyder, *New Directions*, p.89.

9   Bieber, Dehousse. Pinder and Weiler, 'Back to the Future: Policy, Strategy and Tactics of the White Paper on the Creation of a Single European Market', in *1992: One European Market?*, (1988) pp.18–20.

their economic content, are best seen as a long-term and transformative strategy for peace among the states of Western Europe, principally France and Germany.[10] This strategy tried to address the "mischief" embodied in the excesses of the modern nation-state and the traditional model of statal intercourse among them that was premised on full *"sovereignty," "autonomy," "independence"* and a relentless defense and maximization of the national interest. This model was opposed not simply because, at the time, it displayed a propensity to degenerate into violent clashes, but also because it was viewed as unattractive for the task of reconstruction in times of peace.[11] The European Community was to be an antidote to the negative features of the state and statal intercourse; its establishment in 1951 was seen as the beginning of a process[12] that would bring about their elimination.

At this point, the two visions depart. According to the first – unity – vision, the process that started in 1951 was to move progressively through the steps of establishing a common market and approximating economic policies[13] through ever tighter economic integration (economic and monetary union), resulting, finally, in full political union, in some version of a federal United States of Europe. If we link this vision to governance process and constitutional structure, the ultimate model of the Community and the constitutionalized treaties stands as the equivalent, in the European localized context, of the utopian model of "world government" in classical international law. Tomorrow's Europe in this form would indeed constitute the final demise of Member State nationalism and, thus, the ultimate realization of the original objectives through political union in the form of a federalist system of governance.[14]

---

10   See, for example, Schuman Declaration of 9 May 1950, reprinted in 13, *Bull. Eur. Communities*, 5/1980, pp.14–15 (hereinafter Schuman Declaration): "The gathering of the nations of Europe requires the elimination of the age-old opposition of France and the Federal Republic of Germany."; Preamble to 1951 Treaty of Paris, reprinted in Eur. Community Info. Service, *Treaties Establishing the Eur. Communities* (1987): "Considering that world peace can be safeguarded only by creative efforts commensurate with the dangers that threaten it ..."

11   This does not mean that states and leaders were engulfed in some teary-eyed sentimentalism. Signing on to the Community idea was no doubt also a result of cool calculation of the national interest. See A. Milward, *The Reconstruction of Western Europe 1945–51* (1984). But this does not diminish the utility of seeking the overall ethos of the enterprise that they were joining.

12   On the one hand: "In taking upon [it]self for more than 20 years the role of champion of a united Europe, France has always had as [its] essential aim the service of peace." On the other hand: "Europe will not be made all at once, or according to a single... plan." Schuman Declaration, supra note 10, at 15.

13   EEC Treaty, art. 2.

14   Of course, even in this vision, one is not positing a centrist unified Europe but a federal structure of sorts, in which local interests and diversity would be maintained. Thus, although Delors speaks in his 17 Oct 1990 speech of Europe as federation, he is – in good

The alternative – community – vision also rejects the classical model of international law which celebrates statal sovereignty, independence, and autonomy and sees international legal regulation providing a "neutral" arena for states to prosecute their own ("national") goals premised on power and self-interest.[15] The community vision is, instead, premised on limiting, or sharing, sovereignty in a select albeit growing number of fields, on recognizing, and even celebrating, the reality of *interdependence*, and on counterpoising to the exclusivist ethos of statal autonomy a notion of a *community* of states and peoples sharing values and aspirations.

Most recently, it has been shown convincingly, not for the first time, how the classical model of international law is a replication at the international level of the liberal theory of the state.[16] The state is implicitly treated as the analogue, on the international level, to the individual within a domestic situation. In this conception, international legal notions such as self-determination, sovereignty, independence, and consent have their obvious analogy in theories of the individual within the state. The idea of community is thus posited in juxtaposition to the international version of pure liberalism and substitutes a modified communitarian vision.

Since the idea of "community" is currently in vogue and has become many things to many people, I would like to explain the meaning I attach to it in this transnational European context.[17] The importance of the EEC inter-statal notion of *community* rests on the very fact that it does not involve a negation of the state. It is neither state nor community. The idea of community seeks to dictate a different type of intercourse among the actors belonging to it, a type of self-limitation in their self-perception, a redefined self-interest, and, hence, redefined policy goals. To the interest of the state must be added the interest of the community. But crucially, it does not extinguish the separate actors who are fated to live in an uneasy tension with two competing senses of the polity's self, the autonomous self and the self as part of a larger community, and committed to an elusive search for an opti-

---

faith – always careful to maintain respect for "pluralism." See 'Jacques Delors at the College of Europe in Bruges', reprinted in *Europe Doc.* (No. 1576) pp.1–5 (21 Oct 1989) (hereinafter Delors Speech of 17 Oct 1990).

[15] This, of course, is the classical model of international law. It is not monolithic. There are, in international law, voices, from both from within and without, calling for an alternative vision expressed in such notions as "common heritage of humankind". See, for example, P. Sands, *Lessons Learned in Global Environmental Governance*, World Resources Inst., (1990).

[16] M. Koskenniemi, *From Apology to Utopia*, (1989) at XVI *passim*.

[17] I certainly do not find it useful to make an explicit analogy to the theories of community of domestic society, although I would not deny their influence on my thinking. See, for example, M. Sandel, *Liberalism and the Limits of Justice* (1982); M. Walzer, *Spheres of Justice* (1983), and the fierce debates about these, see, for example, Dworkin, 'To Each His Own', *New York Review of Books*, 14 Apr 1983; 'Spheres of Justice: an Exchange', *New York Review of Books*, 21 July 1983.

mal balance of goals and behavior between the community and its actors. I say it is crucial because the unique contribution of the European Community to the civilization of international relations – indeed its civilizing effect on intra-European statal intercourse – derives from that very tension among the state actors and between each state actor and the Community. It also derives from each state actor's need to reconcile the reflexes and ethos of the "sovereign" national state with new modes of discourse and a new discipline of solidarity.[18] Civilization is thus perceived not in the conquering of Eros but in its taming.[19]

Moreover, the idea of Europe as community not only conditions discourse among states, but it also spills over to the peoples of the states, influencing relations among individuals. For example, the Treaty provisions prohibiting discrimination on grounds of nationality, allowing the free movement of workers and their families, and generally supporting a rich network of transnational social transactions may be viewed not simply as creating the optimal conditions for the free movement of factors of production in the common market. They also serve to remove nationality and state affiliation of the individual, so divisive in the past, as the principal referent for transnational human intercourse.

The *unity* vision of the Promised Land sees then as its "ideal type" a European polity, finally and decisively replacing its hitherto warring Member States with a political union of federal governance. The *community* vision sees as its "ideal type" a political union in which Community and Member State continue their uneasy co-existence, although with an ever-increasing embrace. It is important also to understand that the voice of, say, Thatcher is not an expression of this community vision. Thatcherism is one pole of the first vision, whereby Community membership continues to be assessed and re-evaluated in terms of its costs and benefits to a Member State, in this case Great Britain, which remains the ultimate referent for its desirability. The Community is conceived in this way of thinking not as a redefinition of the national self but as an arrangement, elaborate and sophisticated, of achieving long-term maximization of the national interest in an interdependent world. Its value is measured ultimately and exclusively with the coin of national utility and not community solidarity.

---

[18]   Cf. EEC Treaty, art. 5.

[19]   This tension between actor and community finds evocative expression in the Preamble and opening Article of the EEC Treaty, the foundation of the current Community. The Preamble speaks of "an ever closer union among the *peoples* of Europe" (emphasis added) whereas Article 2 speaks of "closer relations between the *States* belonging to it" (emphasis added). Note, too, that the Preamble speaks about the peoples, of Europe rejecting any notion of a melting pot and nation-building. Finally, note the "ever closer union": something which goes on for "ever" incorporates, of course, the "never". See EEC Treaty, preamble.

I do not think that *1992* can be seen as representing a clear preference and choice for one vision over the other. But there are manifestations, both explicit and implicit, suggesting an unprecedented and triumphal resurgence and ascendancy of the unity vision of Europe over the competing vision of community: part and parcel of the *1992* momentum. If indeed the road to European union is to be paved on this unity vision, at the very moment of ascendancy the Community endangers something noble at its very core and, like other great empires, with the arrival of success may sow the seeds of self-destruction.

Why such foreboding? Whence the peril in the unity vision? At an abstract logical level it is easy to challenge the unity vision which sets up a fully united Europe as the pinnacle of the process of European integration. It would be more than ironic if a polity with its political process set up to counter the excesses of statism ended up coming round full circle and transforming itself into a (super) state. It would be equally ironic that an ethos that rejected the nationalism of the Member States gave birth to a new European nation and European nationalism. The problem with the unity vision is that its very realization entails its negation.

But the life of the Community (like some other things) is not logic, but experience. And experience suggests that with all the lofty talk of political union and federalism we are not about to see the demise of the Member States, at least not for a long time. The reports leaking out of the intergovernmental conference suggest fairly modest steps on this road.

That being the case, the unease with the unity vision nonetheless remains. For if the unity ethos becomes the principal mobilizing force of the polity, it may, combined with the praxis and rhetoric of the *1992* single market, compromise the deeper values inherent in the community vision, even if the Community's basic structure does not change for years to come.

I suggested above that these values operated both at the interstate level by conditioning a new type of statal discourse and self-perception and at the societal and individual level by diminishing the importance of nationality in transnational human intercourse. How then would the unity vision and the *1992* praxis and rhetoric corrode these values?

The successful elimination of internal frontiers will, of course, accentuate in a symbolic and real sense the external frontiers of the Community. The privileges of Community membership for states and of Community citizenship for individuals are becoming increasingly pronounced. This is manifest in such phenomena as the diffidence of the Community towards further enlargement (packaged in the notion of the concentric circles),[20] in the inevitable harmonization of external border controls, immigration, and asylum policies, and in policies such as local European content of television broadcasting regulation. It assumes picaresque character with

---

[20] See Delors Speech of 17 Oct 1990, supra.

the enhanced visibility of the statal symbols already adopted by the Community: flag, anthem, Community passport. The potential corrosive effect on the values of the community vision of European integration are self-evident. Nationality as referent for interpersonal relations, and the human alienating effect of *Us* and *Them* are brought back again, simply transferred from their previous intra-Community context to the new inter-Community one. We have made little progress if the *Us* becomes European (instead of German or French or British) and the *Them* becomes those outside the Community or those inside who do not enjoy the privileges of citizenship.

There is a second, slightly more subtle, potentially negative influence in this realm. A centerpiece of the agenda for further integration is the need of Europe to develop the appropriate structures for a common foreign and defense policy.[21] It has indeed been anomalous that despite the repeated calls since the early 1970's for a Europe that will speak with one voice,[22] the Community has never successfully translated its internal economic might to commensurate outside influence. There could be much positive in Europe taking such a step to an enhanced common foreign and security policy. The potential corrosive element of this inevitable development rests in the suspicion that some of the harkening for a common foreign policy is the appeal of strength and the vision of Europe as a new global superpower. Europe is a political and economic superpower and often fails to see this and discharge its responsibilities appropriately. But the ethos of strength and power, even if transferred from the Member State to the European level, is closer to the unity rather than community notion of Europe and, as such, partakes of the inherent contradiction of that vision.

All these images and the previous question marks are not intended as an indictment of *1992* and the future road of European integration. Both in its structure and process, and, in part, its ethos, the Community has been more than a simple successful venture in transnational cooperation and economic integration. It has been a unique model for reshaping transnational discourse among states, peoples, and individuals who barely a generation ago emerged from the nadir of Western civilization. It is a model with acute relevance for other regions of the world with bleak histories or even bleaker present.

Today's Community is impelled forward by the dysfunctioning of its current architecture. The transformation that is taking place has immense, widely discussed

---

[21]   Ibid.; see also Proposals of European Parliament to Intergovernmental Conference, PE 146.824, new art. 130u (proposing full-fledged apparatus for European foreign and security policy).

[22]   On the history of European Political Cooperation and the idea of Europe speaking with one voice, see Stein, 'Towards a European Foreign Policy? The European Affairs System from the Perspective of the United States Constitution', 1:3 *Integration Through Law*, **63**, (1986).

promise. If I have given some emphasis to the dangers, it is not simply to redress a lacuna in the literature. It is also in the hope that as this transformation takes place, that part, limited as it may be, of the Community that can be characterized as the modern contribution of Europe to the civilization of interstatal and intrastatal inter-course shall not be laid by the wayside.

(End of excerpt)

B. NEED AND VALUE OF A EUROPEAN ECONOMIC CONSTITUTION

The existence or non-existence of a 'European State' pre-determines the concept of a European Economic Constitution. Where there is no 'European State', there can be no competences in the hands of the Community outside market integration. Market regulation on the other hand requires a European regulator and, more and more, in one way or another, a 'European State'.

1. The *"Ordnungspolitik"* (Neo-liberal Economic Policy) as European Economic Constitutional Law

German theory of the Community's Economic Constitution has never been merely positivist or pragmatic interpretations of the EC Treaty, but has always striven for a functional understanding of European law and a normatively consistent overall perspective on the integration. The contribution of Manfred Streit and Werner Mussler, *The Economic Constitution of the European Community – From 'Rome' to 'Maastricht'* provides an introduction to what '*Ordnungspolitik*' in economic theory means and what it entails for the legal order of the economy. The authors suggest that the EC Treaty contains a European Economic Constitution along the line of the '*Ordnungspolitik*' and explain, why from their point of view, the Treaty of Maastricht jeopardizes this Constitution.

THE ECONOMIC CONSTITUTION OF THE EUROPEAN COMMUNITY – FROM 'ROME' TO 'MAASTRICHT'*

Manfred Streit and Werner Mussler

[...]
2.2. Functional Properties of the EEC Treaty

A constitution for a market system

Considering the Treaty establishing the European Economic Community (EEC) of 1958 from the perspective of an economic constitution, there is sufficient evidence to argue that the Treaty provides a framework for a common market as a self-organizing system:

1   In order to allow an unimpeded self-coordination of economic actors through market transactions, it belongs to the activities of the Community to eliminate tariff as well as non-tariff barriers to the import and export of goods between Member States (Art. 3(a)) and to abolish "obstacles to freedom of movement for persons, services and capital" (Art. 3(c))[1].
2   In order to allow self-control of economic actors through competition and to contain economic power, the Community establishes "a system ensuring that competition in the common market is not distorted" (Art. 3(f)).
3   As far as the external markets are concerned, the Community not only establishes "a common customs tariff" and "a common commercial policy" (Art. 3(b)) but is also committed "to contribute, in the common interest, to the harmonious development of world trade, the progressive abolition of restrictions on international trade and the lowering of customs barriers" (Art. 110).

As a whole, these activities describe sovereign tasks of the Community with the aim of improving the institutional framework for autonomous economic decisions of private actors. They imply a clear demarcation of the private and the public sphere whereby it is the duty of the Court of Justice to "ensure that in the interpretation and application of this Treaty the law is observed" (Art. 164).

---

*   First published in *Constitutional Political Economy*, 5, 1994, pp.319 *et seq.*, reprinted by permission of *Constitutional Political Economy*, Center for studies of Public Choice, Fairfax, Virginia.
[1]   This was, in fact, already the definition of an internal market, which is covered now in the Treaty of Maastricht by the two largely overlapping provisions of Artt. 3(a) and (c).

Considering this arrangement in isolation, we would argue that it is a constitution which clearly establishes a market system. Thereby, we set aside not only the non-market elements of the EEC Treaty, i.e. the common policies in the sphere of agriculture and transport as well as some uses of the European Social Fund, but also particularly those interventionist practices which are in accordance with the ECSC Treaty (section 2.3).

Safeguards for economic liberties

The liberties quoted in Art. 3 of the Treaty which are constitutive to the autonomy of economic agents are protected in two directions. However, they appear to be at risk in a third one. The first safeguard concerns restrictions imposed upon the freedom to compete by making use of the very liberties. Such restrictions would result from the market system. Private restraints to trade are covered particularly by the rules of Artt. 85 and 86. To the extent to which these rules are per-se rules. they fit – in view of their universalizability – particularly well into the institutional framework for a self-organizing system.

The second safeguard refers to a category of restrictions coming from outside the market system: It concerns the protection against distortions and – consequently – restrictions of competition which result from activities of the Member States[2]. Forming a common market according to Art. 3(c) represents an obligation to remove existing restrictions of trade and hence of competition between Member States. In addition, those distortions of competition are considered incompatible with the Treaty which may result from aids granted by Member States (Artt. 92 ff.), from regulations (Artt. 101 f.) and from measures related to "public undertakings and undertakings to which Member States grant special or exclusive rights" (Art. 90).[3]

The enforcement of the safeguards for economic freedom is not restricted to Community action. This follows from the specific constitutional character of the EEC Treaty. It transforms the obligations of the Member States according to the

---

[2] This has already been required by the "Spaak report" preparing the negotiations on the Treaty in 1956: "Normal conditions of competition" had to be secured by competition rules in order "to obviate the consequences of state interventions and monopolies" (quoted in Mestmäcker (1988/93. 184)). There can be no doubt that the "hands-tying effect" of these rules with regard to the Member States favoured the market forces within the Common Market and was also a driving force for many steps towards deregulation on the national level. For a comprehensive study of limits to regulation of the Member States by European Competition Law. cf. Bach (1992).

[3] This appears almost self-evident when considering the objective of economic integration. But so far, national competition policy turned a blind eye to the fact that the State tends to distort competition within its boundaries and beyond probably more and more lastingly than private actors can achieve on their own.

law of nations into subjective rights of the citizens of the Community which are enforceable by court action.[4] From a functional point of view, the supremacy of European law in all areas which are subjected to the Treaty and the transformation of obligations of the Member States into subjective rights proved to be highly conducive to strengthening the internal market system: It worked as an effective means of deregulation within the Member States and it helped to open the national economic and social systems towards the Community. At the same time, it favoured a "competition of regulations" in the sense of the already mentioned "Cassis de Dijon" decision.

Considering the third direction in which the liberties require protection, a clear impediment of the Community to become itself a source of restrictions imposed upon the economic freedom of its citizens does not exist. At a first glance, there should be no doubt that the constitutionally secured basic liberties and the principle of undistorted competition are also safeguards against Community interference (Petersmann (1993b, 408)). But the Treaty itself does not make sufficiently clear that the principles of open markets and the rules of competition, which have the Member States as addressees, do equally apply to the Community. Particularly the more recent political moves towards European integration make it necessary to recall a fundamental constitutional problem of the nation state again, this time with regard to the Community: "The new (...) challenge consists of the obligation of the Community authorities to the Community law" (Mestmäcker (1992) – our translation).

[...]

2.4. From "Rome" to "Maastricht"

Driving forces: centralization and constitutional displacement

Looking back at the history of European integration, we propose to distinguish two driving forces which manifested themselves in the administrative practice of the Commission and in consecutive changes of the relevant treaties. The first one is centralization. It can be convincingly explained by modern political economy. The European bureaucracy has a self-interest in expanding its discretionary competences[5]. The principle of "compétence d'attribution" was undermined more and

---

[4]   For a more detailed discussion. cf. v.d.Groeben/Mestmäcker (1974) and Mestmäcker (1994b). This "constitutionalization" of individual liberties has been confirmed several times by the European Court. In this context, the EEC Treaty has been called by the Court "the constitutional charter of a community based on the rule of law" (quotation according to Mestmäcker (1994a, p.6)).

[5]   A thorough explanation of this behaviour has been given by Vaubel (1992).

more by efforts of the Community, based on proposals of the Commission, to take measures which were considered "necessary to attain, in the course of the operation of the common market, one of the objectives of the Community" according to the EEC Treaty (Art. 235)[6]. The European Court is not on the record for having opposed the extensive use of this provision. However, it would not be appropriate to blame only the Commission for expanding discretionary action by the Community. It is quite plausible and has been argued by (former) members of the Commission (e.g. Caspari (1993, 132)) that the Community can be and is used by the Member States as a kind of joker to serve special and sometimes public interests via Brussels in view of domestic opposition.

The second force emerged from a kind of constitutional displacement of the original Member States. When considering the EEC Treaty and its interpretation as well as its execution, it appears plausible to argue that the signatories could hardly foresee the restraining effects which the Treaty had regarding their propensity to intervene in general and their ideological inclinations in particular (cf. Mestmäcker (1993)). And consecutive governments had to live with the Treaty anyhow. The enlargement of the Community did have a constitutional displacement effect in the sense that the "acquis communautaire" was partly questioned by the new members. Some of them obtained exemptions, others simply ignored parts of their obligations, following examples set by original Member States. The unforeseen consequences of the Treaty and the experience of the enlargements have probably provided strong incentives to the Member States to reconsider the constitutional situation with regard to the constraining effects of the Treaty. This has to be taken into account when considering the two steps of constitutional recontracting: the Single European Act (SEA) and the Treaty on European Union (EU).

The decisive constitutional step: the SEA

The first step – the SEA – consisted partly of measures which were overdue when considering Artt. 3 and 8 of the EEC Treaty. To establish an internal market that "shall comprise an area (...) in which the free movement of goods, persons, services and capital is ensured" (Art. 13 SEA) has been on the agenda of the Community since 1958. However, the SEA gave a new stimulus in that direction. It was based on the Commission's White Paper on Completing the Internal Market of 1985 and gained political momentum with the Cecchini Report of 1988.

Considering the dichotomy between integration by competition and integration by intervention with regard to regulation, the SEA appears to have established further ambiguities. On the one hand, the White Paper nurtured the hope that the

---

[6] For a more detailed discussion of this development. cf. Weiler (1991) pp.2434 ff. and Mestmäcker (1994b) pp.4.

Commission would follow the competitive approach formally introduced by the "Cassis de Dijon" decision of the Court in 1979. On the other, the SEA authorized the Council to harmonize regulation following corresponding proposals of the Commission (Art. 100a(1)). Thereby, the proposals on "health, safety, environmental protection and consumer protection will take as a base a high level of protection" (Art. 100a(3)). These areas of regulation are extremely difficult to delimit.[7] As a consequence, it is more dubious than before how much room remains for "competition of regulations".

From a constitutional point of view, the SEA was a breakthrough for integration by intervention in several directions. By introducing Art. 100a. the negotiating parties definitely discharged the principle of enumerated powers as they mandated the Community to "adopt the measures for the approximation of the provision laid down by laws, regulations or administrative actions in Member States which have as their object the establishment and functioning of the internal market". This general authorization which had been interpreted extensively by the European Court enabled a new "round" of discretionary Community measures because it was up to the Community to define which rules had as their object the establishment and functioning of the internal market (cf. Petersmann (1993b, 412)).

Furthermore, after several attempts of the Commission to establish a European industrial policy[8], the SEA provided for such a policy in a special form: the promotion of research and technological development (R&TD; Art.24 SEA). It gave a firm legal basis to a policy which had become effective already in 1984: the ESPRIT programme ("European Programme for Research in Information Technology"). At that time, twelve big European firms did not need much encouragement by commissioner Davignon to pool their lobbying activities into forming a "European Information Table" and to assist the Commission in convincing a partly reluctant Council of Ministers that industry was in need of a "European technology community". Half of the European Community's (EC) financial support providing for some 240 projects during the first phase of the programme (1984 – 1988) was given to the "Big 12", the same twelve who also developed the basic concept for ESPRIT. The legal backing of this policy by the SEA initiated a bewildering variety of R&TD programmes of the Community and "an amazing alphabet soup of trendy acronyms" (Curzon Price (1991, 136)). It opened a new field of purpose-

---

[7] Art. 100b seems to establish the principle of mutual recognition of national regulations – i.e. the "Cassis de Dijon" approach – for all provisions not harmonized by the end of 1992 after the Commission having presented a list of such regulations. By the beginning of 1993, however, the Commission had not presented this list (Langhammer, 1993, pp.15f.).

[8] The basic conception of a European industrial policy goes back to the Collonna Memorandum of 1970. Industrial policy was introduced as a "new Community instrument" in 1978 and concretized in an encompassing document in 1982.

oriented sectoral policies favouring anew vested interests at the expense of the European citizens.[9]

Another part of the SEA – on social and economic cohesion (Art. 23 SEA) – widened the legal basis for a policy direction which had been initiated already by the EEC Treaty (Part 3, Title III on social policy) and by the establishment of the European Fund on Regional Development in 1975: The attempt of reducing or removing interregional differences in economic development, which reflect market assessments of different locations.[10] To this respect, the EC authorities have an amazing variety of different "funds" at their disposal. Apart from the dysfunctional, purpose-oriented character of such funds, they reveal another constitutional problem caused by every effort of political discretion: It initiates a redistribution struggle within the Community. The criterion of "social and economic cohesion" can hardly be assessed by the courts because of its lacking material content. It is a "weasel word" opening the field for the EC authorities to start programmes and use funds in the name of almost every conceivable "social" purpose. And it encourages interest groups – but especially in this case, national governments not being able to finance some more or less requisite projects of regional development on the national level – to demand new financial privileges by referring to the objective of economic and social cohesion.

3. THE CONSTITUTIONAL CHANGE OF "MAASTRICHT"

As argued in the previous section, the non-market elements contained in the European economic constitution as well as the provisions allowing discretionary political action on behalf of the Community have been decisively strengthened already by the SEA. In this section, we intend to show that, as a consequence of the Treaty on European Union,[11] control and guidance of private economic activities by competition will be further replaced by corporatist structures.

---

9   Until now, the EC authorities did not try very hard to evaluate the results of the different R&TD policies (for a corresponding systematic concept including empirical results on the record of the SCIENCE programmeme, cf. Vetterlein (1991)). According to empirical evidence, as far as it is available, the success of the different R&TD programmemes was rather small (for corresponding assessments, cf. Starbatty/Vetterlein (1990), Oberender/Fricke (1992)).

10   For a corresponding overview, cf. Klodt/Stehn (1992), Schäfers (1993).

11   We shall not discuss the provisions on Monetary Union (Artt. 105 ff.) which have been and still are the object of well substantiated criticism by many economists. For corresponding analyses, cf. Hauser (1992), Ohr (1993) and Vaubel (1993).

3.1. Ambiguities as a Characteristic Feature

At a first glance, the Treaty of European Union (EU) appears to reaffirm the basic decision with regard to the economic constitution of the Community which can be found in Art. 3 of the EEC Treaty (section 2.2). According to Art. 3a(1) (EU Treaty), the economic policy adopted by the Community and the Member States will be "conducted in accordance with the principle of an open market economy with free competition". Equally, self-coordination of private agents through market transactions and self-control through undistorted competition as well as a further opening-up of the EU towards countries outside are confirmed by Artt. 3c, 3g and 110(1), respectively. -

However, it is very difficult – if not impossible – to see how this basic decision can be upheld in view of the new competences attributed to the Community[12] according to Art. 3. Considering this provision, the new activities are of equal rank when compared with those conducive to "an open market economy with free competition". As we shall argue particularly with regard to industrial policy (Title XIII of the EU Treaty), the additional activities necessarily discriminate, for example, between sectors, enterprises, special activities (e.g. types of applied research) and occupations. This, however, means that distortions of competition are becoming practically unavoidable. And given the material content of the provisions, it is hardly possible to challenge them in court, except for the observance of rules of competence and procedure (cf. Mestmäcker (1991/93, 72 f.)).

Besides its ambiguity, the EU Treaty establishes direct and indirect links between the various fields of interventionist activities. This, again, can be demonstrated by analysing industrial policy. Because of these linkages, Title XIII provides a kind of superstructure to the interventionist policies introduced already by the SEA. However, these policy mandates themselves have been widened by the EU Treaty.

The provisions on R&TD were supplemented by the clause that the Community shall promote "all the research activities deemed necessary by virtue of the Chapters of this Treaty" (Art. 130f(1)). This represents a more or less general authoriza-

---

[12]   In view of the new competences, it is frequently argued that the principle of subsidiarity introduced by the Maastricht Treaty (Art. 3b) represents a powerful safeguard against an overexpansion of the Community (Union) and thus can be interpreted as an important amendment of the SEA. But the effectiveness of "this new, legally binding general principle" (Summit of Lisbon, June 1992) will depend upon its justiciability. The doubts which have been raised to this respect (cf. also Grimm (1992), Mestmäcker (1994a)) have been strongly expressed by the former president of the European Court of Justice, Lord Mackenzie-Stuart: "To decide whether a given action is more appropriate at Community level, necessary at the Community level, effective at Community level is essentially a political topic. It is not the sort of question a Court should be asked to decide" (Mackenzie-Stuart (1991, 42)).

tion for the Community to promote any kind of research activities interpreted as "necessary". The same extension of discretionary Community activities can be observed in the field of economic and social cohesion. First, a new fund – the "cohesion fund" – was added to the already existing funds. Second, a corresponding general authorization for equivalent Community action which was not provided by the SEA can be found now in Art. 130b (EU Treaty): "If specific actions prove necessary outside the Funds and without prejudice to the measures decided upon within the framework of the other Community policies, such actions may be adopted by the Council". Apart from this, the Treaty establishes further new fields of Community action, such as education, vocational training and youth (Art. 126f). culture (Art. 128), public health (Art. 129), consumer protection (Art. 129a), and trans-European networks (Art. 129b and c).

Together with the encompassing authorization to industrial policy, these regulations offer a considerable number of opportunities for the EC authorities to discretionary policies incompatible with the principle of undistorted competition (Art. 3(g) EU Treaty). This changes the constitutional situation profoundly. Before, the Member States were constrained in their discretionary policies in view of the principle of undistorted competition (Art. 3f EEC Treaty), Now, the EC authorities themselves are encouraged to take actions which are likely to be incompatible with this principle. but seemingly compatible with a new objective of the Community: "to ensure that the conditions necessary for the competitiveness of the Community industry exist" (Art. 130(1)). This may even lead to a situation where the Community would have to tolerate an activity by a Member State. e.g. the granting of aid in pursuing an industrial policy, which before could be prevented according to Art. 92 (EEC Treaty).

(End of excerpt)

2. A pragmatic French/British response

The German debate has not really been perceived outside Germany. That is to say, the German example has not led to a Europe-wide discussion on the value and the need of a European Economic Constitution. It is felt only in the position German lawyers take on the reach of market regulation and on the key role of market integration. The response to the theoretical debate is much more pragmatic. Efforts concentrate not so much on the development of a coherent concept but on the compromise character of the treaties unifying different notions on the function of market integration vs. market regulation in one and the same document. There is Article 30 which restricts state action, but Article 36 and 'the rule of reason' Cassis de Dijon allows the state room for manoeuvre. There are Articles 85 and 86 which affect the state as a commercial undertaking – but more important, there is Article 5 read with Articles 85 and 86 which restricts the state's power to regulate the economy where this will produce anti-competitive results. How far does Article 5 go in restricting state action? Of course, Article 5 has elements of both controlling and allowing, so here too there is a kind of balance in the law about what the state can do. Then there is Article 90(1) which controls the state, whereas Article 90(2) gives some limited protection to state functions. So we have Articles 30/37/5/85,86/90(1) which all restrict state powers to intervene in the economy. But we have also Articles 36/5/90(2) which admit that the states have a degree of flexibility in managing their economies. Is it possible to extract from this a single general principle of what the states can and cannot do? Article 3(f) talks of not 'distorting' competition – but what has that come to mean in EC law?

The European Court's caselaw on Article 90 bears witness to the efforts to balance private market freedoms against state monopolies, but the Court has understandably avoided giving definite and final answers. The policy of the Court, if there is any, is not explicitly to prohibit state exclusivity *per se* nor to support private market freedoms *per se*. The court is not overtly advocating privatization against state monopolies, or establishing market freedoms and cutting back national economic policies. So far, one may dare to summarize the jurisprudence in the following way: the existence of exclusive rights receives the green light from the Court, that is to say Member States are allowed to maintain a specific national economic policy, as concretized in a state monopoly, but the exercise of those exclusive rights may receive the red light, that is to say the way in which the state monopoly interferes with market freedoms of private parties. Though this sums up the jurisprudence it is somewhat misleading, because by restricting the exercise of the rights, the court may throw into doubt the very existence of the rights. Accordingly it is possible that there is a hidden – even subconscious! – policy in the Court which is challenging State monopolies with increasing vigour. Thus, although the Court avoids taking a clear cut position, private market freedoms have a priority over state monopolies and social considerations inherent in the building of state monopolies are sacrificed to market freedoms.

One cannot neglect the institutional role of the Commission as policy maker. It (DG IV) has increasingly been prepared to use Article 90 to challenge state monopolies – this was a major policy plank of Commissioner Leon Brittan. This policy has cast doubt on the survival of many state monopolies (energy, postal services, telecommunications and so on) which in the past, although theoretically controllable under Article 90, remained in practice immune from threat. The Commission is tempted to 'feed' the Court with cases which will allow the Court to clarify the scope of its (the Commission's) powers to control state monopolies. For example in the telecommunications case, the Commission adopted a Directive hoping to provoke the states into challenging before the Court the validity of the

Directive in order to allow the Court to set the groundrules for Article 90(3) – Case C-202/88 *France* v. *Commission*. The Court has been cautious, not to say cunning, in meeting the Commission's aspirations without unduly upsetting the Member States – for example in its partial annulment of telecommunications Directive, also in Dutch/ Spanish postal services, courier services, Case C-271/90 *Spain* v. *Council*: Commission acts annulled by Court for faulty procedures, but the principle of control of state monopolies via Article 90 appears well accepted and indeed advanced by the Court (cf. Chapter 5).

C. THE POSITION OF THE INDIVIDUAL IN THE EUROPEAN ECONOMIC CONSTITUTION

The Treaty does not offer any elaboration of the legal position of the individual, even though some provisions, such as Articles 85, 119, refer to him or her. This is due to the fact that the Treaty is a piece of public international law and that the addressee of public international law is usually and normally the state and not the individual, perhaps with the exception of human rights. Community law is different and it is this difference which is characteristic of Community law and which is the real legal revolution in the relationship between national legal orders and a supranational treaty.

1. Supremacy and direct effect

The Court transformed the Treaty of Rome from a piece of international legislation addressed to states into an independent legal order, which grants enforceable rights to individuals flowing directly from the Treaty. The Community legal order provides for rights which the individual by reference to provisions of the Treaty may enforce against both its own state and against other states. The pillars of the Community legal order are *direct effect* and *supremacy*. It started with Case 26/62 *Van Gend en Loos*, where the Court established that rules of the Treaty may have direct effect if they are concise enough to be enforced. From there it was only one step further to dictate that the Community legal order must have supremacy over national law, Case 6/64 *Costa* v. *ENEL*.

The role and importance of *direct effect* and *supremacy* cannot be overestimated. The enforceability of individual rights made the shaping of a European Economic constitution of the Court possible. The technical means for the Court was the Article 177 procedure which was and is instrumentalized by private individuals to challenge statutory trade restrictions by relying on Community law. This is due to a long established characteristic of European Community law, that it is enforced at two levels. This phenomenon is commonly known as the principle of 'dual vigilance'. The first level of enforcement is the 'supranational' level, whereby the European Commission supervises the observance of EC law and if necessary initiates proceedings before the Court in the event of default. The second level of enforcement is at national level, based on the direct effect of Community law.

2. Economic rights and human rights

The legal means for the private individuals were and are most of all the four freedoms. And this is the reason why the case-law of the European Court focuses so much on the interrelationship between private freedoms and state intervention, between market integration and market regulation, between negative integration and positive integration. At bottom, the problems remain the same: what kind of statutory action or statutory intervention into the market may be upheld as compatible with the Community legal order?

The shaping of individual rights is not limited to the enforceability of market freedoms. The economy touches on morality and on human rights – see Chapter 12. A good example of the spillover effect in relation to rights is Case C-159/90 *SPUC* v. *Grogan – Irish Abortion*. Those who want to liberalize public morality in Ireland may win the case if they manage to demonstrate that the individual rights they claim are part of the European economic order – at the very least they would force Ireland to find justification for its laws which is recognized under EC law. Public morality appears in the perspective of EC law as a spillover effect of the market freedoms. It shows that EC law cannot deny its roots, but it shows also that EC law, even if economic in substance, is broadened and opened towards moral categories. EC economic law stands against Irish constitutional law. Who wins and who judges it? The economic rights of the Community legal order are tipped into the realm of public morality.

The same process of interpenetration can be elaborated in the field of human rights, but the other way round. Human rights are moral in substance, but they suffer from a process of economization. This can be demonstrated in *Sigurjonsson* v. *Iceland*, European Court of Human Rights, Strasbourg, 30 June, 1993: state compulsion on a taxi driver to join a private association of taxi drivers is held to violate rights of freedom of association under Article 11 ECHR. The European Community and the European Convention of Human rights are approaching each other, thereby paving the way for interconnection.

What may be especially interesting is that some fact patterns attract very similar responses from EC and ECHR law, whereas others show substantial divergence. In Sigurjonsson both EC and ECHR law would challenge the state monopoly as a restriction of freedom – in Case C-159/90 *Grogan* the focus of EC law is the claimed economic right to trade in information, it is the economic element which lends strength to the right, whereas in ECHR law the economic context actually weakens the strength of the right. In Case C-159/90 *Grogan* a significant gap appears between the purpose of rights: to trade in EC law, to express oneself in ECHR law.

3. Direct effect and social rights

So far individual rights have been understood to a large extent as freedoms given to private entities to be executed against state trade barriers. These rights are negative rights. Social rights derive to a large extent from secondary Community law, not from primary Community law. The Single European Act and the Treaty of Maastricht have introduced environmental protection and consumer protection as Titles in the EC Treaty, but these provisions formulate policy objectives not individual enforceable rights. Social rights may result from secondary Community law which is meant to specify and concretize these policy objectives. It goes without saying that a possible direct effect of secondary Community law rules to the benefit of the private individual goes to the heart of the legal order of the European Community. If individual enforceable rights exist, they balance out economic rights and add to the Economic Constitution of the Community elements of social welfare or social justice.

Chapter 11 includes a discussion of the way these rights are protected under national law. The focus here is on the scope of rights conferred by EC Law. The most complicated issues arise in relation to Directives. This may be understood with reference to Article 189:

Article 189(1)
In order to carry out their task and in accordance with the provisions of this Treaty, the European Parliament acting jointly with the Council, the Council and the Commission shall make regulations and issue directives, take decisions, make recommendations or deliver opinions.

A regulation shall have general application. It shall be binding in its entirety and directly applicable in all Member States.

A directive shall be binding, as to the result to be achieved, upon each Member State to which it is addressed, but shall leave to the national authorities the choice of form and methods.

A decision shall be binding in its entirety upon those to whom it is addressed. Recommendations and opinions shall have no binding force.

The European Court has had no difficulty in finding that sufficiently clearly phrased Treaty provisions, Regulations and Decisions are directly effective. They may therefore create rights which the individual may vindicate before national courts. By contrast, the constitutional impact of the Directive appears restricted. Article 189 envisages no direct relationship between an EC Directive and the individual. National implementing measures will be interposed. This makes Directives fragile. They are vital sources of social rights for individuals. EC social policy, environmental policy and consumer policy have all been developed by important Directives. However, those rights are available only where the state has properly implemented the Directive. It is notorious that implementation of Directives has been patchy throughout the history of the Community.

Over many years the European Court has involved itself in enhancing the practical value of Directives as sources of rights for individuals. It has often seemed to be fighting a battle against Member States' poor record of implementation. The evolution of this judicial attempt to build individual rights out of unimplemented Directives is a lesson in the possibilities and limitations of building a European Constitution involving individual rights out of the EC Treaty.

In Case 152/84 *Marshall* v. *Southampton Area Health Authority* [1986] ECR 723 the Court took the view that an unimplemented Directive was capable of direct effect against the state, though not a private party:

[46] It is necessary to recall that, according to a long line of decisions of the Court (in particular its judgment of 19 January 1982 in Case 8/81 *Becker* v. *Finanzamt Münster-Innenstadt* [1982] ECR 53), wherever the provisions of a directive appear, as far as their subject-matter is concerned, to be unconditional and sufficiently precise, those provisions may be relied upon by an individual against the State where that State fails to implement the directive in national law by the end of the period prescribed or where it fails to implement the directive correctly.

[47] That view is based on the consideration that it would be incompatible with the binding nature which Article 189 confers on the directive to hold as a matter of principle that the obligation imposed thereby cannot be relied on by those concerned. From that the Court deduced that a Member State which has not adopted the implementing measures required by the directive within the prescribed period may not plead, as against individuals, its own failure to perform the obligations which the directive entails.

[48] With regard to the argument that a directive may not be relied upon against an individual, it must be emphasized that according to Article 189 of the EEC Treaty the binding nature of a directive, which constitutes the basis for the possibility of relying on the directive before a national court, exists only in relation to 'each Member State to which it is addressed'. It follows that a directive may not of itself impose obligations on an individual and that a provision of a direc-

tive may not be relied upon as such against such a person. It must therefore be examined whether, in this case, the respondent must be regarded as having acted as an individual.

This ruling demonstrates how the Court has felt able to create rights from Directives despite the wording of Article 189, which seems to place Directives at one remove from the individual. Where the Directive is sufficiently clear and where the defendant is the state, a Directive may exert direct effect. The Court rejected in paragraph 48 the notion of the 'horizontal direct effect' of Directives. Constitutionally, the rights which arise under Directives are not directly enforceable against other private parties in the event of non-implementation. This weakens the vigour of individual rights under Community Directives. It means that individuals enjoy different levels of protection under EC Directives in different parts of the European Union depending on rates of implementation in different States.

This constitutional inequality prompted AG Lenz in Case C-91/92 *Paola Faccini Dori* v. *Recreb SRL*, opinion 9.2.1994 – Dori, [1994], ECR I-3342 *et seq.* at 67–73 to propose that the Court should accept even the horizontal direct effect of Directives.

> 67. The principle of *legitimate expectations* is invoked in favour of private individuals on whom a burden is imposed and against the horizontal effect of directives. Expectations deserving of protection certainly exist, in so far as a private individual does not have to reckon with the imposition of additional burdens provided that he acts lawfully within the context of his national legal system. On the other hand, once a directive has been published and the period for transposition has expired, the burden is foreseeable. I would ask whether the expectation that the national legislature will act contrary to Community law is worthy of protection.
>
> 68. An argument based on the *democratic principle* is put forward against the horizontal effect of directives. According to that argument, the democratic deficit, which is deplored in any event in the context of Community legislation, is increased where national parliaments are by-passed when directives are implemented.
>
> 69. As far as the alleged democratic deficit is concerned, I would observe, on the one hand, that the European Parliament's rights to collaborate in drawing up Community legislation have gradually been increased by the Single European Act and the Maastricht Treaty. On the other hand, it cannot be argued, I submit, that the national legislature is by-passed.
>
> 70. The national legislature has every freedom during the period for transposition to choose the form and means of transposing the directive into national law. Even after the period for transposition has elapsed, the obligation on the national legislature to transpose the directive continues to exist, as well as leeway to fulfil that obligation in one way or another to the extent permitted by the directive. Only provisions of directives or protective rules which are sufficiently

precise to be asserted without being fleshed out in any way and therefore have to be taken over by the national legislature would have legal effects as between the addressees of the legislation in question within the national legal system. To my mind, fears that there will be a hiatus between the legal situation existing during the intermediate period preceding the transposition of the directive into national law and that existing thereafter are groundless, since the provisions suitable for horizontal applicability must also be found in the implementing measure.

71. The objection that recognition of the horizontal direct effect of directives would increase Member States' carelessness in transposing them does not convince me, since the national legislature remains responsible for their implementation in full. Recognition in principle of horizontal effect might possibly encourage Member States to effect transposition within the prescribed period in order to forestall horizontal application by the authorities and courts of the Community and the Member States. In my view, the arguments on the educative effect of horizontal applicability balance themselves out and hence do not tip the balance for or against.

72. Before concluding, I would further observe that, if directives are recognized as having horizontal effect, the necessary consequences should be drawn as regards *legal protection*. Thus they should be capable of being challenged – as regulations and decisions are – under the second paragraph of Article 173.

73. In the final analysis, I consider that for reasons of legal certainty it is not possible to envisage directives having horizontal effect as regards the past. As far as the future is concerned, however, horizontal effect seems to me to be necessary, subject to the limits mentioned, in the interests of the uniform, effective application of Community law. In my view, the resulting burdens on private individuals are reasonable, since they do not exceed the constraints which would have been applied to them if the Member State concerned had acted in conformity with Community law. Lastly, it is the party relying on the unconditional and sufficiently precise provisions of a directive who will have to bear the risk of the court proceedings.

However the Court Case C-91/92, judgment 14.7.1994 – *Paola Faccini Dori* v. *Recreb SRL* [1994]; ECR I-3355 at 19–28, declined this invitation. It maintained its view that Directives are incapable of horizontal direct effect:

Whether the provisions of the directive concerning the right of cancellation may be invoked in proceedings between a consumer and a trader

19   The second issue raised by the national court relates more particularly to the question whether, in the absence of measures transposing the directive within the prescribed time-limit, consumers may derive from the directive itself a right of cancellation against traders with whom they have concluded contracts and enforce that right before a national court.

20   As the Court has consistently held since its judgment in Case 152/84 *Marshall* v. *Southampton and South-West Hampshire Health Authority* [1986] ECR 723, paragraph 48, a directive cannot of itself impose obligations on an individual and cannot therefore be relied upon as such against an individual.

21   The national court observes that if the effects of unconditional and sufficiently precise but untransposed directives were to be limited to relations between State entities and individuals, this would mean that a legislative measure would operate as such only as between certain legal subjects, whereas, under Italian law as under the laws of all modern States founded on the rule of law, the State is subject to the law like any other person. If the directive could be relied on only as against the State, that would be tantamount to a penalty for failure to adopt legislative measures of transposition as if the relationship were a purely private one.

22   It need merely be noted here that, as is clear from the judgment in *Marshall*, cited above (paragraphs 48 and 49), the case-law on the possibility of relying on directives against State entities is based on the fact that under Article 189 a directive is binding only in relation to 'each Member State to which it is addressed'. That case-law seeks to prevent 'the State from taking advantage of its own failure to comply with Community law'.

23   It would be unacceptable if a State, when required by the Community legislature to adopt certain rules intended to govern the State's relation – or those of State entities – with individuals and to confer certain rights on individuals, were able to rely on its own failure to discharge its obligations so as to deprive individuals of the benefits of those rights. Thus the Court has recognized that certain provisions of directives on conclusion of public works contracts and of directives on harmonization of turnover taxes may be relied on against the State (or State entities) (see the judgment in Case 103/88, *Fratelli* Constanzo v. *Comune di* Milano [1989] ECR 1839 and the judgment in Case 8/81 *Becker* v. *Finanzamt Münster-Innenstadt* [1982] ECR 53).

24   The effect of extending that case-law to the sphere of relations between individuals would be to recognize a power in the Community to enact obligations for individuals with immediate effect, whereas it has competence to do so only where it is empowered to adopt regulations.

25   It follows that, in the absence of measures transposing the directive within the prescribed time-limit, consumers cannot derive from the directive itself a right of cancellation as against traders with whom they have concluded a contract or enforce such a right in a national court.

26   It must also be borne in mind that, as the Court has consistently held since its judgment in Case 14/83 *Von Colson and Kamann* v. *Land Nordrhein Westfalen* [1984] ECR 1891, paragraph 26, the Member States' obligation arising from a directive to achieve the result envisaged by the directive and their duty under Article 5 of the Treaty to take all appropriate measures,

whether general or particular, is binding on all the authorities of Member States, including, for matters within their jurisdiction, the courts. The judgments of the Court in Case C-106/89 *Marleasing* v. *La Comercial Internacional de Alimentación* [1990] ECR I-4135, paragraph 8, and Case C-334/92 *Wagner Miret* v. *Fondo de Garantia Salarial* [1993] ECR I-6911, paragraph 20, make it clear that, when applying national law, whether adopted before or after the directive, the national court that has to interpret that law must do so, as far as possible, in the light of the wording and the purpose of the directive so as to achieve the result it has in view and thereby comply with the third paragraph of Article 189 of the Treaty.

27   If the result prescribed by the directive cannot be achieved by way of interpretation, it should also be borne in mind that, in terms of the judgment in Joined Cases C-6/90 and C-9/90 *Francovich and Others* v. *Italy* [1991] ECR I-5357, paragraph 39, Community law requires the Member States to make good damage caused to individuals through failure to transpose a directive, provided that three conditions are fulfilled. First, the purpose of the directive must be to grant rights to individuals. Second, it must be possible to identify the content of those rights on the basis of the provisions of the directive. Finally, there must be a causal link between the breach of the State's obligation and the damage suffered.

28   The directive on contracts negotiated away from business premises is undeniably intended to confer rights on individuals and it is equally certain that the minimum content of those rights can be identified by reference to the provisions of the directive alone (see paragraph 17 above).

This does not mean unimplemented Directives have *no* legal effect in relations between private parties. The Court requires national courts to interpret relevant national law in the light of an improperly unimplemented Directive – a kind of 'indirect effect'.

Case C-106/89 *Marleasing* v. *La Comercial Internacional de Alimentacion* [1990] ECR I-4135

[8] ...[T]he obligation of Member States under a Directive to achieve its objects, and their duty by virtue of Article 5 of the Treaty to take all necessary steps to ensure the fulfilment of that obligation, binds all authorities of Member States, including national courts within their jurisdiction. It follows that in applying national law, whether the provisions concerned pre-date or post-date the Directive, the national court asked to interpret national law is bound to do so in every way possible in the light of the text and the aim of the Directive to achieve the results envisaged by it and thus to comply with Article 189(3) of the Treaty.

This approach promises a subtle penetration of EC law into the national legal order. It does, however, depend heavily for its practical success on the capabilities of the national judiciary. Europeanization of private law will be the cornerstone for the use and usefulness of the concept of 'indirect effect'.

Moreover, where failure to implement a Directive causes loss to an individual, the Court has recognized that individuals may sue the State for compensation. This is the ruling in Cases C-6, C-9/90 *Andrea Francovich and others* v. *Italian State* [1991] ECR I-5357, examined at more length in Chapter 11. This ruling is especially important from the perspective of the protection of individual rights, because it envisages a claim even where direct effect is lacking.

Neither *Marleasing* (interpretation of national law in the light of a Directive) nor *Francovich* (state liability for failure to implement) completely fill the gap caused by refusal to accept that Directives are capable of horizontal direct effect. However, both go some way to alleviating its harshest effects for the individual robbed of EC rights by non-implementation of a Directive. The success or failure of possible effects of Directives to the benefit of the private individual will to a large extent decide on the character of the Economic constitution of the EC, whether it relies on economic rights on the four freedoms alone, or whether it integrates social rights in the concept.

QUESTIONS

1   'As a result of *Van Gend en Loos*, the unique feature of Community law is its ability to impinge directly on the lives of individuals, who are declared to be the "subjects" of the new legal order, entitled as such to invoke rights "which become part of their legal heritage". The effect of *Van Gend en Loos* was to take Community law out of the hands of politicians and bureaucrats and to give it to the people. Of all the Court's democratizing achievements none can rank so highly in practical terms.' (Mancini and Keeling, Democracy and the European Court of Justice, **57**, *Modern Law Review* (1994) pp.175, 183.)

Do you agree with this analysis of *Van Gend en Loos*? How should the ruling in *Dori* be viewed from this perspective?

2   What are the limits that *Dori* places on the development of constitutional rights – is *Dori* a reflection of the Court 'running scared' that it should not be too ambitious in the wake of the *Bundesverfassungsgericht*'s ruling? It seems important that in *Dori* the Court mentioned specifically constitutional limitations on Community competence to adopt acts that bind individuals. This seems to follow the *Bundesverfassungsgericht*'s 'warnings'.

2   Internal Market and Industrial Policy

A. INTRODUCTION TO THE SUBJECT MATTER

The activities of private parties may lead to significant restructuring of the market. This is especially apparent in the field of mergers and takeovers. Changes in corporate control may radically affect the competitive structure of the market. Such market adjustment may attract the attention of the state – either the national states or the 'European State' (cf. Chapter 1), or even both.

An oversimplified example serves to make the point. In a particular sector, the two largest firms in the European Community are French and German. They decide that they will merge. Initially that is a simply a market decision, governed by the EC competition rules (Chapter 4). Why should the state or the Community wish to intervene? Several factors may come into play.

A national state – France or Germany – may wish to intervene to block the merger. The state may consider that the deal will lead to anti-competitive implications. Competition in the market will become significantly restricted. However, the question arises whether the individual Member States should hold competence to regulate a deal which is of wider relevance to the European market. In so far as there are anti-competitive implications, should that not be a matter for the 'European State' to regulate, for it is a matter arising out of the European market?

A second motivation for action by the Member States may be directly linked with the desire to protect the national market. The French or German state may wish to intervene precisely because it does not wish to see the disappearance of 'its' firm into a European firm. Such a policy confronts directly the process of market integration. It would be likely to fall foul of the law of market integration.

The 'European State' – the Community – also has a number of factors to take into account in considering its policy. (It is not at this stage considered precisely what powers the Community possesses in the field: they are constitutionally limited). There are initial attractions in the deal for the Community. It is a vehicle of market integration. It creates a European firm and is confirmation of the process of establishing the European market. There is no rationale for blocking such a market process. However, if the two firms are the most powerful in the sector concerned, the result of the creation of the European firm is a severe reduction in competition. Potentially, the creation of a European firm in a European market may allow that firm to dominate that market. Mergers may produce monopolies. That may be a reason for blocking such a market process.

Another ingredient should be added to the mix. This is the external aspect. The European market does not exist in isolation. It is part of the global market. The creation of a European firm which is not subject to effective competition from other European firms is not a cause for concern where the European market remains open to competition from firms from outside Europe. Only where competition in Europe is restricted for structural or regulatory reasons is it appropriate to assess competition from the perspective of Europe alone. In a perfectly competitive global market the creation through merger of a single powerful European firm is not anti-competitive. In a European market which is not open to external competition, such a merger will be severely anti-competitive.

The final aspect concerns the extent to which Europe should be prepared to accept restrictions on competition internally where they serve to increase the competitiveness of the European firm globally. Put bluntly, should the 'European State' put up with a monopolistic home market if that monopoly producer is thereby given a sufficiently strong economic base to be able to compete effectively in the world market, as a 'European Champion'. The Japanese experience suggests – definitely not.

The examination involves state reaction to market decisions which lead to restructuring of the market. A separate question asks whether the state – national or Community – should intervene to promote, induce or to require such restructuring. This is the subject matter of industrial policy. It suggests a subordination of markets to states, where public authorities take decisions which would not otherwise have been taken by private parties. Such state intervention may be based on economic inadequacy in the market, on strengthening infant industries to make them fit for the market or, more generally, it may involve the pursuit of state social policy.

Where Member States pursue such policies of intervention, the competitive distortion may be addressed under European economic law. There might then be a clash between (national) state and (European) market. What policies can the Member States be allowed to pursue in conformity with the development of the European market? Can they subsidize national industries, directly or indirectly, and what is the role of the European Community and more specifically of the Commission, if Member States do so? This is the difficult issue of the legality and the legitimacy of state aids (cf. Chapter 3).

Where the Community pursues such policies, it is assuming the role of 'European State' in a European market. The development of Community policy making of this type has been hotly contested. The key issue turns around the desirability and the existence of an EC industrial policy. It is disputed how far the Community should have such powers and, even where Community competence has been (grudgingly) accepted, it is disputed how it should exercise them. In particular, there is a fundamental division between the French willingness to see industrial policy developed and the German/British antipathy to such intervention. This argument can be traced both in merger control (Case No IV/M. 053 of 2 October 1991 – *Aerospatiale-Alenia/de Havilland* (91/619/EEC), OJ L 334, 42 *et seq.*) where the question is the response of the Community to private market decisions, but also in industrial policy where the question is how far the Community itself should shape policy.

B. INDUSTRIAL POLICY

Until the adoption of the Maastricht Treaty there had been no power conferred on the Community to regulate industrial policy. The Commission even avoided the term and spoke instead of industrial strategy. Since the early 1970s the Commission had tried nevertheless to build up a European concept of industrial policy, but failed because of the reluctance and sometimes overt resistance of some Member States in the Council of Ministers. If at all, a European industrial policy existed with respect to specific sectors only, like coal and steel, and more recently, space and information technology. *Article 130* paves the way for the development of a European industrial policy on a solid legal basis:

TITLE XIII

INDUSTRY

Article 130

1. The Community and the Member States shall ensure that the conditions necessary for the competitiveness of the Community's industry exist.

For that purpose, in accordance with a system of open and competitive markets, their action shall be aimed at:

- speeding up the adjustment of industry to structural changes;

- encouraging an environment favourable to initiative and to the development of undertakings throughout the Community, particularly small and medium-sized undertakings;

- encouraging an environment favourable to cooperation between undertakings;

- fostering better exploitation of the industrial potential of policies of innovation, research and technological development.

2. The Member States shall consult each other in liaison with the Commission and, where necessary, shall coordinate their action. The Commission may take any useful initiative to promote such coordination.

3. The Community shall contribute to the achievement of the objectives set out in paragraph 1 through the policies and activities it pursues under other provisions of this Treaty. The Council, acting unanimously on a proposal from the Commission, after consulting the European Parliament and the Economic and Social Committee, may decide on specific measures in support of action taken in the Member States to achieve the objectives set out in paragraph 1.

This Title shall not provide a basis for the introduction by the Community of any measure which could lead to a distortion of competition.

The Commission has anticipated the objectives of *Article 130* in its Communication to the Council and to the European Parliament on *'European industrial policy for the 1990s'*, Bulletin of the European Communities, Supplement 3/91. Here the Commission has developed its perspectives for the 1990s, and perhaps more importantly of its understanding of what a European industrial policy should stand for. Here we take a close look at the scope of the Commission's understanding of the industrial policy.

The concept of Community industrial policy

The present communication aims at developing an industrial policy concept for the Community as a whole. It lays the emphasis on the need to concentrate on the creation of the right business environment and on the priority to give to a positive, open and subsidiarity-oriented approach. The case for such a concept for the Community is dictated both by the experience of the recent past and by the main features of the European economy. Sectoral approaches to industry policy can work during a period but they entail inevitably the risk of delaying structural adjustments and thereby creating job losses in the future. Openness to international trade and respect of the rules governing such trade deliver the right signals to the economy and preclude the recourse by the Community to the various types of defensive measures commonly used to protect domestic producers in the furtherance of such policies. By experience, a competitive environment applied to all on the same basis is the best guarantee for a strong and competitive industry.

The industrial policy concept for the Community should therefore be built around an adequate balance between the following key elements:

(i) first, laying down stable and long-term conditions for an efficiently functioning market economy: maintenance of a competitive economic environment, as well as a high level of educational attainment and of social cohesion;

(ii) second, providing the main catalysts for structural adjustment. In this respect, the completion of the internal market has a strategic role to play. The principles on which the internal market programme are based built around the harmonization of essential items and the mutual recognition of Member States' own systems also provide optimal opportunities for industrial development;

(iii) third, developing the instruments to accelerate structural adjustment and to enhance competitiveness.

The Community approach

The internal market itself represents an essential step for business to look, think and act strategically beyond national borders. A number of other measures are necessary to facilitate the process of internationalization by strengthening the ability of European industry to compete both on its own market and globally. The internal market is also open to firms from third countries. Therefore it is all the more important to prepare European industry for stronger competition.

The process by which industry adapts, on a permanent basis, to the signals provided by the market can best be described under the heading of structural adjustment. It comprises the steady shifting of resources in reply to these signals towards the most productive outlets, and thereby enables an ever higher standard of living to be attained. Structural adjustment and international competitiveness are closely linked since the ability to produce effectively for markets comes precisely from that speedy adjustment of resources to demand which is at the basis of structural adjustment. European industry must find its own path, but it must also be willing to learn from others. Therefore, European industrial policy must provide a reasonable framework for industry to compete successfully world-wide. Effective competition, financial and societal incentives for new business formation are the most important conditions for creating the necessary breeding ground for a market economy.

Behind the Community's approach, therefore, to industrial policy lies the will to promote the most efficient functioning of markets. A dynamic industrial policy concerns the effective and coherent implementation of all those policies which impinge on the structural adjustment of industry. Three axes can be used to build an effective industrial approach:

(i) maintaining a favourable business environment

An efficient market economy requires that the main initiative and responsibility for structural adjustment must lie with economic operators. This means that public authorities may take accompanying measures to assist and speed up the process, particularly in the area of infrastructural provision (for example education, energy and telecommunications networks, research and development capacity), but can never substitute for the decisions to be made by business. The link between risk and rewards cannot be separated and must be borne by firms. The necessary environment for industrial development is, however, not always easy to achieve. Special interests are always attempting to obtain favourable treatment at the expense of the free play of market forces. European industrial policy must convince firms that such competition hindering activities prove ultimately counter-productive.

Creation of a favourable business environment also involves ensuring that superfluous and niggling bureaucratic regulation is eliminated. Community policies must also fulfil this requirement. The internal market must be made as unbureaucratic as possible. This includes especially a horizontal approach to harmonization; sector-specific rules should only be made in exceptional cases. Both the Community and the Member States have therefore undertaken actions during the last decade specifically aimed at ensuring that in the development of regulation and procedures account is taken of the need not to impose undue burdens on industry, particularly on smaller businesses. The freer enterprise climate thus created has led to the creation and development of many small businesses which in turn has contributed significantly to the growth in employment.

Such measures must continue to be applied if a healthy business environment is to be maintained. Arrangements for ensuring that representatives of industry, including those of SMEs, are consulted at the earliest possible stage in the preparation of proposals which will affect them in the conduct of their business, are of particular importance. This does not mean that legitimate policy objectives, such as those in the social, environmental and consumer protection areas must be sacrificed to the interests of industry. Their impact on industry must, however, be considered so that a reasonable and balanced approach can be adopted.

(ii) implementing a positive approach to adjustment

A positive approach to industrial adjustment implies the recourse to policy which enables public authorities to avoid 'defensive' industrial policies of a protectionist nature; policies which have resulted in the past from the failure to anticipate in time necessary adjustments or as a manner of easing the adaptation required. This has only partially been successful, for example in steel policy. Most 'sectoral' policies in practice have been directed more towards social objectives than the achievement of adjustment. On the contrary, the Community's industrial approach should be based on the active promotion of positive adjustment. Sectoral policies must promote structural adjustment and not retard it. Sector-specific policies have to be carefully examined and possibly adapted.

(iii) maintaining an open approach to markets

The optimal allocation of resources requires that markets should be open, both outside as well as inside the Community. Without open markets the benefits of competition and specialization cannot be reaped. Therefore, market opening should be generalized and all partners must participate equally in the process on the basis of mutual comprehension and effective implementation of rules which guarantee the proper functioning of trade.

The community will also remain open for direct investment from third countries. Direct investment is an invigorating competitive element by which technical know-how and industrial competence are exchanged and international economic integration put on a broader basis.

Three main areas cover the principal stages of structural adjustment:

(i)   prerequisites required for structural adjustment to get under way:
(ii) catalysts, which act on the willingness of business to undertake adjustment in reply to pressures and opportunities;
(iii) accelerators, which further develop structural adjustment.

Ensuring the necessary prerequisites for adjustment

In order for industry to actively participate in the process of structural adjustment a number of prerequisites need to be met.

Securing a competitive environment: an essential task

In order to achieve competitive conditions the following are essential.

First, the greatest vigilance should be exercised on very large concentrations. Such vigilance should ensure the best combination between the requirements imposed by international competition and the maintenance of balanced and competitive conditions of operation between operators on the domestic market.

Globalization of markets enables not only greater economies of scale to be reaped but also specialization for more defined market segments. At the same time, greater standardization of products places a premium on product innovation, manufacturing excellence, design, reliability compared with the more traditional factors like proximity to markets, distribution systems and customer loyalty. The bases for competition are considerably modified, in particular through rising barriers to entry from higher minimum efficient scales of operations, and more and more intensive research and development expenditure. Competition policy must also take this into account. It is essential for the appreciation of the problem of concentrations that this appreciation should not be limited to the Community market when concentrations are subject to international competition.

Faced by such tendencies towards globalization, European firms must be able to meet the terms of competition as appropriate. In turn, this implies that great care be taken over the definition of the relevant market on which competition must be maintained. Countries with internationally successful industrial sectors have usually been found to possess several competitive firms in the same industry – even when their domestic markets are quite small. Indeed, domestic rivalry between firms can be said to constitute an important element in success overseas. Completion of the internal market should provide the necessary basis both to allow the development of enterprises of sufficient scale and to ensure that competition on that market can be effective. Since the conditions of competition vary considerably between sectors and over time, it will be necessary to analyse such conditions on a permanent basis.

The Regulation on the control of concentrations puts in place the necessary legal instrument for Community treatment of large mergers and acquisitions. The Regulation provides a high degree of the necessary legal security and rapidity for firms in their pursuit of suitable business strategies for competing on the internal market, which must necessarily include the possibility of growth through mergers and acquisitions as long as competition remains effective in the markets concerned. The Regulation will ensure rapid approval of mergers which are not anti-competitive.

Secondly, financial support by public authorities must be rigorously examined and controlled. As other forms of protectionism recede, the importance of State aids as an anti-competitive mechanism tends to grow. Beyond their negative effect on competition, State aids can also have serious implications for economic convergence within the Community. Large and well developed Member States will always be able to outbid less developed Member States on the periphery of the Community. The four largest Member States account for 88% of all aid granted. The objective of industrial policy should be to create the conditions which allow better control of such subsidies.

It is important to ensure that State expenditure, far from representing a positive contribution to the competitiveness of a region, does not become a covert anti-competitive mechanism which inhibits structural adjustment. Moreover, the effectiveness of the Community's policies to promote greater cohesion could be improved by some progressive reduction in aid intensities in the central and more prosperous regions.

The link between the control of State aids and economic convergence covers several aspects. Existing aid ceilings for the purposes of regional development need to be rigorously enforced. It is not so much the quantity of aid granted as the importance of the differential between existing aid schemes which acts as the spur for foot-loose industrial location. Less developed Member States can therefore make significant budgetary savings provided that the appropriate differentials on a low level are maintained. In addition to national State aids, the granting of aid in cash or kind by sub-national (regional or local) authorities needs to be monitored, since it adds to the total volume of aid and probably aggravates counter-cohesive distortions since authorities in more prosperous parts of the Community are able to offer more generous incentives.

The value of regional development grants can also be undermined by continuing State aids of a sectoral character, which by falsifying competition within an industry also alter optimal location decisions. Sector-specific aids must be limited in both duration and value, and made degressive. Their main task lies in easing structural adjustments. Finally, a return to sectoral subsidization must not be allowed to occur through the use made of existing regional development schemes in more developed parts of the Community, in particular for capital intensive investments.

Putting a stop to the international subsidy race is an important prerequisite for a further reduction in State aids in the Community. Stricter disciplines on State aids should be applied by the Community's international partners.

Maintaining a stable economic environment

The return to a stable economic environment ensuring improved functioning of the price mechanism allowed industrial recovery in the Community to occur. The maintenance of such conditions, in particular with regard to savings and investment, will continue to be required.

Fiscal policies also have a strong effect on the capacity of firms to invest, and thereby to adjust to market conditions. On the one hand, public authorities must be able to raise the necessary finance for their activities, which includes the direct taxation of enterprises. On the other hand, fiscal treatment, in particular of profits and depreciation, has an impact on the cost and availability to firms of funds for investment. Of particular importance in this context are the fiscal treatment of depreciation and retained earnings. In a time of greatly increased international competition, the impact on European competitiveness of such measures can no longer be neglected. The capital stock is ever more quickly depreciated by technological innovation. There follows a higher requirement for own capital formation, which should be promoted by fiscal policy, which is already the case in certain Member States.

Ensuring a high level of educational attainment

A high level of educational attainment represents the foundation for the necessary level of human capital which advanced economies require. Increasingly the ability to generate and assimilate new technologies, organizational methods and cultural diversity, rather than the level of knowledge itself, is becoming a prerequisite for effective structural adjustment. Lifelong learning should therefore become an attitude and practice to continuously upgrade skills. Some serious imbalances have also arisen with regard to the supply and demand of trained people. All-round education is an important advantage for European industry which can be further strengthened by greater development of specialized knowledge after school. Permanent market-oriented research and training is necessary to maintain or achieve competitive advantage on specialized markets.

Promoting economic and social cohesion

The diversity of Europe's regions presents challenges as well as advantages. The effectiveness of the large market can be enhanced by greater levels of economic cohesion among its regions. The adjustment of less favoured regions to the 1992 single market is being assisted by the Community's structural Funds, which were enhanced for this purpose. They are operating on the factors which are crucial to the competitiveness of businesses, such as the provision of advanced infrastructures and the quality of human resources. Economic convergence between Member States and greater cohesion between regions occurs more spontaneously among countries and regions which have reached a more mature level of economic development. It is important to ensure that industries in those regions which are significantly less highly developed than the central regions of the Community have access to the sort of infrastructures which will enable them to compete on more equal terms not just with other regions within Europe but also on the global market. Dialogue and partnership between industry and the public authorities have a vital role to play in this process.

Flexible, innovative, knowledge-intensive industry requires strong social cohesion. Employee information, consultation and participation in decision-making facilitates structural adjustment by securing confidence in business decisions and assisting the rapid introduction of new working methods and the re-development of human resources within the enterprise. Appropriate information and consultation practices covering employees at all levels of responsibility within the enterprise will reinforce their motivation and their receptivity to changes. A good balance between the needs of the various parties concerned will play an important constructive role in such processes.

Adjustments can also be carried out easier in those circumstances, where an adequate level of social protection provides a safety net which diminishes the risks of change and so promotes mobility. At the same time the economy and individual enterprises require a good degree of flexibility, which should not be hampered unnecessarily by too restrictive regulatory practices.

Flexible working hours, which can take various forms also of an innovative nature, will be a matter for negotiations and/or agreements, according to the level concerned. This should not only encourage the creation of new jobs, but also facilitate a better utilization of production equipment in accordance with changing market conditions and at the same time contribute to an improvement of working conditions, in particular with a view to the health of the worker and to his possibilities of better organizing his time both within and outside work. although such cohesion cannot be without costs for enterprises, these costs must be viewed in the light of the benefits that they are able to draw from it and as a necessary condition for the normal conduct of their activities. It is crucial for higher social costs to be obtained through higher productivity.

Achieving a high level of environmental protection

Continued economic growth can only be sustained by a high level of protection for the environment. As it is no longer possible to treat environmental resources without due regard to their intrinsic value, it is necessary to ensure that the utilization of natural resources is both prudent and rational. It is also necessary for the utilization cost of these resources to be internalized in the market price of products.

To begin with, the heightened concern for environmental matters led to an increased flow of information, and a complex of legislation in order to protect health and the natural environment. Increasingly, environmental awareness in underlined by growing consumer demand for products and services perceived to be environmentally friendly. Environment has a value in itself. Therefore it must be used sparingly.

In the case of acute dangers to health of the environment, outright prohibition is unavoidable. In the interests of conservation, the environment is being seen as a valuable resource on whose use public authorities must impose a framework to guard against overuse. This market-oriented approach concords with the principle that the polluter pays.

Since it is now certain that the necessity to pay due regard to the environment is imperative throughout the world for all segments of business, a leading position occupied by Community firms in the field of environmental protection can represent a major competitive advantage. Such an advantage, achieved by a high level of environmental standards, must not be allowed to erode. As international competitors to European industry also meet increasingly higher environmental standards, it is imperative that European standards can surpass or at least equal them so that European firms are not hindered in trading freely. Within the single market, it will also be necessary to meet such high levels not only to meet legislative requirements but also to facilitate consumer acceptance and to avoid fragmentation as a result of varying national measures. Having been set at a high level, environmental standards need to be predictable and stable so that industry can produce with sufficient scale to amortize the investments required. [...]

Providing the catalysts for adjustment

Certain policies play a particularly important role in industrial policy by acting as catalysts for change. Those policies which favour firms' initiative and guide them in the direction of a long-term perspective founded on the Community's interests are to be preferred. Establishing a stimulating economic environment thus requires a clear political consensus on the economic policy to be followed and the necessary resulting decisions. Such an industrial policy is anything but a policy of *laissez-faire*.

The internal market as a factor for change

Through providing a home market of the requisite size and quality, the programme to complete the internal market can be considered as industrial policy *par excellence*. It is not at all the case that at a time when competition increasingly takes the form of global competition on the major markets of the world, the importance of the home market diminishes. All competitors require a home base, from which they may subsequently add foreign operations.

The advantages for achieving economies of scale for investments on the domestic market are not only relevant for mass production, but also for the development of specialized products. As important as the size of the home market is its quality. This is based around the composition of domestic demand, for example for specialized products, and the specific elements of the cultural environment which provide special advantages for competing in particular industries. Italian success in design is an example. The way in which the internal market programme is implemented largely through the principle of mutual recognition allows many of these regional features to be exploited effectively by opening up new market opportunities without sacrificing essentially local specific advantages. In this sense the interlocking and competitive nature of the European home market is the very opposite of a homogeneous and undifferentiated mass market for standardized products. Such markets no longer offer great advantages in the face of increasingly sophisticated, quality conscious and individualistic consumers. Different tastes and cultural characteristics also in future guarantee a diversified market. The elimination of internal frontiers can lead to new competitive situations, which bring forth even better and more sophisticated goods. [...]

Standards and product quality

Over the past five years, European standardization has been transformed from a marginal activity to one which is attracting priority attention. The importance that voluntary standards have assumed in the Community's technical legislation has been the driving force behind this change. The development of a European standards system is, however, an on-going process which will take several years to complete.

Under the new approach to technical harmonization and standardization, legislation is confined to laying down the essential requirements to which products must comply in order to ensure the protection of public health or safety, or the protection of the environment or the consumer. European standards provide manufacturers with a set of technical specifications recognized in each directive as giving a presumption of conformity to the essential requirements. The European standards concerned remain voluntary.

Since the adoption of the new approach, the number of new European standards has increased rapidly from 19 in 1985 to 150 in 1989. This is still low compared to that of unharmonized national standards, and compared to the requirements for the implementation of the internal market programme.

European standards are not only required for the purpose of removing technical barriers to trade, but increasingly they are also becoming a key item for the promotion of industrial competitiveness. Standards promote competitiveness by:

–   lowering costs for producers:

- shaping customer preferences for products by their familiarity:
- enabling the emergence of new markets, particularly for developing technologies, where they are becoming a pre-condition for industrial production or marketing.

[...]

Successful standardization implies successful implementation. Credible procedures for certification, inspection and testing play a key role in creating the conditions which allow confidence to grow and mutual recognition of each Member State's procedures to become effective.

Efficient procedures for applying standards entail an added gain for competitiveness when they go beyond certification to cover also conformity assessment – including testing, quality systems and accreditation in addition to certification. It is when control takes place before production (in the course of the development of a prototype or model), or during production (either as surveillance of products or of production processes), that industry gains most advantage. Increasingly, industry is using quality systems as a source of competitive advantage and to diminish costs associated with lack of quality. Third party certification adds credibility to these efforts both internally within the firm and externally for clients.

Public procurement

The great importance of public procurement for industrial competitiveness is threefold:

(i) Firstly, the vast size of public procurement – ECU 600 billion or 16% of GDP in 1987 – means that market access is very important for all firms. Of this vast market, available information for the larger Member States shows that less than 4% is taken by imports – and in some cases less than 1%. Compared with markets in general, for which import penetration is around 20% for these countries, public procurement is still very closed.

(ii) Secondly, public procurement may enhance technological capability when it is directed towards the upgrading of marketable demand for products of the latest technology. In order to increase this effect, invitations to tender should preferably be formulated in an open manner and not fix the 'state of technology'.

(iii) Thirdly, public procurement is heavily concentrated on a relatively small group of sectors, and these industries depend on a competitive market for public procurement to develop the necessary products and skills to be successful internationally. Fewer than 20 subsectors of the 60 surveyed for procurement practices account for more than 85% of public procurement. As a result, public procurement represents a substantial proportion of total sales for power generation equipment, and computers and office machinery (30%), aerospace equipment (50%), and railway rolling stock and telecommunications equipment (90%).

The existence of considerable economies of scale in the manufacture of these products has led to high entry barriers and the creation of oligopolistic structures. The lack of innovative competition has led to a redirection of effort towards meeting existing technical requirements at the expense of product innovation, marketing and achieving value for money.

Governments have often rationalized the need to accept such situations through arguments in favour of 'national champions' in order to guarantee security of supply, to maintain a presence in certain vulnerable areas of high technology or to protect jobs. The failure of such strategies is well illustrated by the date-processing sector where Europe has consistently failed to produce internationally competitive suppliers in spite of massive public support. Without the requirement to adjust in response to the existence of a number of competitors, the necessary spur to innovation is normally lacking. So-called high technology industries quickly lose any competitive advantages provided by protection. It is precisely for these industries, therefore, that the opening-up of public procurement is of greatest importance. It will only be possible to effectively open such markets, however, if the necessary standards at European level are in place. [...]

The abolition of national quotas

Even today, more than 30 years after the Treaty of Rome, Member States continue to apply over 2000 national quotas on imports from third countries, in particular in execution of Article 115 of the Treaty, and a variety of bilateral 'voluntary export restrictions' to protect their industry from third country imports in a number of sectors, including for example automobiles, textiles, toys, porcelain and chemicals. Such arrangements are not consistent with the objectives of the internal market with its freedom for all goods and services to move throughout the Community. The internal market must also be open to goods and services from third countries once they have been legitimately imported into the Community. After completion of the internal market, it will no longer be possible to use border controls at internal frontiers in order to apply such restrictions.

The removal of third country quotas and similar measures represents an important item of industrial policy because it exposes national markets to a greater degree of international competition and by so doing prepares them for global challenges. The necessary structural adjustment which results from the removal of quantitative restrictions should be taken into account by the Community's structural policies, if necessary by horizontal measures. Defensive protective strategies and subsidies to maintain unprofitable capacity are not an appropriate response to strengthen permanently the industrial competitiveness of European industry.

A coherent legal framework for business

The internal market programme also affects the legal framework for doing business in the Community. The appropriate legal instruments need to be available for firms to choose the most appropriate legal form and size for their needs.

As far as mergers are a necessary pre-requisite for optimal company size, the internal market should provide the necessary legal conditions, subject always to the essential requirement of maintaining competition. At present, company mergers across frontiers are made more difficult than necessary from a legal point of view. In fiscal policy, the two directives on mergers, divisions, transfers of assets and exchanges of shares concerning companies of different Member States and on the Community system of taxation applicable in the case of parent companies and subsidiaries of different Member States, which were adopted by the Council on 23 July 1990 and which are due to enter into force on 1 January 1992 will remove the main tax obstacles to cooperation and restructuring of enterprises within the Community. Additional proposals will be put forward before the end of 1990 according to the orientations set out in the Commission communication to the Parliament and to the Council concerning guidelines on reforming taxation of 20 April 1990. From an industrial policy point of view, the possibility for transnational parent companies and subsidiaries to carry forward and backward losses is of outstanding interest. As far as company law is concerned, it is expected that the adoption of the tenth Directive on transnational mergers will remove the remaining obstacles inherent in the existing national legislations. The setting-up of a joint subsidiary involves at least one partner in an unfamiliar legal system while, again, the tax implications may act as a disincentive. When businesses wish to pursue jointly a single activity, they had no appropriate corporate European form.

The entry into force of the European economic interest grouping has gone some way to remedying the problem. The adoption of the European Company Statute, which has been before the Council for several months, will go a step further by allowing companies incorporated in different Member States to merge or to form a holding company or joint subsidiary of a European format, while avoiding the legal and practical constraints arising from the existence of 12 different legal systems. Since the decision to adopt such a statute will be a matter of choice for the firms themselves, and the possibility of using existing nationally constituted corporate forms will remain, this new legal form will have to find its place in competition with national and Community legal instruments. But one can expect its broad acceptance as a result of increasing European industrial cooperation. [...]

Trans-European networks

Trans-European networks form a direct part of the completion of the internal market which contribute to the integration of Community industry and markets by filling in missing links between existing national systems. Beyond the Community, trans-European networks assist in the realization of the European economic area and economic development in Central and Eastern Europe through providing the necessary technical and physical basis for doing business with the Community. Within the Community, networks assist the development of peripheral regions by facilitating their access to central regions.

Mobility of persons and fluid movement of goods calls for dense, rapid and cost-effective transport infrastructure for travellers and goods, and the elimination of remaining bottlenecks and improved integration of different types of carriers (rail-road) are of particular importance. The single market also requires a Europe-wide integrated telecommunications network and properly conceived and executed interlinking national energy distribution systems in the Community. (Work is already in progress in certain areas such as customs, statistics and social security. The third framework programme provides for prenormative research work on system integration to put in place a common methodological and standards base.) Lastly, the establishment of training networks between universities, firms and research centres of the Community has become more and more necessary to provide an international dimension to training.

The Community as a world trade partner

As a necessary complement to internal market opening, an open and vigilant trade policy is required based on the regroups enforcement of agreed international rules. The Community's approach has always been open, both as a result of its historically strong ties with the rest of the world and as a cause of its leading role in international trade. An open approach in turn requires that the rules of the game be respected by all trading partners since the Community's economy will become more sensitive to such practices in line with its even greater openness. A failure to ensure that respect for these rules is maintained would lead to renewed protectionist pressures. The aim of the Community, which is strongly attached to the principle of the balance between rights and obligations, should be to ensure that the markets of the Community's competitors are as open as that of the Community itself.

In this context, the importance of a successful conclusion of the Uruguay Round of negotiations under GATT cannot be overstressed. Such an outcome would present further opportunities for Community industry in foreign markets still protected, such as the Asian NICs, and to sectors not previously covered by the agreement, in particular services. [...]

Accelerating adjustment

A positive approach to industrial adjustment also implies the recourse to policies which can help accelerate the process. These include:

- The development of the technological capacity of the Community. The impact of technology is not limited to a few high technology sectors but affects the whole economy, both in terms of products and production methods. Thus, the mastery of generic technologies such as flexible manufacturing systems and information technologies, new materials and bio-technology possess great importance for the competitiveness of European firms. [...]

The strategic role of the diffusion and exploitation of technology means that isolated measures are inadequate for its promotion. It requires that a number of mutually coherent measures be implemented:

by strengthening the size and cooperative nature of the pre-competitive research effort. It is clear that for the effort of public authorities to bear fruit, firms must remedy the low level of their own investments for technological research, development and innovation. The creation of an appropriate fiscal environment would be of assistance on this matter;

by the promotion of an active policy for innovation based on the rapid transfer of know-how from basic research through to industrial application, by ensuring in particular the SMEs access to this know-how and their possibility to make best use of it. This policy should, as a result, have a significant portion devoted to the circulation of information, including that from abroad;

by the positive effect that a high level of standards, the implementation of technologically advanced trans-European networks and public procurement open to the most sophisticated technologies can have on demand;

by strengthening training, in particular through specialized centres of higher education.

• A dynamic policy towards small and medium-sized enterprises (SMEs). Through their contribution to flexibility in production and their capacity to adapt quickly to new market trends, SMEs play an important role in structural adjustment. Policies aimed at maintaining an enterprise culture and at the creation and development of SMEs must be maintained. Efforts to ensure that burdens for the economy are limited are particularly important for smaller firms, as are information and business services and mechanisms to improve business cooperation. Policies to improve access of smaller enterprises to Community and external markets are also important. [...]

• Better use of human resources, facilitating the introduction of new technologies and working methods through vocational training and more efficient redeployment through retraining. In the face of impending skill shortages and a much faster rate of innovation, the adaptability and quality of human capital has become a key determinant of industrial competitiveness and the one on which developed economies must place greatest reliance in future. It is important to recognize that upgrading of skills must take place throughout industry and should not be restricted merely to so-called high technology industries. The distinction between 'high-tech' and 'low-tech' industries is losing its importance. Also in traditional areas there is a permanent requirement for greater sophistication and further qualifications. European industry in the long run can hardly rely on price alone to remain competitive; it must further improve its product technology and exploit fully its reserves of productivity.

- Ensuring the requisite conditions for the development of business services. The growing complexity of production and management methods requires a dynamic and competitive business services sector. A major objective should be to extend the coverage of the internal market programme to eliminate remaining obstacles to the creation of a common market for these services. The efforts being made to achieve the internal market in the area of financial services will also result in cost-savings to industry.

Ensuring a coherent and effective approach

All policies with consequences for industrial policy must be looked at from a common perspective and be mutually compatible. However, individual policies must be developed and implemented at the appropriate level. Ensuring coherence comprises the following items.

First, as with all Community policies, the principle of subsidiarity by which the Community only tackles those tasks which can be done better at the European level must be applied to industrial affairs. With completion of the internal market, the economically relevant markets in which firms operate often no longer coincide with national boundaries. In this case external economies can be provided at European rather than national level. For instance, large-scale investment in R&D or infrastructure projects may be more efficiently carried out if national resources are more concentrated.

It will be necessary, therefore, for industrial policy to identify the correct mix of Community, national and local responsibilities. For instance, in research and development a division of responsibility between the pre-competitive aspect of Community-financed research and the Eureka projects which are closer to the market has been developed. Programmes for promoting technology transfer and the access of SMEs to research programmes are also important at EC level. Nevertheless, national R&D programmes will continue to be dominant, and the coordination of these programmes with the Community's efforts must be ensured.

Secondly, the experience of the 1970s and 1980s has shown that sectoral policies of an interventionist type do not form an effective instrument to promote structural adaptation. They have failed to make industry competitive by delaying the requirement to implement necessary adjustments, led to grave misallocation of resources and exacerbated problems of budgetary imbalances. Of course, the situation of different industrial sectors in the European economy is not static and from time to time issues affecting specific sectors have to be tackled at Community level. [...]

Special importance has to be attached in this context to coordinated efforts for research. There may also be a case for encouraging industry to set up joint research laboratories (but not necessarily Community financed), in particular to further develop sectoral applications for core technologies. Specialized institutes of higher education have also proved important for providing industry with the necessary skills and to facilitate the transfer of research (which often also takes place in such centres) to industry. Particularly high levels of training in specialized skills are also required in order to facilitate the introduction of modern manufacturing technologies.

Thirdly, greater consultation with the representatives of industry is required in order to strengthen consensus in the Community and to guide European policies towards the real problems. In developing policies and guidelines, it is particularly important that the representatives of industry be fully consulted at the earliest possible stage. This should include consultation with the representatives of SMEs as well as with those of larger enterprises. Also employee representatives must be given sufficient opportunities to make comments.
[...]

Strengthening competition internally and externally

Completion of the internal market should increase competition on the Community market. However, it will be necessary to ensure that the movements towards concentration which are taking place in anticipation of the single market do not obstruct the free play of market forces. The tendency for certain groups to acquire a dominant position under the guise of achieving a sufficient critical size should be checked. In many ways, a series of cross-border mergers which leave no firm in charge of significant markets can lead to stronger competition between the resulting groups than the national champions option. The way in which concentration takes place is therefore as important as the degree. In order to maintain competition on the Community market, the necessary legal basis has now been put in place. It remains to elaborate the appropriate means of evaluating the industrial impact of such concentrations. The implementation of the regulation will entail a full analysis of the markets concerned.

Respecting competition in international markets will become much more important. Globalization of markets and the ever greater dimension of major groups requires that mechanisms be created that can avoid the creation at international level of monopolistic or oligopolistic situations which would be unacceptable at national or regional level. The even greater impetus towards liberalization, and attendant possibilities for international firms, opened up by the Uruguay Round could lead to an increase in those anti-competitive tendencies and dominant positions which are already visible for such markets as data processing and telecommunications equipment or consumer electronics. Reflection on the means to confront this issue is required, both within the Community and at international level.

Promoting the Community's advantages

Industrial integration is to be regarded as an instrument of economic and social cohesion. Regional diversity within the Community is one of its advantages, allowing the creation of new sources of competitive advantage through appropriate specializations. The adaptation of regional industries to completion of the internal market therefore can constitute an important vector for the development of EC industry. In order to achieve this, efforts already undertaken through the structural Funds to ensure that the weakest regions develop the type of infrastructure and quality of human resources essential for the success of their firms in a competitive environment should be pursued. Technical assistance should be supplied to certain parts of industry, for example through programmes of Community initiative which attempt to improve the capacity of SMEs in less developed regions to compete. In a dynamic market, restructuring can take place without the negative consequences on employment and output that occurs in a period of recession. Underutilized resources can be put to work productively and already the advantages of several regions, particularly in the south of the Community, are also attracting investors from elsewhere in the Community.

Conclusions

I – The Commission proposes that the Council approves:

the Commission's analysis of the degree of industrial adjustment achieved so far and of its ongoing character which is required for the global competitiveness of European industry;
the concept that Community industrial policy should promote permanent adaptation to industrial change in an open and competitive market. It is based on the principle of free trade and on the competitive functioning of markets around long-term industrial and technological perspectives;
the principle that this policy be implemented through the creation of a favourable environment for firms' initiative through the coherent recourse to all those Community activities having an impact on industry;
that industrial problems at a regional or sectoral level should increasingly be resolved by horizontal measures.

II – In order to implement these principles in the current competitive context, the Commission proposes that the Community and Member States:

1. Improve the functioning of the internal market:

through ensuring its completion on the basis of the White Paper's approach, properly transposed and enforced at the national level;
through ensuring better control of public financial assistance to industry, in particular when this assistance affects highly capital-intensive investments;
through ensuring more coherence between different Community and national activities as far as they concern industrial policy. In order to achieve this and assure subsidiarity, it is important to develop dialogue and the exchange of information;

through accepting the necessity for this policy to take into consideration developments resulting from the globalization of markets, production and operators, as well as the industrial policies of the Community's main competitors.

2. Improve the functioning of the world market:

through a continuous effort to further open up and strictly implement the multilateral trading system;
through facilitating the flow of international investment;
through vigilance against unfair commercial practices, and the will to deal with them;
through facilitating cooperation with international partners of the Community, amongst others in Central and Eastern Europe;
through ensuring that the markets of the Community's competitors are as open as that of the Community itself on the basis of the principle of balance between rights and obligations.

3. Pursue those positive adjustment policies aimed at building a favourable economic environment for private initiative and investment in the Community:

by maintaining a macroeconomic framework directed towards stability and the facilitation of medium and long-term funding for industrial enterprises. In the current context of growing international economic incertitude, a dependable macroeconomic framework is more and more necessary for business;
by ensuring that the efforts of firms, the Community and Member States for technological research and development are strengthened, through greater cooperation between the parties concerned and in particular between producers and users of new technologies, and through exploiting the industrial potential of innovation and technological research and development policies at national and Community level;
by strengthening policies which take into account the special requirements of SMEs and the promotion of new business formation. In particular, national and Community actions to support intra-Community and international cooperation between SMEs and large firms should be developed;
by directing national and Community structural instruments more towards backing structural adjustment strengthening firms' competitiveness in less developed regions;
by recognizing that a high level of environmental protection offers both challenges and opportunities for industry, and that competitiveness and protection of the environment are not in opposition to one another;
by implementing effective policies to develop human resources, in particular through a life-long approach to the acquisition of skills based on detailed knowledge of industry's requirements;
by supporting the implementation of trans-European networks required for the proper functioning of the Community and wider European markets;

by ensuring that a sufficiently attentive examination of industrial development is made in order to ensure that the necessary requirements for adjustment are met.

Structural adjustment

I. Prerequisites	II. Catalysts	III. Accelerators
• Competition	• Internal market	• Research, development, technology, innovation
• Economic context	• Commercial policy	• Training
• Educational level		• Small and medium-sized enterprises
• Economic and social cohesion		• Business services
• Environmental protection		

The Commission's policy has been strongly criticized because of its interventionist approach. Ordo-liberal thinking (cf. Chapter 1) does not allow for an active industrial policy in the way it is understood by the Commission. There should be much more leeway for private undertakings to develop their own policies without statutory constraints. *Article 130* is seen as the means to put an end to the said prevailing economic constitution of the European Community based on the four freedoms and the competition rules. Ernst Steindorff, *Quo vadis Europa*, underlines below that *Article 130* may have harmful effects on the European Community because of its potential anti-competitive and anti-market effects.

QUO VADIS, EUROPE? FREEDOMS, REGULATION AND FUNDAMENTAL SOCIAL RIGHTS AFTER THE EXPANDED GOALS OF THE EC CONSTITUTION*

Ernst Steindorff

6. INDUSTRIAL POLICY

6.1.1.1 The framework   Industrial policy too is nothing new for the Community. As early as 1970, the Commission presented the Council with a first, 380 page memorandum on the Community's industrial policy. Article 130 EC .. which specially regulated industrial policy (along with numerous other provisions) might just fill the barrel of sovereign intervention to overflowing, and it could lead to the successes achieved in implementing a market-economic system in Germany and in orienting Europe towards a system of free and undistorted competition being thrown on the rubbish heap of EC history. Article 130 calls upon the Community *and* the States to engage in industrial policy. The Scientific Council to the Federal Minister of Economics even proposed taking the new provision back out of the EC Treaty. This is relevant even if it is taken into account that the unanimity provided in its Para. 3 and the final sentence of Para. 3 were first added in Maastricht and serve to restrict industrial policy to modest dimensions. Above all the great efforts which were employed in giving a competition-oriented direction to the merger control regulation could prove post facto to have been wasted. Yet only cautious criticism will be offered here, for two reasons: unlike the situation with respect to the infrastructure and the many measures on health and consumer protection, it is still not sufficiently clear how the Commission and States will use the new provision, and what specific possibilities for action open up in accordance with the future law. The most recent document of the Commission on industrial policy concerns increasing the competitiveness of the textile and clothing industry within the Community. It certainly deserves applause to the extent that it wishes to give other policies a form necessary for industrial development, and in addition work on

---

*   Ernst Steindorf, 'Weiterentwicklung der Europäischen Gemeinschaften und der Marktwirtschaft', (FIW-Schriftenreihe Heft 148, Referate des XXV. FIW-Symposiums), pp.11, 56–66, excerpt, reprinted by permission of Carl Heymann Verlag KG, Köln. Translation by John Blazek, Brussels.

creating an 'environment' favourable to this development. But the document goes further and plans the future industrial structure as though it were a general staff – thus distancing itself rather markedly from the free market economic order. In the meantime, at Maastricht the above-cited new provision was adopted, which depending on the future political composition of the Commission could give rise to more extensive measures. If one looks at the substantive goals of the Community, as they have been discussed on the basis of examples of health and consumer protection as well as with respect to infrastructure, it is no surprise that industrial policy too would be used for their implementation. Initially, however, the consultations about Article 130 focused especially on ensuring the competitiveness of the Community. That this goal is no longer dominant will become clear as we go along.

We will not focus here on other standards which support industrial policy. We will simply mention as an example that the research and development policy conducted in the Community as well as in Germany complements the industrial policy, just as it is also complemented by structural policy. Industrial policy has taken form above all through the operation of Article 92 ff EC.

Here the fundamental faith in industrial policy (as it was most recently implemented in France by Mme. Cresson in the Thomson CEA) case is called into question. In political agreement with Minister Strauss-Kahn (and e.g. Jacques Calvet, the President of Peugeot), Vice-President Bangemann affirms his belief in industrial policy, as well as in individual measures. Here one might mention his proposal for promoting training measures in the automotive industry. He and others want to discredit free-market economic policy as 'fundamentalism' or 'ideology'. Such reproaches were earlier levelled against early proponents of German cartel law such as Franz Böhm. What is really at stake is the opposition between the long-term rationality guaranteed by a competitive economic order and the irrationality of an active industrial policy interventionism, to which the EC is supposed to subscribe.

6.1.1.2 De facto importance   The main thing to emphasize is that industrial policy competences of the Community and the obligations of the states may not be played down as a mere embellishment of Community law. The Commission has in several cases declared its belief in industrial policy; the textile industry is only one example. The Commission believes that it is authorized to examine whether the Community should be active in the restructuring of the armaments industry. According to its Document COM (92) 2000, 'From the Single Act to the Post-Maastricht Period', the Commission will strive to spend 3.5 billion ECU annually between now and 1997 for the promotion of competitiveness.

At the end of 1991, a Council decision approved a programme for setting up a market for information. The Parliament showed that it even exerted pressure for industrial policy measures to be taken. This could have major effects in the future. Two examples may suffice: On 11 July 1991 the Parliament, with respect to a possible takeover offer of Hanson PLC for ICI, called upon the Commission 'to assess the foreseeable consequences of the takeover not only on current competition, but also on future technical and economic progress in the EC and in the United Kingdom, and to present a report on this matter'. And on the same day the Parliament spoke out 'for a coherent, socially and environmentally-compatible industrial policy . . . which takes greater consideration of the interdependencies and goals without losing sight of the requirement of competitiveness'. This constitutes a major step towards industrial policy. Competition is downgraded. Of course the Parliament mentions competitiveness, at least as an afterthought. But no one knows what majorities will be found there after future elections. Therefore it is decisive what authorization the rewritten EC Treaty gives for industrial policy. However, the interpretation necessary for this can here only be offered as a possible one.

The industry itself is motivated by industrial policy activities of the Commission to promote the extension of these activities. Cecimo is doing this for the machine tool industry on the basis of a Bangemann paper from November 1991, characteristically due to a slump in this economic sector. Further activities which signal the de facto importance of industrial policy will be mentioned later.

6.1.1.3 Article 130 EC   According to its wording, the new provision in the EC Treaty is aimed at the competitiveness of companies, and it affirms its faith in a competition-based free market economy. But it expressly permits (e.g. in Paragraph 3) sovereign statutory intervention, and it also provides for entrepreneurial cooperation for this purpose. It by no means limits the powers of the Community to measures for the promotion of framework conditions and for the structuring of the surrounding environment, as would correspond to the Community philosophy on industrial policy addressed above.

In the draft of the Dutch Presidency of 8 November 1991, the promotional measures of Para. 3 were limited to 'especially in favour of future-oriented industries'. The elimination of this reference by the foreign ministers in Noordwijk on 12/13 November 1991 virtually programmed the Community to promote old industries as well, as illustrated by the Commission's concern for the textile industry. This requires no comment.

6.1.2 Competitiveness

In assessing the industrial policy, it has been assumed that the policy sets as its goal the competitiveness of the industry. Does it not therefore, just like infrastructure policy, belong among the elements of the competition-based economic order? This is apparently affirmed by many, yet the answer to the question must be 'no'. The development and structuring of companies belong among the decisive competitive parameters in a competition-based free market economy. Therefore they count as part of the responsibilities of the companies themselves, even if individual members of the Commission (such as Vice-President Bangemann) label this a 'backwards' point of view. Infrastructural measures, by contrast, are those which do not themselves affect the individual companies, and which thus cannot be made into one of their competitive parameters. Here the state can take over responsibility. However, it can also leave the shaping of the infrastructure to private companies. Then it conducts competition-restricting industrial policy, in case it – as the EC is planning to do – intervenes in the private structuring.

Alongside the obligation of the states to engage in competition policy, the new regulation could mean two things above all.

6.2 Community activity on the basis of Article 130 EC

6.2.1 Industrial policy and infrastructure

This does not involve state infrastructural measures such as offering education or building roadways. Those are measures which companies normally cannot take themselves. Here the attention is focused only on measures which companies themselves can also undertake. The Community bodies might also feel themselves authorised to undertake such measures. If necessary, Article 235 EC could provide the required instrument if the measures of paragraphs 2 and 3 do not suffice. The effort focusing on infrastructure show where this can lead. Telecommunications can be adduced as an example for further efforts of the Commission. Mr. van Miert, the Commissioner responsible for transport, has already demonstrated his inclination in favour of the development of 'Euro-champions' of the aviation companies. That German measures are pursuing industrial policy not only in the new federal *Länder*, is a fact that observers outside Germany like to point out.

6.2.2 Mergers and cartels

The Commission might even have to use the new provision under certain circumstances in order – by reference to the policy competence of the Community and the systematic connection of the Community law for merger control and other cartel law – to attain something which the pertinent law had until now denied it: it could (or perhaps would even have to) call upon the new provision in order (e.g.) to approve mergers contrary to the Regulation. After all, Article 130 Para. 3 EC does say that the Community must take into account the industrial policy goals of Para. 1 when setting policy and implementing measures in other areas, that is, also in competition policy. It is telling that Vice-President Bangemann has already, in connection with the De Havilland case, demanded that all departments of the Commission should cooperate with respect to such mergers. This can only mean that points of view other than that of competition policy should also enter into the decision-making process. This modifies Articles 85 and 86 as well as the merger regulation. In a case such as De Havilland, the upper hand could be gained by those Commission members who saw a contribution to the competitiveness of the European aviation industry in the French-Italian acquisition of a Canadian company. It is probably no accident that within the Commission the Vice-President who proclaimed his support for the merger was the former German Minister of Economics who had provided decisive support for the Daimler-Benz/MBB merger. Nor does it appear to be an accident that on 29 November 1991 it was announced in the press that Commission President Delors himself had encouraged Siemens and Philips to unite their semiconductor business with that of the Italian-French group SGS-Thomson. But it is also conceivable that, beyond Article 85 Para. 3 EC, agreements would be approved like those (for example) that the aviation companies regard as necessary to re-establish their competitiveness in the European and global markets. Unnoticed by competition watchdogs, the industrial policy (meaning agricultural policy) motivated draft regulation of the Commission on protection of the geographical and origin characterizations for agricultural products and foods (Article 7 and elsewhere) already expressly provides for agreements among company associations on product qualities: that is, nothing less than the cartel-like elimination of quality competition. What is good enough for agricultural policy must be acceptable for industrial policy as well. On the whole, such consequences would fit into what the Economic and Social Committee in its opinion on the 20th competition report of the Commission set forth (in agreement with the thinking of Vice-President Bangemann), namely that competition policy makes up part of a broader programme of economic, social and financial policy.

6.2.3 Aids

The new provision could also become the basis of a promotional policy which goes beyond what the Community is authorized to do for research and technological development. In the sub-paragraph adopted at Maastricht on the conclusion of Article 130 Para. 3 EC, a limit is set only for competition-distorting measures. This by no means renders all forms of aid impermissible. The creation of a fund is planned. That this must have as its consequence that the Commission will request an increase in its budgetary resources .. is just as inevitable here as it is for other policies. True, Para. 3 sub-para. 2 provides for action on the part of the Community only in support of State measures. But what State will renounce its own promotional measures, if they open to it the opportunity of receiving additional financing from the Community? The German federal government, with its penchant for the industry policy concepts of the Community will only continue the progressive abandonment of market economic principles which can be seen in several areas.

The Parliament remains faithful to its interventionist orientation with respect to aids as well. At the end of 1991 it urged that the aid systems for shipbuilding be retained. It is unrealistic to expect that in principle it would judge admissible indirect aids from the Community any differently.

6.2.4 Distortion of competition as limit

As we have said, the concluding paragraph of Article 130 EC prohibits industrial policy measures which produce distortions of competition. But, far beyond the industrial policy, this norm shows how little is achieved by the legal commitment of the Community to the principle of competition-structured markets.

First, for Article 130 it is especially the case that its half-hearted final sentence with the term 'competition-distorting' excludes only a part of the disturbances of competition which are caused by industry policy.

Secondly, the *Jongeneel Kaas* case (237/82, [1985], ECR 483) shows how little the competition principle is able to achieve in an actual dispute. In that case, the Court found a sharply production-directing provision to be altogether compatible with healthy competition. Thus, one must count on approval for industry policy measures at least when they are aimed at improving the competitiveness of individual enterprises or even entire economic sectors. As long as such provisions are found to be acceptable, a legal commitment of the Community to competition is worthless.

6.3 State measures

Among the competition-promoting developments named above is the judicial case law on Article 5 EC, which prohibits the States from introducing measures which promote cartel law-violating behaviour. Since the new provision on industrial policy provides for state cooperation, it might serve to restrict this case law, if not to repress it altogether. The provision could achieve a limitation on norms that are aimed against state subsidies. Perhaps it could be mobilized in cases involving public companies within the framework of Article 90 EC.

6.4 Uncertainty

The consequences mentioned above are only possibilities. Even if they do not occur in the way that has been sketched here, they will nevertheless contribute to
creating greater uncertainty as to what was addressed here as the logical competition policy of the Community. No one will expect or fear that the Directorate-
General for Competition and the Vice-President of the Commission for competition
policy will be convinced to depart from their previous path. But it cannot be excluded that pursuing this path in the future might provoke greater resistance even
within the Commission.

6.5 Limits

Von Wartenberg (WuW 1991, 863 *et seq.*) has indicated the limits of state industrial policy in a market economy. The new provision does not mean that the Community in the future must (or would) jump over such limits, contrary to its previous
programme. But it does open the door for such a development, since it visibly re-
moves or reduces legal limits.

6.6 Dangers

With respect to infrastructure and industrial policy as well it can be said that these
find their models in the state area. For Germany, one would scarcely dare to hazard
a prediction about whether the needs of the new federal *Länder* will stimulate new
political activity, perhaps promoting federal undertakings for limitations of private
economic areas. Why should the Community deny this to itself? As with legal
harmonization, our reservations about Community law can in the final analysis be
grounded in the fact that Community policy will not eliminate or even coordinate
state policy in many areas, but rather will complement them, so that at least a
growth of sovereign statutory intervention will result. And this will come on top of
the regulations which in the future will serve to implement the basic social rights.

DEMOCRACY, THE STATE UNDER THE RULE OF LAW AND ECONOMIC CONSTITUTION

7.1 The questions

The first purpose of this paper is thus fulfilled. Examples have been offered to make clear to what degree even today and especially in the future EC regulations can be important, and what problems they entail.

As to importance, it should be pointed out that the examples can be multiplied, for example in respect to environmental and in the future the social policy of the Community, research and regional policy and others – to say nothing of agricultural and trade policy.

Problems identified include the insufficiencies of some EC regulations, and the fact that one must also expect regulations whose existence and content appear questionable. Above all, what is often overlooked amidst euphoric evaluation of increased Community competences should have become clear: that the new powers often entail additional regulation.

In view of the scope and the problems the second question becomes urgently important: namely, the limits of permissible regulation. To analyse this issue it is useful to expand it and break it into three questions. All are focused on how future Community regulation can be controlled and its contents influenced. In detail, they focus on 1) the structural qualification of the EC for its regulatory tasks, 2) the legal commitment of the Community bodies, and 3) finally, simply on the proper understanding of the developing system, that is, on the theory underlying it.

7.2 Structure of the EC

The decision-making of the Community in the dense network of its various bodies and their countless committees, as well as in their relationship to the States and to the European Council is too complex a process to allow examination here of the question of in what sense this decision-making in the future will aim at deregulation and make possible better-quality Community regulation. Only individual comments will be offered on the impact on decision-making.

7.2.1 Commission

The fact that widely differing proposals emerge from the Commission, ones which a jurist would tend to regard as systemically incoherent, may well be due to the fact that the initiators adhere to various legal and political traditions and that the individual Directorates-General and Directorates frequently work too independently of one another. This may be further conditioned by the fact that there is no necessarily public (and thus also legal scholarly) discussion which paves the way for law-making initiatives.

An important question in my opinion is whether the scope of the regulation proposed by the Commission is also connected with how the departments of the Commission are organized and structured. Those who set up their own separate department for consumer protection cannot be surprised about activities in this area. Here we can only raise the question whether (for example) the establishment of new Directorates is the consequence of fundamental political decisions in favour of a new policy, or whether it could be influenced by the fact that – as with the German Ministry of Families – tasks simply have to be found for new Commission members and officials. As the Community expands, the second alternative must lead to an increase in regulations. But here we can only mention this problem in passing.

It must undoubtedly be regarded as more important that the Commission under Article 158 EC is only with difficulty becoming an institution supported by a Parliamentary majority, and an institution which must take this majority into consideration. This has both positive and negative consequences. Positively, a Commission supported by a Parliamentary majority must attempt to implement what this majority has promised to its voters as a programme, or what appears electorally effective to this majority. Negatively, and this is the point in our context, the Commission would probably *not* decide in favour of proposals which it can assume run contrary to the ideas of this majority. Thus, for example, the proposal on European works councils or other regulatory proposals might never have seen the light of day. Certainly Commission proposals must secure the approval of the European Parliament to the extent that the Parliament has right of participation. But this does not establish any dependency of the Commission on a Parliamentary majority conscious of its need to be reelected, as is the case in most state constitutions. The independence of the Commission may encourage it to present particularly numerous and occasionally especially radical regulatory proposals. Even the strong involvement of the national bureaucracies in the work of the Commission changes nothing here, since their representatives are able to a certain extent to liberate themselves from nationally effective political ties.

7.2.2 States

The next question involves the influence of the States in the EC. The strong involvement of the States early on in the preparation of Community measures should provide assurance with respect to the quality of regulation. But the necessity of making compromises not simply on the specific topic, but rather between national traditions makes concern about quality more acute. Neither in the Council nor in the Commission does there exist a body which would concern itself at least with the uniformity of the law-making instruments, or even with the policy which defines them.

On the relationship between regulation and deregulation, the great influence of the bureaucracies on law-making could well prove to be regulation-promoting. The influence of individual States may not suffice to counter effectively the wishes for regulation. In the legal battle concerning the television Directive, the German government effectively argued that its participation – objected to by the federal *Länder* who lodged the complaint – was necessary, so as to avoid ending up with an even worse result. This suggests that the states' possibilities for exerting influence with respect to the limits of Community regulation are rather slight.

7.2.3 Parliament

Here we shall not repeat the occasional reproaches made against the qualification of the European Parliament and its tendency to over-production, which in essence say that its mandates generally function as sinecures for veteran political party hacks. Here what is of interest is whether the European Parliament could prove to be a guarantor of quality and restraint in regulation. One might well doubt this, since in many areas it is precisely the Parliament which presses for ever more regulation. This was demonstrated earlier with respect to industrial policy. A further example is provided by advertising, where prohibition or regulation is called for beyond the field of medications for at least the following areas: tobacco, alcohol, financial services and motor vehicles. A data protection Directive should moreover make it more difficult to reach the consumers through advertising. This would simultaneously restrict economic activity. Moreover, anyone who actually reads the committee reports will not gain the impression that a profound examination is conducted with respect to quality. As far as the relationship between regulation and freedom is concerned, the European Parliament may suffer from the fact that there are with respect to regulation or deregulation, no more or less stable majorities and minorities which would adopt the one or the other principle as a guiding ideal. Instead of this, occasions for regulation are taken up on a virtually ad hoc basis, as with the highly ill-considered proposal for state compensation for crime victims. In several areas an exception may be constituted by the Socialist parliamentary group, which on 22 October 1991 opposed the passage of an insurance directive in order thereby to demonstrate against the failure to advance towards a social Europe. The Parliament also does not deal with proposals from a government supported by its majority, a government which can conceive of itself as an expression of either a regulation-friendly or a more liberal policy. Thus from Strasbourg – at least for the time being – one can expect perhaps individual contributions, but no principled orientation with respect to regulation. Probably we must even fear a certain activism along the lines of ill-considered attempts to 'improve the world'.

Moreover, Article 189b EC gives occasion for a critical assessment of the Parliament. It keeps the Parliament's consultation periods so short that qualified examinations by Parliament are virtually excluded, thus encouraging premature decisions.

(End of excerpt)

The years to come will demonstrate whether the Commission succeeds in its efforts to formulate a European industrial policy or whether the unanimity rule allows resisting Member States to opt out and to prevent the Commission from establishing a coherent European industrial policy. E. Steindorff has highlighted the far-reaching implications of the existence and the shaping of a European Community policy. There is more at stake than defining concepts and borderlines, it will be a fight about the 'economic constitution' of the European Community (cf. Chapter 1).

C. INDUSTRIAL POLICY AND COMPETITION POLICY

Whereas the outcome of *Article 130* is far from clear and the conflicts seem to focus around differing understandings of the role and function of industrial policy in a market society (cf. Chapter 1), there is a field in which both objectives, competition policy and industrial policy, clash: the field of the control of mergers, governed by Council Regulation No 4064/89 of 21 December 1989 on the control of concentrations between undertakings. There has been a substantial debate between the Member States since its adoption. We now take an American perspective on the Regulation, J.T. Halverson, Shearman & Sterling New York, N.Y., *EC Merger Control: Competition Policy or Industrial Policy? Views of A US Practitioner*. He is clearly developing the possible tension between competition and industrial policy and the attempts to bring both policy objectives together in one concept.

EC MERGER CONTROL: COMPETITION POLICY OR INDUSTRIAL POLICY? VIEWS OF A US PRACTITIONER*

James T. Halverson

[...] The merger control laws of France, Germany, and the United Kingdom allow for noncompetition concerns to play a greater role in decision-making than is the case under the United States merger control regime. It would be logical that any Community-wide merger regulation would reflect the attitude of the Member States as to the role that noncompetition concerns should play in merger policy. Member States, however, though generally more open than the United States to responding to noncompetition concerns within a merger policy, differ in their beliefs as to what role such concerns should play in merger policy. This of course, leads to the debate between the relative importance of competition and industrial policy.

I now would like to turn to the Merger Regulation,[1] and the debate between industrial and competition policy that has surrounded it. Like the debate between the various schools of economics and antitrust policy in the United States, the debate between the advocates of industrial and competition policy is not simply an academic one, for the outcome of the debate has important implications as to how the law is to be applied. I turn first to an examination of whether or not the Merger Regulation was drafted with a substantive standard incorporating the goals of one policy or another.

At first glance, the question of the goals of the Merger Regulation may seem obvious from the wording of the substantive standard to be used in its application. Article 2, paragraphs 2 and 3 of the Merger Regulation state:

2. A concentration which does not create or strengthen a dominant position as a result of which effective competition would be significantly impeded in the common market or in a substantial part of it shall be declared compatible with the common market.

3. A concentration which creates or strengthen a dominant position as a result of which effective competition would be significantly impeded in the common market or in a substantial part of it shall be declared incompatible with the common market.

---

*   Previously published in *Legal Issues of European Integration*, 1992/2, pp.49 *et seq.*; reprinted by permission of Kluwer Law and Taxation Publishers, Deventer.
1   Regulation No. 4064/89, OJ L 395/1 (1989).

The Merger Regulation goes on, however, to set out a list of criteria to be taken into account in determining the compatibility of a concentration with the common market. Paragraph 1 of Article 2 states,

(a) the need to maintain and develop effective competition within the common market in view of, among other things, the structure of all the markets concerned and the actual or potential competition from undertakings located either within or without the Community;

(b) the market position of the undertakings concerned and their economic and financial power, the alternatives available to suppliers and users, their access to supplies or markets, any legal or other barriers to entry, supply and demand trends for the relevant goods and services, the interests of the intermediate and ultimate consumers, and the development of technical and economic progress provided that it is to consumers' advantage and does not form an obstacle to competition.

From the view of a US practitioner, the substantive standard appears to be principally competition-based, emphasizing the protection of competition and incorporating measures of market definition and market power long accepted in US antitrust analysis, such as product and geographic market definition, and ease of entry.

Not all the criteria listed in paragraphs 1(a) and 1(b), however, neatly fit into traditional antitrust analysis. Many factors, such as the structure of the market, actual and potential competition, and the alternatives available to suppliers and users, clearly are designed to measure concerns typically associated with the protection of free competition. Other criteria, in particular 'the development of technical and economic progress,' seem to address concerns other than those typically associated with competition policy.

The possible use of noncompetition factors caused concern both inside and outside of the Community during the drafting of the regulation and following its adoption. Early drafts of the Regulation were viewed with concern by some Member States, notably Germany and England, because of fear that the Regulation would allow for the approval of mergers that failed competition tests but which provided some other benefit to the Community. The concern of these Member States was that considerations of industrial, regional, or social policy would be allowed to overrule strict competition analysis. Although these states allowed noncompetition factors and political decision-making to enter to some degree into their own merger control, they did not have a history of industrial policy and wanted a merger regulation grounded in competition policy rather than in some amorphous European industrial policy. Other Member States, such as France, Spain, and Portugal, desired the inclusion of such factors in determining whether or not a merger was compatible with the common market.

While the concern of some Member States was that the Merger Regulation might sacrifice free competition at the altar of industrial policy, the concern from outside of the Community was that the Regulation might be used to sacrifice non-EEC competitors in favor of EEC-based firms.[2] Foreign firms wondered whether they would be subjected to a regulation, applied pursuant to an unpredictable substantive standard incorporating industrial policy, that could be used as a protectionist tool under the guise of protecting free competition in the EC. The Act, it was feared, could be used to build and protect European champions, and to keep out aggressive US competitors seeking to compete in a lucrative European market. After all, it would not be outrageous to claim that industrial policy called for the creation and protection of European firms, with the associated benefits to employment and to the economies of Member States.

Concerns over the influence of industrial policy were somewhat alleviated by the eventual wording of the Regulation. Although the 'development of technical and economic progress' wording represents a compromise nod to industrial policy, the language has been strongly limited by the requirement that such progress will only be considered when, 'it is to consumers' advantage and does not form an obstacle to competition'. This caveat seems to provide very little room for exception. There may be few mergers where the parties can prove that their contributions: 1) are, but for the merger, a requirement not directly stated but that is inherent in the caveat; 2) will have real tangible benefit to the consumer rather than to the financial situation of the merging parties; and 3) do not result in some block to future competition.

Worry in some quarters that industrial policy had somehow reappeared in the Regulation has also been alleviated by statements made by Commission officials. In remarks made before the Center for European Studies, EC Commissioner Sir Leon Brittan explained that 'technical and economic progress' was simply one of many factors that make up the 'wider analysis' of mergers:

> Let me stress that no words plucked from the Regulation can give rise to a defense against the finding that there is a dominant position as a result of which competition is significantly impeded. If that is the finding, then the merger may not proceed. If on the other hand, no dominant position is found to exist as a result of which competition is impeded, then the merger may proceed without further ado. The Regulation amounts to no more than that.
>
> It could hardly be otherwise, because I do not see how a dominant position which impedes competition could give rise to technical or economic progress of the sort which competition policy could endorse. There may be some short-term technical progress available to a monopolist, but it would not last for long when one considers the well-known debilitating effect of monopoly. As for economic

---

2   See, for example, Paul D. Callister, 'The December 1989 European Community Merger Control Regulation: A Non-EC Perspective,' 24, *Cornell Int'l L.J.*, p.101 (1991).

progress, apart for monopoly rents which would accrue, there would be no progress at all.[3]

It is clear from his remarks that Sir Leon Brittan views the 'technical and economic progress' wording as extremely limited. The wording clearly, in his view, cannot be used to save a merger which would result in a competitively harmful dominant position. Thus, Sir Leon Brittan has further calmed those who were concerned that industrial policy may have found its way into the language of the Regulation.

The wording of Article 2 seems to reflect a compromise included to insure the adoption of the Regulation by the Member States. The fact that the Regulation includes this compromise does not diminish it as an achievement, however, since it is the very nature of laws that they are forged of compromise and negotiation. Indeed, that a compromise could be found is impressive in itself considering the variant competition policies of the Member States involved in its drafting.

We in the United States have had the benefit of only limited partisan groups with which to work in forming an antitrust policy, and our laws too represent a compromise between different views as to the goals of antitrust laws, and different schools of economic theory. Our experience has taught us that competition law is motivated by a variety of goals, and pristine substantive standards are not a direct result when laws are written based on some combination of values. Thus, that a substantive standard is not firmly grounded in one economic theory, based upon one ultimate goal, nor ideologically pure, does not mean that it will not prove to be effective and beneficial. Any such criticism is unwarranted and premature, especially considering the alternative of no competition regulation at all.

The compromise forged in the Regulation's substantive standard has proven to be a good one. In its drafting, and through its interpretation, the substantive standard rests on competition policy. [...]

Although I do not advocate substantive harmonization, I firmly believe that procedural harmonization of merger control would be extremely beneficial in light of the rapidly developing world economy and the greater number of cross-jurisdictional transactions. Such harmonization would greatly increase the efficiency with which transactions are reviewed, and allow for comity considerations to be discussed in early consultations. Procedural harmonization would still allow states to carry out the goals of their own substantive laws.

In conclusion, discussions such as this one, and public debate concerning the goals of competition law and how those goals should be achieved, are useful endeavors. Generally, debate assists in re-evaluating and prioritizing the goals of competition law, and insures that the law will remain in tune with current condi-

---

[3]   'Brittan Still Wants Treaty With US, Clarifies Misconceptions With Merger Rule', *Antitrust & Trade Reg. Rep.* (BNA) No.59, at 517 (4 October 1990).

tions and needs. Specifically, debate helps to focus on what should be the goals of the Merger Regulation and should, in the end, make its application more predictable.

(End of excerpt)

The Commission Decision of 2 October 1991 declaring the incompatibility with the common market of a concentration (Case No IV/M. 053 of 2 October 1991 – *Aerospatiale-Alenia/de Havilland*, 91/619/EEC) OJ L 334, 5.12.1991, 42 *et seq.* demonstrates the practical difficulties in the process of law enforcement. For J.T. Halverson, it is the test case to check whether the substantive standard on competition policy has been applied in a rational and reasonable manner that is true to competition policy.

The Decision is presented here only as far as the clash between the two policies is of interest. We set aside the extensive analysis of the relevant product markets, the geographical reference market and the market structure (IV. 1–3) and concentrate our interest on the IV.4, the 'Impact of the concentration', where the danger of using competition policy as a disguise for industrial policy purposes is most striking.

COMMISSION DECISION

of 2 October 1991

declaring the incompatibility with the common market of a concentration

(Case No. IV/M.053 – Aérospatiale-Alenia/de Havilland)

Council Regulation (EEC) No 4064/89

(Only the English, French and Italian texts are authentic)

(91/619/EEC)

[...]

The parties

(3)   Aérospatiale is a French company active in the aerospace industries. Its product range includes civil and military aircraft and helicopters, missiles, satellites, space systems and avionics. Alenia is an Italian company predominantly active also in the aerospace industries. Its product range includes civil and military aircraft, satellites, space systems, avionics, and air and maritime traffic control systems. Aérospatiale and Alenia jointly control the Groupment d'Intérêt Economique (GIE) Avions de Transport Régional (ATR) which was set up in 1982 in order jointly to design, develop,

manufacture and sell regional transport aircraft. There are currently two ATR regional turbo-prop aircraft on the market.

(4) De Havilland, which is a Canadian division of Boeing, only manufactures regional turbo-prop aircraft. The former de Havilland Corporation (DHC) was nationalized by the Canadian Government in 1982 and sold to Boeing in 1986. There are currently two de Havilland regional turbo-prop aircraft on the market.

II. THE CONCENTRATION

(5) The notified operation is a concentration in the form of a concentration joint venture within the meaning of Article 3 of the Merger Regulation since:

- de Havilland will be run by an operating company which will be jointly controlled by Aérospatiale and Alenia, and
- the activities of Aérospatiale and Alenia in regional turbo-prop aircraft (commuters) have already been concentrated in the GIE ATR since 1982.

[...]

1. Relevant product markets

(8) The relevant product markets affected by the proposed concentration are those of regional turbo-prop aircraft.

[...]

4. Impact of the concentration

A. Effect on ATR'S position

(27) The proposed concentration would significantly strengthen ATR's position on the commuter markets, for the following reasons in particular:

- high combined market share on the 40 to 59-seat market, and of the overall commuter market
- elimination of de Havilland as a competitor
- coverage of the whole range of commuter aircraft
- considerable extension of the customer base.

(a) Increase in market shares

(28) The proposed concentration would lead to an increase in market shares for ATR in the world market for commuters between 40 to 59 seats from 46% to 63%. The nearest competitor (Fokker) would have 22%. This market, to-gether with the larger market of 60 seats and above where ATR has a world

market share of 76%, is of particular importance in the commuter industry since there is a general trend towards larger aircraft.

(29) ATR would increase its share of the overall worldwide commuter market of 20 to 70 seats from around 30% to around 50%. The nearest competitor (Saab) would only have around 19%. On the basis of this the new entity would have half the overall world market and more than two and a half times the share of its nearest competitor. [...]

(30) [...]

Following a concentration between ATR and de Havilland, the competitors would be faced with the combined strength of two large companies. This would mean that where an airline was considering placing a new order, the competitors would be in competition with the combined product range of ATR and de Havilland. The sales strategy of the formerly separate companies would now be concerted. The combination could enable the new entity ATR/de Havilland to be more flexible in setting its price than its competitors where a sale is contestable, because of their absolute size advantage in terms of sales base. Furthermore, unlike the competitors, the combined entity would have all the advantages of a family of commuters to offer. [...]

The parties themselves expect that the aggregation of ATR and de Havilland marketing and manufacturing forces 'will certainly lead to an improvement of their position in North America and Europe among the regional aircraft producers', so that the position of the combined entity would be stronger than that of ATR and de Havilland currently.

(b) Elimination of de Havilland as competitor

(31) In terms of aircraft sold, de Havilland is the most successful competitor of ATR. In the relevant product market of 40 to 59 seats, Fokker has a higher market share than de Havilland, but Fokker at the end of 1990 had a backlog of only 27 orders for the Fokker 50 whilst de Havilland had a backlog of 72 orders for the Dash 8-300 (second only to ATR with 103 orders for the ATR 42).

Furthermore, de Havilland has plans to develop a new aircraft – the Dash 8-400 – to compete in the top segment (60 seats and over).[1] If the concentration goes ahead, therefore, de Havilland would be eliminated as a potential competitor from this segment where ATR has a market share of 76%.

The parties argue that if the proposed concentration does not proceed, although de Havilland would not be immediately liquidated, its production might be phased out by Boeing so that de Havilland might in any case be eliminated as a competitor in the medium to long term. Without prejudice as

---

[1]   Boeing has currently suspended this programme in order to give the buyer of de Havilland an opportunity to conduct its own programmeme analysis to determine what action would be taken after the sale.

to whether such a consideration is relevant pursuant to Article 2 of the Merger Regulation, the Commission considers that such elimination is not probable. According to a pre-acquisition review of de Havilland carried out for Aéro-spatiale-Alenia at the end of 1990, the following factors, *inter alia*, were identified as critical in assessing the investment decision from a business/financial point of view: de Havilland produces high quality, well-known and highly respected products, the net selling prices of which have been increasing; progress has already been made in reducing excess employees, and relations with trade unions have improved; there is still however scope for further improvement in production management since de Havilland's productivity is relatively poor [...].[2]

On the evidence made available to the Commission, there is therefore no likelihood that de Havilland, in the absence of the proposed concentration, would in any case be phased out. Boeing has however expressed its preference to sell de Havilland rather than continue to operate it. This would seem possible given that the parties are not the only potential buyers. British Aerospace, for example, has expressed an interest to buy de Havilland.

(c) Coverage of the whole range of commuter aircraft

(32) The new entity ATR/de Havilland would be the only commuter manufacturer present in all the various commuter markets as defined above. [...]

According to a study submitted by the parties, it is argued that the inability of a manufacturer to offer a full range of seating capacities under the same umbrella may harm the demand for other existing aircraft of that manufacturer. Thus, a significant regional carrier whose aircraft needs may call for a full complement of aircraft capacities to meet the route needs of that carrier might be dissuaded from purchasing smaller aircraft from a single manufacturer if the needs of the carrier for a larger aircraft could not also be met from the same aircraft manufacturer. This logic flows from the fixed costs borne by the carrier for each aircraft manufacturer dealt with by that carrier. These costs include the fixed costs of pilot and mechanic training as well as the costs of maintaining different in-house inventories of parts and the fixed costs of dealing with several manufacturers when ordering parts stocked only by the individual manufacturers themselves.

One of the stated main strategic objectives of the parties in acquiring de Havilland is to obtain coverage of the whole range of commuter aircraft. The competitive advantages which would arise from this would emerge over time. [...]

B. Assessment of the strength of the remaining competition

(34) In order to be able to assess whether the new combined entity would be able to act independently of its competitors, in view of its strengthened position,

---

[2] Analysis of financial position of de Havilland.

it is necessary to assess the current and expected future strength of the remaining competitors. [...]

The medium-sized competitors

(36) *Fokker* has been a successful competitor in the 40 to 59-seat market in the past. It now produces however only one commuter (the Fokker 50) and does not have a family of products to offer. Because of its relatively limited resources, it has only one other significant product, the Fokker 100 jet. Its military business is very limited.

The Fokker 50 has a relatively low share of 9% of the overall worldwide market of 20 to 70 seats and 22% of the market of 40 to 59 seats where ATR/de Havilland combined would have 63%. [...]

Fokker could be particularly affected by the combined strength of ATR/de Havilland. It has not yet built up a large customer base for the Fokker 50 and has smaller resources than ATR. After a concentration between ATR and de Havilland, it would be more difficult for Fokker to broaden its product range of commuters by producing a stretch version of the Fokker 50 given the outlined competitive advantages of the new entity. The concentration may have in this light a crucial impact on the situation of Fokker as a competitor in the aircraft market. [...]

The large aerospace groups

(39) *British Aerospace* has the resources to broaden its current product range in the commuter markets. Its current market share is however small (4% of the overall world commuter market) and it has only 2% of the worldwide backlog of commuter orders, representing less than one year of its production capacity at the end of 1990. Future investment in the commuter markets by British Aerospace would depend on whether there exist more profitable opportunities elsewhere in the group and whether a stronger commitment to the commuter markets would be rational. Other than its broad aerospace activities. British Aerospace has significant interests in nonaerospace industries including cars, telecommunications and property. [...]

Following the completion of a concentration between ATR and de Havilland, since British Aerospace has only a very small customer base in the commuter markets. it is doubtful that it would focus on these markets. It already has an identifiable gap between its two existing models in the key product market of 40 to 59 seats. Furthermore, the already difficult competitive situation for the 64-seat ATP *vis-à-vis* the 66-seat ATR72 would be worsened after completion of the proposed concentration, given the strength of the new entity.

The proposed concentration will therefore lead to British Aerospace becoming further marginalized as a competitor in the commuter markets.

(40) *Saab* can be expected to stay in the 20 to 39-seat market where it has a relatively healthy position. It is developing a 50-seat fast turbo-prop commuter which is expected to come on the market in two years time. This may to a certain extent only be a limited competitor to ATR and de Havilland since it meets a special need for customers operating regional routes of relatively long distances. The turbo-prop markets generally are short-haul markets with flights of an average of around one hour. Because takeoff and landing times are a relatively high proportion of the overall flight time for short routes, speed is not so relevant since only some five minutes can be shaved off a particular flight by even the 25% increase in speed envisaged for the Saab 2000. It may be therefore that most customers would not be willing to pay a premium for this plane. This implies that this plane, given its technical and cost characteristics, will occupy a niche market which will not compete directly in the market for 40 to 59-seat commuters.

(41) *Dornier*, which is part of the Daimler-Benz group via Deutsche Aerospace (DASA), will enter the small commuter market with a 30-seat type in 1993. In assessing DASA's future competition with ATR, however, it must be noted that a Memorandum of Understanding has been entered into between DASA and Aérospatiale and Alenia as to future development of a regional jet. If the decision is taken to develop this regional jet, it is intended that these companies would then form the joint venture 'International Commuter' for the marketing of the whole range of regional aircraft, including commuters, manufactured by the three companies. If International Commuter is formed in this way, Dornier would not remain a real competitor of ATR/de Havilland. The formation of International Commuter is not, however, yet definitely decided and would be subject to review under the Community competition rules. If DASA does not enter into a final agreement with Aérospatiale and Alenia, then it may become a significant competitor in the 20 to 39-seat market.

Overall evaluation of the remaining competition

(42) It follows from the above that effective competition for the combined entity would only be maintained in the market of 20 to 39-seat commuters, although even here the ability of the competitors to compete with the combined entity would lessen to a certain extent given the overall advantages to ATR/de Havilland arising from a broad sales base and coverage of all the markets. In the markets for commuters of 40 seats and over, apart from the limited competition from the Saab 2000, it is questionable whether the other existing competitors could provide effective competition in the medium to long term. [...]

E. Potential entry into the market

(53) In general terms, a concentration which leads to the creation of a dominant position may however be compatible with the common market within the meaning of Article 2(2) of the Merger Regulation if there exists strong evidence that this position is only temporary and would be quickly eroded because of high probability of strong market entry. With such market entry the dominant position is not likely to significantly impede effective competition within the meaning of Article 2(3) of the Merger Regulation. In order to assess whether the dominant position of ATR/de Havilland is likely to significantly impede effective competition therefore, it is necessary to assess the likelihood of new entry into the market.

(54) Any theoretical attractiveness of entry into the commuter market by a new player must be put into perspective taking into account the forecast demand and the time and cost considerations to enter the market.

Based on the parties' figures, the overall market potential for 20 to 70-seat commuter aircraft over the next 20 years is estimated at around [...] units including the backlog of around 700 units. It is expected that the current level of demand will be maintained only until the mid-1990s, and thereafter decline and stabilize. The average annual level of demand from the mid-1990s onwards could then be estimated at around [...][3] units compared to the current rate of some [...] units.

It follows that in terms of increase in annual deliveries the market appears to have therefore already reached maturity. [...]

(56) It follows from the above that a new entrant into the market would face high risk. Furthermore, given the time necessary to develop a new aircraft and the foreseeable development of the market as described above, a new manufacturer may come too late into the market to catch the expected period of relatively high demand. Any new market entry at this stage could only come when the market would have declined from current levels and have stabilized. It is therefore doubtful whether a break-even level of sales could be achieved by a new entrant since even existing competitors are not yet at break-even point in their product cycles.

(57) For these reasons it is considered that it would not be rational to now enter the commuter aircraft market. This is accepted by the parties. The parties argue however that some newly industrialized countries would decide nonetheless to support the development of a local commuter industry. Even if some time in the future such a local commuter industry were established in the way the parties suggest, it is considered unlikely that significant inroads into the international markets could occur in this way. Such an uncer-

---

3   Substantially lower: around two-thirds of current rate.

tain possibility would not in any case be sufficient to justify a conclusion that the dominant position of ATR/de Havilland is only temporary. [...]

Evaluation of the possibility of new entry

(63) It follows that there is no realistic significant potential competition in the commuter markets in the foreseeable future.

The parties claim that the commuter markets are volatile on the basis that in the early 1980s Fokker and British Aerospace had high market shares and this did not prevent significant market entry, notably of ATR.

A change in market structure from the early 1980s to the early 1990s does not demonstrate that these markets are volatile. The situation in the early 1980s was very different from the current situation.

The markets in the early 1980s were characterized by the following factors:

- there were very few competitors on the markets. In the small commuter market of 20 to 39 seats, there was only Shorts, and in the market of 40 to 59 seats there were only Fokker, British Aerospace and to a limited extent de Havilland,
- the aircraft on the markets and in particular those of Fokker and British Aerospace were very old, even obsolete, products. The markets were ripe for the introduction of new and better performing aircraft,
- forecasts showed that there would be high growth in the markets over the following decade arising from deregulation in North America. These forecasts proved justified,
- the markets were therefore attractive to new entrants and it was rational for entry to occur.

The markets in the early 1990s, in contrast, are characterized by the following factors:

- there are eight competitors altogether already on the markets. The aircraft available are all based on modern technology which fulfils the stringent customer requirements in this respect for the foreseeable future,
- current forecasts as outlined above show that the markets are approaching maturity and will decline and stabilize from the mid-1990s,
- the markets are not therefore attractive to new entrants, and it is not rational to now enter. The expectation is rather that some of the existing competitors will leave.

(64) It is considered therefore that a change in market structure similar to that which took place in the 1980s is unlikely to recur in the 1990s. Furthermore, the possibility of market entry would be further reduced if the proposed concentration goes ahead.

F. Other general conditions

[...]

(67) ATR's current position in the industry is very healthy. Given the relatively high initial costs of development for new aircraft, it is normal for manufacturers in this industry to show losses in the early years of a programme. It takes some time before a sufficient level of sales has been achieved to amortize the development costs. [...].[4]

Since ATR has also established an excellent position in the market, and efficient production management, it does not need to obtain by acquisition further capacity or market shares in order to guarantee its long-term success as a major player in the worldwide commuter industry.

(68) The parties have stated that a competitive advantage (which has not been quantified) will be obtained from acquiring de Havilland by enabling manufacturing in a dollar area to reduce the currency fluctuation risk. For the ATR product range this will only arise, however, to the extent that production could be shifted between Europe and North America.

Although some advantage may be obtained from a dollar manufacturing base, it should be noted that no competitor other than de Havilland has such a base. It is doubtful in practice that production of ATR aircraft would be transferred to Canada in any significant way.

(69) For the above reasons, the Commission does not consider that the proposed concentration would contribute to the development of technical and economic progress within the meaning of Article 2(1)(b) of the Merger Regulation. Even if there was such progress, this would not be to the consumers' advantage.

The consumers will be faced with a dominant position which combines the most popular aircraft families on the market. Choice will be significantly reduced. There is a high risk that in the foreseeable future, the dominant position of ATR/de Havilland would be translated into a monopoly.

Both British Aerospace and Fokker, the two principal competitors in the markets of 40 seats and above, have stated that the concentration would seriously jeopardize the survival of the ATP and Fokker 50 aircraft. These two competitors expect that the proposed concentration would lead to ATR/de Havilland pursuing a strategy of initially lowering prices so as to eliminate the competitors at least in the key markets of 40 seats and above. Neither Fokker nor British Aerospace consider it possible for them to withstand such a price war. Consequently, both would leave the markets.

In evaluating these statements, it is noted that such conduct could be rational since the proposed concentration would mean that ATR/de Havilland would exceed the threshold of market shares which would make such a pricing policy likely given that it would be the optimal profit-maximizing strategy. [...]

---

4   ATR financial projections.

V. CONCLUSION

(72) For the reasons outlined above, it is considered that the proposed concentration would lead to a situation whereby the combined entity ATR/de Havilland could act to a significant extent independently of its competitors and customers on the world markets as defined for commuters of 40 to 59 seats and 60 seats and over. The proposed concentration therefore creates a dominant position on the world markets. Furthermore, according to the above analysis, this dominant position is not merely temporary and will therefore significantly impede effective competition. It is considered that such a dominant position is also created even if the relevant product market is the overall 20 to 70-seat market.

The condition of competition in the Community commuter markets are not appreciably different from those prevailing in the overall world markets. The market shares of the new entity would be similar in both the world and Community markets for commuters of 60 seats and over, and even higher in the Community market for commuters of 40 to 59 seats than in the world market. These markets are also relatively more important in the Community than in the rest of the world. As to the overall market of 20 to 70 seats, the market shares of the new entity would be higher in the Community than in the rest of the world. It is considered therefore that the proposed concentration creates a dominant position which significantly impedes effective competition in the common market within the meaning of Article 2(3) of the Merger Regulation.

HAS ADOPTED THIS DECISION:

Article 1

The proposed concentration between Aérospatiale and Alenia and de Havilland is declared incompatible with the common market.

Article 2

This Decision is addressed to:

Aérospatiale SNI,
37 Boulevard de Montmorency,
F-75781 Paris Cedex 76,

and

Alenia-Aeritalia & Selenia Spa,
P. le V. Tecchio 51/a,
I-80125 Napoli.

Done at Brussels, 2 October 1991,

For the Commission
Leon BRITTAN
Vice-President

QUESTIONS

1   When reading and analysing the reasoning of the Commission, to what extent is it underpinned by the objective of keeping Fokker and British Aerospace alive as competitors in the market?

2   Is the Commission exercising its power to pursue industrial policy objectives with the purpose of keeping intra-European competition alive or even more of fostering competition by protecting Fokker and British Aerospace?

3   Quite another perspective is taken by J.T. Halverson: 'The De Havilland case... seems to have established that the Commission is committed to the notion that the Merger Regulation is based on competition policy, and should not be used as a tool of industrial policy'... Do you share his conclusion? or would you follow E. Steindorff, who does not see Article 130(3) as a guarantee that the competition policy will prevail over industrial policy and that the Merger's Control Regulation has to face these uncertainties?

4   The importance of the role of the industrial policy in a market society reaches beyond the borders of the European Community. The potential clash between competition within Europe and the need for big firms competing in the labour market 'on behalf of Europe' illustrates its international dimension (cf. Chapter 10).

FURTHER READING

Sir Leon Brittan, 'The Law and Policy of Merger Control in the EEC', *ELRev*, **15**, 1990, p.351.

Collins, 'The Coming of Age of EC Competition Policy', *Yale J Intl L*, **17**, 1992, p.249.

T.A. Downes and Davis S. MacDougall, 'Significantly Impeding Effective Competition: Substantive Appraisal under the Merger Regulation', *ELRev*, **19**, 1994, p.286.

Picat and Zachmann, 'Community Monitoring of Concentration Operations: Evaluation after two years' application of Regulation 4064/89', *ECLR*, **6**, 1993, p.240.

Marie Sirgagusa and Romano Subiotto, 'The EEC Merger Control Regulation: the Commission's Evolving Case Law', *CMLRev*, **28**, 1991, p.877.

3 Internal Market and State Aid

A. CONTROL OF STATE AID: INTRODUCTION

State aid is a well established method of regulating the economy. It may appear in different forms, as sectorial policy in order to provide support to ailing industries, as regional policy in order to increase the level of regional development, and as horizontal policy in order to increase investment where it is deemed necessary.

State aid, however, cannot easily be reconciled with a reliance on the market as a mechanism for resource allocation. State aid in whatever form must be seen as being part of industrial policy. There is no agreement within Member States on the role and function of industrial policy within a market economy. This becomes apparent not so much in state aids for ailing industries, but in state aids as a means of regional policy and as an instrument to foster R & D or to set incentives for new environmental technologies.

Community rules on state aid, Articles 92–94, must be seen in the light of the debate on the use and usefulness of an economic constitution. Against that background the differences between Member States and the difficulties in developing a coherent Community system on state aid become abundantly clear (cf. Chapter 1). The Treaty of Rome does not forbid state aid, *per se*. Member States are allowed to give state aids to their national industries. They are, however, obliged to notify the national policy instruments to the Commission. Based on that notification the Commission and the Member States are bound into a process of cooperation. It seems fair to say that the Community rules on state aids are mainly shaped to serve transparency rather than to control national policy instruments.

SECTION 3   AIDS GRANTED BY STATES

Article 92

1. Save as otherwise provided in this Treaty, any aid granted by a Member State or through State resources in any form whatsoever which distorts or threatens to distort competition by favouring certain undertakings or the production of certain goods shall, in so far as it affects trade between Member States, be incompatible with the common market.

2. The following shall be compatible with the common market:

(a) aid having a social character, granted to individual consumers, provided that such aid is granted without discrimination related to the origin of the products concerned;

(b) aid to make good the damage caused by natural disasters or exceptional occurrences;

(c) aid granted to the economy of certain areas of the Federal Republic of Germany affected by the division of Germany, in so far as such aid is required in order to compensate for the economic disadvantages caused by that division.

3.   The following may be considered to be compatible with the common market:

(a) aid to promote the economic development of areas where the standard of living is abnormally low or where there is serious underemployment;

(b) aid to promote the execution of an important project of common European interest or to remedy a serious disturbance in the economy of a Member State;

(c) aid to facilitate the development of certain economic activities or of certain economic areas, where such aid does not adversely affect trading conditions to an extent contrary to the common interest. However, the aids granted to shipbuilding as of 1 January 1957 shall, in so far as they serve only to compensate for the absence of customs protection, be progressively reduced under the same condition as apply to the elimination of customs duties, subject to the provisions of this Treaty concerning common commercial policy towards third countries;

(d) aid to promote culture and heritage conservation where such aid does not affect trading conditions and competition in the Community to an extent that is contrary to the common interest;

(e) such other categories of aid as may be specified by decision of the Council acting by a qualified majority on a proposal from the Commission.

Article 92(1) provides a basic *prohibition*, Article 92(2) supplies a list of types of state aid that *are* compatible with the common market, Article 92(3) contains a list of those policy instruments that *may* be regarded as compatible with the common market. Article 92(1) forbids Member States to discriminate on grounds of nationality. Such measures are seen as a distortion of competition. Article 92(2) legalizes types of aids having a social character or being necessary to overcome damages resulting from a national disaster or to compensate for shortcomings related to the division of Germany. The purposes behind Article 92(2) are clearly political. They are, however, well recognized and commonly agreed. The real problem area starts with Article 92(3). Here all difficult types of state aids are enumerated. The list can even be extended by a Council decision, Article 92(3)(e). The Maastricht Treaty added to the list aid to promote cultural conservation. The

Commission has to decide whether the state aid in question distorts competition or whether it is given to national industries for legitimate reasons. The Treaty of Rome has put much power in the hands of the Commission. The latter has to exercise the considerable discretion carefully and to operate on a clearly shaped community policy. Much of what happens in the Commission and in negotiations between Member States and the Commission never reaches the level of a legal conflict. That is why a clear Community policy is needed in order to increase transparency. The Commission has done so in publishing guidelines and recommendations on differing types of aids (e.g. the general policy of the Commission concerning sectorial aid can be found in a communication to the Council of 5 May 1978, COM (78), 221 *et seq*.).

Article 93 establishes a procedure whereby the Commission may supervise both existing and new aid.

Article 93

1. The Commission shall, in cooperation with Member States, keep under constant review all systems of aid existing in those States. It shall propose to the latter any appropriate measures required by the progressive development or by the functioning of the common market.

2. If, after giving notice to the parties concerned to submit their comments, the Commission finds that aid granted by a State or through State resources is not compatible with the common market having regard to Article 92, or that such aid is being misused, it shall decide that the State concerned shall abolish or alter such aid within a period of time to be determined by the Commission.

If the State concerned does not comply with this decision within the prescribed time, the Commission or any other interested State may, in derogation from the provisions of Articles 169 and 170, refer the matter to the Court of Justice direct.

On application by a Member State, the Council, may, acting unanimously, decide that aid which that State is granting or intends to grant shall be considered to be compatible with the common market, in derogation from the provisions of Article 92 or from the regulations provided for in Article 94, if such a decision is justified by exceptional circumstances. If, as regards the aid in question, the Commission has already initiated the procedure provided for in the first subparagraph of this paragraph, the fact that the State concerned has made its application to the Council shall have the effect of suspending that procedure until the Council has made its attitude known.

If, however, the Council has not made its attitude known within three months of the said application being made, the Commission shall give its decision on the case.

3.   The Commission shall be informed, in sufficient time to enable it to submit its comments, of any plans to grant or alter aid. If it considers that any such plan is not compatible with the common market having regard to Article 92, it shall without delay initiate the procedure provided for in paragraph 2. The Member State concerned shall not put its proposed measures into effect until this procedure has resulted in a final decision.

Article 94

The Council, acting by a qualified majority on a proposal from the Commission *and after consulting the European Parliament*, may make any appropriate regulations for the application of Article 92 and 93 and may in particular determine the conditions in which Article 93(3) shall apply and the categories of aid exempted from this procedure.

Article 92(1) concerns *existing* aids. Article 92(3) concerns plans of Member States to *grant* or *alter* aids. The Commission has to supervise constantly existing aids in cooperation with the Member States. New aids have to be notified to the Commission. The notification duty is the cornerstone of the whole Community system of state aids. The Commission has reminded the Member States of their duty at different occasions. Based on the notification the Commission may initiate an investigation procedure. Interested parties have to be given a right to be heard in the inquiry which is carefully protected by the European Court. Article 93(3) provides for a stand-still obligation. Member States shall not put their proposed measures into effect until the procedure has resulted in a final decision. The Commission may decide within two months (Case 120/73 *Lorenz* v. *Germany* [1979] ECR 1471) that the state concerned shall abolish or alter such aid. Where existing or new aid is perceived to violate such a decision, Article 93(2) allows the Commission to pursue a special infringement procedure in derogation from Article 169.

B. DEFINITION OF STATE AID

The first issue is to define state aids. State aid has been found in the presence of the following:

(a) interventions which, in various forms, mitigate the charges which are normally included in the budget of an undertaking and which without being subsidies are similar in character and have the same effect;

(b) the payment of a proportion of the cost of production by someone other than the purchaser;

(c) an advantage entailing a burden to public finances in the form of either expenditure or reduced revenue;

(d) a grant from the state for no consideration;

(e) assumption by the state of costs which are normally assumed by undertakings;

(f) assumption by the state of part of the risk which is normally assumed by undertakings;

(g) compensation from the state to a company or receipt of reduced revenue by the state;

(h) the grant of resources or advantages by the state to encourage the attainment of economic or social objectives;

(i) any type of support granted by a Member State or through state resources other than for commercial purposes.

(Taken from A. Evans & S. Martin, Socially Acceptable Distortion of Competition: Community Policy on State Aid, *ELRev*, 1991, p.79 *et seq.* 81.)

All these examples are taken from Court rulings. They indicate the broad range of instruments dedicated to providing financial assistance to undertakings. In defining whether a measure comes under the scope of Article 92, the ECR applies the same rules as in defining the reach of Article 30: it is not the objective but the effect, which decides.

Case 173/73 *Italian Republic* v. *Commission* [1974] ECR 709, 715 concerned the legal character of family allowances allowing for temporary and partial reduction of social charges in the textile sector.

Grounds of judgment

By application of 9 October 1973 the Government of the Italian Republic asked, on the basis of Article 173 of the EEC Treaty, that the Court should annul the Commission Decision of 25 July 1973 on Article 20 of the Italian Law No 1101 of 1 December 1971 on the restructuring, reorganization and conversion of the textile industry (OJ of 11 September 1973, No L 254, p.14).

The action is based on three submissions described as 'preliminary', relating to the form and preliminary procedure of the Decision, and three submissions described as 'subsidiary', relating to its substance.

Because of the connection between the first three submissions and that between the three subsidiary submissions they should be examined under two separate headings.

[...]

As to the subsidiary submissions

12 The applicant Government maintains first that, by encroaching upon a field reserved by the Treaty to the sovereignty of Member States – that of the

levying of internal taxation – the Decision is vitiated by reason of abuse of powers.

Secondly, the applicant asserts that the reduction of social charges in issue must be regarded as a measure of a social nature and that accordingly it falls outside the scope of Articles 92 and 93.

Because the system for financing family allowances which was previously in force placed sectors employing a high proportion of female labour in a disadvantageous position, the measure in issue is said simply to make up for a handicap suffered by the Italian textile industry.

Furthermore, this industry is alleged to be at a disadvantage as compared with the textile industries of the other Member States by reason of the fact that the social charges devolving upon employers are appreciably higher in Italy than in the other Member States.

Finally, the partial reduction in social charges is stated not to be such as to affect intra-Community trade or distort competition within the common market. [...]

14   As to the argument that the contested measure has no purpose other than to rectify the amount of charges payable by the textile industry to the state insurance scheme, in this case relating to family allowances, it is clear that the Italian family allowance scheme is intended, as is the case with all similar schemes, to ensure that the worker obtains a salary which meets the needs of his family.

Since in a system of this kind employers' contribution are assessed in accordance with the wage costs of each undertaking, the fact that a relatively small number of the employees of an undertaking can, on the basis of their position as heads of household, claim actual payment of these allowances, cannot constitute either an advantage or a specific disadvantage for the undertaking in question as compared with other undertakings where a higher proportion of employees receive these allowances; the burden of payment of these allowances is rendered exactly the same for all undertakings.

15   The above observations in respect of charges under the family allowance scheme payable out of the profits of an undertaking applies, on the same basis, to the relationship between the different branches of industry.

Consequently, the figures submitted by the applicant Government showing that during 1971 the sum of 65.7 thousand million lire was paid in contributions by the textile sector, whereas the social security benefits pertaining to family allowances in this sector only amounted to 42.4 thousand million lire, cannot prove that, in respect of its production costs, the textile sector was placed in a disadvantageous position in relation to other sectors of industry.

It must be concluded that the partial reduction of social charges pertaining to family allowances devolving upon employers in the textile sector is a measure intended partially to exempt undertakings of a particular industrial sector from the financial charges arising from the normal application of the general social security system, without there being any justification for this exemption on the basis of the nature or general scheme of this system.

16 The argument that the contested reduction is not a 'State aid', because the loss of revenue resulting from it is made good through funds accruing from contributions paid to the unemployment insurance fund, cannot be accepted. As the funds in question are financed through compulsory contributions imposed by State legislation and as, as this case shows, they are managed and apportioned in accordance with the provisions of that legislation, they must be regarded as State resources within the meaning of Article 92, even if they are administered by institutions distinct from the public authorities.

17 As to the argument that the social charges devolving upon employers in the textile sector are higher in Italy than in the other Member States, it should be observed that, in the application of Article 92(1), the point of departure must necessarily be the competitive position existing within the common market before the adoption of the measure in issue.

This position is the result of numerous factors having varying effects on production costs in the different Member States.

Moreover, Articles 92 to 102 of the Treaty provide for detailed rules for the abolition of generic distortions resulting from differences between the tax and social security systems of the different Member States whilst taking account of structural difficulties in certain sectors of industry.

On the other hand, the unilateral modification of a particular factor of the cost of production in a given sector of the economy of a Member State may have the effect of disturbing the existing equilibrium.

Consequently, there is no point in comparing the relative proportions of total production costs which a particular category of costs represents, since the decisive factor is the reduction itself and not the category of costs to which it relates.

18 In addition, the social charges payable by employers are part of the more general category of labour costs.

It emerges from the file that labour costs in the Italian textile sector are, in relation to those in the textile sector in the other Member States, relatively low.

It is clear that the reduction in social charges provided for by Article 20 of Law No 1101 has the effect of reducing labour costs in the Italian textile sector.

19 The Italian textile industry is in competition with textile undertakings in the other Member States, as is shown by the substantial and growing volume of Italian textile exports to other Member States of the Common Market.

The modification of production costs in the Italian textile industry by the reduction of the social charges in question necessarily affects trade between the Member States.

20   Accordingly, the subsidiary submissions must also be dismissed.

C. DISTORTION OF COMPETITION AND EFFECT ON TRADE

Once the state aid is identified the question is whether competition is distorted. It is suggested that a state aid, coming under Article 92 will automatically affect competition. However, Article 92 requires the likelihood of a distortion of competition affecting trade between Member States. What does likelihood mean? Is a quantitative evaluation necessary or a qualitative one? Is an economic analysis required which describes and analyses the possible effects of the state aid on intracommunity trade? Articles 92–94 do not provide an answer. This had to be found by the Court, Case 47/69 *France* v. EC *Commission* [1970] ECR 487, 493:

Grounds of judgment

1   By an application made on 26 September 1969, the Government of the French Republic requested the annulment of the decision of the Commission of 18 July 1968, which in the first place ordered the abolition of the aid given in France to the textile industry and, alternatively, gave its approval to the said aid subject to amendments being made to the quasi-fiscal charge designed to finance it.

The first submission

2   The French Government maintains, first, that the contested decision has no legal foundation and amounts to a misuse of powers since Article 93(2) of the Treaty, which empowers the Commission only to take a decision that aid which is recognized as incompatible with the common market must be abolished or altered, cannot serve as the basis for a decision which is concerned with procuring the alteration of the basis of assessment of a charge intended to finance that aid.

3   Under Article 93(2) of the Treaty, if the Commission finds 'that aid granted by a State or through State resources is not compatible with the Common Market having regard to Article 92 or that such aid is being misused, it shall decide that the State concerned shall abolish or alter such aid within a period of time to be determined by the Commission'.

4   This provision, by thus taking into account the connection which may exist between the aid granted by a Member State and the method by which it is financed through the resources of that State, does not therefore allow the Commission to isolate the aid as such from the method by which it is financed and to disregard this method if, in conjunction with the aid in its narrow sense, it renders the whole incompatible with the Common Market.

5   Under Article 92(1): 'Any aid granted by a Member State or through State resources in any form whatsoever which distorts or threatens to distort competition by favouring certain undertakings or the production of certain goods shall, in so far as it affects trade between Member States, be incompatible with the Common Market'.

6   Nevertheless under Article 92(3)(c): 'The following may be considered to be compatible with the Common Market: ...aid to facilitate the development of certain economic activities or of certain economic areas, where such aid does not adversely affect trading conditions to an extent contrary to the common interest'.

7   In order to determine whether an aid 'affects trade between Member States', 'distorts or threatens to distort competition by favouring certain undertakings or the production of certain goods' and 'adversely affects trading conditions to an extent contrary to the common interest', it is necessary to consider all the legal and factual circumstances surrounding that aid, in particular whether there is an imbalance between the charges imposed on the undertakings or producers concerned on the one hand and the benefits derived from the aid in question on the other.

8   Consequently the aid cannot be considered separately from the effects of its method of financing.

9   The Commission therefore had power to decide whether the French Republic should abolish or alter the disputed system of aid as a whole.

The second submission

10   The French Government claims that Articles 12 and 95 are alone applicable in this case and can afford no grounds for objecting to the charge in question, since it was levied both on national and imported products and did not have any effects equivalent to a customs duty.

11   This argument amounts to asserting that when an aid is financed by internal taxation, this method of financing can only be examined in relation to its compatibility with Article 95 and that the requirements of Articles 92 and 93 must be disregarded.

12   However these two types of provision have different aims in view.

13   The fact that a national measure complies with the requirements of Article 95 does not imply that it is valid in relation to other provisions, such as those of Articles 92 and 93.

14   When an aid is financed by taxation of certain undertakings or certain producers, the Commission is required to consider not only whether the method by which it is financed complies with Article 95 of the Treaty but also whether in conjunction with the aid which it services it is compatible with the requirements of Articles 92 and 93.

15   The French Government further maintains that in admitting that the French textile industry needed aid, the Commission could not refuse it without contradicting itself nor require an alteration of the method whereby it was financed since on the one hand this method does not adversely affect trade to an extent contrary to the common interest, and on the other hand the same result could be achieved if the aid in question, instead of being serviced by a charge designed for the purpose, were serviced by budgetary means financed by the value-added tax.

16   It may be that aid properly so-called, although not in conformity with Community law, does not substantially affect trade between States and may thus be acknowledged as permissible but that the disturbance which it creates is increased by a method of financing it which would render the scheme as a whole incompatible with a single market and the common interest.

17   In its appraisal the Commission must therefore take into account all those factors which directly or indirectly characterize the measure in question, that is, not only aid, properly so-called, for selected national activities, but also the indirect aid which may be constituted both by the method of financing and by the close connection which makes the amount of aid dependent upon the revenue from the charge.

18   If such a system whereby an aid is serviced by a charge designed for that purpose, were to become general, it would have the effect of opening a loophole in Article 92 of the Treaty and of reducing the Commission's opportunities of keeping the position under constant review.

19   In fact it leads to a system of permanent aids, the amount of which is unforeseeable and which would be difficult to review.

20   By automatically increasing the amount of national aid in proportion to the increase in the revenue from the charge and more especially the revenue from the charge levied on competing foreign products, the method of financing in question has a protective effect which goes beyond aid properly so-called.

21   In particular, the more Community undertakings succeed in increasing sales in a Member State by marketing efforts and by price-cutting, the more they have to contribute under the system of the servicing charge to an aid which is essentially intended for those of their own competitors who have not made such efforts.

22 Thus the Commission was entitled to take the view that the fact that foreign undertakings can have access to research work done in France could not eliminate the adverse effects on the Common Market of an aid incorporating a charge designed to service it.

23 Therefore it has rightly decided that this aid, whatever might be the rate of the said charge, has the effect, because of the method by which it is financed, of adversely affecting trade to an extent contrary to the common interest within the meaning of Article 92(3)(c).

24 It follows from these considerations that the Commission in assessing as a whole the aid granted by the French Republic through State resources was justified in considering this aid as contrary to 'the common interest' and in requesting the French Government to abolish it, whilst acknowledging both the useful nature of the aid properly so-called and the fact that it conformed with 'the common interest' if the method whereby it was financed could be modified.

25 Consequently the application must be dismissed.

After this very explicit statement of the Court it seemed to be clear that only a qualitative analysis was needed to define the possible effects of the state aid. Member States, however, were not willing to accept such a low threshold of intervention and brought the issue of 'likelihood' again to Court. Case 730/79 *Philip Morris Holland BV* v. *EC Commission* [1980] ECR 2671, 2687 underlined that no complicated market analysis was required:

Decision

1 By an application of 12 October 1979 the applicant asks the Court, pursuant to Article 173 of the EEC Treaty, to declare void Commission Decision 79/743/EEC of 27 July 1979 on proposed Netherlands Government assistance to increase the production capacity of a cigarette manufacturer (Official Journal 1979, L 217, p. 17).

2 The applicant is the Netherlands subsidiary of a major tobacco manufacturer. The Netherlands Government by a letter of 7 October 1978 informed the Commission of its intention to grant the applicant "the additional premium for major schemes" provided for by the Netherlands Law of 29 June 1978 on the promotion and guidance of investment (Staatsblad No 368, 1978). This premium for investment projects having a value exceeding Hfl 30 000 000 depends on the number of jobs created and may account for up to 4% of the investment in question. According to Article 6 of that Law the premium shall not be granted to the extent to which, in the opinion of the Commission, the grant thereof would be incompatible with the common market under the terms of Articles 92 to 94 of the Treaty.

3   The aim of the aid in question was to help the applicant to concentrate and develop its production of cigarettes by closing one of the two factories which it owns in the Netherlands and by raising the annual production capacity of the second located at Bergen-op-Zoom in the south of the country to 16 000 million cigarettes, thereby increasing the manufacturing capacity of the subsidiary by 40% and total production in the Netherlands by about 13%.

4   After the Commission had reviewed the proposed aid in accordance with the provisions of Article 93 of the Treaty it adopted the disputed decision, which provides that the Kingdom of the Netherlands shall refrain from implementing its proposal, communicated to the Commission by letter dated 4 October 1978, to grant the "additional premium for major schemes" to investment made at Bergen-op-Zoom.

Admissibility of the application

5   The Commission does not dispute the applicant's right as a potential recipient of the aid referred to in the decision to bring an action for a declaration that the decision is void even though it is addressed to a Member State.

Substance

6   The applicant puts forward two grounds for declaring the contested decision to be void. In the first place the Commission Decision (a) is in breach of Article 92(1) of the Treaty, (b) is in breach of one or more general principles of Community law, in particular the principles of good administration, the protection of legitimate expectation and of proportionality, or at least one or more principles of the Commission's competition policy, (c) is in breach of Article 190 of the Treaty in that the Commission's statement of the reasons on which the decision is based is incomprehensible or contradictory.

7   In the second place the decision that the derogating provisions of Article 92(3) of the Treaty do not apply in the circumstances of this case is in breach of the provisions of the Treaty and of the above-mentioned principles of Community law.

First submission

[...]

9   The applicant maintains that, in order to decide to what extent specific aid is incompatible with the common market, it is appropriate to apply first of all the criteria for deciding whether there are any restrictions on competition under Articles 85 and 86 of the Treaty. The Commission must therefore first determine the "relevant market" and in order to do so must take account of the product, the territory and the period of time in question. It must then consider the pattern of the market in question in order to be able to as-

sess how far the aid in question in a given case affects relations between competitors. But these essential aspects of the matter are not found in the disputed decision. The decision does not define the relevant market either from the standpoint of the product or in point of time. The market pattern and moreover for that matter, the relations between competitors resulting therefrom which might in a given case be distorted by the disputed aid, have not been specified at all.

10 It is common ground that when the applicant has completed its planned investment it will account for nearly 50% of cigarette production in the Netherlands and that it expects to export over 80% of its production to other Member States. The "additional premium for major schemes" which the Netherlands Government proposed to grant the applicant amounted to Hfl 6.2 million (2.3 million EUA) which is 3.8% of the capital invested.

11 When State financial aid strengthens the position of an undertaking compared with other undertakings competing in intra-Community trade the latter must be regarded as affected by that aid. In this case the aid which the Netherlands Government proposed to grant was for an undertaking organized for international trade and this is proved by the high percentage of its production which it intends to export to other Member States. The aid in question was to help to enlarge its production capacity and consequently to increase its capacity to maintain the flow of trade including that between Member States. On the other hand the aid is said to have reduced the cost of converting the production facilities and has thereby given the applicant a competitive advantage over manufacturers who have completed or intend to complete at their own expense a similar increase in the production capacity of their plant.

12 These circumstances, which have been mentioned in the recitals in the preamble to the disputed decision and which the applicant has not challenged, justify the Commission's deciding that the proposed aid would be likely to affect trade between Member States and would threaten to distort competition between undertakings established in different Member States.

13 It follows from the foregoing considerations that the first submission must be rejected in substance and also as far as concerns the inadequacy of the statement of reasons on which the decision was based.

Second submission

14 The applicant's second submission criticizes the decision for being based on the inapplicability in this case of the derogations referred to in Article 92(3) on the Treaty and in particular in subparagraphs(a), (b) and (c) thereof. [...]

16 According to the applicant it is wrong for the Commission to lay down as a general principle that aid granted by a Member State to undertakings only falls within the derogating provisions of Article 92(3) if the Commission

can establish that the aid will contribute to the attainment of one of the objectives specified in the derogations, which under normal market conditions the recipient firms would not attain by their own actions. Aid is only permissible under Article 92(3) of the Treaty if the investment plan under consideration is in conformity with the objectives mentioned in subparagraphs (a), (b) and (c).

17   This argument cannot be upheld. On the one hand it disregards the fact that Article 92(3), unlike Article 92(2), gives the Commission a discretion by providing that the aid which it specifies "may" be considered to be compatible with the common market. On the other hand it would result in Member States being permitted to make payments which would improve the financial situation of the recipient undertaking although they were not necessary for the attainment of the objectives specified in Article 92(3).

18   It should be noted in this connection that the disputed decision explicitly states that the Netherlands Government has not been able to give nor has the Commission found any grounds establishing that the proposed aid meets the conditions laid down to enforce derogations pursuant to Article 92(3) of the EEC Treaty.

19   The applicant maintains that the Commission was wrong to hold that the standard of living in the Bergen-op-Zoom area is not "abnormally low" and that this area does not suffer serious "under-employment" within the meaning of Article 92(3)(a). In fact in the Bergen-op-Zoom region the underemployment rate is higher and the *per capita* income lower than the national average in the Netherlands.

20   As far as concerns Article 92(3)(b) the applicant disputes the Commission's assertion that the system of an "additional premium" cannot be compared to aid intended to "remedy a serious disturbance in the economy of a Member State", and that to take any other view would allow the Netherlands in the context of an economic downturn and large-scale unemployment throughout the whole Community to effect to their advantage investments likely to be made in other Member States in a less favourable situation.

21   In the applicant's view it is impossible to answer the question whether there is a serious disturbance in the economy of a Member State and, if so, whether a specific national aid remedies that disturbance by considering, as the Commission has done, whether the investment by the undertaking to which the aid from the particular Member State relates may if necessary be effected in other Member States in a less favourable situation than that Member State.

22   Finally the applicant challenges the Commission's statement in the decision that an examination of the cigarette manufacturing industry in the Community and in the Netherlands shows that market conditions alone and without State intervention seem apt to ensure a normal development and

that the disputed aid cannot therefore be considered as facilitating the development within the meaning of Article 92(3)(c).

23   The applicant takes the view that, in principle, the question whether "without state intervention" market conditions alone are such as to ensure a normal development of production in a Member State and in the Community is irrelevant. The only thing that matters is to ascertain whether the aid facilitates development or not. Furthermore the statement of the reasons on which the decision is based is incomprehensible and contradictory.

24   These arguments put forward by the applicant cannot be upheld. It should be borne in mind that the Commission has a discretion the exercise of which involves economic and social assessments which must be made in a Community context.

25   That is the context in which the Commission has with good reason assessed the standard of living and serious under-employment in the Bergen-op-Zoom area, not with reference to the national average in the Netherlands but in relation to the Community level. As far as concerns the applicant's argument based on Article 92(3)(b) of the Treaty the Commission could very well take the view, as it did, that the investment to be effected in this case was not "an important project of common European interest" and that the proposed aid could not be likened to aid intended "to remedy a serious disturbance in the economy of a Member State", since the proposed aid would have permitted the transfer to the Netherlands, of an investment which could be effected in other Member States in a less favourable economic situation than that of the Netherlands where the national level of un-employment is one of the lowest in the Community.

26   As far as concerns Article 92(3)(c) of the Treaty the arguments submitted by the applicant are not relevant. The compatibility with the Treaty of the aid in question must be determined in the context of the Community and not of a single Member State. The Commission's assessment is based for the most part on the finding that the increase in the production of cigarettes envisaged would be exported to the other Member States, in a situation where the growth of consumption has slackened and this did not permit the view that trading conditions would remain unaffected by this aid to an extent contrary to the common interest. This assessment is justified. The finding that market conditions in the cigarette manufacturing industry seem apt without State intervention, to ensure a normal development, and that the aid cannot therefore be regarded as "facilitating" the development is also justified when the need for aid is assessed from the standpoint of the Community rather than of a single Member State.

27   The application is therefore dismissed.

So, it is relatively easy for the Commission to apply Article 92 and to initiate an investigation procedure. If, however, the Commission wants to take action, that is, if it intends to require the state in question to alter or to abolish the aid, it must state its reasons for action. In Cases 296 and 318/82 *Kingdom of Netherlands and Leeuwarder Papierwarenfabriek BV* v. *EC Commission* [1985], ECR 809 the Court began by saying that 'the statement of reasons for a decision adversely affecting an undertaking must be such as to allow the Court to review its legality and to provide the undertaking concerned with the information necessary to enable it to ascertain whether or not the decision is well-founded'. The Court had annulled the decision in question because it did not contain 'the slightest information concerning the situation in the relevant market, the place of the undertaking in that market, the pattern of trade between Member States in the products in question or the undertaking's exports'. Since then the Commission's decisions have contained market and trade statistics.

Does the Commission gain anything in the end? What does it mean, if the Commission does not need to prove the likelihood of a state aid affecting intra-community trade, but if it has to state its reasons accurately? Is it just a shift from economic analysis to legal grounding?

D. COMPENSATORY JUSTIFICATION

When looking through the Articles on subsidies no rule on the possibility of compensatory justification may be found. Such a logic may be drawn, however, from the interplay between Article 85(1) and Article 85(3). Exemption of certain restrictive agreements from the prohibition of Article 85(3) is allowed, if they fulfil the requirements. In Case 730/79 *Philip Morris Holland BV* v. *EC Commission* (1980) ECR 2671 the Court of Justice endorsed a similar principle in the context of state aids. Advocate General Capotorti (at 2702) tried to draw a borderline between acceptable justification and unacceptable justifications. The reference point is the existence of community policies: 'in authorising derogations from the prohibition of State aid the Commission must strive to co-ordinate national policies towards aids on the basis of common criteria and in terms of the general interest of the Community'. Where should the 'common criteria' and the 'terms of general interest' be found? The basis must be sought in Article 92(3). The policy requirements laid down here are not at all clearly shaped. When it comes down to deciding whether a policy instrument in question matches the requirements of one of the sub-paragraphs, the result will usually be that quite a number of sub-paragraphs come into play.

Andrew Evans and Stephen Martin, *Socially Acceptable Distortion of Competition: Community Policy on State Aid*, have developed a classification, which provides an order which is lacking in the law. This has proven to be helpful. They distinguish between 'sectorial policies', 'regional policy' and 'horizontal policies'.

SOCIALLY ACCEPTABLE DISTORTION OF COMPETITION: COMMUNITY POLICY ON STATE AID*

Andrew Evans and Stephen Martin

[...]
Sectoral policies

The approaches of the Commission to sectoral aid are basically of two kinds. First, such problems may be approached within the framework of a common policy for which the Treaties provide a specific legal basis (such as those for coal and steel, agriculture and fisheries). Here the approach of the Commission has been determined by the general requirements of each policy. [...]

The second approach constitutes the response of the Commission to state interventions in specific sectors. Here the principal concern of the Commission has been to prevent the grant of state aid from exacerbating existing problems or transferring them from one Member State to another. Principles have been formulated regarding aid to the textile, man-made fibre, and automobile industries, as well as air transport.[1]

The general policy of the Commission regarding sectoral aid was defined in a communication to the Council of 5 May, 1978.[2] At this time, sectoral policy was seen as a tool to ease industries with persistent excess capacity through a transitional period:[3]

(i) aids should not be given where their sole effect would be to maintain the status quo;

(ii) while rescue measures may be needed in order to provide a breathing space during which longer-term solutions to a company's difficulties can be worked out, they should not frustrate any necessary reductions in capacity;

---

* First published in *European Law Review*, 1991, pp.79(92) *et seq.*; reprinted by permission of Sweet & Maxwell, London.

[1] The Commission first notified Member States of principles regarding aids to the textile industry in 1971, and these were updated in 1977. Guidelines regarding aid to the automobile sector were introduced in 1988. These principles are not legally binding: see the view of Advocate General Darmon in Case 310/85 *Deufil GmbH & Co. KG* v. *EC Commission* [1978] ECR 901 at 914; [1988] 1 C.M.L.R.553 at 556. Directives on shipbuilding are binding: see Directive 87/167 O.J. 1987 L69/55.

[2] Com (78) 221.

[3] EC Commission, *Eighth Report on Competition Policy*, Brussels, 1978, p.126. Similar language appears in innumerable Commission decisions.

(iii) since it is a common feature of the industries concerned that capacity is excessive, aids should not be given to investment projects which would result in capacity being increased.

[...]

Operating aid. Operating aid is assistance that "has a direct effect on production costs and on the selling price."[4] It is regarded as artificially maintaining excess capacity, and has traditionally been considered by the Commission to be particularly objectionable.[5] Such aid, it is feared, may discourage firms from undertaking the restructuring activity necessary to solve their problems. [...]

Restructuring aid. Aid designed to resolve structural problems is more likely to be found acceptable than aid aimed at cyclical or conjunctural problems,[6]

> As to the exception in Article 92(3)(c) for aid to facilitate the development of certain economic activities or certain economic areas, Noviboch produces and markets quality ceramic sanitary ware on a fairly modest scale, with 269 employees....its output is currently 20 to 30% lower than that of its predecessor...
> The restructuring stemming from the winding-up of Boch has therefore contributed to the reorganisation of a Community industry suffering from surplus production capacity...
> ...the aid in the form of a subscription of Bfrs 400 million of share capital granted in connection with the setting-up of Noviboch therefore qualifies for exemption under Article 92(3)(c).

The amount and intensity of aid must be justified by the restructuring effort involved, taking account of general structural problems of the region where the investment is to take place.[7] [...]

Rescue aid. In a letter to the Member States of January 24, 1979,[8] the Commission elaborated on the conditions under which rescue aid would be regarded as compatible with the common market. Rescue aid must be designed to keep a firm in

---

[4] Commission Decision 82/744 of October 11, 1982, concerning Italian national Law No.423/81 of August 1, 1981, on measures for agriculture O.J.1982 L315/23 at 24.

[5] The attitude of the Commission has the approval of the Court. See Case 310/85 *Deufil GmbH & Co. KG* v. *EC Commission* [1987] E.C.R.901 at 926; [1988] 1 C.M.L.R.553 at 566, regarding investment for the normal modernisation of plant. See, more recently, Case C-86/89 *Italy* v. *EC Commission* (not yet reported).

[6] Commission Decision 87/423 of March 11, 1987, concerning aid which the Belgian Government has granted to a ceramic sanitary ware manufacturer at La Louvière O.J. 1987 L228/39 at 40.

[7] Commission Decision No. 2320/81 of August 7, 1981, establishing Community rules for aids to the steel industry O.J. 1981 L228/14 at 16.

[8] For discussion, see Commission Decision 87/585 of July 15, 1987, on aid granted by the French Government to a producer of textiles, clothing and paper products – Boussac Saint Freres O.J. 1987 L352/42 at 48.

business while the causes of its difficulties are discovered and a remedy is worked out. Compatible rescue aid will have the following characteristics:

1   it is provided in cash and must bear normal interests rates;
2   it is provided only for the time needed to draw up recovery measures (generally six months or less);
3   it does not have adverse effects on industrial activity on other Member States;
4   it is notified to the Commission in advance.

The judgment in *Intermills S.A.* v. *EC Commission*,[9] which involved a Belgian programme of aid to a paper manufacturing firm, is illustrative of the issues raised by rescue aid. Intermills S.A. operated five factories in Wallonia. State aid was linked to a restructuring programme that included a reduction in output, conversion from mass production to high value-added specialty papers, closure of two factories, and creation of three independent companies to manage the remaining factories. The aid took the form of investment by the Walloon Regional Executive in Intermills and in the three manufacturing companies, and a low-interest loan to finance an investment programme by the manufacturing companies. [...]

The Commission, however, distinguished between aid in the form of low-interest loans and aid in the form of capital investment. In the Commission's view, low-interest loans were directly related to the conversion toward specialty paper, and hence justified under Article 92(3)(c). The capital investment (2,350 million Belgian francs in an enterprise whose capital and reserves were 1,250 million Bfrs) was intended mainly to allow the firm to meet its debt-servicing obligations. The Commission was not willing to permit this "rescue aid," and ordered that it be stopped.

Intermills S.A. applied to the Court of Justice to set aside the Commission decision. It argued, among other things, that the Commission had not adequately explained why it was appropriate to distinguish aid in the form of low-interest loans and aid in the form of capital investment. The Court agreed:[10]

the Commission has not shown why the applicant's activities on the market, following the conversion of its production with the assistance of the aid granted, were likely to have such an adverse effect on trading conditions that the undertaking's disappearance would have been preferable to its rescue.

On this ground, the Court annulled the Commission decision. [...]

---

9   Case 323/82 [1984] E.C.R.3809; [1986] 1 C.M.L.R.614.
10   [1984] E.C.R. 3809 at 3832;[1986] 1 C.M.L.R.614 at 646. See Dony, Marianne "La participation des pouvoirs publics au capital des enterprises et le droit de la concurrence," *Cahiers de Droit Européen*, Vol.22, No.2, 1986, pp.161–84.

Regional policy[11]

Regional policy reflects a desire to balance support for the kind of unregulated decision making that characterises a market system with the promotion of economic integration:[12]

> The issue here is the necessary balance between free competition and solidarity. The importance of the latter depends upon the particular case; it is more likely to outweigh considerations of competition in the situations of crisis described in subparagraph (a) than in the cases provided for in subparagraph (c) relating to aid intended to assist the development of certain activities or certain economic regions.

The Commission's objection to regional aid is in part specific to its regional nature:[13]

> In so far as the aid induces firms to choose another location, this also constitutes a distortion of competition ... the institution of a system ensuring that competition in the common market is not distorted ... implies that firms should be allowed to make up their own mind where to locate and that their choice should therefore not be swayed or guided by financial inducements.

In other respects, the Commission's objection to regional aid is quite general:[14]

> The aid in issue in the present case distorts competition because it calculably improves the recipient's return on his investment, thereby strengthening his financial position compared with competitors who do not receive such assistance.

Level of regional development. A 1986 Commission decision, involving a Federal Republic of Germany regional aid programme, makes clear that the standard for regional aid is the level of regional development relative to the Community as a whole, not relative to the average of the state proposing the aid:[15]

---

11   See Commission Communication of June 23, 1971, J.O. 1971 C111/7; Resolution of the Representatives of the Governments of the Member States, meeting within the Council, on general systems of regional aid, of October 20, 1971, J.O. 1971 C111/1; Communication of the Commission on regional aid systems, O.J. 1979 C31/9; Commission Communication of 1988 O.J. 1988, C212/2.

12   Opinion of Advocate General Darmon, Case 248/84 *Germany* v. *EC Commission* [1987] E.C.R.4013 at 4031;[1988] 1 C.M.L.R.591 at 600.

13   Ibid.

14   Commission Decision 87/15 of February 19, 1986, on the compatibility with the common market of aid under the German Federal/Land Government Joint Regional Aid Programmeme (Joint Programmeme for the improvement of regional economic structures) in six labour market regions O.J. 1987 L12/17 at 21.

15   Ibid. at 22. See also Case 248/84 *Germany* v. *EC Commission* [1987] E.C.R.4013 at 4042; [1988] 1 C.M.L.R.591 at 608.

The only circumstances in which the effect on trading conditions caused by regional aid can be regarded as not against the common interest are where it can be shown that the aided region suffers from difficulties that are relatively severe by Community standards, that without the aid market forces would not eliminate these difficulties, that the level of aid is in proportion to the difficulties and that the grant of aid does not unduly distort competition in particular sectors.

The Commission has developed a systematic procedure for the comparison of regional and Community development, based on evaluation of structural unemployment and per capita gross domestic product.[16] The thresholds at which regional aid is deemed acceptable for a given Member State are decided in the light of its relative position in comparison with the Community average. The thresholds for more developed Member States are more restrictive. [...]

Infrastructure investment. A 1987 decision clarifies the import of Community policy toward state aids for a Greek business aid programme, and in so doing provides insight into recent developments regarding aid related to infrastructure investment:[17]

> With regard to the exceptions provided for...aid to promote the economic development of areas where the standard of living is abnormally low or where there is serious under-employment, while Greece may be regarded as meeting these definitions, the concept of regional development to which this exception is linked is based essentially on the provision of aid for new investment or major expansions or conversions of undertakings involving large-scale investments of a physical nature and the costs associated with these....the interventions...in respect of companies that have fallen into financial difficulties and the consequent restoration of their balance cannot be said to fall under the prescriptions of this exception.

Thus Article 92(3)(a) is seen by the Commission as permitting aid to investment programmes that will support regional development. Rescue aid for individual companies does not fall within this category.

The Commission has increasingly stressed that regional aid will only be permissible under Article 92(3)(c) where it involves initial investment or job creation. [...]

Developments related to European unification. The Commission showed considerable concern to secure the abolition of preferential rediscount rates prior to July 1,

---

[16] Commission Decision 87/15 of February 19, 1986, O.J. 1987 L12/17 at 23. See Communication of the Commission on regional aid systems O.J. 1979 C31/9 and Communication of the Commission on the method for the Application of Article 92(3)(a) and (c) to Regional Aids O.J. 1988 C212/2.

[17] Commission Decision 88/167 of October 7, 1987, concerning Law 1386/1983 by which the Greek Government grants aid to Greek industry O.J. 1988 L76/18 at 20.

1968, when the common market was to come into force.[18] One might expect to find corresponding concerns during the period preceding the completion of the internal market. Indeed, in the *Sixteenth Report on Competition Policy*, the Commission stated that

> The Community's efforts to complete a single unified internal market by 1992...lend added weight and importance to the enforcement of the competition rules, and in particular the rules on State aid.[19]

This has meant a refinement of policy regarding regional aid. As the Commission has noted,[20]

> The entry of Spain and Portugal, coming after that of Greece, has made it necessary for the Commission to refine its methods and criteria for assessing regional aid in the so-called 'peripheral' regions of the Community....The economic and social problems of these areas, which are predominantly agricultural, industrially under-developed and have widespread underemployment, call for a certain rethinking of the Commission's policy toward regional aid.

More generally, the Commission now concentrates on issues that have become a matter of priority as a result of the Single European Act. Thus

> The new Title v. of Part Three of the EEC Treaty, Article 130A, requires the Community to 'develop and pursue its actions leading to the strengthening of its economic and social cohesion' and, in particular, to aim at 'reducing disparities between the various regions and the backwardness of the least-favoured regions.'[21]

The willingness to assist severely depressed areas has led the Commission to modify its long-standing hostility toward operating aid.[22]

> Article 92(3)(a) regions are those suffering abnormally low living standards or serious underemployment where the per capita gross domestic product does not exceed 75% of the Community average...the assessment is made relative to the Community average. Given the particularly severe development problems faced in such regions, the Commission has decided that it may allow operating aids in some circumstances.

---

[18] See the facts in Cases 6/69 & 11/69 *EC Commission v. France* [1969] E.C.R. 523; [1970] C.M.L.R.43.
[19] EC Commission, *Sixteenth Report on Competition Policy*, Brussels, 1987, p.135. See also *Completing the Internal Market*, COM (85) 310 at pp.39–40.
[20] Ibid., p.178.
[21] Ibid.
[22] EC Commission, *Eighteenth Report on Competition Policy*, Brussels, 1989, p.147. For an application, see Commission Decision 88/318 of March 2, 1988, on Law No.64 of March 1,1986, on aid to the Mezzogiorno O.J. 1988 L143/37.

[...]

Horizontal policies

The new horizontal policies – environmental policy, the programme for small and medium-sized enterprises, and others – take as their starting-point the desirability of aid to accomplish certain goals. The presumption implied in the formal legal structure of Article 92 and established in past Commission practice may be reversed.

Article 92(3)(b) allows the Commission to exempt state aid related to important projects of common European interest. Projects which for example, seek to protect the environment may meet this qualification:[23]

> "The Commission has based its policy with regard to aid on the view that a project may not be described as being of common European interest for the purposes of Article 92(3)(b) unless it forms part of a transnational European programme supported jointly by a number of governments of the Member States, or arises from concerted action by a number of Member States to combat a common threat such as environmental pollution.
>
> In adopting that policy and in taking the view that the investments envisaged in this case did not fulfill the requisite conditions, the Commission did not commit a manifest error of judgment."

What is problematical, however, is the effect for competition policy. The horizontal policies cannot easily be reconciled with a reliance on the market as a mechanism for resource allocation.

Environmental policy. The first guidelines concerning environmental aid were produced in November 1974.[24] The Commission endorsed the "polluter pays" principle, and indicated that firms should normally bear the cost of investments needed to comply with environmental laws. At the time, however, the Community was perceived as lagging behind in environmental protection. For this reason, the guide-

---

[23] Joined Cases 62/87 and 72/87 *Exécutif Régional Wallon and Glaverbal SA* v. *EC Commission* [1988] E.C.R. 1573 at 1595; [1989] 2 C.M.L.R. 771. See Grabitz, Eberhard and Zacker, Christian "Scope for action by the EC Member States for the improvement of environmental protection under EEC law: the example of environmental taxes and subsidies," (1989) 26 C.M.L.Rev.423.

[24] EC Commission, *Fourth Report on Competition Policy*, Brussels, 1975, pp.101–106.

lines permitted state aid up to a specified ceiling for this purpose during a six-year transitional period (1975–1980).[25] [...]

The 1974 guidelines were supplemented in 1980.[26] At this time, the transitional period was extended through 1986. The guidelines were extended again in 1986, by which time the Commission was beginning to rethink the whole basis of its environmental policy:[27]

> However, developments in the years since 1974 have changed the context of environmental policy. The process has culminated in the environmental provisions of the Single European Act, which states that 'Action by the Community relating to the environment shall be based on the principles that preventive action should be taken, that environmental damage should as a priority be rectified at the source, and that the polluter shall pay. Environmental protection requirements shall be a component of the Community's other policies'... These developments call into question the concept of a purely transitional approach since it is now clear that improvement in the environment and the need to avoid distortions of competition caused by national measures in this field will remain a major task for an indefinite period.

Under present guidelines, environmental aid qualifies for an Article 92(3)(b) exemption as an important project of common European interest if:

(i)   the aid is intended to facilitate the implementation of new environmental standards;

(ii) the net grant equivalent of the aid does not exceed 15 per cent of the value of the aided investment;

(iii) firms receiving aid have had installations in operation for at least two years before the entry into force of the environmental standards in question;

(iv) the eligible firm bears the entire cost of normal replacement investment and operating costs.[28]

These guidelines suggest that market failure no longer has the decisive significance once attributed to it as a condition for the acceptability of state aid. It is notable that the guidelines are broadly interpreted. Listings of instances of state aid to which the Commission does not object (published in the annex of the annual *Report on Competition Policy*) indicate that the Commission permits numerous instances of aid aimed at protecting the environment.

---

25 See EC Commission, *Sixth Report on Competition Policy*, Brussels, 1977, pp.127–131 for instances in which the Commission approved and did not approve aid under these guidelines.
26 EC Commission, *Tenth Report on Competition Policy*, Brussels, 1981, pp.157–158.
27 EC Commission, *Sixteenth Report on Competition Policy*, Brussels, 1987, p.176.
28 Ibid.

Research & development. While the main concern of sectoral policy has been the management of structural excess capacity, a subsidiary purpose has been to promote technological competitiveness. By co-ordinating investment in innovation, the Commission seeks in effect to minimise a kind of "technological excess capacity":

> For other industries the Commission's action has been much more limited, and has been confined to those, such as computers, certain areas of electronics and aerospace, in which, because of the strength of competition from producers in third countries, the Community industry has proved unable to take full advantage of a rapid growth in demand. In these cases the Commission has laid particular stress on the need to avoid a duplication of efforts and has accordingly argued for collaboration between Member States on some projects and more generally for a coordination of national measures. It has in general been favourably disposed to aids which are granted within a coordinated framework of this kind and particularly to those for research and development.[29]

Underlying this policy is an evident belief in market failure, as regards technological advance.[30] State aid is seen as a device for improving on the performance of the unaided market.

Because the market is seen as generating a less-than-optimal level of investment in research and development, there is a general presumption in favour of aid for research and development:[31]

> the Commission has traditionally taken a favourable view...when it has come to scrutinize individual schemes under Article 92...This...is justified by...the aims of such aid, the often considerable financing requirements for R&D, the risks attached and, given the distance from the market place of such projects, the reduced likelihood of distortions of competition or trade between Member States.

Aid for research and development to promote an important project of common European interest may be exempted under Article 92(3)(b). The Commission has approved aid for the development of a common standard for high-definition colour television on this basis.[32]

The Commission has discretion to decide whether or not a project is important and of common European interest. This involves not only an evaluation of the in-

---

[29] EC Commission, *Eighth Report on Competition Policy*, Brussels, 1979, p.126.
[30] See the remarks on state aid to the electronic data processing industry in EC Commission, *Second Report on Competition Policy*, Brussels, 1973, p.93, where it is clear that the market for financial capital is seen as the source of market failure.
[31] Community Framework for State Aids for Research and Development, O.J. 1986 C83/2.
[32] EC Commission, *Eighteenth Report on Competition Policy*, Brussels, 1989, p.151.

novative nature of the project, but also a consideration of market factors:[33] "The mere fact that the investments envisaged enabled new technology to be used does not make the project one of common European interest: that certainly cannot be the case when...the products have to be sold on a saturated market."

Aid which would otherwise fail to qualify for one of the Article 92 exemptions cannot be saved by characterising it as R&D aid. Individual aid packages are carefully scrutinised, to assure that the aided activity is genuinely innovative in character. Modest technical improvements and routine refittings will not qualify.[34]

Small and medium-sized enterprise. Aid for small and medium-sized enterprise was initially seen as a means of assisting such firms to overcome their peculiar difficulties:[35]

1   limited access to markets for financial capital;
2   small size not justified by economic need;
3   greater difficulty adapting to technological, industrial, and commercial developments;
4   lack of information needed to extend operations to the Community scale and beyond.

The Commission has consistently maintained a positive attitude toward small and medium enterprises, because of the role they are seen as playing in a market economy. [...]

Employment. Programmes of state aid designed to increase employment will often be found acceptable, particularly if they also involve the promotion of research and development or small and medium-sized firms. Thus in 1986 the Commission approved portions of a Belgian regional aid programme:[36]

---

[33]   Joined Cases 62/87 and 72/87 *Exécutif Régional Wallon and Glaverbel SA* v. *EC Commission* [1988] ECR 1573 at 1595; [1989] 2 C.M.L.R.771.

[34]   See Commission Decision 87/16 of April 23, 1986, on a proposal by the Italian Government to grant aid to a firm in the chemical industry (producing industrial auxiliaries, intermediates and pesticides) O.J. 1987 L12/27; Commission Decision 87/194 of November 12, 1986, on an FIM (industrial modernisation fund) loan to a mineral-water and glass-water manufacturer O.J 1987 L77/43; Commission Decision 87/303 of January 14, 1987, on an FIM loan to a brevery O.J. 1987 L152/27; Commission Decision 89/254 of November 15, 1988, relating to aid which the Belgian Government has granted to a petrochemicals company at Ottignies/Louvain-la-Neuve (S.A. Belgian Shell) O.J. 1989 L106/34; Commission Decision 89/305 of December 21, 1988, concerning aid from the French Government to an undertaking in the motor vehicle sector--Peugeot S.A. O.J. 1989 L123/53.

[35]   EC Commission, *Sixth Report on Competition Policy*, Brussels, 1977, p.132.

[36]   EC Commission, *Sixteenth Report on Competition Policy*, Brussels, 1987, p.138.

The provisions not contested by the Commission were a partial relief from corporation tax for six years for companies which before 31 December 1987 reduce their weekly working hours by at least 8% and correspondingly increase their workforce, and a partial relief from corporation tax for 10 years for 'innovative' companies employing less than 100 people engaged in the exploitation of new high technologies.

The Commission raised no objection to these parts of the Act, because they were in line with stated Commission policy to encourage employment by reducing working hours and to promote small and medium-sized enterprises, particularly in high-technology sectors.

However, claims are carefully scrutinised. Aid will not be exempted merely because it may indirectly protect employment and the pay levels of employees. In a decision where this issue was raised, the Commission stated:

> The Belgian authorities also pointed out in their comments that the investment would not only maintain the jobs of 336 persons, but would also lead over the next few years to the recruitment of several hundred workers in the district bordering on the Turnhout area, which qualifies for regional assistance and where the rate of unemployment is particularly high. However, this knock-on effect is by no means assured and at this juncture the effect of the aid on the employment situation in the Turnhout area cannot be assessed.[37]

TRENDS IN COMMISSION PRACTICE

[...]

An emerging presumption in favour of certain types of aid?

On the other hand, regional policy as well as the horizontal policies, such as environmental policy and the programme for small and medium-sized enterprises were given a boost by the Single European Act. This boost may be reflected in recent trends in Commission practice.

Horizontal policies take as their starting-point the desirability of aid to accomplish certain goals. The presumption implied in the formal structure of Article 92 EEC and established by past Commission practice may be reversed. Restriction of

---

[37] Commission Decision 81/984 of November 23, 1981, on a Belgian Government proposal to aid certain investments in a refinery at Antwerp O.J. 1981 L361/24 at 25. Even direct effects on employment may be difficult to assess in advance. See C. Hultin, "The effects of state aid on employment and investment in the French textile and clothing industry", *International Journal of Industrial Organisation*, 1989, pp.489–501.

the grant of aid promoting the aims of horizontal policies may be permissible only where unjustified distortion of competition can be established.

State aid is increasingly seen as a vehicle for making the completion of the internal market politically acceptable:

> The problem also has to be seen in the context of wider policies which 1992 will bring about. The most important of these is that of coherence of the economies of the Member States and particularly the development of the more peripheral and poorer regions of the Community. The Commission has recognized this by bringing into play the derogation of Article 92(3)(a) EEC which allows high levels of State aid to be given in these regions.[38]

There appears to be a willingness to permit the use of state aid as a device to resolve political problems. Suitably controlled, state aid can bolster political consensus in favour of economic union, by ensuring that the benefits produced by such a union are distributed in a way that is perceived as fair.

(End of excerpt)

E. PROCEDURAL ASPECTS

The rules on state aid rely for their enforcement mechanism on cooperation between the Member States and the Commission. Cooperation means that the tasks and the responsibilities between the Member States and the Commission are shared. The starting point for a concept of shared responsibilities has been set by the Court of Justice. In Case 120/72 *Lorenz* v. *Germany* [1973] ECR 1471 it denied direct effect to Article 92(1). Undertakings excluded from state aids were not given the right to use community law and to strike down national state aids contrary to Article 92. The consequence may be characterized as a politicization of the decision-making procedure. The decision-making power remains in the hands of the Commission. Direct effect would have led to a judicialization and would have transferred the power from the Commission to the national courts and by way of Article 177 to the European Court of Justice. That is what the Court of Justice did not want. Whether or not a national state aid complies with Community law should be decided by the Commission. If one recalls that the Member States notified in two years 2000 state aid measures and that only a few of them became the subject of litigation between the Commission and the Member States, it becomes abundantly clear that the Commission has considerable political discretion.

---

[38]   EC Commission, *Eighteenth Report on Competition Policy*, Brussels, 1989, p.150.

1. The role of the Court of Justice in shaping Article 93

It has been said that Articles 92–94 rely on cooperation. Member States are obliged to notify their intended new aids to the Commission and they may participate in the negotiations. Their right to be heard as well as the right to be heard of the interested parties have been maintained and constantly defended by the Court of Justice. What remains to be clarified is the role and function of the national courts. The Court of Justice has attributed to them the task of supervising the implementation of Article 93 (3). National courts should rule aid illegal, where it has not been notified under Article 93 (3). Violation of Article 93 (3), however, may be invoked by private individuals. Article 93 (3) is directly effective and it gives rise to rights in favour of private individuals that national courts must protect in the event of implementation without notification.

Although the framework of responsibilities is set, Member States and the Commission are constantly struggling over the extent of their rights and duties under Article 93. The Commission tries to extend its rights and to give more weight to a violation of the notification duty. Quite to the contrary, Member States maintain their sovereignty and reject any effort of the Commission to strengthen its impact on the assessment of Member States' state aids. The Court of Justice has to balance the conflicting interest and to keep cooperation going. Recent trends within the Court's jurisprudence deserve attention as a number of open questions in the Article 93 procedure have been clarified.

In Case 301/87, *France* v. *Commission* [1990] ECR I-307 the Court rejected the Commission's contention that aid granted in breach of the procedure laid down in Article 93 (3) cannot subsequently be declared compatible with the common market. The Commission was given the power to issue an interim order requiring the Member State to suspend immediately the payment of the illegal aid. If procedural defects cannot make an aid measure illegal *per se*, the question then is, and it had been raised by the *Conseil d'Etat*, whether national courts should unreservedly continue to give effect to the prohibition of Article 93 (3), Case C-354/90, 21.11.1991 *Fédération National du Commerce Extérieur des Produits Alimentaires et Syndicat National des Négociants et Transformateurs de Saumon* v. *France*, ECR 1991, I-5505).

C-261/89, *Italy* v. *Commission*, ECR 1991 I-4437 and Case C-294/90, *British Aerospace plc. & Rover Group Holdings* v. *Commission* ECR I-493 throw light on the legal means available to the Commission where a Member State does not comply with the conditions under which aid has been authorized in an earlier decision. The point at stake was the kind of procedure the Commission has to initiate when implementing conditional decisions adopted under Article 93 (2). In the case of a breach of an adopted decision, the Commission may go directly to Court without re-opening the investigation procedure. If, however, a Member State has paid a new aid which has not been examined, the Commission has to initiate the special procedure provided for by the first subparagraph of Article 93 (2) and give notice to the parties concerned to submit their comments.

2. Repayment of unlawful state aids

In particular the last series of judgments must be seen in relation to the requirement under which state aid must be repaid. As a rule, one may say, repayment of illegally granted aid may be required. Where does the illegality derive from? Must it be illegality in substance? The Court of Justice ruled in Case C-301/87 *France* v. *Commission* [1990] ECR I-307, that an unnotified new aid is not rendered illegal *per se* just because of the procedural flaw. The firm, however, cannot legitimately rely on the compliance of the state measure with Community law. It is up to the firm to check whether the aid runs counter to Community law. The firm cannot shelter behind the Member States' ignorance or unwillingness to respect Community law, which is quite the opposite of Case C-91/92, *Paola Faccini Dori* v. *Recreb Srl* dealing with horizontal direct effect of Directives (cf. Chapter 1). The Commission insists that the illegal aid is repaid and that the Member States have to use national procedure to remedy the damage done to the economy by the illegal subsidy. It goes without saying that there are difficulties to overcome: could there not be a situation where the expectations are legitimate?

What exactly must the Member States do to ensure that the firms repay the illegal aid? All these questions have been investigated by Thomas Jestaedt, *The risk of repayment in cases of 'formally unlawful' aid.*

THE RISK OF REPAYMENT IN CASES OF 'FORMALLY UNLAWFUL' AID*

Thomas Jestaedt

[...]

IV. 'FORMALLY UNLAWFUL' AIDS

'Formally unlawful' aids are those which were not notified to the Commission or which were paid out in violation of the suspensive effect of the examination proceeding before a final decision by the Commission.

1. Procedural rights of the Commission

If a Member State has granted an aid without first notifying the Commission, the Commission can, after hearing the Member State involved, order through a decision an immediate discontinuation of the aid. At the same time it can demand from the Member State all the information which it needs in order to assess whether the aid is compatible with the Common Market. If the Member State does not comply with this demand, the Commission can immediately issue a decision through which it finds the compatibility or incompatibility of the aid on the basis of the information available to it. If the Member State does not comply with the demand to discontinue payment of the aid, the Commission can immediately bring an action before the ECJ. Meanwhile, the examination of the aid with respect to its compatibility with the Common Market can continue. The Commission has the same rights if an aid was granted after notification, but prior to the conclusion of the examination proceeding.

2. Demand for repayment in case of a finding of incompatibility with the Common Market

It is undisputed that the Commission has the right to insist upon a repayment if it finds with respect to a 'formally unlawful' aid in the examination proceeding according to Article 93 EC that the aid is incompatible with the Common Market. It is true that Article 93(2) EC speaks only of a right of the Commission to decide

---

*   Extract from 'Das Rückzahlungsrisiko bei "formell rechtswidrigen" Beihilfen', *Europäische Zeitschrift für Wirtschaftsrecht*, 1993, pp.49–52, reprinted by permission of the author. Translation by John Blazek, Brussels.

that the affected State must 'abolish' or 'alter' the aid within a specified period. However, it is generally recognized that this provision also includes the ordering of repayment. Article 93(2) EC gives the Commission discretion in determining the measures it finds appropriate. This discretion is thus accorded to the Commission in the decision about repayment as well.

The demand for repayment itself is made in accordance with national law. Article 5 EC obliges the Member States to give EC law the broadest possible application and effect. According to this provision, the Member States are obliged to demand back, in accordance with their national law, aids which the Commission has determined are incompatible with the Common Market. In Germany, the demand for repayment is made in accordance with the regulations on revocation of unlawful administrative actions contained in § 48 *Verwaltungsverfahrensgesetz* (VwVfG – the Law on Administrative Procedure), or the corresponding regulations of the given *Land*. In the event of 'formally unlawful' aid, the authorities of the Member State involved can initiate repayment demand procedures even without a prior decision of the Commission.

3. No repayment demand without examination of compatibility with the Common Market

Can the Commission order the repayment of an aid solely on the basis of a procedural violation – that is, failure to give notification or violation of the suspensive effect? The prevailing opinion in the literature is 'no'. This view is often defended on the basis of two 1990 ECJ decisions.[1] Looked at more closely, however, these decisions require only one thing: that the Commission must, *in all cases*, proceed with examining the compatibility of the aid with the Common Market.

Both decisions involve the repayment of aids which had not been notified in advance, and which the Commission in an examination proceeding then declared to be incompatible with the Common Market. The Commission in each case took the position that it already followed from the omitted notification alone that the aid was unlawful and thus had to be paid back. The Commission therefore believed that a substantive law examination was unnecessary. The European Court of Justice rejected this position with the following reasoning, which is virtually identical in both decisions:[2]

> –   If the Commission learns of an aid which was not notified to it, it must demand of the Member State involved an explanation and information.

---

1   Case C-301/87, *France* v. *Commission*, [1990] ECR 307; Case C-142/87, *Belgium* v. *Commission*, [1990] ECR 959.
2   (1990) ECR 307 at 356; [1990] ECR 959 at 1010.

- If the Member State complies with this demand, then the Commission is *obliged* to examine its compatibility.
- If the Member State does *not* comply with the demand for information, the Commission must decide about the aid's compatibility with the Common Market on the basis of the knowledge that it does have. Such a decision may also include an order to demand the return of the aid.

In the final analysis, the European Court thus demanded that the Commission *in any event* decide about the compatibility of the aid with the Common Market. For a repayment demand procedure, the Commission cannot simply content itself with a reference to the omitted notification as long as the substantive law examination has not yet been performed.

4. Demand for repayment in case of mere 'formal unlawfulness'?

In both its 1990 decisions, the ECJ says nothing about how the Commission has to decide, in terms of results, about unnotified aid, if it embarked upon the examination of the compatibility with the Common Market. In particular, the Court says nothing about the question of whether the Commission can demand repayment of the portion of an ultimately approved aid which was paid out before the notification or during the examination proceeding, that is, the 'formally unlawful' part. This question is relevant for aids which are granted over a longer period of time.

a) No curing of the formal unlawfulness. The ECJ decision in the case *Fédération National du Commerce Extérieur des Produits Alimentaires and Syndicat National des Négociants et Transformateurs de Saumon* v. *France* of 21 November 1991[3] gives an indication of how mere 'formally unlawful' aids or aid components might be treated in the future. The decision was rendered in response to a submission by the French *Conseil d'État* using the procedure under Article 177 EC. The plaintiffs in the initial procedure were two French food associations. In 1982, the French government had established an intervention fund for the promotion of the French deep-sea fishing industry, and introduced public duties in favour of this fund. The French government failed to notify the Commission that it had created the fund. The Commission informed the French government of its intention to initiate a proceeding under Article 93(2) EC, which it did on 27 July 1984. Nevertheless, the French government on 15 April 1985 issued an inter-ministerial decree setting the level of the duties. The plaintiffs of the initial procedure attacked the inter-ministerial decree before the *Conseil d'État*. In their view, the decree – as a measure for the implementation of an aid which required approval in accordance with the EEC Treaty – was already unlawful because it ignored the suspensive effect of the examination proceeding before the Commission. On 25 October 1985 the

---

[3] Case C-301/87, [1990] ECR I-307.

Commission informed the participants that it had decided to stop the aid examination proceeding under Article 93(2) EC, since it regarded the aid as compatible with the Common Market. The *Conseil d'État* then submitted to the ECJ a question as to whether Article 93(3) EC imposes upon the authorities of the Member States an obligation whose violation leads to the ineffectiveness of all actions undertaking to implement the aid measures at issue, regardless of a subsequent positive decision by the Commission declaring the measures to be compatible with the Common Market.

The ECJ responded that a violation of the suspensive effect of the Article 93(3) EC makes the aid measures *per se* unlawful. Nor can this error be cured *a posteriori* by the Commission's later finding in the examination proceeding under Article 93(2) EC that the aid is compatible with the Common Market. In other words: the substantive lawfulness of the aid does not cure its formal unlawfulness.

The ECJ based its decision on the requirement of practical enforceability ('*effet utile*') of the procedural rules of the aid law, as well as on the division of competences between the Commission and the national courts in the monitoring of Articles 92, 93 EC. The Commission has the monopoly on determining whether a given aid is compatible with the Common Market. The national courts may not and cannot make this finding. According to the ECJ, they can thus effectively enforce the aid rules of Articles 92, 93 EC only if they are authorized to invalidate aid measures on the basis of procedural law defects alone. According to the ECJ, a subsequent curing of the procedural defect through a compatibility decision by the Commission is excluded, since this would effectively encourage the Member States to ignore the procedural rules, and in that case, the violation of the procedural provisions would go completely unsanctioned.

b) Effects on the repayment demand procedure under national law. It can be directly drawn from the decision that all measures of national law which have been initiated on the basis of a violation of the notification requirement and the suspensive effect remain unaffected by the subsequent approval of the aid by the Commission. This includes in particular: (1) provisional measures under national law (e.g. for suspension); (2) repayment demand procedures which are initiated by state authorities; (3) complaints by competitors against the granting of the aid.

In the case of aid which is not notified or which is granted in violation of the suspensive effect, the aid recipient runs a significantly increased risk of being required to pay back the aid in a national procedure. Even if the Commission later declares the aid to be compatible with the Common Market, a repayment decision of the national court continues to have effect. Thus, without incurring any risk, competitors can sue before the national courts against 'formally unlawful' aids favouring their competitors.

c) Possible effects on the practice of the Commission. The Commission had, in the 16th Competition Report in 1987, announced that it would 'gradually apply' its policy of demanding repayment of aids 'also to aids which are only regarded as unlawful on the basis of procedural law'. The two 1990 ECJ decisions put a damper on this intention. This may be the reason why the Commission has still not made aggressive use of the possibilities contained in the decision of 21 November 1991. For if the finding of substantive legality by the Commission does not subsequently cure the formal unlawfulness in the judgment of an aid in a procedure before the national courts, it is unclear why something else should apply for the Commission procedure. In other words: it would be altogether logical for the Commission, in reliance upon the ECJ decision, to demand the repayment of the 'formally unlawful' portions of an aid, namely the allocations made prior to conclusion of the examination proceeding. In any event, such a demand would not stand in contradiction to the ECJ's two 1990 decisions, as long as the Commission does ultimately come to a decision about the compatibility of the aid with the Common Market.

It appears that until now the Commission has not demanded repayment of the part of the aid which is merely 'in violation of procedural law'. Typical in this regard is the decision on the purchase of the property on Potsdamer Platz by Daimler-Benz AG. In its examination proceeding, the Commission decided that the *Land* of Berlin *had* given Daimler-Benz AG aid which could be regarded as only partially compatible with the Common Market. Although the aid as a whole was given in violation of the procedural provisions of Article 93(3) EC, the Commission only obliged the German federal government to pay back the part of the aid which was incompatible with the Common Market. In the reasons it offered for its decision, the Commission was apparently making reference to the ECJ decision of 21 November 1991 when it found that the aid was unlawful already because of the violation of Article 93(3) EC, and that this unlawfulness cannot be subsequently cured. Nevertheless, it did not order repayment of the 'formally unlawful' part.

In another case, the Commission suspended a procedure against the French government in connection with aids for the French deep-sea fishing fleet. Although the French government, in violation of Article 93(3) EC, had already granted the aid before the Commission reached its final decision, the Commission did not demand repayment, but merely 'regretted deeply the failure of the French authorities to fulfil their obligations under Art. 93(3) EC', and 'reserved the right to take appropriate measures in order to ensure the observance of these provisions'. In the final analysis, therefore, the violation of the duties under Article 93(3) EC remained unsanctioned. (End of excerpt)

CONCLUSION

1.   The Commission must be notified about the introduction of new aid or the alteration of existing aids. A violation of this obligation makes the aid 'formally unlawful'.
2.   If the Commission finds that a Member State has granted a 'formally unlawful' aid, it must ask the Member State for further information. Based on the results of

the information procedure, the Commission must *in all cases* decide whether or not the aid is compatible with the Common Market.

3.   Within the framework of its decision about the compatibility of a 'formally unlawful' aid with the Common Market, the Commission may order the repayment of the aid.

4.   In the decision of 21 November 1991, the ECJ found for the national procedures that a subsequent approval does not *a posteriori* cure the formal unlawfulness. With respect to 'formally unlawful' aid, the authorities of the Member States or competitors of the aid recipients could in the future (and at no risk to themselves) initiate repayment complaints.

5.   It is possible that, on the basis of the ECJ decision, the Commission will change its practice so as to order the repayment of merely 'formally unlawful' aid. However, it has not yet taken this step.

QUESTION

State aids have not been reduced, they have increased in number and in expenditure. There is considerable disharmony between the Member States on the role and function of state aids. This is even more so after Maastricht. Criticism has been voiced that the Member States foster state aid competition and that the Commission gives way to state aids being used more and more as an integral part of industrial policy. Political reasons to justify politically state aids are easy at hand: They are necessary in old industries to save employment and they are needed in new industries and new technologies to get them started and to keep them going. What adjustments to Articles 92–94 EC do you think could improve the control mechanism? Is the balance between the role of the Commission and that of the national courts appropriate?

FURTHER READING

L. Hancher, State Aids and Judical Control in the European Community, *ECLR*, **3**, 1994, p.134 *et seq.*

L. Hancher, T. Ottervanger and P.J. Slot, *EC State Aids*, London, New York, Chichester, Brisbane, Toronto, Singapore 1993.

P. Slot, 'Procedural aspects of State aids: the guardian of competition v. the subsidiary villains', *CMLRev*, **27**, 1990, p.741 *et seq.*

J.A. Winter, 'Supervision of State Aid: article 93 in the Court of Justice', *CMLRev*, **30**, 1993, p.311 *et seq.*

4 Internal Market and Competition

A. COMPETITION

The market economy is founded on the process of competition. Competition law serves that process. It is vital for the lawyer to develop an understanding of the economic theory which underpins the market system within which competition law operates.

ECONOMIC CONCEPTS OF COMPETITION*

John Agnew

THE OPTIMAL ALLOCATION OF RESOURCES

At its simplest level, the rationale for policy towards competition is based on the argument that an economy performs better if the industries within it operate in a competitive way than if they do not. However, such a statement is not self-evident and can only be justified with reference to some clear idea of what is meant by 'better performance'. Such a framework is provided by the economic analysis outlined in this section.

Every economy, no matter how it is organized, has to produce the answer to three basic questions. These are:

1   Which goods and services should be produced, and how much of each should be provided? While this can be put as a single question, it involves producing detailed answers to tens of millions of other questions, one for each commodity which the economy is capable of producing;

2   How should each of these commodities be produced? Answering this question most obviously involves choosing the appropriate technique for each commodity (labour-intensive production or capital-intensive methods) but it also involves decisions on where to locate production and decisions on which individual workers should be involved in the production of which commodities; and

3   Who gets what? How are the goods and services produced to be distributed between the different participants in the economic process.

There are essentially three ways in which these questions could be answered. First, they could be answered through 'custom' – society could have some pre-ordained set of rules which allowed the questions to be answered by reference to previous practice. Secondly, they could be answered by 'command', where those holding power simply decree their preferred answers to each question. Thirdly, they could be answered through a 'market mechanism'. It is this last method which dominates in unplanned economies, and whose workings are central to the whole debate on

---

*   First published in *Competition Law*, London: Allen and Unwin, 1985; selected passages from Chapter 2; reprinted by permission of International Thomson Publishing Services Ltd., Hampshire.

competition policy. It is therefore important to take a very brief look at the outlines of a market economy.

In a market economy the resource allocation decisions are not taken by any individual. Rather it is the case that the answers emerge from a decentralized decision-making process. The economy consists of millions of households and hundreds of thousands of firms. Households are concerned to distribute their available time, wealth and skills across a range of different activities in the ways which suit them best. Firms are mainly concerned to make profits. These two groups of economic factors are linked together through two sets of markets. First, there are the markets for goods and services. In these markets, firms supply those goods which are demanded by households who are willing to sacrifice part of their income and time in order to acquire them. Second, there are the markets for factors of production, including all the different types of resource which can be used to produce goods and services. In these markets, households are the suppliers, seeking to earn income, and firms are the demanders, seeking to buy or hire the resources they need in order to produce products. Out of this apparent chaos (some would say real chaos) come the detailed answers to the resource allocation questions outlined above. The fundamental question about such a social mechanism, and the one which underlies the whole range of issues concerning competition policy is simply 'How well does it work?'

Such a question can only be answered if there is some clear idea of what the system's objectives are and what constitutes 'good' performance. This is an obvious question, but an extremely difficult one to answer, without being too partial or specific or simply producing a long list of conflicting desiderata. Economists identify two basic objectives for any system of resource allocation. The first is that it should be 'efficient', the second is that it should be 'equitable'. Each of these objectives is important for competition policy and each requires elaboration.

'Efficiency' may be simply defined as getting maximum output from the resources available to the economy, and that definition is very similar to the definitions of efficiency used in engineering or physics. However, the economy's output consists of tens of millions of different items so that there is a problem in deciding what exactly is meant by 'maximum output'. In principle this can be resolved by noting that the real output of the economy is not goods and services, but rather the satisfaction which households and individuals derive from those goods and services. In that case 'economic efficiency' means organizing the economy in such a way that households derive maximum satisfaction from the combination of goods and services produced. [...]

The second aim for any system of resource allocation is 'equity', or fairness. However, unlike efficiency, equity is not a concept on which economic analysis has very much to contribute. The economist has no definition of equity from which to derive optimal conditions, and the economic analysis of competition and monopoly is, therefore, almost entirely concerned with questions of efficiency. Clearly, this imposes limits on the ability of the economist to guide policy when equity is a major objective and this is particularly true of competition policy where many of the legal issues are framed in terms of the 'fairness' of prices or of agreements reached between companies and individuals. It is important to bear in mind that when an economist refers to 'a social optimum', or to the 'optimal allocation of resources', he is almost always referring to an efficient allocation of resources, without any further consideration of its equity.

(End of excerpt)

B. COMPETITION LAW AND THE EUROPEAN MARKET

In Europe, competition law is a major component of the Internal Market project. It has already been seen in Chapter 1 how competition stands alongside the four freedoms as a building block of the European economic constitution. Competition law, seen from the perspective of *Ordnungspolitik*, acts as a framework which defines the rules which economic actors have to respect in their behaviour on the market.

EC competition law serves to integrate markets under one and the same doctrine, the doctrine of competition. There is one basic difference between the four freedoms and competition. The four freedoms are implemented negatively. They eliminate barriers to trade and in this sense they promote pure market integration. This is not true for competition, nor for competition law. Competition law is a form of regulation of the market. The critical question is always how far such regulation should reach. Cross border agreements between firms might contribute to the integration of markets, but they may distort competition. What is needed is a borderline between what is required to integrate markets and what must be regulated in order to maintain competition. The freedom of the parties must be restricted for the sake of the maintenance of an efficient European market structure.

The twin pillars of the Treaty competition law system are Articles 85 and 86. These apply to private parties. They are extended into the sphere of public undertakings by Article 90, which is examined in the next Chapter. The phenomenon of Mergers is the subject of a special Regulation which came into force in 1990, Regulation 4064/89. These rules set the framework for assessing the behaviour of private actors in order to decide whether an agreement or market behaviour distorts competition unacceptably. In a fashion quite distinct from any other field of Community law (with the exception of agriculture), powers are conferred on the Commission to supervise the market and to intervene directly, 'top down', from Brussels into the activities of private firms. It may behave like a regulating agency and it may issue orders. This lends to this area of law a critically important capacity to shape the nature of the economic process in Europe.

ARTICLE 85

1. The following shall be prohibited as incompatible with the common market: all agreements between undertakings, decisions by associations of undertakings and concerted practices which may affect trade between Member States and which have as their object or effect the prevention, restriction or distortion of competition within the common market, and in particular those which:

(a) directly or indirectly fix purchase or selling prices or any other trading conditions;
(b) limit or control production, markets, technical development, or investment;
(c) share markets or sources of supply;
(d) apply dissimilar conditions to equivalent transactions with other trading parties, thereby placing them at a competitive disadvantage;
(e) make the conclusion of contracts subject to acceptance by the other parties of supplementary obligations which, by their nature or according to commercial usage, have no connection with the subject of such contracts.

2. Any agreements or decisions prohibited pursuant to this Article shall be automatically void.

3. The provisions of paragraph 1 may, however, be declared inapplicable in the case of

– any agreement or category of agreements between undertakings;
– any decision or category of decisions by associations of undertakings;
– any concerted practice or category of concerted practices;

which contributes to improving the production or distribution of goods or to promoting technical or economic progress, while allowing consumers a fair share of the resulting benefit, and which does not:

(a) impose on the undertakings concerned restrictions which are not indispensable to the attainment of these objectives;
(b) afford such undertakings the possibility of eliminating competition in respect of a substantial part of the products in question.

ARTICLE 86

Any abuse by one or more undertakings of a dominant position within the common market or in a substantial part of it shall be prohibited as incompatible with the common market in so far as it may affect trade between Member States. Such abuse may, in particular, consist in:

(a) directly or indirectly imposing unfair purchase or selling prices or unfair trading conditions;

(b) limiting production, markets or technical development to the prejudice of consumers;

(c) applying dissimilar conditions to equivalent transactions with other trading parties, thereby placing them at a competitive disadvantage;

(d) making the conclusion of contracts subject to acceptance by the other parties of supplementary obligations which, by their nature or according to commercial usage, have no connection with the subject of such contracts.

Articles 85 and 86 exercise control over the activities of private economic actors. At the same time they have a significant impact on domestic commercial law. They place a European overlay on the status of agreements and other practices under domestic private law. Article 85 may require a national court to rule an agreement void even though it is perfectly acceptable under domestic private law. Article 86 controls the freedom of economically powerful firms. It may even be used to require them to conclude contracts. Articles 85 and 86 are part of the development of a European policy on the structure of commercial relations in the market.

The Merger Regulation 4064/89 plays an additional role in this pattern of regulation. The Commission is required to examine mergers with a Community dimension against a criterion of compatibility with the common market. Here too commercial decisions are subjected to control under European law. The precise nature of the control mechanism placed in the hands of the Commission has attracted comment. In particular, the extent to which mergers may be controlled for reasons of industrial policy has stimulated fierce controversy. Such issues are central to the debate about the function of legal intervention in the European market. The reader should (re-)consult Chapter 2 for the debate about the role of industrial policy in merger control.

THE CONTRIBUTION OF EC COMPETITION POLICY TO THE SINGLE MARKET*

Claus-Dieter Ehlermann

1. INTRODUCTION: THE CONTRIBUTION OF THE SINGLE MARKET TO COMPETITION POLICY

The main thrust of EC competition policy will be determined in the years ahead by the Single Market programme. I have taken as my title "The contribution of EC competition policy to the Single Market". However, by way of introduction, let me turn the question round.

With the entry into force of the Single European Act, the Single Market exercise was enshrined with "constitutional" force in the Treaty itself. The competition rules laid down in Articles 85 to 94 of the EEC Treaty were left untouched by the amendments incorporated into the Treaty by the Single European Act. However, the Single European Act added a number of accompanying policies to Part Three of the EEC Treaty under the headings "Economic and social cohesion", "Research and technological development", and "Environment".

The policy on "Economic and social cohesion" in particular has implications for competition policy. It has a particular bearing on the control of state aid. Although Article 130a of the EEC Treaty is referred to in the recitals (No.13) of the merger control Regulation,[1] it has not as yet played any role in the practice of applying this Regulation.

The Single Market programme has greatly increased the importance of competition policy. This has been emphasized not only in academic studies. Its growing importance is also recognized by Community bodies and Member States.

The importance which the Council attaches to competition policy may be illustrated by its extension of the competition rules to include areas to which they did not previously apply (such as air and sea transport)[2] and its adoption of the merger control Regulation, by the conclusions it adopted on the Community's industrial

---

* First published in *Common Market Law Review*, **29**, 1992 pp.257–67; reprinted by permission of *Common Market Law Review*, Kluwer Academic Publishers, AA Dordrecht.

[1] Council Regulation (EEC) No.4064/89 of 21 Dec. 1989 on the control of concentrations between undertakings (O.J. 1989, L 395; corrigendum: O.J. 1990, L 257).

[2] Council Regulation (EEC) No. 4056/86 of 22 Dec. 1986, O.J. 1986, L 378/4; Council Regulation (EEC) No. 3975/87 of 14 Dec. 1987, O.J. 1987, L 374/1.

policy[3] and by the – unsuccessful – attempt by the Italian Presidency to get the Commission's aid policy discussed within the Council.

That Member States individually are attaching greater importance to competition policy may be seen from the moves which have already been successfully completed (in some cases after decades of efforts), such as the setting up of an independent cartel office in Italy[4] and Ireland[5] and the reform of the Belgian Law on competition,[6] or will probably shortly be successfully completed, as in Ireland. The process of spontaneous, autonomous legal alignment through the adoption of legal provisions modelled on Articles 85 and 86 of the EEC Treaty is thus continuing.

Lastly, mention must be made of the attention with which Community competition policy is being followed by the public at large. Never before have the decisions taken by the Commission and the opinions of the Commission Member with special responsibility for competition, Sir Leon Brittan, been so widely reported in the national and international media.

The Single Market programme is a gigantic programme of deregulation. It improves the opportunities for firms to compete on markets in other Member States; this applies in particular to public tenders, especially in hitherto inaccessible areas, such as energy, transport and telecommunications. It is also resulting in the opening-up of markets in services, particularly in banking and insurance, but also in air transport, where international competition has hitherto played little or no role.

Experience in recent years shows that business has not only recognized these opportunities, but has seized them with alacrity. Through the increase in cross-frontier activities, business and industry have given additional impetus to integration and have injected unprecedented dynamism into the competition process. As a result, the conditions for maintaining and developing effective competition within the Community on a broad basis have improved.

Fair competition based on the principle of performance results in an increase in the economic efficiency of firms. It enables them to compete both within the Community and with firms outside the Community. The international competitiveness of European industries is an essential precondition for the opening-up of the Single Market to the world market or, to put it another way, for maintaining and further developing a liberal competition-based trade policy.

While the European Single Market acts as the driving force for economic growth and hence also for the raising of living standards in the Member States, it

---

3   Bull. EC 11-1990, points 1.3.109 *et seq.*
4   Italian Law on the protection of competition and the market, Law No. 287 of 10 Oct. 1989, *Official Gazette of the Italian Republic* No. 240, 13.10.1989; see Siragusa and Scassellati, "Italian and EC competition law: a new relationship-reciprocal exclusivity and common principles", 29 *CML Rev.*, pp.93–131.
5   Competition Bill 1991, in force since 1 Oct. 1991.
6   Law of July 1991 on the protection of economic competition.

must not be forgotten that the complete dismantling of internal frontiers will create serious adjustment problems for certain firms, sectors and regions in the Community. The pressure of increasing competition will force a whole series of non-viable firms to be merged into larger economic units or to withdraw from the market. Most of the remaining firms will have to modernize their production plant, improve the marketing of their products and step up their research and development activities.

As the burden of cost increases, firms are faced with a growing temptation to resort to anti-competitive agreements and practices so as to gain a breathing space in the competitive struggle or an artificial advantage in penetrating new markets. The governments of the Member States are persuaded to provide assistance for their firms (sometimes in an effort to maintain jobs, particularly in structurally weak areas, sometimes as part of a policy to strengthen their own industrial base) by delaying the dismantling of obstacles, introducing protectionist measures or distorting competition through the granting of subsidies.

In such situations, there is an overriding need for competition policy. Its role is to ensure that the opening-up of markets brings about the macroeconomic advantages pursued. It must ensure that the barriers that have been removed in intra-Community trade in goods are not replaced by other types of market partitioning of private or state provenance.

The Single Market programme has resulted in the stricter application of existing rules, particularly the control of aid, in the application of such rules being extended to areas which were previously more or less outside their scope, such as banking, insurance, transport, energy and telecommunications, and in new instruments, primarily the merger control Regulation, being implemented for the first time.

Another consequence of the Single Market programme is that discussions in some policy areas have shifted from national to Community level. Let me cite energy policy as an example.[7] The Single Market programme is forcing the opening-up of national energy markets, where rules have hitherto been based on national concepts of security of supply. A Community-wide energy market will not come

---

[7] On 29 Oct. 1991, the Commission presented its liberalization programmeme to the Council of Ministers. The latter approved the general orientations which are founded on a three-stage approach on the basis of Art.100A; Cf. Ehlermann, "Grundfreiheiten und Wettbewerbsregeln des EWG-Vertrages-Bedeutung für die Stromversorgungsunternehmen", in: *Energiewirtschafiliche Tagesfragen* (1992), pp.96 *et seq.*; see most recently the proposals adopted by the Commission for directives towards the completion of the Internal Market in gas and electricity, Commission press release IP 92/5 of 22 January 1992. In a more general context, reference is made to the signature of the European Energy Charter in the Hague on 16/17 Dec. 1991 by the 35 parties that negotiated it, including the EC, EC Member States, 9 former Soviet Republics, 2 Baltic States, the US and Canada, published in *Europe, Documents* No. 1754, of 21 Dec. 1991.

about unless there is discussion of security of supply at Community level. Consequently, security of supply will in future have to be defined not just nationally, but also as a Community concept.

A further example is industrial policy. Discussion of the future of the European micro-electronics industry, for instance, can no longer be properly carried out at national level. An industrial policy for microelectronics can be effectively defined and shaped only at Community level.

Lastly, the growing importance of competition policy was reflected in the two intergovernmental conferences on Economic and Monetary Union and on Political Union. This is evident in the German proposals on economic policy principles and on the setting up of a European cartel office, and in the proposals put forward by several Member States on the inclusion of a chapter on industrial policy in the Treaty. The latter has finally been agreed upon, albeit with the proviso that this does not provide a basis for the introduction by the Community of any measure which may distort competition.

2. BASIC FEATURES OF EXISTING COMPETITION POLICY

The changes which have taken place since the entry into force of the Single European Act do not require any radical change in the general aims of competition policy. The elimination of national frontiers and the creation of competitive market structure, while maintaining a balance between enforcing prohibitions on the one hand and granting exemptions on the other, were from the outset amongst its basic objectives. These have, since the 1960s, determined not only legislative and decision-making practice in competition law, but have also significantly influenced the Community's supervisory activity regarding state measures *vis-à-vis* private and public sector undertakings.

The Commission has from the start pursued a hardline policy under Article 85 against market sharing agreements, cartels related to prices, quotas and investments and collective mutual exclusive dealing arrangements between manufacturers and traders. Selling syndicates have also been viewed unfavourably. Such agreements and arrangements are in direct contradiction to the principle of a single market based on effective competition; logically, it was necessary to eliminate them. The Commission's practice *vis-à-vis* abuses of dominant positions by undertakings has developed along the same lines. The decisions adopted under Article 86 reflect clearly the Commission's determination to prevent suppliers, customers or consumers being exploited as a result of inadequate competition, to ensure that there is no unfair prevention of actual or potential competition and to prevent any further weakening of residual competition. However, most of the decisions have, over and above that, the specific aim of promoting integration.[8]

The positive side of existing competition policy towards firms is evident primarily in the Commission's readiness to exempt agreements on the specialization of production, cooperation between companies in research, development and the exploitation of results, and cooperative joint ventures. Experience here has resulted in the adoption of two block exemption Regulations.[9]

Initially, the main problem in dealing with vertical agreements, particularly distribution and licensing agreements, was the sheer quantity of notifications. With the help of the block exemptions, embodied in specific regulations on exclusive dealing agreements, exclusive purchasing agreements (including beer supply and service-station agreements), motor vehicle distribution and servicing agreements, franchising agreements, patent licensing agreements and know-how licensing agreements,[10] not only was the mountain of some 30,000 notifications cut down to size. In addition, the Commission provided firms with an approved arena within which they could pursue their business and exploit their intellectual property without fear of breaching the competition rules. At the same time, the requirements of the efficiency of the distribution system and of protecting industrial property rights, had to be balanced against the principles of the Single Market and of effective, undistorted competition. The compromise consisted essentially in the acceptance of territorial protection clauses at the first marketing stage accompanied by guaranteed freedom in intra-Community trade at the following distribution stages.

In its policy on competition-distorting measures taken by Member States to assist firms, the Commission has also been guided by the general objectives of competition policy. Its efforts as regards the control of state aid under Articles 92 and 93 have been directed both to developing a system of control covering all the aid falling within the scope of the EEC Treaty and to giving practical effect to the substantive legal provisions through individual decisions and general guidelines in which the scope of the incompatibility rule (Article 92(1)) and the conditions for applying the exemptions (Article 92(2) and (3)) are explained. This latter objective

---

[8]   Recent decisions include the soda ash Decision of 19 Dec. 1990. O.J.1991, 1,152, and the Tetra Pak Decision of 24 July 1991, Commission press release IP(91)715.

[9]   Commission Regulation (EEC) No.417/85 of 9 Dec. 1984, O.J.1985, L53/1; Commission Regulation (EEC) No. 418/85 of 19 Dec. 1984, O.J. 1985, L53.

[10] Commission Regulation (EEC) 1983/83 of 22 June 1983, O.J. 1983, L173/1; Commission Regulation (EEC) No.1984/83 of 22 June 1983, O.J. 1983, L173/5; Commission Regulation (EEC) No.123/85 of 12 Dec. 1984, O.J. 1985, L15/16; Commission Regulation (EEC) No. 4087/88 of 30 Nov. 1988, O.J.1988, L359/46; Commission Regulation (EEC) No.2349/84 of 23 July 1984, O.J.1984, L219/15, corrigendum O.J. 1985, L280/32; Commission Regulation (EEC) No.556/89 of 30 Nov. 1988, O.J.1989, L61/1.

is pursued particularly in the form of the so-called Community frameworks.[11] General rules and criteria were established for the types of aid which are particularly important in practice, namely aid to assist regions, research and development aid, environmental protection aid and aid to rescue firms in difficulties.[12] Specific Community rules apply to certain sectors that are faced with crises (such as synthetic fibres, shipbuilding, and the steel and motor vehicle industries).[13]

The twin aims of Community policy in this area are reflected, firstly, in the ban on operating aid, which is used to maintain non-viable firms in operation, and on export aid in trade between Member States and, secondly, in the authorization of grants for the development of economically backward regions, the restructuring of branches of industry, the easing of social difficulties and the promotion of projects serving the interests of the Community as a whole. So as to ensure that there is effective, undistorted competition, the Commission ensures that the aid granted by Member States remains restricted to what is essential in order to solve the relevant problem and that it is limited in time and if possible degressive. The aid should be a means of helping recipients to help themselves. In addition, it must not result either in economically sound firms in other Member States being jeopardized or in the partitioning of national markets, since this would run counter to the principle of a unified market.

The unity of the market is also the concern underlying the adjustment of state monopolies of a commercial character pursuant to Article 37, involving the removal of the exclusive rights granted to such monopolies as regards imports, exports and the marketing of foreign products. Integration of the market is also the objective underlying the provisions of Article 90, which is directed against state measures taken in favour of public undertakings, where such measures run counter to the rules on unrestricted trade. Article 90 ensures the protection of effective, undistorted competition by prohibiting in particular measures that infringe the competition rules. Up until the entry into force of the Single European Act, Article 90 was rarely applied, but has recently become a key Treaty provision in connection with the deregulation of certain sectors and in terms of the equal treatment of private and public undertakings. We will return to this point later.

In conclusion, it may thus be seen that the competition rules and the policies based on them have already been serving the creation and shaping of the common market and hence also of the Single Market.

---

[11] On the general principles, see the communication to the Council on Commission policy on sectoral aid schemes, COM(78) 221 final (May 1978).

[12] See the compendium published by the Commission under the title *Competition law in the European Communities, Volume II: Rules applicable to State aids*, Brussels. Luxembourg, 1990. The compendium is to be updated in 1992.

[13] See the compendium referred to in note 12.

3. COMPETITION POLICY AS A MEANS OF COMPLETING THE SINGLE MARKET

3.1 Concentrating on the application of existing rules

The experiences acquired over a quarter of a century provide a broad basis for the further development of competition policy in the years ahead. Initially, the principle of *continuity* will predominate. Adjustment to new tasks will follow gradually, with a shift of emphasis in administrative practice, but without any basic changes in the legal instruments.

The period of active *legislation* is essentially over for DG IV. However, this does not mean that it will not be necessary in certain areas to revise and in some cases supplement the existing rules. It is, for example, inconvenient to have the competition rules on *transport* set out in different instruments. The three regulations on land, sea and air transport[14] should soon be combined into a single regulation. The multimodal cooperation agreements that are being concluded in increasing numbers require an overall assessment that is possible only on the basis of a single legal instrument.

At the same time, the remaining *gaps* in the legislative framework (tramp shipping, air transport within Member States and between the Community and third countries) need to be filled. Consideration should also be given to the question of whether the block exemptions applying to liner conferences[15] and commercial cooperation between airlines[16] still meet present requirements.

3.2 Competition policy priorities

An efficient competition policy that operates both as the engine for completing the Single Market and as its essential element must be based on the appropriate choice of *priorities*. Given the Commission's limited staff resources, previous activities can be successfully continued and further developed only if there is a clear dividing line between important and less important matters. Priorities must therefore be set for future activities, with account being taken not only of specific competition pol-

---

[14] Council Regulation (EEC) No. 1017/68 of 19 July 1968, O.J. 1968, L175/1; Council Regulation (EEC) No.4056/86 of 22 Dec. 1986, O.J. 1986, L378/4; Council Regulation (EEC) No. 3975/87 of 14 Dec. 1987, O.J. 1987, L374/1.

[15] Council Regulation (EEC) No. 4056/86 of 22 Dec. 1986, O.J. 1986, L378/4.

[16] Council Regulation (EEC) No. 3976/87 of 14 Dec. 1987, O.J. 1987, L374/9, as amended by Council Regulation (EEC) No.2344/90 of 24 July 1990, O.J. 1990, L217/15 and by Regulation (EEC) Nos. 82, 83 and 84/91 of 5 Dec. 1990, O.J. 1991, L10/7, *et seq.*

icy objectives but also of the need to combine and reconcile various Community policies so as to achieve the joint "Single Market" objective.

3.3 Application of Articles 85 and 86 to undertakings

Measures to combat *restrictive practices* and *abuses of dominant positions* that threaten the unity of the Single Market or the effectiveness of the system of competition will be pursued with vigour. Just how serious the Commission is in carrying out this task may be seen from the "*soda ash*" Decisions[17] adopted at the end of 1990, under which record fines amounting to ECU 48 million were imposed on the three companies concerned, namely Solvay, ICI and the BASF subsidiary CFK. The Decision is also a good example of the combined application of Article 85(1) and Article 86 of the EEC Treaty. It involves, on the one hand, the almost perfect division of the common market into a northern and a southern half by the two leading European manufacturers, with a smaller competitor having to be compensated with a given market quota, and, on the other, abuse of a dominant position by the two main partners against smaller competitors in order to drive them from the market or hinder their access to it.

Similar problems arise in the "*razor blades*" case, examined in detail in a report by the United Kingdom Mergers and Monopolies Commission,[18] in which Gillette, the leading world manufacturer of razor blades, acquired through a leveraged buy-out a minority holding in its main competitor, Wilkinson, and subsequently concluded with Wilkinson *inter alia* a trademark assignment agreement for the dividing up of markets at world level. This case also raises the very interesting question of the scope of the "Philip Morris" doctrine. It was notified to the Commission before the entry into force of the EC merger control regulation. The Commission is presently considering the operation under Art. 86 as well as under Art. 85.

Particular thought is given to *cooperative joint ventures* (JVs). In so far as these represent associations performing a partial function, in other words do not form an independent economic unit, they will in principle be assessed under competition law on the basis of the relevant object of the cooperation (buying/selling, research and development, production), so that it is difficult to make general pronouncements. Matters are different when it comes to joint ventures that represent undertakings in their own right. Their establishment usually results in an increase in the number of competitors on the market. Where they are caught by Article 85 (1),

---

[17]   See note 8 *supra*. The fines in the Tetrapak Decision amounted to a total of 75 million ECU.
[18]   Produced on 12 Dec. 1990.

therefore, such joint ventures should in most cases be viewed positively and exempted under Article 85 (3).

However, this would not apply to joint ventures which are primarily an instrument for coordinating the competitive behaviour of the parent companies (a sort of surrogate form of cartel) or which, by combining the market power of the participants, threaten the maintenance of effective competition. In 1990, in various individual decisions (Elopak/Metal Box-Odin, Konsortium ECR, Cekacan),[19] the Commission made it clear that in principle it takes a favourable view of joint ventures. It will maintain this attitude. Its policy in this area will be set out in a notice to be published in the *Official Journal* in 1992. We are currently examining whether the existing block exemptions for specialization and research and development agreements can be extended to apply to cooperative joint ventures operating as fully fledged undertakings.

A favourable attitude is also taken to agreements on *technical cooperation between firms*, particularly where it promotes the development, utilization or dissemination of new processes, products or services. The same applies (within the limits set by Article 85(3)(b)) to cooperation between competitors in opening up new markets. Such cooperation contributes to the integration of economies within the European Single Market. It does not occasion any fundamental misgivings where residual competition remains strong.

Firms can also expect the Commission to continue to adopt a favourable position on *vertical agreements*. Any legal uncertainty was largely removed during the early years of Community competition policy through general notices and block exemption regulations. The Community will continue to require this sort of legal framework once the Single Market has been completed. However, this does not mean that there will not have to be some adjustment of the rules to the changes in the legal and economic circumstances. Accordingly, the Commission intends in the near future to update its notice on contracts with commercial agents. We are also considering whether, at least in the medium term, the current block exemptions for vertical agreements should not be amended so as to give firms greater freedom of manoeuvre in drawing up agreements.

(End of excerpt)

---

[19] Decision of 13 July 1990, O.J. 1990, L209/15; Decision of 27 July 1990, O.J. 1990, L228/31; Decision of 15 Oct. 1990, OJ 1990, L299/64.

C. DISTRIBUTION AGREEMENTS AND THE INTEGRATION OF THE EUROPEAN MARKET

1. Policy

The structure of Article 85 is such that it may catch all manner of agreements between commercial parties, no matter what their subject matter may be. 'Vertical' agreements – between traders at different levels in the production and marketing chain – may be caught. 'Horizontal' agreements – between traders at the same level – may also be caught. Indeed horizontal deals will more frequently be caught than vertical deals in view of their inherently greater potential for exerting anti-competitive effects. The key to the application of Articles 85 is the effect of an agreement, not its form. Article 85 shares this characteristic with Articles 30 and 59.

The treatment of one particular type of agreement under Article 85 is especially instructive. The following examination focuses on distribution agreements. An agreement under which one party agrees to distribute goods made by another appears perfectly unobjectionable. The distribution network brings a product on to the market and thereby enhances competition and consumer choice. If the agreement is between a producer in one state and a distributor in another state the advantages are increased. It is then not simply a case of enhanced competition. There is an additional cross-border element to the enhancement and the agreement serves to promote market integration. Accordingly such agreements should be positively welcomed by a system dedicated to competition and to integration.

The difficulties arise when clauses are added to the agreement which are supplementary to the basic fact of distribution. The distributor is likely to want protective clauses in the deal. Where the distributor has made an investment in building up a market for the product in the new territory, for example by paying for an advertising campaign, that investment will be wasted if, once the market has been built up, other distributors are then able to enter the market. The newcomers will be able to sell the product without having to bear the costs of the investment. They will be able to 'free-ride' on the distributor's investment. To forestall this, it will therefore be in the interest of the distributor to include in the deal clauses restraining the producer from supplying other sources in the territory directly or indirectly. An exclusive distributorship would offer the required protection. The producer is likely to concede such an exclusive arrangement where, without the conferral of the protection of exclusivity, no distributor would be willing to embark on the deal.

For these reasons the parties may have incentives to set up a distributorship involving territorial exclusivity. What of the public interest? Competition law must hold the ring. On the one hand such deals may properly include exclusivity because otherwise the parties would not conclude the deal at all and the enhancement of competition and integration consequent on the deal will be lost to the consuming public. However, if the parties include excessive restrictions on competition the advantages may come to be outweighed by the disadvantages. It may be in the public interest to forbid certain clauses even where that refusal leads to the parties abandoning the whole deal.

There is a margin between lawful and unlawful restraints and it has to be set by the Community competition law authorities. It is a difficult balance to strike and, in striking it, the authorities are obliged to develop an important policy stance on the (potentially conflicting) roles of competition and integration in the market and the impact on private commercial freedoms. Private parties must align their plans to the European competition law system. This process of legal Europeanization has a significant impact on the structure of developing European commercialization.

The first major statement of the margin between lawful and unlawful clauses in a distribution agreement is found in the Court's ruling in *Consten and Grundig* v. *Commission*. The Court accepts that parties are permitted to enforce certain provisions guaranteeing exclusivity, but subjects that freedom to control inspired by the process of market integration.

Cases 56 & 58/64 *Consten and Grundig* v. *Commission* [1966] ECR 299

An arrangement was concluded between Consten, the French distributor, and Grundig, the German producer. Consten agreed to act as the exclusive dealer in France for the electrical products made in Germany by Grundig and was for these purposes permitted to register Grundig's trademark GINT under French law. Consten promised not to handle competing brands. Grundig, for its part, supplied only Consten in France and made sure that other dealers which it supplied outside France undertook not to resell Grundig products in France or to a French customer. The net result of the arrangement between Consten and Grundig was that on the French market Consten enjoyed absolute protection from competition by other suppliers of Grundig goods. The Commission decided that this absolute territorial protection meant that the agreement violated Article 85. The parties challenged the Commission's decision before the Court.

The complaints concerning the criterion of restriction on competition

The applicants and the German Government maintain that since the Commission restricted its examination solely to Grundig products the decision was based upon a false concept of competition and of the rules on prohibition contained in Article 85(1), since this concept applies particularly to competition between similar products of different makes; the Commission, before declaring Article 85(1) to be applicable, should, by basing itself upon the 'rule of reason', have considered the economic effects of the disputed contract upon competition between the different makes. There is a presumption that vertical sole distributorship agreements are not harmful to competition and in the present case there is nothing to invalidate that presumption. On the contrary, the contract in question has increased the competition between similar products of different makes.

The principle of freedom of competition concerns the various stages and manifestations of competition. Although competition between producers is generally more noticeable than that between distributors of products of the same make, it does not thereby follow that an agreement tending to restrict the latter kind of competition should escape the prohibition of Article 85(1) merely because it might increase the former.

Besides, for the purpose of applying Article 85(1), there is no need to take account of the concrete effects of an agreement once it appears that it has as its object the prevention, restriction or distortion of competition.

Therefore the absence in the contested decision of any analysis of the effects of the agreement on competition between similar products of different makes does not, of itself, constitute a defect in the decision.

It thus remains to consider whether the contested decision was right in founding the prohibition of the disputed agreement under Article 85(1) on the restriction on competition created by the agreement in the sphere of the distribution of Grundig products alone. The infringement which was found to exist by the contested decision results from the absolute territorial protection created the said contract in favour of Consten on the basis of French law. The applicants thus wished to eliminate any possibility of competition at the wholesale level in Grundig products in the territory specified in the contrast essentially by two methods.

First, Grundig undertook not to deliver even indirectly to third parties products intended for the area covered by the contract. The restrictive nature of that undertaking is obvious if it is considered in the light of the prohibition on exporting which was imposed not only on Consten but also on all the other sole concessionaires of Grundig, as well as the German wholesalers. Secondly, the registration in France by Consten of the GINT trade mark, which Grundig affixes to all its products, is intended to increase the protection inherent in the disputed agreement, against the risk of parallel imports into France of Grundig products, by adding the protection deriving from the law on industrial property rights. Thus no third party could import Grundig products from other Member States of the Community for resale in France without running serious risks.

The defendant properly took into account the whole distribution system thus set up by Grundig. In order to arrive at a true representation of the contractual position the contract must be placed in the economic and legal context in the light of which it was concluded by the parties. Such a procedure is not to be regarded as an unwarrantable interference in legal transactions or circumstances which were not the subject of the proceedings before the Commission.

The situation as ascertained above results in the isolation of the French market and makes it possible to charge for the products in question prices which are sheltered from all effective competition. In addition, the more producers succeed in their efforts to render their own makes of product individually distinct in the eyes of the consumer, the more the effectiveness of competition between producers tends to diminish. Because of the considerable impact of distribution costs on the aggregate cost price, it seems important that competition between dealers should also be stimulated. The efforts of the dealer are stimulated by competition between distributors of products of the same make. Since the agreement thus aims at isolating the French market for Grundig products and maintaining artificially, for products of a very well-known brand, separate national markets within the Community, it is therefore such as to distort competition in the Common Market.

It was therefore proper for the contested decision to hold that the agreement constitutes an infringement of Article 85(1). No further considerations, whether of economic data (price differences between France and Germany, representative character of the type of appliance considered, level of overheads borne by Consten) or of the corrections of the criteria upon which the Commission relied in its comparisons between the situations of the French and German markets, and no possible favourable effects of the agreement in other respects, can in any way lead, in the face of abovementioned restrictions, to a different solution under Article 85(1).

The complaints relating to the extent of the prohibition

The applicant Grundig and the German Government complain that the Commission did not exclude from the prohibition, in the operative part of the contested decision, those clauses of the contract in respect of which there was found no effect capable of restricting competition, and that it thereby failed to define the infringement.

It is apparent from the statement of the reasons for the contested decision, as well as from Article 3 thereof, that the infringement declared to exist by Article 1 of the operative part is not to be found in the undertaking by Grundig not to make direct deliveries in France except to Consten. That infringement arises from the clauses which, added to this grant of exclusive rights, are intended to impede, relying upon national law, parallel imports of Grundig products into France by establishing absolute territorial protection in favour of the sole concessionaire.

The provision in Article 85(2) that agreements prohibited pursuant to Article 85 shall be automatically void applies only to those parts of the agreement which are subject to the prohibition, or to the agreement as a whole if those parts do not appear to be severable from the agreement itself. The Commission should, therefore, either have confined itself in the operative part of the contested decision to declaring that an infringement lay in those parts only of the agreement which came within the prohibition, or else it should have set out in the preamble to the decision the reasons why those parts did not appear to it to be severable from the whole agreement.

It follows, however, from Article 1 of the decision that the infringement was found to lie in the agreement as a whole, although the Commission did not adequately state the reasons why it was necessary to render the whole of the agreement void when it is not established that all the clauses infringed the provisions of Article 85(1). The state of affairs found to be incompatible with Article 85(1) stems from certain specific clauses of the contract of 1 April 1957 concerning absolute territorial protection and from the additional agreement on the GINT trade mark rather than from the combined operation of all the clauses of the agreement, that is to say, from the aggregate of its effects.

Article 1 of the contested decision must therefore be annulled in so far as it renders void, without any valid reason, all the clauses of the agreement by virtue of Article 85(2).

It is important to appreciate that there is a collision embedded in this ruling between the function of competition law as a system dedicated to regulating the competitive market and competition law as a system dedicated to achieving integration. Consten was *not* necessarily achieving a monopoly in France in economic terms. It achieved a monopoly over the supply of Grundig goods in France, but this need not be a cause for concern if we assume the availability to French consumers of other brands of such goods. From that point of view the agreement did not damage competition in the market even though it conferred absolute territorial protection for Consten in France. This is the argument presented in the first paragraph of the above extract. Yet this line of argument is rejected by the Court. The motivation for the ruling appears to derive from the pursuit of integration, which dictates a need to secure the flow of parallel trade across borders. This is an important current in European competition policy and it intrudes into private commercial autonomy.

Parallel trade is perceived as the driving force in European market integration. European competition policy is motivated by the desire to curtail restrictions on parallel trade in pursuit of a European market. Sustaining interbrand competition alone may not satisfy the European policymaker. The Commission wants cross-border intrabrand competition too, even where that may undermine the distributor's exclusivity and even where that may accordingly threaten the willingness of traders to enter into such deals in the first place.

2. Block Exemption of Distribution Agreements

The Commission has exclusive powers conferred by Regulation 17/62 to exempt agreements caught by Article 85(1) by means of adopting decisions under Article 85(3). It has chosen to issue a series of block exemptions to avoid the need to make hundreds of decisions on individual cases. These block exemptions crystallize the requirements for exemption under Article 85(3) in relation to particular types of deal.

After the decision in *Consten and Grundig* the Commission chose to issue a Block Exemption Regulation to cover the phenomenon of the Exclusive Distribution agreement. The current version is Regulation 1983/83. The instrument appears to be part codification and part amplification of the Court's ruling in *Consten and Grundig*. The underlying theme of fostering market integration emerges in support for parallel importers. Article 1 concedes the permissibility of exclusivity in the relationship. This may also be traced through Article 2. Article 3, especially (c) and (d), reflects the importance of parallel trade and the abhorrence of absolute territorial protection.

COMMISSION REGULATION (EEC) No. 1983/83

of 22 June 1983

on the application of Article 85(3) of the Treaty to categories of exclusive distribution agreements

(Corrected in accordance with Corrigenda OJ 1983 L281/24)

THE COMMISSION OF THE EUROPEAN COMMUNITIES,

Having regard to the Treaty establishing the European Economic Community,
Having regard to Council Regulation No 19/65/EEC of 2 March 1965 on the application of Article 85(3) of the Treaty to certain categories of agreements and concerted practices,[1] as last amended by the Act of Accession of Greece, and in particular Article 1 thereof,

Having published a draft of this Regulation,[2]

Having consulted the Advisory Committee on Restrictive Practices and Dominant Positions,

(1) Whereas Regulation No 19/65/EEC empowers the Commission to apply Article 85(3) of the Treaty by regulation to certain categories of bilateral exclusive distribution agreements and analogous concerted practices falling within Article 85(1);

(2) Whereas experience to date makes it possible to define a category of agreements and concerted practices which can be regarded as normally satisfying the conditions laid down in Article 85(3);

(3) Whereas exclusive distribution agreements of the category defined in Article 1 of this Regulation may fall within the prohibition contained in Article

---

[1] OJ No 36, 6.3.1965, pp.533/65.
[2] OJ No C 172, 10.7.1982, p.3.

85(1) of the Treaty; whereas this will apply only in exceptional cases to exclusive agreements of this kind to which only undertakings from one Member State are party and which concern the resale of goods within that Member State; whereas, however, to the extent that such agreements may affect trade between Member States and also satisfy all the requirements set out in this Regulation there is no reason to withhold from them the benefit of the exemption by category;

(4) Whereas it is not necessary expressly to exclude from the defined category those agreements which do not fulfil the conditions of Article 85(1) of the Treaty;

(5) Whereas exclusive distribution agreements lead in general to an improvement in distribution because the undertaking is able to concentrate its sales activities, does not need to maintain numerous business relations with a larger number of dealers and is able, by dealing with only one dealer, to overcome more easily distribution difficulties in international trade resulting from linguistic, legal and other differences;

(6) Whereas exclusive distribution agreements facilitate the promotion of sales of a product and lead to intensive marketing and to continuity of supplies while at the same time rationalizing distribution; whereas they stimulate competition between the products of different manufacturers; whereas the appointment of an exclusive distributor who will take over sales promotion, customer services and carrying of stocks is often the most effective way, and sometimes indeed the only way, for the manufacturer to enter a market and compete with other manufacturers already present; whereas this is particularly so in the case of small and medium-sized undertakings; whereas it must be left to the contracting parties to decide whether and to what extent they consider it desirable to incorporate in the agreements terms providing for the promotion of sales;

(7) Whereas, as a rule, such exclusive distribution agreements also allow consumers a fair share of the resulting benefit as they gain directly from the improvement in distribution, and their economic and supply position is improved as they can obtain products manufactured in particular in other countries more quickly and more easily;

(8) Whereas this Regulation must define the obligations restricting competition which may be included in exclusive distribution agreements; whereas the other restrictions on competition allowed under this Regulation in addition to the exclusive supply obligation produce a clear division of functions between the parties and compel the exclusive distributor to concentrate his sales efforts on the contract goods and the contract territory; whereas they are, where they are agreed only for the duration of the agreement, generally necessary in order to attain the improvement in the distribution of goods sought through exclusive distribution; whereas it may be left to the contracting parties to decide which of these obligations they include in their agree-

ments; whereas further restrictive obligations and in particular those which limit the exclusive distributor's choice of customers or his freedom to determine his prices and conditions of sale cannot be exempted under this Regulation;

(9) Whereas the exemption by category should be reserved for agreements for which it can be assumed with sufficient certainty that they satisfy the conditions of Article 85(3) of the Treaty;

(10) Whereas it is not possible, in the absence of a case-by-case examination, to consider that adequate improvements in distribution occur where a manufacturer entrusts the distribution of his goods to another manufacturer with whom he is in competition; whereas such agreements should, therefore, be excluded from the exemption by category; whereas certain derogations from this rule in favour of small and medium-sized undertakings can be allowed;

(11) Whereas consumers will be assured of a fair share of the benefits resulting from exclusive distribution only if parallel imports remain possible; whereas agreements relating to goods which the user can obtain only from the exclusive distributor should therefore be excluded from the exemption by category; whereas the parties cannot be allowed to abuse industrial property rights or other rights in order to create absolute territorial protection; whereas this does not prejudice the relationship between competition law and industrial property rights, since the sole object here is to determine the conditions for exemption by category;

(12) Whereas, since competition at the distribution stage is ensured by the possibility of parallel imports, the exclusive distribution agreements covered by this Regulation will not normally afford any possibility of eliminating competition in respect of a substantial part of the products in question; whereas this is also true of agreements that allot to the exclusive distributor a contract territory covering the whole of the common market;

(13) Whereas, in particular cases in which agreements or concerted practices satisfying the requirements of this Regulation nevertheless have effects incompatible with Article 85(3) of the Treaty, the Commission may withdraw the benefit of the exemption by category from the undertakings party to them;

(14) Whereas agreements and concerted practices which satisfy the conditions set out in this Regulation need not be notified; whereas an undertaking may nonetheless in a particular case where real doubt exists, request the Commission to declare whether its agreements comply with this Regulation;

(15) Whereas this Regulation does not affect the applicability of Commission Regulation (EEC) No 3604/82 of 23 December 1982 on the application of

Article 85(3) of the Treaty to categories of specialization agreements;[3] whereas it does not exclude the application of Article 86 of the Treaty,

HAS ADOPTED THIS REGULATION:

Article 1

Pursuant to Article 85(3) of the Treaty and subject to the provisions of this Regulation, it is hereby declared that Article 85(1) of the Treaty shall not apply to agreements to which only two undertakings are party and whereby one party agrees with the other to supply certain goods for resale within the whole or a defined area of the common market only to that other.

Article 2

1. Apart from the obligation referred to in Article 1 no restriction on competition shall be imposed on the supplier other than the obligation not to supply the contract goods to users in the contract territory.

2. No restriction on competition shall be imposed on the exclusive distributor other than:

(a) the obligation not to manufacture or distribute goods which compete with the contract goods;

(b) the obligation to obtain the contract goods for resale only from the other party;

(c) the obligation to refrain, outside the contract territory and in relation to the contract goods, from seeking customers, from establishing any branch and from maintaining any distribution depot.

3. Article 1 shall apply notwithstanding that the exclusive distributor undertakes all or any of the following obligations:

(a) to purchase complete ranges of goods or minimum quantities;

(b) to sell the contract goods under trade marks, or packed and presented as specified by the other party;

(c) to take measures for promotion of sales, in particular:
   - to advertise,
   - to maintain a sales network or stock of goods,
   - to provide customer and guarantee services,
   - to employ staff having specialized or technical training.

Article 3

Article 1 shall not apply where:

(a) manufacturers of identical goods or of goods which are considered by users as equivalent in view of their characteristics, price and intended use enter

---

[3]   OJ No L 376, 31.12.1982, p.33.

into reciprocal exclusive distribution agreements between themselves in respect of such goods;

(b) manufacturers of identical goods or of goods which are considered by users as equivalent in view of their characteristics, price and intended use enter into a non-reciprocal exclusive distribution agreement between themselves in respect of such goods unless at least one of them has a total annual turnover of no more than 100 million ECU;

(c) users can obtain the contract goods in the contract territory only from the exclusive distributor and have no alternative source of supply outside the contract territory;

(d) one or both of the parties makes it difficult for intermediaries or users to obtain the contract goods from other dealers inside the common market or, in so far as no alternative source of supply is available there, from outside the common market, in particular where one or both of them:

1. exercises industrial property rights so as to prevent dealers or users from obtaining outside, or from selling in, the contract territory properly marked or otherwise properly marketed contract goods;

2. exercises other rights or takes other measures so as to prevent dealers or users from obtaining outside, or from selling in, the contract territory contract goods.

Article 4

1. Article 3(a) and (b) shall also apply where the goods there referred to are manufactured by an undertaking connected with a party to the agreement.

2. Connected undertakings are:

(a) undertakings in which a party to the agreement, directly or indirectly:
    - owns more than half the capital or business assets, or
    - has the power to exercise more than half the voting rights, or
    - has the power to appoint more than half the members of the supervisory board, board of directors or bodies legally representing the undertaking, or
    - has the right to manage the affairs;

(b) undertakings which directly or indirectly have in or over a party to the agreement the rights or powers listed in (a);

(c) undertakings in which an undertaking referred to in (b) directly or indirectly has the rights or powers listed in (a).

3. Undertakings in which the parties to the agreement or undertakings connected with them jointly have the rights or powers set out in paragraph 2(a) shall be considered to be connected with each of the parties to the agreement.

Article 5

1. For the purpose of Article 3(b), the ECU is the unit of account used for drawing up the budget of the Community pursuant to Articles 207 and 209 of the Treaty.

2. Article 1 shall remain applicable where during any period of two consecutive financial years the total turnover referred to in Article 3(b) is exceeded by no more than 10 %.

3. For the purpose of calculating total turnover within the meaning of Article 3(b), the turnovers achieved during the last financial year by the party to the agreement and connected undertakings in respect of all goods and services, excluding all taxes and other duties, shall be added together. For this purpose no account shall be taken of dealings between the party to the agreement and its connected undertakings or between its connected undertakings.

Article 6

The Commission may withdraw the benefit of this Regulation, pursuant to Article 7 of Regulation No 19/65/EEC, when it finds in a particular case that an agreement which is exempted by this Regulation nevertheless has certain effects which are incompatible with the conditions set out in Article 85(3) of the Treaty, and in particular where:

(a) the contract goods are not subject, in the contract territory, to effective competition from identical goods or goods considered by users as equivalent in view of their characteristics, price and intended use;

(b) access by other suppliers to the different stages of distribution within the contract territory is made difficult to a significant extent;

(c) for reasons other than those referred to in Article 3(c) and (d) it is not possible for intermediaries or users to obtain supplies of the contract goods from dealers outside the contract territory on the terms there customary;

(d) the exclusive distributor:

    1. without any objectively justified reason refuses to supply in the contract territory categories of purchasers who cannot obtain contract goods elsewhere on suitable terms or applies to them differing prices or conditions of sale;

    2. sells the contract goods at excessively high prices.

Article 7

In the period 1 July 1983 to 31 December 1986, the prohibition in Article 85(1) of the Treaty shall not apply to agreements which were in force on 1 July 1983 or entered into force between 1 July and 31 December 1983 and which satisfy the exemption conditions of Regulation No 67/67/EEC.[4]

---

[4] OJ No 57, 25.3.1967, pp.849/67.

Article 8

This Regulation shall not apply to agreements entered into for the resale of drinks in premises used for the sale and consumption of drinks or for the resale of petroleum products in service stations.

Article 9

This Regulation shall apply *mutatis mutandis* to concerted practices of the type defined in Article 1.

Article 10

This Regulation shall enter into force on 1 July 1983.

It shall expire on 31 December 1997.

This Regulation shall be binding in its entirety and directly applicable in all Member States.

Done at Brussels, 22 June 1983.

For the Commission

Frans ANDRIESSEN

Member of the Commission

3. The Court's persisting policy on the maintenance of parallel imports in distribution systems

The Court has consistently supported the Commission in its policy of insisting on the maintenance of channels for parallel imports as part of the approach to the freedom of firms to shape their distribution systems. Exclusive distribution, selective distribution and franchising are different forms of commercial collaboration, yet the Court's attitude has remained basically the same. The 'Europeanized' concern to achieve both regulation and integration remains visible, especially in relation to the support offered to the parallel trader. Private contractual autonomy must yield to the policy of the European market.

The next decision is a particularly good example of the difficult balance which the Community authorities endeavour to strike in adjudicating on deals which have an ambiguous impact on the market. In Case 258/78 *Nungesser* v. *Commission* [1982] ECR 2015, the contested decision found that Article 85(1) had been infringed as a result of the conclusion of contracts entered into between Eisele, majority shareholder of Nungesser, and INRA. INRA, a French research institute, assigned plant breeders' rights for German territory over varieties of hybrid maize seeds which INRA had developed. Also granted were exclusive propagating and selling rights over the seeds.

The Court was forced to undertake a close examination of the application of Article 85 to exclusive licences. It found that exclusive licences could take at least two distinct forms which attracted different legal consequences.

53   It should be observed that those two sets of considerations relate to two legal situations which are not necessarily identical. The first case concerns a so-called open exclusive licence or assignment and the exclusivity of the licence relates solely to the contractual relationship between the owner of the right and the licensee, whereby the owner merely undertakes not to grant other licences in respect of the same territory and not to compete himself with the licensee on that territory. On the other hand, the second case involves an exclusive licence or assignment with absolute territorial protection, under which the parties to the contract propose, as regards the products and the territory in question, to eliminate all competition from third parties, such as parallel importers or licensees for other territories.

54   That point having been clarified, it is necessary to examine whether, in the present case, the exclusive nature of the licence, in so far as it is an open licence, has the effect of preventing or distorting competition within the meaning of Article 85(1) of the Treaty.

55   In that respect the Government of the Federal Republic of Germany emphasized that the protection of agricultural innovations by means of breeders' rights constitutes a means of encouraging such innovations and the grant of exclusive rights for a limited period, is capable of providing a further incentive to innovative efforts.

From that it infers that a total prohibition of every exclusive licence, even an open one, would cause the interest of undertakings in licences to fall away, which would be prejudicial to the dissemination of knowledge and techniques in the Community.

56   The exclusive licence which forms the subject-matter of the contested decision concerns the cultivation and marketing of hybrid maize seeds which were developed by INRA after years of research and experimentation and were unknown to German farmers at the time when the cooperation between INRA and the applicants was taking shape. For that reason the concern shown by the interveners as regards the protection of new technology is justified.

57   In fact, in the case of a licence of breeders' rights over hybrid maize seeds newly developed in one Member State, an undertaking established in another Member State which was not certain that it would not encounter competition from other licensees for the territory granted to it, or from the

owner of the right himself, might be deterred from accepting the risk of cultivating and marketing that product; such a result would be damaging to the dissemination of a new technology and would prejudice competition in the Community between the new product and similar existing products.

58 Having regard to the specific nature of the products in question, the Court concludes that, in a case such as the present, the grant of an open exclusive licence, that is to say a licence which does not affect the position of third parties such as parallel importers and licensees for other territories, is not in itself incompatible with Article 85(1) of the Treaty.

59 Part B of the third submission is thus justified to the extent to which it concerns that aspect of the exclusive nature of the licence.

60 As regard to the position of third parties, the Commission in essence criticizes the parties to the contract for having extended the definition of exclusivity to importers who are not bound to the contract, in particular parallel importers. Parallel importers or exporters, such as Louis David KG in Germany and Robert Bomberault in France who offered INRA seed for sale to German buyers, had found themselves subjected to pressure and legal proceedings by INRA, Frasema and the applicants, the purpose of which was to maintain the exclusive position of the applicants on the German market.

61 The Court has consistently held (cf. Joined Cases 56 and 58/64 *Consten and Grundig* v. *Commission* [1966] ECR 299) that absolute territorial protection granted to a licensee in order to enable parallel imports to be controlled and prevented results in the artificial maintenance of separate national markets, contrary to the Treaty.

62 The Government of the United Kingdom advanced the view that a contract between two undertakings could not impede the freedom of importers to buy seeds in the country of the owner of the breeder's rights with a view to exporting them to the country of the licensee since, according to previous decisions of the Court, a commercial or industrial property right cannot be invoked against the marketing of a product which has been lawfully placed in circulation on the market of another Member State by the owner of that right or with his consent. Therefore such a contract cannot be regarded as an agreement prohibited by Article 85(1) of the Treaty.

63 However, that view fails to take into account the fact that one of the powers of the Commission is to ensure, pursuant to Article 85 of the Treaty and the regulations adopted in implementation thereof, that agreements and concerted practices between undertakings do not have the object or the effect of restricting or distorting competition, and that that power of the Commission is not affected by the fact that persons or undertakings subject to such restrictions are in a position to rely upon the provisions of the Treaty relating to the free movement of goods in order to escape such restrictions.

64 It is clear from the documents in the case that the contracts in question were indeed intended to restrict competition from third parties on the German

market. In fact under Clause 5 of the 1965 contract INRA promises that it and those deriving rights through it will do "everything in their power to prevent the export" of the varieties of seeds in question to Germany.

65 In the contested decision that clause is interpreted as seeking to prevent third parties who purchase INRA seeds in France from exporting them to Germany (II, No. 3(b)). It may be inferred from the obstructions which the parties to the contracts have placed in the way of the efforts of Louis David KG and Robert Bomberault to sell INRA seeds in Germany that that interpretation is correct.

66 Article 1(b) of the decision expressly refers to Clause 5 of the 1965 contract and to the exercise of breeders' rights by Mr Eisele so as to prevent the marketing of INRA seeds in Germany by third parties. Therefore, to that extent Part B of the third submission is unfounded.

67 An examination of Part B of the third submission therefore leads to the conclusion that that submission is well-founded in part and that Article 1(b) of the decision must be declared void to the extent to which it relates to Clause 1 of the 1965 contract and in so far as that contract imposes:

An obligation upon INRA or those deriving rights through INRA to refrain from having the relevant seeds produced or sold by other licensees in Germany, and

An obligation upon INRA or those deriving rights through INRA to refrain from producing or selling the relevant seeds in Germany themselves.

The Court proceeded to address the question of whether an arrangement involving absolute territorial protection could benefit from exemption under Article 85(3).

76 It must be remembered that under the terms of Article 85(3) of the Treaty an exemption from the prohibition contained in Article 85(1) may be granted in the case of any agreement between undertakings which contributes to improving the production or distribution of goods or to promoting technical progress, and which does not impose on the undertakings concerned restrictions which are not indispensable to the attainment of those objectives.

77 As it is a question of seeds intended to be used by a large number of farmers for the production of maize, which is an important product for human and animal foodstuffs, absolute territorial protection manifestly goes beyond what is indispensable for the improvement of production or distribution or the promotion of technical progress, as is demonstrated in particular in the present case by the prohibition, agreed to by both parties to the agreement, of any parallel imports of INRA maize seeds into Germany even if those seeds were bred by INRA itself and marketed in France.

78 It follows that the absolute territorial protection conferred on the licensee, as established to exist by the contested decision, constituted a sufficient reason for refusing to grant an exemption under Article 85(3) of the Treaty. It is therefore no longer necessary to examine the other grounds set out in the decision for refusing to grant such an exemption.

The message is that competition policy as an exercise in economic assessment of individual transactions may have to yield to competition policy in the much wider context of European market integration. The European policymakers seem unwilling to accept absolute territorial protection of a national market; certainly this cannot be cleared under Article 85(1). It is conceivable that the economic risks of being undermined by parallel importers might dissuade a party from entering into a deal. Yet it seems that in Europe there is a preference for seeing such a transaction fall rather than sustaining it by permitting absolute territorial protection which compartmentalizes the European market.

Case 161/84 *Pronuptia de Paris GmbH* v. *Pronuptia de Paris Irmgard Schillgalis* [1986] ECR 353 concerns a franchising arrangement. The Court was asked by the referring court, the German *Bundesgerichtshof*, to rule on the application of Article 85(1).

14 The compatibility of franchise agreements for the distribution of goods with Article 85(1) cannot be assessed *in abstracto* but depends on the provisions contained in such agreements. In order to make its reply as useful as possible to the Bundesgerichtshof the Court will concern itself with contracts such as that described above.

15 In a system of distribution franchises of that kind an undertaking which has established itself as a distributor on a given market and thus developed certain business methods grants independent traders, for a fee, the right to establish themselves in other markets using its business name and the business methods which have made it successful. Rather than a method of distribution, it is a way for an understanding to derive financial benefit from its expertise without investing its own capital. Moreover, the system gives traders who do not have the necessary experience access to methods which they could not have learned without considerable effort and allows them to benefit from the reputation of the franchisor's business name. Franchise agreements for the distribution of goods differ in that regard from dealerships or contracts which incorporate approved retailers into a selective distribution system, which do not involve the use of a single business name, the application of uniform business methods or the payment of royalties in return for the benefits granted. Such a system, which allows the franchisor to profit from his success, does not in itself interfere with competition. In order for the system to work two conditions must be met.

16   First, the franchisor must be able to communicate his know-how to the franchisees and provide them with the necessary assistance in order to enable them to apply his methods, without running the risk that that know-how and assistance might benefit competitors, even indirectly. It follows that provisions which are essential in order to avoid that risk do not constitute restrictions on competition for the purposes of Article 85(1). That is also true of a clause prohibiting the franchise during the period of validity of the contract and for a reasonable period after its expiry, from opening a shop of the same or a similar nature in an area where he may compete with a member of the network. The same may be said of the franchisee's obligation not to transfer his shop to another party without the price approval of the franchisor, that provision is intended to prevent competitors from indirectly benefiting from the know-how and assistance provided.

17   Secondly, the franchisor must be able to take the measures necessary for maintaining the identity and reputation of the network bearing his business name of symbol. It follows that provisions which establish the means of control necessary for that purpose do not constitute restrictions on competition for the purposes of Article 85(1).

18   The same is true of the franchisee's obligation to apply the business methods developed by the franchisor and to use the know-how provided.

19   That is also the case with regard to the franchisee's obligation to sell the goods covered by the contract only in premises laid out and decorated according to the franchisor's instructions, which is intended to ensure uniform presentation in conformity with certain requirements. The same requirements apply to the location of the shop, the choice of which is also likely to affect the network's reputation. It is thus understandable that the franchisee cannot transfer his shop to another location without the franchisor's approval.

20   The prohibition of the assignment by the franchisee of his rights and obligations under the contract without the franchisor's approval protects the latter's right freely to choose the franchisees, on whose business qualifications the establishment and maintenance of the network's reputation depend.

21   By means of the control exerted by the franchisor on the selection of goods offered by the franchisee, the public is able to obtain goods of the same quality from each franchisee. It may in certain cases – for instance, the distribution of fashion articles – be impractical to lay down objective quality specifications. Because of the large number of franchisees it may also be too expensive to ensure that such specifications are observed. In such circumstances a provision requiring the franchisee to sell only products supplied by the franchisor or by suppliers selected by him may be considered necessary for the protection of the network's reputation. Such a provision

may not however have the effect of preventing the franchisee from obtaining those products from other franchisees.

22 Finally, since advertising helps to define the image of the network's name or symbol in the eyes of the public, a provision requiring the franchisee to obtain the franchisor's approval for all advertising is also essential for the maintenance of the network's identity, so long as that provision concerns only the nature of the advertising.

23 It must be emphasized on the other hand that, far from being necessary for the protection of the know-how provided or the maintenance of the network's identity and reputation, certain provisions restrict competition between the members of the network. That is true of provisions which share markets between the franchisor and franchisees or between franchisees or prevent franchisees from engaging in price competition with each other.

24 In that regard, the attention of the national court should be drawn to the provision which obliges the franchisee to sell goods covered by the contract only in the premises specified therein. That provision prohibits the franchisee from opening a second shop. Its real effect becomes clear if it is examined in conjunction with the franchisor's undertaking to ensure that the franchisee has the exclusive use of his business name or symbol in a given territory. In order to comply with that undertaking the franchisor must not only refrain from establishing himself within that territory but also require other franchisees to give an undertaking not to open a second shop outside their own territory. A combination of provisions of that kind results in a sharing of markets between the franchisor and the franchisees or between franchisees and thus restricts competition within the network. As is clear from the judgment of 13 July 1966 (Joined Cases 56 and 58/64 *Consten and Grundig* v. *Commission* [1966] ECR 299), a restriction of that kind constitutes a limitation of competition for the purposes of Article 85(1) if it concerns a business name or symbol which is already well-known. It is of course possible that a prospective franchisee would not take the risk of becoming part of the chain, investing his own money, paying a relatively high entry fee and undertaking to pay a substantial annual royalty, unless he could hope, thanks to a degree of protection against competition on the part of the franchisor and other franchisees, that his business would be profitable. That consideration, however, is relevant only to an examination of the agreement in the light of the conditions laid down in Article 85(3).

25 Although provisions which impair the franchisee's freedom to determine his own prices are restrictive of competition, that is not the case where the franchisor simply provides franchisees with price guidelines, so long as there is no concerted practice between the franchisor and the franchisees or between the franchisees themselves for the actual application of such prices. It is for the national court to determine whether that is indeed the case.

26   Finally, it must be added that franchise agreements for the distribution of goods which contain provisions sharing markets between the franchisor and the franchisees or between the franchisees themselves are in any event liable to affect trade between Member States, even if they are entered into by undertakings established in the same Member State, in so far as they prevent franchisees from establishing themselves in another Member State.

27   In view of the forgoing, the answer to the first question must be that:

(1)   The compatibility of franchise agreements for the distribution of goods with Article 85(1) depends on the provisions contained therein and on their economic context.

(2)   Provisions which are strictly necessary in order to ensure that the know-how and assistance provided by the franchisor do not benefit competitors do not constitute restrictions of competition for the purposes of Article 85(1).

(3)   Provisions which establish the control strictly necessary for maintaining the identity and reputation of the network identified by the common name or symbol do not constitute restrictions of competition for the purposes of Article 85(1).

(4)   Provisions which share markets between the franchisor and the franchisees or between franchisees constitute restrictions of competition for the purposes of Article 85(1).

(5)   The fact that the franchisor makes price recommendations to the franchisee does not constitute a restriction of competition, so long as there is no concerted practice between the franchisor and the franchisees or between the franchisees themselves for the actual application of such prices.

(6)   Franchise agreements for the distribution of goods which contain provisions sharing markets between the franchisor and the franchisees or between franchisees are capable of affecting trade between Member States.

The message of the Court is largely the same in its refusal to accept territorial restriction as a component in a deal which can escape Article 85(1). The decision leaves open the possibility that territorial restriction might be exempted under Article 85(3). There is now a Block Exemption Regulation applicable to franchising, 4087/88 OJ 1988 L359/46. This envisages limited territorial restriction only as part of the franchising arrangement.

4. Distinct trends in European and American policy

The drive to sustain parallel trade dictates that European competition policy must eliminate contractual schemes which cement existing market fragmentation. Competition policy must play its part in the long march towards the creation of a European common market. One might expect competition policy in a territory which is already regarded as a common market to be less intrusive. There, one might anticipate a sharper focus on the economic motivation for the particular agreement and on the underlying structure of interbrand competition. Concern for cross-border intrabrand competition emerges clearly from European policy making, but one might suppose that that would not be an issue in a territory lacking economically significant borders. A brief glance at US antitrust policy reveals something of this difference in policy. European economic law seems more interventionist than US law because of the pressing desire to 'force' market integration through competition policy.

In the United States the Sherman Act performs the control function which is in Europe the preserve of Article 85. However, the structure of the Sherman Act is not identical to Article 85, because it has no in-built exemption procedure comparable to Article 85(3). The US courts have, however, interpreted the Act with some flexibility. They have read a rule of reason into the Sherman Act which serves a comparable function to the Article 85(3) exemption procedure. In 433 US 36 *Continental TV Inc* v. *GTE Sylvania Inc* (1977), the US Supreme Court was forced to reassess its own earlier decision in 388 US 365 *United States* v. *Arnold, Schwinn & Co* to the effect that, under the Sherman Act, it is unreasonable for a manufacturer to seek to restrict and confine areas or persons with whom an article may be traded after the manufacturer has parted with title to it, but that the rule of reason applies when the manufacturer exercises such control having retained title. In *Continental TV Inc* v. *GTE Sylvania Inc* title had passed to the franchisee, Continental. Each franchisee was able to sell the products only from the location at which the retailer was franchised. The clause restricted locations from which resale could occur. The arrangement violated the Sherman Act as interpreted in *Schwinn*. It is important that the Supreme Court, in overruling *Schwinn*, took full account of the economic considerations which underpin distribution agreements.

> The traditional framework of analysis under §1 of the Sherman Act is familiar and does not require extended discussion. Section 1 prohibits "[e]very contract, combination...., or conspiracy, in restraint of trade or commerce." Since the early years of this century a judicial gloss on this statutory language has established the "rule of reason" as the prevailing standard of analysis. *Standard Oil Co.* v. *United States*, 221 US 1, 55 L Ed 619, 31 S Ct 502 (1911). Under this rule, the factfinder weighs all of the circumstances of a case in deciding whether a restrictive practice should be prohibited as imposing an unreasonable restraint on competition. Per se rules of illegality

[433 US 50]

are appropriate only when they relate to conduct that is manifestly anticompetitive. As the Court explained in *Northern Pac. R. Co.* v. *United States*, 356 US 1, 5, 2 L Ed 2d 545, 78 S Ct 514 (1958), "there are certain agreements or practices which because of their pernicious effect on competition and lack of any redeeming virtue are conclusively presumed to be unreasonable and therefore illegal without elaborate inquiry as to the precise harm they have caused or the business excuse for their use."

In essence, the issue before us is whether Schwinn's per se rule can be justified under the demanding standards of Northern Pac. R. Co. The Court's refusal to endorse a per se rule in White Motor Co. was based on its uncertainty as to whether vertical restrictions satisfied those standards. Addressing this question for the first time, the Court stated:

"We need to know more than we do about the actual impact of these arrangements on competition to decide whether they have such a 'pernicious effect on competition and lack...any redeeming virtue' (Northern Pac. R. Co. v. United States, supra, p 5, [2 L Ed 2d 545, 78 S Ct 514]) and therefore should

[433 US 51]

be classified as per se violations of the Sherman Act." 372 US, at 263, 9 L Ed 2d 738, 83 S Ct 696.

Only four years later the Court in Schwinn announced its sweeping per se rule without even a reference to Northern Pac. R. Co. and with no explanation of its sudden change in position. We turn now to consider Schwinn in light of Northern Pac. R. Co.

The market impact of vertical restrictions is complex because of their potential for a simultaneous reduction of intrabrand competition and stimulation of interbrand competition.

[433 US 52]

Significantly, the Court in Schwinn did not distinguish among the challenged restrictions on the basis of their individual potential for intrabrand harm or interbrand benefit. Restrictions that completely eliminated intrabrand competition among Schwinn distributors were analyzed no differently from those that merely moderated intrabrand competition among retailers. The pivotal factor was the passage of title: All restrictions were held to be per se illegal where title had passed, and all were evaluated and sustained under the rule of reason where it had not. The location restriction at issue here would be subject to the same pattern of analysis under Schwinn.

It appears that this distinction between sale and nonsale transactions resulted from the Court's effort to accommodate the perceived intrabrand harm and interbrand benefit of vertical restrictions. The per se rule for sale transactions reflected the view that vertical restrictions are "so obviously destructive" of intrabrand competition that their use would "open the door to exclusivity of outlets and limitation of territory

[433 US 53]

further than prudence permits." 388 US, at 379–380, 18 L Ed 2d 1249, 87 S Ct 1856. Conversely, the continued adherence to the traditional rule of reason for nonsale transactions reflected the view that the restrictions have too great a potential for the promotion of interbrand competition to justify complete prohibition.

[433 US 54]

The Court's opinion provides no analytical support for these contrasting positions. Nor is there even an assertion in the opinion that the competitive impact of vertical restrictions is significantly affected by the form of the transaction. Nonsale transactions appear to be excluded from the per se rule, not because of a greater danger of intrabrand harm or a greater promise of interbrand benefit, but rather because of the Court's unexplained belief that a complete per se prohibition would be too "inflexibl[e]." Id., at 379, 18 L Ed 2d 1249, 87 S Ct 1856.

Vertical restrictions reduce intrabrand competition by limiting the number of sellers of a particular product competing for the business of a given group of buyers. Location restrictions have this effect because of practical constraints on the effective marketing area of retail outlets. Although intrabrand competition may be reduced, the ability of retailers to exploit the resulting market may be limited both by the ability of consumers to travel to other franchised locations and, perhaps more importantly, to purchase the competing products of other manufacturers. None of these key variables, however, is affected by the form of the transaction by which a manufacturer conveys his products to the retailers.

Vertical restrictions promote interbrand competition by allowing the manufacturer to achieve certain efficiencies in the distribution of his products. These "redeeming virtues" are implicit in every decision sustaining vertical restrictions under the rule of reason. Economists have identified a number

[433 US 55]

of ways in which manufacturers can use such restrictions to compete more effectively against other manufacturers. See, e.g., Preston, Restrictive Distribution Arrangements: Economic Analysis and Public Policy Standards, 30 *Law & Contemp Prob* 506, 511 (1965). For example, new manufacturers and manufacturers entering new markets can use the restrictions in order to induce competent and aggressive retailers to make the kind of investment of capital and labor that is often required in the distribution of products unknown to the consumer. Established manufacturers can use them to induce retailers to engage in promotional activities or to provide service and repair facilities necessary to the efficient marketing of their products. Service and repair are vital for many products, such as automobiles and major household appliances. The availability and quality of such services affect a manufacturer's goodwill and the competitiveness of his product. Because of market imperfections such as the so-called "free rider" effect, these services might not be provided by retailers in a purely competitive situation, despite the fact that each retailer's benefit would be greater if all provided the services than if none did. Posner, supra, n 13, at 285; cf. P. Samuelson, *Economics* 506–507 (10th ed 1976).

[433 US 56]

Economists also have argued that manufacturers have an economic interest in maintaining as much intrabrand competition as is consistent with the efficient distribution of their products. Bork, The Rule of Reason and the Per Se Concept: Price Fixing and Market Division [II], 75 *Yale LJ* 373, 403 (1966); Posner, supra, n 13, at 283, 287–288. Although the view that the manufacturer's interest necessarily corresponds with that of the public is not universally shared, even the leading critic of vertical restrictions concedes that Schwinn's distinction between sale and nonsale transactions is essentially unrelated to any relevant economic impact. Comanor, Vertical Territorial and Customer Restrictions: White Motor and Its Aftermath, 81 *Harv L Rev* 1419, 1422 (1968). Indeed, to the extent that the form of the transaction is related to interbrand benefits, the Court's distinction is inconsistent with its articulated concern for the ability of smaller firms to compete effectively with larger ones. Capital requirements and administrative expenses may prevent smaller firms from using the exception for nonsale transactions. See, e.g., Baker, supra, n 13, at 538; Philips, Schwinn Rules and the "New Economics" of Vertical

[433 US 57]

Relation, 44 Antitrust LJ 573, 576 (1975); Pollock, supra, n 13, at 610.

[7] We conclude that the distinction drawn in Schwinn between sale and nonsale transactions is not sufficient to justify the application of a per se rule in one situation and a rule of reason in the other. The question remains whether the per se rule stated in Schwinn should be expanded to include nonsale transactions or abandoned in favor of a return to the rule of reason. We have found no persuasive support for expanding the per se rule. As noted above, the Schwinn Court recognized the undesirability of "prohibit[ing] all vertical restrictions of territory and all franchising...." 388 US, at 379–380, 18 L Ed 2d 1249, 87 S Ct 1856. And even Continental does not urge us to hold that all such restrictions are per se illegal.

[8, 9a, 10a, 11a, 12a, 13] We revert to the standard articulated in Northern Pac. R. Co., and reiterated in White Motor, for determining whether vertical restrictions must be "conclusively presumed to be unreasonable and therefore illegal without elaborate inquiry as to the precise harm they have caused or the business excuse for their use." 356 US, at 5, 2 L Ed 2d 545, 78 S Ct 514. Such restrictions, in varying forms, are widely used in our free market economy. As indicated above, there is substantial scholarly and judicial authority

[433 US 58]

supporting their economic utility. There is relatively little authority to the contrary. Certainly, there has been no showing in this case, either generally or with respect to Sylvania's agreements, that vertical restrictions have or are likely to have a "pernicious effect on competition" or that they "lack ... any redeeming virtue." Ibid. Accordingly, we conclude that the per se rule stated in Schwinn must be overruled. In so holding we do not foreclose the possibility that particular applications of vertical restrictions might justify per se prohibition under Northern Pac. R. Co. But we do make clear that departure from the rule-of-reason standard

[433 US 59]

must be based upon demonstrable economic effect rather than – as in Schwinn – upon formalistic line drawing.

It is striking that the policy issues identified in this passage as relevant to control of vertical restraints can be directly transplanted to Europe. Yet the Supreme Court here is unwilling to interfere with a deal which promotes interbrand competition. What is missing from this judgment is the concern for market integration which extends in Europe even to a desire to retain cross-border intrabrand trade. European competition policy has a distinctive flavour drawn from the political and economic context in which it operates.

QUESTIONS

1   Outline the differences between the approaches taken in Europe and America to the relevance of the interplay between intrabrand and interbrand competition in assessing the permissibility of distribution deals. Do you consider that the differences are objectively justified?

2   In the light of the historical association between EC competition policy and market integration, consider the role that may be played by competition policy in the developing pattern of economic relationships between firms in the EC Member States and firms in European states that are aiming to join the European Union. (You might consider, for example, whether an acquisition by a

large German firm of a monopoly supplier in Poland should be regarded as a desirable step towards European market integration or as an undesirable extension of private market power.)

3   Should the power to develop European competition policy that is currently held by the European Commission be transferred to an independent Competition Agency?

4   To what extent is competition policy an instrument for enhancing the position of the private consumer? Should the role of the consumer interest be made more explicit in the framework of competition policy?

FURTHER READING

J.A. Fairburn and J.A. Kay (eds), *European Mergers and Merger Policy*, Oxford: Oxford University Press, 1993.

T. Frazer, 'Competition Law after 1992: the Next Step', *Modern Law Review*, **53**, 1990, p.609.

D. Hay, 'The Assessment: Competition Policy', *Oxford Review of Economic Policy*, **9**, 1993, p.1.

V. Korah, 'EEC Competition Policy – Legal Form or Economic Efficiency', *Current Legal Problems*, **39**, 1986, p.85.

J. Lonbay, *Frontiers of Competition Law*, Chichester, UK: Wiley Chancery Law Publishing, 1994.

H. Page, 'Ideological Conflict and the Origins of Antitrust Policy', *Tulane Law Review*, **66**, 1991, p.1.

R. Whish and B. Sufrin, 'Article 85 and the Rule of Reason', *Yearbook of European Law*, **7**, 1987, p.1.

5   State Intervention in the Market

A. THE CONTROL OF STATE INTERVENTION IN THE MARKET

The previous Chapter explained that competition policy forms a major component of the Internal Market project. Competition in the market counts as a pillar of the European economic constitution. The focus in the previous Chapter was on private actors. Yet the state involves itself in the economy in many different ways. It too may affect the process of competition. It too needs to be subjected to the rules of the European economic constitution.

State actions may come into conflict with the rules of the 'four freedoms'. A state measure which obstructs cross-border trade in goods falls to be considered in the light of Article 30. Where the obstruction is to services, Article 59 is the relevant provision. However, beyond the trade barrier, the state may act in other ways which affect the competitive process. In the modern mixed economy the opportunities for private parties to compete are affected by the extent to which the state has intervened in the market. State laws may lead to the creation or maintenance of the type of distorted market which would certainly be the subject of challenge by Community law had it been the product of private action. The state may create special or exclusive rights which insulate a particular undertaking from competition. This may be done for social policy reasons, yet it will reduce competition. Therefore, anti-competitive action attributable to the state may need to be controlled as much as anti-competitive behaviour by private actors.

There are a number of Treaty provisions which operate as controls over the state's capacity to affect the competitive process. Article 3(g) EC declares that 'the activities of the Community shall include... a system ensuring that competition in the internal market is not distorted'. This is the successor to Article 3(f) EEC which applied before the coming into force of the Treaty on European Union, which stated that 'the activities of the Community shall include... (f) the institution of a system ensuring that competition in the common market is not distorted'. This provision has been combined with Article 5 to create a basis for subjecting the Member States to a control drawn from the competitive ethos of the European economic constitution. Article 5 declares that;

> 'Member States shall take all appropriate measures, whether general or particular, to ensure fulfilment of the obligations arising out of this Treaty or resulting from action taken by the institutions of the Community. They shall facilitate the achievement of the Community's tasks.

They shall abstain from any measure which could jeopardise the attainment of the objectives of the Treaty.'

The combination of Articles 3(g) and 5 provides a basis for control. Much remains to be elaborated. What is meant by the notion of a distortion of competition in Article 3(g)? It is in the amplification of this imprecise notion that the European policy makers have had the chance to establish a European control over state intervention in the market. A major issue is the extent to which EC law represents simply a collection of basic instruments such as the provisions on free movement or whether, much more ambitiously, there are certain key economic and legal principles, such as undistorted competition, which underpin the whole notion of the Community market and which control the activities of all entities, public and private. If the latter analysis is even only partially correct, then it suggests the growth of an Economic Constitution of which individual Treaty provisions are merely specific manifestations.

Article 90 is of direct relevance to undertakings with which the state has defined links.

1. In the case of public undertakings and undertakings to which Member States grant special or exclusive rights, Member States shall neither enact nor maintain in force any measure contrary to the rules contained in this Treaty, in particular to those rules provided for in Article 6 and Articles 85 to 94.

2. Undertakings entrusted with the operation of services of general economic interest or having the character of a revenue-producing monopoly shall be subject to the rules contained in this Treaty, in particular to the rules on competition, in so far as the application of such rules does not obstruct the performance, in law or in fact, of the particular tasks assigned to them. The development of trade must not be affected to such an extent as would be contrary to the interests of the Community.

3. The Commission shall ensure the application of the provisions of this Article and shall, where necessary, address appropriate directives or decisions to Member States.

The structure of Article 90 deserves careful attention. Its first paragraph accepts the existence of public undertakings and undertakings to which special or exclusive rights have been granted. It then asserts the control of the Treaty rules over Member States where such undertakings exist. There is here a suggestion of a balance to be struck, between the fact of the existence of such undertakings and the scope of the activities in which they are permitted to engage on the market. This is an issue where there is scope for developing from Article 90(1) a European approach to the place in the market of public undertakings and undertakings to which Member States grant special or exclusive rights. The second paragraph of Article 90 provides an exception from the general rule. In defined circumstances, an undertaking may be able to shelter from the application of the Treaty rules. This reflects the idea that state intervention in the market may serve beneficial and necessary social ends. Article 90(2) promises to be an element in developing a European notion of permissible curtailment of competition in pursuit of other social objectives. The third paragraph of Article 90 empowers the Commission to legislate in this field. This is unusual in the structure of the Treaty. The Council, the representative of the Member States, is normally responsible for the adoption of legislation in the Community. Article 90(3) gives the Commission unusual leverage over the states in this area.

The intermingling of these several Treaty provisions places a significant European control over state participation in the market. There is, however, scope for confusion consequent on this intermingling. An example may be taken from the situation which arises when a state grants exclusive rights to an undertaking. Where this confers a dominant position on the firm it falls under an obligation not to act abusively – Article 86. The state's grant of exclusivity needs to be checked against Article 90(1). Where the exclusivity obstructs cross-border trade, account must be taken of Article 30 where goods are in issue, Article 59 where services are in issue. There appears to be an accumulation of relevant legal provisions, yet it is not clear whether all apply as controls or whether, in the event of overlap, some are overridden by others. This may be especially important where the state seeks to justify the grant of exclusivity. If, for example, an undertaking is granted exclusive rights over the supply of goods for reasons of social need, should justification be sought under Article 90(2) or Article 36 – or both? The Community pursuit of market integration does not inevitably and necessarily lead to the ejection of the state from the market. There remains scope for market regulation by the states themselves. The policies of market integration and competition have to find a *modus vivendi* with the role of the state in the market – and, more broadly still, with the role of the state in society.

The Europeanization of the control of state intervention in the market presents the Community institutions with some problems of achieving coherence within the Treaty itself. Is there a general European theory of what the state can and cannot do? Markets in which competition is artificially restricted or in which parallel trade or indeed any kind of cross-border trade is impeded as a result of state intervention are prime candidates for scrutiny under Community law. The Commission and Court are developing a basis for control which is flavoured by the familiar themes of market integration and market regulation. The result is an increasing emphasis on cross-border competition which substantially curtails the regulatory powers of the Member States on their own territory, even, indeed especially, in respect of markets which have in many Member States traditionally been run as national monopolies. Such legal developments may be taken as pointers towards the shaping of a European Economic Constitution, but, in so far as there is a movement in this direction, it is a markedly erratic one.

The majority of the decisions which follow involve clear violations by the state. The result is that the state is 'ejected' from the market leading to·increased competition.

B. STATE MONOPOLIES SUBJECTED TO THE PRINCIPLES OF ARTICLE 86

In Case C-41/90 *Höfner and Elser* v. *Macrotron* [1991] ECR I-1979 Höfner and Elser had provided Macrotron with a candidate for a post as a sales director. Macrotron did not appoint the person despite his suitability and refused to pay Höfner and Elser. German law granted exclusive rights relating to employee recruitment to a public agency. Therefore the contract on which Höfner and Elser sued Macrotron was void. Höfner and Elser relied on Community law to challenge the German law which excluded them from the market for supplying staff.

In its decision the Court declined to examine the law in question from the perspective of Article 59, dealing with the free movement of services, because on the facts of the case there was no cross-border element involved. However, it drew out of Article 86 an obligation on the state not to sustain a market which was uncompetitive. The decision amounts to a strong message in favour of liberalization through which the structure of the market should be settled by private market decisions (supply and demand) and not by state regulation. It also shows powerfully how European economic law is directed at the structure of national markets even where no point arising directly out of the 'four freedoms' is in issue.

The interpretation of Articles 86 and 90 of the EEC Treaty

16   In its fourth question, the national court asks more specifically whether the monopoly of employment procurement in respect of business executives granted to a public employment agency constitutes an abuse of a dominant position within the meaning of Article 86, having regard to Article 90(2). In order to answer that question, it is necessary to examine that exclusive right also in the light of Article 90(1), which is concerned with the conditions that the Member States must observe when they grant special or exclusive rights. Moreover, the observations submitted to the Court relate to both Article 90(1) and Article 90(2) of the Treaty.

17   According to the appellants in the main proceedings, an agency such as the Bundesanstalt is both a public undertaking within the meaning of Article 90(1) and an undertaking entrusted with the operation of services of general economic interest within the meaning of Article 90(2) of the Treaty. The Bundesanstalt is therefore, they maintain, subject to the competition rules to the extent to which the application thereof does not obstruct the perform-

ance of the particular task assigned to it, and it does not in the present case. The appellants also claim that the action taken by the Bundesanstalt, which extended its statutory monopoly over employment procurement to activities for which the establishment of a monopoly is not in the public interest, constitutes an abuse within the meaning of Article 86 of the Treaty. They also consider that any Member State which makes such an abuse possible is in breach of Article 90(1) and of the general principle whereby the Member States must refrain from taking any measure which could destroy the effectiveness of the Community competition rules.

18 The Commission takes a somewhat different view. The maintenance of a monopoly on executive recruitment constitutes, in its view, an infringement of Article 90(1) read in conjunction with Article 86 of the Treaty where the grantee of the monopoly is not willing or able to carry out that task fully, according to the demand existing on the market, and provided that such conduct is liable to affect trade between Member States.

19 The respondent in the main proceedings and the German Government consider on the other hand that the activities of an employment agency do not fall within the scope of the competition rules if they are carried out by a public undertaking. The German Government states in that regard that a public employment agency cannot be classified as an undertaking within the meaning of Article 86 of the Treaty, in so far as the employment procurement services are provided free of charge. The fact that those activities are financed mainly by contributions from employers and employees does not, in its view, mean that they are not free, since those contributions are general and have no link with each specific service provided.

20 Having regard to the foregoing considerations, it is necessary to establish whether a public employment agency such as the Bundesanstalt may be regarded as an undertaking within the meaning of Articles 85 and 86 of the Treaty.

21 It must be observed, in the context of competition law, first that the concept of an undertaking encompasses every entity engaged in an economic activity, regardless of the legal status of the entity and the way in which it is financed and, secondly, that employment procurement is an economic activity.

22 The fact that employment procurement activities are normally entrusted to public agencies cannot affect the economic nature of such activities. Employment procurement has not always been, and is not necessarily, carried out by public entities. That finding applies in particular to executive recruitment.

23 It follows that an entity such as a public employment agency engaged in the business of employment procurement may be classified as an undertaking for the purpose of applying the Community competition rules.

24   It must be pointed out that a public employment agency which is entrusted, under the legislation of a Member State, with the operation of services of general economic interest, such as those envisaged in Article 3 of the AFG, remains subject to the competition rules pursuant to Article 90(2) of the Treaty unless and to the extent to which it is shown that their application is incompatible with the discharge of its duties (see judgment in Case 155/73 *Sacchi* [1974] ECR 409).

25   As regards the manner in which a public employment agency enjoying an exclusive right of employment procurement conducts itself in relation to executive recruitment undertaken by private recruitment consultancy companies, it must be stated that the application of Article 86 of the Treaty cannot obstruct the performance of the particular task assigned to that agency in so far as the latter is manifestly not in a position to satisfy demand in that area of the market and in fact allows its exclusive rights to be encroached on by those companies.

26   Whilst it is true that Article 86 concerns undertakings and may be applied within the limits laid down by Article 90(2) to public undertakings or undertakings vested with exclusive rights or specific rights, the fact nevertheless remains that the Treaty requires the Member States not to take or maintain in force measures which could destroy the effectiveness of that provision (see judgment in Case 13/77 *Inno* [1977] ECR 2115, paragraphs 31 and 32). Article 90(1) in fact provides that the Member States are not to enact or maintain in force, in the case of public undertakings and the undertakings to which they grant special or exclusive rights, any measure contrary to the rules contained in the Treaty, in particular those provided for in Articles 85 to 94.

27   Consequently, any measure adopted by a Member State which maintains in force a statutory provision that creates a situation in which a public employment agency cannot avoid infringing Article 86 is incompatible with the rules of the Treaty.

28   It must be remembered, first, that an undertaking vested with a legal monopoly may be regarded as occupying a dominant position within the meaning of Article 86 of the Treaty (see judgment in Case 311/84 *CBEM* [1985] ECR 3261) and that the territory of a Member State, to which that monopoly extends, may constitute a substantial part of the common market (judgment in Case 322/81 *Michelin* [1983] ECR 3461, paragraph 28).

29   Secondly, the simple fact of creating a dominant position of that kind by granting an exclusive right within the meaning of Article 90(1) is not as such incompatible with Article 86 of the Treaty (see Case 311/84 *CBEM*, above, paragraph 17). A Member State is in breach of the prohibition contained in those two provisions only if the undertaking in question, merely by exercising the exclusive right granted to it, cannot avoid abusing its dominant position.

30   Pursuant to Article 86(b), such an abuse may in particular consist in limiting the provision of a service, to the prejudice of those seeking to avail themselves of it.

31   A Member State creates a situation in which the provision of a service is limited when the undertaking to which it grants an exclusive right extending to executive recruitment activities is manifestly not in a position to satisfy the demand prevailing on the market for activities of that kind and when the effective pursuit of such activities by private companies is rendered impossible by the maintenance in force of a statutory provision under which such activities are prohibited and non-observance of that prohibition renders the contracts concerned void.

32   It must be observed, thirdly, that the responsibility imposed on a Member State by virtue of Articles 86 and 90(1) of the Treaty is engaged only if the abusive conduct on the part of the agency concerned is liable to affect trade between Member States. That does not mean that the abusive conduct in question must actually have affected such trade. It is sufficient to establish that that conduct is capable of having such an effect (see Case 322/81 *Michelin*, above, paragraph 104).

33   A potential effect of that kind on trade between Member States arises in particular where executive recruitment by private companies may extend to the nationals or to the territory of other Member States.

34   In view of the foregoing considerations, it must be stated in reply to the fourth question that a public employment agency engaged in employment procurement activities is subject to the prohibition contained in Article 86 of the Treaty, so long as the application of that provision does not obstruct the performance of the particular task assigned to it. A Member State which has conferred an exclusive right to carry on that activity upon the public employment agency is in breach of Article 90(1) of the Treaty where it creates a situation in which that agency cannot avoid infringing Article 86 of the Treaty. That is the case, in particular, where the following conditions are satisfied:

- the exclusive right extends to executive recruitment activities;
- the public employment agency is manifestly incapable of satisfying demand prevailing on the market for such activities;
- the actual pursuit of those activities by private recruitment consultants is rendered impossible by the maintenance in force of a statutory provision under which such activities are prohibited and non-observance of that prohibition renders the contracts concerned void;
- the activities in question may extend to the nationals or to the territory of other Member States.

The interpretation of Article 59 of the EEC Treaty

35   In its third question, the national court seeks essentially to determine whether a recruitment consultancy company in a Member State may rely on Articles 7 and 59 of the Treaty regarding the procurement of nationals of that Member State for posts in undertakings in the same State.

36   It must be recalled, in the first place, that Article 59 of the EEC Treaty guarantees, as regards the freedom to provide services, the application of the principle laid down in Article 7 of that Treaty. It follows that where rules are compatible with Article 59 they are also compatible with Article 7 (judgment in Case 90/76 *Van Ameyde* [1977] ECR 1091, paragraph 27).

37   It must then be pointed out that the Court has consistently held that the provisions of the Treaty on freedom of movement cannot be applied to activities which are confined in all respects within a single Member State and that the question whether that is the case depends on findings of fact which are for the national court to make (see, in particular, the judgment in Case 52/79 *Debauve* [1980] ECR 833, paragraph 9).

38   The facts, as established by the national court in its order for reference, show that in the present case the dispute is between German recruitment consultants and a German undertaking concerning the recruitment of a German national.

39   Such a situation displays no link with any of the situations envisaged by Community law. That finding cannot be invalidated by the fact that a contract concluded between the recruitment consultants and the undertaking concerned includes the theoretical possibility of seeking German candidates resident in other Member States or nationals of other Member States.

40   It must therefore be stated in reply to the third question that a recruitment consultant in a Member State may not rely on Article 7 and 59 of the Treaty regarding the procurement of nationals of that Member State for posts in undertakings in the same State.

41   In view of the above answer, it is unnecessary to consider the first two questions and the part of the fourth question concerned with the question whether Article 59 of the Treaty precludes a statutory prohibition of the pursuit, by private recruitment consultancy companies in a Member State, of the business of executive recruitment.

It is difficult to disagree with the actual result of this case. There seems no particular reason why the state should arrange in advance the structure of such a market. However, the Court's approach may be open to a more general criticism that it offers little opportunity to a state to show a justification for its intervention. This could be of importance in a case involving a law more deserving that that at issue here.

N. Reich, 'Competition between Legal Orders: a New Paradigm of EC Law?', *Common Market Law Review*, **29**, (1992) pp.861, 886 comments that the Court adopts 'a *narrow* reading of Article 59, excluding purely internal restrictions of services... but at the same time *extend[s]* the sphere of application of Articles 86/90 to state activities which become undertakings [in the sense of Arts. 85/86] by the simple fact that, as a necessary corollary of the exercise of their statutory powers, they close market entry to private ... competitors'. In this way EC law controls state regulation of the market even in the absence of any trans-border element in the case. From this perspective, the ruling in *Höfner* v. *Macrotron* seems to count as a rather strong expression of a European internal market regulated by a European economic law which applies even where the subject matter of the dispute is internal to a single Member State. However, it will be seen below (especially in the ruling in *Meng* at p.213) that there are limits to the control of a European Economic Law which is exercised over internal state laws which do not fall under the control of the rules on free movement. The fact that a law affects the market is not always enough to engage EC law. The European Economic Constitution does not seem to be comprehensive in its coverage of Member State laws which affect the market. However, before examining these issues further, the following extract from a paper presented by N. Reich in Bremen to ZERP (Centre for European Legal Policy), translated from the German for this book, offers further reflection on the powerfully interventionist flavour of the ruling in *Höfner* v. *Macrotron*. It is followed by further cases in which the state is ejected from the market by the application of EC law.

THE SINGLE MARKET AND 'PUBLIC SERVICE' – REFLECTIONS ON A CURRENT CONTROVERSY*

Norbert Reich

Allow me to begin my brief contribution to the topic of this symposium by quoting from Heine's 'Germany – A Winter's Tale' some lines which I found in Caput I and which accord well with the topic:

'The virgin Europe is engaged with the handsome spirit of freedom, they lie in one another's arms and revel in their first kiss.'

I do not intend to dwell at length on Heine's obviously political allusions, for it was surely *political* freedom that he had in mind when he was writing. But today it is *economic* freedom with which the – now rather mature – 'virgin Europe' is engaged, in order, upon completion of the Single Market, to enter into a late marriage.

Just as political freedom in the 19th century was perceived as a threat to nation-state – and heavily authoritarian – traditions, so today economic freedom attacks the unjust and obsolete vested property interests, social privileges and entire 'systems of acquired rights' as these were understood by Lasalle. And we 'Bremen jurists' in particular have every reason to engage critically with this movement. After all, ZERP was founded in order, through its research, to offer as an alternative to a 'Europe of businessmen' the paradigm of a 'Europe of citizens', to borrow the terms used by a well-known Bremen politician. In the very first ZERP DP 1/82 – ambitiously entitled 'Concepts, Projects, Persons' – we read under the heading 'social integration' as a research topic for the just-established institute:

'In view of the asymmetry between the development of economic and social integration – to a certain extent, the free flow of capital, goods and services made possible by the EC exacerbates existing social differences – major questions are dealt with in until-now largely neglected areas of European legal policy'.

How has Europe, how has ZERP comported itself with respect to this development, which can be paraphrased in Heine's sense as 'spirit', 'pleasure' or 'kiss of freedom' (in the economic sense, of course)? Here rather than summing up almost ten years' of dealing with this question, I would prefer – by focusing on a current ex-

---

* Norbert Reich, 'Binnenmarkt und "Service-Public" - Einige Überlegungen zu einer aktuellen Kontroverse', in *Zentrum für Europäische Rechtspolitik* (ZERP), DP 7/91, pp.15-22, reprinted by permission of ZERP. Translation by John Blazek, Brussels.

ample – to illustrate the relevance of the economic law-theoretical research approach that was developed with the founding of ZERP.

The starting point for a situation which should be regarded rather as a paradigm *confirmation* than as a 'paradigm shift' in Community law was, as so often, a quite trivial civil law suit, one tried before the Munich *Oberlandesgericht* (OLG – Higher Regional Court) and involving a fee claimed by two management consultants (the plaintiffs Mr. Höfner and Mr. Elser) against defendant Macrotron Co. for the (ultimately unsuccessful) recruitment of a sales manager. The defendant opposed the claim by arguing that the contract was invalid because it violated the placement monopoly of the *Bundesanstalt für Arbeit* (BfA – Federal Employment Office) under the *Arbeitsförderungsgesetz* (AFG – Employment Promotion Law). The plaintiffs received support from Prof. Emmerich, one of the most tireless fighters against public service monopolies, and represented by Atty Dr. Müller, who had done his doctoral work under Emmerich on this very topic and flatly asserted that such monopolies were contrary to European law. They saw in just this legal consequence a violation of Article 90 EEC, which – to put it in non-technical terms – prohibits public enterprises from abusing their monopoly power outside of their recognized area of exclusive authority.

In its decision of 23 April 1991, the Court did not spend much time on the scope of the BfA's AFG-based placement monopoly justified on social-policy grounds. Rather it subsumed the placement monopoly under the private law category of abuse of its position by a market-dominating (public!) enterprise. Even this need not have caused undue concern, since the 1974 Sacchi decision had expressly declared that the government radio monopoly *was* compatible with the EEC Treaty. Sacchi stated that the EEC Treaty in no way hindered the Member States 'for reasons that lie in the public interest from giving public bodies the exclusive right to broadcast television programmes'.

However, later case law shows clear tendencies to understand state action in the economic area not according to criteria of *public service*, that is, not as the performance of social integration entrusted to Member States because of a lack of Community harmonization, but rather as interference with market integration. The area of application of Community competition rules to state entrepreneurial or state regulating action is being drawn ever more broadly by the ECJ, although this development cannot be described here in detail. The result is a type of reversal in the perception of Member State social policy as service monopolies: their competition-interfering function is shaken by the vigorous 'kiss of freedom' of Community law, in order to open up new, lucrative markets for the private sector. This can also be seen quite clearly in Commission's various *deregulation initiatives* (details of which are of course hotly contested), whether these involve the fields of telecommunications, insurance monopolies, energy and water supply, government procurement systems, and so on. It almost appears as though the Court wishes to offer legal flanking protection here.

The Court has shown little concern about the limiting criteria of Article 90 EEC or the legislative decisions of the Member States which legitimize the placement monopoly. While abuse may not exist *per se* as a result of the creation of the market-dominating position implied by the placement monopoly, it *is* brought about through the exercise of the monopoly, to which the governmental regulation contributes. This is already the case when the service monopoly extends to areas where the monopolist obviously could not itself satisfy the demand for services – here: the placement of business-sector executives – and thus private business consultants would be hindered in their market activities, for example through the invalidity of the placement contract they conclude.

The tautology – in terms of economic policy evidently intended by the Court – is thus perfect: exercise of a placement monopoly is already abusive if this impedes private placement activities, although it is of course precisely the logic of a placement monopoly to prevent such activities. Earlier decisions had only found 'abuse' in extensions of the area of exclusivity to other markets not covered by the monopoly. The new decision goes well beyond this, because it sees the abuse as commencing already in the exercise of the monopoly power within the framework provided by the law; since, according to the statements of the Court, the monopoly of the BfA in principle also covered the placement of executives, although this may never have been rigidly implemented.

Thus, 'abuse' as a central category of the law of competition restrictions is not aimed (for example) at the monopolist who exploits his consumers and restricts his competitors, but rather at an exclusivity right created by democratically elected legislators and implemented in a state under the rule of law in order to achieve social policy goals! To exaggerate only slightly: the only time the public enterprise does *not* act abusively is when, owing to the need for state subsidy, no demand exists for private services; but then there could also exist no supply and thus no market, so that a case of conflict never arises. According to this logic, every service monopoly would be abusive by definition: either it impedes private suppliers, when the factual situation objected to by the Court is present; or there is no market – and then the service monopoly is superfluous in any event.

Naturally, even a democratically legitimated legislature must respect the provisions of Community law, and ever since the celebrated *Cassis* decision this discussion has been a topic of extensive research in ZERP's work as well. In the present case, it would have to have been examined to what extent the placement monopoly granted by the legislature – as well as other service monopolies – violates the principle of freedom of service transactions in accordance with Article 59 EEC. By making concrete Articles 3c and 8a of the EEC, this provision is intended to protect free service transactions against discriminating or disproportionate state-sovereign restrictions which are not in the general interest. The Court only briefly touches upon this problematic (which it has developed in extensive case law that secures a broad consensus, and which was the main question posed to it by the submitting court), but ultimately rejects it by noting that the legal dispute lacks an international aspect. Why this does not then also apply for Article 90 remains a mystery, since this provision in any case only finds application with respect to impairment of the international action, no matter how broadly this is interpreted. Obviously, Article 90 has the function of allowing the Court to omit the balancing paradigm developed by the Court itself for distinguishing permissible and forbidden restrictions on the freedom to provide services. The delicate navigating between the Community interest in market integration and the citizens' interest in social integration is thus exposed to market and private law-shaped concepts. The attention of the Community, and now obviously that of the Court as well, is concentrated not on the existence of 'public service' reservations of the Member States, but rather on the development of market opportunities that run counter to them.

From legal policy and legal theory perspectives, the consequences of this decision (here more hinted at than thoroughly criticized) for public service monopolies, as well as for the concept of 'public service' are extraordinarily broad: after the already eliminated radio monopoly and the swiftly disappearing telecommunications and (in several countries still defended) insurance monopolies, other monopolies are beginning to slip, such as the placement monopoly of the BfA, the entire community monopolies in the area of the so-called 'existential services', educational monopolies and supply and disposal monopolies. According to this logic, state activity should be restricted to a core of highly subsidized 'public service' institutions. Such a consequence has been in the air ever since the earlier *Humbel* decision from 1988, where application of the service provisions to the educational system was rejected by noting that it lacked the characteristic of equivalent payment, since most of the costs are covered by the taxpayers. On the other hand, following this same logic, the lucrative marginal areas should be opened to the play of competitive forces. Theoretically we are experiencing a new phase of 'legal privatization' of public law categories, which reminds one of 19th century discussions and appears to be a revival of the night-watchman state – or will even the state's monopoly on the use of force ultimately be subject to the criteria of Article 90 EEC as a 'service monopoly for the disposal of criminality'? In the coming decade, ZERP will find a rich field of research questions, and I particularly recommend them to my successor, and to all ZERP colleagues interested in economic law, for further study-work in which I will gladly take part (as an outsider)!

In closing my small contribution let me return to Heine's metaphor: the Member States (and thus also the *Land* of Bremen) can certainly not elude the spirit of freedom, the pleasure of freedom and the kiss of freedom of a Europe conceived in

terms of economic competition. However, the embrace should not be quite as turbulent as the Court apparently thinks is necessary. Otherwise, Heine continues, the marriage will lack the 'blessings of the parson' and his concluding wish threatens to go unfulfilled: 'Long live the bride and groom and their future children!'
(End of excerpt)

Case C-179/90 *Porto di Genova* v. *Siderurgica Gabrielli* [1991] ECR I-5889 stands alongside Case C-41/90 as an example of state exclusivity being readily found to have no merit. The market is liberalized through the application of Community law. The case also stands for the potential crossover of Community competition law into national labour law. European Economic law cannot be confined to a narrow area.

Judgment

1   By order dated 6 April 1990, which was received at the Court on 7 June 1990, the Tribunale di Genova (District Court, Genoa) referred to the Court for a preliminary ruling under Article 177 of the EEC Treaty two questions on the interpretation of Articles 7, 30, 85, 86 and 90 of the Treaty.

2   The questions arose in the course of proceedings between Merci Convenzionali Porto di Genova SpA (hereinafter referred to as 'Merci') and Siderurgica Gabrielli SpA (hereinafter referred to as 'Siderurgica') concerning the unloading of goods in the port of Genoa.

3   It appears from the documents sent to the Court that in Italy the loading, unloading, transhipment, storage and general movement of goods or material of any kind within the port are reserved, under Article 110 of the Codice della Navigazione (Navigation Code), to dock-work companies whose workers, who are also members of these companies, must, under Articles 152 and 156 of the Regolamento per la Navigazione Marittima (Regulation on Maritime Navigation), be of Italian nationality. Any failure to respect the exclusive rights vested in the dock-work companies results in the imposition of the penalties laid down by Article 1172 of the Codice della Navigazione.

4   Article 111 of the Codice della Navigazione grants to dock-work undertakings the right to organize dock work on behalf of third parties. For the performance of dock work such undertakings, which are, as a general rule, companies established under private law, must rely exclusively on the dockwork companies.

5   Siderurgica, under the Italian rules, applied to Merci, an undertaking enjoying the exclusive right to organize dock work in the Port of Genoa for ordinary goods, for the unloading of a consignment of steel imported from the Federal Republic of Germany, although the ship's crew could have per-

formed the unloading direct. For the unloading Merci in turn called upon the Genoa dock-work company.

6   As a result of a delay in the unloading of the goods, due in particular to strikes by the dock-work company's workforce, a dispute arose between Siderurgica and Merci in the course of which Siderurgica demanded compensation for the damage it had suffered as a result of the delay, and the reimbursement of the charges it had paid, which it regarded as unfair having regard to the services performed. The Tribunale di Genova, before which the dispute was brought, decided to stay the proceedings and to refer the following questions to the Court of Justice for a preliminary ruling:

'(1) In the present state of Community law, where goods from a Member State of the Community are imported by sea into the territory of another Member State, does Article 90 of the EEC Treaty, together with the prohibitions contained in Articles 7, 30, 85 and 86 thereof, confer on persons subject to Community law rights which the Member States must respect, where a dockwork undertaking and/or company formed solely of national dock workers enjoys the exclusive right to carry out at compulsory standard rates the loading and unloading of goods in national ports, even when it is possible to perform those operations with the equipment and crew of the vessel?

(2) Does a dock-work undertaking and/or company formed solely of national dock workers, which enjoys the exclusive right to carry out at compulsory standard rates the loading and unloading of goods in national ports constitute, for the purposes of Article 90(2) of the EEC Treaty, an undertaking entrusted with the operation of services of general economic interest and liable to be obstructed in the performance by the workforce of the particular tasks assigned to it by the application of Article 90(1) or the prohibitions under Articles 7, 30, 85 and 86 thereof?'

7   Reference is made to the Report for the Hearing for a fuller account of the facts in the main proceedings, the course of the procedure and the written observations submitted to the Court, which are hereinafter mentioned only in so far as is necessary for the reasoning of the Court.

The first question

8   By its first question the national court is essentially asking whether Article 90(1) of the Treaty, in conjunction with Articles 7, 30 and 86 thereof, precludes rules of a Member State which confer on an undertaking established in that State the exclusive right to organize dock work and require it, for the performance of such work, to have recourse to a dockwork company formed exclusively of nationals, and whether those articles give rise to rights for individuals which the national courts must protect.

9   To answer this question, as it has been reformulated, it should be noted *in limine* that a dock-work undertaking enjoying the exclusive right to organize dock work for third parties, as well as a dock-work company having the exclusive right to perform dock work must be regarded as undertakings to which exclusive rights have been granted by the State within the meaning of Article 90(1) of the Treaty.

10   That article provides that in the case of such undertakings Member States shall neither enact nor maintain in force any measure contrary to the rules contained in the Treaty, in particular those provided for in Article 7 and the articles relating to competition.

11   As regards, in the first place, the nationality condition imposed on the workers of the dock-work company, it should be recalled, to begin with, that according to the case-law of the Court, the general prohibition of discrimination on grounds of nationality laid down in Article 7 of the Treaty applies independently only to situations governed by Community law in regard to which the Treaty lays down no specific prohibition of discrimination (see for example Case 305/87 *Commission* v. *Greece* [1989] ECR 1461, paragraphs 12 and 13; Case C-10/90 *Masgio* v. *Bundesknappschaft* [1991] ECR I1119, paragraph 12).

12   As regards workers, that principle has been specifically applied by Article 48 of the Treaty.

13   In this respect it should be recalled that Article 48 of the Treaty precludes, first and foremost, rules of a Member State which reserve to nationals of that State the right to work in an undertaking of that State, such as the Port of Genoa company which is at issue before the national court. As the Court has already declared (see for example, the judgment in Case 66/85 *Lawrie-Blum* v. *Land Baden-Württemberg* [1986] ECR 2121, paragraph 17) the concept of 'worker' within the meaning of Article 48 of the Treaty presupposes that for a certain period of time a person performs services for and under the direction of another person in return for which he receives remuneration. That description is not affected by the fact that the worker, whilst being linked to the undertaking by a relationship of employment, is linked to other workers by a relationship of association.

14   In the second place, as to the existence of exclusive rights, it should be stated first that with regard to the interpretation of Article 86 of the Treaty the Court has consistently held that an undertaking having a statutory monopoly over a substantial part of the common market may be regarded as having a dominant position within the meaning of Article 86 of the Treaty (see the judgments in Case C-41/90 *Höfner and Elser* v. *Macrotron* [1991] ECR I-1979, paragraph 28; Case C-260/89 *ERT* v. *DEP* [1991] ECR I-2925, paragraph 31).

15   As regards the definition of the market in question, it may be seen from the order for reference that it is that of the organization on behalf of third per-

sons of dock work relating to ordinary freight in the Port of Genoa and the performance of such work. Regard being had in particular to the volume of traffic in that port and its importance in relation to maritime import and export operations as a whole in the Member State concerned, that market may be regarded as constituting a substantial part of the common market.

16   It should next be stated that the simple fact of creating a dominant position by granting exclusive rights within the meaning of Article 90(1) of the Treaty is not as such incompatible with Article 86.

17   However, the Court has had occasion to state, in this respect, that a Member State is in breach of the prohibitions contained in those two provisions if the undertaking in question, merely by exercising the exclusive rights granted to it, cannot avoid abusing its dominant position (see the judgment in Case C-41/90 *Höfner*, cited above, paragraph 29) or when such rights are liable to create a situation in which that undertaking is induced to commit such abuses (see the judgment in Case C-260/89 *ERT*, cited above, paragraph 37).

18   According to subparagraphs (a), (b) and (c) of the second paragraph of Article 86 of the Treaty, such abuse may in particular consist in imposing on the persons requiring the service in question unfair purchase prices or other unfair trading conditions, in limiting technical development, to the prejudice of consumers, or in the application of dissimilar conditions to equivalent transactions with other trading parties.

19   In that respect it appears from the circumstances described by the national court and discussed before the Court of Justice that the undertakings enjoying exclusive rights in accordance with the procedures laid down by the national rules in question are, as a result, induced either to demand payment for services which have not been requested, to charge disproportionate prices, to refuse to have recourse to modern technology, which involves an increase in the cost of the operations and a prolongation of the time required for their performance, or to grant price reductions to certain consumers and at the same time to offset such reductions by an increase in the charges to other consumers.

20   In these circumstances it must be held that a Member State creates a situation contrary to Article 86 of the Treaty where it adopts rules of such a kind as those at issue before the national court, which are capable of affecting trade between Member States as in the case of the main proceedings, regard being had to the factors mentioned in paragraph 15 of this judgment relating to the importance of traffic in the Port of Genoa.

21   As regards the interpretation of Article 30 of the Treaty requested by the national court, it is sufficient to recall that a national measure which has the effect of facilitating the abuse of a dominant position capable of affecting trade between Member States will generally be incompatible with that article, which prohibits quantitative restrictions on imports and all measures

having equivalent effect (see the judgment in Case 13/77 *GB-INNO-BM* v. *ATAB* [1977] ECR 2115, paragraph 35) in so far as such a measure has the effect of making more difficult and hence of impeding imports of goods from other Member States.

22   In the main proceedings it may be seen from the national court's findings that the unloading of the goods could have been effected at a lesser cost by the ship's crew, so that compulsory recourse to the services of the two undertakings enjoying exclusive rights involved extra expense and was therefore capable, by reason of its effect on the prices of the goods, of affecting imports.

23   It should be emphasized in the third place that even within the framework of Article 90, the provisions of Articles 30, 48 and 86 of the Treaty have direct effect and give rise for interested parties to rights which the national courts must protect (see in particular, as regards Article 86 of the Treaty, the judgment in Case 155/73 *Sacchi* [1974] ECR 409, paragraph 18).

24   The answer to the first question, as reformulated, should therefore be that:

Article 90(1) of the EEC Treaty, in conjunction with Articles 30, 48 and 86 of the Treaty, precludes rules of a Member State which confer on an undertaking established in that State the exclusive right to organize dock work and require it for that purpose to have recourse to a dock-work company formed exclusively of national workers;

Articles 30, 48 and 86 of the Treaty, in conjunction with Article 90, give rise to rights for individuals which the national courts must protect.

The second question

25   In its second question the national court is in essence asking whether Article 90(2) of the Treaty must be interpreted as meaning that a dock-work undertaking and/or company in the situation described in the first question must be regarded as being entrusted with the operation of services of general economic interest within the meaning of that provision.

26   For the purpose of answering that question it should be borne in mind that in order that the derogation to the application of the rules of the Treaty set out in Article 90(2) thereof may take effect, it is not sufficient for the undertaking in question merely to have been entrusted by the public authorities with the operation of a service of general economic interest, but it must be shown in addition that the application of the rules of the Treaty obstructs the performance of the particular tasks assigned to the undertaking and that the interests of the Community are not affected (see the judgments in Case 311/84 *CBEM* v. *Compagnie Luxembourgeoise* [1985] ECR 3261, paragraph 17, and in Case C-41/90 *Höfner*, cited above, paragraph 24).

27   In that respect it must be held that it does not appear either from the documents supplied by the national court or from the observations submitted to

the Court of Justice that dock work is of a general economic interest exhibiting special characteristics as compared with the general economic interest of other economic activities or, even if it were, that the application of the rules of the Treaty, in particular those relating to competition and freedom of movement, would be such as to obstruct the performance of such a task.

28   The answer to the second question should therefore be that Article 90(2) of the Treaty must be interpreted as meaning that a dock-work undertaking and/or company in the position described in the first question may not be regarded, on the basis only of the factors set out in that description, as being entrusted with the operation of services of general economic interest within the meaning of that provision.

Costs

29   The costs incurred by the Commission of the European Communities, which has submitted observations to the Court, are not recoverable. Since these proceedings are, for the parties to the main proceedings, a step in the action pending before the national court, the decision on costs is a matter for that court.

In this decision, the Court is remarkably explicit in its explanation of the type of market which it is seeking to create through the application of Community law. Paragraphs 19 and 22 of the judgment deserve particular attention.

Case C-260/89 *Elliniki Radiophonia Tileorassi AE (ERT)* v. *Dimotiki Etairia Pliroforissis and Sotirios Kouvelas* [1991] ECR I-2925 provides a further illustration of the difficulty in maintaining state restrictions on competition in the face of the application of EC law. EC law forces a restructuring of the national economy. It also forces a reassessment of the division between the private and the public sector. The decision is particularly illuminating by virtue of the fact that the Court considers not only several Treaty provisions but also looks beyond the EC Treaty to the European Convention on Human Rights. This breadth of vision promises the development of a European law, not simply a European Community law.

Judgment

1   By judgment of 11 April 1989, which was received at the Court on 16 August 1989, the Monomeles Protodikeio Thessaloniki [Thessaloniki Regional Court], in proceedings for interim measures, referred to the Court for a preliminary ruling under Article 177 of the EEC Treaty, several questions on the interpretation of the EEC Treaty, in particular Articles 2, 3(f), 9, 30, 36, 85 and 86, and also of Article 10 of the European Convention for the Protection of Human Rights and Fundamental Freedoms for November

1950 in order to determine the compatibility with those provisions of a national system of exclusive television rights.

2   Those questions were raised in proceedings between Elliniki Radiophonia Tileorassi Anonimi Etairia (hereinafter referred to as 'ERT'), a Greek radio and television undertaking, to which the Greek State had granted exclusive rights for carrying out its activities, and Dimotiki Etairia Pliroforissis (hereinafter referred to as 'DEP'), a municipal information company at Thessaloniki, and S. Kouvelas, Mayor of Thessaloniki. Notwithstanding the exclusive rights enjoyed by ERT, DEP and the Mayor, in 1989, set up a television station which in that same year began to broadcast television programmes.

3   ERT was established by Law No 1730/1987 (*Official Journal of the Hellenic Republic* No 145 A of 18 August 1987, p.144). According to Article 2(1) of that Law, ERT's object is, without a view to profit, to organize, exploit and develop radio and television and to contribute to the information, culture and entertainment of the Hellenic people. Article 2(2) provides that the State grants to ERT an exclusive franchise, in respect of radio and television, for any activity which contributes to the performance of its task. The franchise includes in particular the broadcasting by radio or television of sounds and images of every kind from Hellenic territory for general reception or by special closed or cable circuit, or any other form of circuit, and the setting up of radio and stations. Under Article 2(3) ERT may produce and exploit by any means radio and television broadcasts. Article 16(1) of the same Law prohibits any person from undertaking, without authorization by ERT, activities for which ERT has an exclusive right.

4   Since it took the view that the activities of DEP and the Mayor of Thessaloniki fell within its exclusive rights, ERT brought summary proceedings before the Thessaloniki Regional Court in order to obtain, on the basis of Article 16 of Law No 1730/1987, an injunction prohibiting any kind of broadcasting and an order for the seizure and sequestration of the technical equipment. Before that court, DEP and Mr Kouvelas relied mainly on the provisions of Community law and the European Convention on Human Rights.

5   Since it took the view that the case raised important questions of Community law, the national court stayed the proceedings and referred the following questions to the Court of Justice for a preliminary ruling:
  '(1)Does a law which allows a single television broadcaster to have a television monopoly for the entire territory of a Member State and to make television broadcasts of any kind is consistent with the provisions of the EEC Treaty and of secondary law.[1]

---

[1]   Grammatical error in original text.

(2) If so, whether and to what extent the fundamental principle of free movement of goods laid down in Article 9 of the EEC Treaty is infringed in view of the fact that the enjoyment by a single broadcaster of an exclusive television franchise entails a prohibition for all other Community citizens on the export, leasing or distribution, by whatever means, to the Member State in question of materials, sound recordings, films, television documentaries or other products which may be used to make television broadcasts, except in order to serve the purposes of the broadcaster who has the exclusive television franchise, when, of course, that broadcaster also has the discretionary power to select and favour national materials and products in preference to those of other Member States of the Community.

(3) Whether and to what extent the grant of a television franchise to a single broadcaster constitutes a measure having equivalent effect to a quantitative restriction on imports, expressly prohibited under Article 30 of the EEC Treaty.

(4) If it is accepted that it is lawful to grant by law to a single broadcaster the exclusive right, for the entire national territory of a Member State, to make television broadcasts of any kind, on the ground that the grant falls within the provisions of Article 36 of the EEC Treaty as it has been interpreted by the European Court, and given that that grant satisfies a mandatory requirement and serves a purpose in the public interest – the organization of television as a service in the public interest – whether and to what extent that intended purpose is exceeded, that is to say whether that purpose, the protection of the public interest, is attained in the least onerous manner, in other words in the manner which offends least against the principle of the free movement of goods.

(5) Whether and to what extent the exclusive rights granted by a Member State to an undertaking (a broadcaster) in respect of television broadcasts, and the exercise of those rights, are compatible with the rules on competition in Article 85 in conjunction with Article 3(f) of the EEC Treaty when the performance by the undertaking of certain activities, in particular the exclusive (a) transmission of advertisements, (b) distribution of films, documentaries and other television material produced within the Community, (c) selection, in its own discretion, distribution and transmission of television broadcasts, films, documentaries and other material, prevents, restricts or distorts competition to the detriment of Community consumers in the sector in which it operates and throughout the national territory of the Member State, even though it is entitled by law to carry out those activities.

(6) Where the Member State uses the undertaking entrusted with the operation of the television service – even with regard to its commercial activities, particularly advertising – as an undertaking entrusted with the operation of services of general economic interest, whether and to

what extent the rules on competition contained in Article 85 in conjunction with Article 3(f) are incompatible with the performance of the task assigned to the undertaking.

(7) Whether such an undertaking which has been granted under the law of the Member State a monopoly on television broadcasting of any kind throughout the national territory of that State may be considered to occupy a dominant position in a substantial part of the Common Market, and,

(8) If so, whether and to what extent the imposition (owing to the absence of any other competition in the market) of monopoly prices for television advertisements and of such preferential treatment, at its discretion, to the detriment of Community consumers, and the performance by that undertaking of the activities mentioned above in question (5), pursued in the absence of competition in the field in which it operates, constitute an abuse of a dominant position.

(9) Whether and to what extent the grant by law to a single broadcaster of a television monopoly for the entire national territory of a Member State, with the right to make television broadcasts of any kind, is compatible today with the social objective of the EEC Treaty (preamble and Article 2), the constant improvement of the living conditions of the peoples of Europe and the rapid raising of their standard of living, and with the provisions of Article 10 of the European Convention for the Protection of Human Rights of 4 November 1950.

(10) Whether the freedom of expression secured by Article 10 of the European Convention for the Protection of Human Rights of 4 November 1950 and the abovementioned social objective of the EEC Treaty, set out in its preamble and in Article 2, impose *per se* obligations on the Member States, independently of the written provisions of Community law in force, and if so what those obligations are.'

6   Reference is made to the report for the hearing for a fuller account of the legal background and facts of the main proceedings, the procedure and the written observations submitted to the Court, which are mentioned or discussed hereinafter only in so far as is necessary for the reasoning of the Court.

7   It emerges, in substance, from the judgment making the reference that by its first question the national court is seeking to ascertain whether a television monopoly held by a single company to which a Member State has granted exclusive rights for that purpose is permissible under Community law. The second, third and fourth questions relate to the point whether the rules on the free movement of goods, in particular Article 9 and Article 30 and 36 of the Treaty, preclude such a monopoly. Since these questions concern a monopoly in services, they are to be regarded as referring not only to the rules of the Treaty in relation to the free movement of goods but also to those

relating to the freedom to provide services, in particular Article 59 of the Treaty.

8   The fifth, sixth, seventh and eighth questions relate to the interpretation of the rules on competition applicable to undertakings. In that respect the national court seeks to ascertain in the first place whether Article 3(f) and Article 85 of the Treaty preclude the grant by the State of exclusive rights in the field of television. Secondly, the national court inquires whether an undertaking which has an exclusive right in relation to television throughout the territory of a Member State holds, as a result, a dominant position in a substantial part of the market within the meaning of Article 86 of the Treaty and whether certain conduct constitutes an abuse of that dominant position. Thirdly, the national court asks whether the application of the rules on competition precludes the performance of the particular task entrusted to such an undertaking.

9   The ninth and tenth questions are concerned with an examination of the monopoly situation in the field of television in the light of Article 2 of the Treaty and Article 10 of the European Convention on Human Rights.

The television monopoly

10   In Case C-155/73 Sacchi [1974] ECR 409, paragraph 14, the Court held that nothing in the Treaty prevents Member States, for considerations of a non-economic nature relating to the public interest, from removing radio and television broadcasts from the field of competition by conferring on one or more establishments an exclusive right to carry them out.

11   Nevertheless, it follows from Article 90(1) and (2) of the Treaty that the manner in which the monopoly is organized or exercised may infringe the rules of the Treaty, in particular those relating to the free movement of goods, the freedom to provide services and the rules on competition.

12   The reply to the national court must therefore be that Community law does not prevent the granting of a television monopoly for considerations of a non-economic nature relating to the public interest. However, the manner in which such a monopoly is organized and exercised must not infringe the provisions of the Treaty on the free movement of goods and services or the rules on competition.

Free movement of goods

13   It should be observed *in limine* that it follows from the *Sacchi* judgment that television broadcasting falls within the rules of the Treaty relating to services and that since a television monopoly is a monopoly in the provision of services, it is not as such contrary to the principle of the free movement of goods.

14   However it follows from the same judgment that trade in material, sound recordings, films, and other products used for television broadcasting is subject to the rules on the free movement of goods.

15   In that respect, the grant to a single undertaking of exclusive rights in relation to television broadcasting and the grant for that purpose of an exclusive right to import, hire or distribute material and products necessary for that broadcasting does not as such constitute a measure having an effect equivalent to a quantitative restriction within the meaning of Article 30 of the Treaty.

16   It would be different if the grant of those rights resulted, directly or indirectly in discrimination between domestic products and imported products to the detriment of the latter. It is for the national court, which alone has jurisdiction to determine the facts, to consider whether that is so in the present case.

17   As regards Article 9 of the Treaty it is sufficient to observe that that article contains a prohibition between Member States of customs duties on imports and exports and of all charges having equivalent effect. Since the documents before the Court contain nothing to show that the legislation in question involves the levying of a charge on import or export, Article 9 does not appear to be relevant for the purpose of appraising the monopoly in question from the point of view of the rules on the free movement of goods.

18   It is therefore necessary to reply that the articles of the EEC Treaty on the free movement of goods do not prevent the granting to a single undertaking of exclusive rights relating to television broadcasting and the granting for that purpose of exclusive authority to import, hire or distribute materials and products necessary for that broadcasting, provided that no discrimination is thereby created between domestic products and imported products to the detriment of the latter.

Freedom to provide services

19   Article 59 of the Treaty provides that restrictions on freedom to provide services within the Community are to be progressively abolished during the transitional period in respect of nationals of Member States who are established in a State of the Community other than that of the person for whom the services are intended. The requirements of that provision entail, in particular, the removal of any discrimination against a person providing services who is established in a Member State other than that in which the services are to be provided.

20   As has been indicated in paragraph 12 of this judgment, although the existence of a monopoly in the provision of services is not as such incompatible with Community law, the possibility cannot be excluded that the monopoly may be organized in such a way as to infringe the rules relating to the freedom to provide services. Such a case arises, in particular, where the mo-

nopoly leads to discrimination between national television broadcasts and those originating in other Member States, to the detriment of the latter.

21   As regards the monopoly in question in the main proceedings, it is apparent from Article 2(2) of Law No 1730/1987 and the case-law of the Hellenic Council of State that ERT's exclusive franchise comprises both the right to broadcast its own programmes (hereinafter referred to as 'broadcasts') and the right to receive and retransmit programmes from other Member States (hereinafter referred to as 'retransmissions').

22   As the Commission has observed, the concentration of the monopolies to broadcast and retransmit in the hands of a single undertaking gives that undertaking the possibility both to broadcast its own programmes and to restrict the retransmissions of programmes from other Member States. That possibility, in the absence of any guarantee concerning the retransmission of programmes from other Member States, may lead the undertaking to favour its own programmes to the detriment of foreign programmes. Under such a system equality of opportunity as between broadcasts of its own programmes and the retransmission of programmes from other Member States is therefore liable to be seriously compromised.

23   The question whether the aggregation of the exclusive right to broadcast and the right to retransmit actually leads to discrimination to the detriment of programmes from other Member States is a matter of fact which only the national court has jurisdiction to determine.

24   It should next be pointed out that the rules relating to the freedom to provide services preclude national rules which have such discriminatory effects unless those rules fall within the derogating provision contained in Article 56 of the Treaty to which Article 66 refers. It follows from Article 56, which must be interpreted strictly, that discriminatory rules may be justified on grounds of public policy, public security or public health.

25   It is apparent from the observations submitted to the Court that the sole objective of the rules in question was to avoid disturbances due to the restricted number of channels available. Such an objective cannot however constitute justification for those rules for the purposes of Article 56 of the Treaty, where the undertaking in question uses only a limited number of the available channels.

26   Accordingly the reply to the national court must be that Article 59 of the Treaty prohibits national rules which create a monopoly comprising exclusive rights to transmit the broadcasts of the holder of the monopoly and to retransmit broadcasts from other Member States, where such a monopoly gives rise to discriminatory effects to the detriment of broadcasts from other Member States, unless those rules are justified on one of the grounds indicated in Article 56 of the Treaty, to which Article 66 thereof refers.

The rules on competition

27   As a preliminary point, it should be observed that Article 3(f) of the Treaty states only one objective for the Community which is given specific expression in several provisions of the Treaty relating to the rules on competition, including in particular Articles 85, 86 and 90.

28   The independent conduct of an undertaking must be considered with regard to the provisions of the Treaty applicable to undertakings, such as, in particular, Articles 85, 86 and 90(2).

29   As regards Article 85, it is sufficient to observe that it applies, according to its own terms, to agreements 'between undertakings'. There is nothing in the judgment making the reference to suggest the existence of any agreement between undertakings. There is therefore no need to interpret that provision.

30   Article 86 declares that any abuse of a dominant position within the common market or in any substantial part of it is prohibited as incompatible with the common market in so far as it may affect trade between Member States.

31   In that respect it should be borne in mind that an undertaking which has a statutory monopoly may be regarded as having a dominant position within the meaning of Article 86 of the Treaty (see the judgment in Case C-311/84 *CBEM* v. *CLT and IBP* [1985] ECR 3261, paragraph 16) and that the territory of a Member State over which the monopoly extends may constitute a substantial part of the common market (see the judgment in Case C-322/81 *Michelin* v. *Commission* [1983] ECR 3461, paragraph 28).

32   Although Article 86 of the Treaty does not prohibit monopolies as such, it nevertheless prohibits their abuse. For that purpose Article 86 lists a number of abusive practices by way of example.

33   In that regard it should be observed that, according to Article 90(2) of the Treaty, undertakings entrusted with the operation of services of general economic interest are subject to the rules on competition so long as it is not shown that the application of those rules is incompatible with the performance of their particular task (see in particular, the judgment in *Sacchi*, cited above, paragraph 15).

34   Accordingly it is for the national court to determine whether the practices of such an undertaking are compatible with Article 86 and to verify whether those practices, if they are contrary to that provision, may be justified by the needs of the particular task with which the undertaking may have been entrusted.

35   As regards State measures, and more specifically the grant of exclusive rights, it should be pointed out that while Articles 85 and 86 are directed exclusively to undertakings, the Treaty none the less requires the Member States not to adopt or maintain in force any measure which could deprive

those provisions of their effectiveness (see the judgment in Case C-13/77 *INNO* v. *ATAB* [1977] ECR 2115, paragraphs 31 and 32).

36 Article 90(1) thus provides that, in the case of undertakings to which Member States grant special or exclusive rights, Member States are neither to enact nor to maintain in force any measure contrary to the rules contained in the Treaty.

37 In that respect it should be observed that Article 90(1) of the Treaty prohibits the granting of an exclusive right to retransmit television broadcasts to an undertaking which has an exclusive right to transmit broadcasts, where those rights are liable to create a situation in which that undertaking is led to infringe Article 86 of the Treaty by virtue of a discriminatory broadcasting policy which favours its own programmes.

38 The reply to the national court must therefore be that Article 90(1) of the Treaty prohibits the granting of an exclusive right to transmit and an exclusive right to retransmit television broadcasts to a single undertaking, where those rights are liable to create a situation in which that undertaking is led to infringe Article 86 by virtue of a discriminatory broadcasting policy which favours its own programmes, unless the application of Article 86 obstructs the performance of the particular tasks entrusted to it.

Article 2 of the Treaty

39 As the Court has consistently held (see, in particular, the judgment in Case C-339/89 *Alsthom Atlantique* v. *Compagnie de Construction Mécanique* [1991] ECR I-107), Article 2 of the Treaty, referred to in the ninth and tenth preliminary questions, describes the task of the European Economic Community. The aims stated in that provision are concerned with the existence and functioning of the Community and are to be achieved through the establishment of a common market and the progressive approximation of the economic policies of Member States.

40 The reply to the national court must therefore be that no criteria for deciding whether a national television monopoly is in conformity with Community law can be derived from Article 2.

Article 10 of the European Convention on Human Rights

41 With regard to Article 10 of the European Convention on Human Rights, referred to in the ninth and tenth questions, it must first be pointed out that, as the Court has consistently held, fundamental rights form an integral part of the general principles of law, the observance of which it ensures. For that purpose the Court draws inspiration from the constitutional traditions common to the Member States and from the guidelines supplied by international treaties for the protection of human rights on which the Member States have collaborated or of which they are signatories (see, in particular, the judgment in Case C-4/73 *Nold* v. *Commission* [1974] ECR 491, paragraph 13).

The European Convention on Human Rights has special significance in that respect (see in particular Case C-222/84 *Johnston* v. *Chief Constable of the Royal Ulster Constabulary* [1986] ECR 1651, paragraph 18). It follows that, as the Court held in its judgment in Case C-5/88 *Wachauf* v. *Federal Republic of Germany* [1989] ECR 2609, paragraph 19, the Community cannot accept measures which are incompatible with observance of the human rights thus recognized and guaranteed.

42   As the Court has held (see the judgment in Joined Cases C-60 and C-61/84 *Cinéthèque* v. *Fédération Nationale des Cinémas Français* [1985] ECR 2605, paragraph 25, and the judgment in Case C-12/86 *Demirel* v. *Stadt Schwäbisch Gmund* [1987] ECR 3719, paragraph 28), it has no power to examine the compatibility with the European Convention on Human Rights of national rules which do not fall within the scope of Community law. On the other hand, where such rules do fall within the scope of Community law, and reference is made to the Court for a preliminary ruling, it must provide all the criteria of interpretation needed by the national court to determine whether those rules are compatible with the fundamental rights the observance of which the Court ensures and which derive in particular from the European Convention on Human Rights.

43   In particular, where a Member State relies on the combined provisions of Articles 56 and 66 in order to justify rules which are likely to obstruct the exercise of the freedom to provide services, such justification, provided for by Community law must be interpreted in the light of the general principles of law and in particular of fundamental rights. Thus the national rules in question can fall under the exceptions provided for by the combined provisions of Articles 56 and 66 only if they are compatible with the fundamental rights the observance of which is ensured by the Court.

44   It follows that in such a case it is for the national court, and if necessary, the Court of Justice to appraise the application of those provisions having regard to all the rules of Community law, including freedom of expression, as embodied in Article 10 of the European Convention on Human Rights, as a general principle of law the observance of which is ensured by the Court.

45   The reply to the national court must therefore be that the limitations imposed on the power of the Member States to apply the provisions referred to in Articles 66 and 56 of the Treaty on grounds of public policy, public security and public health must be appraised in the light of the general principle of freedom of expression embodied in Article 10 of the European Convention on Human Rights.

Costs

46   The costs incurred by the French Government and the Commission, which have submitted observations to the Court, are not recoverable. As these proceedings are, for the parties to the main proceedings, a step in the action

pending before the national court, the decision as to costs is a matter for that court.

On those grounds,

THE COURT,

in answer to the questions referred to it by the Monomeles Protodikeio de Thessalonique by judgment of 11 April 1989, hereby rules:

(1) Community law does not prevent the granting of a television monopoly for considerations of a non-economic nature relating to the public interest. However, the manner in which such a monopoly is organized and exercised must not infringe the provisions of the Treaty on the free movement of goods and services or the rules on competition;

(2) The articles of the EEC Treaty on the free movement of goods do not prevent the granting to a single undertaking of exclusive rights relating to television broadcasting and the granting for the purpose of exclusive authority to import, hire or distribute materials and products necessary for that broadcasting, provided that no discrimination is thereby created between domestic products and imported products to the detriment of the latter;

(3) Article 59 of the Treaty prohibits national rules which create a monopoly comprising exclusive rights to transmit the broadcasts of the holder of the monopoly and to retransmit broadcasts from other Member States, where such a monopoly gives rise to discriminatory effects to the detriment of broadcasts from other Member States, unless those rules are justified on one of the grounds indicated in Article 56 of the Treaty, to which Article 66 thereof refers;

(4) Article 90(1) of the Treaty prohibits the granting of an exclusive right to transmit and an exclusive right to retransmit television broadcasts to a single undertaking, where those rights are liable to create a situation in which that undertaking is led to infringe Article 86 by virtue of a discriminatory broadcasting policy which favours its own programmes, unless the application of Article 86 obstructs the performance of the particular tasks entrusted to it;

(5) No criteria for deciding whether a national television monopoly is in conformity with Community law can be derived from Article 2 of the Treaty; (6) The limitations imposed on the power of the Member States to apply the provisions referred to in Articles 66 and 56 of the Treaty on grounds of public policy, public security and public health must be appraised in the light of the general principle of freedom of expression embodied in Article 10 of the European Convention on Human Rights.

Delivered in open court in Luxembourg on 18 June 1991.

The industry in question has an impact felt beyond the commercial sphere. The economic restructuring which is required in the wake of this decision must spill over into the social sphere too. The decision sharpens awareness that European economic law may have implications beyond the economy as narrowly understood.

This decision also provides material for consideration of the relationship between European Community law and European Human Rights law. Is there a 'European law' which may be drawn from the common features of both systems? Or are there fundamentally different conceptions of rights in society under the two systems? These are interesting theoretical questions. They are simultaneously important practical questions. There can be no sharp distinction between the field of economic law and the field of human rights law. The two overlap. Because the modern state's functions are many and varied, it is inevitable that European economic law will confront state social policy. Economic policy spills over into other areas. So if the purposes of the systems are distinct, there is scope for conflict between them. The law must develop a basis for resolving such a conflict. The question of the spillover of economic law into state social policy and then into Human Rights law is further addressed below in Chapters 6 and 12. However, the final case in this section makes the point.

Sigurjonsson v. *Iceland* (Case No 24/1992/369/443 judgment of 30 June 1993) concerned compulsion imposed under Icelandic law on a taxicab driver to be a member of a specific organization for taxicab operators. Non-membership would result in a loss of licence. The European Court of Human Rights found this to be an interference with Article 11 of the Convention's protection of freedom of association. Here, the application of the European Convention on Human Rights seems to run in parallel to the thrust of Article 90. State restriction of action is ruled incompatible with the Convention. Social and economic rights to operate free of state intervention can be seen to converge. In Chapter 6, more difficult cases will be addressed, where economic rights and social rights may yield rather different interpretations.

C. THE COMPETITION RULES AND THE FREE MOVEMENT RULES: CASE C-18/88 RTT V. GB INNO [1991] ECR I-5941

In a case of a state monopoly which obstructs cross-border trade in goods, the Court may consider the application of not only the competition rules but also Article 30. This decision makes clear how the law governing the four freedoms may be used to challenge state monopolies. The result is the injection of competition into a market previously protected by the state. This decision, added to those above, helps to paint a broader picture of the policy thrust of the Treaty in favour of market integration and competition.

[...]

The competition rules

14   The national court asks whether Articles 3(f), 90 and 86 of the EEC Treaty preclude a Member State from granting to the company operating the public telecommunications network the power to lay down the standards for telephone equipment and to check that economic operators meet those standards when it is competing with those operators on the market for terminals.

15   Under Belgian law, the RTT holds a monopoly for the establishment and operation of the public telecommunications network. Moreover, only equipment supplied by the RTT or approved by it can be connected to the network. The RTT thus has the power to grant or withhold authorization to connect telephone equipment to the network, the power to lay down the technical standards to be met by that equipment, and the power to check whether the equipment not produced by it is in conformity with the specifications that it has laid down.

16   At the present stage of development of the Community, that monopoly, which is intended to make a public telephone network available to users, constitutes a service of general economic interest within the meaning of Article 90(2) of the Treaty.

17   The Court has consistently held that an undertaking vested with a legal monopoly may be regarded as occupying a dominant position within the meaning of Article 86 of the Treaty and that the territory of a Member State to which that monopoly extends may constitute a substantial part of the common market (judgments in Case C-41/90 *Höfner* [1991] ECR I-1979, paragraph 28, and in Case C-260/89 *ERT* [1991] ECR I-2925, paragraph 31).

18   The Court has also held that an abuse within the meaning of Article 86 is committed where, without any objective necessity, an undertaking holding a dominant position on a particular market reserves to itself an ancillary activity which might be carried out by another undertaking as part of its activities on a neighbouring but separate market, with the possibility of eliminating all competition from such undertaking (judgment in Case 311/84 *CBEM* [1985] ECR 3261).

19   Therefore the fact that an undertaking holding a monopoly in the market for the establishment and operation of the network, without any objective necessity, reserves to itself a neighbouring but separate market, in this case the market for the importation, marketing, connection, commissioning and maintenance of equipment for connection to the said network, thereby eliminating all competition from other undertakings, constitutes an infringement of Article 86 of the Treaty.

20   However, Article 86 applies only to anti-competitive conduct engaged in by undertakings on their own initiative (see judgment in Case C-202/88

France v. *Commission* 'Telecommunications terminals', [1991] ECR I-1223), not to measures adopted by States. As regards measures adopted by States, it is Article 90(1) that applies. Under that provision, Member States must not, by laws, regulations or administrative measures, put public undertakings and undertakings to which they grant special or exclusive rights in a position which the said undertakings could not themselves attain by their own conduct without infringing Article 86.

21 Accordingly, where the extension of the dominant position of a public undertaking or undertaking to which the State has granted special or exclusive rights results from a State measure, such a measure constitutes an infringement of Article 90 in conjunction with Article 86 of the Treaty.

22 The exclusion or the restriction of competition on the market in telephone equipment cannot be regarded as justified by a task of a public service of general economic interest within the meaning of Article 90(2) of the Treaty. The production and sale of terminals, and in particular of telephones, is an activity that should be open to any undertaking. In order to ensure that the equipment meets the essential requirements of, in particular, the safety of users, the safety of those operating the network and the protection of public telecommunications networks against damage of any kind, it is sufficient to lay down specifications which the said equipment must meet and to establish a procedure for type-approval to check whether those specifications are met.

23 According to the RTT, there could be a finding of an infringement of Article 90(1) of the Treaty only if the Member State had favoured an abuse that the RTT itself had in fact committed, for example by applying the provisions on type-approval in a discriminatory manner. It emphasizes, however, that the order for reference does not state that any abuse has actually taken place, and that the mere possibility of discriminatory application of those provisions by reason of the fact that the RTT is designated as the authority for granting approval and is competing with the undertakings that apply for approval cannot in itself amount to an abuse within the meaning of Article 86 of the EEC Treaty.

24 That argument cannot be accepted. It is sufficient to point out in this regard that it is the extension of the monopoly in the establishment and operation of the telephone network to the market in telephone equipment, without any objective justification, which is prohibited as such by Article 86, or by Article 90(1) in conjunction with Article 86, where that extension results from a measure adopted by a State. As competition may not be eliminated in that manner, it may not be distorted either.

25 A system of undistorted competition, as laid down in the Treaty, can be guaranteed only if equality of opportunity is secured as between the various economic operators. To entrust an undertaking which markets terminal equipment with the task of drawing up the specifications for such equip-

ment, monitoring their application and granting type-approval in respect thereof is tantamount to conferring upon it the power to determine at will which terminal equipment may be connected to the public network, and thereby placing that undertaking at an obvious advantage over its competitors (judgment in Case C-202/88, paragraph 51).

26 In those circumstances, the maintenance of effective competition and the guaranteeing of transparency require that the drawing up of technical specifications, the monitoring of their application, and the granting of type-approval must be carried out by a body which is independent of public or private undertakings offering competing goods or services in the telecommunications sector (judgment in Case C-202/88, paragraph 52).

27 Moreover, the provisions of the national regulations at issue in the main action may influence the imports of telephone equipment from other Member States, and hence may affect trade between Member States within the meaning of Article 86 of the Treaty.

28 Accordingly, it must first be stated, in reply to the national court's questions, that Article 3(f), 90 and 86 of the EEC Treaty preclude a Member State from granting to the undertaking which operates the public telecommunications network the power to lay down standards for telephone equipment and to check that economic operators meet those standards when it is itself competing with those operators on the market for that equipment.

The free movement of goods

29 The national court asks secondly whether Article 30 prevents a public undertaking from being given the power to approve telephone equipment which is intended to be connected to the public network and which it has not supplied if the decisions of that undertaking cannot be challenged before the courts.

30 As the Court has consistently held (see in particular the judgment in Case 120/78 *REWE-Zentrale* [1979] ECR 649, 'Cassis de Dijon'), in the absence of common rules applying to the products concerned, the obstacles to free movement within the Community resulting from disparities between national provisions must be accepted in so far as those national provisions, which are applicable without distinction to national products and to imported products, can be justified as being necessary in order to satisfy imperative requirements of Community Law. The Court has, however, held that such rules must be proportionate to the object to be achieved and that, where a Member State has a choice between a number of measures suited to achieving the same purpose, it must choose the means that least hinders the free movement of goods.

31 In the absence of Community rules on the establishment of public telecommunications networks, and in view of the technical diversity of the networks in the Member States, the Member States retain, on the one hand, the

power to lay down technical specifications which telephone equipment must meet to be capable of being connected to the public network and, on the other, the power to examine whether the said equipment is fit to be connected to the network in order to satisfy the imperative requirements regarding the protection of users as consumers of services and the protection of the public network and its proper functioning.

32   It is true that the requirement that telephone equipment must be granted type-approval to be capable of being connected to the network does not absolutely exclude the importation into the Member State concerned of products from other Member States. But that requirement does nonetheless render the sale of such equipment more difficult or more onerous. Such a requirement means that a manufacturer in the Member State of exportation has to take into account, when manufacturing the products concerned, the criteria for type-approval laid down in the Member State of importation. Moreover, the procedure for obtaining type-approval necessarily entails delay and expense, even where the imported products meet the criteria for approval.

33   An exception to the principle of the free movement of goods based on an imperative requirement is justified only if the national rules are proportionate to the object to be achieved.

34   It is apparent from the judgment in Case 178/84 *Commission* v. *Germany* [1987] ECR 1227, paragraph 46, that it must be open to traders to challenge before the courts an unjustified failure to grant authorization for imports. The same possibility must exist with regard to decisions refusing to grant type-approval since they can lead in practice to denial of access to the market of a Member State to telephone equipment imported from another Member State and hence to a barrier to the free movement of goods.

35   If there were no possibility of any challenge before the courts, the authority granting type-approval could adopt an attitude which was arbitrary or systematically unfavourable to imported equipment. Moreover, the likelihood of the authority granting type-approval adopting such an attitude is increased by the fact that the procedures for obtaining type-approval and for laying down the technical specifications do not involve the hearing of any interested parties.

36   The second answer to be given to the national court is, therefore, that Article 30 of the Treaty precludes a public undertaking from being given the power to approve telephone equipment which is intended to be connected to the public network and which it has not supplied if the decisions of that undertaking cannot be challenged before the courts.

It is notable that in this ruling the Court places reliance on Article 3(f) of the Treaty, which is now, since the coming into force of the Treaty on European Union, Article 3(g). This reference to the Principles found in Part 1 of the Treaty suggests, but does not conclusively prove, an interest in the scope for the construction of a general theoretical basis for the role of Community law, as distinct from simply and more narrowly applying individual Treaty provisions to the cases which arise. In 1986 Pescatore explained that if Community competition policy were a tree, 'the trunk is formed by the general rule of fair competition expressed in... letter (f) of Article 3'. He went on to explain that there are two groups of branches, those which apply to private action and those which apply to public action (see Further Reading list below).

It should be recognized that the use of Article 30 to challenge a state monopoly leaves open the possibility of a state seeking justification for its intervention by relying on Article 36. In Case C-271/92 *Société Laboratoire de Prothèses Oculaires* v. *Union Nationale des Syndicats d'Opticiens de France and Others* judgment of 25 May 1993, the Court held that

(i) national legislation which prohibits the sale of contact lenses and ancillary products in commercial establishments, thereby reserving sale to specialist agents, acts as an obstacle to trade in such goods: but
(ii) where this restriction applies to establishments which are not run or managed by persons fulfilling the necessary conditions to practise as opticians, it is justified on grounds of protection of public health.

The Court is prepared to concede that there are limits to liberalization of sectors which affect interests other than those of a purely commercial nature.

D. STATE SUPPORT FOR PRIVATE ANTI-COMPETITIVE PRACTICES

In Case 311/85 *Vereniging van Vlaamse Reisbureaus* v. *Sociale Dienst* [1987] ECR 3801, the background is different from those above. It involves state support for an existing private anti-competitive agreement rather than intervention by the state to sustain or create a monopoly. However, it shares with the decisions already considered the common feature that Community rules are used to 'eject' the state from the market and to promote competition in the market.

[...]

Question A

9 Although the first question refers expressly only to Article 85(1) of the Treaty, it must be understood, as the Belgian and French Governments and the Commission have suggested, as seeking to ascertain whether legislative provisions or regulations of a Member State requiring travel agents to observe the prices and tariffs for travel set by tour operators, prohibiting them

from sharing commissions paid in respect of the sale of such travel with their customers or granting rebates to their customers and· regarding such acts as contrary to fair commercial practice are incompatible with the obligations of the Member States pursuant to Article 5, in conjunction with Articles 3(f) and 85, of the EEC Treaty.

10   As the Court has consistently held (see, most recently, the judgment of 30 April 1986 in Joined Cases 209 to 213/84 *Ministère public* v. *Asjes* [1986] ECR 1425), while it is true that Articles 85 and 86 of the Treaty concern the conduct of undertakings and not laws or regulations of the Member States, the Treaty nevertheless imposes a duty on Member States not to adopt or maintain in force any measure which could deprive those provisions of their effectiveness. The Court has held that that would be the case, in particular, if a Member State were to require or favour the adoption of agreements, decisions or concerted practices contrary to Article 85 or to reinforce their effects.

11   In order to reply in a useful manner to the national court it is necessary first of all to determine whether the documents before the Court disclose the existence of agreements, decisions or concerted practices of that kind in the area of activities concerned by the question referred, and then to determine whether provisions such as the Belgian provisions at issue are intended to reinforce the effects of such agreements, decisions or concerted practices, or have that effect.

12   The documents before the Court show that the Belgian provisions form part of a structure involving agreements at various levels intended to oblige travel agents to observe the prices of tours fixed by tour operators.

13   First of all, according to information provided by the Commission, which was not disputed, in 1963 the Belgische Beroepsvereniging voor Reisbureaus (Union of Belgian Travel Agents, hereinafter referred to as the 'BBR') adopted a code of conduct binding on its members. Article 22 of that code, the content of which was incorporated in Article 22 of the Royal Decree of 30 June 1966, at issue in the main proceedings, treated the sharing of commissions with customers and the granting to them of prohibited rebates or rebates contrary to commercial usage as unfair competition.

14   Secondly, again according to the information provided by the Commission, in 1975 a framework agreement was concluded within the BBR regarding cooperation between the council of travel agents and the group of charter flight operators belonging to the BBR. Article 8(b) of that agreement provides that an agent may not transfer part of his commission to a third party in any form and must observe the price and conditions of sale laid down by the organizer.

15   With regard to contractual relations between tour operators and travel agents, the standard-form contract attached to the observations of the Belgian Government provides under point 1 of the general conditions of coop-

eration that a tour operator 'may refuse to sell [tours] to agents who refuse to comply with the rules of commercial practice and act contrary to the spirit of the legislation'. That wording allows tour operators to rescind their contracts with travel agents who do not observe the rules of commercial practice applicable to them, including those prohibiting the sharing of commissions and the granting of rebates.

16 The existence of a system of agreements intended to prevent such practices is confirmed, moreover, by the very wording of Article 22 of the Royal Decree of 30 June 1966, at issue in the main proceedings. Article 22(2)(d), concerning the obligations of a travel agent 'with regard to suppliers', states that the agent must 'observe the agreed prohibition on the sharing of commissions with clients'.

17 It must therefore be concluded, on the basis of the documents before the Court, that with regard to the activities of travel agents there is a system of agreements both between travel agents themselves and between agents and tour operators intended to oblige agents to observe the prices for travel set by tour operators, and having that effect. Such agreements have the object and effect of restricting competition between travel agents. That is to say, they prevent travel agents from competing on prices by deciding, on their own initiative, to pass on to their customers some portion of the commission which they receive.

18 Furthermore, such agreements may affect trade between Member States in several respects. First of all, travel agents operating in one Member State may sell travel organized by tour operators established in other Member States. Secondly, these agents may sell travel to customers residing in other Member States. Thirdly, the travel in question is often to other Member States.

19 The Belgian Government denied that Article 85(1) can apply to the relationship between a tour operator and a travel agent, arguing that the relationship is one of principal and agent. A travel agent must therefore be regarded as an auxiliary organ of the tour operator. In support of its argument the Belgian Government emphasized that a travel agent does not enter into contracts with clients in his own name but in the name and on behalf of the tour operator organizing the travel in question.

20 However, a travel agent of the kind referred to by the national court must be regarded as an independent agent who provides services on an entirely independent basis. He sells travel organized by a large number of different tour operators and a tour operator sells travel through a very large number of agents. Contrary to the Belgian Government's submissions, a travel agent cannot be treated as an auxiliary organ forming an integral part of a tour operator's undertaking.

21 It follows from those considerations that agreements such as those at issue in the main proceedings are incompatible with Article 85(1) of the Treaty.

22   It remains to be determined whether provisions such as those at issue before the national court, viewed in this context, are of such a nature as to reinforce the effects of the agreements between travel agents and tour operators.

23   First of all, by transforming an originally contractual prohibition into a legislative provision a provision such as Article 22 of the Royal Decree of 1966 reinforces the effect of the agreements in question between the parties, inasmuch as the rule acquires a permanent character and can no longer be rescinded by the parties. Secondly, by treating the failure to observe agreed prices and tariffs or the prohibition on the sharing of commissions with clients as contrary to fair commercial practice it allows travel agents who comply with the agreed rules of commercial practice to bring proceedings for a restraining order against travel agents who are not party to the agreement and do not comply with those rules. Thirdly, with regard both to parties to the agreements and to third parties the possible withdrawal of the licence to operate as a travel agent in the event of failure to observe the agreed rules of commercial practice constitutes a highly effective sanction.

24   The answer to Question A referred by the national court must therefore be that legislative provisions or regulations of a Member State requiring travel agents to observe the prices and tariffs for travel set by tour operators, prohibiting them from sharing the commission paid in respect of the sale of such travel with their clients or granting rebates to their clients and regarding such acts as contrary to fair commercial practice are incompatible with the obligations of the Member States pursuant to Article 5, in conjunction with Articles 3(f) and 85, of the EEC Treaty, where the object or effect of such national provisions is to reinforce the effects of agreements, decisions or concerted practices which are contrary to Article 85.

The role of Article 5 as a means of preventing the state from supporting anti-competitive practices is potentially highly significant. However, the development of these European controls is at a relatively early stage. In Case C-2/91 *WW Meng* judgment of 17 November 1993 the European Court was relatively cautious in its handling of the scope of European economic law's control over state legislation which does not affect the 'four freedoms'. The decision in *Meng* was mentioned above as one in which the Court is not prepared to use the Treaty as a generally applicable constitutional control over (allegedly) anti-competitive state measures. Instead, the Court adheres to jurisdictional limitations on EC law which it considers arise from the scope of individual provisions of the Treaty.

ARRÊT DE LA COUR

du 17 novembre 1993

«Intermédiaires en assurances – Réglementation étatique interdisant d'accorder des ristournes – Interprétation des articles 3, sous n, 5, deuxième alinéa, et 85, paragraphe 1,du traité »

1   Par ordonnance du 26 novembre 1990, parvenue à la Cour le 3 janvier 1991, le Kammergericht Berlin a posé, en vertu de l'article 177 du traité CEE, une question préjudicielle relative à l'interprétation des articles 3, sous n, 5, deuxième alinéa, et 85, paragraphe 1, du traité en vue d'apprécier la conformité avec ces dispositions d'une réglementation étatique qui a pour effet de restreindre la concurrence entre opérateurs économiques.

2   Cette question a été posée dans le cadre d'un recours introduit par M. Meng contre un jugement par lequel l'Amtsgericht Tiergarten (République Fédérale d'Allemagne) lui a infligé une amende pour infraction à la réglementation sur les assurances qui interdit les cessions de commissions aux clients.

3   Il ressort de l'ordonnance de renvoi que M. Meng a pour profession de donner des conseils en matière financière et notamment sur des contrats d'assurance. C'est dans le cadre de cette activité qu'à six reprises, entre mars 1987 et juillet 1988, lors de la conclusion de contrats d'assurance, il a cédé à ses clients la commission qui lui avait été versée par la compagnie d'assurance. Trois de ces contrats avaient trait à l'assurance maladie et trois autres à l'assurance défense et recours.

4   La cession de commission est interdite en République fédérale d'Allemagne, pour ce qui concerne l'assurance maladie, par l'Anordnung über das Verbot der Gewährung von Sondervergütungen und des Abschlusses von Begünstigungsverträgen in der Krankenversicherung (ordonnance relative à l'interdiction des mesures préférentielles et des contrats de faveur dans le domaine de l'assurance maladie, ci-après "Anordnung", publiée au Deutscher Reichsanzeiger und Preussischer Staatsanzeiger no 129 du 6 juin 1934, p.3), qui a été édictée le 5 juin 1934 par le Reichsaufsichtsamt für Privatversicherung (office allemand de contrôle des assurances, ci-après "office de contrôle"). Le point I de l'Anordung dispose:

> "Il est interdit aux sociétés d'assurance et aux intermédiaires intervenant dans la conclusion de contrats d'assurance d'accorder au preneur d'assurance des bonifications spéciales sous quelque forme que ce soit."

5   La même interdiction est applicable dans le domaine de l'assurance dommage ainsi que dans celui de l'assurance défense et recours en vertu de la Verordnung über das Verbot von Sondervergütungen und Begünstigungsverträgen in der Schadenversicherung (règlement relatif à

l'interdiction des mesures préférentielles et des contrats de faveur dans le domaine de l'assurance dommage, ci-après "Verordnung", publiée au Bundesgesetzblatt I, p.1243) qui, quant à elle, a été adoptée le 17 août 1982 par le Bundesaufsichtsamt für das Versicherungswesen (office allemand de contrôle des assurances, qui a repris les fonctions du Reichsaufsichtsamt für Privatversicherung, ci-après également "office de contrôle"). La Verordnung prévoit en son article 2:

> "1) Il est interdit aux entreprises d'assurance soumises au contrôle fédéral et aux personnes agissant comme intermédiaires pour les contrats d'assurance souscrits auprès d'elles et couvrant les risques d'assurance dommage, d'assurance contre les accidents, d'assurance crédit, d'assurance caution et d'assurance défense et recours, de consentir des mesures préférentielles, quelle qu'en soit la forme, aux preneurs d'assurance.
>
> 2)　Est une mesure préférentielle tout avantage direct ou indirect accordé en sus des prestations résultant du contrat d'assurance, notamment toute cession de commission."

6　L'Anordnung et la Verordnung ont été adoptées par l'office de contrôle sur la base de la Gesetz über die Beaufsichtigung der Versicherungsunternehmen du 12 mai 1901 (loi sur le contrôle des entreprises d'assurances, RGB1. S. 139). L'article 81, paragraphe 2, troisième phrase, de cette loi, telle qu'elle résulte de la version codifiée du 13 octobre 1983 (BGB1. I S. 1261), dispose que l'office de contrôle

> "peut, de manière générale ou pour certains secteurs d'assurance, interdire aux sociétés d'assurance et aux intermédiaires en assurance d'accorder des avantages spéciaux sous quelque forme que ce soit."

7　Estimant qu'en cédant sa commission à ses clients M. Meng avait enfreint la réglementation mentionnée ci-dessus, l'Amtsgericht Tiergarten lui a infligé une amende de 1850 DM. L'intéressé a alors fait appel de ce jugement devant le Kammergericht Berlin, en faisant valoir que la réglementation était contraire aux articles 3, sous n, 5, deuxième alinéa, et 85, paragraphe 1, du traité.

8　C'est dans ces conditions que le Kammergericht Berlin, considérant que l'issue du litige dépendait de l'interprétation du droit communautaire, a déféré à la Cour la question préjudicielle suivante:

> "Les dispositions du point I de l'ordonnance du Deutshes Reichsaufsichtsamt für Privatversicherung du 5 juin 1934 relative à l'interdiction des mesures préférentielles et des contrats de faveur dans le domaine de l'assurance maladie (no 129 du Deutscher Reichsanzeiger und Preussischer Staatsanzeiger du 6 juin 1934) et de l'article 1er du règlement du Bundesaufsichtsamt für das Versicherungswesen du 17 août 1982 relatif à l'interdiction des mesures préférentielles et des contrats de faveur dans le domaine de l'assurance dommage (BGB1. I, p. 1243 –

VerBAV 1982, p. 456), en vertu desquelles il est interdit – également – aux intermédiaires indépendants en assurances d'accorder un traitement préférentiel par cession de la commission, sont-elles incompatibles avec les articles 3, sous n, 5 et 85 paragraphe 1 du traité CEE ..."

9 Pour un plus ample exposé des faits du litige au principal, du déroulement de la procédure ainsi que des observations écrites présentées devant la Cour, il est renvoyé au rapport d'audience. Ces éléments du dossier ne sont repris ci-dessous que dans la mesure nécessaire au raisonnement de la Cour.

10 A titre liminaire, il convient de relever qu'il n'appartient pas à la Cour de se prononcer, dans le cadre d'une procédure introduite en vertu de l'article 177 du traité, sur la compatibilité de normes de droit interne avec les dispositions du droit communautaire, mais que la Cour est compétente pour fournir à la juridiction nationale tous les éléments d'interprétation relevant du droit communautaire qui permettent à celle-ci d'apprécier la compatibilité de ces normes avec la réglementation communautaire.

11 Dans ces conditions, la question posée par le Kammergericht Berlin doit être comprise, en substance, comme visant à savoir si les articles 3, sous n, 5, deuxième alinéa, et 85 du traité font obstacle à ce qu'une réglementation étatique interdise aux intermédiaires en assurance de céder à leurs clients tout ou partie des commissions versées par les compagnies d'assurance.

Sur le caractère étatique de la réglementation

12 A titre liminaire, il convient de relever que l'office de contrôle est une autorité administrative, qu'il dépend d'un ministère (à l'heure actuelle le ministère fédéral des Finances) et qu'il est chargé par la loi de contrôler l'activité des entreprises d'assurance. A cette fin, l'office est notamment habilité à prendre des mesures réglementaires visant à interdire des comportements susceptibles de porter atteinte aux intérêts des consommateurs. C'est sur cette base qu'il a édicté en 1934 et en 1982 les mesures litigieuses.

13 Du statut et des pouvoirs de l'office, il y a lieu de déduire que lesdites mesures présentent un caractère étatique. Il convient donc d'examiner si, ainsi que le soutient M. Meng, l'article 85 lu en liaison avec les articles 3, sous n, et 5, deuxième alinéa, du traité s'oppose à une telle réglementation.

Sur l'interprétation des articles 3, sous n, 5, deuxième alinéa, et 85 du traité

14 Pour ce qui est de l'interprétation des articles 3, sous n, 5, deuxième alinéa, et 85 du traité, il y a lieu de rappelller que, par lui-même, l'article 85 du traité concerne uniquement le comportement des entreprises et ne vise pas des mesures législatives ou réglementaires émanant des Etats membres. Il résulte cependant d'une jurisprudence constante que l'article 85, lu en combinaison avec l'article 5 du traité, impose aux Etats membres de ne pas prendre ou maintenir en vigueur des mesures, même de nature législative ou

réglementaire, susceptibles d'éliminer l'effet utile des règles de concurrence applicables aux entreprises. Tel est le cas, envertu de cette même jurisprudence, lorsqu'un Etat membre soit impose ou favorise la conclusion d'ententes contraires à l'article 85 ou renforce les effets de telles ententes, soit retire à sa propre réglementation son caractère étatique en déléguant à des opérateurs privés la responsabilité de prendre des décisions d'intervention en matière économique (voir arrêt du 21 septembre 1988, Van Eycke, 267/86, Rec. p. 4769, point 16).

15 A cet égard, il convient de constater tout d'abord que la réglementation allemande sur les assurances n'impose ni ne favorise la conclusion d'une entente illicite par les intermédiaires en assurances, puisque l'interdiction qu'elle édicte se suffit à elle-même.

16 Il y a lieu de vérifier ensuite si la réglementation a eu pour effet de renforcer un accord anticoncurrentiel.

17 A cet égard, il est constant que cette réglementation n'a été précédée d'aucun accord dans les secteurs qu'elle couvre, à savoir ceux de l'assurance maladie, de l'assurance dommage et de l'assurance défense et recours.

18 La Commission a toutefois fait valoir que certaines entreprises avaient conclu un accord visant à interdire les cessions de commissions dans le secteur de l'assurance vie et qu'en rendant cet accord applicable à d'autres secteurs, la réglementation en a renforcé la portée.

19 Ce point de vue ne saurait être retenu. Une réglementation applicable à un secteur d'assurance déterminé ne saurait être regardée comme renforcant les effets d'une entente préexistante que si elle se borne à reprendre les éléments d'une entente intervenue entre les opérateurs économiques de ce secteur.

20 Enfin, il convient de relever que la réglementation formule elle-même l'interdiction d'accorder des avantages aux preneurs d'assurances et ne délègue pas à des opérateurs privés la responsabilité de prendre des décisions d'intervention en matière économique.

21 Des considérations qui précèdent il résulte qu'une réglementation comme celle en cause dans le litige au principal n'entre pas dans les catégories de réglementations étatiques qui, selon la jurisprudence de la Cour, portent atteinte à l'effet utile des articles 3 sous n, 5 deuxième alinéa, et 85 du traité.

22 Dès lors, il y a lieu de répondre à la question posée par la juridiction nationale que les articles 3, sous n, 5, deuxième alinéa, et 85 du traité CEE ne font pas obstacle à ce que, en l'absence de tout lien avec un comportement d'entreprises visé par l'article 85, paragraphe 1, du traité, une réglementation étatique interdise aux intermédiaires en assurance de céder à leurs clients tout ou partie des commissions versées par les compagnies d'assurance.

Sur les dépens

23 Les frais exposés par les gouvernements belge, danois, allemand, hellénique, espagnol, français, irlandais, italien, néerlandais, portugais et du Royaume-Uni, ainsi que par la Commission des Communautés européennes, qui ont soumis des observations à la Cour, ne peuvent faire l'object d'un remboursement. La procédure revêtant, à l'égard des parties au principal, le caractère d'un incident soulevé devant la juridiction nationale, il appartient à celle-ci de statuer sur les dépens.

Par ces motifs,

LA COUR,

statuant sur la question à elle soumise par le Kammergericht Berlin, par ordonnance du 26 novembre 1990, dit pour droit:

Les articles 3, sous n, 5, deuxième alinéa, et 85 du traité CEE ne font pas obstacle à ce que, en l'absence de tout lien avec un comportement d'entreprises visé par l'article 85, paragraphe 1, du traité, une réglementation étatique interdise aux intermédiaires en assurance de céder à leurs clients tout ou partie des commissions versées par les compagnies d'assurance.

E. JUSTIFICATION FOR STATE MONOPOLIES

The increase in competition which results from the decisions in the majority of the preceding group of cases has been achieved through the application of a range of Treaty provisions. Articles 3, 5, 30, 59, 85, 86 and 90 all have roles to play. The principal theme which emerges is that, irrespective of the specific Treaty provision in issue, the Court typically possesses a general conception of the kind of market it wishes to see develop. Its objective is to secure that the market should be integrated and that it should operate competitively. Accordingly, barriers to entry into markets which result from state acts will be challenged. Chapter 4 showed how Community law also challenges barriers to entry raised by private agreements. The Court is in pursuit of the competitive, integrated Community market. It remains an open question whether that pursuit represents a quest for something as bold as a European Economic Constitution.

The Court maintains the principle that the existence of exclusive rights is not unlawful, but that the exercise of those rights may be unlawful. That seems to be a constitutional principle enshrined in Article 90(1). It preserves state competence to grant exclusive rights. However, this divide between the existence and the exercise of rights is not sharp in practice. The Court's unfavourable view of the anticompetitive impact of exclusive rights makes it inevitable in many sectors that exclusive rights will be indefensible under Community law, save in situations expressly recognized by the Treaty such as Article 90(2). Ehlermann refers to this as the idea of exclusivity leading to an 'inevitable abuse' ([1993] 2 *European Competition Law Review* 61, 63).

This raises the question as to the circumstances in which state intervention in markets may be ruled permissible under Community law. Obstacles to the free circulation of goods or services may be justified under Articles 36 and 55/66 respectively (Case C-271/92 above). Article 90(2) provides for a further exception. However, Article 90(2) has been interpreted restrictively. Some discussion of the circumstances in which it may be employed is found in Case 66/86 *Ahmed Saeed Flugreisen and Silver Line Reisebüro GmbH* v. *Zentrale zur Bekämpfung unlauteren Wettbewerbs e.V.* [1989] ECR 803.

[...]

(d) Articles 5 and 90

47   The third question is concerned with the legality of approval by the supervisory body of a Member State of tariffs contrary to Article 85(1) or Article 86 of the Treaty. The national court asks in particular whether such approval is not incompatible with the second paragraph of Article 5 and Article 90(1) of the Treaty, even if the Commission has not objected to such approval under Article 90(3).

48   In that connection it should be borne in mind in the first place that, as the Court has consistently held, while it is true that the competition rules set out in Articles 85 and 86 concern the conduct of undertakings and not measures of the authorities in the Member States, Article 5 of the Treaty nevertheless imposes a duty on those authorities not to adopt or maintain in force any measure which could deprive those competition rules of their effectiveness. That would be the case, in particular, if a Member State were to require or favour the adoption of agreements, decisions or concerted practices contrary to Article 85 or reinforce their effects (see, most recently, the judgment of 1 October 1987 in Case 311/85 *Vereniging van Vlaamse Reisbureaus* v. *Sociaale Dienst van de plaatselijke en gewestelijke Overheidsdiensten* [1987] ECR 3801).

49   It must be concluded as a result that the approval by the aeronautical authorities of tariff agreements contrary to Article 85(1) is not compatible with Community law and in particular with Article 5 of the Treaty. It also follows that the aeronautical authorities must refrain from taking any measure which might be construed as encouraging airlines to conclude tariff agreements contrary to the Treaty.

50   In the specific case of tariffs for scheduled flights that interpretation of the Treaty is borne out by Article 90(1) of the Treaty, which provides that in the case of undertakings to which Member States grant special or exclusive rights – such as rights to operate on an air route alone or with one or two other undertakings – Member States must not enact or maintain in force any measure contrary to the competition rules laid down in Article 85 and 86, Moreover, it is stated in the preambles to Council Regulations Nos. 3975 and 3976/87 that those regulations do not prejudice the application of Article 90 of the Treaty.

51   Admittedly, in the preamble to Regulation No 3976/87 the Council expressed a desire to increase competition in air transport services between Member States gradually so as to provide time for the sector concerned to adapt to a system different from the present system of establishing a network of agreements between Member States and air carriers. However, that concern can be respected only within the limits laid down by the provisions of the Treaty.

52   Whilst, as a result, the new rules laid down by the Council and the Commission leave the Community institutions and the authorities in the Member States free to encourage the airlines to organize mutual consultations on the tariffs to be applied on certain routes served by scheduled flights, such as the consultations provided for in Directive 87/601/EEC, the Treaty nevertheless strictly prohibits them from giving encouragement, in any form whatsoever, to the adoption of agreements or concerted practices with regard to tariffs contrary to Article 85(1) or Article 86, as the case may be.

53   The national court also refers to Article 90(3), but that provision appears to be of no relevance for the purpose of resolving the problems raised by this case. That provision places the Commission under a duty to ensure the application of the provisions of Article 90 and to address, where necessary, appropriate directives or decisions to Member States; it does not, however, preclude the application of paragraphs (1) and (2) of that article where the Commission fails to act.

54   In contrast, Article 90(2) might entail consequences for decisions by the aeronautical authorities with regard to the approval of tariffs. That provision provides *inter alia* that undertakings entrusted with the operation of services of general economic interest are to be subject to the competition rules contained in the Treaty, in so far however as the application of such rules does not obstruct the performance of the particular tasks assigned to them.

55   That provision may be applied to carriers who may be obliged, by the public authorities, to operate on routes which are not commercially viable but which it is necessary to operate for reasons of the general interest. It is necessary in each case for the competent national administrative or judicial authorities to establish whether the airline in question has actually been en-

trusted with the task of operating on such routes by an act of the public authority (judgment of 27 March 1974 in Case 127/73 *Belgische Radio en Televisie* v. *Sabam* ('BRT-II') [1974] ECR 313).

56   However, for it to be possible for the effect of the competition rules to be restricted pursuant to Article 90(2) by needs arising from performance of a task of general interest, the national authorities responsible for the approval of tariffs and the courts to which disputes relating thereto are submitted must be able to determine the exact nature of the needs in question and their impact on the structure of the tariffs applied by the airlines in question.

57   Indeed, where there is no effective transparency of the tariff structure it is difficult, if not impossible, to assess the influence of the task of general interest on the application of the competition rules in the field of tariffs. It is for the national court to make the necessary findings of fact in that connection.

58   It follows from the foregoing considerations that it should be stated in reply to the third question submitted by the national court that Article 5 and 90 of the EEC Treaty must be interpreted as:

(i)   prohibiting the national authorities from encouraging the conclusion of agreements on tariffs contrary to Article 85(1) or Article 86 of the Treaty, as the case may be;

(ii) precluding the approval by those authorities of tariffs resulting from such agreements;

(iii) not precluding a limitation of the effects of the competition rules in so far as it is indispensable for the performance of a task of general interest which air carriers are required to carry out, provided that the nature of that task and its impact on the tariff structure are clearly established.

The Court has been markedly quicker to find that the requirements of Article 90(2) are *not* satisfied than that they are satisfied. Most of the Court's decisions under Article 90 strike down state distortions of competition incompatible with the rules of the Treaty without finding the justification envisaged by Article 90(2).

What is lacking is any general idea of the circumstances in which state intervention in pursuit of, for example, social objectives may be acceptable under Community law. In 1974 the Court declared firmly that Member States remained competent to grant exclusive rights 'for considerations of public interest of a non-economic nature' (Case 155/73 *Sacchi* [1974] ECR 409). It remains unclear how this notion should be interpreted in practice. It is an issue of prime importance in shaping a European notion of the role of public intervention in markets. It seems clear that a narrow interpretation of Article 90(2)'s concession to the Member States has lately been firmly in vogue. This is especially significant in the light of the wide interpretation – the 'inevitable abuse' notion – placed on Article 90(1).

The more state practices are found to fall within Article 90(1), the more critical becomes the scope of the Article 90(2) exception.

F. A CASE STUDY: POSTAL SERVICES

The Commission has in recent years given a much higher priority to control of state distortions of the market than in the early development of the Community when its focus was private commercial activities. This increased scepticism about state intervention has been in part due to the personal support for such a policy provided by Commissioner Leon Brittan, who held the Competition portfolio in the Commission from 1989 until the start of 1993. The Commission has lately jolted Article 90 out of the dormant state into which it had slipped over many years. This has stirred up some acutely sensitive political and economic issues concerned with the nature of the modern mixed economy.

Case C-320/91 *Paul Corbeau* judgment of 19 May 1993 concerns a monopoly over postal services in Belgium. The decision contributes to the role of Article 90 read with Article 86 in lopping off ancillary rights reserved to state monopolies and opening them up to competition. It is a decision which raises many of the core issues about the shape of European Economic Law which have permeated this Chapter. In *Paul Corbeau,* the most difficult and important questions revolve around the monopoly in the core postal service. If that monopoly is lost, the social function of the service will be jeopardized. In this ruling the Court recognizes the role of cross subsidy as a means of maintaining the viability of loss-making but socially worthwhile services. Article 90(2) is capable of justifying restrictions on competition in such circumstances. It opposes remorseless deregulation. This represents an important statement of the existence of limits to the liberalization of the market. However, it leaves as yet undefined the precise location of those limits. This case was an Article 177 preliminary ruling so the Court did not have the task of deciding the case, merely of interpreting Community law.

Assuming that the scope of Article 90(1) remains broad, the scope of Article 90(2) is the crucial issue for the future defence of such state monopolies. Just when and why should the limits of the ejection of the state from the market be reached? When is the general interest served by restrictions on competition?

[...]

7   With regard to the facts in the main proceedings, the questions referred to the Court must be understood as meaning that the national court is substantially concerned with the question whether Article 90 of the Treaty must be interpreted as meaning that it is contrary to that article for the legislation of

a Member State which confers on a body such as the Régie des Postes the exclusive right to collect, carry and distribute mail to prohibit an economic operator established in that State from offering, under threat of criminal penalties, certain specific services on that market.

8   To reply to that question, as thus reformulated, it should first be pointed out that a body such as the Régie des Postes, which has been granted exclusive right as regards the collection, carriage and distribution of mail, must be regarded as an undertaking to which the Member State concerned has granted exclusive rights within the meaning of Article 90(1) of the Treaty.

9   Next it should be recalled that the Court has consistently held that an undertaking having a statutory monopoly over a substantial part of the common market may be regarded as having a dominant position within the meaning of Article 86 of the Treaty (see the judgments in Case C-179/90 *Merci Convenzionali Porto di Genova* [1991] ECR I-5889 at paragraph 14 and in Case C-18/88 *RTT* v. *GB-Inno-BM* [1991] ECR I-5941 at paragraph 17).

10   However, Article 86 applies only to anti-competitive conduct engaged in by undertakings on their own initiative, not to measures adopted by States (see the *RTT* v. *GB-Inno-BM* judgment, cited above, paragraph 20).

11   The Court has had occasion to state in this respect that although the mere fact that a Member State has created a dominant position by the grant of exclusive rights is not as such incompatible with Article 86, the Treaty none the less requires the Member States not to adopt or maintain in force any measure which might deprive those provisions of their effectiveness (see the judgment in Case C-260/89 *ERT* [1991] ECR I-2925, paragraph 35).

12   Thus Article 90(1) provides that in the case of public undertakings to which Member States grant special or exclusive rights, they are neither to enact nor to maintain in force any measure contrary to the rules contained in the Treaty with regard to competition.

13   That provision must be read in conjunction with Article 90(2) which provides that undertakings entrusted with the operation of services of general economic interest are to be subject to the rules on competition in so far as the application of such rules does not obstruct the performance, in law or in fact, of the particular tasks assigned to them.

14   That latter provision thus permits the Member States to confer on undertakings to which they entrust the operation of services of general economic interest, exclusive rights which may hinder the application of the rules of the Treaty on competition in so far as restrictions on competition, or even the exclusion of all competition, by other economic operators are necessary to ensure the performance of the particular tasks assigned to the undertakings possessed of the exclusive rights.

15   As regards the services at issue in the main proceedings, it cannot be disputed that the Régie des Postes is entrusted with a service of general eco-

nomic interest consisting in the obligation to collect, carry and distribute mail on behalf of all users throughout the territory of the Member State concerned, at uniform tariffs and on similar quality conditions, irrespective of the specific situations or the degree of economic profitability of each individual operation.

16 The question which falls to be considered is therefore the extent to which a restriction on competition or even the exclusion of all competition from other economic operators is necessary in order to allow the holder of the exclusive right to perform its task of general interest and in particular to have the benefit of economically acceptable conditions.

17 The starting point of such an examination must be the premise that the obligation on the part of the undertaking entrusted with that task to perform its services in conditions of economic equilibrium presupposes that it will be possible to offset less profitable sectors against the profitable sectors and hence justifies a restriction of competition from individual undertakings where the economically profitable sectors are concerned.

18 Indeed, to authorize individual undertakings to compete with the holder of the exclusive rights in the sectors of their choice corresponding to those rights would make it possible for them to concentrate on the economically profitable operations and to offer more advantageous tariffs than those adopted by the holders of the exclusive rights since, unlike the latter, they are not bound for economic reasons to offset losses in the unprofitable sectors against profits in the more profitable sectors.

19 However, the exclusion of competition is not justified as regards specific services dissociable from the service of general interest which meet special needs of economic operators and which call for certain additional services not offered by the traditional postal service, such as collection from the senders' address, greater speed or reliability of distribution or the possibility of changing the destination in the course of transit, in so far as such specific services, by their nature and the conditions in which they are offered, such as the geographical area in which they are provided, do not compromise the economic equilibrium of the service of general economic interest performed by the holder of the exclusive right.

20 It is for the national court to consider whether the services at issue in the dispute before it meet those criteria.

21 The answer to the questions referred to the Court by the Tribunal Correctionnel de Liège should therefore be that it is contrary to Article 90 of the EEC Treaty for legislation of a Member State which confers on a body such as the Régie des Postes the exclusive right to collect, carry and distribute mail, to prohibit, under threat of criminal penalties an economic operator established in that State from offering certain specific services dissociable from the service of general interest which meet the special needs of economic operators and call for certain additional services not offered by the

traditional postal service, in so far as those services do not compromise the economic equilibrium of the service of general economic interest performed by the holder of the exclusive right. It is for the national court to consider whether the services in question in the main proceedings meet those criteria.

G. CONCLUSION

The final extract in this Chapter provides a valuable attempt to draw together the principal issues and to rationalize the Court and Commission's policy. It should be read in the light of the suggestion at the start of this Chapter that the search is on for a constitutional framework of European economic law which will determine the scope of state intervention in the integrating European market. Has a reliable notion of 'distortion of competition' (Article 3(g)) been developed?

ARTICLE 90: COMPETING FOR COMPETENCE*

Marc van der Woude

THE RELATION BETWEEN COMPETITION RULES AND PROVISIONS ON FREE CIRCULATION

France v. *Commission* shows that the grant of exclusive import and selling rights necessarily constitutes a measure of equivalent effect within the meaning of Article 30, but may be justified by Article 36 or mandatory requirements. It results from *RTT* that the right of a public telephone company to decide which telephones may be connected to its network is also contrary to Article 30.[1] The Court accepted as a principle that the protection of the consumer and the good operation of the network were mandatory requirements which may justify a regulation which imposes approval of the telephones before they are put on the market. It considered, however, that the right of the Belgian telephone company to grant such authorisations was disproportionate in comparison to its restrictive effects on trade. In the absence of any right of appeal against RTT's decision before a jurisdiction, RTT could in effect block the access to the Belgian telephone market.

Article 59 is the Treaty provision which corresponds in the services sector to Article 30. In *Höfner* the Court did not examine the validity of the monopoly of the German federal employment agency in the light of Article 59, because the facts of his case were of a purely national nature.[2] This reasoning is understandable if one considers that the provisions on free circulation relate to the integration of markets and not to their functioning. It is not, if Article 59 has to be interpreted in the light of Article 3F which determines the functioning of the market.

In *ERT*, however, the Court did examine a service monopoly under Article 59.[3] It concerned the exclusive rights of the Greek national television company to broadcast and retransmit programmes in Greece. The Court held that such rights would be incompatible with Article 59 if they lead to discrimination against foreign programmes. It should be noted that the scope of this provision is wider than a mere prohibition of discrimination. In the Dutch television cases the Court explicitly ruled that even indistinctly applicable regulations may be caught by Article 59

---

* First published in Robin White (ed.), *European Law Review*, **17**, 1992, Competition Law Checklist, 1991, pp.60–80; reprinted by permission of Sweet & Maxwell, London.

1 *RTT*, 13 December 1991, Case C-18/88, [1991] ECR I 5941.
2 *Höfner*, 23 April 1991, Case C-41/90, [1991] ECR I 1979.
3 *ERT*, 18 June 1991, Case C-260/89, [1991] ECR I 2925.

if they restrict the free circulation of services.[4] The Dutch legislation in question imposed indistinctly applicable conditions for the transmission on the cable network of television programmes containing commercials. The Court held that these conditions restricted free access of foreign programmes and that these restrictions were not necessary for the maintenance of a varied television system which in itself is a legitimate cultural policy objective.

The broad scope of Article 30 and 59 implies that every exclusive import or sales right is forbidden unless it is justified by Articles 36 and 56 or by mandatory requirements. This means that such an exclusive right should in principle be suppressed to allow free access of goods and services from other Member States. This is a very far reaching conclusion which even affects local or regional monopolies. Some examples may again be useful. If a French commune grants an exclusive right to a French company for local funeral services, foreign companies will not be able to provide these services.[5] Therefore, such a concession is contrary to Article 59 unless justified by Article 56 or some kind of mandatory requirement. The same holds true for concessions concerning public transport, water and gas supplies.

It is unclear whether the Court is aware of these very far reaching consequences of its case law. The *Merci* case seems to indicate that it is not or at least not willing to accept them.[6] The case concedes the grant of a monopoly for dock facilities in the port of Genoa. All activities related to the loading or unloading of ships had to be carried out by certain Italian companies which were only allowed to employ Italian nationals. Because of strikes by dock workers the monopolists did not unload a German ship. The exclusive rights prohibited the crew to unload the ship themselves. The owner of the cargo sued the monopolist for damages incurred by the delays. The Italian judge asked the Court whether the exclusive rights and the obligation to employ Italian nationals were compatible with Articles 7, 30, 85, 86 and 90. The Court's answer is primarily based on the combined application of Articles 86 and 90. Before discussing this answer, the Court's reaction under the provisions on free circulation should be examined first.

The Court considered first the obligation to employ Italian nationals. Such an obligation is manifestly contrary to Article 7. However, this article can only be relied upon in situations which are not governed by other specific Treaty provisions. The Court therefore turned to Article 48 and declared that the contested obligation infringed this provision. The Court subsequently dealt with Article 86. Why did it not mention Article 59, another specific Treaty provision which implements the general principle of Article 7? Article 59 was in the author's view the most

---

[4] *Commission* v. *Netherlands*, 25 July 1991, Case C-353/89, [1991] ECR I 4069; *Gouda*, 25 July 1991, Case C-288/89 [1991] ECR I 4007.

[5] Compare with *Bodson*, 4 May 1988, Case 30/87, [1988] ECR 2507.

[6] *Merci*, 10 December 1991, Case C-179/90, [1991] ECR I 5889.

suitable provision to solve the case, since the monopoly made it impossible for the German ship itself to provide the necessary services. What is a more characteristic restriction of the freedom to provide services than a prohibition to help oneself? Moreover, it could also have been argued that the monopoly was contrary to Article 52, because it made it impossible for companies from other Member States to establish themselves in the port of Genoa.[7]

A similar reaction of the Court to avoid the assessment of exclusive rights in the light of the provisions on free circulation can be seen in *RTT*. The Court's analysis under Article 30 is confined in that case to RTT's right to decide which telephones may be connected to the network. RTT's rights to establish and supervise the technical norms for telephones were only examined under Articles 86 and 90, although the national judge had explicitly referred to Article 30 in its preliminary questions. In the light of *France* v. *Commission* the Court could have ruled that the legal possibility for the RTT with producers from other Member States, is a potential restriction of trade, forbidden by Article 30.

Merci and *RTT* indicate under these circumstances that the Court has refused to accept the consequences of *France* v. *Commission* when assessing exclusive rights under the provisions on free circulation. Instead of using these provisions it relies upon a combined application of Articles 86 and 90. In doing so the Court seems to prefer to control the exercise of monopolies rather than the admissibility of their existence. However, the application of Articles 86 and 90 also has far reaching consequences for the public sector. *Höfner*, *ERT*, *Merci*, and *RTT* show that in some respects the grant of exclusive rights becomes almost impossible under these Articles, if the exercise of such rights necessarily leads to an abuse by the company concerned or if a situation is created in which this company could not place itself autonomously without infringing Article 86.

In *Höfner* the Court held that grant of an exclusive right to the federal employment office for headhunting services is contrary to Articles 86 and 90(1), if several cumulative conditions are fulfilled. First, this office should be unable to satisfy the demand for these services. The law thereby creates a situation envisaged by Article 86(b). Secondly, the law should make it impossible for private companies to provide headhunting services. Third, these services should not be confined to the territory Member State and its nationals. Headhunting activities should potentially

---

[7] In *Costa* v. *Enel*, 15 July 1964, Case 6/64, [1964] ECR 545, the Court ruled that the nationalisation of the Italian electricity was not contrary to Article 52, because it was not discriminatory. In the light of the recent case law on Article 52 one could challenge the exclusive right of a nation wide electricity company, because it impedes primary or secondary establishment, see *Klopp*, 14 July 1984, Case 107/83, [1984] ECR2971, *Vlassopoulou*, 7 May 1991, Case C-340/89, ECR 2357.

relate to foreign nationals or companies to Germans living abroad.[8] In short, a Member State infringes Articles 86 and 90(1), if the exercise of the exclusive rights leads unavoidably to an abuse.

ERT concerned the grant of an exclusive retransmission right to a company which already enjoyed an exclusive broadcasting right. The Court ruled that this is contrary to Article 90(1), if these rights create a situation in which this company is induced to infringe Article 86 by a discriminatory transmission policy on behalf of its own programmes. This finding corresponds to the Court's conclusion under Article 59, according to which the grant of these rights restricts the free circulation of services if the monopoly discriminates against foreign programmes. One may therefore wonder why the Court still bothered to analyse these rights under Articles 86 and 90.

As already mentioned above this question also arises in *RTT* and *Merci*. In the latter case the Court applied the principles developed in *Höfner* and *ERT*. A Member State creates a situation contrary to Article 86 if it adopts a regulation which induces the docker companies concerned to claim the payment of services which were not provided, to charge disproportionate prices, to refuse the application of modern technology thereby increasing costs and delays, or to discriminate between customers. The Court subsequently specified that such a regulation is also contrary to Article 30, because it makes imports more expensive. Why did it bother then to make a complicated analysis of the regulation under Articles 86 and 90(1)?

In *RTT* the Court ruled that the operation of a public telephone network is a service of general economic interest within the meaning of Article 90(2). The right to operate this service on a nationwide scale leads to the existence of a dominant position. A company abuses this position if it extends its monopoly without objective justification to ancillary markets.[9] Article 90(1) is infringed if a public regulation makes such monopolisation possible. This occurs if it grants to RTT the right to establish the technical norms for telephones which may be connected to its network and its power to supervise the respect of these norms. Such rights obviously distort the competitive relations between RTT and other telephone suppliers in favour of RTT.

It results from *RTT* and the other case law of the Court after *France* v. *Commission* that the Court is reluctant to assess the admissibility of exclusive rights under the provisions on free circulation. It relies instead on a combined application of Articles 86 and 90(1). However, its approach under these Articles is of a structural nature, in that sense that the existence of exclusive rights can be challenged under

---

[8]   This does not mean that *Höfner* could rely upon Article 59. According to the Court's case law the provisions on free circulation do not apply in purely internal situations; see n. 30, *supra*.

[9]   *Télémarketing*, 3 October 1985, Case 311/84, [1985] ECR 3261.

these rules by "the automatic abuse theory." According to this theory the grant of an exclusive right is only authorized if the Member States ensure that its exercise will not lead to an abuse within the meaning of Article 86, In other words, the monopolist should be just as efficient as a company which operates under normal competitive conditions. If it is not, it loses its exclusive right.[10] This approach therefore allows Member States to intervene in the market place but not in the functioning of the market mechanism, except when justified under Article 90(2).

This approach is surprising because in *France* v. *Commission* the Court exclusively relied upon Article 30. This provision and the other provisions on free circulation enable a comprehensive control of the admissibility of exclusive rights, without the burdens of market analysis required by Article 86. The reasons why the Court nevertheless preferred the competition rules remain unclear. One explanation lies perhaps in the fact that the Court has developed one of the competition rules into the fundamental norm for the assessment of the admissibility of exclusive rights.

THE JUSTIFICATION OF EXCLUSIVE RIGHTS

In *France* v. *Commission* the Court explicitly discarded Article 90(2) from the case. Its examination of the French application was entirely focused on Articles 90(1) & (3) in conjunction with Article 30. It therefore only examined whether the contested exclusive rights were justified by Article 36 or mandatory requirements. However, if the French government had argued that the exclusive rights on terminal equipment were justified by Article 90(2), the Court should also have examined whether this provision justified an infringement of Article 90(1). In other words the Court should have examined twice whether the exclusive rights were justified or not. It could be argued that the Court tried to avoid this problem of double justification in its case law after *France* v. *Commission* by focusing on the competition rules. Article 90(2) is indeed the only exception to the application of these rules.

In *Höfner* the problem of double justification did not occur, because Article 59 was held not to be applicable in purely internal situations. As regards the justification of an infringement of Articles 86 and 90(1) by virtue of Article 90(2), the Court held that the application of Article 86 to the monopoly of the federal employment office could not obstruct the proper fulfilment of the particular tasks as-

---

10 A comparison could be made in this respect with the establishment of a dominant position under Art. 86. A 100 per cent, market share, which corresponds to a factual monopoly, will not necessarily prove dominance, if the firm concerned is obliged to maintain a competitive price level under the pressure from potential competitors which can enter the market without being hampered by entry barriers.

signed to it, because it was manifestly not capable to satisfy the demand for head-hunting services and because it in fact tolerated the activities of private headhunters.

In *ERT* the problem did occur, because the Court examined the Greek television monopoly from the angles of both Articles 59 and Articles 86 and 90(1). In respect of Article 59 it held that the exclusive rights in question were not justified by Article 56. However, as regards Article 90(2) it merely replied to the national judge that it was his duty to assess whether a particular task was assigned to the Greek television company and whether its practices were necessary for the fulfilment of this task.[11] If this judge were to decide that Article 90(2) was applicable, what would be the relation between this justification and the Court's finding under Article 56?

In the author's view the rules on the freedom to provide services should prevail in this case. As mentioned here above, these rules concern the creation of the common market and govern the admissibility of exclusive rights. Competition rules which relate to the functioning of the market only come into play when exclusive rights are allowed under Article 56 or when justified by mandatory requirements. Therefore, Article 90(2) becomes without object if the existence of an exclusive right is in itself contrary to the rules on free circulation.[12] It is doubtful, however, whether this reasoning will be followed by the Court, since it abandoned the distinction between the control of the existence and exercise of exclusive rights in *France* v. *Commission.*

Merci remains unclear on the relation between Article 90(2) and the possible justifications of exclusive rights under the provisions on free circulation. This judgment has two parts. In the first part the Genoese port monopoly is held to be contrary to Article 90(1) in conjunction with Article 48, 86 and 30. The Court does not at this stage examine the applicability of Articles 48, paragraphs 3 and 4, and 36. Nor does it assess the admissibility of the monopoly in the light of mandatory requirements. In the second part of the judgment the Court deals with Article 90(2). It considered that the port monopoly did not provide a service of general economic interest and even if it did the application of the rules on competition *and* free circu-

---

[11] This delegation to the national judge is understandable in the light of the facts of the case, as reported in the Report for the Hearing. The Court did not dispose of any elements which indicated that the Greek television company actually abused its dominant position or not. An assessment of Art. 90(2) could therefore only be abstract and thus useless. Compare with *Merci* and *Höfner* in which the Court rules itself on the justification of the rights under Art. 90(2).

[12] For the sake of completeness, it should be noted that the problem of double justification also occurs when Art. 90(1) is used in conjunction with Art. 30 for the appraisal of ancillary restraints accompanying the exercise of an exclusive right, which in itself is justified.

lation would not obstruct its performance.[13] This refusal to apply Article 90(2) concerns all the provisions mentioned in the first part of the judgment. However, even if *Merci* seriously restricts the possibility for the Italian authorities to maintain the Genoese monopoly, it does not make it completely impossible. So, one could still argue that the Court's reasoning on Article 90(2) only concerns the abusive exercise of the monopoly.

However, this reasoning cannot be upheld any more after *RTT*. This judgment also has two parts. The first part relates to *RTT's* right to set the technical norms for the telephone market on which it competes with other producers. The second part concerns its right to decide which telephones may be connected to its network. The first part starts with a statement. A monopoly on the basic telephone network is a service of general economic interest within the meaning of Article 90(2). Its extension to the market of terminal equipment is an act of monopolisation which is not justified by this provision. The Court states in this respect that the protection of essential requirements such as the safety of the user of the terminal equipment, the safety of the employees of the public telephone network and the protection of the network itself, could be ensured by less restrictive alternatives. These requirements, advanced as possible justifications under Article 90(2), correspond exactly to those mentioned in *France* v. *Commission* as justifications under Article 30. This finding is confirmed by the second part of the judgment in *RTT* in which the Court assesses *RTT's* right in the light of Article 30 and mandatory requirements such as the protection of the user of the network and the good operation of the network.

It results from *RTT* that Article 90(2) absorbs all the interests of a non economic nature which according to *Sacchi* justify the existence of monopolies under the rules of free circulation. In contrast with the view expressed by the author, Article 90(2) therefore not only relates to the exercise of exclusive rights but also to their existence. Exclusive rights are only allowed in so far as they are covered by this provision. If they are not, they either infringe Articles 86 and 90(1) on the basis of the automatic abuse theory or by virtue of the Treaty's provisions on free circulation. Exclusive import and sales rights restrict by their very nature the freedom for other companies than the holder of the rights to import or sell goods and services. Exclusive production rights infringe Article 52, because they make it impossible for other producers to establish themselves in the Member State concerned.

Article 90(2) has thus become the fundamental norm for the assessment of exclusive rights. The Court developed this norm in conjunction with the application of Articles 86 and 90(1). It would have been surprising if it had directly used Article 90(2) in conjunction with Articles 30 and 59 outside the context of competition rules and without referring to Articles 36 and 56 or mandatory requirements. It

---

13 Compare with ground 11 of *Müller*, 14 July 1971, Case 10/71, [1971] ECR 821, in which a port was declared to be a service of general economic interest.

implicitly results from *Merci*, however, that this step in the Court's case law on Article 90 has already been made in a stealthy way. Indeed, the part of the judgment relating to Article 90(2) relates to all provisions mentioned in its first part, including those on free circulation.

(End of excerpt)

QUESTIONS

1   Do the competition rules have an 'effet utile'? What might it be? To what extent do the cases examined in this Chapter and Chapter 4 disclose a European notion of 'distortion of competition' which is the subject of supervision?

FURTHER READING

C. Bright, 'Article 90, Economic Policy and the Duties of Member States', *ECLR*, 6, 1993, p.263.

B. Van der Esch, 'Deregulation, Autoregulation et Le Regime de Concurrence non Fausse dans la CEE', *Cahiers de Droit Europeen*, 1990, p.499.

L. Gyselen, 'State Action and the Effectiveness of the EEC Treaty's Competition Provisions', *CMLRev*, 26, 1989, p.33.

A. Hoffman, 'Anti-Competitive State Legislation Condemned under Articles 5, 85 and 86 of the EEC Treaty: How far should the Court go after Van Eycke?', *ECLR*, 1, 1990, p.11.

A. Pappalardo, 'State Measures and Public Undertakings: Article 90 of the EEC Treaty Revisited', *ECLR*, 1, 1991, p.29.

P. Pescatore, 'Public and Private Aspects of Community Competition Law', *Annual Proceedings of the Fordham Corporate Law Institute*, 1987.

N. Reich, 'The 'November Revolution' of the European Court of Justice: Keck, Meng and Audi Revisited', *CMLRev*, 31, 1994, p.459.

P.J. Slot, 'Energy and Competition', *CMLRev*, 31, 1994, p.511.

6 Advertising and Commercial Free Speech

A. ADVERTISING, THE CONSUMER AND MARKET INTEGRATION

The first and obvious task of a manufacturer is to produce goods which will attract the interest of consumers. However, it has long been common for a marketing strategy to cover much more than simply the product in question. Advertising techniques are in effect part of the whole product package. Advertising is a form of consumer information. It is a method whereby the producer is able to explain to the consumer the purpose of the product. Equally it is a method whereby a producer might seek to distinguish his or her product in the eyes of consumers from that of a competitor. This may involve stressing quality differences or price variations, or it may involve attempts to impress the consumer in order to build consumer loyalty to a brand.

As a market is integrated across borders the producer will wish to export advertising and other marketing techniques along with the products themselves. In some areas, the development of a Europe-wide marketing strategy is likely to parallel the development of a Europe-wide production strategy. The market for advertising is in this sense simply another candidate for economic integration.

Is there a 'European' consumer at whom an integrated European marketing strategy may be directed? If the advertising industry believes the European consumer exists, that may begin to provide a justification for the Community institutions to respond by developing a common regulatory strategy.

THE ELUSIVE EURO-CONSUMER*

Ruth Schmidt and Elke Pioch

The Single European Market (SEM) has in theory been upon us for over a year now. The breaking down of barriers to trade has been driven by the desire to reap the benefits of greater economies of scale through supplying to a much enlarged marketplace of consumers. But is there really a single market to be supplied? Or, more precisely, is there such a thing as a Euro-consumer?

Commercial distribution, at the interface between suppliers and end users, has found even less attention than consumers in the SEM framework – the Commission asserts that distribution is by its very nature local in character and therefore does not warrant any specific EU wide legislation, apart from very limited cases.[1] Yet if distribution is assumed to be national, regional or local in character, is the same not likely to be true for the customers it serves? A number of marketing-led approaches have sought to address this and are explored below.

THE DEVELOPMENT OF EURO-BRANDS

Marketers have long been excited about the idea of a unified de-regulated market, as it consists of 340 million consumers, with an estimated consumer spend of $4.4 trillion in 1993.[2] However, the existence of 12 nation states, with nine key languages, 40 regional variations[3] and widely differing cultural values and traditions, casts doubt on the homogeneity assumed for a single market, thus posing a number of challenges as to how these differences can be overcome.

Nevertheless, multinational companies have for some time, predating the 1992 programme, tried to penetrate these diverse consumer markets, not least by launching new products across the whole of Europe. This increasing trend has been accompanied by the search for the identity of a putative Euro-consumer. Euro-brands have been described in various ways. Marketing, for example, defines a pan-European brand as one 'which is advertised in two or more European coun-

---

*   Previously published in *Consumer Policy Review*, **4**(1), 1994 pp.4–9; reprinted by permission of the author.
1   In 'Towards a single market in commercial distribution', *COM* (91) 41 final, 11 March 1991.
2   'The Myth of the Euro-consumer', *The Economist*, 4 November 1989.
3   V. Matthews, 'The EEC citizen is a nonsense in any language', *The Daily Telegraph*, 4 December 1989.

tries'.[4] This very wide definition means that a great variety of products could be included, with many differences in, for example, pricing, packaging and advertising at a local level. A narrower definition can be adapted from Keegan's definition of world brands, as cited by Castlelow and Doole: 'A world brand is...guided by the same strategic principles, is positioned the same in every market, and follows the same marketing approach in every market with the caveat that the marketing mix may vary'.[5]

Although the development of a successful Euro-brand has been described as the ultimate marketing nightmare, their numbers are increasing. Companies such as Ford, Mars, Swatch, British Airways and American Express all run European-wide campaigns.[6] Standardisation of products and packaging sizes are particularly common in the area of personal care products eg Gillette, Unilever.

It has been argued that, in the SEM, companies confining themselves to their home territories will find greatly increased competition for their customers. One way of addressing that challenge is by attempting to sell their products over a wider area to maintain sales volume.[7] Increasing sales of existing Euro-brands or introducing new ones to their merchandise portfolio is one option. However, the concept of pan-European brands predates 1992 and has to be seen in the wider context of the globalisation of industries, accompanied by global marketing strategies, of which Euro-branding can be regarded as a subset.

Jones and Ramsden[8] state that whilst during the '50s, '60s and '70s companies built their brands via a saturation strategy, in the '80s brand acquisition and increasing concentration on a multinational level was the key to success. They predict that growth in the 1990s 'will come from the much more complex task of managing an existing brand portfolio and doing so on an international or global basis'.

Advantages of globalisation, and likewise Euro-branding, include economies of scale in research and development, purchasing, manufacturing and marketing. This can be a crucial factor where the investment required for product development and innovation is such that it can only be recovered on a multinational scale. For the

---

4 'Marketing Eurobrands – Top Ten spending pan-European Brands; White Goods', *Marketing,* 23 April 1992. This identifies Moulinex as the company with the largest pan-European advertising expenditure.

5 D. Castlelow and I. Doole, 'Can global marketing strategies still meet the needs of local consumers?', 'Marketing in the new Europe and beyond Conference', Loughborough, *MEG* 1992.

6 P. Kierman, 'The European Promotion comes of age', *Marketing Week*, 18 September 1992.

7 A. Wolfe, 'The single European market: National or Euro-brands?' *International Journal of Advertising,* vol. 10, 1991.

8 B. Jones and R. Ramsden, 'Big-name products are increasingly flexing their muscles on the world market', *Management Today,* September 1991.

multinationals in 'power brands' developing are often bigger in their own right than the national subsidiaries. In theory, a virtuous cycle is created as: 'Innovation leads to brand growth and the power brand umbrella reduces the cost and risk of innovation, permitting an increase in its level and frequency'.[9]

The logic of Euro-branding clearly implies the need for quality information on a 'Euro-consumer' which would allow for more effective targeting of that potential customer base. Therefore the question needs to be addressed as to whether there is evidence of the existence of this elusive creature.

UNDERSTANDING THE EUROPEAN CONSUMER

Before engaging in more detailed discussion of existing approaches to classification and segmentation, the two main stands in the academic debate surrounding the putative existence of the Euro-consumer will be outlined briefly. Wolfe[10] and Treadgold[11] discount the idea of a Euro-consumer for the foreseeable future and stress that pan-European differences are more compelling than the similarities. Similarly, Reichel[12] maintains that EU consumers' preferences have not been Europeanised or internationalised. Reasons given for this are identified as language, history, climate, religion and work habits.[13]

The arguments of this group of authors have recently been supported by the findings of a 'European Lifestyles 1993' study published by Mintel.[14] Based on research conducted in seven major European countries, the study's findings highlight differences rather than similarities in spending and consumption patterns. For example, the British emerge as the least well-dressed, except where underwear is concerned; Belgians have the highest expenditure on food, drink and tobacco; and the Germans and the British are the most dedicated TV watchers. The report concludes that a typical Euro-consumer is unlikely to emerge for some time. A 1989 Henley Centre report came to the same conclusion,[15] pointing to the predominantly American, rather than distinctly European, roots of any commonalities in consumption and behaviour patterns, as evidenced in the pervasiveness of American

---

9   Ibid.
10   A. Wolfe, 'The single European market: National or Euro-brands?' Op cit.
11   A. Treadgold, 'The developing internationalization of retailing', *International Journal of Retail and Distribution Management*, vol. 18, no.2, 1990.
12   J. Reichel, 'How can marketing be successfully standardised for the European market?', *European Journal of Marketing*, vol. 23, no.7, 1989.
13   A. Wolfe, 'The single European market: National or Euro-brands?' Op cit.
14   N. Watt, 'Marketing Men Grapple with the Elusive Euro-Consumer – Mintel', *The Times*, 22 June 1993.
15   See V. Matthews, 'The EEC citizen is a nonsense in any language', Op cit.

feature films and McDonald's, for example. National differences are also identified by Purnell[16], who points out that expenditure on household appliances is very varied throughout the EU: British citizens are more likely to own a microwave oven than the German or the French but lag behind all other EU countries in terms of fridge and freezer ownership. Luxembourg leads in the dishwasher league, Germans have the highest level of car ownership and the Irish boast the highest concentration of pubs and off-licences.

In contrast, a range of studies believes to have detected a certain degree of pan-European convergence in consumer habits.[17,18,19] They have adopted a more pluralist view, that is they have not tried to identify the homogeneous Euro-consumer, but have allowed for various European consumer segments. Willis[20] summarises this view by denouncing the existence of a homogeneous market and arguing that the directional movement is more towards segmentation than singularisation.

The two main approaches followed by marketing practitioners and academics to establish the possible existence and characteristics of segments of Euro-consumers are the use of socio- and geo-demographic indicators on the one hand and that of psychographic measures on the other. Both are used to describe consumer groups on the basis of commonalities, using a range of variables as likely indicators of consumer behaviour. Furthermore they aim to establish tentative causal links between the characteristics measured and consumption behaviour thus offering predictive value to potential commercial users.

Socio- and geo-demographic trends and classification systems

Burt[21] argues that a certain degree of convergence across Europe can be identified in the form of a number of demographic, socio-economic and lifestyle trends associated with the development of a post-industrial society. These pan-European trends are identified as a decline in population growth, a changing age profile, an increase in unemployment and part-time labour, an increase in female employment, falling family size associated with declining birth rates and increasing numbers of divorce, plus a polarisation of household income distribution. However, whilst

---

16 S. Purnell, 'British are hot on microwaves', *The Daily Telegraph*, 6 March 1993.
17 'Marketing Futures – Nielsen; European Shoppers', *Marketing*, 1 November 1990.
18 S. Burt, 'Trends and Management Issues in European Retailing' (Section 1: The European Consumer), *International Journal of Retailing*, vol. 4, 1989.
19 C. Still, 'Ideas... and resourcing in 1992' *The Implications for Marketing, Advertising and the Media*, London: Economist Conference Unit, Rooster, 1989.
20 G. Willis, 'The single market and national marketing thinking', *European Journal of Marketing*, vol. 25, no.4, 1991.
21 S. Burt, 'Trends and Management Issues in European Retailing', Op cit.

these commonalities provide the common ground for analysis, local variations call for further segmentation of the market.

Historically, it could be argued that geographic subdivisions on the continent were always predominantly centred around regions rather than national borders. Due to the absence of strongly-defined natural boundaries, people in frontier regions traditionally had more in common with each other than they did with their fellow nationals in geographically-remote parts of the country. Common traits included local dialects, tastes and purchasing behaviour. It should also be remembered that 'nationality' may not always have been that clearly defined in border regions, which over the centuries may have changed hands frequently.

At the simplest level, European geo-demographic segmentation may make a north/south divide.[22] Looking at both geographical and lifestyle factors. Still quotes a Euriko study, whereby Spain, Italy and France share similar lifestyles and the Roman language. German-speaking Switzerland, Austria and West Germany are seen as aligned with the UK and the Scandinavian states. Alongside such geographical clusters, he stresses age as well as educational and economic groupings. He suggests that differences between the young are subsiding, and that wealthier and highly-educated Europeans share similarities.[23]

Others look at 'golden circles' of affluence and spending patterns which may overlap national boundaries.[24] Vandermerwe states:

> Instead of either one single homogeneous market or a collection of small specialized markets, the most likely model for the future mass Europe is a market... of regional Euro-clusters with customers geographically close but not necessarily living in the same country [and] the same or similar economic, demographic and/or lifestyle characteristics, which cut across cultural and national boundaries... Differences... will not be nationally determined... consumers in a cluster will be closer to each other in their purchasing tastes and behaviour than to consumers with the same national origin.[25]

Vandermerwe suggests a hierarchy of clusters ranging from regional mass clusters over regional niche clusters to local and specialised clusters.

A well established system encompassing both geo-demographic and behavioural lifestyle factors is the ACORN/MOSAIC system. Developed by CCN Marketing, MOSAIC was originally pioneered in the UK and now exists in 11 European markets. CCN has recently entered into partnership with a US software company for a

---

[22]   H. Bell, 'Special Report on Top European Advertisers: Advertisers' jeux sans frontières', *Campaign*, 27 November 1992.
[23]   C. Still, 'Ideas and resourcing', Op cit.
[24]   'The Myth of the Euro-consumer', Op cit.
[25]   S. Vandermerwe, 'A Framework for constructing Euro-networks', *European Management Journal*, vol. 11, no.1, March 1993.

joint launch of a European database marketing system. Despite initial difficulties in standardisation of raw data between countries, the development of pan-European classifications was pushed by national worries about the implications of EU data protection legislation. It was regarded as important to have an independent database in place before any potentially restrictive legislation could jeopardise such a venture. In addition multinational clients were increasingly looking for a common and consistent European based consumer targeting system.[26]

EuroMOSAIC identifies ten pan-European geo-demographic consumer types[27] but recognises differences between countries (e.g. Germany and Sweden exhibit more clear-cut divisions between city centre and suburb locations than the UK) and in purchasing behaviour:

> Fashion magazines and home computers will sell well in smart apartment districts in central Madrid. Lotteries and tobacco sell better in the suburbs of Bilbao. Hunting is popular among office workers in Orebro, whilst long haul holidays sell better in the smart single neighbourhoods of central Stockholm.[28]

Psychographic trends and classification systems

Whilst demographic and socio-economic trends give a broad indication of likely demand and consumption patterns it could be argued that consumer behaviour is at least as strongly influenced by consumer attitudes, opinions and values, as well as individual personalities. Burt argues that:

> The broad-scale changes taking place in attitudes and value structures amongst European society reflect a retreat from those found in the conflict-based hierarchical or 'pyramid' society of the industrial phase – in which roles and relationships are clearly defined – to those derived from the more variable and multidimensional relationships within the 'matrix' society of post-industrial Europe.[29]

As individualism increases, the market becomes more diverse. However, there are some similarities in the changes in attitudes observed across Europe. Gibson and Barnard identified five key consumer trends which result from the interaction of demographic, socio-economic, consumer lifestyle and activity changes –

---

[26] 'Geodemographics and Target Marketing: Will the Continent Catch On and Catch Up?', *MOSAIC Today*, Autumn 1993.
[27] These are: elite suburbs; average areas; luxury flats; low-income innercity; hi-rise social housing; industrial communities; dynamic families; low-income families; rural/ agricultural and vacation/retirement.
[28] CCN Marketing, 'EuroMOSAIC' (brochure).
[29] S. Burt, 'Trends and Management Issues in European Retailing', Op cit.

'wellness', 'home centredness', 'search for time, information and identity', 'expertism' and 'euro-ness'.[30] The latter is supported by Nelson[31] who sees the changing attitude towards open European citizenship as one of the key changes in attitude going hand in hand with the establishment of the single European market:

> people at the forefront of social trends no longer feel that they are citizens of one country, but often citizens of Europe or the world....There is a feeling of being able to belong to one's own country and at the same time to the world-wide space of modernity in all of its various facets – pop music, ethnic food, films, arts etc. One feels closer to people in other countries who share the same interests or tastes than to follow countrymen who do not.

Consequently, psychographic approaches are concerned with designing measures of consumer motivations which can be linked to purchasing behaviour. Most psychographic measures use an AIO (attitudes/interests/opinions) framework. The majority of national as well as European based typologies of this nature are in essence variations of the US VALS (Value Lifestyle) typology developed in the late '70's/early '80s. Such approaches may prove a very valuable addition to the socio-demographic systems discussed above. However, unlike them, psychographic analysis hardly ever starts from an existing database. This means that due to the resource implications involved in any methodologically rigorous attempt at a pan-European psychographic consumer typology, this work has largely been restricted to a few large commercial agencies.[32]

Two well-known psychographic classifications are the result of the work of the International Research Institute on Social Change (RISC) and of Europanel. RISC uses a longitudinal approach examining consumer response to change within Europe. Based on three central dimensions of change, 'individualism', 'hedonism' and 'flexibility', three key groups are identified and monitored. This establishes the basic framework for analysis, within which further segmentation is possible. By comparison, the Europanel typology makes use of a cross-sectional design to identify 16 distinct Euro-lifestyles, which can be plotted along three dimensions, labelled 'movement', 'value' and 'emotion'. The study concludes that the positioning of the Euro-styles is identical across all European nations but with differences in the percentage of the population classified under each style heading. In addition, Europanel are reported to have recently launched something called 'Eurawbase', which compiles European wide raw data on demographics, purchase frequencies and penetration levels on a basis which allows cross-country compari-

---

30   G. Gibson and P. Barnard, 'Consumer trends in the EC – how can retailers respond?', Section 4 in *Responding to 1992 – key factors for retailers*, Oxford: OXIRM, 1989.
31   E. Nelson, 'A diverging or converging community?', *Survey*, Spring 1990.
32   'Mafo-Instrumente fuer das Euromarketing', *Absatzwirtschaft*, May 1989.

son and aggregate analysis.[33] Within the same school of thought, advertising agency Horner Collis and Kirvan's 'Consumer Europe' lifestyle study identifies four main groups which are classified by psychological attitudes rather than demographics. They advocate a psychographic approach towards the assessment of the pan-European potential of brands.[34]

In addition to European-wide attempts at consumer typologies, a multitude of national lifestyle segmentation systems exist. The issue is further complicated by the diverse range of customer typologies developed for particular products and services, ranging from pubs to garden products.

But all this analysis is not without its detractors. Burt[35] questions the validity and reliability of lifestyle systems in view of the secrecy surrounding indicators and measures used in commercially developed typologies. This is confounded by a possible lack of theoretical underpinning:

> Notwithstanding these failings, the lifestyle literature focuses attention on those determinants of consumer behaviour and consumer activity other than simple economic and demographic criteria. Attitudes and values play an important role in influencing consumer activity. Furthermore these attitudes and values change over time and for different product markets. The wide range of schemes devised and numerous subgroups identified within consumer markets serve to emphasise fragmentation of the mass consumer market.[36]

IMPLICATIONS AND CONCLUSIONS

A Henley centre report discussed in the Financial Times[37] concludes that there is no single way of clustering consumers and that the appropriate clustering strategy depends on the issue under investigation. Thus the unitarist mass-marketing 'e pluribus unum' philosophy, using 'one sight, one sound, one sell', is increasingly replaced by pluralist micro-marketing strategies which rely on sophisticated market segmentation.[38]

Having identified clusters of Euro-consumer groups, what are the benefits for both the manufacturer and the customer? Vandermerwe[39] suggests that Euro-

---

33 'Research firms bump up Euro data services: Databases', *Marketing*, 1 July 1993.
34 'Psychology not demographics holds the key to the single European market', *Marketing Week*, 5 July.
35 S. Burt, 'Trends and management issues in European retailing', Op cit.
36 Ibid.
37 'Finding the definitive "Euroshopper" proves elusive', *The Financial Times*, 19 September 1991.
38 'The Myth of the Euro-consumer', Op cit.
39 S. Vandermerwe, 'A Framework for constructing Euro-networks', Op cit.

structuring, based on business customer and end-user demand for panEuropean goods, together with reliable country-to-country service, is beneficial for companies. This approach, based on an understanding of perceived customer needs, aims at maximising the performance of the whole system, rather than that of nation-based profit centres. This view is further supported by Jones et al:[40]

> 'The organisation whose centre is responsible for supervision and co-ordination, with country-based units retaining profit and loss responsibility, is built on the assumption that market differences are more important than similarities. The fast-moving innovator... while recognising that differences exist, will allow the similarities to guide decisions'.

Castelow and Doole arrive at the conclusion that:

> Very few examples of global marketing in fact demonstrate completely universal products, nor do they exhibit disregard for local consumer preferences and their evident success is probably based on this. What they do show is a recognition of those aspects of business activity which can benefit from a global approach. The importance of operating as an insider in markets is also evident. It can therefore be argued that global strategies can be responsive to customer needs if there is an acceptance that a global strategy may take many forms and it may well be only some aspect of a strategy that is purely global.[41]

In terms of the search for the elusive Euro-consumer this means that the striving for ever more sophisticated segmentation will continue. Global, and as a subset pan-European marketing, will expand attempts to segment from a national base to world- or European-wide proportions. For the individual European consumer it could mean greater choice and scope for individualism, as well as membership in a wider community of like-minded fellow-shoppers. However, the market-led approach to identifying Euro-consumers does not address issues such as customer protection issues in cross-border shopping nor does it per se encourage or facilitate such trans-frontier activities. If the consumer is to make use of the unified market, regulating safeguards have to be imbedded into the SEM framework.

(End of excerpt)

---

[40] B. Jones and R. Ramsden, 'Big name products are increasingly flexing their muscles on the world market', Op cit.

[41] D. Castelow and I. Doole, 'Can global marketing strategies still meet the needs of local consumers?', Op cit.

B. COMMUNITY LEGISLATION

In the early stages of the development of the European Community, the legal regulation of advertising was the preserve of national authorities just as the legal regulation of product markets was also principally a national matter. Driven by the process of market integration, European law has been obliged to develop an approach to advertising law just as it has developed an approach to general market regulatory law.

The Community has put in place a partial strategy for the regulation of advertising in the Community. Directive 84/450 controls misleading advertising. This Community strategy is described as only partial in two principal respects. First, it regulates only misleading advertising. There are other aspects of advertising which might be thought appropriate for Community intervention as part of the process of developing European regulatory strategies in supplement to or replacement for national measures. These other aspects are discussed further below. Second, much of the detailed implementation of the Community Directive rests with national procedures and will vary state by state. This is especially apparent in relation to enforcement. Accordingly, the regulation of advertising in the European Community is a responsibility shared between the Community and its Member States.

The following extract is from Directive 84/450 relating to the approximation of the laws, regulations and administrative provisions of the Member States concerning misleading advertising OJ 1984 L250/17.

Article 1

The purpose of this Directive is to protect consumers, persons carrying on a trade or business or practising a craft or profession and the interests of the public in general against misleading advertising and the unfair consequences thereof.

Article 2

For the purposes of this Directive:

1. 'advertising' means the making of a representation in any form in connection with a trade, business, craft or profession in order to promote the supply of goods or services, including immovable property, rights and obligations;
2. 'misleading advertising' means any advertising which in any way, including its presentation, deceives or is likely to deceive the persons to whom it is addressed or whom it reaches and which, by reason of its deceptive nature, is likely to affect their economic behaviour or which, for those reasons, injures or is likely to injure a competitor;

3.   'person' means any natural or legal person.

Article 3

In determining whether advertising is misleading, account shall be taken of all its features, and in particular of any information it contains concerning:

(a)   the characteristics of goods or services, such as their availability, nature, execution, composition, method and date of manufacture or provision, fitness for purpose, uses, quantity, specification, geographical or commercial origin or the results to be expected from their use, or the results and material features of tests or checks carried out on the goods or services;

(b)   the price or the manner in which the price is calculated, and the conditions on which the goods are supplied or the services provided;

(c)   the nature, attributes and rights of the advertiser, such as his identity and assets, his qualifications and ownership of industrial, commercial or intellectual property rights or his awards and distinctions.

Article 4

1. Member States shall ensure that adequate and effective means exist for the control of misleading advertising in the interests of consumers as well as competitors and the general public.

Such means shall include legal provisions under which persons or organizations regarded under national law as having a legitimate interest in prohibiting misleading advertising may:

(a)   take legal action against such advertising; and/or

(b)   bring such advertising before an administrative authority competent either to decide on complaints or to initiate appropriate legal proceedings.

It shall be for each Member State to decide which of these facilities shall be available and whether to enable the courts or administrative authorities to require prior recourse to other established means of dealing with complaints, including those referred to in Article 5.

2. Under the legal provisions referred to in paragraph 1, Member States shall confer upon the courts or administrative authorities powers enabling them, in cases where they deem such measures to be necessary taking into account all the interests involved and in particular the public interest:

–   to order the cessation of, or to institute appropriate legal proceedings for an order for the cessation of misleading advertising, or

–   if misleading advertising has not yet been published but publication is imminent, to order the prohibition of, or to institute appropriate legal proceedings for an order for the prohibition of, such publication, even without proof of actual loss or damage or of intention or negligence on the part of the advertiser.

Member States shall also make provision for the measures referred to in the first subparagraph to be taken under an accelerated procedure:

- either with interim effect, or
- with definitive effect,

on the understanding that it is for each Member State to decide which of the two options to select.

Furthermore, Member States may confer upon the courts or administrative authorities powers enabling them, with a view to eliminating the continuing effects of misleading advertising the cessation of which has been ordered by a final decision:

- to require publication of that decision in full or in part and in such form as they deem adequate,
- to require in addition the publication of a corrective statement.

3. The administrative authorities referred to in paragraph 1 must:

(a) be composed so as not to cast doubt on their impartiality;

(b) have adequate powers, where they decide on complaints, to monitor and enforce the observance of their decisions effectively;

(c) normally give reasons for their decisions.

Where the powers referred to in paragraph 2 are exercised exclusively by an administrative authority, reasons for its decisions shall always be given. Furthermore in this case, provision must be made for procedures whereby improper or unreasonable exercise of its powers by the administrative authority or improper or unreasonable failure to exercise the said powers can be the subject of judicial review.

Article 5

This Directive does not exclude the voluntary control of misleading advertising by self-regulatory bodies and recourse to such bodies by the persons or organizations referred to in Article 4 if proceedings before such bodies are in addition to the court or administrative proceedings referred to in that Article.

Article 6

Member States shall confer upon the courts or administrative authorities powers enabling them in the civil or administrative proceedings provided for in Article 4:

(a) to require the advertiser to furnish evidence as to the accuracy of factual claims in advertising if, taking into account the legitimate interests of the advertiser and any other party to the proceedings, such a requirement appears appropriate on the basis of the circumstances of the particular case; and

(b) to consider factual claims as inaccurate if the evidence demanded in accordance with (a) is not furnished or is deemed insufficient by the court or administrative authority.

Article 7

This Directive shall not preclude Member States from retaining or adopting provisions with a view to ensuring more extensive protection for consumers, persons carrying on a trade, business, craft or profession, and the general public.

Article 8

Member States shall bring into force the measures necessary to comply with this Directive by 1 October 1986 at the latest. They shall forthwith inform the Commission thereof.

Member States shall communicate to the Commission the text of all provisions of national law which they adopt in the field covered by this Directive.

Article 9

This Directive is addressed to the Member States.

Done at Brussels, 10 September 1984.

For the Council

The President

P. O'TOOLE

The Directive is based on some rather imprecise notions. For example, although the notion of 'misleading' is amplified in Articles 2(2) and 3 of the Directive, much will depend on the circumstances surrounding a particular advertisement. Article 4(1) refers to the unelaborated notion of 'adequate and effective means' for the control of misleading advertising. Therefore the application of the Directive will be in part dictated by national responses. However, even after implementation at national level, these notions remain strictly European in meaning and are subject to the interpretation of the European Court. It should not be assumed that traditional national interpretative techniques should be applied to them. Their European context is of vital importance to their proper interpretation. The European Court has had the opportunity to begin to develop a 'Europeanized' approach to these terms in Case C-373/90 *Procureur de la République* v. *X* [1992] ECR I-131.

Judgment

1   By a letter of 12 December 1990, which was received at the Court on 17 December 1990, the Juge d'Instruction (Examining Magistrate) at the Tribunal de Grande Instance (Regional Court), Bergerac, referred to the Court for a preliminary ruling under Article 177 of the EEC Treaty a question on the interpretation of Council Directive 84/450/EEC of 10 September 1984

relating to the approximation of the laws, regulations and administrative provisions of the Member States concerning misleading advertising (Official Journal L 250, p.17).

2 The question arose in the context of a complaint lodged against X, together with a claim for civil indemnity, by Jean-Pierre Richard, the Chairman of the Board of Directors of the Societe Richard-Nissan, which enjoys an exclusive importation contract for Nissan vehicles on French territory. The complaint, brought under Article 44 of French Law No 73-1193 of 27 December 1973 on the Orientation of Business and Crafts, known as the '*Loi Royer*', alleges untruthful and unlawful advertising.

3 The French legal provision in question was communicated by the French Government to the Commission as the legislative measure implementing the directive.

4 The complaint concerned a garage in Bergerac which placed display advertisements in the press with the words 'buy your new vehicle cheaper', followed by the words 'one year manufacturer's guarantee'. It transpires from the letter containing the reference that the advertising refers to vehicles imported from Belgium, registered for import purposes but never having been driven, being sold in France below local dealers' prices because Belgian basic models have fewer accessories than the basic models sold in France.

5 On those facts, the Examining Magistrate dealing with the dispute at the Tribunal de Grande Instance of Bergerac decided to stay the proceedings pending a preliminary ruling from the Court of Justice on the question 'whether such a marketing practice is in compliance with the European rules currently in force'.

6 Reference is made to the Report for the Hearing for a fuller account of the facts of the main proceedings, the course of the procedure and the written observations submitted to the Court, which are mentioned or discussed hereinafter only in so far as is necessary for the reasoning of the Court.

7 It should be recalled at the outset that, by a line of authority now well-established by the Court, the Member States' obligation arising from a directive to achieve the result envisaged by the directive and their duty under Article 5 of the Treaty to take all appropriate measures, whether general or particular, to ensure the fulfilment of that obligation is binding on all the authorities of Member States including, for matters within their jurisdiction, the courts, and that, in applying national law, the national court is therefore required to interpret it in the light of the wording and purpose of the directive in order to achieve the result pursued by the latter and thereby comply with the third paragraph of Article 189 of the Treaty (see Case 14/83 *Von Colson and Kamann* [1984] ECR 1891, paragraph 26, and Case C-106/89, *Marleasing* [1990] ECR I-4135, paragraph 8).

8 The national court's question must therefore be understood as asking whether or not Council Directive 84/450, referred to above, precludes advertising of the type at issue in the main proceedings.

9 As is clear from the preamble, this directive, adopted under Article 100 of the Treaty, aims to improve consumer protection and to put an end to distortions of competition and hindrances to the free movement of goods and services arising from disparities between the Member States' laws against misleading advertising. With those objectives in mind, it seeks to establish minimum and objective criteria as a basis for determining whether advertising is misleading.

10 Article 2(2) of the directive defines 'misleading advertising' as:

> 'any advertising which in any way, including its presentation, deceives or is likely to deceive the persons to whom it is addressed or whom it reaches and which, by reason of its deceptive nature, is likely to affect their economic behaviour or which, for those reasons, injures or is likely to injure a competitor'.

11 In interpreting this provision in relation to the features of advertising such as that at issue in the main proceedings, one must consider in turn the three claims made in the advertising, namely that the cars in question are new, that they are cheaper, and that they are guaranteed by the manufacturer.

12 Before embarking on such an examination, it should be emphasised that these aspects of the advertising are of great practical importance for the business of parallel car importers, and that, as the Advocate General has pointed out in paragraphs 5 and 6 of his Opinion, parallel imports enjoy a certain amount of protection in Community law because they encourage trade and help reinforce competition.

13 On the first point, concerning the claim that the cars in question are new, it should be noted that such advertising cannot be considered misleading within the meaning of Article 2 just because the cars were registered before importation.

14 It is when a car is first driven on the public highway, and not when it is registered, that it loses its character as a new car. Moreover, as the Commission has pointed out, registration before importation makes parallel import operations considerably easier.

15 It is for the national court, however, to ascertain in the circumstances of the particular case and bearing in mind the consumers to which the advertising is addressed, whether the latter could be misleading in so far as, on the one hand, it seeks to conceal the fact that the cars advertised as new were registered before importation and, on the other hand, that fact would have deterred a significant number of consumers from making a purchase, had they known it.

16   On the second point, concerning the claim that the cars are cheaper, such a claim can only be held misleading if it is established that the decision to buy on the part of a significant number of consumers to whom the advertising in question is addressed was made in ignorance of the fact that the lower price of the vehicles was matched by a smaller number of accessories on the cars sold by the parallel importer.

17   Thirdly and finally, regarding the claim about the manufacturer's guarantee, it should be pointed out that such information cannot be regarded as misleading advertising if it is true.

18   It should be remembered in this respect that in Case 31/85 *ETA* v. *DK Investment* [1985] ECR 3933 the Court held that a guarantee scheme under which a supplier of goods restricts the guarantee to customers of his exclusive distributor places the latter and the retailers to whom he sells in a privileged position as against parallel importers and distributors and must therefore be regarded as having the object or effect of restricting competition within the meaning of Article 85(1) of the Treaty (paragraph 14).

19   In answer to the question referred to the Court for a preliminary ruling it must therefore be held that Council Directive 84/450/EEC of 10 September 1984 must be interpreted as meaning that it does not preclude vehicles from being advertised as new, less expensive and guaranteed by the manufacturer when the vehicles concerned are registered solely for the purpose of importation, have never been on the road, and are sold in a Member State at a price lower than that charged by dealers established in that Member State because they are equipped with fewer accessories.

It seems probable that the Court's readiness to find that these practices fall outside the meaning of 'misleading' was to some extent motivated by the desire not to obstruct the cross-border 'parallel' trade in cars which was occurring in a sector notoriously fragmented along national lines. Paragraph 12 of the ruling deserves special attention. Clearly the European meaning of the terms of the Directive is strongly flavoured by the aim of market integration. Nonetheless, it should be appreciated that this decision is addressed not only to Member State authorities responsible for securing the implementation of the Directive, but also to parallel traders, who are given guidance as to their room for manoeuvre in planning a cross-border trading strategy.

The Court's capacity to set the terms for parallel trade by restricting the possibilities for state action under the Directive is to some extent limited by Article 7 of the Directive. This is the 'minimum harmonization' formula. It permits Member States to set stricter rules than those contained in the Directive should they so wish. Those stricter rules must be compatible with the Treaty. In so far as they impede the free movement of goods they must comply with Articles 30–36. In effect Directive 84/450 sets a floor of regulation, which all states must lay down, but the ceiling for state action is set not by the Directive but by the rules of primary Community law. The application of those Treaty rules then allows the Court to subject national regulatory initiatives to the control of the law of market integration.

The extension of Community intervention in this field has been on the agenda for many years. In fact the 1984 Directive emerged from more ambitious earlier proposals to regulate unfair advertising as well as misleading advertising, and to liberalize comparative advertising. The general perception in favour of Community action in the field is that disparity between national laws obstructs market integration and that accordingly Community laws are called for. However the Member States, which display a variety of techniques in the regulation of advertising, were unable to agree Community rules other than Directive 84/450. Other cross-border advertising was subject not to positive Community rules, but to national law applied subject to the law of market integration.

In 1991 the Commission issued a Proposal for a Council Directive concerning comparative advertising and amending Directive 84/450 on misleading advertising (OJ 1991 C180/14). In the Second Commission Three Year Action Plan for 1993–1995, 'Placing the Single Market at the Service of European Consumers' (COM (93) 378), adoption is presented as a priority. However the Council has not adopted legislation.

The Three Year Action Plan makes specific reference to the implementation of Directive 84/450 in all twelve Member States, but accepts that there are many problems in its application to transfrontier practices. It is a general theme that the European market has proved to be more readily integrated from the perspective of traders than from that of consumers. In Chapter 11, matters of access to justice are considered further.

Other Community legislative initiatives have touched on the advertising industry. Directive 89/552 OJ 1989 L298/23 coordinates national rules concerning the pursuit of television broadcasting activities. It is designed to liberalize the market for broadcasting and distribution of television services. As part of the regime established by the Community rules, Chapter IV of the Directive, Articles 10–21, regulates Television Advertising and Sponsorship; and Chapter V, Article 22, concerns the protection of minors. In both cases, controls over freedom to advertise are envisaged.

CHAPTER IV

Television advertising and sponsorship

Article 10

1.   Television advertising shall be readily recognizable as such and kept quite separate from other parts of the programme service by optical and/or acoustic means.

2.   Isolated advertising spots shall remain the exception.

3.   Advertising shall not use subliminal techniques.

4.   Surreptitious advertising shall be prohibited.

Article 11

1.   Advertisements shall be inserted between programmes. Provided the conditions contained in paragraphs 2 to 5 of this Article are fulfilled, advertisements may also be inserted during programmes in such a way that the integrity and value of the programme, taking into account natural breaks in and the duration and nature of the programme, and the rights of the rights holders are not prejudiced.

2.   In programmes consisting of autonomous parts, or in sports programmes and similarly structured events and performances comprising intervals, advertisements shall only be inserted between the parts or in the intervals.

3.   The transmission of audio-visual works such as feature films and films made for television (excluding series, serials, light entertainment programmes and documentaries), provided their programmed duration is more than 45 minutes, may be interrupted once for each complete period of 45 minutes. A further interruption is allowed if their programmed duration is at least 20 minutes longer than two or more complete periods of 45 minutes.

4.   Where programmes, other than those covered by paragraph 2, are interrupted by advertisements, a period of at least 20 minutes should elapse between each successive advertising break within the programme.

5.   Advertisements shall not be inserted in any broadcast of a religious service. News and current affairs programmes, documentaries, religious programmes, and children's programmes, when their programmed duration is less than 30 minutes shall not be interrupted by advertisements. If their programmed duration is of 30 minutes or longer, the provisions of the previous paragraphs shall apply.

Article 12

Television advertising shall not:

(a)   prejudice respect for human dignity:

(b)   include any discrimination on grounds of race, sex or nationality;

(c)   be offensive to religious or political beliefs;

(d)   encourage behaviour prejudicial to health or to safety;

(e)   encourage behaviour prejudicial to the protection of the environment.

Article 13

All forms of television advertising for cigarettes and other tobacco products shall be prohibited.

Article 14

Television advertising for medicinal products and medical treatment available only on prescription in the Member State within whose jurisdiction the broadcaster falls shall be prohibited.

Article 15

Television advertising for alcoholic beverages shall comply with the following criteria:

(a) it may not be aimed specifically at minors or, in particular, depict minors consuming these beverages;

(b) it shall not link the consumption of alcohol to enhanced physical performance or to driving;

(c) it shall not create the impression that the consumption of alcohol contributes towards social or sexual success;

(d) it shall not claim that alcohol has therapeutic qualities or that it is a stimulant, a sedative or a means of resolving personal conflicts;

(e) it shall not encourage immoderate consumption of alcohol or present abstinence or moderation in a negative light;

(f) it shall not place emphasis on high alcoholic consent as being a positive quality of the beverages.

Article 16

Television advertising shall not cause moral or physical detriment to minors, and shall therefore comply with the following criteria for their protection:

(a) it shall not directly exhort minors to buy a product or a service by exploiting their inexperience or credulity;

(b) it shall not directly encourage minors to persuade their parents or others to purchase the goods or services being advertised;

(c) it shall not exploit the special trust minors place in parents, teachers or other persons;

(d) it shall not unreasonably show minors in dangerous situations.

Article 17

1.   Sponsored television programmes shall meet the following requirements:

(a) the content and scheduling of sponsored programmes may in no circumstances be influenced by the sponsor in such a way as to affect the responsibility and editorial independence of the broadcaster in respect of programmes;

(b) they must be clearly identified as such by the name and/or logo of the sponsor at the beginning and/or the end of the programmes;

(c) they must not encourage the purchase or rental of the products or services of the sponsor or a third party, in particular by making special promotional references to those products or services.

2. Television programmes may not be sponsored by natural or legal persons whose principal activity is the manufacture or sale of products, or the provision of services, the advertising of which is prohibited by Article 13 or 14.

3. News and current affairs programmes may not be sponsored.

Article 18

1. The amount of advertising shall not exceed 15% of the daily transmission time. However, this percentage may be increased to 20% to include forms of advertisements such as direct offers to the public for the sale, purchase or rental of products or for the provision of services, provided the amount of spot advertising does not exceed 15%.

2. The amount of spot advertising within a given one-hour period shall not exceed 20%.

3. Without prejudice to the provisions of paragraph 1, forms of advertisements such as direct offers to the public for the sale, purchase or rental of products or for the provision of services shall not exceed one hour per day.

Article 19

Member States may lay down stricter rules than those in Article 18 for programming time and the procedures for television broadcasting for television broadcasters under their jurisdiction, so as to reconcile demand for televised advertising with the public interest, taking account in particular of:

(a) the role of television in providing information, education, culture and entertainment;

(b) the protection of pluralism of information and of the media.

Article 20

Without prejudice to Article 3, Member States may, with due regard for Community law, lay down conditions other than those laid down in Article 11(2) to (5) and in Article 18 in respect of broadcasts intended solely for the national territory which may not be received, directly or indirectly, in one or more other Member States.

Article 21

Member States shall, within the framework of their laws, ensure that in the case of television broadcasts that do not comply with the provisions of this chapter, appropriate measures are applied to secure compliance with these provisions.

CHAPTER V

Protection of minors

Article 22

Member States shall take appropriate measures to ensure that television broadcasts by broadcasters under their jurisdiction do not include programmes which might seriously impair the physical, mental or moral development of minors, in particular those that involve pornography or gratuitous violence. This provision shall extend to other programmes which are likely to impair the physical, mental or moral development of minors, except where it is ensured, by selecting the time of the broadcast or by any technical measure, that minors in the area of transmission will not normally hear or see such broadcasts.

Member States shall also ensure that broadcasts do not contain any incitement to hatred on grounds of race, sex, religion or nationality.

C. NATIONAL ADVERTISING REGULATION

The Community has made a start in developing a regulatory strategy for the integrated market. However, it is a familiar theme that the process of market integration has moved much more quickly than the process of Community regulation. Accordingly many cross-border advertising campaigns will be subject to several different national legal controls. The question which is addressed in this section is how far national powers to act against cross-border trade are affected by the law of market integration contained in primary Community law.

The case law of the Court acts as a demonstration of the flexibility inherent in the application of primary Community law to national measures which act as trade barriers. National regulation of marketing and advertising techniques which obstructs cross-border trade is compatible with Article 30 only where it is 'recognized as being necessary in order to satisfy mandatory requirements relating in particular to the effectiveness of fiscal supervision, the protection of public health, the fairness of commercial transactions and the defence of the consumer'. This phrase is drawn from the fundamentally important ruling of the European Court in Case 120/78 *Rewe Zentrale* v. *Bundesmonopolverwaltung fur Branntwein* – *'Cassis de Dijon'* – [1979] ECR 649. It then falls to the Court to determine whether particular national schemes meet this requirement. National market regulation is subject to the law of market integration, but within the law of market integration there remains scope for lawful national action even where that may cause impediments to trade. Accordingly the Court has composed a formula within which it tests national initiatives against the broader idea of market integration. It must, therefore, develop a European notion of the value of national initiatives in order to balance them against the objective of European market integration. This can be most effectively illustrated by examining selected case law of the European Court.

1. National laws as lawful trade barriers

Case 286/81 *Oosthoek's Uitgeversmaatschappij* [1982] ECR 4575

Under Dutch law it was forbidden to use particular types of inducement in product promotion. The consequence was that a firm which used such techniques in another Member State where they were permitted was forced to adopt a different strategy for the Dutch market. An integrated cross-border marketing strategy could not be pursued as a result of the disparity in national laws.

Although the Dutch rule acted as a trade barrier, potentially contrary to Article 30, it was motivated by the need to regulate the market in order to ensure free and fair competition. It fell to the European Court to determine how European law reflects these competing concerns.

Decision

1   By judgment of 9 October 1981 which was received at the Court on 3 November 1981 the Gerechtshof [Regional Court of Appeal], Amsterdam, referred to the Court of Justice for a preliminary ruling under Article 177 of the EEC Treaty a question on the interpretation of Articles 30 and 34 of the EEC Treaty in order to enable it to determine whether Netherlands legislation intended to restrict the freedom to offer or give free gifts within the framework of a commercial activity was compatible with Community law.

2   The question was raised in proceedings brought by the Netherlands company Oosthoek's Uitgeversmaatschappij BV (hereinafter referred to as "Oosthoek") against a judgment of the Arrondissementsrechtbank [District Court], Utrecht, imposing three fines of HFL 85 each on Oosthoek for infringement of the Wet Beperking Cadeaustelsel 1977 [Law on the restriction of free gift schemes].

3   Article 2(1) of that Law prohibits the offering or giving of products as free gifts within the framework of a commercial activity. There are, however several exceptions to that prohibition, in particular that provided for in Article 4(3) of the Law which permits a free gift to be offered or given provided that it is usually used or consumed at the same time as all the product in respect of the purchase of which it is offered or given (a criterion usually described as related consumption or use – in Dutch "consumptievet wantschap"), if it bears a mark which is indelible and clearly visible when it is used in the normal way and which clearly shows that it is intended for ad-

vertising purposes, and if its value does not exceed 4% of the sale price of all the products in respect of the purchase of which it is offered or given. Oosthoek markets in the Netherlands, in Belgium and in a small part of northern France, various encyclopaedias in the Dutch language, which are typeset and manufactured partly by Oosthoek in the Netherlands and partly by a company affiliated to Oosthoek in Belgium. Since 1974, in its newspaper and magazine advertisements and advertising brochures, Oosthoek has offered a dictionary, a universal atlas or a small encyclopaedia as a free gift to all subscribers to an encyclopaedia. Following the entry into force of the Wet Beperking Cadeaustelsel 1977 and in the light of that practice, proceedings were instituted against Oosthoek in the Netherlands for infringement of that Law.

4   According to Oosthoek, that practice is compatible with the provisions of the relevant Belgian legislation which, whilst it also prohibits the offering of free gifts for sales promotion purposes and provides for an exception similar to that contained in Article 4(3) of the Wet Beperking Cadeaustelsel 1977, does not make the application of that exception subject to compliance with the criterion of related consumption or use.

5   The Gerechtshof, Amsterdam, taking the same view as that taken by the Arrondissementsrechtbank, Utrecht, in the judgment contested in the main proceedings, considered that there was no related consumption or use, as required by Article 4(3) of the Wet Beperking Cadeaustelsel, in the case of encyclopaedias sold and the books offered as free gifts and that the sales promotion scheme operated by Oosthoek therefore constituted an infringement of that Law. However, since Oosthoek claimed that the Wet Beperking Cadeaustelsel 1977 was incompatible with Article 30 and 34 of the EEC Treaty, the Gerechtshof, Amsterdam, considered it necessary to request the Court to give a preliminary ruling on the following question:

6   "Is it compatible with Community law (especially with the principle of the free movement of goods) for a publisher who, by offering free goods in the form of books, seeks to promote sales of various reference works, which are intended for the entire Dutch-speaking area and originate partly in the Netherlands and partly in Belgium, to have to discontinue in the Netherlands that method of promoting sales, which is allowed in Belgium, owing to the Netherlands Wet Beperking Cadeaustelsel solely because that Law requires a relationship to exist between the consumption or use of the free gift and the product which constitutes the basis for the offering of the free gift?"

7   In its question, the national court seeks in substance to ascertain whether Articles 30 and 34 of the EEC Treaty preclude the application by a Member State to products from, or intended for, another Member State of national legislation which prohibits the offering or giving, for sales promotion purposes, of free gifts in the form of books to purchasers of an encyclopaedia

and requires, for the application of an exception to that prohibition, the existence of a relationship between the consumption or use of the free gift and the product sold.

8   In their observations, the Netherlands, German and Danish Governments express the view, *in limine*, that national legislation such as that at issue has no particular impact on intra-Community trade and does not fall within the scope of Articles 30 and 34 of the EEC Treaty.

9   In that regard, it must be stated that the application of the Netherlands legislation to the sale in the Netherlands of encyclopaedias produced in that country is in no way linked to the importation or exportation of goods and does not therefore fall within the scope of Articles 30 and 34 of the EEC Treaty. However, the sale in the Netherlands of encyclopaedias produced in Belgium and the sale in other Member States of encyclopaedias produced in the Netherlands are transactions forming part of intra-Community trade. In the view of the question raised by the national court, it is therefore necessary to determine whether provisions of the type contained in the Netherlands legislation are compatible with both Article 30 and Article 34 of the EEC Treaty.

10   Oosthoek maintains that the Netherlands legislation obliges it to adopt different sales promotion schemes in the various Member States which constitute a single market, involves it in additional costs and further difficulties and thus hinders the importation and exportation of the encyclopaedias in question. The requirement of related consumption or use is not justified by the need either to protect consumers or to safeguard competition.

11   The Commission considers that although the possibility that such a measure may indirectly hinder the importation of encyclopaedias cannot be ruled out, it is not contrary to Article 30 since it applies to all products without distinction and is justified by the objectives of consumer protection and organization of the economy.

12   In order to answer the question raised by the national court, it is necessary to consider the question relating to exportation separately from that relating to importation.

13   As regards exportation, Article 34 is concerned with national measures the aim or effect of which is specifically to restrict the flow of exports and thus establish a difference in treatment between the domestic trade of a Member State and its export trade, in such a way as to confer a particular advantage on domestic production or on the domestic market of the State in question. That is evidently not the position in the case of legislation such as that at issue as regards the sale in other Member States of the Community of encyclopaedias produced in the Netherlands. That legislation merely imposes certain restrictions on marketing conditions within the Netherlands without affecting the sale of goods intended for exportation.

14   As regards the restrictions on imports referred to in Article 30 of the EEC Treaty, it must be remembered that the Court has repeatedly held, since its judgment of 20 February 1979 in Case 120/78 *Rewe* [1979] ECR 649, that in the absence of common rules relating to marketing, obstacles to movement within the Community resulting from disparities between national rules must be accepted in so far as those rules, being applicable to domestic products and imported products without distinction, are justifiable as being necessary in order to satisfy mandatory requirements relating, *inter alia*, to consumer protection and fair trading.

15   Legislation which restricts or prohibits certain forms of advertising and certain means of sales promotion may, although it does not directly affect imports, be such as to restrict their volume because it affects marketing opportunities for the imported products. The possibility cannot be ruled out that to compel a producer either to adopt advertising or sales promotion schemes which differ from one Member State to another or to discontinue a scheme which he considers to be particularly effective may constitute an obstacle to imports even if the legislation in question applies to domestic products and imported products without distinction.

16   It is therefore necessary to consider whether a prohibition of a free gift scheme, such as that contained in the Netherlands legislation, may be justified by requirements relating to consumer protection and fair trading.

17   In that regard, it is clear from the evidence before the Court that the Wet Beperking Cadeaustelsel 1977 pursues a twofold objective which is, in the first place, to prevent the disruption of normal competition by undertakings which offer products as free gifts or at very low prices with a view to promoting the sale of their own range of goods and, secondly, to protect consumers by the attainment of greater market transparency.

18   It is undeniable that the offering of free gifts as a means of sales promotion may mislead consumers as to the real prices of certain products and distort the conditions on which genuine competition is based. Legislation which restricts or even prohibits such commercial practices for that reason is therefore capable of contributing to consumer protection and fair trading.

19   The question raised by the national court with regard to legislation of that kind concerns, in particular, the criterion of related consumption or use the purpose of which, in the present case, is to define the scope of one of the exceptions relaxing the rule which in principle prohibits the offering of free gifts.

20   Even though no such criterion has been incorporated in the laws of other Member States, and in particular that of Belgium, it does not appear to be unrelated to the above-mentioned objectives of the Netherlands legislation or, in particular, to the desire to achieve market transparency to the extent considered necessary for the protection of consumers and to ensure law trading. Accordingly, the incorporation of such a criterion in national legis-

lation in order to define the scope of an exception to a rule which prohibits the offering of free gifts does not exceed what is necessary for the attainment of the objectives in question.

21 The answer to the question raised must therefore be that Article 30 and 34 of the EEC Treaty do not preclude the application by a Member State to products from, or intended for, another Member State of national legislation which prohibits the offering or giving, for sales promotion purposes, of free gifts in the form of books to purchasers of an encyclopaedia and requires, for the application of an exception to that prohibition, the existence of a relationship between the consumption or use of the free gift and the product constituting the basis for the offering of the gift.

The problem which the Court had to confront in this case can be neatly captured in the phrase 'Market without a State'. The trader was attempting to operate on the basis of an integrated European 'Market'. But the existence of such a market is impeded by the absence of a single Community regulatory authority – a 'State' – with the result that there is a complex interplay between the development of the market, the lack of Community state and the persistent place of the regulatory choices of the Member States. The market then goes unregulated where Member State intervention is ruled incompatible with Article 30 and where the Community has not itself legislated; alternatively, where Member State intervention is ruled lawful under Article 30, the market is not fully integrated, nor can it be until the Community/state assumes regulatory competence in the field. The Court becomes a key player in this maze through its development of the law of market integration under Articles 30–36.

The next case is comparable to the ruling in *Oosthoek*. It too involves a finding by the Court that national regulation of marketing techniques is compatible with Article 30 despite the impediment to trade. It is Case 382/87 *Buet* v. *Ministère public* [1989] ECR 1235. French law prohibited 'doorstep selling'. This technique arises where the trader calls on the consumer unannounced to try to sell something. The perceived danger in such deals is that the consumer will be unprepared and underinformed and may be lured or pressured into a deal which he or she has not properly considered.

Judgment

1 By a judgment of 27 November 1987, which was received at the Court on 23 December 1987, the cour d'appel de Paris referred to the Court of Justice for a preliminary ruling under Article 177 of the EEC Treaty a question concerning the interpretation of Article 30 of the Treaty in order to enable it to determine whether a prohibition on canvassing in connection with the sale of educational material was compatible with that provision.

2   The question was raised in proceedings between the Ministère public and Mr Buet, the manager of the French company Educational Business Services (hereinafter referred to as 'EBS'). Representatives of that company went to the homes of potential clients for the purpose of selling them English language teaching material. EBS earned 90% of its turnover in this way and the remainder at trade fairs and exhibitions.

3   The tribunal de grande instance (Regional Court), Paris, sentenced Mr Buet to a term of imprisonment and a fine and held EBS liable in civil law for having infringed Article 8 II of Law No 72-1137 of 22 December 1972 on the protection of consumers with respect to canvassing and to selling at private dwellings (JORF, 23.12.1972, p.13348), which prohibits canvassing for the purpose of selling educational material. That provision was intended to supplement a prohibition of canvassing for the subscription to a contract of instruction contained in Article 13 of Law No 71-556 of 12 July 1971 on the establishment and functioning of private bodies providing home study courses and on advertising and canvassing by educational establishments (JORF, 13.7.1971, p.6907). Some of those establishments had attempted to circumvent that prohibition by proposing at private dwellings, not subscription to a contract of instruction, but the sale of educational material.

4   Mr Buet, EBS and the Ministère public appealed against the judgment of the tribunal de première instance. The essence of Mr Buet's contentions before the cour d'appel de Paris was that in the absence of pedagogical supervision by the vendor, the home sale of material for learning a foreign language did not fall under the prohibition of canvassing laid down in Article 8 II of the aforementioned Law No 72-1137. He also claimed that application of the prohibition on canvassing to his case was contrary to the provisions of Article 30 *et seq.* of the Treaty inasmuch as it forced him to abandon a particularly effective sales technique and thus restricted the marketing in France of products from another Member State.

5   The cour d'appel rejected Mr Buet's argument relating to the scope of the prohibition in question but nevertheless stayed the proceedings and requested a preliminary ruling on the compatibility with Article 30 of the Treaty of the prohibition of canvassing laid down in Article 13 of Law No 71-556 of 12 July 1971 and Article 8 II of Law No 72-1137 of 22 December 1972.

6   Reference is made to the Report for the Hearing for a fuller statement of the relevant legislation and the facts of the main proceedings, the course of the procedure and the written observations lodged before the Court, which are mentioned or discussed hereinafter only in so far as is necessary for the reasoning of the Court.

(a) The existence of an obstacle to the free movement of goods

7   As the Court held in its judgment of 15 December 1982 in Case 286/81 *Oosthoek* [1982] ECR 4575, the possibility cannot be ruled out that to com-

pel a trader either to adopt advertising or sales promotion schemes which differ from one Member State to another or to discontinue a scheme which he considers to be particularly effective may constitute an obstacle to imports even if the legislation in question applies to domestic and imported products without distinction.

8 That finding applies *a fortiori* when the rules in question deprive the trader concerned of the possibility of using not a means of advertising but a method of marketing whereby he realizes almost all his sales.

9 Application of a prohibition on canvassing in order to sell foreign language teaching material from another Member State must therefore be regarded as constituting an obstacle to imports.

(b) The possibility of justifying the obstacle in question by the need to protect consumers

10 The Court has consistently held (see primarily the judgment of 20 February 1979 in Case 120/78 *Rewe-Zentrale AG* v. *Bundesmonopolverwaltung für Branntwein* [1979] ECR 649) that in the absence of common rules, obstacles to movement within the Community resulting from disparities between the national rules must be accepted, provided the rules are applied without distinction to domestic and imported products, as being necessary in order to satisfy mandatory requirements such as the protection of consumers and fair trading.

11 It is common ground that the French legislature adopted the prohibition of canvassing in question out of concern to protect consumers against the risk of ill-considered purchases. However, as the Court has repeatedly held (see in particular the judgment of 14 July 1988 in Case 407/85 3 *Glocken GmbH* [1988] ECR 4233) such rules must be proportionate to the goals pursued, and if a Member State has at its disposal less restrictive means of obtaining the same goals, it is under an obligation to make use of them.

12 In that respect canvassing at private dwellings exposes the potential customer to the risk of making an ill-considered purchase. To guard against that risk it is normally sufficient to ensure that purchasers have the right to cancel a contract concluded in their home.

13 It is necessary, however, to point out that there is greater risk of an ill-considered purchase when the canvassing is for enrolment for a course of instruction or the sale of educational material. The potential purchaser often belongs to a category of people who, for one reason or another, are behind with their education and are seeking to catch up. That makes them particularly vulnerable when faced with salesmen of educational material who attempt to persuade them that if they use that material they will have better employment prospects. Moreover, as is apparent from the documents, it is as a result of numerous complaints caused by such abuses, such as the sale

of out-of-date courses, that the legislature enacted the ban on canvassing at issue.

14   Finally, it needs to be stressed that since teaching is not a consumer product in daily use, an ill-considered purchase could cause the purchaser harm other than mere financial loss that could be longer lasting. Thus it has to be acknowledged that the purchase of unsuitable or low-quality material could compromise the consumer's chances of obtaining further training and thus consolidating his position on the labour market.

15   In those circumstances it is permissible for the national legislature of the Member State to consider that giving consumers a right of cancellation is not sufficient protection and that it is necessary to ban canvassing at private dwellings.

16   Moreover, while the Council Directive of 20 December 1985 on the protection of consumers in respect of contracts negotiated away from business premises (Official Journal 1985, L 372, p.31) requires Member States to ensure that consumers have the right to cancel a contract of sale concluded at their home, Article 8 allows the State to adopt or maintain more favourable provisions to protect consumers. In the last recital in the preamble to the directive the Council expressly recognized that Member States might introduce or maintain a total or partial prohibition on the conclusion of contracts away from business premises.

17   In those circumstances the answer to the question submitted by the national court must be that the application to imported products of a prohibition on canvassing in relation to the sale of educational material, such as that laid down by the law on the protection of consumers with respect to canvassing and to selling at private dwellings, is not incompatible with Article 30 of the Treaty.

The first point to make is that there is Community legislation in the field. Directive 85/577 requires states to have in place certain controls over the practice of doorstep selling. These include the requirement that a consumer should have at least seven days after the conclusion of the contract within which to exercise a right to withdraw. France, however, had gone far beyond this level of consumer protection and had chosen to ban the practice altogether. As in *Oosthoek*, this impeded trade from other Member States where the practice was employed.

Directive 85/577 contains the minimum harmonization formula. Moreover its Preamble explicitly declares that states shall remain free to prohibit completely the practice of doorstep selling. It was accordingly clear that the Directive did not forestall the taking of further measures by France. This is itself of interest. Where the technique of minimum harmonization applies, even where the Community has acted in a field, the states remain free to set stricter rules compatible with the Treaty. The market may be regulated by two 'States'!

In *Buet*, the Directive set the floor of regulation, but the ceiling, above which a state could not regulate, was judged with reference to Article 30.

2. National laws as unlawful trade barriers

The next pair of cases follow basically comparable fact patterns to those in Cases 286/81 *Oosthoek* and 382/87 *Buet*. National market regulation collides with the process of European market integration. However, the result of the following two cases is quite different. In these two cases the Court is not prepared to accept that the national laws pursue objectives of sufficient weight to defeat the process of market integration.

In Case C-362/88 *GB-INNO* v. *CCL* [1990] ECR I-667 a Belgian trader was unable to penetrate the Luxembourg market because of restrictive rules imposed in Luxembourg. The Luxembourg laws prohibited the types of price comparisons which the Belgian trader was accustomed to making as part of advertising campaigns commonly employed in Belgium.

Judgment

1   By judgment of 8 December 1988, which was received at the Court on 14 December 1988, the Cour de cassation of the Grand Duchy of Luxembourg referred to the Court for a preliminary ruling under Article 177 of the EEC Treaty a question on the interpretation of Article 30, the first paragraph of Article 31 and Article 36 of the EEC Treaty in order to enable it to assess the compatibility with those provisions of national legislation on advertising.

2   The question was raised in proceedings between the Confédération du commerce luxembourgeois (hereinafter referred to as 'CCL'), a non-profit-making association which claims to represent the interests of Luxembourg traders, and GB-INNO-BM, which operates supermarkets in Belgian territory, *inter alia* in Arlon, near the Belgian-Luxembourg border. The Belgian company had distributed advertising leaflets on Luxembourg territory as well as on Belgian territory and CCL applied to the Luxembourg courts for an injunction against the company to stop the distribution of those advertising leaflets. CCL claimed that the advertising contained in the leaflets was contrary to the Grand-Ducal Regulation of 23 December 1974 on unfair competition (*Mémorial* A 1974, p. 2392), according to which sales offers involving a temporary price reduction may not state the duration of the offer or refer to previous prices.

3   The presiding judge of the tribunal d'arrondissement (District Court), Luxembourg, competent for commercial matters granted the injunction, taking

the view that the distribution of the leaflets in question constituted a sales offer prohibited by the Grand-Ducal Regulation of 1974 and an unfair practice prohibited by the same regulation. The cour d'appel upheld the injunction, whereupon GB-INNO-BM appealed to the Cour de cassation. It argued that the advertising contained in the leaflets complied with the Belgian provisions on unfair competition and that it would thus be contrary to Article 30 of the EEC Treaty to apply to it the prohibitions laid down in the Luxembourg legislation.

4   The Cour de cassation stayed proceedings and submitted the following question to the Court of Justice for a preliminary ruling:

'Is a legislative provision of a Member State whereby the offering of goods for retail sale at a temporarily reduced price, other than in special sales or clearance sales, is permitted only on condition that the offers may not state their duration and that there may be no reference to previous prices contrary to Article 30, the first paragraph of Article 31 and Article 36 of the EEC Treaty, properly construed?'

5   Reference is made to the Report for the Hearing for a fuller account of the facts of the case, the course of the procedure and the observations submitted to the Court, which are mentioned or discussed hereinafter only in so far as is necessary for the reasoning of the Court.

6   As a preliminary point, an argument that was raised by CCL and the German and Luxembourg Governments calls for examination. That argument is to the effect that the provisions of Articles 30, 31 and 36 of the Treaty have no relevance to the subject-matter of the main proceedings, which solely concern advertising, not the movement of goods between Member States. Moreover, it is said, GB-INNO-BM sells its wares only on Belgian territory.

7   That argument cannot be accepted. The Court has already held, in its judgment of 15 December 1982 in Case 286/81 *Oosthoek's Uitgeversmaatschappij* [1982] ECR 4575, that legislation which restricts or prohibits certain forms of advertising and certain means of sales promotion may, although it does not directly affect trade, be such as to restrict the volume of trade because it affects marketing opportunities.

8   Free movement of goods concerns not only traders but also individuals. It requires, particularly in frontier areas, that consumers resident in one Member State may travel freely to the territory of another Member State to shop under the same conditions as the local population. That freedom for consumers is compromised if they are deprived of access to advertising available in the country where purchases are made. Consequently a prohibition against distributing such advertising must be examined in the light of Articles 30, 31 and 36 of the Treaty.

9   It is therefore clear that the question referred to the Court for a preliminary ruling concerns the compatibility with Article 30 of the Treaty of an obsta-

cle to the free movement of goods resulting from disparities between the applicable national legislation. It is apparent from the documents before the Court that the advertising of sales offers involving a price reduction and stating the duration of the offer and the prices previously charged is prohibited by the Luxembourg legislation but permitted by the provisions in force in Belgium.

10 The Court has consistently held that in the absence of common rules relating to marketing, obstacles to the free movement of goods within the Community resulting from disparities between national laws must be accepted in so far as such rules, applicable to domestic and imported products without distinction, may be justified as being necessary in order to satisfy mandatory requirements relating *inter alia* to consumer protection or the fairness of commercial transactions (see, in particular, the judgments of 20 February 1979 in Case 120/78 *Rewe* [1979] ECR 649, and of 26 June 1980 in Case 788/79 *Gilli and Andres* [1980] ECR 2071).

11 According to CCL and the Luxembourg Government, the two prohibitions in question – against stating the duration of a special offer and against specifying the previous price – are justified on the grounds of consumer protection. The purpose of the prohibition concerning the duration of the special offer is to avoid the risk of confusion between special sales and half-yearly clearance sales the timing and duration of which is restricted under Luxembourg legislation. The prohibition against allowing the previous price to appear in the offer is justified, they say, by the fact that the consumer is not normally in a position to check that a previous reference price is genuine. In addition, the marking of a previous price might exert excessive psychological pressure on the consumer. In substance the German Government shares that point of view.

12 That view is contested by GB-INNO-BM and the Commission, who point out that any normally aware consumer knows that annual sales take place only twice a year. As regards comparison of prices the Commission has submitted an overview of the relevant legislation in various Member States and concludes that, with the exception of the Luxembourg and German provisions, they all allow both prices to be indicated if the reference price is genuine.

13 The question thus arises whether national legislation which prevents the consumer from having access to certain information may be justified in the interest of consumer protection.

14 It should be observed first of all the Community policy on the subject establishes a close link between protecting the consumer and providing the consumer with information. Thus the 'preliminary programme' adopted by the Council in 1975 (Official Journal 1975, C 92, p. 1) provides for the implementation of a 'consumer protection and information policy'. By a Resolution of 19 May 1981 (Official Journal 1981, C 133, p. 1), the

Council approved a 'second programme of the European Economic Community for a consumer protection and information policy' the objectives of which were confirmed by the Council Resolution of 23 June 1986 concerning the future orientation of the policy of the Community for the protection and promotion of consumer interests (Official Journal 1986, C 167, p. 1).

15   The existence of a link between protection and information for consumers is explained in the introduction to the second programme. There it is stressed that measures taken or scheduled in accordance with the preliminary programme contribute towards improving the consumer's situation by protecting his health, his safety and his economic interest, by providing him with appropriate information and education, and by giving him a voice in decisions which involve him. It is stated that often those same measures have also resulted in harmonizing the rules of competition by which manufacturers and retailers must abide.

16   The introduction goes on to specify that the purpose of the second programme is to continue and intensify the measures in this field and to help establish conditions for improve consultation between consumers on the one hand and manufacturers and retailers on the other. To that end the programme sets out five basic rights to be enjoyed by the consumer, amongst which appears the right to information and education. One of the measures proposed in the programme is the improvement of consumer education and information (paragraph 9D). The part of the programme which lays down the principles which must govern the protection of the economic interests of consumers includes passages which aim to ensure the accuracy of information provided to the consumer, but without refusing him access to certain information. Thus, according to one of the principles (Paragraph 28(4)), no form of advertising should mislead the buyer; an advertiser must be able to 'justify, by appropriate means, the validity of any claims he makes'.

17   As the Court has held, a prohibition against importing certain products into a Member State is contrary to Article 30 where the aim of such a prohibition may be attained by appropriate labelling of the products concerned which would provide the consumer with the information he needs and enable him to make his choice in full knowledge of the facts (judgments of 9 December 1981 in Case 193/80 *Commission* v. *Italy* [1981] ECR 3019, and of 12 March 1987 in Case 178/84 *Commission* v. *Germany* [1987] ECR 1227).

18   It follows from the foregoing that under Community law concerning consumer protection the provision of information to the consumer is considered one of the principal requirements. Thus Article 30 cannot be interpreted as meaning that national legislation which denies the consumer access to certain kinds of information may be justified by mandatory requirements concerning consumer protection.

19 In consequence, obstacles to intra-Community trade resulting from national rules of the type at issue in the main proceedings may not be justified by reasons relating to consumer protection. They thus fall under the prohibition laid down in Article 30 of the Treaty. The exceptions to the application of that provision contained in Article 36 are not applicable; indeed, no reliance was placed on them during the proceedings before the Court.

20 Since Article 30 is applicable, there is no need to interpret Article 31 of the Treaty, which was also mentioned in the reference for a preliminary ruling.

21 The reply to the question posed must therefore be that under Article 30 and 36 of the EEC Treaty, properly interpreted, advertising lawfully distributed in another Member State cannot be made subject to national legislation prohibiting the inclusion, in advertisements relating to a special purchase offer, of a statement showing the duration of the offer or the previous price.

The Court's emphasis on the Consumer Policy Programmes is interesting from the constitutional point of view. Those Programmes are 'soft law' in the sense that they do not conform to the list of formal Community legal acts contained in Article 189 of the Treaty. Nonetheless the Court is prepared to draw on such partly informal sources in developing the law of market integration. Of more direct interest in the present context is the way in which the Court is shaping a model European 'informed consumer'. In this ruling the Court makes certain assumptions about the nature of a consumer in the European market. The consumer is to be informed in order to be able to make efficient and autonomous decisions. Therefore laws which suppress the provision of information, such as the Luxembourg law in issue, cannot serve the consumer. They fall foul of the law of market integration.

The decision is therefore an important boost in the integration of the market for information, which acts as a complement to the market for goods themselves. Public suppression of information is prohibited, thereby releasing private methods of providing information.

The next case is in essence a further application of the ruling in Case C-362/88 *GB-INNO* v. *CCL*. A German law introduced in 1986 prohibited advertisements in which individual prices were compared except where the comparison was not eye-catching ('blickfangmässig'). Rocher relied on Article 30 to challenge this restriction on its ability to develop an integrated cross-border marketing strategy. A preliminary ruling was sought by the Bundesgerichtshof. A summary of Case C-126/91 *Schutzverband gegen Unwesen in der Wirtschaft* v. *Yves Rocher* judgment of 18 May 1993 follows.

By order of 11 April 1991, which was received at the Court on 30 April 1991, the Bundesgerichtshof referred to the Court for a preliminary ruling a question on the interpretation of Articles 30 and 36 of the Treaty to establish the compatibility with those provisions of a national rule concerning commercial advertising.

That question had been raised in the course of a dispute between the Schutzverband gegen Unwesen in der Wirtschaft e.V., registered in Munich, and Yves Rocher GmbH, a subsidiary of the French company, Laboratoires de biologie végétale Yves Rocher. That dispute concerned an advertisement circulated by Yves Rocher comparing old and new prices for its products.

Prior to 1986, advertising by way of comparisons between the prices of the same undertaking was lawful provided that it was not unfair or liable to mislead the consumer. At the request of certain groups of retailers, the German legislature included in Article 6(e) of the Gesetz gegen den unlauteren Wettbewerb (Law on unfair competition) the prohibition of advertising in which individual prices are compared. That prohibition is intended to protect consumers and competitors against advertising by way of price comparison. Nevertheless, the prohibition laid down in Article 6(e) of the UWG is not absolute. A derogation is provided for price comparisons which are not "eye-catching" (*blickfangmässig*) as well as for advertising in catalogues.

The court stated that, in the absence of common rules relating to marketing, obstacles to the free movement of goods within the Community resulting from disparities between national laws had to be accepted in so far as such rules were applied to domestic and imported products without distinction and in so far as they could be justified as being necessary in order to satisfy mandatory requirements relating *inter alia* to consumer protection or the fairness of commercial transactions. However, as the Court had stated on numerous occasions, the rules had to be in proportion to the objective pursued.

The protection of consumers against misleading advertising was regarded by Community law as a legitimate objective, and it had therefore to be considered whether the national provisions were likely to achieve the intended objectives and did not go beyond what was necessary for that purpose.

In that respect, the Court noted that a prohibition of the kind in question in the main proceedings applied when the price comparisons were eye-catching, irrespective of whether they were correct or not. Thus, that prohibition did not apply to price comparisons which were not eye-catching. In the case in point, the advertising was not forbidden because of its alleged inaccuracy but because it was eye-catching. It followed that all eye-catching advertising using price comparisons was forbidden, whether it was true or false.

Moreover, the prohibition in question went beyond the requirements of the objective pursued in so far as it affected advertising that was in no way misleading and contained comparisons of prices actually charged; the latter could be extremely useful to enable the consumer to make his choice in full knowledge of the facts.

The Court stated that the prohibition of the type in question in the main proceedings was therefore not in proportion to the objective pursued.

With regard to the protection of fair trading, and consequently of competition, the Court stated that correct price comparisons, prohibited by a rule of the type in question, could in no way distort competitive conditions. On the other hand, a rule, the effect of which was to prohibit such comparisons, was liable to restrict competition.

The Court held:

> Article 30 of the EEC Treaty must be interpreted as rendering inapplicable legislation of Member State A which prohibits an undertaking established in that State and engaged in the mail order sale by catalogue or prospectus of goods imported from Member State B from advertising by means of prices when a new price is contrasted in an eye-catching manner with a higher price indicated in an earlier catalogue or sales prospectus.

The Court focuses on the way in which the law restricted the provision of accurate and useful information. It is clear that once again the Court was not prepared to accept that information suppression could be justified in the integrated market. It does, however, exclude from its ruling national action against information which is apt to mislead the consumer. This is permissible regulation of the market. Such measures fall within the scope of Directive 84/450, above.

Some of the implications of the ruling are examined in the next article, which has been translated from the German for this book.

COMMENT ON THE DECISION OF THE EUROPEAN COURT OF JUSTICE OF 18 MAY 1993, CASE C-126/91[*][1]

Norbert Reich

The outcome of the preliminary ruling issued in response to a question submitted by the Bundesgerichtshof (BGH – the German Federal Supreme Court), a question which dealt once again with the classic issue of the application of Article 30 EC to Member State marketing restrictions – here the prohibition of attention-grabbing price comparisons in catalogues in accordance with 6e I, II No. 2 of the *Gesetz gegen den unlauteren Wettbewerb* (UWG – German Unfair Competition Act) came as no real surprise to anyone: in the area of cross-border trade, the prohibition may no longer be applied, while with respect to purely 'national' factual situations, the ECJ acknowledged that it had no authority to decide. Here the BGH must either continue its tendency of interpreting 'attention-grabbing advertising' in a restrictive manner, thus gradually interpreting away the prohibition, or finally call for judicial review by the *Bundesverfassungsgericht* (BVerfG – the German Federal Constitutional Court) because of the unequal treatment which results from the 'reverse discrimination' against the German entrepreneur, in violation of Article 3 I of Germany's Basic Law.

Although both the direction and reasoning of the decision met with broad approval, several comments may be permitted to set its relevance for European law and consumer policy in a broader context:

1.   Several times now since its 1986 amendment the hybrid protective goal of 6e UWG has been the focus of a controversy which has not died out: on the one hand, the creation of an *abstract* deceptive situation, in order to overcome the supposed evidentiary difficulties in combating deception through price comparisons; on the other hand, the confounding of the attractive effect of any advertisement with a prohibition which is not clearly limited to the deception. While the ECJ within the framework of its proportionality examination finds the first line of reasoning to be legitimate – a very important finding for consumer protection – it rejects the second line of justification as disproportionate. The German legislature is reproached for equating the *attractive effect* of the (attention-grabbing) advertising with *deception*. In the ECJ's penetrating analysis, however, the prohibition of 6e is not, as

---

[*]   First published in *Verbraucher und Recht* 1993, pp.254–257, reprinted by permission of the author. Translation by John Blazek, Brussels.
[1]   *Schutzverband gegen Unwesen in der Wirtschaft* [Protective Association against Pernicious Economic Practices] v. *Yves Rocher GmbH*.

the German government argued, directed against the (abstract) deception, but rather in reality against the attraction, regardless of whether it rests on facts which are false or true.

2. This criticism of the confounding of sub-rationales which, taken cumulatively, are intended to justify a prohibition (something one unfortunately finds quite often in the UWG) was made even clearer in the closing arguments of French Advocate-General Darmon delivered on 15 September 1992. With biting irony he reproached the German legislature for prohibiting an advertisement precisely because it was designed to attract attention:

> We cannot conceal our puzzlement here. Without wishing to push paradox too far, couldn't one argue that it is precisely an advertisement's ability to attract attention which is the criterion of a good ad? After all, what good is an ad which *doesn't* attract attention? Isn't prohibiting an advertisement which captures one's attention equivalent to prohibiting advertising altogether? (Figure 44, NR)

3. Furthermore, the decision emphasizes the consumer's freedom to receive information precisely through the admission of attention-grabbing, non-deceptive price comparisons. Once again, the principle of freedom of choice – which has run through the decisions of the ECJ ever since the celebrated Cassis decision, and which the GB-INNO decision virtually elevated to the status of a fundamental right – is confirmed.

Following the decision, however, the reader is forced to ask how, despite the freedom of choice principle, the consumer can be protected against the undeniable danger of deception through what are, after all, frequently false price comparisons. The complaining consumer association or – as in this case – the association for promotion of trade interests (which rather fatuously calls itself the 'Protective Association against Pernicious Economic Practices'!) will frequently fail to meet the burden of proof. The ECJ recognizes this dilemma very clearly, but does not allow the legislature to make, as it were, a disproportionate 'preemptive' strike by equating the mere *probability* of deception with an abstract *factual situation* of deception. Instead the ECJ says that one must follow the path laid out by Article 6 of the Misleading Advertising Directive 84/450/EEC, with which the German legislature however asserts – contrary to the Community – that it does not have to comply, i.e. the introduction of a general *duty to provide substantiation* for assertions of fact contained in the advertisement, especially with respect to price reductions, health- or environment-related data, and so on. While the decisions of the BGH reflect an awareness of such easing of evidence, for example with respect to the unique position and price comparison advertising, it focuses primarily on competition protection, not consumer protection. Here it would be fully sufficient if this duty to provide substantiation were to apply not *vis-à-vis* competitors and trade associations, but only *vis-à-vis consumer associations*, so that they could use their standing to sue in the general interest more effectively than before. 'Protective Associations against Pernicious Economic Practices' would not be able to claim this privilege, since it would first be necessary to clarify whether their complaint did not itself constitute a 'pernicious practice' because it is improperly raised (see 13 V UWG).

4.   From the perspective of the advertising entrepreneur, the ECJ refers to yet another important principle: Community-law protection against being forced, through application of Member State advertising laws, to abandon an advertising and sales promotion system which 'the entrepreneur regards as particularly effective' (text number 10). Behind this stands a clear affirmation of the so-called 'country of origin principle', which however – as is implicitly assumed here, and as I have demonstrated in detail in another context – requires that the advertising in the country of origin – here France – also be conducted in a lawful manner. Otherwise, the Single Market could lead to a 'dumping' of protective standards, which is exactly what the ECJ wants to avoid with its careful review of proportionality and the express reference to the *Buet* decision (admissibility of a prohibition – backed by criminal sanctions – of door-to-door sales of educational materials).

5.   The ECJ does not examine the fair advertising practices aspect of the prohibition of attention-grabbing price comparisons, which played a role when the UWG amendment law was passed in 1986 for reasons of 'protecting small and medium-sized companies', although this aspect was not argued by the German government before the ECJ. And indeed, it is hard to see how the Community law, with its affirmation of a system of undistorted competition (Art. 3f EC), can allow a form of structural policy to be achieved via the UWG.

6.   In the future, the task of the German lawyer will be to review the UWG, together with the supplementary statutes and the differentiated judicial decisions, in order to identify where at least within the field of cross-border goods and – it must be added – services there exist disproportionate prohibitions which could not be justified either from the consumer perspective or from precisely-defined fair practices perspectives.

   This suspicion of a prohibition which cannot be justified under Community law exists generally for the special provisions of 6a-e UWG, which – except for the factual situation of progressive soliciting of customers in 6c UWG – contain 'abstract deceptive factual situations' which however cannot be examined in detail here. The same is true for the Rabattgesetz [Rebate Law]. But even the classical deception and unconscionability case law under 3,1 UWG must be examined more closely than before to see whether – for example, in the area of the parallel imports of motor vehicles through intermediaries as permitted under Community law – it measures advertising against an artificially established deception threshold, or regards comparative advertising which is *not* misleading to be an unconscionable 'reliance' when it makes a correct (!) reference to the bio-equivalence of the imitation preparation to the 'standard preparation' which is no longer protected by patent. The protection – emphasized perhaps somewhat optimistically by the ECJ – of the mature and well-informed consumer is steadily gaining ground against the model – still embraced by the German UWG – of the uninformed citizen, a model which above all serves as a pretext for restricting competition. Here, too, one sees that Community law is penetrating traditional reservations of the civil law of Member States, something they would be only too happy to ward off by employing the 'subsidiarity principle'.

(End of excerpt)

3. The Court's concept of unfair advertising – the development of substantive autonomous European legal rules

Decisions such as *GB-INNO* and *Rocher* have different resonances in different Member States. In states with well-developed controls over techniques such as comparative advertising, they will require a significant liberalization of national regulatory policy. This seems to be true of, for example, Germany. This emerges clearly from Reich's discussion in the previous extract. In other states, which already possess legal regimes which place little constraint on comparative advertising, the decisions will have relatively little direct impact. This is true of the United Kingdom.

That disparity is itself of interest. It shows that the Court is developing the scope of its concept of consumer protection in a manner distinct from that prevailing in at least some Member States. Its 'European' consumer will have some features in common with the view taken of the consumer in a national legal system, but in other respects the Court's consumer is capable of assuming a distinctive identity.

The four cases discussed above show that the Court is moving towards the development of a 'European consumer' whose interests are to be taken into account in assessing the legitimacy of national market regulation which impedes trade. That 'European consumer' was entitled to protection in *Oosthoek* and in *Buet*, but not in *GB-INNO* and in *Rocher*. As Reich asserts in the closing paragraph of the previous extract, the Court displays a certain conception of an informed consumer as a participant in the market. This is also reflected in the limited amount of Community legislation which exists in the field. In fact where the Court's rulings restrict the scope of national regulation they tend to act as a prompt to further discussion of the desirability of legislative intervention to set clearer Community rules. The *GB-INNO* ruling was a stimulus to further discussion of the value of a Community Directive on comparative advertising. A Commission proposal followed in 1991, although, as is mentioned above, the proposal has not secured adoption in Council.

One should be careful not to overstate the process of 'Europeanization' in this area. National laws remain in place, subject to the impact of Article 30, and those national laws vary significantly state by state. Questions of redress for consumers of improper advertising are notoriously 'under-Europeanized'. This is considered in Chapter 11 of this book.

There are limits to the extent to which the Court can elaborate a notion of the European consumer. The Article 30 cases which reach it arise directly out of national legislation adopted to protect the national consumer. In *Buet* the Court was concerned to examine the legitimacy of protection of the French consumer. Its ruling in favour of the French prohibition could be seen as odd in the sense that it upheld protective measures on behalf of French consumers which consumers in other Member States did not seem to need. This may be taken to mean there is *no* European consumer. In fact, it is more a reflection of the limits of the Court's role in applying 'negative law' under Article 30. It must judge national measures, which vary state by state, against a broader common standard. It cannot create a European consumer, but it can set a standard based on a notional 'European consumer' which then becomes part of the law of market integration which exercises control over national regulatory measures which restrict trade.

There is every likelihood that clashes will develop between the European Court's perception and those of national systems. From a strict constitutional standpoint, any clash must be resolved with reference to the principle of supremacy, which ensures the primacy of Community law over national law in the event of conflict in an area of Community competence. However, the practical operation of this hierarchy will require close attention. More subtly, the problems of reconciling European economic law with national law will deepen where there are significant fundamental conceptual differences between the systems in their appreciation of the role of the consumer in the market. The German law in *Rocher*, for which the European Court showed little regard, provides a glimpse of this potential for divergence. This issue is developed in the two extracts that follow, both of which have been translated from the German for this book. Meyer analyses the gulf between EC and German notions; Piper is severely critical of that gulf.

THE CONSUMER MODEL OF THE EUROPEAN COURT OF JUSTICE: TURNING AWAY FROM THE 'FLEETING CONSUMER'*

Alfred Hagen Meyer

CONSUMER MODEL

The degree of consumer protection that is required depends on the ideas one holds about consumers and their habits. Unlike German competition law, Community law has until now not been marked by an explicitly defined consumer model. Of course, a uniform European consumer model cannot exist outside the binding secondary Community law, for in the absence of a Community-wide binding regulation of deceptive advertising, it remains within the authority of the Member States to issue such competition regulations. The extent of consumer protection must nevertheless be oriented on the Common Market, since consumer protection is subordinated to the principle of free trade. While it is true that each given national consumer model is not replaced by a Community-wide model, in assessing the admissibility of import-restricting measures which employ labelling requirements, the national model can be qualified by the Community law in concrete cases. The question therefore arises as to what relevance threshold is permissible under Community law on misrepresentation dangers in connection with cross-border trade.

The degree of protection in cross-border trade can only be determined by focusing on the meaning and goal of the Community, above all on the objectives specified in the EEC Treaty, such as the four freedoms of the Common Market. The most important aid here is recourse to the law-making systems of the Community's Member States.

This recourse to the legal systems of the Member States is a consequence of the rudimentary development of Community law, and the resulting dynamic-teleological interpretation of the EEC Treaty by the European Court of Justice (ECJ), which orients itself on the meaning and goal of the Community, the Single European Market. To realize and strengthen the Common Market, the Court seeks, on a case by case basis and within the framework of the submission procedure or the Treaty violation procedure, to derive general legal principles for the Community from the legal systems of the Community's Member States. This generates a

---

*   First published in 'Das Verbraucherleitbild des Europäischen Gerichtshofes – Abkehr vom "flüchtigen Verbraucher"', *Wettbewerb in Recht und Praxis*, 1993, pp.215-224, reprinted by permission of the author. Translation by John Blazek, Brussels.

Community law interpretation with autonomous legal principles, which could be drawn retrospectively from the totality of the individual decisions. In this way, the Court mirrors the overall process of European integration.

Although the European Court of Justice may still not have pronounced in favour of any specific consumer model, a review of the Court's Cassis decisions on labelling and competition regulations nevertheless allows one to conclude that it has oriented itself on the model of the 'critical', not the 'fleeting' consumer. In the light of the model of an attentive and critical consumer which predominates in most Member States, this may not be surprising. Several cases decided by the Court support this conclusion.

THE 'MATURE' VERSUS THE 'FLEETING' CONSUMER

From the foregoing analysis, one may conclude that the Court orients its decisions on a critical and attentive consumer, what others have referred to as a 'mature' or 'prudent' citizen. Leisner[1] accurately remarks here that the ECJ does not presuppose a consumer who contentedly sticks to his habits; rather, it demands that the consumer be open to new developments and willing to test critically statements made about products.

This is illustrated by the ECJ decision in the *Nissan* case [*Procureur de la Republique* v. *X*]. In the conception of the ECJ, a parallel importer would have a duty to point out explicitly the lower level of equipment of the imported vehicle only if it can be demonstrated that, at the moment of the purchase decision, a significant part of the targeted consumer group was actually labouring under a mistaken impression on this point. The national and the supranational European consumer models thus diverge not only on the requirements about the burden of proof for establishing the existence of deception, but also on the prerequisites for the relevance threshold on dangers of misrepresentation.

The consumer model employed by German national competition law is the so-called 'fleeting consumer', the person who perceives advertising statements in a casual and uncritical manner. The justification given for this is that in fact commercial announcements directed at the general public are rarely read with either attention or a critical eye as to their contents. A fleeting observer would be incapable of making a precise, complete and critical assessment of the advertising data, nor could he subject them to grammatical or philological reflection. In substantive law terms, the intent is to protect underprivileged classes of consumers. The particular stringency of the German competition case law is often met with incomprehension. The ECJ's *Bocksbeutel* decision quotes one of the participants in the procedure who described the model adopted in German competition law decisions

---

[1]   Walter Leisner, 'Der mündige Verbraucher in der Rechtsprechung des EuGH', *EuZW*, 1991, pp.498.

as that of an '*absolutely immature, almost pathologically stupid and negligently inattentive average consumer*'.

The model of the 'fleeting consumer' is not undisputed. Recently, an increasing number of voices have called for German competition law to adapt to European legal developments. After Keilholz[2] – following the Directive on deceptive advertising issued in 1984 – prematurely concluded that the high prohibition level of German competition law decisions was obsolete, Streinz (in a lecture published in 1991 taking a broad view of future legal developments) asserted that, in view of the *Cassis* decision of the European Court of Justice, it would be necessary to modify German national consumer expectations. Until now, however, these voices have remained largely ignored in the literature and judicial decisions.

EFFECTS AND SUMMARY

The normative stabilization of received consumer notions about low levels of misrepresentation which characterizes German competition law makes it necessary to shut off the national market from foreign products and marketing systems. The stringency of the German advertising law, which is unequalled in other parts of Europe, could force advertisers to orient the form and content of their advertising – regardless of the requirements of their own national market regulations – on the requirements of the advertising law in Germany. This runs contrary to the penetration of the national markets which is necessary for creating a single European market.

Accordingly, to establish the permissible limits of advertising within the Single Market, we must resolve the central question: what consumer model will be used to set the standard for defining the danger of deception? Analysis of the relevant case law of the ECJ and the resultant parameters of admissible advertising restrictions show that the ECJ's decisions employ the model of the critical and attentive consumer. Providing information to the consumer takes precedence over provisions offering substantive protection. In the view of the ECJ, in order to protect the consumer it is generally sufficient to provide for suitable labelling with respect to the type, contents and properties of the product being sold (so-called 'appropriate labelling'). The labelling of a product thus receives indirectly an informative function, because the consumer is called upon to develop a clear notion about the range of European products by inspecting and comparing labels. The 'fleeting consumer' merely preserves his prejudices against foreign goods, and thus runs counter to an effective realization of the Single European Market.

(End of excerpt)

---

2   Kurt Keilholz, 'Die mißlungene Harmonisierung des Verbots der irreführenden Werbung in der EG und ihre Konsequenzen für die deutsche Rechtsprechung', *GRUR int*, 1987, pp.390.

THE EFFECTS OF THE EC SINGLE MARKET ON GERMANY'S UNFAIR COMPETITION LAW*

Henning Piper

In its decision of 5 December 1991, Germany's *Bundesgerichtshof* (the BGH – Federal Supreme Court) announced that it is deceptive to advertise on the domestic market imported motor vehicles which were manufactured abroad for a foreign market, and which feature equipment and furnishings of lesser value than do vehicles that the same manufacturer produced for the domestic market, unless this lesser value is explicitly mentioned within the advertisement. The rationale behind this decision is that, absent such notice, consumers will generally assume that the vehicles being advertised have the same quality equipment and furnishings as are otherwise offered on the domestic market.

This judgment of the Federal Supreme Court appears to be so self-evident that the decision would not even bear mentioning, were it not for the fact that the European Court of Justice (ECJ) a short time later, upon submission of a French court concerning a similar set of factual circumstances, rendered a different and far more limited decision. As in the legal dispute resolved by the BGH, the ECJ case involved vehicles which were manufactured for a foreign market and imported into the domestic market – in this case, manufactured in Belgium and imported into France – and were advertised as being cheaper – without making reference to the fact that they featured lower-value equipment than the domestic (i.e. French) models. The ECJ decided that such advertising could be described as deceptive only if a not-insignificant number of the consumers to whom the advertising was addressed could be demonstrated to have made their purchase decisions without knowing that the lower price was due to the inferior equipment of the vehicles being offered by the advertiser. Thus, according to the decision of the ECJ, deception is only present if it was actually produced in the mind of the consumer and this is proven against the advertiser.

This decision is remarkable in several respects. First, the question arises as to whether it corresponds with the minimum requirements and criteria of the Misleading Advertising Directive 84/450/EEC of the Council. In its decision, of course, the ECJ starts from the definition of misleading advertising contained in Article 2 of

---

* First published in 'Zu den Auswirkungen des EG-Binnenmarktes auf das deutsche Recht gegen den unlauteren Wettbewerb', *Wettbewerb in Recht und Praxis*, 11, 1992, pp.685-91; reprinted by permission of Verlagsgruppe Deutscher Fachverlag GmbH, Frankfurt/M. Translation by John Blazek, Brussels.

the Directive. Yet the body of the opinion does not make clear that its decision actually corresponds to this definition. According to Article 2 of the Directive, an advertisement is deceptive not only when it actually deceives consumers (which was the only possibility referred to by the ECJ), but also when it is susceptible to mislead them.

As the use of the conceptual pair 'deception' and 'susceptibility to mislead' in the Misleading Advertising Directive shows, just as in cases under 3 of the *Gesetz gegen den unlauteren Wettbewerb* (UWG – the German Unfair Competition Act), it is sufficient for a finding of deception that there exist a concrete danger that such deception *might* occur. It is not of vital importance that such deception *actually* occur in the mind of the person targeted by the advertisement. It is thus altogether logical that Article 4 of the Directive does not expressly demand proof of actual loss or damage in order to challenge or prohibit such deceptive advertising.

There can be no doubt that a 'susceptibility to mislead' is intrinsic to any advertisement which offers new cars for sale at a 'cheaper price' without mentioning that the equipment these cars feature is of lesser value than that of the vehicles which are otherwise produced by the same manufacturer and offered on its domestic market. After the advertisement, the solicited consumer will generally have no reason to pose questions to the seller on this subject, and the (more or less accidental) possibility that the customer might learn of the difference during the sales discussions does not eliminate the susceptibility to mislead.

However, it is also unclear that – or why – the German advertising prohibition contained in 3 UWG in such a case – measured against the *Cassis-de-Dijon* decision of the ECJ – should be supplanted by operation of Article 30 of the EEC Treaty. This matter does not involve trimming back an excessive national protective standard (something which might be acceptable in the interest of harmonization) in favour of the free circulation of goods from the perspective of proportionality of means, or recourse to measures which are less restrictive of free trade. At issue is nothing more and nothing less than whether the prohibition of a concrete danger of deception, a prohibition which expresses Germany's legal culture and convictions as they have developed over a period of many years, may be inhibited in principle and generally in all cases of action in the field of commercial trade for purposes of competition on the basis of Article 30 of the EEC Treaty. The fact that the Council in 1984 held the creation of the Misleading Advertising Directive to be necessary, as well as the content of this Directive and its history, all argue against such an interpretation of Article 30, as does the basic idea behind the Treaty of giving great weight to the interest of consumer protection (see Article 100a, Para. 3, EEC Treaty).

Finally, one cannot view as desirable a harmonization which, even in a case such as that discussed here, puts the free circulation of goods ahead of competition law provisions of the individual Member States designed to protect consumers and ensure fair commercial practices. Such a harmonization runs contrary to both effective assurance of consumer protection and the requirements of fair commercial practices, as well as the necessity of interpreting Treaty provisions in such a way as to produce a balanced relationship between the Community and its Member States.

Of course, as already mentioned, harmonization of the laws should not and may not consist merely of placing one's own values as the basis of Community law judgments or legislation. What must be sought and found are consensus and balance in a legal order which, beyond mere loyal respect, is based on a conviction that the legal foundations supporting the Community are correct. However, this can only be achieved if the legal traditions of the Member States in their fundamental structures are recognizable within the legal order of the Community.

(End of excerpt)

4. A retreat in the control exercised by European law

The cases examined above proceeded on the basis that it had been shown that differences in national advertising laws restricted trade and that therefore it fell to the regulating state to show a justification for its rules. The nature of the trade barrier concerned can be understood from a reading of paragraph 15 in *Oosthoek*, paragraph 7 of *Buet* and paragraph 8 of *GB-INNO* v. *CCL*. The finding of such a barrier to trade then triggers the application of the law of European market integration which exercises control over national regulatory measures. However in its ruling in Joined Cases C-267 and C-268/91 *Keck and Mithouard* judgment of 24 November 1993 the Court has signalled clearly how important it is that a restrictive effect felt peculiarly by imports shall be shown to flow from the national rule in question. Only where that is shown will the Court be prepared to allow the invocation of Article 30.

Keck and Mithouard had resold goods at a loss in violation of a French law forbidding such practices. The two traders submitted that the law restricted the volume of sales of imported goods and that it therefore fell for consideration in the light of Article 30. It was, however, plain that any restrictive effect on trade affected all goods and not simply imports. The European Court commented on the increasing tendency of commercial parties to invoke Article 30 to attack rules which limit commercial freedom even where those rules are not directed at imported products. The Court, unusually and remarkably, declared that it would reexamine and refine its jurisprudence. The Court stated that

> the application to products from other Member States of national provisions restricting or prohibiting certain selling arrangements is not such as to hinder, di-

rectly or indirectly, actually or potentially, trade between Member States, provided that the provisions apply to all affected traders operating within the national territory and provided that they affect in the same manner, in law and in fact, the marketing of domestic products and those from other Member States.

In the absence of the necessary restrictive effect the Article 30 control does not apply. National market regulation is unaffected by Article 30 in such circumstances. This ruling sets limits to 'Europeanization' of trade regulation via Article 30. The ruling in *Keck and Mithouard* should also be considered in conjunction with that in Case C-2/91 *Meng*, examined in Chapter 5. The decisions have in common a reluctance to use European Economic Law to control matters which seem to be perceived by the Court to fall outside the proper scope of that law. It is an unresolved question whether these rulings represent a careful shift in the ambit of European Economic Law or whether, less ambitiously, they represent a pragmatic attempt by the Court to reduce the level of litigation by commercial parties making unmeritorious use of EC law as a 'last-resort'.

FURTHER READING ON THE IMPLICATIONS OF THE *KECK AND MITHOUARD* RULING

D. Chalmers, 'Repackaging the Internal Market', *ELRev*, **19**, 1994, p.385.
L. Gormley, 'Reasoning Renounced? The Remarkable Judgment in Keck & Mithouard' *European Business Law Review*, 1994, p.63.
M. Poiares Maduro, 'Keck: the end? the beginning of the end? or just the end of the beginning?', *Irish Jnl of European Law*, **1**, 1994, p.30.
N. Reich, 'The "November Revolution" of the European Court of Justice: Keck, Meng and Audi Revisited', *CMLRev*, **31**, 1994, p.459.

D. BEYOND THE ECONOMY: THE SCOPE OF COMMERCIAL FREE SPEECH IN EUROPE

Both Community legislation and the decisions of the European Court reveal an impetus in favour of the free flow of information, but there is no absolute right of commercial free speech recognized under Community law. On the legislative plane, advertising is controlled where it is misleading under Directive 84/450; and Directive 89/552 envisages, *inter alia*, the protection of minors from corrupting influences. As far as the European Court is concerned, cases such as *Oosthoek* and *Buet* demonstrate the continued validity of some national supervisory rules. *Keck and Mithouard* show that, absent the necessary restriction felt by imports in particular, national market regulation remains a matter untouched by Article 30.

Traders cannot invoke Community law of market integration as an indefeasible weapon for opening up markets throughout the Community. The market does not go totally unregulated. Commercial free speech is not absolute. Nevertheless, the application of Community law has reduced the scope for national action which obstructs cross-border advertising campaigns. States are obliged to find justification under Community law for rules which restrict trade. Commercial free speech is a powerful current.

1. Irish Abortion

The potential scope of Community law in this area was vividly demonstrated in Case C-159/90 *Society for the Protection of Unborn Children (SPUC)* v. *Grogan* [1991] ECR I-4685. This litigation arose against the background of the right to life of the unborn under the Irish Constitution. Thousands of Irish women travel annually to London to receive abortion services because they are unable to receive such services in Ireland. A Students' Union in Dublin provided information about services available in London. This practice was challenged before the Irish courts by SPUC. The Students' Union claimed that as a matter of Community law they were entitled to provide such information because it formed part of the cross-border provision of services, guaranteed under Articles 59–66 of the Treaty.

Accordingly, the essence of the claim was a right to commercial free speech under Community law which overrode national constitutional norms. Abortion is in any event a problem of ranking rights (of the mother, of the unborn child), yet Community law adds yet another right to the complex picture – the right of European economic integration.

In its ruling, the Court evaded the issue. It accepted that abortion was a commercial service, but observed that the Students' Union had no commercial interest in distributing information about the service available in another Member State. The Union provided the information with no intent to profit thereby. This was therefore not a question of *commercial* free speech and was untouched by Community law.

One can appreciate the Court's interest in avoiding ruling on such a sensitive issue. However, were litigation of this type to involve a *paid* advertisement, the Court would be unable to deny the commercial context. In such litigation, the economic process of European market integration would collide with moral choices made by one Member State. The Court would have to choose! Must a State surrender its moral preferences to free trade when it is out of step with the rest of Europe?

In *SPUC* v. *Grogan*, Advocate General van Gerven, in an Opinion which is rather braver than the ruling of the Court, would have resolved such a conflict by permitting the Irish rules to remain in place.

However, the very fact that in such circumstances a Court might find itself obliged to choose between competing interests in defining the scope of commercial free speech under EC law shows the depth of the intrusion of Community law into national life. The issue of defining the scope of commercial free speech under Community law has very far reaching implications. European *Economic* Law cannot be properly understood in a narrow sense!

This impression is deepened when it is realized that advertising need not simply be viewed as an economic process, but itself as a form of right of expression. This perception points towards a linkage between EC economic law and the protection afforded by the European Convention on Human Rights. The distinct motivations of the two systems render the linkage difficult to define. The next extract explores some of these issues in the context of the ruling in *SPUC* v. *Grogan*. The author identifies differences between the two systems, which, moreover, may be widened by the ruling. Immediately after the extract, attention is devoted to the subsequent ruling of the European Court of Human Rights which arose out of Irish abortion laws. Unlike the European Court in *Grogan*, the European Court of Human Rights was unable to evade the issue by relying on a non-economic context.

ABORTION, SPEECH AND THE EUROPEAN COMMUNITY*

Elisabeth Spalin

[...]

C. AVOIDING THE EUROPEAN CONVENTION ON HUMAN RIGHTS

The *Grogan* decision avoided facing the applicable European Convention on Human Rights provisions regarding both abortion and the freedom of expression issues presented in the case by construing the facts as "outside" of Community law under Article 59.

> 31. According to *inter alia*, the judgment of June 18, 1991 in *Elliniki Radiophonia Tileorasi* (Case C-260/89 *Elliniki Radiophonia Tileorasi* v. *Dimotiki Elairia Pliroforissis* (not yet reported). para. 42), where national legislation falls within the field of application of Community law the Court, when requested to give a preliminary ruling, must provide the national court with all the elements of interpretation which are necessary in order to enable it to assess the compatibility of that legislation with the fundamental rights – as laid down in particular in the European Convention on Human Rights – the observance of which the Court ensures. However, the Court has no such jurisdiction with regard to national legislation lying outside the scope of Community law. In view of the facts of the case and of the conclusions which the Court has reached above with regard to the scope of Articles 59 and 62 of the Treaty, that would appear to be true of the prohibition at issue before the national court.
>
> 32. The reply to the national court's second and third questions must therefore be that it is not contrary to Community law for a Member State in which medical termination of pregnancy is forbidden to prohibit students' associations from distributing information about the identity and location of clinics in another Member State where voluntary termination of pregnancy is lawfully carried out and the means of communicating with those clinics, where the clinics in question have no involvement in the distribution of the said information.

By inventing the new "economic interest of the speaker test" to distinguish Irish students from Belgian grocery stores, the Court was able to avoid (temporarily) applying European Community law to the problem of cross frontier reproductive consumer information. Because the economic interest of the speaker test is a new legal test, and finds no support in the Opinion of Mr. Advocate General Van Ger-

---

*   First published in *Journal of Social Welfare and Family Law*, **17**, 1992, pp.26–30; reprinted by permission of Sweet & Maxwell Ltd., London.

ven, the Court may not have had the opportunity to consider carefully the full implications of this strategy.

My thesis is that the new economic versus non-economic speech dichotomy of *Grogan* has inadvertently created conflicts between the European Court of Justice and the European Court of Human Rights on the question of whether freedom of expression is interpreted in conflicting manners under the European Convention on Human Rights and the European Community treaties. In trying to avoid the problems of a European Community system of open borders for medical services, the Court created legal dissonance regarding protections for freedom of expression between the two most significant European legal institutions. The Court may also have opened itself to collateral review by the European Convention institutions.

1. The ECJ and Human Rights Law

The problem of human rights arises in *Grogan* because SPUC asserted a derogation from the normal Community requirements of Article 59 open frontiers for advertising based upon the public policy protecting human rights for the unborn as codified in the Irish Constitution (the abortion problem). The problem of human rights was not avoided by the European Court of Justice in its Article 59 holding. Rather the Court simply swapped one human rights problem (abortion) for another (free expression). The *Grogan* case, therefore, presents a challenging situation in which to examine the boundaries between the European Community and its Member States on issues involving human rights. *Grogan* also presents the question of the boundaries between the European Community itself and a related European institutional system – the European Convention on Human Rights (ECHR).

It is commonplace to view the two European systems (Community and Convention) as quite separate and distinct. Traditionally the European Community is seen as primarily focused on economic matters and operates under a system normally characterized as "supranational" or "federal". The ECHR is seen as quite distinct on several important levels. It is a creature of the Council of Europe and operates as an international treaty under traditional doctrines of international law. Furthermore "Europe" as constituted by the ECHR includes as Contracting States several nations which are not Member States of the European Community. All Member States of the European Community, however, are also Contracting States under the ECHR.

The boundaries between the separate systems of the European Community and the ECHR are less sharply defined, however, than one might expect. As the *Grogan* case illustrates, the relationship between the two systems arises in two significant ways. First, the European Court of Justice has utilized the heritage of the ECHR in developing general principles of human rights law for the European

Community. Secondly, the ECHR itself provides legal forums for examining activities of Contracting States, which if acting under authorization of the European Community, could involve Community institutions or policies.

The development of human rights standards as part of European Community law by the Court is closely related to, and indeed arises in large measure out of, the German and Italian constitutional courts' resistance to the concept of the supremacy of European Community law in the absence of any substantive human rights limitations on Community institutions. "It is probably fair to say that the conversion of the European Court to a specific doctrine of human rights has been as much a matter of expediency as conviction." (Hartley 1988: 132). "The acceptance of an express doctrine of fundamental rights was prompted by the desire to persuade the German courts to accept the supremacy of Community law even in the case of an alleged conflict with the fundamental rights provisions of the [state constitution]." (Hartley 1988: 132).

Human rights as part of European Community law are generally accepted as applying to actions by European Community institutions. The question of whether human rights developed as part of European Community law apply to Member States raises quite different issues:

> [T]he Community concept of human rights has so far been applied only against the Community itself. Member States are not affected by it, though the same principles may be binding on a Member State on some other basis. The only exception is where the matter is covered by a provision of written Community law, such as a provision in one of the Treaties or in a regulation. In such case, the provision will be interpreted in the light of the Community concept.... Any derogations thus made by the national governments should not violate the Community concept of human rights. The reason is that, in derogating from the right, the Member States are acting under a power granted by the Community and are therefore subject to the same restrictions as the Community itself. (Hartley 1988: 138 to 139).

The primary concern of the Court, therefore, is jurisdictional. Allowing a Member State unilaterally to determine the scope of a public policy derogation based on human rights to a protected Community provision will undermine the supremacy of European Community law. Nor can the Court permit a Member State unilaterally to derogate from a human right because it could be claimed that the Member State is acting under authority from the European Community, particularly if a Treaty such as the European Convention on Human Rights were thereby to be violated. If the public policy derogation by a Member State were permitted by the Court and subsequently challenged under the European Convention on Human Rights, the effect would be to raise the European Court of Human Rights *above* the European Court of Justice.

The distinction between a human rights law developed by the European Court which applies to Community organs and one which applies to Member States is thus presented directly by SPUC's assertion of a public policy exception to Article 59. The key to analysing the action by a European Community institution versus action by a Member State dichotomy is to focus on the respective competences of the local and Community interests asserted, according to Weiler's analysis of the *Cinétheque/Klensch* line of cases:

> There are subject-matters which are predominately within an area which comes under the Community jurisdiction, even if incidental Member State action is not always barred. In these cases, it is submitted, the Court will have the power to review State action for violation of Community human rights. There are, by contrast, areas which are predominately within the jurisdiction of the Member States, even though incidental Community action, or control is not precluded. (Weiler, 1987: 827).

The Court would not be asked to review the entire Bavarian educational policy, or the entire French cultural policy, but only those measures which affect a Community fundamental freedom (Weiler 1988, 833). Similarly it would be possible to define the core area of Community competence as open borders, open frontiers for movement of persons seeking medical services and information regarding those medical services, without directly reviewing the entire Irish abortion policy.

When Ireland prohibits its own citizens from abortion medical services based on its view of public policy, it may or may not violate substantive ECHR standards. When Ireland erects a frontier to prevent its citizens from learning about British medical services, the European Community treaty provision is directly involved. If the Court permits Ireland to exempt itself out of Article 59 on the basis of local public policy, a subsequent case under the ECHR may be the subject of an Irish claim that the censorship was "authorized" by the ECJ.

2. Freedom of Expression

Grogan limits Article 59 to cross-frontier advertising in which the speaker has an economic interest. Article 10(1) ECHR, extends European protection to the freedom of expression including "to receive and impart information and ideas without interference by public authority and regardless of frontiers." This provision has been interpreted by the Commission of Human Rights as extending to economically motivated expression, and prohibiting state injunctions against such expression. (Van Dijk and Van Hoof 1990: 426 citing *Markt Intern Verlag and Klaus Beerman*, Report of 18 December, 1987, paras. 224–252).

Commercially motivated speech, however, is generally treated less favourably under the Convention than non-commercial expression (see Van Dijk and Van Hoof 1990: 425–427 and cases cited therein). Indeed the Convention has been interpreted repeatedly and very clearly by the Court and Commission on Human Rights as protecting "non-economic" speech at a higher level than economic speech.

> [I]t is essential in a democratic society that a pluralism of opinions including those which shock or offend is in principle recognized. In order to secure effectively the freedom of expression, any restrictions must be applied in a spirit of pluralism, tolerance and broadmindedness, in particular where freedom of expression in political matters is involved. (Van Dijk and Van Hoof 1990, 415–417 citing Lingens, Report of 11 October 1984. A. 103 (1986) p. 34.)

Assuming, *arguendo*, that the motivation of the Irish students was not "economic" but was primarily "political" then it arguably receives higher levels of protection under the Convention against state interference such as an injunction banning the speech. The Court decision in *Grogan* views the "economic" versus "political" speech hierarchy quite differently.

Thus even if Article 59 of the EEC itself is limited to "economic" speech, the *Grogan* court still needed to consider the applicability of Article 10(1) ECHR since this includes both "economic" and "non-economic" expression. Accepting *Grogan*'s second holding for the sake of this argument, having determined that Article 59 did not apply to the students' speech, that does not render the case "outside" of applicable European legal limits. The Court still needed to address the scope of Article 59 in the context of the Convention's provisions of Article 10, in the interests of harmonious interpretations between the European Community and the Convention. The Court also needed to address the Convention speech provisions to prevent SPUC from claiming the injunction was "authorized" action by a Member State under the European Community by the Court.

This difference of interpretation regarding speech protections also raises the possibility of the European Court on Human Rights sitting in review of the decision of the European Court of Justice in *Grogan*. If the Irish students now take their "non-economic" speech to the Human Rights Court, the European Court of Justice will have opened itself to collateral review. Although not free from difficulty, the current stance of the Court is to "incorporate" limits based, *inter alia*, on the ECHR where an organ of the European Community itself (or a Member State acting under the auspices of the European Community) may have violated human rights. It would be ironic indeed if the European Community organ alleged to have authorized a violation of human rights were to be the Court itself. If SPUC defends its version of the Irish standards by sheltering behind the Court decision in *Grogan* before the Court of Human Rights, it will indeed open a new chapter in the development of the European Community.

It would appear, however, that the better view of *Grogan* is not of the European court opening itself to possible collateral review by the Court of Human Rights, but rather of the Court's narrow construction of Article 59 speech as a method to delay the abortion state border conflicts until more classically "economic" facts are presented.

(End of excerpt)

The European Court of Human Rights ruling of October 1992 in *Open Door and Dublin Well Woman* v. *Ireland* (Case No. 64/1991/316/387-388) deserves attention in the light of the European Court's ruling in *Grogan* and the analysis provided above by Spalin. Irish court orders restrained the applicant counselling agencies from providing pregnant women with information concerning abortion facilities abroad. A violation of Article 10 of the Convention which governs freedom of expression was found by the European Court of Human Rights. The validity of the moral choice itself was not struck down, but the Court was unreceptive to the disproportionate nature of the control;

[...]

Was the restriction necessary in a democratic society?

64.   The Government submitted that the Court's approach to the assessment of the "necessity" of the restraint should be guided by the fact that the protection of the rights of the unborn in Ireland could be derived from Articles 2, 17 and 60 of the Convention. They further contended that the "proportionality" test was inadequate where the rights of the unborn were at issue. The Court will examine these issues in turn.

1. Article 2

65.   The Government maintained that the injunction was necessary in a democratic society for the protection of the right to life of the unborn and that Article 10 should be interpreted *inter alia* against the background of Article 2 of the Convention which, they argued, also protected unborn life. The view that abortion was morally wrong was the deeply held view of the majority of the people in Ireland and it was not the proper function of the Court to seek to impose a different viewpoint.

66.   The Court observes at the outset that in the present case it is not called upon to examine whether a right to abortion is guaranteed under the Convention or whether the foetus is encompassed by the right to life as contained in Article 2. The applicants have not claimed that the convention contains a right to abor-

tion, as such, their complaint being limited to that part of the injunction which restricts their freedom to impart and receive information concerning abortion abroad (see paragraph 20 above).

Thus the only issue to be addressed is whether the restrictions on the freedom to impart and receive information contained in the relevant part of the injunction are necessary in a democratic society for the legitimate aim of the protection of morals as explained above (see paragraph 63). It follows from this approach that the Government's argument based on Article 2 of the Convention does not fall to be examined in the present case. On the other hand, the arguments based on Articles 17 and 60 fall to be considered below (see paragraphs 78 and 79).

2. Proportionality

67.   The Government stressed the limited nature of the Supreme Court's injunction which only restrained the provision of certain information (see paragraph 20 above). There was no limitation on discussion in Ireland about abortion generally or the right of women to travel abroad to obtain one. They further contended that the convention test as regards the proportionality of the restriction was inadequate where a question concerning the extinction of life was at stake. The right to life could not, like other rights, be measured according to a graduated scale. It was either respected or it was not. Accordingly, the traditional approach of weighing competing rights and interests in the balance was inappropriate where the destruction of unborn life was concerned. Since life was a primary value which was antecedent to and a prerequisite for the enjoyment of every other right, its protection might involve the infringement of other rights such as freedom of expression in a manner which might not be acceptable in the defence of rights of a lesser nature.

The Government also emphasised that, in granting the injunction, the Supreme Court was merely sustaining the logic of Article 40.3.3 of the Constitution. The determination by the Irish courts that the provision of information by the relevant applicants assisted in the destruction of unborn life was not open to review by the Convention institutions.

68.   The Court cannot agree that the State's discretion in the field of the protection of morals is unfettered and unreviewable (see, *mutatis mutandis*, for a similar argument, the *Norris* v. *Ireland* judgment of 26 October 1988, Series A no. 142, p. 20, § 45).

It acknowledges that the national authorities enjoy a wide margin of appreciation in matters of morals, particularly in an area such as the present which touches on matters of belief concerning the nature of human life. As the Court has observed before, it is not possible to find in the legal and social orders of the Contracting States a uniform European conception of morals, and the State authorities are, in principle, in a better position than the international judge to give an opinion on the exact content of the requirement of morals as well as on the "necessity" of a "restriction" or "penalty" intended to meet them (see, *inter alia*, the *Handyside* v. *the United Kingdom* judgment of 7 December 1976, Series A no. 24, p. 22, § 48, and the *Müller and Others* v. *Switzerland* judgment of 24 May 1988, Series A no. 133, p. 22, § 35).

However this power of appreciation is not unlimited. It is for the Court, in this field also, to supervise whether a restriction is compatible with the Convention.

69.   As regards the application of the "proportionality" test, the logical consequence of the Government's argument is that measures taken by the national authorities to protect the right to life of the unborn or to uphold the constitutional guarantee on the subject would be automatically justified under the Convention where infringement of a right of a lesser stature was alleged. It is, in principle, open to the national authorities to take such action as they consider necessary to respect the rule of law or to give effect to constitutional rights. However, they must do so in a manner which is compatible with their obligations under the Convention and subject to review by the Convention institutions. To accept the Government's pleading on this point would amount to an abdication of the Court's responsibility under Article 19 "to ensure the observance of the engagements undertaken by the High Contracting Parties ...".

70.   Accordingly, the Court must examine the question of "necessity" in the light of the principles developed in its case-law (see, *inter alia, the Observer and Guardian* v. *the United Kingdom* judgment of 26 November 1991, Series A no. 216, pp. 29–30, § 59). It must determine whether there existed a pressing social need for the measures in question and, in particular, whether the restriction complained of was "proportionate to the legitimate aim pursued" (ibid).

71.   In this context, it is appropriate to recall that freedom of expression is also applicable to "information" or "ideas" that offend, shock or disturb the State or any sector of the population. Such are the demands of that pluralism, tolerance and broadmindedness without which there is no "democratic society" (see, *inter alia*, the above-mentioned *Handyside* v. *the United Kingdom* judgment, Series A no. 24, p. 23, § 49).

72.   While the relevant restriction, as observed by the Government, is limited to the provision of information, it is recalled that it is not a criminal offence under Irish law for a pregnant woman to travel abroad in order to have an abortion. Furthermore, the injunction limited the freedom to receive and impart information with respect to services which are lawful in other Convention countries and may be crucial to a woman's health and well-being. Limitations on information concerning activities which, notwithstanding their moral implications, have been and continue to be tolerated by national authorities, call for careful scrutiny by the Convention institutions as to their conformity with the tenets of a democratic society.

73.   The Court is first struck by the absolute nature of the Supreme Court injunction which imposed a "perpetual" restraint on the provision of information to pregnant women concerning abortion facilities abroad, regardless of age or state of health or their reasons for seeking counselling on the termination of

pregnancy. The sweeping nature of this restriction has since been highlighted by the case of *The Attorney General* v. *X and Others* and by the concession made by the Government at the oral hearing that the injunction no longer applied to women who, in the circumstances as defined in the Supreme Court's judgment in that case, were now free to have an abortion in Ireland or abroad (see paragraph 25 above).

74.   On that ground alone the restriction appears over broad and disproportionate. Moreover, this assessment is confirmed by other factors.

75.   In the first place, it is to be noted that the corporate applicants were engaged in the counselling of pregnant women in the course of which counsellors neither advocated nor encouraged abortion, but confined themselves to an explanation of the available options (see paragraphs 13 and 14 above). The decision as to whether or not to act on the information so provided was that of the women concerned. There can be little doubt that following such counselling there were women who decided against a termination of pregnancy. Accordingly, the link between the provision of information and the destruction of unborn life is not as definite as contended. Such counselling had in fact been tolerated by the State authorities even after the passing of the Eighth Amendment in 1983 until the Supreme Court's judgment in the present case. Furthermore, the information that was provided by the relevant applicants concerning abortion facilities abroad was not made available to the public at large.

76.   It has not been seriously contested by the Government that information concerning abortion facilities abroad can be obtained from other sources in Ireland such as magazines and telephone directories (see paragraph 23 and 27 above) or by persons with contacts in Great Britain. Accordingly, information that the injunction sought to restrict was already available elsewhere although in a manner which was not supervised by qualified personnel and thus less protective of women's health. Furthermore, the injunction appears to have been largely ineffective in protecting the right to life of the unborn since it did not prevent large numbers of Irish women from continuing to obtain abortions in Great Britain (see paragraph 26 above).

77.   In addition, the available evidence, which has not been disputed by the Government, suggests that the injunction has created a risk to the health of those women who are now seeking abortions at a later stage in their pregnancy, due to lack of proper counselling, and who are not availing of customary medical supervision after the abortion has taken place (see paragraph 26 above). Moreover, the injunction may have had more adverse effects on women who were not sufficiently resourceful or had not the necessary level of education to have access to alternative sources of information (see paragraph 76 above). These are certainly legitimate factors to take into consideration in assessing the proportionality of the restriction.

3. *Articles 17 and 60*

78. The Government, invoking Articles 17 and 60 of the Convention, have submitted that Article 10 should not be interpreted in such a manner as to limit, destroy or derogate from the right to life of the unborn which enjoys special protection under Irish law.

79. Without calling into question under the Convention the regime of protection of unborn life that exists under Irish law, the Court recalls that the injunction did not prevent Irish women from having abortions abroad and that the information it sought to restrain was available from other sources (see paragraph 76 above). Accordingly, it is not the interpretation of Article 10 but the position in Ireland as regards the implementation of the law that makes possible the continuance of the current level of abortions obtained by Irish women abroad.

4. *Conclusion*

80. In the light of the above, the Court concludes that the restraint imposed on the applicants from receiving or imparting information was disproportionate to the aims pursued. Accordingly there has been a breach of Article 10.

2. Commercial Free Speech

The extract from Spalin's article, p.282 above, concludes that the European Court in *Grogan* was concerned to delay deciding the conflicts in such a case until a more classically economic situation presented itself. The European Court of Human Rights opens up the 'market' for non-commercial speech in *Open Door*, but how does the Court of Human Rights view the role of Article 10 in the setting of commercial free speech?

The European Court of Human Rights has had relatively little opportunity to consider freedom of expression in the commercial context. The following judgment represents the most important statement by the European Court of Human Rights on the scope of commercial free speech under Article 10 of the Convention. Although no violation of Article 10 was found, this result was achieved only on the casting vote of the President, after the 18 judges were evenly divided. This confirms the complexity of the issue of defining the ambit of commercial free speech protected by law. The judgment below should be read for its own sake. It should also be read bearing in mind the question of whether the German law would be ruled compatible with EC law were it to be challenged on that basis.

In *Markt Intern and Beermann* v. *Germany* judgment of 20 November 1989 12 EHRR 161; Eur. Court H.R. Series A No. 165, the applicants were a publishing company and one of its editors. The company defends the interests of small and medium sized retailers against more powerful economic actors. For example, it supports test cases and lobbies. It sends out bulletins, in one of which it published the dissatisfaction of a consumer who had been unable to get reimbursement for cosmetics from a mail-order firm. The bulletin sought information from readers about the practices of the firm in question. A German court issued an order restraining repetition of the statements on the basis that they infringed the German Unfair Competition Act 1909. The applicants claimed that this violated Article 10 of the Convention governing freedom of expression. The judgment found that the rules on freedom of expression were in principle applicable to the circumstances of the case, but the following extract focuses on the approach to Article 10(2) of the Convention, which permits restrictions of the exercise of the freedom 'as are prescribed by law and are necessary in a democratic society...'

"Necessary in a democratic society"

32.   The applicants argued that the injunction in question could not be regarded as "necessary in a democratic society". The Commission agreed with this view.

The Government, however, disputed it. In their view, the article published on 20 November 1975 did not contribute to a debate of interest to the general public, but was part of an unlawful competitive strategy aimed at ridding the beauty products market of an awkward competitor for specialist retailers. The writer of the article had sought, by adopting aggressive tactics and acting in a way contrary to usual practice, to promote the competitiveness of those retailers. The Federal Court of Justice and the Federal Constitutional Court had ruled in accordance with well established case-law, having first weighed all the interests at stake (*Güter- und Interessenabwägung*).

In addition, in the field of competition, States enjoyed a wide discretion in order to take account of the specific situation in the national market and, in this case, the national notion of good faith in business. The statements made "for purposes of competition" fell outside the basic nucleus protected by the freedom of expression and received a lower level of protection than other "ideas" or "information".

33.   The Court has consistently held that the Contracting States have a certain margin of appreciation in assessing the existence and extent of the necessity of an interference, but this margin is subject to a European supervision as regards both the legislation and the decisions applying it, even those given by an independent court (see, as the most recent authority, the Barfod judgment of 22 February 1989, Series A no. 149, p. 12, § 28). Such a margin of appreciation is essential in commercial matters and, in particular, in an area as complex and fluctuating as that of unfair competition. Otherwise, the European Court of Human Rights would have to undertake a re-examination of the facts and all the circumstances of each case. The Court must confine its review to the question whether the measures taken on the national level are justifiable in principle and

proportionate (see, *inter alia*, the above-mentioned Barthold judgment, Series A no. 90, p. 25, § 55).

34.   In this case, in order to establish whether the interference was proportionate it is necessary to weigh the requirements of the protection of the reputation and the rights of others against the publication of the information in question. In exercising its power of review, the Court must look at the impugned court decision in the light of the case as a whole (see the above-mentioned Barfod judgment, Series A no. 149, p. 12, § 28).

Markt intern published several articles on the Club criticising its business practices and these articles, including that of 20 November 1975, were not without a certain effect (see paragraph 12 above). On the other hand, the Club honoured its promises to reimburse dissatisfied customers and, in 1975, 11,870 of them were reimbursed (see paragraph 20 above).

The national courts did weigh the competing interests at stake. In their judgments of 2 July 1976 and 31 March 1977, the Hamburg Regional Court and the Hanseatic Court of Appeal explicitly referred to the right to freedom of expression and of the press, as guaranteed by Article 5 of the Basic Law (see paragraph 15 and 16 above) and the Federal Constitutional Court, in its decision of 9 February 1983, considered the case under that provision (see paragraph 19 above). The Federal Court of Justice based its judgment of 16 January 1980 on the premature nature of the disputed publication and on the lack of sufficient grounds for publicising in the information bulletin an isolated incident and in doing so took into consideration the rights and legal interests meriting protection (see paragraph 18 above).

35.   In a market economy an undertaking which seeks to set up a business inevitably exposes itself to close scrutiny of its practices by its competitors. Its commercial strategy and the manner in which it honours its commitments may give rise to criticism on the part of consumers and the specialised press. In order to carry out this task, the specialised press must be able to disclose facts which could be of interest to its readers and thereby contribute to the openness of business activities.

However, even the publication of items which are true and describe real events may under certain circumstances be prohibited: the obligation to respect the privacy of others or the duty to respect the confidentiality of certain commercial information are examples. In addition, a correct statement can be and often is qualified by additional remarks, by value judgments, by suppositions or even insinuations. It must also be recognized that an isolated incident may deserve closer scrutiny before being made public; otherwise an accurate description of one such incident can give the false impression that the incident is evidence of a general practice. All these factors can legitimately contribute to the assessment of statements made in a commercial context, and it is primarily for the national courts to decide which statements are permissible and which are not.

36.   In the present case, the article was written in a commercial context; *Markt intern* was not itself a competitor in relation to the Club but it intended – legitimately – to protect the interests of chemists and beauty product retailers. The article itself undoubtedly contained some true statements, but it also expressed doubts about the reliability of the Club, and it asked the readers to report "similar experiences" at a moment when the Club had promised to carry out a prompt investigation of the one reported case.

According to the Federal Court of Justice (see paragraph 18 above), there was not sufficient cause to report the incident at the time of the publication. The Club had agreed to undertake an immediate investigation in order to clarify the position. Furthermore, the applicants had been aware that criticisms of the Club could not be fully justified before further clarification had been sought, as they themselves had described the reply of the Club as a provisional answer. In the opinion of the Federal Court they should therefore have taken into consideration that any such premature publication of the incident was bound to have adverse effects on the Club's business because it gave the specialised retailers an effective argument capable of being used against the Club with their customers, and one which could be used even if the incident should turn out to be an isolated mishap from which no conclusion could be drawn as to the Club's business policy.

37.   In the light of these findings and having regard to the duties and responsibilities attaching to the freedoms guaranteed by Article 10, it cannot be said that the final decision of the Federal Court of Justice – confirmed from the constitutional point of view by the Federal Constitutional Court – went beyond the margin of appreciation left to the national authorities. It is obvious that opinions may differ as to whether the Federal Court's reaction was appropriate or whether the statements made in the specific case by *Markt intern* should be permitted or tolerated. However, the European Court of Human Rights should not substitute its own evaluation for that of the national courts in the instant case, where those courts, on reasonable grounds, had considered the restrictions to be necessary.

38.   Having regard to the foregoing, the Court reaches the conclusion that no breach of Article 10 has been established in the circumstances of the present case.

The following dissenting Opinion deserves attention.

JOINT DISSENTING OPINION OF JUDGES GÖLCÜKLÜ, PETTITI, RUSSO, SPIELMANN, DE MEYER, CARRILLO SALCEDO AND VALTICOS

(Translation)

I.

In the field of human rights, it is the exceptions, and not the principles, which "[are] to be interpreted narrowly".[1]

This proposition is especially true in relation to the freedom of expression.

That principle constitutes "one of the essential foundations" of a democratic society ,[2] "one of the basic conditions for its progress and for the development of every man";[3] "it is applicable not only to 'information' or 'ideas' that are favourably received or regarded as inoffensive or as a matter of indifference, but also to those that offend, shock or disturb ...".[4]

"Due regard being had to the importance of freedom of expression in a democratic society",[5] any interference with it must correspond to a "pressing social need", "be proportionate to the legitimate aim pursued" and be justified on grounds which are not merely "reasonable", but "relevant and sufficient".[6]

In the present case these conditions, which the Court has affirmed on several occasions in previous judgments, were not satisfied.

In any event, in the light of the criteria which the Court has applied hitherto, the "necessity" of the measures taken against the applicants was not "convincingly established".[7]

It is just as important to guarantee the freedom of expression in relation to the practices of a commercial undertaking as it is in relation to the conduct of a head of government, which was at issue in the *Lingens* case. Similarly the right thereto must be able to be exercised as much in the interests of the purchasers of

---

[1] See *inter alia, Klass and Others* judgment, 6 September 1978, Series A no. 28, p. 21, § 42, and *Sunday Times* judgment, 26 April 1979, Series A no. 30, p. 41, § 65.

[2] *Handyside* judgment, 7 December 1976, Series A no. 24, p. 23, § 49; *Sunday Times,* cited above, p. 40, § 65; *Barthold* judgment, 25 March 1985, Series A no. 90, p. 26, § 58; *Lingens* judgment, 8 July 1986, Series A no. 103, p. 26, § 41; and *Müller and Others* judgment, 24 May 1988, Series A no. 133, p. 22, § 33.

[3] Above-mentioned judgments, *Handyside, loc. cit.; Barthold, loc. cit.; Lingens, loc. cit.;* and *Müller and Others, loc. cit.*

[4] Above-mentioned judgments, *Handyside, loc. cit.; Sunday Times, loc. cit.; Lingens, loc. cit.;* and *Müller and Others, loc. cit.*

[5] *Barfod* judgment, 22 February 1989, Series A no. 149, p. 12, § 28; see also *Barthold* judgment, cited above, *loc. cit.*

[6] Above-mentioned judgments, *Handyside,* p. 22-24, §§ 48–50; *Sunday Times,* pp. 36 and 38, §§ 59 and 62; *Barthold,* p. 25, § 55; *Lingens,* pp. 25–26, §§ 39–40; and *Müller and Others,* p. 21, § 32.

[7] *Barthold* judgment, cited above, p. 26, § 58.

beauty products as in those of the owners of sick animals, the interests at stake in the Barthold case. In fact, freedom of expression serves, above all, the general interest.

The fact that a person defends a given interest, whether it is an economic interest or any other interest, does not, moreover, deprive him of the benefit of freedom of expression.

In order to ensure the openness of business activities,[8] it must be possible to disseminate freely information and ideas concerning the products and services proposed to consumers. Consumers, who are exposed to highly effective distribution techniques and to advertising which is frequently less than objective, deserve, for their part too, to be protected, as indeed do retailers.

In this case, the applicants had related an incident which in fact occurred, as has not been contested,[9] and requested retailers to supply them with additional information. They had exercised in an entirely normal manner their basic right to freedom of expression.

This right was, therefore, violated in their regard by the contested measures.

II.

Having said this, we consider it necessary to make three further observations in relation to the present judgment.

We find the reasoning set out therein with regard to the "margin of appreciation" of States[10] a cause for serious concern. As is shown by the result to which it leads in this case, it has the effect in practice of considerably restricting the freedom of expression in commercial matters.

By claiming that it does not wish to undertake a re-examination of the facts and all the circumstances of the case,[11] the Court is in fact eschewing the task, which falls to it under the Convention,[12] of carrying out "European supervision"[13] as to the conformity of the contested "measures" "with the requirements" of that instrument.[14]

---

[8] § 35 of the judgment.
[9] Moreover it was not an "isolated" case (§ 36 of the judgment), because in 1975 the undertaking in question had to reimburse 11,870 of its clients (§§ 20 and 34 of the judgment).
[10] §§ 33 and 37 of the judgment.
[11] § 33 of the judgment.
[12] Above-mentioned judgments in *Handyside*, p. 23, § 49; *Sunday Times*, p. 36, § 59, and § 33 of the present judgment.
[13] Article 19 of the Convention.
[14] Judgment in the case "relating to certain aspects of the laws on the use of languages in education in Belgium", 23 July 1968, Series A no. 6, p. 35, § 10.

On the question of the need to "weigh the competing interest at stake",[15] it is sufficient to note that in this case the interests which the applicants sought "legitimately" to protect[16] were not taken into consideration at all.[17]

The rulings of the European Court of Human Rights in *Open Door*, involving Ireland, and in *Markt Intern*, involving Germany, extracted above, appear to have rather different emphases. That involving Ireland is significantly more rigorous in its assessment of national methods than that in the case originating in Germany. The two judgments (and the dissent in *Markt Intern*) present rather different perceptions of the appropriate scope of 'Europeanization'. It seems plausible that this difference is attributable to the commercial context which is present in the German but not the Irish case. Given the commercial element in *Markt Intern* the Court seems less prepared to deepen the application of Article 10. This seems to accord with Spalin's comment, p.282 above, that the European Convention lends more weight to freedom of expression where it has a non-commercial motivation.

3. Broadcasting

Broadcasting provides a further area in which to test the scope for the development of notions of freedom of expression, broadly construed, in European law (meaning both EC and ECHR law). European Community law in the field of broadcasting clearly recognizes the connection with the principles of the European Convention. This is plain in both legislative and judicial statements. The Preamble to Directive 89/552 on television broadcasting declares that:

Whereas this right as applied to the broadcasting and distribution of television services is also a specific manifestation in Community law of a more general principle, namely the freedom of expression as enshrined in Article 10(1) of the Convention for the Protection of Human Rights and Fundamental Freedoms ratified by all Member States; whereas for this reason the issuing of Directives on the broadcasting and distribution of television programmes must ensure their free movement in the light of the said Article and subject only to the limits set by paragraph 2 of that Article and by Article 56(1) of the Treaty.

Case C-260/89 *ERT* v. *Dimotiki* [1991] ECR I-2925 was considered in Chapter 5 of this book. The Court dealt with Greek restrictions on free movement of services in

---

[15] § 34 of the judgment.
[16] § 36 of the judgment.
[17] For the rest, we agree substantially with the arguments put forward in §§ 3 to 7 of the dissenting opinion of Judge Martens to which Judge Macdonald has given his approval (see pp. 21–23 below).

the broadcasting sector, *inter alia* with reference to Article 10 of the European Convention on Human Rights. Paragraphs 42-45 of the ruling deserve repetition in the present context.

42   As the Court has held (see the judgment in Joined Cases C-60 and C-61/84 *Cinethèque* v. *Fédération Nationale des Cinémas Français* [1985] ECR 2605, paragraph 25, and the judgment in Case C-12/86 *Demirel* v. *Stadt Schwäbisch Gmund* [1987] ECR 3719, paragraph 28), it has no power to examine the compatibility with the European Convention on Human Rights of national rules which do not fall within the scope of Community law. On the other hand, where such rules do fall within the scope of Community law, and reference is made to the Court for a preliminary ruling, it must provide all the criteria of interpretation needed by the national court to determine whether those rules are compatible with the fundamental rights the observance of which the Court ensures and which derive in particular from the European Convention on Human Rights.

43   In particular, where a Member State relies on the combined provisions of Articles 56 and 66 in order to justify rules which are likely to obstruct the exercise of the freedom to provide services, such justification, provided for by Community law must be interpreted in the light of the general principles of law and in particular of fundamental rights. Thus the national rules in question can fall under the exceptions provided for by the combined provisions of Articles 56 and 66 only if they are compatible with the fundamental rights the observance of which is ensured by the Court.

44   It follows that in such a case it is for the national court, and if necessary, the Court of Justice to appraise the application of those provisions having regard to all the rules of Community law, including freedom of expansion, as embodied in Article 10 of the European Convention of Human Rights, as a general principle of law the observance of which is ensured by the Court.

45   The reply to the national court must therefore be that the limitations imposed on the power of the Member States to apply the provisions referred to in Articles 66 and 56 of the Treaty on grounds of public policy, public security and public health must be appraised in the light of the general principle of freedom of expression embodied in Article 10 of the European Convention on Human Rights.

In November 1993, the European Court of Human Rights considered the impact of Article 10 of the Convention on public broadcasting monopolies in the case of *Informationsverein Lentia* v. *Austria* (Case No 36/1992/381/455-459). The Austrian monopoly was adjudged incompatible with the Convention.

38.   The Court has frequently stressed the fundamental role of freedom of expression in a democratic society, in particular where, through the press, it serves

to impart information and ideas of general interest, which the public is moreover entitled to receive (see, for example, *mutatis mutandis, the Observer and Guardian* v. *the United Kingdom* judgment of 26 November 1991, Series A no. 216, pp. 29-30, § 59). Such an undertaking cannot be successfully accomplished unless it is grounded in the principle of pluralism, of which the State is the ultimate guarantor. This observation is especially valid in relation to audio-visual media, whose programmes are often broadcast very widely.

39.   Of all the means of ensuring that these values are respected, a public monopoly is the one which imposes the greatest restrictions on the freedom of expression, namely the total impossibility of broadcasting otherwise than through a national station and, in some cases, to a very limited extent through a local cable station. The far-reaching character of such restrictions means that they can only be justified where they correspond to a pressing need.

As a result of the technical progress made over the last decades, justification for these restrictions can no longer today be found in considerations relating to the number of frequencies and channels available; the Government accepted this. Secondly, for the purposes of the present case they have lost much of their *raison d'être* in view of the multiplication of foreign programmes aimed at Austrian audiences and the decision of the Administrative Court to recognise the lawfulness of their retransmission by cable (see paragraph 21 above). Finally and above all, it cannot be argued that there are no equivalent less restrictive solutions; it is sufficient by way of example to cite the practice of certain countries which either issue licences subject to specified conditions of variable content or make provision for forms of private participation in the activities of the national corporation.

40.   The Government finally adduced an economic argument, namely that the Austrian market was too small to sustain a sufficient number of stations to avoid regroupings and the constitution of "private monopolies".

41.   In the applicant's opinion, this is a pretext for a policy which, by eliminating all competition, seeks above all to guarantee to the Austrian Broadcasting Corporation advertising revenue, at the expense of the principle of free enterprise.

42.   The Court is not persuaded by the Government's argument. Their assertions are contradicted by the experience of several European States, of a comparable size to Austria, in which the coexistence of private and public stations, according to rules which vary from country to country and accompanied by measures preventing the development of private monopolies, shows the fears expressed to be groundless.

43.   In short, like the Commission, the Court considers that the interferences in issue were disproportionate to the aim pursued and were, accordingly, not necessary in a democratic society. There has therefore been a violation of Article 10.

An attempt to develop a real 'European' law must involve an inquiry into how the two systems might work together. The European Court in *ERT* v. *Dimotiki* plainly envisages a congruence of approach and in many instances this will be readily achievable. There are indeed superficial similarities in that both EC law and the European Convention seem to embody a presumption in favour of freedom, yet neither EC law nor the European Convention recognize absolute rights. Limitations exist. However, there are divergences between the systems, which, after all, have different histories, different objectives and different institutions. If, as Spalin's examination suggests, it is correct to see *SPUC* v. *Grogan* as exposing a gulf between EC law and the European Convention, then the European Court's comments above in *ERT* v. *Dimotiki* may appear rather over-optimistic.

The European Court's quest to align EC law with Article 10 of the Convention will have to confront these tensions. This imposes on the European Court the task of accommodating political and social aspects of freedom of expression within the economic constitution envisaged by the EC Treaty. The forbidding complexity of that process may be measured by the Court's decision to 'escape' the need to rule on the merits of the case in *Grogan* via a very narrow 'economics only' focus. However, the potential exists in the future for litigation which will, unlike *Grogan*, have the required economic content and yet which will draw in the social and political aspects of freedom of expression which underpin Article 10 of the Convention. The European Court will then have to digest the European Court of Human Rights' jurisprudence under Article 10.

This tale stands as further confirmation of two overarching principles of this book. First, a real 'European' law is under construction. The EC and ECHR systems cannot be neatly demarcated one from the other. There are interlinking channels along which legal principles flow. The second and connected point is that 'Economic' law cannot be confined to a narrow commercial area alone. True, in individual cases such as *Grogan* limits may be imposed, but the impact of the economy on the structure of society and its moral choices means that a broader theory must be developed.

The potential for a harmonious development of a European law which draws on both European Community law and the law of the European Convention on Human Rights is reassessed in Chapter 12.

QUESTIONS

1   Divergent rules governing tobacco advertising in different Member States have prompted the Community to initiate a process of harmonization. Directive 89/622 OJ 1989 L359/1 is based on Article 100a. It concerns the labelling of tobacco products. For example, products must carry specified warnings. The

Directive was amended and extended to all tobacco products by Directive 92/41 OJ 1992 L158. In addition, Article 13 of Directive 89/552 provides that; 'All forms of television advertising for cigarettes and other tobacco products shall be prohibited.'

A Commission proposal in April 1992 (OJ 1992 C129/5) envisaged the introduction of a complete ban on advertising, except within tobacco retail outlets. This was based on Article 100a. The Council has not adopted the proposal and it is fiercely opposed by some Member States such as the United Kingdom.

Is Article 100a a valid base for the adoption of such legislation? What role might be played by Articles 129 EC (Public Health) and Article 129a EC (Consumer Protection), both introduced by the Treaty on European Union?

2   Would such legislation be susceptible to challenge for violation of the subsidiarity principle under Article 3b?

3   Would such legislation be susceptible to challenge for violation of rights of commercial free speech? If so, how?

FURTHER READING LIST

A. M. Collins, 'Commercial Speech and the Free Movement of Goods and Services at Community Law', in J. O'Reilly (ed.), *Human Rights and Constitutional Law*, Dublin: Butterworths, 1992.

P. van Dijk and G. van Hoof, *Theory and Practice of the European Convention on Human Rights*, 2nd ed., Deventer: Klüwer, 1990.

T. Hartley, *The Foundations of Community Law*, 2nd ed.

S. O'Leary, 'The Court of Justice as a reluctant constitutional adjudicator', *European Law Review*, **17**, 1992, p.138.

R. Pearce, 'Abortion and the Right to Life under the Irish Constitution', *Journal of Social Welfare and Family Law*, 1993, p.386.

D. Phelan, 'Right to Life of the Unborn v. Promotion of Trade in Services: the European Court of Justice and the Normative Shaping of the European Union', *Modern Law Review*, **55**, 1992, p.670.

B. Schmitz, 'Advertising and Commercial Communications – Towards a Coherent and Effective EC Policy', *Journal of Consumer Policy*, **16**, 1993, p.387.

J. Weiler, 'The European Court at Crossroads: Community Human Rights and Member State Action' in Capotoriti, Ehlermann and other (eds), *Du Droit International au Droit de l'Integration*, Baden-Baden: Nomos, 1987, p.828.

B. Wilkinson, 'Abortion, the Irish Constitution and the EEC', *Public Law*, 1992, p.20.

7   Intellectual Property Rights

A. THE FORMS AND FUNCTIONS OF INTELLECTUAL PROPERTY RIGHTS

The key common feature of intellectual property rights is the exclusive rights which they confer on their holder. The right involves exclusivity over a defined period of time within a defined geographic area. The holder is entitled to market the product which is protected by the intellectual property right without being subjected to competition from other producers using the same design.

The patent and the copyright offer to the inventor a reward for his or her skill in developing a new product, technique or design. The inventor is enabled to reap a reward for time and money invested in research without fear that a rival who has made no such investment will be able to copy the idea and share in the profits. That rival is constrained by law from competing and therefore may not take a 'free ride' on the inventor's skill.

The trademark has a rather different function although the idea of legally protected exclusivity runs parallel to that available under the patent and the copyright. The trademark guarantees the origin of the product to the consumer. It is the guarantee of a link between product and producer and therefore it must be exclusive to an individual producer in order accurately to inform the consumer.

There are other rights which are analogous to the patent, copyright and trademark. The details vary under different national systems. Under English law, for example, there exist exclusive design rights. However, the essential feature is the exclusivity conferred on the holder and it is that which is relevant in assessing the impact of European law.

The functions of each of these intellectual property rights may be distinguishable, but the nature of the legal regime is basically similar. Ownership of these rights involves the right to stop imitation. National law may be invoked to suppress competition which violates the exclusive rights which are the core of the intellectual property right. Intellectual property law involves the creation of private rights which may be used to isolate the holder from potential competitors.

B. THE 'BALANCE' UNDER NATIONAL LAW: THE NEED TO PROTECT INVENTORS

Under any national law system a careful balance has to be struck in fixing the scope of protection for the intellectual property right holder. The advantages of granting exclusive rights lie in the reward for innovation and protection from competition by 'free-riders'. This acts as an encouragement to further innovation and investment in research and development. The disadvantage lies in the suppression of competition. Much of this book examines material in which the message is that restriction on competition is undesirable, whether it is the result of state intervention or of agreement among private parties. Yet in the field of intellectual property the very objective of the law is suppression of competition, in so far as that is necessary to reward and encourage innovation.

In this area, there is a tension between the advantages and disadvantages of competition in the market. The result of this tension is that national law is typically prepared to grant exclusive rights under intellectual property law, but will set limits to the scope of those rights. Exclusivity is conferred as far as is necessary to stimulate innovation, but no further. So rights are limited in time. Moreover, there is a body of law concerned with the limits of what is capable of forming the subject of an intellectual property right. Beyond the limits of protectability competition cannot be restricted. In this vein, most systems have had to grapple with the question of whether genetically engineered animals can be patented. The classic example is the 'Harvard mouse', a mouse which develops cancer and which can then be used in research. Furthermore, in some circumstances the enjoyment of exclusive rights may be curtailed. In English law, for example, ineffective exploitation of a patent may lead to the compulsory award of a licence to a third party, who is then permitted to exploit the invention subject to payment of royalties to the original right owner. The public interest in the availability of the invention may limit the exercise of the private right where exclusivity, as a suppression of competition, is viewed as unduly damaging to the market.

C. THE 'BALANCE' UNDER EC LAW: ARTICLE 222 AND THE INVIOLABILITY OF NATIONAL PROPERTY LAWS

National Intellectual Property law restricts trade, but only so far as is necessary to ensure that the advantages of encouraging innovation outweigh the disadvantages of suppressing competition. EC law of market integration collides with the exclusivity granted for a national territory under intellectual property law. Here too a balance has to be struck between the advantages of free trade and the respect which must be shown to national rights.

1. The Background to EC law of intellectual property

There is no complete system of EC-wide intellectual property. Part V of this Chapter explains that the EC is making slow legislative progress in this direction. However, as yet, EC intellectual property law is essentially national intellectual property law operating in the context of and subject to the EC law of market integration and regulation. The starting point must be Article 222 of the EC Treaty: 'This Treaty shall in no way prejudice the rules on Member States governing the system of property ownership.' On its face, Article 222 is a severe impediment to the development of a European intellectual property law. At the very least it seems to deprive the European Court of responsibility for such a development.

The dynamics of the Treaty structure draw the Court into the task of placing a European interpretation on national legal concepts. This is a constant theme. It is especially marked in the area of intellectual property. The Court has not been prepared to view Article 222 as an instruction to leave national intellectual property law untouched. In fact the process of market integration through law makes it impossible for the Court to avoid the elaboration of a Community notion of intellectual property. In the Treaty, 'There is no constitutionally protected nucleus of residual State sovereignty' (K. Lenaerts (1990) 38 A.J.C.L. 205). Article 222 alone cannot change this fundamental characteristic of the Community constitution. It cannot act as a 'hands-off' sign directed at the Court.

However, the Court must tread warily in developing the process of market integration. Article 222 suggests a constitutional sensitivity to interference with private law rights. In part this sensitivity may be met by controlling national intellectual property law by means of the subjection of Member State laws to Articles 30–36, rather than by affecting private rights directly. In this sense the national legal systems are interposed between the European Court's capacity to elaborate a European intellectual property law and the influence which this may ultimately exert on private parties who hold rights under national law. However in practice the enjoyment of private rights in this area is intimately bound to their potential for enforcement through state mechanisms, especially the courts. So the European Court's development of a European notion of intellectual property has significant implications for both public and private parties. Both are addressees of the Court's jurisprudence.

Beyond these constitutional considerations the Court needs also to be cautious in sweeping away protected rights on a tide of market integration. There are good reasons for granting exclusivity to inventors. Research and innovation needs to be encouraged and the grant of intellectual property rights is one method, albeit not the only one. Trademarks offer to consumers a guarantee of the origin of products. Accordingly, an over-eager undermining of protected national rights could cause undesirable economic consequences. The state cannot be simply ejected from this market. So the Court is required to develop a rather sophisticated conception of European intellectual property law, in which national law is shaped with care towards a type of European intellectual property law suitable for the internal market. This consideration is, in fact, a valuable reminder of the much broader point that 'Europeanization' has many varied implications which must be closely monitored and, where possible, managed.

2. The Court's developing formula

The suppression of competition which is inherent in intellectual property law presents the same problem in EC law as in national law. A balance needs to be achieved, through which the detrimental aspects of suppressing competition can be controlled. Where an intellectual property right confers a dominant position on its owner which affects cross-border trade, the exercise of that right may be subject to control under EC law. Article 86 EC forbids the abuse of a dominant position. There is in this sense a developing European notion of the limits within which national intellectual property rights can be exercised. National law is unavoidably and irreversibly affected by the spread of the requirements of the common European legal system, trailing in the wake of the development of the European market.

Apart from the basic problem of suppression of competition inherent in intellectual property law, which is confronted by EC law as much as by national law, there is a further problem in the structure of intellectual property law which is peculiar to EC law. National intellectual property law is based on geographical limitation of the scope of the exclusive right. Typically, an exclusive right is enforceable within the territory of a single Member State. The result is that a national intellectual property right has the effect of securing a national market for a right holder who is immune from competition, but more specifically from cross-border competition. The geographic limitation of the national intellectual property right is a problem for EC economic law because of the obstacle to the free movement of goods. The process of market integration collides with the very structure of national intellectual property law. It has therefore proved necessary to develop an EC law approach to the scope of permissible trade restriction which is consequent upon the territorial protection offered by national intellectual property law.

Neither primary nor secondary EC law offers the Court any detailed blueprint for the resolution of this problem. It has been for the Court itself to develop the balance appropriate to European intellectual property law through its case law. The tensions within intellectual property law itself manifest themselves in this line of cases.

3. The Court admits the legitimate existence of national intellectual property rights, but controls the exercise of those rights

In cases where national intellectual property law comes into conflict with the law of the free movement of goods, the core of the Court's approach lies in an acceptance of the existence of national intellectual property law, but balanced by a determination to subject the exercise of those rights to control inspired by the process of market integration. This implies the pursuit of a compromise solution in pursuit of market integration, but it clearly envisages potential interference in private rights granted under national law. In this sense there is a European intellectual property law which affects the content of national intellectual property law.

The Court issued a basic statement of its stance in Case 119/75 *Terrapin* v. *Terranova* [1976] ECR 1039. This extract spells out the specific circumstances in which reliance on national rights to prevent importation may be lost.

[...]

5   As a result of the provisions in the Treaty relating to the free movement of goods and in particular of Article 30, quantitative restrictions on imports and all measures having equivalent effect are prohibited between Member States. By Article 36 these provisions nevertheless do not preclude prohibitions or restrictions on imports justified on grounds of the protection of industrial or commercial property. However, it is clear from that same article, in particular the second sentence, as well as from the context, that whilst the Treaty does not affect the existence of rights recognized by the legislation of a Member State in matters of industrial and commercial property, yet the exercise of those rights may nevertheless, depending on the circumstances, be restricted by the prohibitions in the Treaty. Inasmuch as it provides an exception to one of the fundamental principles of the common market, Article 36 in fact admits exceptions to the free movement of goods only to the extent to which such exceptions are justified for the purpose of safeguarding rights which constitute the specific subject-matter of that property.

6   It follows from the above that the proprietor of an industrial or commercial property right protected by the law of a Member State cannot rely on that law to prevent the importation of a product which has lawfully been marketed in another Member State by the proprietor himself or with his consent. It is the same when the right relied on is the result of the subdivision, either by voluntary act or as a result of public constraint, of a trade-mark right which originally belonged to one and the same proprietor. In these cases the basic function of the trade-mark to guarantee to consumers that the product has the same origin is already undermined by the subdivision of the original right. Even where the rights in question belong to different pro-

prietors the protection given to industrial and commercial property by national law may not be relied on when the exercise of those rights is the purpose, the means or the result of an agreement prohibited by the Treaty. In all these cases the effect of invoking the territorial nature of national laws protecting industrial and commercial property is to legitimize the insulation of national markets without this partitioning within the common market being justified by the protection of a legitimate interest on the part of the proprietor of the trade-mark or business name.

7   On the other hand in the present state of Community law an industrial or commercial property right legally acquired in a Member State may legally be used to prevent under the first sentence of Article 36 of the Treaty the import of products marketed under a name giving rise to confusion where the rights in question have been acquired by different and independent proprietors under different national laws. If in such a case the principle of the free movement of goods were to prevail over the protection given by the respective national laws, the specific objective of industrial and commercial property rights would be undermined. In the particular situation the requirements of the free movement of goods and the safeguarding of industrial and commercial property rights must be so reconciled that protection is ensured for the legitimate use of the rights conferred by national laws, coming within the prohibitions on imports 'justified' within the meaning of Article 36 of the Treaty, but denied on the other hand in respect of any improper exercise of the same rights of such a nature as to maintain or effect artificial partitions within the common market.

The Court's approach has been refined since this decision. It is explained below that the meaning of the proprietor's 'consent', in the first sentence of paragraph 6 of the judgment, has been developed in case law; and the second sentence of paragraph 6 no longer represents the Court's view. Nevertheless, the basic overall pattern mapped out in the ruling holds true. The Court considers that national intellectual property rights may be enforced *subject to* the requirements of the law of market integration and market regulation.

D. THE EXERCISE OF INTELLECTUAL PROPERTY RIGHTS IN THE INTERNAL MARKET

1. The place of parallel trade

There is as yet no single system of EC intellectual property rights. It is therefore necessary for the inventor to take out one or more separate national intellectual property rights. The rights are tied to individual national markets. The right holder must then make the commercial decision whether to pursue a marketing strategy confined by individual national markets or whether to pursue a wider strategy within the integrated Community market. At one extreme the right holder who wishes to exploit a right on a single national market alone will wish to maintain the exclusive protection from competition on that market which is characteristic of intellectual property. This is entirely permissible. However where the trader chooses to exploit the product in the wider integrated market, he or she will still be tempted to try to retain exclusive rights to exploit the individual national markets, even against parallel traders who export the protected goods from states where they have been marketed by the right holder across borders to other states. The right holder will be attracted by the prospect of operating free from competition in each state and will seek to rely on national rights to stop the parallel trading. However, parallel traders are the driving force of market integration. They cause harmonization in prices and other trading conditions between states simply by taking advantage of any discrepancies in different national markets, by, for example, exporting goods from low price states to high price states where they will force prices down. Their activities stop right holders setting different prices and conditions for the markets of different States.

There is a collision between the interests of parallel traders and the interests of the right holder determined to maintain exclusive rights to the home market. It is in fact representative of the basic clash between the free trade principle of EC law and the exclusive national protection characteristic of intellectual property.

The Court has developed a European law notion of what limits should be placed on the exercise of national intellectual property rights by a trader who has opted to take advantage of the wider European market.

2. Cases where rights to obstruct the free movement of goods are exhausted

The national right holder has commercial threats and opportunities consequent upon European market integration. Viewing the process as a threat, he or she might protect a national market by relying on national intellectual property rights to keep out infringing imports. Viewing the process as an opportunity, he or she might sell the protected goods throughout the wider market. The difficult questions arise where the right holder attempts to do *both*: to sell the products outside the State where the right is held but then also to secure that State against reimportation by third party parallel traders through reliance on the intellectual property right. In Case 15/74 *Centrafarm BV* v. *Sterling Drug Inc* [1974] ECR 1147 Sterling Drug was trying to do both. Its activities were considered incompatible with the law of market integration and it could not rely on national protection. This litigation is a perfect example of the clash between the interests of the right holder and the parallel trader, which is emblematic of the more general clash between national intellectual property law and European law of market integration.

Sterling Drug held patents for pharmaceuticals in several Member States. At issue was the patent it held for NEGRAM in both the UK and the Netherlands. Centrafarm bought stocks of NEGRAM in the UK and exported them to the Netherlands. It claimed a right under EC law of market integration to undertake such trade. Sterling Drug claimed a right under national patent law to maintain an exclusive right to sell NEGRAM on the Dutch market.

[...]

[10] An obstacle to the free movement of goods may arise out of the existence, within a national legislation concerning industrial and commercial property, of provisions laying down that a patentee's right is not exhausted when the product protected by the patent is marketed in another Member State, with the result that the patentee can prevent importation of the product into his own Member State when it has been marketed in another State.

[11] Whereas an obstacle to the free movement of goods of this kind may be justified on the ground of protection of industrial property where such protection is invoked against a product coming from a Member State where it is not patentable and has been manufactured by third parties without the consent of the patentee and in cases where there exist patents, the original proprietors of which are legally and economically independent, a derogation from the principle of the free movement of goods is not, however, justified where the product has been put onto the market in a legal manner, by the patentee himself or with his consent, in the Member State from which it has been imported, in particular in the case of a proprietor of parallel patents.

[12] In fact, if a patentee could prevent the import of protected products marketed by him or with his consent in another Member State, he would be able to partition off national markets and thereby restrict trade between Member States, in a situation where no such restriction was necessary to guarantee the essence of the exclusive rights flowing from the parallel patents.

[13] The plaintiff in the main action claims, in this connection, that by reason of divergences between national legislations and practice, truly identical or parallel patents can hardly be said to exist.

[14] It should be noted here that, in spite of the divergences which remain in the absence of any unification of national rules concerning industrial property, the identity of the protected invention is clearly the essential element of the concept of parallel patents which it is for the courts to assess.

[15] The question referred should therefore be answered to the effect that the exercise, by a patentee, of the right which he enjoys under the legislation of a Member State to prohibit the sale, in the State, of a product protected by the pat-

ent which has been marketed in another Member State by the patentee or with his consent is incompatible with the rules of the EEC Treaty concerning the free movement of goods within the Common Market.

The incentive for the parallel trader arose because there were significant price differentials between the Dutch market and the British market for the product. These arose because the price was depressed in the UK by the strength of a dominant buyer, the National Health Service. The result of the case is that the parallel trader can proceed and that, more generally, price differences between states will be removed in pursuit of more even market conditions.

The Court is careful not to deny the fruits of invention to the right holder. The holder is able to maintain its exclusive rights under national law on the terms set out in paragraph 11 of the judgment. However, European law places limits on the enjoyment of those rights. Those limits are inspired by the process of market integration. They are expressed in paragraph 15 of the judgment. Once the right holder has chosen to place the product on the wider market, he or she cannot then prevent parallel trade in the product concerned. European law provides the national right holder with a choice, but the exercise of national law rights can be undertaken only with due account for the limitations prescribed by the law of market integration.

The decision in Cases 55 & 57/80 *Musik-Vertrieb Membran* v. *GEMA* [1981] ECR 147 is a further illustration of the inability of a national right holder to enjoy the advantages of the wider market while simultaneously maintaining a national monopoly. The fact pattern to this decision is largely comparable to that in Case 15/74 *Centrafarm* v. *Sterling Drug* above. In Case 15/74 a patent was at issue; here, the exclusive right arose under the German *Urheberrechtsgesetz*, which creates rights comparable in function to the English copyright. However, the precise nature of the exclusive right makes no material difference to the Court's approach. The parallel trader is taking advantage of price differences between the UK and Germany. The prices of the protected product are lower in the UK, so trade flows from the UK to Germany, undercutting prices on German territory. Of course, this is desirable from the perspective of market integration because it will lead to the erosion of those price differentials. The principal interest in the case is the argument of the German right holder that these price differentials are attributable to state intervention and are not the product of market conditions. Therefore, the right holder is demanding an extra payment on importation to take account of the higher rates payable under German law:

[...]

16 GEMA has argued that such an interpretation of Article 30 and 36 of the Treaty is not sufficient to resolve the problem facing the national court

since GEMA's application to the German courts is not for the prohibition or restriction of the marketing of the gramophone records and tape cassettes in question on German territory but for equality in the royalties paid for any distribution of those sound recordings on the German market. The owner of a copyright in a recorded musical work has a legitimate interest in receiving and retaining the benefit of his intellectual or artistic effort regardless of the degree to which his work is distributed and consequently it is maintained that he should not lose the right to claim royalties equal to those paid in the country in which the recorded work is marketed.

However the Court is not prepared to allow this factor to alter the principle which it established in Case 15/74 *Centrafarm* v. *Sterling Drug.*

[...]

18   It should be observed next that no provision of national legislation may permit an undertaking which is responsible for the management of copyrights and has a monopoly on the territory of a Member State by virtue of that management to charge a levy on products imported from another Member State where they were put into circulation by or with the consent of the copyright owner and thereby cause the Common Market to be partitioned. Such a practice would amount to allowing a private undertaking to impose a charge on the importation of sound recordings which are already in free circulation in the Common Market on account of their crossing a frontier; it would therefore have the effect of entrenching the isolation of national markets which the Treaty seeks to abolish.

19   It follows from those considerations that this argument must be rejected as being incompatible with the operation of the Common Market and with the aims of the Treaty. [...]

25   It should further be observed that in a common market distinguished by free movement of goods and freedom to provide services an author, acting directly or through his publisher, is free to choose the place, in any of the Member States, in which to put his work into circulation. He may make that choice according to his best interests, which involve not only the level of remuneration provided in the Member State in question but other factors such as, for example, the opportunities for distributing his work and the marketing facilities which are further enhanced by virtue of the free movement of goods within the Community. In those circumstances, a copyright management society may not be permitted to claim, on the importation of sound recordings into another Member State, payment of additional fees based on the difference in the rates of remuneration existing in the various Member States.

The Court's theme is that once the right holder has chosen to market the product in another Member State, it must accept the consequences of market integration. This is a stronger decision than Case 15/74 *Centrafarm* v. *Sterling Drug* in the sense that it promotes the impetus of European market integration over national exclusive protection even where, in truth, the market is *not* common because of the existence of different state systems. The Court commented at paragraph 24 of its judgment that '... the existence of a disparity between national laws which is capable of distorting competition between Member States cannot justify a Member State's giving legal protection to practices of a private body which are incompatible with the rules concerning free movement of goods'. The message here is that private parties cannot delay the strengthening of market integration law by using the excuse of slow progress on the part of public authorities. The creation of the European market precedes the creation of the European 'State'.

3. Cases where rights to obstruct the free movement of goods are not exhausted

In some cases the Court has found it necessary to limit the incursion of Community trade law into national intellectual property law. In the next two cases the holder of a national intellectual property right in more than one Member State is allowed to assert that right to defeat cross-border trade. The result is therefore in direct contrast to that in Cases 15/74 and 55 & 57/80 above.

In Case 19/84 *Pharmon BV* v. *Hoechst AG* [1985] ECR 2281 Hoechst owned a patent for a drug, Frusemide, in Germany, the Netherlands and the UK. It had chosen not to manufacture the drug in the UK. The public authorities in the UK granted a compulsory licence to a third party under which that third party could manufacture Frusemide subject to payment of a royalty to Hoechst. The products made in the UK under the compulsory licence were exported to the Netherlands and marketed there by Pharmon. Hoechst sought to rely on their intellectual property right under Dutch law in order to maintain exclusive rights on the Dutch market. This would plainly obstruct free trade. Pharmon claimed a right under EC law of market integration to sell the product in the Netherlands.

The fact pattern follows that in Case 15/74 *Centrafarm* v. *Sterling Drug* and Cases 55 & 57/80 *Musik-Vertrieb Membran* v. *GEMA*, excepting only that in those cases the product had been marketed in another state with the consent of the party wishing to rely on the exclusive right in the state where the litigation occurred, whereas in Case 19/84 that party, Hoechst, had not consented to marketing in the other State, the UK.

[...]

[25]   It is necessary to point out that where, as in this instance, the competent authorities of a Member State grant a third party a compulsory licence which allows him to carry out manufacturing and marketing operations which the patentee would normally have the right to prevent, the patentee cannot be deemed to have consented to the operation of that third party. Such a measure deprives the patent proprietor of his right to determine freely the conditions under which he markets his products.

[26]   As the Court held most recently in its judgment of 14 July 1981 (*Merck* v. *Stephar*, cited above), the substance of a patent right lies essentially in according the inventor an exclusive right of first placing the product on the market so as to allow him to obtain the reward for his creative effort. It is therefore necessary to allow the patent proprietor to prevent the importation and marketing of products manufactured under a compulsory licence in order to protect the substance of his exclusive rights under his patent.

Because here, unlike in Case 15/74 *Centrafarm* v. *Sterling Drug* and Cases 55 & 57/80 *Musik-Vertrieb Membran* v. *GEMA*, the goods were not marketed in the UK with the consent of the holder of the patent, the Court ruled that it was possible to rely on the patent to maintain exclusive rights on the Dutch market in order to keep out goods originating in the UK. Pharmon had argued unsuccessfully that Hoechst had chosen to take out the UK patent and should be taken to accept the full consequences, including the possibility of compulsory licensing. The Court was not prepared to interpret the law of market integration in a way which would intrude so deeply into the exercise of national intellectual property law. For the Court, the key was that Hoechst had not consented to marketing the goods in the UK. Here, then, the limits of European law control over national intellectual property rights are reached.

In Case 19/84 *Pharmon* v. *Hoechst* the German right holder had consented to the registration of the right in the UK, but not to the marketing of the goods. In Case 341/87 *EMI Electrola* v. *Patricia Import* [1989] ECR 79 the situation is different again. A parallel trader had imported goods from Denmark to Germany but was opposed by the holder of an exclusive right under German law. That German right holder had also been the Danish right holder in respect of the goods, but the Danish right had expired with the result that the goods were being freely manufactured in Denmark by third parties. The goods in question which had been exported from Denmark to Germany had not been manufactured in Denmark by the German right holder nor with its consent, except in the indirect sense that the right holder knew on acquiring the Danish right that third parties would be able to use the design once the period of protection under Danish law had expired.

In fact the problem would not have arisen had the period of protection been the same in both Denmark and Germany. However Danish law set a shorter period for protection than German law. It was the disparity in the length of protection which gave an incentive to the parallel trader. So the question for the Court was whether the absence of a common European legal system should be allowed to prevent the development of a common European market.

[...]

9   In previous decisions the Court has accordingly concluded that a copyright owner may not rely on the exclusive exploitation right conferred by copyright to prevent or restrict the importation of sound recordings which have been lawfully marketed in another Member State by the owner himself or with his consent (judgment of 20 January 1981 in Joined Cases 55 and 57/80 *Musik-Vertrieb Membran GmbH and Another* v. *GEMA* [1981] ECR 147).

10   However, such a situation is different from the one described by the national court. As its preliminary question indicates, the fact that the sound recordings were lawfully marketed in another Member State is due, not to an act or the consent of the copyright owner or his licensee, but to the expiry of the protection period provided for by the legislation of that Member State. The problem arising thus stems from the differences between national legislation regarding the period of protection afforded by copyright and by related rights, those differences concerning either the duration of the protection itself or the details thereof, such as the time when the protection period begins to run.

11   In that regard, it should be noted that in the present state of Community law, which is characterized by a lack of harmonization or approximation of legislation governing the protection of literary and artistic property, it is for the national legislatures to determine the conditions and detailed rules for such protection.

12   In so far as the disparity between national laws may give rise to restrictions on intra-Community trade in sound recordings, such restrictions are justified under Article 36 of the Treaty if they are the result of differences between the rules governing the period of protection and this is inseparably linked to the very existence of the exclusive rights.

13   No such justification would exist if the restrictions on trade imposed or accepted by the national legislation relied on by the owner of the exclusive rights or his licensee were of such a nature as to constitute a means of arbitrary discrimination or a disguised measure to restrict trade. However, there is nothing in the documents before the Court to suggest that such a situation might exist in a case such as the present one.

14   Consequently, the reply to the question referred to the Court must be that Articles 30 and 36 of the Treaty must be interpreted as not precluding the application of a Member State's legislation which allows a producer of sound recordings in that Member State to reply on the exclusive rights to reproduce and distribute certain musical work of which he is the owner in order to prohibit the sale, in the territory of that Member State, of sound recordings of the same musical works when those recordings are imported from another Member State in which they were lawfully marketed without the consent of the aforesaid owner or his licensee and in which the producer of those recordings had enjoyed protection which has in the mean time expired.

The Court's unwillingness to curtail the German exclusive right in this case shows its sensitivity to the value of national intellectual property rights. It also shows the Court's reluctance in this case to use market integration law to solve problems caused by the lack of a common European intellectual property law. The result is that the development of the European market is inhibited by the absence of common European laws.

The four cases discussed above illustrate the possibilities and the limitations of the law of market integration in this area. The exclusive rights granted under national intellectual property law are subject to control. The Court has fixed on the idea of consensual marketing in another Member State as the key event. Once this occurs, the enforceability of the national exclusive right is subordinated to the law of market integration. The immediate addressee of this principle is the national right holder who is able to make a commercial choice about how to exploit the rights. The would-be parallel trader is also able to follow the Court's principle in determining the opportunities for trading across borders to take advantage of price differentials.

Cases 15/74 *Centrafarm* v. *Sterling Drug* and 55 & 57/80 *Musik-Vertrieb Membran* v. *GEMA* are illustrations of the capacity of the law of market integration to reduce the scope of national rights. Cases 19/84 *Pharmon* v. *Hoechst* and 341/87 *EMI Electrola* v. *Patricia Import* are instances of the persisting capacity of national intellectual property rights to block cross-border trade.

A separate addressee of the Court's jurisprudence in this area is the Member States and the Community institutions. The Court is setting limits on how far the Court will go in creating a European economic law of free trade without explicit legislative support. If trade barriers such as those which emerge from consideration of Cases 19/84 *Pharmon* v. *Hoechst* and 341/87 *EMI Electrola* v. *Patricia Import* are to be abolished, the contribution of the political institutions to the development of positive European law is required.

The Court chose to make this point explicitly in Case C-9/93 *IHT Internationale Heiztechnik GmbH* v. *Ideal Standard GmbH* [1994] ECR I-2789. The American Standard group held the trademark 'Ideal Standard' through subsidiaries in France and in Germany. In 1984 the French subsidiary sold the trade mark to an independent third party buyer. IHT, a German subsidiary of the buyer, began to sell French-made goods in Germany that bore the (French) 'Ideal Standard' trademark. It found itself sued before German courts by Ideal Standard for infringement of the German 'Ideal Standard' trademark.

There were 'Ideal Standard' trademarks in both France and Germany and they had the same source. But they were held by economically independent firms. The European Court ruled that reliance on the German trade mark to exclude French-made goods impeded trade (Article 30), but that it was nevertheless justified (Article 36). The Court was not prepared to regard a voluntary assignment of a trademark to an independent third party as sufficient 'consent' to cause exhaustion of the assignor's right to protect its home (here, German) territory from goods made by the assignee. The Court ruled that consent implicit in an assignment is less than the consent required to exhaust rights – contrary to the Commission's submissions in the case. As mentioned at page 308 above, this represents a rejection of the second sentence of Case 119/75 *Terrapin* v. *Terranova*. The Court had already moved in this direction in Case C-10/89 *SA CNL-SUCAL* v. *HAG* [1990] ECR I-3711, which concerned division of a trademark by governmental action, and *Ideal Standard* confirms that a division caused by voluntary act is equally insufficient automatically to exclude reliance on the right to exclude goods made by an independent third party using the trademark that happens to have a common origin. The Court focuses on the consumer interest in the trademark as a guarantor of origin rather than on the consumer interest in market integration and wider choice.

In the *Ideal Standard* ruling, there is a strong flavour of the need to respect legislative diversity between the Member States despite the unfavourable consequences for integration. The Court made explicit its perception of the margin between its own role and that of the Community legislature.

[...]

49   IHT has further argued that the French subsidiary, Ideal-Standard SA, has adjusted itself in France to a situation where products (such as heating equipment and sanitary fittings) from different sources may be marketed under the same trade mark on the same national territory. The conduct of the German subsidiary of the same group which opposes the marketing of the heating equipment in Germany under the trade mark 'Ideal Standard' is therefore abusive.

50   That argument cannot be upheld either.

51   First of all, the assignment was made only for France. The effect of that argument, if it were accepted, would, as the German Government points out, be that assignment of the right for France would entail permission to use the device in Germany, whereas assignments and licences always relate, having regard to the territorial nature of national trade-mark rights, to a specified territory.

52   Moreover, and most importantly, French law, which governs the assignment in question here, permits assignments of trade marks confined to certain products, with the result that similar products from different sources may be in circulation on French territory under the same trade mark, whereas German law, by prohibiting assignments of trade marks confined to certain products, seeks to prevent such co-existence. The effect of IHT's argument, if it were accepted, would be to extend to the importing State whose law opposes such co-existence the solution prevailing in the exporting State despite the territorial nature of the rights in question.

53   Starting from the position that assignment to an assignee having no links with the assignor would lead to the existence of separate sources within a single territory and that, in order to safeguard the function of the trade mark, it would then be necessary to allow prohibition of export of the assignee's products to the assignor's territory and vice versa, unified laws, to avoid creating such obstacles to the free movement of goods, render void assignments made for only part of the territory covered by the rights they create. By limiting the right to dispose of the trade mark in this way, such unified laws ensure single ownership throughout the territory to which they apply and guarantee free movement of the product.

54   Thus, the Uniform Benelux Law on Trade Marks for Goods, whose objective was to unify the territory of the three States for trade-mark purposes (statement of grounds, *Bulletin Benelux*, 1962-2, pp. 3 and 4), provided that, from the date of its entry into force, a trade mark could be granted only for the whole of Benelux (statement of grounds, *Bulletin Benelux*, 1962-2, p. 14). To that end it further provided that trade-mark assignments not effected for the whole of Benelux were void.

55   The regulation on the Community trade mark referred to above also creates a right with a unitary character. Subject to certain exceptions (see in this respect Article 106 on the prohibition of use of Community trade marks and Article 107 on prior rights applicable to particular localities), the Community trade mark 'shall have equal effect throughout the Community: it shall not be registered, transferred or surrendered or be the subject of a decision revoking the rights of the proprietor or declaring it invalid, nor shall its use be prohibited, save in respect of the whole Community' (Article 1(2)).

56   However, unlike the Benelux Law, 'the Community law relating to trade marks... does not replace the laws of the Member States on trade marks' (fifth recital in the preamble to the regulation on the Community trade

mark). The Community trade mark is merely superimposed on the national rights. Undertakings are in no way obliged to take out Community trade marks (fifth recital). Moreover, the existence of earlier national rights may be an obstacle to the registration of a Community trade mark since, under Article 8 of the regulation, the owner of a trade mark in a single Member State may oppose the registration of a Community trade mark by the proprietor of national rights for identical or similar products in all the other Member States. That provision cannot be interpreted as precluding the assignment of national trade marks for one or more States of the Community only. It is therefore apparent that the regulation on the Community trade mark does not render void assignments of national marks which are confined to certain States of the Community.

57 That sanction cannot be introduced through case-law. To hold that the national laws are measures having equivalent effect which fall under Article 30 and are not justified by Article 36, in that, given the independence of national rights (see paragraphs 25 to 32 above), they do not, at present, make the validity of assignments for the territories to which they apply conditional on the concomitant assignment of the trade mark for the other States of the Community, would have the effect of imposing on the States a positive obligation, namely to embody in their laws a rule rendering void assignments of national trade marks made for part only of the Community.

58 It is for the Community legislature to impose such an obligation on the Member States by a directive adopted under Article 100a of the EEC Treaty, elimination of the obstacles arising from the territoriality of national trade marks being necessary for the establishment and functioning of the internal market, or itself to enact that rule directly by a regulation adopted under the same provision.

59 It should be added that, where undertakings independent of each other make trade-mark assignments following a market-sharing agreement, the prohibition of anti-competitive agreements under Article 85 applies and assignments which give effect to that agreement are consequently void. However, as the United Kingdom rightly pointed out, that rule and the accompanying sanction cannot be applied mechanically to every assignment. Before a trade-mark assignment can be treated as giving effect to an agreement prohibited under Article 85, it is necessary to analyse the context, the commitments underlying the assignment, the intention of the parties and the consideration for the assignment.

60 In view of the foregoing, the answer to the Oberlandesgericht Düsseldorf's question must be that there is no unlawful restriction on trade between Member States within the meaning of Articles 30 and 36 where a subsidiary operating in Member State A of a manufacturer established in Member State B is to be enjoined from using as a trade mark the name 'Ideal Standard' because of the risk of confusion with a device having the same origin,

even if the manufacturer is lawfully using that name in his country of origin under a trade mark protected there, he acquired that trade mark by assignment and the trade mark originally belonged to a company affiliated to the undertaking which, in Member State A, opposes the importation of goods bearing the trade mark 'Ideal Standard'.

4. Trademarked, repackaged goods

A special problem arises in relation to trademarked goods. Where there are different trademarks in different states for the same product it is lawful for the parallel trader simply to export a product from one state to another, in order to take advantage of any price differences between the states. That is clear from Case 15/74 *Centrafarm* v. *Sterling Drug*. However, it would be pointless to undertake such trade, because in the target state the product will be unfamiliar and difficult to market. The parallel trader will want to change the trademark to that which is used on the target state's market, without changing the product itself. The holder of the trademark in the target state will seek to rely on that trademark to exclude the repackaged import. The question arises as to how far European law of market integration restricts the right of the trademark holder to enjoy exclusive use of the trademark on the national market.

The same problem arises even where trademarks are the same in different states if different types of package are preferred on the different markets. The parallel trader will want to alter neither product nor trademark, but will want to alter the package.

This was the situation in Case 102/77 *Hoffman La Roche* v. *Centrafarm* [1978] ECR 1139. Prices for a pharmaceutical were lower in the UK than in Germany. The patent was held in both countries by the Roche group. This was an obvious inducement for parallel trade from the UK to Germany, in accordance with the Court's ruling in favour of such trade in Case 15/74 *Centrafarm* v. *Sterling Drug*. However, normal packaging in the UK was not normal in Germany, so the parallel trader changed the packaging and was confronted by Roche's reliance on German patent law to exclude the repackaged goods from the German market.

[...]

7   In relation to trade-mark, the specific subject-matter is in particular to guarantee to the proprietor of the trade-mark that he has the exclusive right to use that trade-mark for the purpose of putting a product into circulation for the first time and therefore to protect him against competitors wishing to

take advantage of the status and reputation of the trademark by selling products illegally bearing that trade-mark. In order to answer the question whether that exclusive right involves the right to prevent the trade-mark being affixed by a third person after the product has been repackaged, regard must be had to the essential function of the trade-mark, which is to guarantee the identity of the origin of the trademarked product to the consumer or ultimate user, by enabling him without any possibility of confusion to distinguish that product from products which have another origin. This guarantee of origin means that the consumer or ultimate user can be certain that a trade-marked product which is sold to him has not been subject at a previous stage of marketing to interference by a third person, without the authorization of the proprietor of the trade-mark, such as to affect the original condition of the product. The right attributed to the proprietor of preventing any use of the trade-mark which is likely to impair the guarantee of origin so understood is therefore part of the specific subject-matter of the trade-mark right.

8   It is accordingly justified under the first sentence of Article 36 to recognize that the proprietor of a trade-mark is entitled to prevent an importer of a trade-marked product, following repackaging of that product, from affixing the trade-mark to the new packaging without the authorization of the proprietor.

9   It is, however, necessary to consider whether the exercise of such a right may constitute a 'disguised restriction on trade between Member States' within the meaning of the second sentence of Article 36. Such a restriction might arise, *inter alia*, from the proprietor of the trade-mark putting onto the market in various Member States an identical product in various packages while availing himself of the rights inherent in the trade-mark to prevent repackaging by a third person even if it were done in such a way that the identity of origin of the trade-marked product and its original condition could not be affected. The question, therefore, in the present case is whether the repackaging of a trade-marked product such as that undertaken by Centrafarm is capable of affecting the original condition of the product.

10   In this respect the answer must vary according to the circumstances and in particular according to the nature of the product and the method of repackaging. Depending on the nature of the product repackaging in many cases inevitably affects its condition, while in others repackaging involves a more or less obvious risk that the product might be interfered with or its original condition otherwise affected. Nevertheless, it is possible to conceive of the repackaging being undertaken in such a way that the original condition of the product cannot be affected. This may be so where, for example, the proprietor of the trade-mark has marketed the product in a double packaging and the repackaging affects only the external packaging, leaving the internal packaging intact, or where the repackaging is inspected by a public authority for the purpose of ensuring that the product is not adversely af-

fected. Where the essential function of the trade-mark to guarantee the origin of the product is thus protected, the exercise of his rights by the proprietor of the trade-mark in order to fetter the free movement of goods between Member States may constitute a disguised restriction within the meaning of the second sentence of Article 36 of the Treaty if it is established that the use of the trade-mark right by the proprietor, having regard to the marketing system which he has adopted, will contribute to the artificial partitioning of the markets between Member States.

11   Although this conclusion is unavoidable in the interests of freedom of trade, it amounts to giving the trader, who sells the imported product with the trade-mark affixed to the new packaging without the authorization of the proprietor, a certain licence which in normal circumstances is reserved to the proprietor himself. In the interests of the proprietor as trade-mark owner and to protect him against any abuse it is therefore right to allow such licence only where it is shown that the repackaging cannot adversely affect the original condition of the product.

12   Since it is in the proprietor's interest that the consumer should not be misled as to the origin of the product, it is moreover right to allow the trader to sell the imported product with the trade-mark affixed to the new packaging only on condition that he gives the proprietor of the mark prior notice and that he states on the new packaging that the product has been repackaged by him.

The Court is clearly motivated by the need to help parallel importers, who play a major role in the development of the integrated market. It is also careful to pay attention to the interests of the right holder and of the consumer, which are based on the function of the trademark as a guarantee of the origin of the product. It reached this conclusion;

1. (a) The proprietor of a trade-mark right which is protected in two Member States at the same time is justified pursuant to the first sentence of Article 36 of the EEC Treaty in preventing a product to which the trade-mark has lawfully been applied in one of those States from being marketed in the other Member State after it has been repacked in new packaging to which the trade-mark has been affixed by a third party.

    (b) However, such prevention of marketing constitutes a disguised restriction on trade between Member States within the meaning of the second sentence of Article 36 where:

        – It is established that the use of the trade-mark right by the proprietor, having regard to the marketing system which he has adopted, will contribute to the artificial partitioning of the markets between Member States;

- It is shown that the repackaging cannot adversely affect the original condition of the product;
- The proprietor of the mark receives prior notice of the marketing of the repackaged product; and
- It is stated on the new packaging by whom the product has been repackaged.

2. To the extent to which the exercise of a trade-mark right is lawful in accordance with the provisions of Article 36 of the Treaty, such exercise is not contrary to Article 86 of the Treaty on the sole ground that it is act of an undertaking occupying a dominant position on the market if the trade-mark right has not been used as an instrument for the abuse of such a position.

5. Some Concluding Comments on the Exhaustion of Rights

'Consensual' marketing of products outside the state in which an intellectual property right is held exhausts the right holder's capacity to stop reimportation of those goods by third party parallel traders. But, in the absence of consent, reliance on the right remains possible to prevent importation of infringing products. Definition of 'consent' is therefore critical. As explained, the Court has devoted much attention to this issue. In cases such as Case 19/84 *Pharmon* v. *Hoechst*, Case 341/87 *EMI Electrola* v. *Patricia Import* and Case C-9/93 *IHT Internationale Heiztechnik GmbH* v. *Ideal Standard GmbH* the Court was not willing to adopt an extensive notion of 'consent', with the result that market segregation persisted.

Once it is established that the right-holder has not exhausted those rights by 'consent', it is in principle permissible to rely on the national right to exclude infringing goods from the territory covered by the right. This is plain from paragraph 7 of the decision in *Terrapin* v. *Terranova*, p.308 above, which concedes that

in the present state of Community law an industrial or commercial property right legally acquired in a Member State may legally be used to prevent under the first sentence of Article 36 of the Treaty the import of products marketed under a name giving rise to confusion where the rights in question have been acquired by different and independent proprietors under different national laws.

For trademarks, infringement arises where there is confusion between the protected goods and other goods. Only where there is such confusion is reliance on the right justified. The extent to which the European Court might be tempted to develop a Europeanized notion of 'confusion' was tested in Case C-317/92 *Deutsche Renault AG* v. *Audi AG*, judgment of 30 November 1993. The Court was in cautious mood. It chose not to deepen the process of 'Europeanization' of legal concepts in this area. Both parties were motor manufacturers. Audi held two trade marks for the term 'Quattro' under German law and had been marketing four-wheel drive vehicles since 1980 under that designation. In 1988 Renault began to market in Germany a four-wheel drive vehicle made in France under the designation 'Espace Quadra'. Audi sought to restrain Renault from using the designation Quadra, which it considered likely to lead to confusion. The European Court ruled that the determination of the criteria for deciding on the risk of confusion was a matter for the national system. The scope of protection against risk of confusion was an aspect of the scope of the right itself. Community law did not impose strict criteria of interpretation of the risk of confusion.

In Case C-9/93 *IHT Internationale Heiztechnik GmbH* v. *Ideal Standard GmbH* the Court confirmed that it was for national law to determine the criteria relevant to assessment of the risk of confusion. However, the Court also made clear that the national court must comply with the prohibition against arbitrary discrimination and disguised restrictions on trade between Member States set out in the second sentence of Article 36. According to paragraph 19 of the ruling, 'There would, in particular, be a disguised restriction if the national court were to conduct an arbitrary assessment of the similarity of products'.

6. Abuse of a Dominant Position

The previous section examined the problems of geographical exclusivity in national intellectual property law. At the European level, these typically give rise to problems in the law of the free movement of goods contained in Articles 30–36 of the Treaty. Also of significance in economic law is the extent to which an intellectual property right may create a monopoly. Intellectual property rights confer monopolies over the specific protected product. They may not be monopolies on a strict economic definition. A patented pharmaceutical may be subject to competition from other pharmaceuticals which have a different composition, but comparable medicinal properties. However, in other situations the intellectual property right holder may be effectively immunized from competition. He or she may possess a legal and economic monopoly. Where this monopoly affects cross-border trade, the holder is subject to control under Article 86. The existence of a monopoly or dominant position is not itself challenged under Article 86, but the exercise of economic power by a dominant right holder must not amount to an 'abuse'. Here too European law sets limits to the exercise of exclusive rights under national law.

In the next case the Court upheld the Commission's condemnation under Article 86 of a refusal to license a third party to use a copyright. Three television firms, RTE, BBC and ITP, held copyright protection in the UK and Ireland over listings for future programmes. Each produced its own guides to its own programmes. There was no single guide to all programmes available on the market, because the television companies declined to produce one themselves. Nor, despite requests, would they licence a third party to use the copyright on payment of a fee in order to produce a guide. The Commission found the practices of the television firms to be abusive and in violation of Article 86 (OJ 1989 L78/43). Applications by the television firms for the annulment of the Commission Decision was rejected by the Court of First Instance (Case T-69/89 *Radio Telefis Eireann* v. *Commission* [1991] ECR II-485). The following extracts are taken from judgment on appeal to the European Court, Cases C-241/91P, C-242/91P *RTE and ITP* v. *Commission* [1995] ECR I-743:

[...]

51 In the present case, the conduct objected to is the appellants' reliance on copyright conferred by national legislation so as to prevent Magill – or any other undertaking having the same intention – from publishing on a weekly basis information (channel, day, time and title of programmes) together with commentaries and pictures obtained independently of the appellants.

52 Among the circumstances taken into account by the Court of First Instance in concluding that such conduct was abusive was, first, the fact that there was, according to the findings of the Court of First Instance, no actual or potential substitute for a weekly television guide offering information on the programmes for the week ahead. On this point, the Court of First Instance confirmed the Commission's finding that the complete lists of programmes for a 24-hour period – and for a 48-hour period at weekends and before public holidays – published in certain daily and Sunday newspapers, and the television sections of certain magazines covering, in addition, 'highlights' of the week's programmes, were only to a limited extent substitutable for advance information to viewers on all the week's programmes. Only weekly television guides containing comprehensive listings for the week ahead would enable users to decide in advance which programmes they wished to follow and arrange their leisure activities for the week accordingly. The Court of First Instance also established that there was a specific, constant and regular potential demand on the part of consumers (see the *RTE* judgment, paragraph 62, and the *ITP* judgment, paragraph 48).

53 Thus the appellants – who were, by force of circumstance, the only sources of the basic information on programme scheduling which is the indispensable raw material for compiling a weekly television guide – gave viewers wishing to obtain information on the choice of programmes for the week ahead no choice but to buy the weekly guides for each station and draw from each of them the information they needed to make comparisons.

54 The appellants' refusal to provide basic information by relying on national copyright provisions thus prevented the appearance of a new product, a

comprehensive weekly guide to television programmes, which the appellants did not offer and for which there was a potential consumer demand. Such refusal constitutes an abuse under heading (b) of the second paragraph of Article 86 of the Treaty.

55 Second, there was no justification for such refusal either in the activity of television broadcasting or in that of publishing television magazines (*RTE* judgment, paragraph 73, and *ITP* judgment, paragraph 58).

56 Third, and finally, as the Court of First Instance also held, the appellants, by their conduct, reserved to themselves the secondary market of weekly television guides by excluding all competition on that market (see the judgment in Joined Cases 6/73 and 7/73 *Commercial Solvents* v. *Commission* [1974] ECR 223, paragraph 25) since they denied access to the basic information which is the raw material indispensable for the compilation of such a guide.

57 In the light of all those circumstances, the Court of First Instance did not err in law in holding that the appellants' conduct was an abuse of a dominant position within the meaning of Article 86 of the Treaty.

This amounts to a significant control over the nature of the copyright conferred by national law. Article 86 is used to create a competitive market despite the existence of intellectual property rights. The copyright owner is forced under the influence of European law to surrender exclusive rights. This is a radical adjustment of the whole basis of exclusivity which is characteristic of the intellectual property right.

7. Licensing Intellectual Property Rights

The owner of a national intellectual property right may seek to exploit that right throughout the Community market using several different commercial methods. A common technique is the establishment of a licensing system, whereby the right holder sells licences to traders in other Member States which permit them to exploit the right under the terms of the licensing agreement.

The freedom of the owner of the right to license the right is affected by the process of market integration. The owner must to a defined extent respect the demands of economic integration. It is clear that once the licensor has agreed to permit the marketing of products by the licensee in another Member State, it is no longer possible to prevent parallel trading in the goods in question. That is the outcome of the Court's case law since Case 15/74 *Centrafarm* v. *Sterling Drug*, examined above. Separate questions arise about the permissible scope of restrictions on action which can be included in the deal between the licensor and the licensee.

The licensing deals are agreements between undertakings which affect cross-border trade and they are therefore subject to the control of Article 85(1). Nevertheless such deals extend the availability of valuable knowledge throughout the

Community and there are compelling reasons for taking a favourable view of such deals in accordance with Article 85(3). A balance between the anti-competitive and the pro-competitive aspects of such deals was mapped out in Regulation 2349/84, the Block Exemption on Patent Licensing Agreements (OJ 1984 L219/15 corrected OJ 1985 L113/34 and amended by Regulation 151/93 OJ 1992 L21/8.

The licensing of rights under national law occurs in the context of European market integration law and is affected by European law. The Commission takes a similar approach to the application of Article 85 to the licensing of other intellectual property rights, even though there is no Block Exemption covering trademark or copyright licensing. The Patent Licensing Block Exemption Regulation expired at the end of 1994. It was the intention of the Commission to replace it by a Regulation exempting technology transfer agreements. This would be wider in scope than the Patent Licensing Regulation. In particular, it would cover Know-How agreements, which had previously been subject to a separate Regulation, Regulation 556/89. The Commission also proposed adjustments to the nature and scope of the Exemption. This stimulated a sufficiently fierce debate to force delay of the date for entry into force of the new regime.

From the end of 1994, control of Patent Licensing underwent a transitional period of subjection to the 'old' rules of Regulation 2349/84 until such time as agreement could be reached on the new text.

E. LEGISLATIVE HARMONISATION

The European Court has developed a partial concept of the European intellectual property right. The starting point is national intellectual property law, but the enjoyment of those national rights is significantly affected by the process of European market integration. Articles 30–36, 85 and 86 shape the nature of the rights enjoyed under national intellectual property law, despite the apparent protection afforded such rights by Article 222 EC. There is a body of European intellectual property law which demands respect for the integrated market. Even national law which has in no sense been comprehensively transformed into European law changes shape under the imperatives of the evolving European market. However, there is no comprehensive set of European intellectual property rights.

It is simple to provide the prescription for the transformation of the present pattern of national rights affected by European law into a true European law of intellectual property. There should be as a first stage a harmonization of national intellectual property law, so that rights in each state are equivalent. Then, Community-wide rights should replace national rights. In this way the advantages of a system of intellectual property protection would be achieved without the distortions presently caused by the confinement of rights to national territories in a market which is integrating.

There is severe difficulty in developing a 'true' European intellectual property right. The problems which confront the realization of such a prescription can be readily appreciated. They can be summarized with reference to the idea that the regulation of the Community market, which already exists, should be achieved by the Community state, which does not exist. It has proved impossible to secure the political agreement to replace national rights with Community rights. In fact, it has proved impossible to make more than limited progress in that direction. Regulation 40/94 on the Community Trade Mark (OJ 1994 L11/1) represents a limited break-through in the 'Europeanization' of this area. It deserves attention for the way it incorporates the Court's case law, discussed above, and for the way it envisages that a European trade mark will co-exist with national rights. The Regulation con-sists of thirteen Titles and 143 Articles. It is not reproduced here in full. Instead the Preamble and the first two Titles are reproduced. These contain the core provisions of substance.

COUNCIL REGULATION (EC) No. 40/94

of 20 December 1993

on the Community trade mark

THE COUNCIL OF THE EUROPEAN UNION,

Having regard to the Treaty establishing the European Community, and in par-ticular Article 235 thereof,

Having regard to the proposal from the Commission,[1]

Having regard to the opinion of the European Parliament,[2]

Having regard to the opinion of the Economic and Social Committee,[3]

Whereas it is desirable to promote throughout the Community a harmonious de-velopment of economic activities and a continuous and balanced expansion by completing an internal market which functions properly and offers conditions which are similar to those obtaining in a national market; whereas in order to create a market of this kind and make it increasingly a single market, not only must barriers to free movement of goods and services be removed and arrange-ments be instituted which ensure that competition is not distorted, but, in addi-tion, legal conditions must be created which enable undertakings to adapt their

---

[1]   OJ No C 351, 31. 12. 1980, p.1 and OJ No C 230, 31. 8. 1984, p.1.
[2]   OJ No C 307, 14. 11. 1983, p.46 and OJ No C 280, 28. 10. 1991, p.153.
[3]   OJ No C 310, 30. 11. 1981, p.22.

activities to the scale of the Community, whether in manufacturing and distributing goods or in providing services; whereas for those purposes, trade marks enabling the products and services of undertakings to be distinguished by identical means throughout the entire Community, regardless of frontiers, should feature amongst the legal instruments which undertakings have at their disposal;

Whereas action by the Community would appear to be necessary for the purpose of attaining the Community's said objectives; whereas such action involves the creation of Community arrangements for trade marks whereby undertakings can by means of one procedural system obtain Community trade marks to which uniform protection is given and which produce their effects throughout the entire area of the Community; whereas the principle of the unitary character of the Community trade mark thus stated will apply unless otherwise provided for in this Regulation;

Whereas the barrier of territoriality of the rights conferred on proprietors of trade marks by the laws of the Member States cannot be removed by approximation of laws; whereas in order to open up unrestricted economic activity in the whole of the common market for the benefit of undertakings, trade marks need to be created which are governed by a uniform Community law directly applicable in all Member States;

Whereas since the Treaty has not provided the specific powers to establish such a legal instrument, Article 235 of the Treaty should be applied;

Whereas the Community law relating to trade marks nevertheless does not replace the laws of the Member States on trade marks; whereas it would not in fact appear to be justified to require undertakings to apply for registration of their trade marks as Community trade marks; whereas national trade marks continue to be necessary for those undertakings which do not want protection of their trade marks at Community level;

Whereas the rights in a Community trade mark may not be obtained otherwise than by registration, and registration is to be refused in particular if the trade mark is not distinctive, if it is unlawful or if it conflicts with earlier rights;

Whereas the protection afforded by a Community trade mark, the function of which is in particular to guarantee the trade mark as an indication of origin, is absolute in the case of identity between the mark and the sign and the goods or services; whereas the protection applies also in cases of similarity between the mark and the sign and the goods or services; whereas an interpretation should be given of the concept of similarity in relation to the likelihood of confusion; whereas the likelihood of confusion, the appreciation of which depends on numerous elements and, in particular, on the recognition of the trade mark on the market, the association which can be made with the used or registered sign, the degree of similarity between the trade mark and the sign and between the goods of services identified, constitutes the specific condition for such protection;

Whereas it follows from the principle of free flow of goods that the proprietor of a Community trade mark must not be entitled to prohibit its use by a third party in relation to goods which have been put into circulation in the Community, under the trade mark, by him or with his consent, save where there exist legitimate reasons for the proprietor to oppose further commercialization of the goods;

Whereas there is no justification for protecting Community trade marks or, as against them, any trade mark which has been registered before them, except where the trade marks are actually used;

Whereas a Community trade mark is to be regarded as an object of property which exists separately from the undertakings whose goods or services are designated by it; whereas accordingly, it must be capable of being transferred, subject to the overriding need to prevent the public being misled as a result of the transfer. It must also be capable of being charged as security in favour of a third party and of being the subject matter of licences;

Whereas administrative measures are necessary at Community level for implementing in relation to every trade mark the trade mark law created by this Regulation; whereas it is therefore essential, while retaining the Community's existing institutional structure and balance of powers, to establish an Office for Harmonization in the Internal Market (trade marks and designs) which is independent in relation to technical matters and has legal, administrative and financial autonomy; whereas to this end it is necessary and appropriate that it should be a body of the Community having legal personality and exercising the implementing powers which are conferred on it by this Regulation, and that it should operate within the framework of Community law without detracting from the competencies exercised by the Community institutions;

Whereas it is necessary to ensure that parties who are affected by decisions made by the Office are protected by the law in a manner which is suited to the special character of trade mark law; whereas to that end provision is made for an appeal to lie from decisions of the examiners and of the various divisions of the Office; whereas if the department whose decision is contested does not rectify its decision it is to remit the appeal to a Board of Appeal of the Office, which is to decide on it; whereas decisions of the Boards of Appeal are, in turn, amenable to actions before the Court of Justice of the European Communities, which has jurisdiction to annul or to alter the contested decision;

Whereas under Council Decision 88/591/ECSC, EEC, Euratom of 24 October 1988 establishing a Court of First Instance of the European Communities,[4] as amended by Decision 93/350/Euratom, ECSC, EEC of 8 June 1993,[5] that Court shall exercise at the first instance the jurisdiction conferred on the Court of Justice by the Treaties establishing the Communities – with particular regard to appeals lodged under the second subparagraph of Article 173 of the EC Treaty – and by the acts adopted in implementation thereof, save as otherwise provided in an act setting up a body governed by Community law; whereas the jurisdic-

---

[4] OJ No L 319, 25. 11. 1988, p.1 and corrigendum in OJ No L 241, 17. 8. 1989, p.4.
[5] OJ No L 144, 16. 6. 1993, p.21.

tion which this Regulation confers on the Court of Justice to cancel and reform decisions of the appeal courts shall accordingly be exercised at the first instance by the Court in accordance with the above Decision;

Whereas in order to strengthen the protection of Community trade marks the Member States should designate, having regard to their own national system, as limited a number as possible of national courts of first and second instance having jurisdiction in matters of infringement and validity of Community trade marks;

Whereas decisions regarding the validity and infringement of Community trade marks must have effect and cover the entire area of the Community, as this is the only way of preventing inconsistent decisions on the part of the courts and the Office and of ensuring that the unitary character of Community trade marks is not undermined; whereas the rules contained in the Brussels Convention of Jurisdiction and the Enforcement of Judgments in Civil and Commercial Matters will apply to all actions at law relating to Community trade marks, save where this Regulation derogates from those rules;

Whereas contradictory judgments should be avoided in actions which involve the same acts and the same parties and which are brought on the basis of a Community trade mark and parallel national trade marks; whereas for this purpose, when the actions are brought in the same Member State, the way in which this is to be achieved is a matter for national procedural rules, which are not prejudiced by this Regulation, whilst when the actions are brought in different Member States, provisions modelled on the rules on *lis pendens* and related actions of the abovementioned Brussels Convention appear appropriate;

Whereas in order to guarantee the full autonomy and independence of the Officer, it is considered necessary to grant it an autonomous budget whose revenue comes principally from fees paid by the users of the system; whereas however, the Community budgetary procedure remains applicable as far as any subsidies chargeable to general budget of the European Communities are concerned; whereas moreover, the auditing of accounts should be undertaken by the Court of Auditors;

Whereas implementing measures are required for the Regulation's application, particularly as regards the adoption and amendment of fees regulation and an Implementing Regulation; whereas such measures should be adopted by the Commission, assisted by a Committee composed of representatives of the Member States, in accordance with the procedural rules laid down in Article 2, procedure III(b), of Council Decisions 87/373/EEC of 13 July 1987 laying down the procedures for the exercise of implementing powers conferred on the Commission (1),[6]

HAS ADOPTED THIS REGULATION:

---

[6] OJ No L 197, 18. 7. 1987, p.33.

TITLE I

GENERAL PROVISIONS

Article 1

Community trade mark

1. A trade mark for goods or services which is registered in accordance with the conditions contained in this Regulation and in the manner herein provided is hereinafter referred to as a 'Community trade mark'.

2. A Community trade mark shall have a unitary character. It shall have equal effect throughout the Community: it shall not be registered, transferred or surrendered or be the subject of a decision revoking the rights of the proprietor or declaring it invalid, nor shall its use be prohibited, save in respect of the whole Community. This principle shall apply unless otherwise provided in this Regulation.

Article 2

Office

An Office for Harmonization in the Internal Market (trade marks and designs), hereinafter referred to as 'the Office', is hereby established.

Article 3

Capacity to act

For the purpose of implementing this Regulation, companies of firms and other legal bodies shall be regarded as legal persons if, under the terms of the law governing them, they have the capacity in their own name to have rights and obligations of all kinds, to make contracts or accomplish other legal acts and to sue and be sued.

TITLE II

THE LAW RELATING TO TRADE MARKS

SECTION 1

DEFINITION OF A COMMUNITY TRADE MARK
OBTAINING A COMMUNITY TRADE MARK

Article 4
Signs of which a Community trade mark may consist

A Community trade mark may consist of any signs capable of being represented graphically, particularly words, including personal names, designs, letters, numerals, the shape of goods or of their packaging, provided that such signs are capable of distinguish the goods or services of one undertaking from those of other undertakings.

Article 5
Persons who can be proprietors of Community trade marks

1. The following natural or legal persons, including authorities established under public law, may be proprietors of Community trade marks:

(a) nationals of the Member States; or

(b) nationals of other States which are parties to the Paris Convention for the protection of industrial property, hereinafter referred to as 'the Paris Convention'; or

(c) nationals of States which are not parties to the Paris Convention who are domiciled or have their seat or who have real and effective industrial or commercial establishments within the territory of the Community or of a State which is party to the Paris Convention; or

(d) nationals, other than those referred to under subparagraph (c), of any State which is not party to the Paris Convention and which, according to published findings, accords to nationals of all the Member States the same protection for trade marks as it accords to its own nationals and, if nationals of the Member States are required to prove registration in the country of origin, recognizes the registration of Community trade marks as such proof.

2. With respect to the application of paragraph 1, stateless persons as defined by Article 1 of the Convention relating to the Status of Stateless Persons signed at New York on 28 September 1954, and refugees as defined by Article 1 of the Convention relating to the Status of Refugees signed at Geneva on 28 July 1951 and modified by the Protocol relating to the Status of Refugees signed at New York on 31 January 1967, shall be regarded as nationals of the country in which they have their habitual residence.

3. Persons who are nationals of a State covered by paragraph 1(d) must prove that the trade mark for which an application for a Community trade mark has been submitted is registered in the State of origin, unless, according to published findings, the trade marks of nationals of the Member States are registered in the State of origin in question without proof of prior registration as a Community trade mark or as a national trade mark in a Member State.

Article 6
Means whereby a Community trade mark is obtained

A Community trade mark shall be obtained by registration.

Article 7
Absolute grounds for refusal

1. The following shall not be registered:

(a)   signs which do not conform to the requirements of Article 4;

(b)   trade marks which are devoid of any distinctive character;

(c)   trade marks which consist exclusively of signs or indications which may serve, in trade, to designate the kind, quality, quantity, intended purpose, value, geographical origin or the time of production of the goods or of rendering of the service, or other characteristics of the goods or service;

(d)   trade marks which consist exclusively of signs or indications which have become customary in the current language or in the bona fide and established practices of the trade;

(e)   signs which consist exclusively of:
   (i)   the shape which results from the nature of the goods themselves; or
   (ii) the shape of goods which is necessary to obtain a technical result; or
   (iii) the shape which gives substantial value to the goods;

(f)   trade marks which are contrary to public policy or to accepted principles of morality;

(g)   trade marks which are of such a nature as to deceive the public, for instance as to the nature, quality or geographical origin of the goods or service;

(h)   trade marks which have not been authorized by the competent authorities and are to be refused pursuant to Article 6ter of the Paris Convention;

(i)   trade marks which include badges, emblems or escutcheons other than those covered by Article 6ter of the Paris Convention and which are of particular public interest, unless the consent of the appropriate authorities to their registration has been given.

2. Paragraph 1 shall apply notwithstanding that the grounds of non-registrability obtain in only part of the Community.

3. Paragraph 1(b), (c) and (d) shall not apply if the trade mark has become distinctive in relation to the goods or services for which registration is requested in consequence of the use which has been made of it.

Article 8
Relative grounds of refusal

1. Upon opposition by the proprietor of an earlier trade mark, the trade mark applied for shall not be registered:

(a) if it is identical with the earlier trade mark and the goods or services for which registration is applied for are identical with the goods or services for which the earlier trade mark is protected;

(b) if because of its identity with or similarity to the earlier trade mark and the identity or similarity of the goods or services covered by the trade marks there exists a likelihood of confusion on the part of the public in the territory in which the earlier trade mark is protected; the likelihood of confusion includes the likelihood of association with the earlier trade mark.

2. For the purposes of paragraph 1, 'Earlier trade marks' means:

(a) trade marks of the following kinds with a date of application for registration which is earlier than the date of application for registration of the Community trade mark, taking account, where appropriate, of the priorities claimed in respect of those trade marks:
    (i)   Community trade marks;
    (ii) trade mark registered in a Member State, or, in the case of Belgium, the Netherlands or Luxembourg, at the Benelux Trade Mark Office;
    (iii) trade marks registered under international arrangements which have effect in a Member State;

(b) applications for the trade marks referred to in subparagraph (a), subject to their registration;

(c) trade marks which, on the date of application for registration of the Community trade mark, or, where appropriate, of the priority claimed in respect of the application for registration of the Community trade mark, are well known in a Member State, in the sense in which the words 'well known' are used in Article 6 bis of the Paris Convention.

3. Upon opposition by the proprietor of the trade mark, a trade mark shall not be registered where an agent or representative of the proprietor of the trade mark applies for registration thereof in his own name without the proprietor's consent, unless the agent, or representative justifies his action.

4. Upon opposition by the proprietor of a non-registered trade mark or of another sign used in the course of trade of more than mere local significance, the trade mark applied for shall not be registered where and to the extent that, pursuant to the law of the Member State governing that sign,

(a) rights to that sign were acquired prior to the date of application for registration of the Community trade mark, or the date of the priority claimed for the application for registration of the Community trade mark;

(b) that sign confers on its proprietor the right to prohibit the use of a subsequent trade mark.

5. Furthermore, upon opposition by the proprietor of an earlier trade mark within the meaning of paragraph 2, the trade mark applied for shall not be registered where it is identical with or similar to the earlier trade mark and is to be registered for goods or services which are not similar to those for which the earlier trade mark is registered, where in the case of an earlier Community trade mark the trade mark has a reputation in the Community and, in the case of an earlier national trade mark, the trade mark has a reputation in the Member State concerned and where the use without due cause of the trade mark applied for would take unfair advantage of, or be detrimental to, the distinctive character or the repute of the earlier trade mark.

SECTION 2

EFFECTS OF COMMUNITY TRADE MARKS

Article 9

Rights conferred by a Community trade mark

1. A Community trade mark shall confer on the proprietor exclusive rights therein. The proprietor shall be entitled to prevent all third parties not having his consent from using in the course of trade:

(a) any sign which is identical with the Community trade mark in relation to goods or services which are identical with those for which the Community trade mark is registered;

(b) any sign where, because of its identity with or similarity to the Community trade mark and the identity or similarity of the goods or services covered by the Community trade mark and the sign, there exists a likelihood of confusion on the part of the public; the likelihood of confusion includes the likelihood of association between the sign and the trade mark;

(c) any sign which is identical with or similar to the Community trade mark in relation to goods or services which are not similar to those for which the Community trade mark is registered, where the latter has a reputation in the Community and where use of that sign without due cause takes unfair advantage of, or is detrimental to, the distinctive character or the repute of the Community trade mark.

2. The following, *inter alia*, may be prohibited under paragraph 1:

(a) affixing the sign to the goods or to the packaging thereof;

(b) offering the goods, putting them on the market or stocking them for these purposes under that sign, or offering or supplying services thereunder;

(c) importing or exporting the goods under that sign;

(d) using the sign on business papers and in advertising.

3. The rights conferred by a Community trade mark shall prevail against third parties from the date of publication of registration of the trade mark. Reasonable compensation may, however, be claimed in respect of matters arising after the date of publication of a Community trade mark application, which matters would, after publication of the registration of the trade mark, be prohibited by virtue of that publication. The court seized of the case may not decide upon the merits of the case until the registration has been published.

Article 10
Reproduction of Community trade marks in dictionaries

If the reproduction of a Community trade mark in a dictionary, encyclopaedia or similar reference work gives the impression that it constitutes the generic name of the goods or services for which the trade mark is registered, the publisher of the work shall, at the request of the proprietor of the Community trade mark, ensure that the reproduction of the trade mark at the latest in the next edition of the publication is accompanied by an indication that it is a registered trade mark.

Article 11
Prohibition on the use of a Community trade mark registered in the name of an agent or representative

Where a Community trade mark is registered in the name of the agent or representative of a person who is the proprietor of that trade mark, without the proprietor's authorization, the latter shall be entitled to oppose the use of his mark by his agent or representative if he has not authorized such use, unless the agent or representative justifies his action.

Article 12
Limitation of the effects of a Community trade mark

A Community trade mark shall not entitle the proprietor to prohibit a third party from using in the course of trade:

(a) his own name or address;

(b) indications concerning the kind, quality, quantity, intended purpose, value, geographical origin, the time of production of the goods or of rendering of the service, or other characteristics of the goods or service; (c) the trade mark where it is necessary to indicate the intended purpose of a product or service, in particular as accessories or spare parts, provided he uses them in accordance with honest practices in industrial or commercial matters.

Article 13

Exhaustion of the rights conferred by a Community trade mark

1. A Community trade mark shall not entitle the proprietor to prohibit its use in relation to goods which have been put on the market in the Community under that trade mark by the proprietor or with his consent.

2. Paragraph 1 shall not apply where there exist legitimate reasons for the proprietor to oppose further commercialization of the goods, especially where the condition of the goods is changed or impaired after they have been put on the market.

Article 14

Complementary application of national law relating to infringement

1. The effects of Community trade marks shall be governed solely by the provisions of this Regulation. In other respects, infringement of a Community trade mark shall be governed by the national law relating to infringement of a national trade mark in accordance with the provisions of Title X.

2. This Regulation shall not prevent actions concerning a Community trade mark being brought under the law of Member States relating in particular to civil liability and unfair competition.

3. The rules of procedure to be applied shall be determined in accordance with the provisions of Title X.

SECTION 3

USE OF COMMUNITY TRADE MARKS

Article 15

Use of Community trade marks

1. If, within a period of five years following registration, the proprietor has not put the Community trade mark to genuine use in the Community in connection with the goods or services in respect of which it is registered, or if such use has been suspended during an uninterrupted period of five years, the Community trade mark shall be subject to the sanctions provided for in this Regulation, unless there are proper reasons for non-use.

2. The following shall also constitute use within the meaning of paragraph 1:

(a) use of the Community trade mark in a form differing in elements which do not alter the distinctive character of the mark in the form in which it was registered;

(b) affixing of the Community trade mark to goods or to the packaging thereof in the Community solely for export purposes.

3. Use of the Community trade mark with the consent of the proprietor shall be deemed to constitute use by the proprietor.

SECTION 4

COMMUNITY TRADE MARKS AS OBJECTS OF PROPERTY

Article 16

Dealing with Community trade marks as national trade marks

1. Unless Articles 17 to 24 provide otherwise, a Community trade mark as an object of property shall be dealt with in its entirety, and for the whole area of the Community, as a national trade mark registered in the Member State in which, according to the Register of Community trade marks,

(a) the proprietor has his seat or his domicile on the relevant date; or

(b) where subparagraph (a) does not apply, the proprietor has an establishment on the relevant date.

2. In cases which are not provided for by paragraph 1, the Member State referred to in that paragraph shall be the Member State in which the seat of the Office is situated.

3. If two or more persons are mentioned in the Register of Community trade marks as joint proprietors, paragraph 1 shall apply to the joint proprietor first mentioned; failing this, it shall apply to the subsequent joint proprietors in the order in which they are mentioned. Where paragraph 1 does not apply to any of the joint proprietors, paragraph 2 shall apply.

Article 17

Transfer

1. A Community trade mark may be transferred, separately from any transfer of the undertaking, in respect of some or all of the goods or services for which it is registered.

2. A transfer of the whole of the undertaking shall include the transfer of the Community trade mark except where, in accordance with the law governing the transfer, there is agreement to the contrary or circumstances clearly dictate otherwise. This provision shall apply to the contractual obligation to transfer the undertaking.

3. Without prejudice to paragraph 2, an assignment of the Community trade mark shall be made in writing and shall require the signature of the parties to the contract, except when it is a result of a judgment; otherwise it shall be void.

4. Where it is clear from the transfer documents that because of the transfer the Community trade mark is likely to mislead the public concerning the nature, quality or geographical origin of the goods or services in respect of which it is registered, the Office shall not register the transfer unless the successor agrees to limit registration of the Community trade mark to goods or services in respect of which it is not likely to mislead.

5. On request of one of the parties a transfer shall be entered in the Register and published.

6. As long as the transfer has not been entered in the Register, the successor in title may not invoke the rights arising from the registration of the Community trade mark.

7. Where there are time limits to be observed *vis-à-vis* the Office, the successor in title may make the corresponding statements to the Office once the request for registration of the transfer has been received by the Office.

8. All documents which require notification to the proprietor of the Community trade mark in accordance with Article 77 shall be addressed to the person registered as proprietor.

Article 18
Transfer of a trade mark registered in the name of an agent

Where a Community trade mark is registered in the name of the agent or representative of a person who is the proprietor of that trade mark, without the proprietor's authorization, the latter shall be entitled to demand the assignment in his favour of the said registration, unless such agent or representative justifies his action.

Article 19
Rights in rem

1. A Community trade mark may, independently of the undertaking, be given as security or be the subject of rights in rem.

2. On request of one of the parties, rights mentioned in paragraph 1 shall be entered in the Register and published.

Article 20
Levy of execution

1. A Community trade mark may be levied in execution.

2. As regards the procedure for levy of execution in respect of a Community trade mark, the courts and authorities of the Member States determined in accordance with Article 16 shall have exclusive jurisdiction.

3. On request of one of the parties, levy of execution shall be entered in the Register and published.

Article 21
Bankruptcy or like proceedings

1. Until such time as common rules for the Member States in this field enter into force, the only Member State in which a Community trade mark may be involved in bankruptcy or like proceedings shall be that in which such proceedings are first brought within the meaning of national law or of conventions applicable in this field.

2. Where a Community trade mark is involved in bankruptcy or like proceedings, on request of the competent national authority an entry to this effect shall be made in the Register and published.

Article 22
Licensing

1. A Community trade mark may be licensed for some or all of the goods or services for which it is registered and for the whole or part of the Community. A licence may be exclusive or non-exclusive.

2. The proprietor of a Community trade mark may invoke the rights conferred by that trade mark against a licensee who contravenes any provision in his licensing contract with regard to its duration, the form covered by the registration in which the trade mark may be used, the scope of the goods or services for which the licence is granted, the territory in which the trade mark may be affixed, or the quality of the goods manufactured or of the services provided by the licensee.

3. Without prejudice to the provision of the licensing contract, the licensee may bring proceedings for infringement of a Community trade mark only if its proprietor consents thereto. However, the holder of an exclusive licence may bring such proceedings if the proprietor of the trade mark, after formal notice, does not himself bring infringement proceedings within an appropriate period.

4. A licensee shall, for the purpose of obtaining compensation for damage suffered by him, be entitled to intervene in infringement proceedings brought by the proprietor of the Community trade mark.

5. On request of one of the parties the grant or transfer of a licence in respect of a Community trade mark shall be entered in the Register and published.

Article 23
Effects *vis-à-vis* third parties

1. Legal acts referred to in Articles 17, 19 and 22 concerning a Community trade mark shall only have effects *vis-à-vis* third parties in all the Member States after entry in the Register. Nevertheless, such an act, before it is so entered, shall have effect *vis-à-vis* third parties who have acquired rights in the trade mark after the date of that act but who knew of the act at the date on which the rights were acquired.

2. Paragraph 1 shall not apply in the case of a person who acquires the Community trade mark or a right concerning the Community trade mark by way of transfer of the whole of the undertaking or by any other universal succession.

3. The effects *vis-à-vis* third parties of the legal acts referred to in Article 20 shall be governed by the law of the Member State determined in accordance with Article 16.

4. Until such time as common rules for the Member States in the field of bankruptcy enter into force, the effects *vis-à-vis* third parties of bankruptcy or like proceedings shall be governed by the law of the Member State in which such proceedings are first brought within the meaning of national law or of conventions applicable in this field.

Article 24
The application for a Community trade mark as an object of property

Articles 16 to 23 shall apply to applications for Community trade marks.

QUESTION

To what extent is legislative harmonization a more effective and justified approach to the development of a Community-wide system of intellectual property than the work of the European Court?

8 Internal Market and Consumer Protection: EC and Civil Law

A. INTRODUCTION: THE ROLE OF CIVIL LAW IN THE EC; EC RULES DRAWN FROM SECONDARY COMMUNITY LAW

1. Civil law and market integration

There is no policy statement in the Treaty of Rome on whether and, if so, how civil law should become the subject of Community law. One might even read the Treaty in such a way as to confirm the Member States' exclusive competence in the shaping of civil law. The European market would then resemble the American market where there are no or only limited common civil law rules. The differences within the United States have to be balanced out with the help of international private law rules. And indeed the American experience is often used to prove the feasibility of divergent civil legal orders within one European market.

That starting point has been revised by neither the Single European Act, nor the Maastricht Treaty. Nevertheless there are two conventions to be mentioned which determine the relationship between national civil law and the EC law. First of all there is the so called Rome Convention (OJ 1980 L 266, 19.6.1989, 1 *et seq.*) intended to harmonize the Member States' international private law rules. The Rome Convention has not been adopted under the provisions of the Treaty of Rome. It is a piece of public international law and the Member States have insisted on the need to transform the Rome Convention into national law. The Rome Convention is not directly part of EC law. The second important piece in that field is the Brussels Convention, adopted under Article 220 OJ L 285, 30.10.1989, 1 *et seq.* (Convention on Jurisdiction and the Enforcement of Judgements in Civil and Commercial Law Matters). As the title indicates it is not aiming at the harmonization of civil law, but at the execution of foreign decisions. The general idea of the Convention is that judicial decisions shall be mutually recognized i.e. the court in charge of the execution shall not re-examine the subject matter. The Member States have agreed on the necessity to put both Conventions under the jurisdiction of the Court of Justice, so as to guarantee a common reading of the Conventions.

The only Community organ which has taken a clear position on the relationship between civil law and EC law is the European Parliament (OJ 1989 C 158, 400 *et seq.*). It calls for a European civil law, that is, one and the same law governing the relationships between private individuals in the European Community. The Commission has not taken a clear position yet. It is to some extent involved in the academic attempts to elaborate such a European civil code, but it has not officially accepted the European Parliament's request, nor has it adopted a policy decision.

This does not mean, however, that the Community has not tried to harmonize the civil law by way of secondary Community law. However, efforts remain fragmented and concerns where partial harmonization is felt necessary to prevent distortion of competition, or to remove barriers to trade, or where harmonization of civil law is part of a particular Community policy. Under the first category come the different Directives on company law. Here the Community is trying to develop a common frame for the organization of private entities. These Directives are not the subject of our book. Much more important for us is the second category, civil law harmonization as part of social policy. Again, labour law can be set aside, as there is a case-book in this series dealing with that subject (L. Betten, C. Kollonay-Lehoczik, J. Rojot, *European Labour Law and Industrial Relations*), so what remains is consumer policy and consumer law.

2. EC law and consumer law

Modern consumer protection began in the United States with the famous Kennedy Declaration on consumer rights in 1962. Since then the distinction between the consumers' economic rights and his or her right to health and safety is well established and made its way through the Member States consumer policy in the sixties and seventies. The Council of Ministers adopted the first consumer programme as early as 1975 (OJ C 92, 25.4.1995) and the second consumer programme in 1981 (OJ C 133, 3.6.1981), thereby following the line of the Kennedy Declaration. These two programmes have been updated (New Impulse on Consumer Protection OJ C 167, 5.7.1986, 1 *et seq.*), and integrated into so-called action plans (COM (90) 98, 3.5.1990, COM (93) 378, 28.7.1993) and COM (95) 519, 31.10.1995. The two programmes, however, still form the starting point of the European Consumer Policy.

In 1975 consumer policy was not part of the Treaty of Rome and the Council had to base the adoption of the programme on the Treaty generally and on Article 2 in particular. The Single European Act changed the situation to the benefit of consumer protection which was indirectly accepted in Article 100a(3).

I. By way of derogations from Article 100 and save where otherwise provided in this Treaty, the following provisions shall apply for the achievement of the objectives set out in Art. 7 a. The Council shall, acting in accordance with the procedure referred to in Art. 189 b and after consultation of the Economic and Social Committee adopt the measures for the approximation of the provisions laid down by law, regulation or administrative action in Member States which have as their objective the establishment and functioning of the internal market.

[...]

III. The Commission in its proposals envisaged in paragraph 1 concerning health safety and environmental protection and consumer protection, will take as a base a high level of protection.

The legal basis remained Article 100 a, completion of the Internal Market, but the Commission was bound to respect a high level of protection, a principle which is not yet concretized, though legal doctrine favours an understanding of providing for the 'best possible' protection. The recognition of consumer protection came with the Maastricht Treaty which gives consumer policy a full legal status in primary Community law, Article 129 a:

TITLE XI

CONSUMER PROTECTION

Article 129a

1. The Community shall contribute to the attainment of a high level of consumer protection through:

(a) measures adopted pursuant to Article 100a in the context of the completion of the internal market;

(b) specific action which supports and supplements the policy pursued by the Member States to protect the health, safety and economic interests of consumers and to provide adequate information to consumers.

2. The Council, acting in accordance with the procedure referred to in Article 189b and after consulting the Economic and Social Committee, shall adopt the specific action referred to in paragraph 1(b).

3. Action adopted pursuant to paragraph 2 shall not prevent any Member State from maintaining or introducing more stringent protective measures. Such measures must be compatible with this Treaty. The Commission shall be notified of them.

What interests us here is not so much the intricacies of the interpretation from Article 129a, its differences from Article 100a and the need to shape a borderline between both provisions with respect to the different role of the European Parliament. Our focus is the measures the European Community has taken pursuant to the two programmes to harmonize consumer law in the field of civil law. The lack of a clear cut competence has not prevented the European Community from adopting Directives, first on the basis of Article 100 and with the adoption of the

Single European Act on Article 100a, whereas Article 129a has not yet been applied. Two areas are of major concern in civil law: contract law and tort law. Most of the activities of the Community concern contract law. In 1985 the Council adopted the Directive on doorstep selling (OJ 1985 L 372, 31.12.1985, 31 *et seq.*). In 1986 the Directive on consumer credit (OJ L 42, 12.2.1987, 48 *et seq.*, as revised OJ 1990 L 61, 10.3.1990, 14 *et seq.*), in 1990 the Directive on package tours (OJ 1990 L 158, 23.6.1990, 59 *et seq.*), in 1993 the Directive on unfair contract terms (OJ L 95, 21.4.1993, 29 *et seq.*) and in 1994 the Directive on time sharing (OJ L 280, 29.10.1994, 83 *et seq.*). Other projects are under consideration: a Directive on distant selling (OJ 1995 C 288, 30.10.1995, 1 *et seq.*) and on consumer guarantees where a first draft is supposed to be published in the course of the year pursuant to the Green Paper on Guarantees on Consumer Goods and After Sales Services, COM (93) 509 final 15 November 1993).

There is a common characteristic in all Community activities: market regulation aims at the harmonization of specific types of risks to consumers, or specific types of contracts. But even where harmonization regulates a particular contract, it does not cover the area as a whole. Harmonization is not meant to integrate markets but to set incentives, to introduce new areas of law in the civil law code for the better protection of the consumer. There is only one area of concern where the Community has tried to regulate a specific market for a specific type of service as a whole. This area is financial services where a series of Directives has been adopted to create a common market for insurance services.

3. Contract law and tort law

The most important piece of community legislation in contract law is the Directive on unfair contract terms, which had to be implemented into national law by 1 January 1995. The Directive is intended to harmonize Member States' unfair contract terms legislation at a minimum level. At the core of the Directive lies the introduction of a general fairness test supplemented by an indicative and non-exhaustive list of unfair terms against which pre-formulated standard terms or pre-formulated individual terms in consumer contracts have to be measured. Enforcement may be guaranteed either by way of a collective action given to consumer organizations or by way of administrative control. It is worthwhile quoting here the leading recitals explaining the purpose of the directive as well as the provisions, as they will probably determine the debate on an emerging European civil law over the years to come:

COUNCIL

COUNCIL DIRECTIVE 93/13/EEC

of 5 April 1993

on unfair terms in consumer contracts

THE COUNCIL OF THE EUROPEAN COMMUNITIES,

Having regard to the Treaty establishing the European Economic Community, and in particular Article 100 A thereof,

Having regard to the proposal from the Commission.[1]

In cooperation with the European Parliament.[2]

Having regard to the opinion of the Economic and Social Committee.[3]

Whereas it is necessary to adopt measures with the aim of progressively establishing the internal market before 31 December 1992; whereas the internal market comprises an area without internal frontiers in which goods, persons, services and capital move freely;

Whereas the laws of Member States relating to the terms of contract between the seller of goods or supplier of services, on the one hand, and the consumer of them, on the other hand, show many disparities, with the result that the national markets for the sale of goods and services to consumers differ from each other and that distortions of competition may arise amongst the sellers and suppliers, notably when they sell and supply in other Member States;

Whereas, in particular, the laws of Member States relating to unfair terms in consumer contracts show marked divergences;

Whereas it is the responsibility of the Member States to ensure that contracts concluded with consumers do not contain unfair terms; [...]

Whereas the two Community programmes for a consumer protection and information policy[4] underlined the importance of safeguarding consumers in the matter of unfair terms of contract; whereas this protection ought to be provided by laws and regulations which are either harmonized at Community level or adopted directly at that level;

Whereas in accordance with the principle laid down under the heading 'Protection of the economic interests of the consumers', as stated in those pro-

---

[1] OJ No C 73, 24. 3. 1992, p.7.
[2] OJ No C 326, 16. 12. 1991, p.108 and OJ No C 21, 25. 1. 1993.
[3] OJ No C 159, 17.6. 1991, p.34.
[4] OJ No C 92, 25. 4. 1975, p.1 and OJ No C 133, 3. 6. 1981, p.1.

grammes: 'acquirers of goods and services should be protected against the abuse of power by the seller or supplier, in particular against one-sided standard contracts and the unfair exclusion of essential rights in contracts'; [...]

Whereas the assessment, according to the general criteria chosen, of the unfair character of terms, in particular in sale of supply activities of a public nature providing collective services which take account of solidarity among users, must be supplemented by a means of making an overall evaluation of the different interests involved; whereas this constitutes the requirement of good faith; whereas, in making an assessment of good faith, particular regard shall be had to the strength of the bargaining positions of the parties, whether the consumer had an inducement to agree to the term and whether the goods or services were sold or supplied to the special order of the consumer; whereas the requirement of good faith may be satisfied by the seller or supplier where he deals fairly and equitably with the other party whose legitimate interests he has to take into account; [...]

Whereas, for the purposes of this Directive, assessment of unfair character shall not be made of terms which describe the main subject matter of the contract nor the quality/price ratio of the goods or services supplied; whereas the main subject matter of the contract and the price/quality ratio may nevertheless be taken into account in assessing the fairness of other terms; whereas it follows, *inter alia*, that in insurance contracts, the terms which clearly define or circumscribe the insured risk and the insurer's liability shall not be subject to such assessment since these restrictions are taken into account in calculating the premium paid by the consumer;

Whereas contracts should be drafted in plain, intelligible language, the consumer should actually be given an opportunity to examine all the terms and, if in doubt, the interpretation most favourable to the consumer should prevail; [...]

Whereas persons or organizations, if regarded under the law of a Member State as having a legitimate interest in the matter, must have facilities for initiating proceedings concerning terms of contract drawn up for general use in contracts concluded with consumers, and in particular unfair terms, either before a court or before an administrative authority competent to decide upon complaints or to initiate appropriate legal proceedings; whereas this possibility does not, however, entail prior verification of the general conditions obtaining in individual economic sectors;

Whereas the courts or administrative authorities of the Member States must have at their disposal adequate and effective means of preventing the continued application of unfair terms in consumer contracts.

HAS ADOPTED THIS DIRECTIVE:

Article 1

1. The purpose of this Directive is to approximate the laws, regulations and administrative provisions of the Member States relating to unfair terms in contracts concluded between a seller or supplier and a consumer.

2. The contractual terms which reflect mandatory statutory or regulatory provisions and the provisions or principles of international conventions to which the Member States or the Community are party, particularly in the transport area, shall not be subject to the provisions of this Directive.

Article 2

For the purposes of this Directive:

(a) 'unfair terms' means the contractual terms defined in Article 3;

(b) 'consumer' means any natural person who, in contracts covered by this Directive, is acting for purposes which are outside his trade, business or profession;

(c) 'seller or supplier' means any natural or legal person who, in contracts covered by this Directive, is acting for purposes relating to his trade, business or profession, whether publicly owned or privately owned.

Article 3

1. A contractual term which has not been individually negotiated shall be regarded as unfair if, contrary to the requirement of good faith, it causes a significant imbalance in the parties' rights and obligations arising under the contract, to the detriment of the consumer.

2. A term shall always be regarded as not individually negotiated where it has been drafted in advance and the consumer has therefore not been able to influence the substance of the term, particularly in the context of a preformulated standard contract.

The fact that certain aspects of a term or one specific term have been individually negotiated shall not exclude the application of this Article to the rest of a contract if an overall assessment of the contract indicates that it is nevertheless a pre-formulated standard contract.

Where any seller or supplier claims that a standard term has been individually negotiated, the burden of proof in this respect shall be incumbent on him.

3. The Annex shall contain an indicative and non-exhaustive list of the terms which may be regarded as unfair.

Article 4

1.   Without prejudice to Article 7, the unfairness of a contractual term shall be assessed, taking into account the nature of the goods or services for which the contract was concluded and by referring, at the time of conclusion of the contract, to all the circumstances attending the conclusion of the contract and to all the other terms of the contract or of another contract on which it is dependent.

2.   Assessment of the unfair nature of the terms shall relate neither to the definition of the main subject matter of the contract nor to the adequacy of the price and remuneration, on the one hand, as against the services or goods supplies in exchange, on the other, in so far as these terms are in plain intelligible language.

Article 5

In the case of contracts where all or certain terms offered to the consumer are in writing, these terms must always be drafted in plain, intelligible language. Where there is doubt about the meaning of a term, the interpretation most favourable to the consumer shall prevail. This rule on interpretation shall not apply in the context of the procedures laid down in Article 7 (2).

Article 6

1.   Member States shall lay down that unfair terms used in a contract concluded with a consumer by a seller or supplier shall, as provided for under their national law, not be binding on the consumer and that the contract shall continue to bind the parties upon those terms if it is capable of continuing in existence without the unfair terms.

2.   Member States shall take the necessary measures to ensure that the consumer does not lose the protection granted by this Directive by virtue of the choice of the law of a non-Member country as the law applicable to the contract if the latter has a close connection with the territory of the Member States.

Article 7

1.   Member States shall ensure that, in the interests of consumers and of competitors, adequate and effective means exist to prevent the continued use of unfair terms in contracts concluded with consumers by sellers or suppliers.

2.   The means referred to in paragraph 1 shall include provisions whereby persons or organizations, having a legitimate interest under national law in protecting consumers, may take action according to the national law concerned before the courts or before competent administrative bodies for a decision as to whether contractual terms drawn up for general use are unfair, so that they can apply appropriate and effective means to prevent the continued use of such terms.

3.   With due regard for national laws, the legal remedies referred to in paragraph 2 may be directed separately or jointly against a number of sellers or suppliers from the same economic sector or their associations which use or recommend the use of the same general contractual terms or similar terms.

Article 8

Member States may adopt or retain the most stringent provisions compatible with the Treaty in the area covered by this Directive, to ensure a maximum degree of protection for the consumer.

Article 9

The Commission shall present a report to the European Parliament and to the Council concerning the application of this Directive five years at the latest after the date in Article 10 (1).

Article 10

1.   Member States shall bring into force the laws, regulations and administrative provisions necessary to comply with this Directive no later than 31 December 1994. They shall forthwith inform the Commission thereof.

These provisions shall be applicable to all contracts concluded after 31 December 1994.

2.   When Member States adopt these measures, they shall contain a reference to this Directive or shall be accompanied by such reference on the occasion of their official publication. The methods of making such a reference shall be laid down by the Member States.

3.   Member States shall communicate the main provisions of national law which they adopt in the field covered by this Directive to the Commission.

Article 11

This Directive is addressed to the Member States.

Done at Luxembourg, 5 April 1993.

For the Council

The President

N. HELVEG PETERSEN

QUESTIONS ON THE DIRECTIVE ON UNFAIR TERMS IN CONSUMER CONTRACTS:

1   What is the notion of a 'consumer', which the directive introduces? Is there a concept behind, and if so, what is it? And how can it be reconciled with civil law?

2   Article 3 states that a clause is supposed to be unfair, 'if, contrary to the requirement of good faith, it causes a significant imbalance' of the parties' rights and duties, to the detriment of the consumer. Good faith is a well-known concept in most of the continental civil law codes, but how does it fit into common law thinking? The Directive provides for a 'content control' executed by the courts, which runs contrary to the doctrine of freedom of contract. Good faith shall be interpreted in a European perspective, where shall the Court of Justice as the ultimate instance take the criteria from?

These are all complicated questions in the building of a European civil law. The same holds true for the second area, where the Community substantially intervenes, in tort law. Strong and comprehensive legislation on product liability formed one of the key issues of consumer protection policies in the 1960s and 1970s. Contrary to unfair standard terms legislation Member States refrained from adopting national legislation and instead favoured the elaboration of a European solution, which should not cover the EC alone but also most of the then EFTA countries. After lengthy discussions lasting more than ten years the Council adopted in 1985 the product liability Directive (OJ 1985 L 210, 7.8.1985, 29 *et seq.*). A draft Directive for the liability of services (OJ 1991 C 1, 18.1.1991, 8 *et seq.*) faces, however, fierce objection by the Member States and it is not all clear, whether it will be adopted or not. Both Directives aim at the protection of consumers. The product liability directive introduces the concept of strict liability, i.e. a liability without fault although the detailed meaning of the Directive's liability regime remains controversial. Except France, Member States have implemented the product liability Directive into national law. Now the question remains whether and to what extent the Directive will gain importance in the national legal systems.

COUNCIL DIRECTIVE

of 25 July 1985

on the approximation of the laws, regulations and administrative provisions of the Member States concerning liability for defective products

(85/374/EEC)

[...]

Whereas approximation of the laws of the Member States concerning the liability of the producer for damage caused by the defectiveness of his products is necessary because the existing divergences may distort competition and affect the movement of goods within the common market and entail a differing degree of protection of the consumer against damage caused by a defective product to his health or property;

Whereas liability without fault on the part of the producer is the sole means of adequately solving the problem, peculiar to our age of increasing technically, of a fair apportionment of the risks inherent in modern technological production; [...]

Whereas protection of the consumer requires that all producers involved in the production process should be made liable, in so far as their finished product, component part or any raw material supplied by them was defective; whereas, for the same reason, liability should extend to importers of products into the Community and to persons who present themselves as producers by affixing their name, trade mark or other distinguishing feature or who supply a product the producer of which cannot be identified; [...]

Whereas, to protect the physical well-being and property of the consumer, the defectiveness of the product should be determined by reference not to its fitness for use but to the lack of the safety which the public at large is entitled to expect; whereas the safety is assessed by excluding any misuse of the product not reasonable under the circumstances; [...]

Whereas, since the exclusion of primary agricultural products and game from the scope of this Directive may be felt, in certain Member States, in view of what is expected for the protection of consumers, to restrict unduly such protection, it should be possible for a Member State to extend liability to such products;

Whereas, for similar reasons, the possibility offered to a producer to free himself from liability if he proves that the state of scientific and technical knowledge at the time when he put the product into circulation was not such as to enable the existence of a defect to be discovered may be felt in certain Member States to restrict unduly the protection of the consumer; whereas it should therefore be possible for a Member State to maintain in its legislation or to provide by new legislation that this exonerating circumstance is not admitted; whereas, in the case of new legislation, making use of this derogation should, however, be subject to a Community stand-still procedure, in order to raise, if possible, the level of protection in a uniform manner throughout the Community;

Whereas, taking into account the legal traditions in most of the Member States, it is inappropriate to set any financial ceiling on the producer's liability without fault; whereas, in so far as there are, however, differing traditions, it seems possible to admit that a Member State may derogate from the principle of unlimited liability by providing a limit for the total liability of the producer for damage resulting from a death or personal injury and caused by identical items with the same defect, provided that this limit is established at a level sufficiently high to guarantee adequate protection of the consumer and the correct functioning of the common market;

Whereas the harmonization resulting from this cannot be total at the present stage, but opens the way towards greater harmonization; whereas it is therefore necessary that the Council receive at regular intervals, reports from the Commission on the application of this Directive, accompanied, as the case may be, by appropriate proposals;

Whereas it is particularly important in this respect that a re-examination be carried out of those parts of the Directive relating to the derogations open to the Member States, at the expiry of a period of sufficient length to gather practical experience on the effects of these derogations on the protection of consumers and on the functioning of the common market [the Council]

HAS ADOPTED THIS DIRECTIVE:

Article 1

The producer shall be liable for damage caused by a defect in his product.

Article 2

For the purpose of this Directive 'product' means all movables, with the exception of primary agricultural products and game, even though incorporated into another movable or into an immovable. 'Primary agricultural products' means the products of the soil, of stock-farming and of fisheries, excluding products which have undergone initial processing. 'Product' includes electricity.

Article 3

1. 'Producer' means the manufacturer of a finished product, the producer of any raw material or the manufacturer of a component part and any person who, by putting his name, trade mark or other distinguishing feature on the product presents himself as its producer.

2. Without prejudice to the liability of the producer, any person who imports into the Community a product for sale, hire, leasing or any form of distribution in the course of his business shall be deemed to be a producer within the meaning of this Directive and shall be responsible as a producer.

3. Where the producer of the product cannot be identified, each supplier of the product shall be treated as its producer unless he informs the injured person, within a reasonable time, of the identity of the producer or of the person who supplied him with the product. The same shall apply, in the case of an imported product, if this product does not indicate the identity of the importer referred to in paragraph 2, even if the name of the producer is indicated.

Article 4

The injured person shall be required to prove the damage, the defect and the causal relationship between defect and damage.

Article 5

Where as a result of the provisions of this Directive, two or more persons are liable for the same damage, they shall be liable jointly and severally, without prejudice to the provisions of national law concerning the rights of contribution or recourse.

Article 6

1. A product is defective when it does not provide the safety which a person is entitled to expect, taking all circumstances into account, including:

(a) the presentation of the product;

(b) the use to which it could reasonably be expected that the product would be put;

(c) the time when the product was put into circulation.

2. A product shall not be considered defective for the sole reason that a better product is subsequently put into circulation.

Article 7

The producer shall not be liable as a result of this Directive if he proves:

(a) that he did not put the product into circulation; or

(b) that, having regard to the circumstances, it is probable that the defect which caused the damage did not exist at the time when the product was put into circulation by him or that this defect came into being afterwards; or

(c) that the product was neither manufactured by him for sale or any form of distribution for economic purpose nor manufactured or distributed by him in the course of his business; or

(d) that the defect is due to compliance of the product with mandatory regulations issued by the public authorities; or

(e) that the state of scientific and technical knowledge at the time when he put the product into circulation was not such as to enable the existence of the defect to be discovered; or

(f) in the case of a manufacturer of a component, that the defect is attributable to the design of the product in which the component has been fitted or to the instructions given by the manufacturer of the product.

Article 8

1. Without prejudice to the provisions of national law concerning the right of contribution or recourse, the liability of the producer shall not be reduced when the damage is caused both by a defect in product and by the act or omission of a third party.

2. The liability of the producer may be reduced or disallowed when, having regard to all the circumstances, the damage is caused both by a defect in the product and by the fault of the injured person or any person for whom the injured person is responsible.

Article 9

For the purpose of Article 1, 'damage' means:

(a) damage caused by death or by personal injuries;

(b) damage to, or destruction of, any item of property other than the defective product itself, with a lower threshold of 500 ECU, provided that the item of property:
   (i) is of a type ordinarily intended for private use or consumption, and
   (ii) was used by the injured person mainly for his own private use or consumption.

This article shall be without prejudice to national provisions relating to non-material damage.

Article 10

1. Member States shall provide in their legislation that a limitation period of three years shall apply to proceedings for the recovery of damages as provided for in this Directive. The limitation period shall begin to run from the day on which the plaintiff became aware, or should reasonably have become aware, of the damage, the defect and the identity of the producer.

2. The laws of Member States regulating suspension or interruption of the limitation period shall not be affected by this Directive.

Article 11

Member States shall provide in their legislation that the rights conferred upon the injured person pursuant to this Directive shall be extinguished upon the expiry of a period of 10 years from the date on which the producer put into circulation the actual product which caused the damage, unless the injured person has in the meantime instituted proceedings against the producer.

Article 12

The liability of the producer arising from this Directive may not, in relation to the injured person, be limited or excluded by a provision limiting his liability or exempting him from liability.

Article 13

This Directive shall not affect any rights which an injured person may have according to the rules of the law of contractual or non-contractual liability or a special liability system existing at the moment when this Directive is notified.

Article 14

This Directive shall not apply to injury or damage arising from nuclear accidents and covered by international conventions ratified by the Member States.

Article 15

1. Each Member State may:

(a) by way of derogation from Article 2, provide in its legislation that within the meaning of Article 1 of this Directive 'product' also means primary agricultural products and game;

(b) by way of derogation from Article 7(e), maintain or, subject to the procedure set out in paragraph 2 of this Article, provide in this legislation that the producer shall be liable even if he proves that the state of scientific and technical knowledge at the time when he put the product into circulation was not such as to enable the existence of a defect to be discovered.

2. A Member State wishing to introduce the measure specified in paragraph 1(b) shall communicate the text of the proposed measure to the Commission. The Commission shall inform the other Member States thereof.

The Member State concerned shall hold the proposed measure in abeyance for nine months after the Commission is informed and provided that in the meantime the Commission has not submitted to the Council a proposal amending this Directive on the relevant matter. However, if within three months of receiving the said information, the Commission does not advise the Member State concerned that it intends submitting such a proposal to the Council, the Member State may take the proposed measure immediately.

If the Commission does submit to the Council such a proposal amending this Directive within the aforementioned nine months, the Member State concerned shall hold the proposed measure in abeyance for a further period of 18 months from the date on which the proposal is submitted.

3. Ten years after the date of notification of this Directive, the Commission shall submit to the Council a report on the effect that rulings by the courts as to the application of Article 7(e) and of paragraph 1(b) of this Article have on consumer protection and the functioning of the common market. In the light of this report the Council, acting on a proposal from the Commission and pursuant to the terms of Article 100 of the Treaty, shall decide whether to repeal Article 7(e).

Article 16

1. Any Member State may provide that a producer's total liability for damage resulting from a death or personal injury and caused by identical items with the same defect shall be limited to an amount which may not be less than 70 million ECU.

2. Ten years after the date of notification of this Directive, the Commission shall submit to the Council a report on the effect on consumer protection and the functioning of the common market of the implementation of the financial limit on liability by those Member States which have used the option provided for in paragraph 1. In the light of this report the Council, acting on a proposal from the Commission and pursuant to the terms of Article 100 of the Treaty, shall decide whether to repeal paragraph 1.

Article 17

This Directive shall not apply to products put into circulation before the date on which the provisions referred to in Article 19 enter into force.

Article 18

1. For the purposes of this Directive, the ECU shall be that defined by Regulation (EEC) No 3180/78,[1] as amended by Regulation (EEC) No 2626/84.[2] The

---

[1] OJ No L 379, 30.12.1978, p.1.
[2] OJ No L 247, 16.9.1984, p.1.

equivalent in national currency shall initially be calculated at the rate obtaining on the date of adoption of this Directive.

2. Every five years the Council, acting on a proposal from the Commission, shall examine and, if need be, revise the amounts in this Directive, in the light of economic and monetary trends in the Community.

Article 19

1. Member States shall bring into force, not later than three years from the date of notification of this Directive, the laws, regulations and administrative provisions necessary to comply with this Directive. They shall forthwith inform the Commission thereof.[3]

2. The procedure set out in Article 15 (2) shall apply from the date of notification of this Directive.

Article 20

Member States shall communicate to the Commission the texts of the main provisions of national law which they subsequently adopt in the field governed by this Directive.

Article 21

Every five years the Commission shall present a report to the Council on the application of this Directive and, if necessary, shall submit appropriate proposa

ls to it.

Article 22

This Directive is addressed to the Member States.

Done at Brussels, 25 July 1985.

For the Council

The President

J. POOS

---

[3]   This Directive was notified to the Member States on 30 July 1985.

QUESTIONS ON THE PRODUCT LIABILITY DIRECTIVE

1   Is it correct to say that the Directive introduces a concept of strict liability, if the producer is given the possibility to escape strict liability, if he or she can prove that the state of scientific and technical knowledge at the time when the product was put into circulation was not such as to enable the existence of the defect to be discovered (Article 7 (e)'s so-called development risk defence)?

2   A key issue of the Directive is the definition of a 'defect'. Article 6 declares a product to be defective if it is not fit for the use 'to which it could reasonably be expected that the product would be put'. What are reasonable expectations of consumers? Is it on the consumer to decide on the reasonableness or on the manufacturer who by way of users' instructions can design the expectations of the consumer?

Bear in mind that the ultimate instance to interpret the notion of 'reasonableness' rests on the Court of Justice. As already discussed in connection with 'good faith' under the Directive on unfair terms, the question is, where should it take the yardsticks from?

4. EC law and *Gemeinschaftsprivatrecht* – Communitarian private law v. a European Consumer law

The Product Liability Directive was seen as a unique effort at harmonizing a specific and relatively narrow part of tort law. Its practical importance seems to be limited as Member States' courts rely on the rules they have applied for decades and it might be a matter for academic research to find out whether the Directive has had an indirect impact on these courts in that they have tightened product liability standards. The different directives on doorstep selling, on package tours, on timesharing and on consumer credit concern civil law matters, but again their impact on the national civil laws has remained marginal. The recently adopted Directive on unfair terms changed the situation dramatically. It is not so much that the directive requires revolutionary changes in the national law systems. The reason for the excitement that the adoption has triggered in politics and law, seems to lie in the fact that Community law, by way of the unfair contract terms Directive interferes for the first time with the basics of the Member States' civil law system. Member States' civil law is based to a large extent on 'Privatautonomie' (cf. Chapter 1), the Directive on unfair contract terms formulates a different, a genuine European concept of consumer protection in private law. THEREFORE concern has been raised that a European civil law is in the offing which differs considerably from the Member States' civil law. THEREFORE consumer law is linked to the economic constitution of the European Community. THEREFORE the notion of a European civil law is linked to the question where the European Community will lead to.

There is a theoretical side to the debate which revolves around the question of the extent to which the unity of civil law should and must be defended against special private law rules. Continental civil law is based historically on the idea of unity of private law. This concept has been challenged since the emergence of consumer law, when it has become necessary to adopt legislation to protect those whose rights are not safeguarded under the idea of unity of private law. Consumer legislation started in the 1970s. Most of the legislative pieces have not been integrated into the civil law code, but have been left outside the so-far coherent body of private law. The unity of private law stands against the so-called Sonderprivatrecht, the idea that all these consumer laws form a coherent legal concept which is not compatible with the unity of private law. The conflict is firmly expressed in the 9th recital of the unfair terms directive, when the protection of the consumer is justified with reference to the 'abuse of power' which is exercised by suppliers. That debate reaches far beyond legal thought, it has practical political implications at the Community level. Depending on one's viewpoint, some fear that the adoption of the Directive on unfair terms will be the starting point for the elaboration of a 'European Code on Consumer Law'. Others may interpret exactly such a perspective as a chance to realize at the European level, what they failed to manage at the national level, with the single exception of France, where a 'Code de la Consommation' was adopted in 1993. Whatever the outcome, the debate may contribute to strengthening the importance of consumer protection policy within the European Community.

Peter Hommelhoff, *Zivilrecht unter dem Einfluß europäischer Rechtsangleichung*, discusses from a German point of view the perspective of such a codification. He starts with an analysis of the inconsistencies of the notion of 'consumer' within the different directives which may provide the ground for the development of a consistent European approach.

CIVIL LAW UNDER THE INFLUENCE OF EUROPEAN LEGAL HARMONIZATION*

Peter Hommelhoff

VI. EFFECTS ANALYSIS AND CATEGORIZATION

In the final analysis, we can probably retain this finding: the European harmonization of legislation exerts an influence on German civil law in a wide variety of ways – even though the harmonization acts are still limited to individual problem fields and areas of life, and there is no intention of creating a Community civil code. Nevertheless (indeed, precisely therefore) this process of isolated, fragmentary legal harmonization harbours two major dangers: first, the individual harmonization acts are not necessarily well-harmonized with one another; and secondly, as specialized technical regulations, the link with fundamental civil law principles can easily be lost. This was made clear in the field of consumer protection. Therefore it must be asked whether one can effectively counter these dangers by attempting to consolidate the harmonized legal material (plus that existing prior to the harmonization) in their own individual categories.

Consumer protection law and its regulatory approaches

The first thing to be noted about the consumer protection directives is that they follow divergent protection approaches: for example, the Directive on the Doorstep Selling focuses on situations classified as 'dangerous for consumers', as do the draft directives on teleshopping and sales trips, and the proposal for a Directive on Unfair Terms (to the extent that standardized contract clauses are involved). Other Directives diverge from this 'situational protection' concept, instead proceeding from a (in the view of the Council of Ministers) 'dangerous contract' type: examples of this are the Directives on consumer credit and package tours. And, finally, there is the role-specific protection approach: the contracting party is protected in his capacity as consumer, as the party of the individual contract under the Unfair Terms Directive. Or: someone is viewed as the victim of a product defect or as the

---

*   First published in 'Zivilrecht unter dem Einfluß europäischer Rechtsangleichung', *Archiv für civilistische Praxis*, **192**, 1992, pp.72 *et seq.* (102–107), reprinted by permission of J.C.B. Mohr (Paul Siebeck), Tübingen. Translation by John Blazek, Brussels.

victim of a defective service as under this future Directive, or as a victim of waste-related harm, for which yet another Directive is currently being prepared.

These protection concepts are not systematically harmonized at the Community level; at any rate, no such harmonization is apparent to outside observers. Here the consolidation of all consumer protection Directives into a uniform category could contribute to better legal doctrinal penetration and greater legal-systemic order. Their hierarchic classification appears to be particularly indicated since the protective approaches have different scopes, targets, intensities and effects: proceeding from the model of the consumer who is given the most extensive possible support for his own protection, situation-related protective approaches should be pursued first, then contract type-related approaches, and only as a final measure, when the desired consumer protection cannot be achieved any other way, should role-specific approaches be selected, given their undifferentiated and potentially unlimited effects. Establishing such a hierarchy would also make it possible to better grasp and control the effects of consumer protection on other legal positions and principles, above all on freedom of contract – an advantage which should not be underestimated given the excessiveness prohibition.

At least at the Community law level, therefore, an argument can be made for forming a legal-systemic independent category of consumer protection law. In the Member States this would by no means have as its unavoidable consequence a multi-track civil law – e.g. a first track for the interaction of economic subjects with one another, a strictly separate second track for the interaction between economic subjects and those deserving legal protection, and finally a third track for legal relations between private parties, i.e. without participation of economic subjects. For the task always remains to coordinate, during the process of drafting Directives (i.e. prior to their adoption), the intended consumer protection instruments with the traditional civil law of the Member States – through legal-systemic 'advance thinking' by the European legislator in the full community dimension. It must be left to others to say whether the legal-systemic independent categorization of an EC labour law should be undertaken in similar fashion.

Private market law and foundation

But what is the purpose of legal harmonization in areas other than labour and consumer protection law? It serves primarily (or even exclusively) to establish the Single Market and make it function. One could consolidate this legal material in the category of a 'private market law'. But where would be the epistemological advantage?

a) 'Private market law' would signify for its components that they serve the free exchange of goods, services and capital, and therefore build upon the common foundation of private autonomy and freedom of contract in the Member States. From this one might wish to conclude that this foundation should be raised to the Community level, and there be subject to comprehensive legal harmonization. And in fact prominent legal comparativists have for decades been calling for broad civil law harmonization in and for the Common Market. The proposals range from the transfer of ownership of movable property and retention of title to the general rules of contract and tort law and all the way to the major step of a civil law codification for the entire Community, with harmonization of obligation and property law as its centrepiece – scientifically prepared by a *Jus Commune Europae*.

But will the European legislator – the Council of Ministers or later, perhaps, the Council and the Parliament – on its own ever find the power to implement such extensive proposals? The evolution of the Uniform Law on the Sale of Goods and the controversies surrounding the codification idea suggest that a healthy measure of scepticism is necessary: 'private market law' is scarcely suitable as a brand name for intensified harmonization policy.

b) And yet the precept applies to integrate the disparate components of the 'private market law' in the civil law and ground it on its fundamental principles already today. To spell this out for the German legal sphere: for every harmonization project in Brussels one must carefully consider from the very outset how its elements could be integrated into the law already existing in Germany and brought into agreement with its principles. Systemic coherence should be thought out before and during the negotiations in Brussels, and not just after the EC Directive has been adopted and has to be implemented in Bonn (or soon: Berlin). The balance sheet directive which had been conceived in terms of large-scale stock companies and its unanticipated consequences on middle-sized GmbH's, as well as the GmbH & Co as a temporary national solution, illustrate the dire consequences of thinking afterwards instead of beforehand. 'In the UK, there has been a growing realization that government departments involved in the development of proposed Community rules may underestimate the incidental impact of such rules on other departments – until the rule is agreed in Brussels and it is too late to object.'

Only anticipatory thinking in systemic contexts will clearly reveal the incompatibilities or the potentially disastrous implications of a given harmonization project. Therefore, an independent category 'private market law' could be a quite reasonable thing; it indicates the necessity of carefully adapting its planned regulations from the start to the traditional civil law system of the Member States. In this effort, generalists (including those from the academic world) must work together with the specialists in the ministries and associations.

In 1964, Günther Beitzke concluded his treatise on 'Problems of private law harmonization in the European Economic Community' with a call for greater awareness that the goal to be served is not an isolated legal–technical task, but rather *European* law. This is quite true; but in the final analysis, the unity of the

European Community is achieved through the small change of the Directives, and we cannot afford to stand on the sidelines.
(End of excerpt)

B. NATIONAL CIVIL LAW RULES AS BARRIERS TO TRADE UNDER PRIMARY COMMUNITY LAW?

Despite the adoption of consumer protection Directives in the field of contract and tort law, the regulation of civil law matters remains in the hands of the Member States. Harmonization has been achieved in bits and pieces only. The interpretation of the Directive has been put in the hands of the Court of Justice, which will become involved in civil law matters eventually. So far, there are a few cases only dealing with civil law matters, none of which concerns the definition of the legal concept in the product liability directive. Step by step, however, the Court might intervene in private law matters and develop a European connotation of basic civil law terms, such as 'defect' in the product liability Directive or 'good faith' in the unfair terms Directive. Whether the Court's legitimatory basis suffices to obtain respect from the national courts will have to be demonstrated. Legal doctrine seems to be quite critical about the application of supremacy in civil law matters. There is an overall tendency in academic writing to protect civil law matters against Community law.

The few cases decided so far in civil law matters deal with the relationship of primary Community law and national civil law. They demonstrate a certain reluctance of the Court of Justice to step into the field and underline the position taken by legal doctrine. It is not at all surprising that the issue has come up first in primary Community law. The fast integration of the Community, accelerated by the Internal Market project, has shed light on differences in the Member States' civil law legislation supposedly as 'barriers to trade'. The extensive court rulings on Articles 30 and 59 quite necessarily led to the question whether and to what extent divergent liability rules or divergent contract provisions could be treated as barriers to trade whose maintenance would then have to be justified with reference to Article 36.

Case C-339/89 *Alsthom Atlantique* v. *Compagnie de construction mécanique Sulzer SA*, [1991] ECR I-107 provided the first opportunity for the Court to investigate whether national rules concerning a vendor's liability for defective products which are stricter than those in force in the other Member States are affected by Article 34. The answer is yes, but only if the civil law rules have as their specific object or effect the restriction of patterns of exports. What sort of civil law rules could come under that definition?

Judgment

1   By judgment of 10 May 1989, which was received at the Court Registry on 3 November 1989, the Tribunal de commerce, Paris, referred to the Court for a preliminary ruling under Article 177 of the EEC Treaty a question on the interpretation of Articles 2, 3(f), 34 and 85(1) of the EEC Treaty.

2   Those questions were raised in a dispute between Alsthom Atlantique SA (hereinafter referred to as 'Alsthom') and Compagnie de construction mécanique Sulzer SA (hereinafter referred to as 'Sulzer'), the latter serving third-party notice on the Union des assurances de Paris, in connection with the defective functioning of ships' engines supplied by Sulzer to Alsthom and fitted in two cruise vessels delivered to the Dutch company Holland and America Tours (hereinafter referred to as 'HAT').

3   One of the main issues which arose before the national court concerns Article 1643 of the French Civil Code, which is worded as follows:

'The vendor shall be liable for any latent defects, even if he is unaware of those defects, unless he stipulates that he shall not be liable.'

4   In its case-law the French Court of Cassation has interpreted that article as raising an irrebuttable presumption that a manufacturer or trader is aware of any defects in the goods sold which he can avoid only if the contract is concluded with a trader in the same specialized field.

5   In the proceedings instituted before the national court by Alsthom for payment of the costs incurred to remedy the latent defects in the engines sold by Sulzer, the latter argues that there is no case-law similar to that of the French Court of Cassation in any other Member State and that such case-law may distort competition and hinder the free movement of goods.

6   Taking the view that the dispute raised a number of questions concerning the interpretation of Article 2, 3(f), 34 and 85(1) of the EEC Treaty, the Tribunal de commerce, Paris, decided to refer the following question to the Court for a preliminary ruling:

'Are the provisions of Articles 2 and 3(f), read together with those of Articles 85(1) and 34, of the EEC Treaty to be interpreted as prohibiting the application of a Member State's case-law which, by not allowing persons selling goods by way of trade to prove that on the date on which the goods were delivered they were unaware of a defect in the goods, has the effect of preventing them from relying on Article 1643 of the French Civil Code, which allows them to limit their liability when unaware of the defect, in the same way as their competitors in the other Member States may do under the provisions of their own national law?' [...]

8   It should be borne in mind first of all that Article 2 of the Treaty describes the task of the European Economic Community. The aims laid down in that provision are concerned with the existence and functioning of the Community and are to be achieved through the establishment of the Common

Market and the progressive approximation of the economic policies of Member States, which are also aims whose implementation is the essential object of the Treaty (see, to that effect, the judgment in Case 126/86 *Gimenez Zaera* v. *Instituto Nacional de la Seguridad Social* [1987] ECR 3697, at paragraph 10).

9   Those aims, on which the establishment of the Community is based, and more particularly the aim of promoting a harmonious development of economic activities throughout the Community, cannot have the effect either of imposing legal obligation on the Member States or of conferring rights on individuals. It follows that the provisions of Article 2 of the Treaty cannot be relied upon by an individual before a national court.

10   The institution of a system ensuring that competition in the Common Market is not distorted, as envisaged by Article 3(f) of the Treaty, is an objective specified more closely in several other provisions relating to the rules of competition (see to that effect in particular the judgments in Case 85/76 *Hoffman-La Roche* v. *Commission* [1979] ECR 461, and in Case 322/81 *Michelin* v. *Commission* [1983] ECR 3461, at paragraph 29), including Article 85 of the Treaty, which prohibits agreements and concerted practices between undertakings which may affect trade between Member States and which have as their object or effect the prevention, restriction or distortion of competition within the Common Market.

11   It must be borne in mind that, as the Court has consistently held (see, in particular, the judgment in Case 311/85 *Vereniging van Vlaamse Reisbureaus v Sociale Dienst van de Plaatselijke en Gewestelijke Overheidsdiensten* [1987] ECR 3801, at paragraph 10), Articles 85 and 86 of the Treaty concern the conduct of undertakings and not measures adopted by the authorities of the Member States. Nevertheless the Treaty imposes a duty on Member States not to adopt or maintain in force any measure which could deprive those provisions of their effectiveness. That would be the case, in particular, if national case-law were to favour the adoption of agreements, decisions or concerted practices contrary to Article 85 of the Treaty or to reinforce their effects.

12   With regard to this case, it must be stated that the irrebuttable presumption that a trader is aware of any defects in the goods sold, to which the national court refers, has been developed in the case-law for reasons connected with the protection of buyers and is unlikely to favour or facilitate the adoption of agreements contrary to Article 85.

13   According to Article 34 of the Treaty, quantitative restrictions on exports and all measures having equivalent effect are prohibited between Member States.

14   As the Court has consistently held (see, most recently, the judgment in Case C-9/89 *Spain* v. *Council* [1990] ECR 1383, at paragraph 21), Article 34 of the Treaty concerns only those measures which have as their specific object

or effect the restriction of patterns of exports and thereby the establishment of a difference in treatment between the domestic trade of a Member State and its export trade in such a way as to provide a particular advantage for national production or for its domestic market at the expense of the production or of the trade of other Member States.

15   It must be held that the case-law of the French Court of Cassation, to which reference is made in this case, applies without distinction to all commercial relations governed by French law and does not have as its specific object or effect the restriction of patterns of exports thereby favouring domestic production or the domestic market. Furthermore, the parties to an international contract of sale are generally free to determine the law applicable to their contractual relations and can thus avoid being subject to French law.

16   In the light of all those considerations, the answer to the question submitted for a preliminary ruling must be that the provisions of Articles 2 and 3(f) of the EEC Treaty, read together with those of Article 34 and 85(1) thereof, must be interpreted as meaning that they do not prohibit the application of a Member State's case-law which, by not allowing persons selling goods by way of trade to prove that on the date on which the goods were delivered they were unaware of a defect in the goods, has the effect of preventing them from relying on provisions of national legislation which allow them to limit their liability when unaware of the defect, in the same way as their competitors in the other Member States may do.

There is only one case to be reported on the relationship between Article 30 and contract law. In Case C-93/92 *CMC Motorradcenter GmbH* v. *Pelin Baskiciogullari*, 13 March 1993 [1993] ECR, I-5009 the German civil law rules on *culpa in contrahendo* have been tested under Community law. *Culpa in contrahendo* concerns the liability of the supplier before the contract is concluded. The doctrine has been developed by the German courts over decades. It has become a multi-facetted regulatory approach dealing basically with pre-contractual liability resulting from violation of information duties or of the general duty to take care of the party's interests in the pre-contractual stage. In *CMC Motorradcenter* the Court had to decide on the civil law effects resulting from parallel-imported bicycles. German law obliges the seller to inform the buyer on foreseeable difficulties in realizing the manufacturer's guarantee. The *Landgericht Augsburg* raised the question whether such a duty violates Article 30.

Arrêt

1   Par ordonnance du 10 mars 1992, parvenue à la Cour le 23 mars suivant, le Landgericht Augsburg a posé, en vertu de l'article 177 du traité CEE, une question préjudicielle portant sur l'article 30 du traité.

2 La question a été soulevée dans le cadre d'un litige entre la firme CMC Motorradcenter (ci-après «Motorradcenter»), établie en Allemagne, et Mme Pelin Baskiciogullari.

3 Motorradcenter, qui exploite un commerce de motocyclettes sans toutefois être concessionnaire d'aucune marque, a acquis une motocyclette de la marque Yamaha auprès d'un importateur allemand qui, lui-même, l'avait achetée à un concessionnaire français. Lors de cette acquisition, l'importateur allemand a obtenu l'assurance que les acheteurs pourraient se prévaloir de la garantie auprès de tout concessionnaire de la marque Yamaha.

4 Motorradcenter a vendu l'une de ces motos à Mme Baskigiocullari. Les conditions générales du contrat spécifiaient que l'acheteur pourrait faire valoir ses droits à la garantie auprès du vendeur ou bien auprès d'entreprises agréées par le fabricant ou par l'importateur. Quoiqu'elle connût ce fait, Motorradcenter n'a pas informé l'intéressée que, en dépit de ces conditions, les concessionnaires allemands refusent généralement d'effectuer des réparations au titre de la garantie sur des motocyclettes importées par la voie parallèle. Ils considèrent en effet que ce type d'importation fait naître un avantage injustifié en matière de concurrence, vu que les prix nets en France sont inférieurs à ceux pratiqués en Allemagne.

5 Ayant eu connaissance de ce comportement, Mme Baskigiocullari a réfuse de prendre possession de la motocyclette en question. Motorradcenter a intenté un recours devant l'Amtsgericht Nördlingen, qu'il'a rejeté. La firme a alors fait appel devant le Landgericht Augsburg. Estimant que le demandeur devait attirer l'attention de son acheteur sur le comportement des concessionnaires allemands mais se demandant si cette obligation ne constituait pas une mesure d'effect équivalant à une restriction quantitative, le Landgericht a sursis à statuer et posé à la Cour la question préjudicielle suivante:

> «Est-il compatible avec l'article 30 du traité CEE d'imposer à un importateur allemand l'obligation d'informer l'acheteur d'une motocyclette de marque Yamaha de ce que les concessionnaires allemands de cette firme refusent fréquemment d'effectuer les réparations au titre de la garantie lorsque les véhicules proviennent d'importations parallèles? »

[...]

7 A titre liminaire, il convient d'observer qu'il ressort du dossier que, en droit allemand, une relation de confiance entre les deux parties à un contrat est présumée dès le début des négociations. Selon une jurisprudence constante, cette relation fait naître une obligation d'information en ce sens que chacune des parties est tenue de communiquer à l'autre les circonstances dont elle a connaissance et qui, bien qu'elles ne prèsentent aucun rapport avec l'objet de la vente ou ses qualités, sont de nature à déterminer la décision de son cocontractant. Selon la jurisprudence allemande, la faute qui est

commise lors de la négociation du contrat (culpa in contrahendo) et qui engendre un dommage pour le cocontractant doit faire l'objet d'une réparation.

8 Par sa question préjudicielle, le juge national vise, en substance, à savoir si une telle obligation d'information constitue une mesure d'effet équivalent au sens de Particle 30 du traité CEE.

9 A cet égard, il y a lieu de rappeler que, selon une jurisprudence constante (voir arrêt du 11 Juillet 1974, Dassonville, 8/74, Rec. p.837), constitue une mesure d'effet équivalent toute règle susceptible d'entraver directement ou indirectement, actuellement ou potentiellement le commerce intracommunautaire.

10 En l'occurrence, il convient d'observer d'abord que l'obligation précontractuelle d'information imposée par le droit allemand des obligations s'applique, à tout le moins en ce qui concerne les produits provenant de la Communauté, indistinctement à toutes les relations contractuelles relevant de ce droit et qu'elle n'a pas pour objet de régir les échanges.

11 Quant à la question de savoir si la libre circulation des marchandises risque d'être entravée, il y a lieu de constater que, en tout etat de cause, ce n'est pas l'obligation d'information qui serait à l'origine de ce risque mais la circonstance que certains concessionnaires de la marque concerneé refusent d'effectuer des prestations relevant de la garantie sur les motocyclettes qui ont fait l'objet d'une importation parallèle.

12 Il en résulte que les effets restrictifs que l'obligation d'information en question pourrait produire sur la libre circulation des marchandises sont trop aléatoires et trop indirects pour que cette obligation puisse être regardée comme étant de nature à entraver le commerce entre les Etats membres (voir arrêt du 7 mars 1990, Krantz, C-69/88, Rec. p. I-583).

13 Il y a lieu dès lors de répondre à la question préjudicielle posée que l'article 30 du traité CEE doit être interprété en ce sens qu'il ne s'oppose pas à une règle jurisprudentielle d'un Etat membre qui impose une obligation d'information dans les relations précontractuelles.

Both the above judgments demonstrate a clear reluctance by the court to intervene in national civil matters by reference to primary Community rules, mainly by reference to Article 30. The Court is obviously not willing to understand national civil law rules as barriers-to-trade. In order to comply with the Community law rules, it seems to suffice that the national rules are applied in a non-discriminatory way. *CMC-Motorradcenter* seems to have foreshadowed the *Keck* decision (Chapter 6).

QUESTIONS ON THE CASES

The two decisions have in common that the 'barriers-to-trade' result from rules which have been developed by national courts, i.e. by the Member States' third power. Both parties claimed likewise a distortion of competition. Would it be possible to consider the applicability of competition law? Reference might be made to Article 85 (1) in connection with Articles 5, 3(g) and to interpret the Court rulings in *Alsthom Atlantique* and *CMC Motorradcenter* as 'statutory behaviour', which have to be measured against Community law? Case C-2/91 *W.W. Meng* could be read along these lines (cf. Chapter 6). Look carefully at *Alsthom Atlantique* at I-123, No. 11.

C. EC LAW, ROME AND BRUSSELS CONVENTION AND INTERNATIONAL PRIVATE LAW

With the completion of the Internal Market business has become easier, more legal transactions will be conducted across borders not only between business, but also between business and consumers. It is one of the objectives of the Commission's consumer policy to strengthen the consumer thrust in transborder transactions by providing him or her with rights against business. Whenever consumers make crossborder transactions, the question is, what law applies, 'his' or 'her law' or the law of the then foreign supplier. Harmonization of civil law rules will guarantee to consumers that there is a minimum protection of rights all over the Community. But even the harmonized law cannot easily be identified as it has to be implemented into national law. Often the rules provide minimum standards and the national standards are higher and even more often the rules in question are not at all harmonized which is the case in consumer sales contracts or in contracts for services. What law applies in transborder transactions is decided by international private law rules. The term is somewhat misleading. International private law rules are national in their origin and they differ between the Member States. The so-called Rome Convention (Convention on the Law Applicable to Contractual Obligations, opened for signature on June 1980) is an international law treaty without any direct link to the Treaty of Rome. It provides for the introduction of common rules on international private law in contract law. Its legal effect depends on the readiness of the Member States to translate the international treaty into national law. As the Treaty of Rome does not apply, the implementation procedure is governed by the general rules in the Member States governing the implementation of public international law treaties. The counter part to the Rome Convention is the Brussels Convention (Convention on Jurisdiction and the Enforcement of Judgments in Civil and Commercial Law Matters). As early as 1968 the Member States fulfilled the mandate of Article 220. Both conventions provide a common basis for the determination of the applicable law, for the decision on the jurisdiction and the enforcement of judgments across Community borders.

1. Extent and reach of jurisdiction under the Rome and Brussels Convention

Right from the beginning it has been the intention of the Commission to put the jurisdiction into the hands of the European Court of Justice. Agreement was reached in the 1971 Protocol on the interpretation of the Brussels Convention. Since its entering into force the national courts are determined which may request the Court of Justice to give preliminary rulings on questions of interpretation. This protocol served as the basis for the two protocols on the interpretation and jurisdiction of the Rome Convention by the European Court of Justice in 1989. However, the two protocols are not identical. While according to Article 3 I of the Brussels Convention Protocol, the Supreme Courts must submit disputed issues to the Court of Justice, Article 2 of the Rome Convention's Protocol provides that the courts entitled to submit disputes are conceded only the possibility of appealing to the Court of Justice, but they are not obliged to take this step.

The interpretation of the Brussels Convention by the Court of Justice is constantly gaining importance. The Convention has awakened from its Sleeping Beauty-like slumbers. The Court is actively making use of its powers and enhancing impact on national procedural law rules. The situation with respect to the Rome Convention is different. The interpretation and the jurisdiction protocols are coupled to one another through a complicated mechanism which should push back the time it enters into effect considerably. While the interpretation protocol must be ratified by only six Member States, the jurisdiction protocol requires the approval of all former twelve Member States.

The still uncertain future of the Rome Convention may explain the extremely wide scope of application of Article 30 by the Court. It suffices to recall the GB-INNO decision (cf. Chapter 6). The case concerned the reach of unfair competition rules across Community borders. Such a conflict has normally to be decided with the help of international private law rules. By confirming the applicability of Article 30, the Court has made impossible a solution under international private law.

2. Transborder consumer conflicts under the Rome Convention

How complicated the interrelationship between national law, international private law, Community law and the Rome Convention is, may be demonstrated by reference to a subject which has gained increasing importance over recent years: the solution of transborder consumer conflicts arising out of so-called *Kaffeefahrten*, where German consumers on holiday in Spain, Italy or Turkey or who are taken to one of these countries were offered German goods for sale in the context of an organized tour to which in theory the German Act on Doorstep Sales would apply. However, the contracts which were concluded provided for the applicability of Spanish or Italian law, countries in which the EC Directive had not been transformed into national law at that time. The key point of the legal construction resulted from the right to withdraw, which was granted by the German law implementing the Doorstep Selling Directive, but still denied under Spanish law. One might expect a solution within the Rome Convention and indeed Article 5 states under the heading of 'Certain consumer contracts':

1. This article applies to a contract the object of which is the supply of goods and services to a person ('the consumer') for a purpose which can be regarded as being outside his trade or profession, or a contract for the provision of credit for that object.

2. Notwithstanding the provisions of Article 3 (freedom of choice), a choice of law made by the parties shall not have the result of depriving the consumer of the protection afforded to him by the mandatory rules of the law of the country in which he has his habitual residence:

- if in that country the conclusion of the contract was preceded by a specific invitation addressed to him or by advertising, and he had taken in that country all the steps necessary on his part for the conclusion of the contract, or,
- if the other party or his agent received the consumer's order in that country, or,
- if the contract for the sale of goods and the consumer travelled from that country to another country and there gave his order, provided that the consumer's journey was arranged by the seller for the purpose of inducing the consumer to buy.

3. Notwithstanding the provision of Art. 4 (applicable law in the absence of choice), a contract to which this article applies shall, in the absence of choice in accordance with Article 3, be governed by the law of the country in which the consumer has his habitual residence if it is entered into the circumstances described in paragraph 2 of this Article.

4. This Article shall not apply to:

(a) a contract for carriage;

(b) a contract for the supply of services where the services are to be supplied to the consumer exclusively in a country other than that in which he has his habitual residence.

Germany has integrated the provisions of the Rome Convention into the EGBGB (Einführungsgesetz zum Bürgerlichen Gesetzbuch). Article 29 of the EGBGB complies with Article 5 of the Convention. German courts and German doctrine discussed the applicability of Article 29 I 3 (Art 5 (1) (3)) to the so-called *Kaffee-fahrten*. The problem is whether this rule applies because the consumers are normally not taken to Spain and Italy just for the purpose of selling them goods. Some lower courts and legal writers pleaded for an analogous interpretation of Article 29 I 3. The circumstances are said to be similar if the consumer is invited while being in Spain and Italy to undertake such an excursion. If the way to the Court of Justice had been free, the case would have certainly ended up in Luxembourg. As this is not the case, the national courts had to decide on how Article 5 of the Convention must be interpreted and may thereby develop quite different approaches. This is to show how necessary the delegation of jurisdiction to the Court of Justice is, even if the Rome Convention provides for information exchange mechanisms of court decisions between the signatory states and if the Rome Convention obliges the signatory states in Article 18 to a 'unified interpretation'.

3. The notion of the consumer under the Brussels Convention – the Courts' definition

The Brussels Convention determines in section 4 jurisdiction over consumer contracts, thereby allowing the consumer to file an action in the country where he has his domicile if only the foreign based undertaking has a branch or an agency there:

Section 4

Jurisdiction over consumer contracts

ARTICLE 13

In proceedings concerning a contract concluded by a person for a purpose which can be regarded as being outside his trade or profession, hereinafter called "the consumer," jurisdiction shall be determined by this section, without prejudice to the provisions of Articles 4 and 5(5), if it is:

(1) a contract for the sale of goods on instalment credit terms, or

(2) a contract for a loan repayable by instalments, or for any other form of credit, made to finance the sale of goods, or

(3) any other contract for the supply of goods or a contract for the supply of services, and
   (a) in the State of the consumer's domicile the conclusion of the contract was preceded by a specific invitation addressed to him or by advertising, and
   (b) the consumer took in that State the steps necessary for the conclusion of the contract.

Where a consumer enters into a contract with a party who is not domiciled in a Contracting State but has a branch, agency or other establishment in one of the Contracting States, that party shall, in disputes arising out of the operations of the branch, agency or establishment, be deemed to be domiciled in that State.

This Section shall not apply to contracts of transport.

ARTICLE 14

A consumer may bring proceedings against the other party to a contract either in the courts of the Contracting State in which that party is domiciled or in the courts of the Contracting State in which he is himself domiciled.

Proceedings may be brought against a consumer by the other party to the contract only in the courts of the Contracting State in which the consumer is domiciled.

These provisions shall not affect the right to bring a counterclaim in the court in which, in accordance with this Section, the original claim is pending.

ARTICLE 15

The provisions of this Section may be departed from only by an agreement:

(1) which is entered into after the dispute has arisen, or

(2) which allows the consumer to bring proceedings in courts other than those indicated in this Section, or

(3) which is entered into by the consumer and the other party to the contract, both of whom are at the time of the conclusion of the contract domiciled or habitually resident in the same Contracting State, and which confers jurisdiction on the courts of the State, provided that such an agreement is not contrary to the law of that State.

[...]

The need to develop within Community law a coherent notion of what a 'consumer' means has already been stressed. That is why case C-89/91 *Shearson Lehmann Hutton Inc.* v. *TVB Treuhandgesellschaft für Vermögensverwaltung und Beteiligung mbH*, 19.1.1993 [1993] ECR, I-139, 186 is so important, where the Court of Justice gave for the first time a definition of what consumers are. The Court rejected an attempt of the German *Bundesgerichtshof* to apply section 4 of the Rome Convention to business activities:

European Court of Justice (ECJ): Consumer status under the European Civil Jurisdiction Convention (ECJC)

In so-called "consumer matters", the ECJC offers to the plaintiff who is a consumer the possibility of suing before the court of his own state of residence (Art. 13, 14 ECJC). The plaintiff of the initial procedure which is pending before the *Bundesgerichtshof* (BGH – German Federal Supreme Court) is a GmbH for asset management and participating interests. It is making in its own place of jurisdiction, claims for compensation against an American brokerage company which were assigned to it by a German private individual. The BGH believed that, for the determination of the place of jurisdiction, Art. 13 ECJC might be relevant, and it therefore applied to the ECJ for a preliminary decision. The ECJ determined that Art. 13 and following are not applicable to the present case, since the plaintiff is pursuing its complaint within the framework of its business activity, and thus is not a "consumer" within the meaning of the ECJC.

Operative provisions of the Court's decision:

Art. 13 of the Convention dated 27.9.1968 concerning the Jurisdiction and Enforcement of Judgements in Civil and Commercial Matters (ECJC) is to be interpreted so that a plaintiff who is acting in the exercise of his professional or business activity and thus is not the consumer participating in one of the contracts listed in Art. 13 I ECJC, may not benefit from the special jurisdictional rules provided by the Convention for consumer matters.

ECJ, decision of 19.1.1993 – Case C-89/91 (Shearson Lehman Hutton Inc./*TVB Treuhandgesellschaft für Vermögensverwaltung und Beteiligungen mbH*)

Facts: The BGH (EuZW 1991, 544 L = NJW 1991, 1632 L) submitted to the *European Court of Justice* four questions concerning the interpretation of Art. 13 I, II ECJC for preliminary decision. These questions arose in a legal dispute between the *TVB Treuhandgesellschaft für Vermögensverwaltung und Beteiligungen mbH*, with headquarters in Munich (in the following referred to as Pl.), and the E.F. Hutton & Company Inc., with headquarters in New York (USA), which in the meantime was taken over by Shearson Lehman Hutton Inc., also located in New York (hereinafter referred to as De.). The Pl. in Germany had brought a complaint against the De. based on an assigned right. The assignor, a German judge, had assigned the De. to perform on a commission basis certain foreign exchange, securities and commodity future transactions. For this, he paid significant margin requirements in 1986 and 1987, amounts which were almost entirely consumed through these transactions. The De. had offered its services in newspaper advertisements in the Federal Republic of Germany. Its contractual relationship with the assignor came into existence via the E.F. Hutton & Company GmbH located in Germany (hereinafter: Hutton GmbH), which is dependent on the De. and performs for it advisory functions vis-à-vis its clients. The Hutton GmbH was involved at least as an intermediary in all the sales and purchase assignments ordered by the assignor. Its shares belong to a sole subsidiary of the De. with headquarters in New York. Moreover, several persons hold leading positions both at the De. and at Hutton GmbH. The Pl. is demanding from the De. the lost margin payments of the assignor. It bases its demand on claims of unjust enrichment and on damage compensation claims due to the violation of contractual and preliminary-contractual duties, as well as due to tortious behaviour, because the De. did not give sufficient information to the assignor concerning the risks of the commodity future transactions. The Munich *Landgericht* (LG – District Court) applied to by the Pl. declared that it lacked jurisdiction and dismissed the complaint as inadmissible. The Munich *Oberlandesgericht* (Higher Regional Court) as appellate court reversed this decision and affirmed the jurisdiction of the LG. The De. appealed against this decision to the BGH. The BGH stayed the proceedings and submitted four questions to the ECJ concerning the regulatory scope of Art. 13 ECJC.

The ECJ decided that Art. 13 ECJC does not apply to fact situations of this type.

From the reasons for the decision:

9. As a preliminary matter, it must be established that all questions of the submitting court involve the interpretation of Art. 13 I, II ECJC, which belongs to the 4th section ("Jurisdiction for consumer matters") of the Convention's Title II concerning court jurisdiction.

10. First, it must be examined whether the prerequisites for the application of this provision in a case such as the present one are fulfilled, since questions concerning the area of application of the jurisdictional rules of the Convention must be examined *ex officio*.

11. As the submission decision makes clear, in this case the complaint for repayment was not raised by the contractual partner of the De., a private individual, but rather by a company to whom this private individual had assigned his claims.

12. Consequently, it must be examined whether a Pl. like that of the initial procedure can be accorded the status of a "consumer" within the meaning of the Convention, and whether it can thus benefit from the special jurisdictional rules of the Convention for consumer matters.

13. To answer this question, reference is made to the Principle established in the judicial decisions (see, among others, ECJ, 1978 Report, 1431 text numbers 14–15 and 19 – Société Bertrand; ECJ, decision of 17.6.1992 – Case C-26/91, text number 10 – Handte, not yet published in the official report) that the concepts used in the Convention – which may have a different significance depending on the national law of the contracting states –, in order to ensure that the Convention will be uniformly applied in all contracting states, are to be autonomously interpreted, whereby primary consideration should be given to the systematic structure and goals of the Convention. This is especially true for the concept of the "consumer" within the meaning of Art. 13 ff. of the Convention as the decisive criterion for court jurisdiction.

14. With respect to this, one must first note that in the system of the Convention the general principle set down in Art. 2 I applies that the courts of the contracting state within whose sovereign territory the De. has his residence have jurisdiction.

15. Only as an exception to this general principle does the Convention in the 2nd through 6th sections of Title II list the cases in which a person who lives or has settled within the sovereign territory of a contracting state can be sued before the courts of another contracting state – i.e. when the factual situation falls under a provision on a special jurisdiction – or must be sued – i.e. when the factual situation falls under a provision on exclusive jurisdiction or if an agreement exists concerning jurisdiction.

16. Consequently, the jurisdictional rules which deviate from this general principle are not amenable to an interpretation going beyond the cases provided for in the Convention (see ECJ, 1978 Report, 1431, text number 17 – Société Bertrand; ECJ, decision of 17.6.1992 – Case C-26/91, text number 14 – Handte).

17. Such an interpretation is all the more appropriate for a jurisdictional provision such as that of Art. 14 ECJC, which allows a consumer within the meaning of the Art. 13 ECJC to sue a person before the courts of the contracting state within whose sovereign territory the Pl. has his residence. With the exception of expressly listed cases, the Convention unambiguously rejects a jurisdiction of the courts at the residence of the Pl. (see ECJ, I 1990 Report, 49 = NJW, 631 = EuZW 1990, 34, text number 16 and 19 – Dumez France, among others).

18. Second, it must be stated that the special regulation of Art. 13 ff. ECJC is intended to protect the consumer as the economically weaker and legally less experienced contracting partner, and that therefore the decision on judicial recognition of his rights may not make it more difficult for the consumer by requiring that he sue in the courts of the state within whose sovereign territory his contracting partner has his place of business.

19. From the protective goal of these provisions it results that the special jurisdictional rules, to the extent they are provided in the Convention, may not be extended to persons who do not require such protection.

20. On the one hand, Art. 13 I ECJC defines the consumer as a person who "[acts] for a purpose . . . which cannot be attributed to the professional or business activity of this person", and provides that the various types of contract it names, and for which the provisions of the 4th section of Title II of the Convention apply, must be concluded by the consumer.

21. On the other hand, Art. 14 I ECJC specifies that the courts of the contracting state in which the consumer has his residence are competent for "the complaint of a consumer against the other contracting party".

22. According to this wording and their purpose, these provisions relate only to private end consumers who are not acting professionally or commercially (see

in this sense also ECJ, 1978 Report, 1431, text number 21 – Société Bertrand, and the expert report prepared upon the occasion of the accession of the Kingdom of Denmark, Ireland and the United Kingdom of Great Britain and Northern Ireland to the Convention, ABIEG 1979 No. C 59, page 71, No. 153), which concluded one of the contracts listed in Art. 13 ECJC and is a party in a legal dispute in accordance with Art. 14 ECJC.

23. As the Advocate-General explained under text number 26 of his closing arguments, the Convention protects the consumer only in so far as he is personally a Pl. or a De. in a procedure.

24. Thus Art. 13 ECJC must be interpreted so that a Pl. who is acting in the exercise of his professional or business activity, and thus is not himself a consumer who participates in one of the contracts listed in Art. 13 I ECJC, cannot benefit from the special jurisdictional rules of the Convention for consumer matters.

25. On the basis of the above considerations, we conclude that it is unnecessary to decide about the specific questions posed by the BGH.

EC law and civil law will certainly be one of the most fascinating areas of legal inquiry for the years to come. This is all the more true if one looks at other matters of civil law, such as company law and financial services. Much will depend on the willingness of the national courts to take their roles as 'trustees' of Community law seriously and on the European Court of Justice's courage to step into the field of civil law, whether on the basis of the Brussels Convention or primary and secondary Community law. There is a vital need for enhanced cooperation between the European Court of Justice and the national courts. The legal basis could be Article 5, but much depends on judicial mood.

FURTHER READING

M. Dauses, 'Empfiehlt es sich, das System des Rechtsschutzes und der Gerichtsbarkeit in der Europäischen Gemeinschaft, insbesondere die Aufgaben der Gemeinschaftsgerichte und der nationalen Gerichte, weiterzuentwickeln?' *Gutachten D zum 60. Deutschen Juristentag Münster*, München: CH Beck, 1994.

G. Howells, *Comparative Product Liability Law*, Aldershot: Dartmouth, 1993.

Ch. Joerges and G. Brüggemeier, 'Europäisierung des Vertragsrechts und Haftungsrechts', in Ch.P. Müller-Graff (ed.), *Gemeinsames Privatrecht in der Europäischen Gemeinschaft*, Baden-Baden: NOMOS, 1993, p.233.

P.-Ch. Müller-Graff, Europäisches Gemeinschaftsrecht and Privatrecht, *NJW*, 1993, pp.13 *et seq.*

P.-Ch. Müller-Graff (ed.), *Gemeinsames Privatrecht in der Europäischen Gemeinschaft*, Baden-Baden: NOMOS, 1993.

J.P. Pizzio (ed.), *Code de la Consommation*, Paris: Montchrestien, 1995.

P. Schlosser, 'Prozeßkostensicherheitsleistung durch Ausländer und gemein-schaftsrechtliches Diskriminierungsverbot', *EuZW*, 1993, p.659.

E. Steindorff, 'Privatrecht und Europäischer Binnenmarkt', in G. Brüggemeier (ed.), *Verfassungen für ein ziviles Europa*, ZERP-Schriftenreihe, Band 20, Baden-Baden: NOMOS, 1994, p.131.

9 External Relations and Common Commercial Policy

The treaties establishing the European Community provide that the foreign commercial and trade policies are to be conducted by the Community itself, not by the Member States acting individually, Article 113. At the Intergovernmental Conference on Political Union in 1991, the Commission had proposed to replace the notion of a Common Commercial Policy with that of a 'common policy on external relations, comprising in particular economic and trade measures in respect of services, capital, intellectual property, investment, establishment and competition', but failed. The Member States were not willing to confer more powers on the European Community, outside the still very strong commitment in Article 113 to define and develop a *Common Commercial Policy*. Such an extension might have put an end to striking conflicts between the Member States and the organs of the European Community on the reach of the competence under Article 113, on the scope of powers under Article 113 and on the meaning of Article 115 to justify restrictions on international free trade. This conflict is guided by one and the same problem: does the Community have exclusive competence in external economic relations or have the Member States and the Community to act jointly?

The key actor in the field is again the European Court of Justice. There are only some fifteen to twenty judgments dealing with the Common Commercial Policy. Most of them are quite outspoken and require an acceptance of the rulings laid down as 'acquis communautaire' – basic principles valid far beyond the subject at stake. This handful of judgments cannot be regarded as a well developed concept of external relations law and policy. The strength and the weaknesses of Article 113 have been duly analysed by the Court of Justice in its recent *Opinion 1/94 [1994] ECR, I-5276 on the competence of the Community to conclude the Agreement establishing the World Trade Organisation and, in particular, the General Agreement on Trade in Services (GATS) and the Agreement on Trade-Related Aspects of Intellectual Property Rights, including trade in counterfeit products (TRIPs).*

The primary Community rules have been supplemented by secondary Community law regulations on import, on export and on illicit trade. These provisions are of great practical importance for the trade of the Member States with countries outside the EU. They have become more and more the subject of litigation, as the banana conflict shows (Chapter 10).

A. THE SYSTEM OF THE EEC TREATY PROVISIONS ON EXTERNAL RELATIONS POWER IN INTERNATIONAL AGREEMENTS: ARTICLES 113 (3), ART. 238 AND ART. 228

There are provisions to be found in the Treaty which bestow express and clear powers on the Community. They relate most of all to the conclusion of international agreements. Article 113 (3) says:

> Where agreements with third countries need to be negotiated, the Commission shall make recommendations to the Council, which shall authorize the Commission to open necessary negotiations.
> The Commission shall conduct these negotiations in consultation with a special committee appointed by the Council to assist the Commission in this task and within the framework of such directives as the Council may issue to it.

It is evident from the text that the Commission has a crucial role to play; that it is, however, dependent on the Council. The Commission always needs a mandate from the Council, thereby putting the ultimate responsibility into the hands of the Member States in the Council.

The Treaty confers express powers on the Community to enter into international association agreements. Article 238 provides that the Community may conclude agreements 'establishing an association involving reciprocal rights and obligations, common action and special procedures with other countries or international organisations'. Quite recently Article 238 has gained an ever growing role in defining the relations with the Central and East European Countries (Chapter 10). Since the adoption of the Single European Act, association agreements must be approved by an absolute majority of the European Parliament.

Beyond Article 113 (3) and Article 238, there are a number of external relation powers which have been introduced by the Single European Act and by the Maastricht Treaty; Article 130 n on research and development agreements; Article 130 r on environmental protection; and lately Article 130 y on development cooperation.

International agreements are subject to an approval procedure under Article 228, whatever their legal basis may be. That is why the procedure laid down in Article 228 applies to Article 113 (3) as well as to Article 238. Since the adoption of the Maastricht Treaty, the European Parliament has to be consulted under the rules of Articles 189 b and Article 189 c, with the exception of agreements concluded under Article 113 (3).

Two further important features of Article 228 have to be mentioned. First it establishes that agreements concluded under the Article 228 procedure are binding on the Community and on the Member States. Second it provides for a reference procedure under which the Council, the Commission or the Member States may ask for an opinion of the Court of Justice in order to know whether the agreements are compatible with the Treaty. Quite recently the Court has been asked twice to give its opinion on the agreement to establish the European Economic Area (Chapter 10).

B. THE COURT OF JUSTICE AND THE QUESTION OF COMPETENCE ON A COMMON COMMERCIAL POLICY

Article 113 does not define what Common Commercial Policy means. Does it have a broad scope similar to Article 30 and Article 59, thereby covering trade in goods and services? Does it therefore cover more or less each and every sector as long as it affects external relations, coming near to what the Commission intended to get from the Intergovernmental Conference? The explanation will start with the debate on the scope of Article 113, a debate which is well-known from the early days of Article 30 and which has been discussed in relation to state aids, a debate focusing on whether the *effects* or the *purpose* is critical in deciding whether Article 113 is affected. This involves a conflict on competence between the Community invoking Article 113 and the Member States claiming sovereignty.

1. Scope of the Community powers in Common Commercial Policy – effect or purpose?

The ECJ had rejected attempts to reduce the scope of application of Article 113 in *Opinion 1/75* (*Understanding on Local Costs Standards*; [1975] ECR 1355 at 1356). Accordingly a Common Commercial Policy must have: 'in the Community sphere a meaning which cannot be construed more narrowly than in the context of the international action of a State and which no doubt covers export policy, including the matters of export credits which were at stake here'. Opinion 1/75 triggered off a lasting debate between the Commission and the Council on the scope of Community power in the Common Commercial Policy. The Commission with its intention to extend the scope began with the idea that Article 113 covers all measures, being a specific *instrument* to regulate international trade. The Council on the contrary, guided by its concept of narrowing the scope down, concentrated on the *purpose* and *aim* of the measure.

The political implications of the diverging attitudes held by the Commission and Council became clear in *Opinion 1/78* (*International Agreement on Natural Rubber* [1979] ECR 2871). The Commission had asked to be informed 'whether the international agreement on rubber comes as a whole or at least in essentials within the sphere of the "Common Commercial Policy" referred to in Article 113 of the Treaty'. The Council argued that Article 113 should not be interpreted so as to render meaningless other provisions of the Treaty, in particular those dealing with *general economic policy*, including the supply of raw materials within the power of the Member States and for which the Council has only, under Article 145, a power of 'co-ordination' and more specifically 'the agreements contain elements of "non-reciprocity" which are typical for *development aid* (policy)'. The Court rejected at that time the Council's attempt to restrict the scope of Article 113 by construing links between *commercial policy* and *development problems*:

> It is not possible to lay down, for *Article 113* of the EEC treaty, an interpretation the effect of which would be to restrict the Common Commercial Policy to the use of instruments intended to have an effect only on the traditional aspects of external trade to the exclusion of more highly developed mechanisms such as appear in the agreement envisaged. A Common Commercial Policy understood in that sense would be destinated to become nugatory in the course of time. Although it may be thought that at the time when the Treaty was drafted liberalization of trade was the dominant idea, the Treaty nevertheless does not form a barrier to the possibility of the Community's developing a commercial policy aiming at a regulation of the world market for certain products rather than at a mere liberalization of trade. Art. 113 empowers the Community to formulate a commercial policy based on uniform principles thus showing that the question of external trade must be governed from a wide point of view and not having regard to the administration of precise systems such as customs and quantitative restrictions. The same conclusion may be deduced from the fact that the enumeration in *Article 113* of the subjects covered by commercial policy ... is conceived as a non-exhaustive enumeration.

Then the Court refuted the Council's attempts to withdraw the Community's competence by referring to the exclusive competence of the Member States in *general economic policy*:

> ... the considerations set out above form to some extent an answer relating to the distinction to be drawn between the spheres of general economic policy and those of the Common Commercial Policy since international co-operation would be confused with the domain of general economic policy. If it appears that it comes, at least in part, under the Common Commercial Policy, as has been indicated.., it follows clearly that it could not, under the name of general economic policy, be withdrawn from the competence of the Community.

The opinion gave the impression that the Court was willing, at the time, to follow the Commission in a wide understanding of the Commercial Policy per Article 113. The Court refuted the Council's intention of focusing entirely on the purpose of the respective measure, but did not go as far as the Commission. The Commission's interpretation, that was the Court's argument already in 1979, would lead to an extremely broad notion of the Common Commercial Policy covering all measures which only indirectly affect the international trade. This restriction was the starting point for *Opinion 1/94* [1994] ECR, I-5276 at 54, 56–58, where it denied exclusive competence of the Commission under Article 113 in the field of intellectual property rights:

B. *TRIPs*

54 The Commission's argument in support of its contention that the Community has exclusive competence under Article 113 is essentially that the rules concerning intellectual property rights are closely linked to trade in the products and services to which they apply. [...]

56 However, as regards matters other than the provisions of TRIPs on the release into free circulation of counterfeit goods, the Commission's arguments cannot be accepted.

57 Admittedly, there is a connection between intellectual property and trade in goods. Intellectual property rights enable those holding them to prevent third parties from carrying out certain acts. The power to prohibit the use of a trade mark, the manufacture of a product, the copying of a design or the reproduction of a book, a disc or a videocassette inevitably has effects on trade. Intellectual property rights are moreover specifically designed to produce such effects. That is not enough to bring them within the scope of Article 113. Intellectual property rights do not relate specifically to international trade; they affect internal trade just as much as, if not more than, international trade.

58 As the French Government has rightly observed, the primary objective of TRIPs is to strengthen and harmonize the protection of intellectual property on a worldwide scale. The Commission has itself conceded that, since TRIPs lays down rules in fields in which there are no Community harmonization measures, its conclusion would make it possible at the same time to achieve harmonization within the Community and thereby to contribute to the establishment and functioning of the common market.

QUESTIONS

The Court seems to approach in Opinion 1/94 the understanding given to Article 113 by the Council in Opinion 1/78, although it does not make use of the terms 'purpose' and 'effect'. Let us remember: Opinion 1/78 started from the idea that only a *Common* Commercial Policy can implement the objectives of the Internal Market. It was this relationship between the rules on the Internal Market and the rules on external relations which had been used in the legal doctrine as a starting point for defining the scope of application of Article 113. The competence in external matters should be coextensive with the Community's powers for internal purposes. This idea, as expressed in the Latin phrase: *in foro interno, in foro externo*, dates back to 1953 (Pescatore (1979) 16 CMLRev 618). It claims a parallelism of the Community's powers in regulating the Internal Market and shaping external relations.

One may assume that the Court has maintained the idea of parallelism in Opinion 1/94, though in a much more narrower sense. The restricted scope of Article 113 as defined in Opinion 1/94 goes along with the most recently restricted scope of Article 100 a in Case C-155/91 *Commission* v. *Council*, judgment of 17 March 1993, [1993] ECR I-939. Here the Court shifted from Article 100 a to Art. 130s, from the general competence to a specific competence as the appropriate legal basis for directive 91/156 on the disposal of waste. Do you share the Court's conclusion with respect to intellectual property rights, Opinion 1/94 [1994] ECR I-5276 at 71?

> In the light of the foregoing, it must be held that, apart from those of its provisions which concern the prohibition of the release into free circulation of counterfeited goods (Council Regulation No 3842/86 of 1 December 1986), TRIPs does not fall within the scope of the Common Commercial Policy.

2. Explicit and implied powers in the field of external economic relations outside Article 113

There is a common tendency to enlarge the competences of the European Community by way of Treaty amendment. Articles 130 q and n, inserted by the Single European Act, confers powers on the Community to regulate R&D in the Internal Market, Article 130 q and in external relations, Article 130 n. The Treaty of the European Union has added powers along that line of thinking on international agreements in the context of monetary union, Article 109, and of the development of cooperation, Article 130 y.

Much more important for the reach of the competence of the Community has been the Court's so-called 'implied powers' doctrine, developed within the *ERTA* decision, Case 22/70, [1971] ECR 274, at 16:

> Such authority (to enter into international agreements – H.-W.M.) arises not only from the express conferment by the Treaty – as in the case of Article 113 and 114 for tariffs and trade agreements and with Article 228 for association agreements – but may flow equally from other provisions of the Treaty and measures adopted, within the framework of those provisions by the Community institutions.

The underlying idea of this doctrine is that the Community's powers to take action in external economic relations flow implicitly from the provisions of the Treaty establishing its internal competence, or from the existence of legislative acts of the institutions giving effect to that internal competence, or else from the need to enter into commitments with a view to achieving an internal Community objective. This doctrine contributes to avoiding differences between an internal market policy and a common commercial policy. Whenever Article 113 falls short from covering measures under Article 113, the Commission has referred to the implied powers doctrine to justify its exclusive competence.

3. Services, intellectual property rights, health and safety in a Common Commercial Policy

Legal doctrine has advocated the integration of services in the notion of a Common Commercial Policy. In Opinion 1/94 [1994] ECR I-5276 at 37–47 the Court investigated whether and to what extent the European Community has the power to conclude GATS on the basis of Article 113.

37   It is appropriate to consider, first, services other than transport and, subsequently, the particular services comprised in transport.

38   As regards the first category, it should be recalled at the outset that in Opinion 1/75 the Court, which had been asked to rule on the scope of Community competence as to the arrangements relating to a local cost standard, held that 'the field of the common commercial policy, and more particularly that of export policy, necessarily covers systems of aid for exports and more particularly measures concerning credits for the financing of local costs linked to export operations' [1975] ECR 1362). The local costs in question concerned expenses incurred for the supply of both goods and services. Nevertheless, the Court recognized the exclusive competence of the Community, without drawing a distinction between goods and services.

39   In its Opinion 1/78, cited above (paragraph 44), the Court rejected an interpretation of Article 113 'the effect of which would be to restrict the common commercial policy to the use of instruments intended to have an effect only on the traditional aspects of external trade'. On the contrary, it considered that 'the question of external trade must be governed from a wide point of view', as is confirmed by 'the fact that the enumeration in Article 113 of the subjects covered by commercial policy ... is conceived as a non-exhaustive enumeration' (Opinion 1/78, cited above, paragraph 45).

40   The Commission points out in its request for an opinion that in certain developed countries the services sector has become the dominant sector of the economy and that the global economy has been undergoing fundamental structural changes. The trend is for basic industry to be transferred to de-

veloping countries, whilst the developed economies have tended to become, in the main, exporters of services and of goods with a high value-added content. The Court notes that this trend is borne out by the WTO Agreement and its annexes, which were the subject of a single process of negotiation covering both goods and services.

41   Having regard to this trend in international trade, it follows from the open nature of the common commercial policy, within the meaning of the Treaty, that trade in services cannot immediately, and as a matter of principle, be excluded from the scope of Article 113, as some of the Governments which have submitted observations contend.

42   In order to make that conclusion more specific, however, one must take into account the definition of trade in services given in GATS in order to see whether the overall scheme of the Treaty is not such as to limit the extent to which trade in services can be included within Article 113.

43   Under Article I(2) of GATS, trade in services is defined, for the purposes of that agreement, as comprising four modes of supply of services: (1) cross-frontier supplies not involving any movement of persons; (2) consumption abroad, which entails the movement of the consumer into the territory of the WTO member country in which the supplier is established; (3) commercial presence, i.e. the presence of a subsidiary or branch in the territory of the WTO member country in which the service is to be rendered; (4) the presence of natural persons from a WTO member country, enabling a supplier from one member country to supply services within the territory of any other member country.

44   As regards cross-frontier supplies, the service is rendered by a supplier established in one country to a consumer residing in another. The supplier does not move to the consumer's country; nor, conversely, does the consumer move to the supplier's country. That situation is, therefore, not unlike trade in goods, which is unquestionably covered by the common commercial policy within the meaning of the Treaty. There is thus no particular reason why such a supply should not fall within the concept of the common commercial policy.

45   The same cannot be said of the other three modes of supply of services covered by GATS, namely, consumption abroad, commercial presence and the presence of natural persons.

46   As regards natural persons, it is clear from Article 3 of the Treaty, which distinguishes between 'a common commercial policy' in paragraph (b) and 'measures concerning the entry and movement of persons' in paragraph (d) that the treatment of nationals of non-member countries on crossing the external frontiers of Member States cannot be regarded as falling within the common commercial policy. More generally, the existence in the Treaty of specific chapters on the free movement of natural and legal persons shows that those matters do not fall within the common commercial policy.

47 It follows that the modes of supply of services referred to by GATS as 'consumption abroad', 'commercial presence' and the 'presence of natural persons' are not covered by the common commercial policy.

Such an interpretation goes along with intellectual property rights coming under Article 113 only as far as they have been subject to community action in internal market relations.

The position of the Court seems to be less consistent with regard to health and safety in international agreements. The Court saw no difficulties in Opinion 1/94 in understanding the GATT Agreement on Technical Barriers to Trade as well as the GATT Agreement on the Application of Sanitary and Phytosanitary Measures as being covered by Article 113. The Commission had invoked Article 43 as the appropriate legal basis. The Court rejected such an understanding and concluded (I-5276 at 31 and 33):

30 The Council further contends that, for the same reasons as were put forward in relation to the Agreement on Agriculture, it will also be necessary to rely on Article 43 of the EC Treaty as the basis for its decision to conclude the Agreement on the Application of Sanitary and Phytosanitary Measures.

31 That contention must be rejected. The Agreement on the Application of Sanitary and Phytosanitary Measures is confined, as stated in its preamble, to 'the establishment of a multilateral framework of rules and disciplines to guide the development, adoption and enforcement of sanitary and phyto-sanitary measures in order to minimize their negative effects on trade'. Such an agreement can be concluded on the basis of Article 113 alone.

32 According to the Netherlands Government, the joint participation of the Community and the Member States in the WTO Agreement is justified, since the Member States have their own competence in relation to technical barriers to trade by reason of the optional nature of certain Community directives in that area, and because complete harmonization has not been achieved and is not envisaged in that field.

33 That argument cannot be accepted. The Agreement on Technical Barriers to Trade, the provisions of which are designed merely to ensure that technical regulations and standards and procedures for assessment of conformity with technical regulations and standards do not create unnecessary obstacles to international trade (see the preamble and Articles 2.2 and 5.1.2 of the Agreement), falls within the ambit of the common commercial policy.

34 It follows that the Community has exclusive competence, pursuant to Article 113 of the EC Treaty, to conclude the Multilateral Agreements on Trade in Goods.

The Court took a different view in its *Opinion 2/91 Convention No 170 of the International Labour Organisation concerning safety in the use of chemicals at work*, [1993] ECR I-1061. The Convention is designed to protect workers against harmful effects of using chemicals in the workplace. Its field led the Court to the conclusion that the Convention falls within the 'social policy provisions' of the Treaty, although the Community has adopted a number of directives (mainly 67/548/EED of 27 June 1967 on the approximation of laws, regulations and administrative practices relating to the classification, packaging and labelling of dangerous substances, *Official Journal* English Special Edition 1967, 234) which are related to health and safety at work and which were based on Article 100 a. The Court assumed competence of the European Community to conclude the ILO Convention under the implied powers doctrine within the meaning of Article 118 a, Opinion 2/91 at 17. It did not investigate the applicability of Article 113 in the field of workers' safety.

17   The Community thus enjoys an internal legislative competence in the area of social policy. Consequently, Convention No 170, whose subject-matter coincides, moreover, with that of several directives adopted under Article 118a, falls within the Community's area of competence.

4. Virtual capacity or factual capacity of the Community

The European Community might have more powers in external relations mainly due to the implied powers doctrine as it has already made use of. Then the question arises whether the virtual capacity of the Community pre-empts the Member States from taking action in a field where the Community is supposed to enter into international agreements.

In the Cases 3, 4 and 6/76, *Kramer* [1976] ECR 1279 at 1305 the Court concluded that 'the Community has authority to enter into international commitments', although it had not made use of the *virtual* external relations powers provided for in the framework of the North-East Atlantic Fisheries Convention. Perhaps the most outspoken dictum of the Court relating to the problem of *virtual* versus *factual* powers of the Community under Art. 113 can still be found in *Opinion 1/76 (Draft agreement establishing a European laying-up fund for inland waterway vessels*, [1977] ECR 741 at 754):

... The Court has concluded *inter alia* that whenever Community law has created for the institutions of the Community powers within its internal system for the purpose of attaining a specific objective, the Community has authority to enter into international commitments necessary for the attainment of that objective even in the absence of an express provision in that connection.

This is particularly so in all cases in which internal power has already been used to adopt measures which come within the attainment of common policies. It is, however, not limited to that eventuality. Although the internal Community measures are only adopted when the international agreement is concluded and made enforceable, as is envisaged in the present case.., the power to bind the Community *vis-à-vis* third party countries nevertheless flows by implication from the provisions of the Treaty creating the internal power and in so far as the participation of the Community in international agreement is, as here, necessary for the attainment of one of the objectives of the Community.

The Commission has invoked this strong statement of the Court to justify its implied power under Articles 100 a and 235 to conclude the GATS agreement. It was faced by the problem that the GATS reaches much further than the already existing rules on the establishment of an internal market for services. The Court in Opinion 1/94 [1994] ECR I-5276 at 73–77 after referring to the Commission's statement, rejected the argument by requiring that implied powers may exist only, where common rules have been established at an internal level:

73 With particular regard to GATS, the Commission cites three possible sources for exclusive external competence on the part of the Community: the powers conferred on the Community institutions by the Treaty at internal level, the need to conclude the agreement in order to achieve a Community objective, and, lastly, Articles 100a and 235.

74 The Commission argues, first, that there is no area or specific provision in GATS in respect of which the Community does not have corresponding powers to adopt measures at internal level. According to the Commission, those powers are set out in the chapters on the right of establishment, freedom to provide services and transport. Exclusive external competence flows from those internal powers.

75 That argument must be rejected.

76 It was on the basis of Article 75(1)(a) which, as regards that part of a journey which takes place on Community territory, also concerns transport from or to non-member countries, that the Court held in the *AETR* judgment (at paragraph 27) that 'the powers of the Community extend to relationships arising from international law, and hence involve the need in the sphere in question for agreements with the third countries concerned'.

77 However, even in the field of transport, the Community's exclusive external competence does not automatically flow from its power to lay down rules at internal level. As the Court pointed out in the *AETR* judgment (paragraph 17 and 18), the Member States, whether acting individually or collectively,

only lose their right to assume obligations with non-member countries as and when common rules which could be affected by those obligations come into being. Only in so far as common rules have been established at internal level does the external competence of the Community become exclusive. However, not all transport matters are already covered by common rules.

The Court then comes back to the Commission's interpretation of Opinion 1/76:

82 Referring to Opinion 1/76 (paragraphs 3 and 4), the Commission submits, second, that the Community's exclusive external competence is not confined to cases in which use has already been made of internal powers to adopt measures for the attainment of common policies. Whenever Community law has conferred on the institutions internal powers for the purposes of attaining specific objectives, the international competence of the Community implicitly flows, according to the Commission, from those provisions. It is enough that the Community's participation in the international agreement is necessary for the attainment of one of the objectives of the Community.

83 The Commission puts forward here both internal and external reasons to justify participation by the Community, and by the Community alone, in the conclusion of GATS and TRIPs. At internal level, the Commission maintains that, without such participation, the coherence of the internal market would be impaired. At external level, the European Community cannot allow itself to remain inactive on the international stage: the need for the conclusion of the WTO Agreement and its annexes, reflecting a global approach to international trade (embracing goods, services and intellectual property), is not in dispute.

84 That application of Opinion 1/76 to GATS cannot be accepted.

85 Opinion 1/76 related to an issue different from that arising from GATS. It concerned rationalization of the economic situation in the inland waterways sector in the Rhine and Moselle basins, and throughout all the Netherlands inland waterways and the German inland waterways linked to the Rhine basin, by elimination of short-term overcapacity. It was not possible to achieve that objective by the establishment of autonomous common rules, because of the traditional participation of vessels from Switzerland in navigation on the waterways in question. It was necessary, therefore, to bring Switzerland into the scheme envisaged by means of an international agreement (see Opinion 1/76, paragraph 2). Similarly, in the context of conservation of the resources of the seas, the restriction, by means of internal legislative measures, of fishing on the high seas by vessels flying the flag of a Member State would hardly be effective if the same restrictions were not to apply to vessels flying the flag of a nonmember country bordering on the same seas. It is understandable, therefore, that external powers may be ex-

ercised, and thus become exclusive, without any internal legislation having first been adopted.

86 That is not the situation in the sphere of services: attainment of freedom of establishment and freedom to provide services for nationals of the Member States is not inextricably linked to the treatment to be afforded in the Community to nationals of non-member countries or in non-member countries to nationals of Member States of the Community.

87 Third, the Commission refers to Articles 100a and 235 of the Treaty as the basis of exclusive external competence.

88 As regards Article 100a, it is undeniable that, where harmonizing powers have been exercised, the harmonization measures thus adopted may limit, or even remove, the freedom of the Member States to negotiate with non-member countries. However, an internal power to harmonize which has not been exercised in a specific field cannot confer exclusive external competence in that field on the Community.

89 Article 235, which enables the Community to cope with any insufficiency in the powers conferred on it, expressly or by implication, for the achievement of its objectives, cannot in itself vest exclusive competence in the Community at international level. Save where internal powers can only be effectively exercised at the same time as external powers (see Opinion 1/76 and paragraph 85 above), internal competence can give rise to exclusive external competence only if it is exercised. This applies *a fortiori* to Article 235.

90 Although the only objective expressly mentioned in the chapters on the right of establishment and on freedom to provide services is the attainment of those freedoms for nationals of the Member States of the Community, it does not follow that the Community institutions are prohibited from using the powers conferred on them in that field in order to specify the treatment which is to be accorded to nationals of non-member countries. Numerous acts adopted by the Council on the basis of Articles 54 and 57(2) of the Treaty – but not mentioned by it – contain provisions in that regard. The Commission has listed them in response to a question from the Court.

91 It is evident from an examination of those acts that very different objectives may be pursued by incorporation of external provisions.

92 The directives on coordination of disclosure requirements and company accounts applied only to companies as such and not to their branches. That gave rise to some disparity, as regards the protection of members and third parties, between companies operating in other Member States by setting up branches and companies operating there by setting up subsidiaries. Consequently, Council Directive 89/666/EEC of 21 December 1989 concerning disclosure requirements in respect of branches opened in a Member State by certain types of company governed by the law of another State (OJ 1989 L 395, p. 36), which is based on Article 54 of the Treaty, was introduced to

regulate the disclosure requirements applying to such branches. In order to avoid any discrimination based on a company's country of origin, that directive also had to cover branches established by companies governed by the laws of non-member countries.

93 Moreover, the Second Council Directive (89/646/EEC) of 15 December 1989 on the coordination of laws, regulations and administrative provisions relating to the taking up and pursuit of the business of credit institutions and amending Directive 77/780/EEC (OJ 1989 L 386, p. 1), which is based on Article 57(2) of the Treaty, contains a Title III on 'relations with third countries'. That directive established a system of uniform authorization and requires the mutual recognition of controls.

94 Once it is authorized in one Member State, a credit institution may pursue its activities in another Member State (for example, by setting up a branch there) without having to seek fresh authorization from that State. In those circumstances, it was enough for a credit institution having its seat in a non-member country to establish a subsidiary in a Member State or to acquire control of an establishment having its seat there to enable it to set up branches in all the Member States of the Community without having to seek further authorizations. For that reason, Title III of that directive provides for a series of measures, including negotiation procedures, with a view to obtaining comparable competitive opportunities for Community credit institutions in non-member countries. Similar provisions have been adopted in the field of insurance (Article 4 of Council Directive 90/618/EEC of 8 November 1990 amending, particularly as regards motor vehicle liability insurance, Directive 73/239/EEC and Directive 88/357/EEC which concern the coordination of laws, regulations and administrative provisions relating to direct insurance other than life assurance (OJ 1990 L 330, p. 44); Article 8 of the Second Council Directive (90/619/EEC) of 8 November 1990 on the coordination of laws, regulations and administrative provisions relating to direct life assurance, laying down provisions to facilitate the effective exercise of freedom to provide services and amending Directive 79/267/EEC (OJ 1990 L 330, p. 50)) and in the field of finance (Article 7 of Council Directive 93/22/EEC of 10 May 1993 on investment services in the securities field (OJ 1993 L 141, p. 27)).

95 Whenever the Community has included in its internal legislative acts provisions relating to the treatment of nationals of non-member countries or expressly conferred on its institutions powers to negotiate with nonmember countries, it acquires exclusive external competence in the spheres covered by those acts.

96 The same applies in any event, even in the absence of any express provision authorizing its institutions to negotiate with non-member countries, where the Community has achieved complete harmonization of the rules governing access to a self-employed activity, because the common rules thus

adopted could be affected within the meaning of the *AETR* judgment if the Member States retained freedom to negotiate with non-member countries.

97 That is not the case in all service sectors, however, as the Commission has itself acknowledged.

QUESTIONS AND OBSERVATIONS

1 The Court insists on the different issues at stake in Opinion 1/76 and Opinion 1/94. Do you share the view that the Court has narrowed down its implied powers doctrine considerably, thereby strengthening the position of the Member States?

2 Has the Community competence in external relations only when it has established common rules at the internal level? The Court might pave the way here for a new line of arguments brought forward by the Member States, which may simply stress that there are no common rules which guide the internal market!

C. THE COURT OF JUSTICE AND THE CONCEPT OF EXCLUSIVE OR SHARED POWERS

The applicability of Article 113 *entails as a possible consequence* that (1) the Community has become the only competent organ under Community law, and that Member States are eliminated or (2) that a joint competence been formed. The case law of the ECJ on the so called mixed procedure, as well as on the exclusive power of the Community, displayed for more than twenty years a common tendency. The first statements, set out in the early seventies, started from the distinct perspective of restricting mixed procedures and extending the Community's exclusive powers (*Opinion 1/76 Draft Agreement establishing a European laying fund for inland waterway vessels*, [1977] ECR 741 at 754).

Later cases indicated a growing preparedness to respect the Member States authority in external relations and to come to joint solutions. Opinion 1/94, however, establishes firmly the role of the Member States as partners of the European Community in external economic relations. This consequence follows suit from the restrictions placed upon the scope of Article 113 as well as from the limits to the implied powers doctrine.

1. Exclusive competence of the Community

In Case 22/70, *Commission* v. *Council*, better known as the ERTA judgment, [1971] ECR 263 at 270, the Court, on concluding that the subject-matter of the contemplated agreement fell within the ambit of the Community, said:

> These Community powers exclude the possibility of concurrent powers on the part of the Member States, since any steps taken outside the framework of the Community institutions would be incompatible with the unity of the Common Market and the uniform application of Community law.

In its *Opinion 1/75 Understanding on Local Cost Standard* [1975] ECR 1355 at 1356 the Court reiterated its broad and outspoken interpretation of the Community's competence in external relations:

> ... It cannot therefore be accepted that, in a field such as that governed by the Understanding (on Local Cost Standard) in question, which is covered by export policy and more generally by the Common Commercial Policy, the Member States should exercise a power concurrent to that of the Community, in the Community sphere and in the international sphere. The provisions of Articles 113 and 114 concerning the conditions under which, according to the Treaty, agreements on commercial policy must be concluded show clearly that the exercise of concurrent powers by the Member States and the Community is impossible.

The judgment triggered off a flood of comments, including critical ones on the exclusive nature of the Community's competence in the Common Commercial Policy. In the late seventies one might indeed have assumed an acquis communautaire just like Pescatore by saying: 'in other words, whenever and so far as the matter belongs to the Community's sphere, jurisdiction over it is exclusive of any concurrent power of Member States.'

The *Kramer* judgment, Case 3,4 and 6/76, [1976] ECR 1279 at 1305, however, modified the ERTA doctrine. The Court considered the Community the proper authority to enter into the North-East Atlantic Fisheries Convention signed in London in 1959. All present members of the Community except Italy and Luxembourg were initial parties to the Convention. The Court based its judgment on a thoroughgoing analysis of the primary and secondary Community law and concluded by saying:

> ... In these circumstances it follows from the very duties and powers which Community law has established and assigned to the institutions of the Community on the internal level that the Community had the authority to enter into international commitments for the conservation of the resources of the sea.

Such a reading followed the common approach of the Court to parallelize internal and external powers of the Community. The Court then, however, turned to the question 'whether the Community institutions in fact assumed the functions and obligations arising from the Convention and from the decisions taken thereunder' – and denied it, thereby upholding the competences of the Member States.

QUESTIONS

Look back at Opinion 1/94 at 77, 95–96 where the Court referred to the reach of the ERTA doctrine in the context of whether the Community may conclude the GATS agreement on the basis of Articles 100 a and 235. Is the whole opinion guided by a different policy? Is it no longer exclusive competence of the Community which is seen as the ultimate objective, but cooperation between the Community and the Member States?

2. Joint competence of the Member States and the Community

The same policy shift will have to be recognized in the role and importance attributed to joint competences. The Court started with strong statements on the limited role of joint competences which are overcome by the two recent opinions on the ILO Convention (Opinion 2/1991) and on the World Trade Organisation (1/94).

In its *Opinion 1/76, Draft Agreement establishing a European laying fund for inland water vessels* [1977] ECR 741, the Court struck a critical note on the concept of shared powers. The participation of the Member States as contracting partners alongside the Community in an agreement contemplated with Switzerland, could be justified only in view of the necessity for removing legal obstacles arising from prior Conventions. However:

> The participation of these States in the Agreement must be considered as being solely for this purpose and not as necessary for the attainment of other features of the system....It may therefore be said that, except for the special undertaking mentioned above, the legal effects of the Agreement with regard to the Member States result in accordance with Art. 228, para 2 of the Treaty, exclusively for the conclusion of the latter by the Community.

Pescatore summarizes: 'in other words, apart from one very particular aspect of the matter, Member States had no right to participate in the contemplated agreement and the "mixed procedure" was therefore to be ruled out in principle' (1979) 16 CMLR 623). The next occasion for the Court to develop further the relationship between Member States and the Community concerned *Opinion 1/78 on the Inter-*

national Agreement on Natural Rubber [1979] ECR 2871). After giving a relatively wide notion to the Common Commercial Policy under Article 113 the Court had to decide whether the participation of the Member States in the agreement was necessary. The crucial point concerned the financing of international trade measures, here financing of the so-called buffer-stock.

> [...] The Council and those of the governments which have supported its views state that since those negotiating the agreement have opted for financing by means of public funds, the finances of the Member States will be involved in the execution of the agreement so that it cannot be accepted that such undertakings could be entered into without their participation. The Commission for its part takes the view that the question of competence precedes that of financing and that the question of Community powers can therefore not be made dependant on the choice of financial arrangements.
>
> ...The Court feels bound to have regard to two possible situations: one which the financial burdens envisaged by the agreement would be entered into the Community budget and one in which the burdens would directly be charged to the budgets of the Member States. The Court itself is in no position to make any choice between the two alternatives.

The Council had transformed the Rubber judgment into a generally applicable rule, the so-called PROBA 20 formula, as proposed by the Commission (Translation from the French text in Völker/Steenbergen, *Leading cases and Materials on the External Relations Law of the E.C*, 1985 p.48). The basic principles concerning participation in international negotiation on Raw Materials have been defined as follows:

> The essential element upon which the deal put forward by the Commission is based consists in the leaving out of any legal or institutional consideration with regard to the respective powers of the Community and the Member States.
> It has been agreed that
> – there shall be joint participation of the Commission and the Member States in all agreements in which both wish to participate;
> – this participation shall be in the form of a joint delegation which will express the common position through a single spokesman.

One could have summarized the Council's and even the Court's attitude as follows: 'he who pays the piper calls the tune!'. Opposition had been voiced against the possibility of extracting general principles from the judgment as well as against the Council's rules. The Opinion 1/78 had been heavily criticized for leaving it to the Member States to decide whether an agreement comes under the exclusive competence of the Community. The PROBA agreement reflected neither the Treaty nor the early case-law of the ECJ. The agreement has set out the framework upon which a joint shaping of the Common Commercial Policy could be achieved which, though perhaps not legally required, was nevertheless politically sound. Opinion 1/78 paved the way for a joint approach by the Member States and Community.

Against that background it cannot be surprising that the Portuguese Government invoked Opinion 1/78 to justify a joint competence in the conclusions of the WTO agreement, Opinion 1/94 I-5276 at 19–21:

V. Budgetary and financial matters

19   The Portuguese Government refers to Article VII of the WTO Agreement, which provides that each member is to contribute to the expenses of the WTO, and submits that, given that the Member States of the Community are to acquire the status of original members of the WTO (see Article XI(1)), that is enough to justify the participation of the Member States in the conclusion of the agreement, even though financing is not as crucially important as it was in the International Agreement on Natural Rubber which gave rise to Opinion 1/78, cited above. The Portuguese Government also advances a reason based on its own constitutional law, under which the national parliament is required to approve international treaties providing for the participation of the Portuguese Republic in international organizations.

20   In reply to that latter argument, suffice it to say that internal rules of law, even of a constitutional nature, cannot alter the division of international powers between the Member States and the Community as laid down by the Treaty.

21   Nor can the first argument be accepted. Given that the WTO is an international organization which will have only an operating budget and not a financial policy instrument, the fact that the Member States will bear some of its expenses cannot, on any view, of itself justify participation of the Member States in the conclusion of the WTO Agreement.

The Court has grounded the joint competence of the Member States and the European Community in the conclusion of the WTO agreement basically in the piecemeal approach of the European Community in the regulation of services and intellectual property rights.

The same type of reasoning can be found in *Opinion 2/91 ILO Convention* at 24. Here the Court confers powers upon the European Community with reference to the implied powers doctrine derived from the 'social provisions' in the Treaty of Rome. It denies, however, the existence of exclusive competence because the scope of the ILO Convention is wider than that of the respective directives. This is particularly true for the provisions in the Convention on workers' representation:

30   Admittedly, as Community law stands at present, social policy and in particular cooperation between both sides of industry are matters which fall predominantly within the competence of the Member States.

31   This matter, however, has not been entirely withdrawn from the competence of the Community. It should be noted, in particular, that, according to Art. 118b of the Treaty, the Commission is required to endeavour to develop the dialogue between industry and labour at European level.

The Court then concludes:

VII

36   At points 34 to 36 in Ruling 1/78 [1978] ECR 2151, the Court pointed out that when it appears that the subject-matter of an agreement or contract falls in part within the competence of the Community and in part within that of the Member States, it is important to ensure that there is a close association between the institutions of the Community and the Member States both in the process of negotiation and conclusion and in the fulfilment of the obligations entered into. This duty of cooperation, to which attention was drawn in the context of the EAEC Treaty, must also apply in the context of the EEC Treaty since it results from the requirement of unity in the international representation of the Community.

3. Is there still an evolutive character of Community case-law in Common Commercial Policy?

The Court had originally underlined in several judgments what is known as the evolutive character of Community law. The Court emphasized the transitional character of joint competence and the long-term perspective of the Community's exclusive jurisdiction. The *Kramer* case may serve as an example of the former Court's attitude. After conferring the power on the Member States, it continued by saying:

> ... it should be stated first that this authority which the Member States have is only of a transitional nature and secondly that the Member States are now bound by Community obligations in their negotiations within the framework of the Convention and of other comparable agreements.

Similar wording can be found in the *ERTA* judgment. Both judgments may be considered as a type of prospective ruling insofar as the Court has found that the actual facts had to be judged from the point of view of a transitional situation where the transfer of powers to the Community had not yet been accomplished.

Against the background of the ECJ case-law on the so-called mixed procedure, as well as on the exclusive power of the Community, one might have come to the following conclusions. First, the Court begins from the idea that the transfer of powers from the Member States to the Community must be seen as a process involving three stages of development:

1   in the beginning, exclusive competence of the Member States – mostly in fields where the Community has not yet vested powers;
2   in a transitional phase, shared powers between the Member States and the Community – the division might be the result of political self-restraint or of overlapping competences between the Community and the Member States; and
3   in the end, exclusive powers of the Community. The Community is empowered to regulate the commercial activities under Art. 113.

The second message of the former ECJ case law concerned the conditions under which the change from the second to the third stage, that is from the concept of shared powers to the concept of exclusive Community powers, might occur. Having the two Opinions 1/76 and 1/78 in mind, one might have had the impression that the Court was willing to accept a certain autonomy of the Member States in deciding whether they accept the transfer of the regulatory power to the Community alone. Even if measures relating to the Common Commercial Policy led principally to a transfer of power from the Member States to the Community, the Member States were permitted to escape the exclusive competence of the Community by retaining financing in their hands.

These perspectives have all been overcome by the recent Opinion 1/94 I-5276 at 106–109 in which the Court reconsidered and refined its position in the shaping of external relation powers. There are no outspoken statements on the future concept of that the Community shall have exclusive powers in external economic relations. The Court proceeds quite cautiously, admits the still limited completion of the Internal Market and harmonizes this view with the even more limited scope of a *common* commercial policy. The Court relies on cooperation for an approach which will open new ground for discussion in the years to come.

IX. The duty of cooperation between the Member States and the Community institutions

106 At the hearing, the Commission drew the Court's attention to the problems which would arise, as regards the administration of the agreements, if the Community and the Member States were recognized as sharing competence to participate in the conclusion of the GATS and TRIPs agreements. While it is true that, in the negotiation of the agreements, the procedure under Article 113 of the Treaty prevailed subject to certain very minor adjustments,

the Member States will, in the context of the WTO, undoubtedly seek to express their views individually on matters falling within their competence whenever no consensus has been found. Furthermore, interminable discussions will ensue to determine whether a given matter falls within the competence of the Community, so that the Community mechanisms laid down by the relevant provisions of the Treaty will apply, or whether it is within the competence of the Member States, in which case the consensus rule will operate. The Community's unity of action *vis-à-vis* the rest of the world will thus be undermined and its negotiating power greatly weakened.

107 In response to that concern, which is quite legitimate, it must be stressed, first, that any problems which may arise in implementation of the WTO Agreement and its annexes as regards the coordination necessary to ensure unity of action where the Community and the Member States participate jointly cannot modify the answer to the question of competence, that being a prior issue. As the Council has pointed out, resolution of the issue of the allocation of competence cannot depend on problems which may possibly arise in administration of the agreements.

108 Next, where it is apparent that the subject-matter of an agreement or convention falls in part within the competence of the Community and in part within that of the Member States, it is essential to ensure close cooperation between the Member States and the Community institutions, both in the process of negotiation and conclusion and in the fulfilment of the commitments entered into. That obligation to cooperate flows from the requirement of unity in the international representation of the Community (Ruling 1/78 [1978] ECR 2151, paragraphs 34 to 36, and Opinion 2/91, cited above, paragraph 36).

109 The duty to cooperate is all the more imperative in the case of agreements such as those annexed to the WTO Agreement, which are inextricably interlinked, and in view of the cross-retaliation measures established by the Dispute Settlement Understanding. Thus, in the absence of close cooperation, where a Member State, duly authorized within its sphere of competence to take crossrelation measures, considered that they would be ineffective if taken in the fields covered by GATS or TRIPs, it would not, under Community law, be empowered to retaliate in the area of trade in goods, since that is an area which on any view falls within the exclusive competence of the Community under Article 113 of the Treaty. Conversely, if the Community were given the right to retaliate in the sector of goods but found itself incapable of exercising that right, it would, in the absence of close cooperation, find itself unable, in law, to retaliate in the areas covered by GATS or TRIPs, those being within the competence of the Member States.

D. DEFLECTIONS OF TRADE: JUSTIFICATIONS UNDER ARTICLE 115

Article 115 could be understood as the counterpart of Article 113, just as Article 36 in relation to Article 30. It allows the Member States to derogate from the Common Commercial Policy in order to protect their home industries against economic difficulties resulting from certain imports of non-Member State origin in free circulation, if so authorized by the Commission. A parallel should be drawn with Article 92 (3) which allows for state aids but binds the Member States to pursue a specific procedure (cf. Chapter 3). At least two major questions have arisen:

1   Are the Member States entitled to justify national rules under Article 115 in order to protect their industries against economic difficulties resulting from an open competitive market in which the undertakings of other Member States, of EFTA countries and of third countries like the United States and Japan participate?
2   What type of explanation should be allowed to justify derogations from primary Community law?

Article 115 has to balance the conflicting objectives of the overall principle of free trade with 'legitimate' protectionism. There is little or no case-law at hand contributing to the solution of this problem. The number of authorizations given by the Commission under Article 115 has steadily increased until recently and underlines the importance of Article 115 in shaping the Common Commercial Policy. The reasons for the key role Article 115 has gained in protecting the Member States from deflections of trade are manifold: the crumbling situation of some home industries in the Member States which were not competitive on the international level; the Member States' efforts to protect their home industries in order to ensure job security and fight against unemployment and to build up an industry competitive with the United States and Japan.

1. Has Art. 115 become obsolete through secondary Community law?

The European Community has started two attempts to fight down the number of exemptions granted under Article 115. Both attempts were guided by the idea to delegate the decision-making power under Article 115 from the Member States to the European Community. Centralization of power is obviously seen as an appropriate means to reduce the importance of Article 115 in external trade matters. The first (OJ No L 238/26 ff of 21.8.1987; as amended JO No L 36/23 of 8.2.1989) did not substantially challenge the Member States' decision autonomy under Art. 115. That is why the Commission has used the completion of the Internal Market as an incentive to urge the Member States in establishing a common authorization scheme under its responsibility (Regulation 518/94 (OJ No 67/77, 10.3.1994)).

Two assumptions may be admissible: (1) One may be tempted to interpret Regulation 518/94 as marking an end to the Member States' autonomy granted within Article 115. Regulation 518/94 would then pave the way for reviewing 'legitimate protectionist authorizations' under international economic law, such as GATT. (2) One may, however, draw the conclusion from the constant struggle over competences between the Commission and the Member States, that the Member States are not willing to understand Regulation 518/94 as a substitute to Article 115, which confers exclusive competence to the Commission.

2. Member States' competence under Article 115 and the European Community's competence under Article 113

The relationship between the contradictory distribution of competence under Articles 113 and 115 was *first* considered in the Court's judgment in Case 41/76 *Donckerwolke* [1976] ECR 1921. The Court made an either/or decision. As long as the Common Commercial Policy had not been accomplished Member States were given the right to refer to their competence under Article 115. – Has it been accomplished with the adoption of Regulation 518/94? – In Cases 59/84 and 242/84 *TEZI* [1986] ECR, 887 at 923, the Court reconsidered the 'either/or' philosophy of the Donckerwolke case and took a compromise approach. The Court had to decide whether the Community had already established a Common Commercial Policy in the field of textiles, under the auspices of the second Multi-Fibre Arrangement, thereby excluding the applicability of Article 115 in the trade of textiles or alternatively whether the Multi-Fibre Arrangement must be understood as an incomplete agreement thereby leaving room for the application of Article 115.

The Advocate General struck a rather critical note on the Member State's attempt to safeguard the application of Article 115 notwithstanding the conclusion of the Multi-Fibre Arrangement. He went beyond existing case law and formulated as a proposed rule that Article 113 must be understood as a legal obligation to establish a Common Commercial Policy:

> I do not regard the attainment of a genuinely uniform commercial policy pursuant to *Art. 111* and the Court's decisions.. as an ultimate ideal and an objective for the future *but as a legal duty which ought to have been fulfilled by the end of the transitional period* (emphasis by H.-W.M.).

The Advocate General thereby refuted the argument put forward by the Commission and some Governments to the effect that disparities in commercial policies brought about by the Community itself might justify the application of Article 115.

The Common Commercial Policy is supposed to be complete – by an act of law! Under the counter-position the authorization procedure of Article 115 remains applicable as long as the rules of the Second Multi-Fibre Arrangement provide for the possibility of allowing distortions to the Common Commercial Policy. The Court struck a compromise.

In Case 59/84 *TEZI* [1986] ECR 887 it took a rather pragmatic view of the controversy. It avoided intervening in the highly political field of protectionism and free trade, and whilst it upheld the rulings laid down in the Donckerwolke case, it came to the conclusion that a Common Commercial Policy which is 'incomplete' allows for the application of Article 115 even *after* the expiry of the transitional period:

> In the same judgment (Donckerwolke), after observing that, despite the expiry of the transitional period, a Common Commercial Policy based, in accordance with *Art 113. (1)* of the Treaty, on uniform principles had not yet been fully achieved, the Court recognized that the incompleteness of the Common Commercial Policy, together with other circumstances, was likely to maintain differences in Common Commercial Policy between Member States capable of causing deflections of trade or economic difficulties in some Member States (1986 ECR 887 at 923 No. 32).

QUESTIONS

Following the Court's approach, the problem of completeness turns out to be the crucial point for the relationship between Articles 113 and 115. Such an interpretation of the Treaty confers a wide discretionary power on the Commission outside of judicial control. Here we are in a similar debate to that relating to the function of state aids, Article 92 (3). Completeness of the Common Commercial Policy opens up opportunities to decide that a Common Commercial Policy has not yet been achieved, whenever it appears to be politically wise for the Community organs not to interfere with Member States' autonomy. Could it provide the ground for the Member States to escape Regulation 518/94?

E. IMPORT MEASURES

For more then ten years Council Regulation 288/82 (OJ L 35, 5.2.1982, 1 *et seq.*) has shaped the import policy of the Community, before being replaced by Council Regulation 518/94. It is applicable to all products other than certain textile products and products from certain state trading countries. The underlying philosophy of both regulations is that import to the Community should be free of quantitative restrictions. Quite contrary to Regulation 288/82, Regulation 518/94 establishes a common information and consultation procedure, a common investigation procedure, a surveillance procedure and a common procedure for taking protective measures. Competences have shifted from the Member States to the Community. Member States have to notify the Commission whenever they think protective measures have to be taken. After consultation the Commission may start an investigation procedure on the presumed adverse effects. The result may be the introduction of surveillance measures. Member States would then have to inform the Commission on imports. If Member States' industries are really endangered, the Commission may take action to restrict the import or define import quotas. Member States may invoke the Council, if they do not comply with the decision of the Commission. Once confirmed, imports would be put into free circulation in the Community only on production of an import document. The import document must be free of charge and must cover any quantity requested.

Outside strict legal rules, there are a number of informal safeguard arrangements, namely the voluntary export restraints (VER's) or voluntary restraint agreements (VRA's). The term voluntary is somewhat misleading as the exporting countries are more or less forced to accept the restraints. The EC is operating with voluntary export restraints, because they may be kept informal and be made applicable to one country only. So far, a number of mainly Japanese products have been subject to import restrictions.

F. EXPORT ARRANGEMENTS

The common rules for export are contained in Regulation 2603/69 (OJ L 324, 20.12.1969, 25 *et seq.*, as amended 1934/82 OJ L 211, 12.7.1982, 1 *et seq.*). The basic principle is that export of products from the Community to third countries shall be free of quantitative restrictions. A number of products are exempted, particularly oil products and products which are subject to a Community decision.

The counterpart to the freedom to export is export control. By far the most important debate on the feasibility of export controls focuses on the export of hazardous products. Background for the debate on export control in this field is the so-called dumping, the export of pesticides and chemicals whose marketing is forbidden or restricted domestically to mainly lesser developed countries. The European Community has adopted Council Regulation No. 1734/88 (OJ L 155, 22.6.1988, 2 *et seq.*), concerning the export from and import into the Community of certain dangerous chemicals, as replaced by Regulation 2455/92 (OJ L 251, 29.8.1992, 13 *et seq.*).

1. International background to the EC Regulation 2455/92

Regional efforts to regulate the export issue lag behind the overwhelming interests of international organizations in pushing for some form of harmonized regulation on the export and import of banned and severely restricted chemicals and pesticides. This has been important for the shaping of the EC's role. Most notably, reference should be made to the:

OECD Recommendation C (84) 37 Information Exchange related to Export of Banned or Severely Restricted Chemicals, 1984;

OECD Guiding Principles on Information Exchange related to Export of Banned or Severely Restricted Chemicals, 1984;

UNEP amended London Guidelines for the Exchange of Information on Chemicals in International Trade, 1989;

FAO International Code of Conduct on the Distribution and Use of Pesticides, 1986, as amended in 1989;

UNEP Convention on the Control of Transboundary Movements of Hazardous Wastes and their Disposal, 1989.

The very first initiative to develop *international* rules notably within the OECD derives from the Unites States' policy in the late '70s and early '80s to regulate export and import from a human rights perspective. But national efforts to get a grip on the export/import issue slowed down and have more or less been substituted by attempts of different international regulations to find some form of harmonized procedure. The original intention to establish some form of internationally harmonized export/import rules was to bridge the gap between differences in nation states' efforts to protect their citizens and the environment against risks resulting from pesticides and chemicals. There has not been any intention to harmonize the international rules on the production, use and marketing of chemicals and pesticides. One might even go so far as to conclude that the original intention was not to regulate the trade of banned and severely restricted chemicals and pesticides but to find rules under which the trade in these categories of products should and could be legitimated.

The OECD adopted in 1984 its Recommendation on the Information Exchange related to Export of Banned or Severely Restricted Chemicals, and the Guiding Principles. The consensus found within the OECD countries determined for a number of years the discussion in the broader fora such as UNEP and FAO. The regulatory model, based on a clear distinction between *information exchange* on the one hand and *export notification* on the other, was superseded in the last few years, when under pressure from less developed countries, supported by non-governmental organizations, these regulatory models of the OECD were further developed and supplemented by the so-called *Prior Informed Consent (PIC) procedure*.

2. The regulatory mechanism

The PIC procedure indicates an important shift in the perspective of regulating hazardous, not simply banned and severely restricted, chemicals and pesticides. These rules might be the starting point for the development of international rules on the production, use and marketing of chemicals and pesticides. This is true for two reasons: first of all, the PIC procedure establishes a mechanism under which it is guaranteed that all actions taken by countries to restrict or ban chemicals or pesticides can be integrated. Secondly, the rules on classification, labelling and on technical assistance integrated within the UNEP amended London Guidelines not only back the scope of the more narrow rules on banned and severely restricted chemicals and pesticides, but must be understood as an effort to lay down world-wide minimum standards, applicable for all chemicals and pesticides. The EC has translated the London Guidelines into Regulation 2455/92 OJ L 251, 29.8.1992, 13 *et seq.*

Article 4

Exports to third countries

1. When a chemical subject to notification is due to be exported from the Community to a third country for the first time following the date as of which it becomes subject to the provisions of this Regulation, the exporter shall provide the designated authority of the Member State in which he is established, no later than 30 days before the export is due to take place, with the information contained in Annex III necessary to enable the designated authority to effect a notification. The designated authority shall take the necessary measures to ensure that the appropriate authorities of the country of destination receive notification of the intended export. Such notification, which shall as far as possible be made at least 15 days before export, must comply with the requirements set out in Annex III.

Where the export of a chemical relates to an emergency situation in which any delay may endanger public health or the environment in the importing country, the provisions referred to above may be waived wholly or partly at the discretion of the designated authority of the exporting Member State.

The designated authority shall send a copy of the notification to the Commission, which shall forward it to the designated authorities of the other Member States and to the International Register of Potentially Toxic Chemicals (IRPTC).

The Commission shall assign a reference number to each notification received and communicate it immediately to the designated authorities of the Member States. It shall periodically publish a list of these reference numbers in the *Official Journal of the European Communities*, stating the chemical concerned and the third country of destination. Until a relevant reference number is published in the *Official Journal of the European Communities*, the exporter shall assume that such an export has not previously taken place unless he can obtain from the designated authority of the Member State in which he is established the relevant reference number previously assigned by the Commission.

2. The designated authority of the relevant Member State shall inform the Commission as soon as possible of any significant reaction from the country of destination. The Commission shall ensure that the other Member States are informed as soon as possible of that country's reaction.

3. For every subsequent export of the chemical concerned from the Community to the same third country, the exporter shall ensure that the export is accompanied by reference to the number of the notification either published in the *Official Journal of the European Communities* or obtained by it from the designated authority of the Member State in which he is established pursuant to the fourth subparagraph of paragraph 1.

4. New notification according to paragraph 1 must be given for exports which take place subsequent to major changes to Community legislation concerning the marketing and use or labelling of the substances in question or whenever the composition of the preparation in question changes to such an extent that the labelling of such preparation is altered. The new notification must comply with the requirements set out in Annex III and must indicate that it is a revision of a previous notification. Information to the effect that a new notification is needed shall be published in the *Official Journal of the European Communities*.

The Commission shall send new notification to the designated national authorities of countries which have received notification of the export from the Community of the substance or preparation in question in the six months prior to the relevant changes to Community legislation.

5. As regards the transmission of information within the meaning of paragraph 1, the Member States and the Commission shall take account of the need to protect the confidentiality of data and ownership in both the Member States and the countries of destination.

The following shall not be regarded as confidential:
–   the names of the substance;
–   the names of the preparation;
–   the names of substances in Annex I contained in the preparation and their percentage in the preparation;
–   the names of the main impurities in the substances in Annex I;
–   the name of the manufacturer or exporter;

- information on the precautions to be taken, including the category of danger, the nature of the risk and the relevant warnings;
- physico-chemical data concerning the substances;
- the summary results of the toxicological and ecotoxicological tests;
- the possible ways of rendering the substance harmless;
- the information contained in the safety data sheet;
- the country of destination.

Article 5

Participation in the international notification and 'prior informed consent' (PIC) procedure

1. The Commission shall notify the competent bodies dealing with the international PIC procedure of the chemicals which are banned or severely restricted in the Community (Annex I). It shall provide all relevant information, especially on the identity of the chemicals, their dangerous properties, Community labelling requirements and necessary precautionary measures. It shall also identify the relevant control actions and the reasons for them.

2. The Commission shall forward forthwith to the Member States information which it receives regarding chemicals subject to the PIC procedure and the decisions of third countries regarding the imposition of bans or import conditions on these chemicals. The Commission shall evaluate in close cooperation with the Member States the risks posed by the chemicals. The Commission shall take its decision, including interim decisions, in accordance with the procedure laid down in Article 21 of Directive 67/548/EEC. It shall then inform the IRPTC whether import into the Community of each of the chemicals is allowed, prohibited or restricted.

When such a decision is taken, the following principles shall be observed:

(a) in the case of a substance or preparation banned by Community legislation: import consent for the banned use shall be refused;

(b) in the case of a substance or preparation severely restricted by Community legislation: import consent shall be subject to conditions; the appropriate conditions shall be decided on a case by case basis;

(c) in the case of a substance or preparation not banned or severely restricted by Community legislation: import consent shall not normally be refused; however, if the Commission, in consultation with Member States, considers that a proposal should be made to the Council to ban or severely restrict a substance or preparation not produced in the Community, interim import conditions, set on a case by case basis, may be imposed until the Council has taken a decision on the proposed severe restriction or permanent ban.

In the case of a substance or preparation banned or severely restricted by legislation of one or more Member States, the Commission shall, at the written request of the Member State concerned, prepare its decision on the reply to be made to the IRPTC, taking into consideration that Member State's bans or severe restrictions.

The Commission shall, whenever practicable, make use of existing Community procedures and shall ensure that the response does not conflict with existing Community legislation.

3. Annex II shall comprise the following:

(a) the international list of banned and severely restricted chemicals subject to the PIC procedure established by the UNEP and FAO;

(b) a list of the countries participating in the PIC scheme; and

(c) the decisions of these countries (including the Community Member States) regarding the import of the chemicals listed in (a) above.

The Commission shall immediately notify the Member States of information which it receives regarding changes to the above. It shall periodically publish these changes in the *Official Journal of the European Communities*.

4. The exporter shall be required to comply with the decision of the country of destination participating in the PIC procedure.

5. If a participating importing country does not make a response or responds with an interim decision which does not address importation, the status quo with respect to imports of the chemical should continue. This means that the chemical should not be exported without the explicit consent of the importing country, unless it is a pesticide which is registered in the importing country or is a chemical the use or importation of which has been allowed by other action of the importing country.

The likelihood of the further development of the international rules on the export of banned and severely restricted pesticides and chemicals seemed to have been strengthened by the fact that GATT had included the issue in the Uruguay Round. With the establishment of the working group on trade and domestically prohibited goods and other hazardous substances, the international scenario was supposed to have been changed. However, in the end GATT failed and the Uruguay Round did not integrate the export issue into the agenda. That is why much will depend on national and regional activities. It may be a basis for action by the European Community.

G. EC RULES ON ILLICIT COMMERCIAL PRACTICE

In 1984, the Community adopted Regulation 2641/84 (OJ L 252/17.9.1984, 1 *et seq.*) aimed at strengthening the Common Commercial Policy against illicit commercial practice. The Regulation must be understood as a direct response to the US

301 legislation (allowing for trade sanctions). The core of the regulation is to be found in Articles 1 and 2:

COUNCIL REGULATION (EEC) NO 2641/84 ON THE STRENGTHENING OF THE COMMON COMMERCIAL POLICY WITH REGARD IN PARTICULAR TO PROTECTION AGAINST ILLICIT COMMERCIAL PRACTICES

Eur. Comm. O.J. L 252/1 (Sept. 20, 1984)

ARTICLE 1 – AIMS

This Regulation establishes procedures in the matter of commercial policy which, subject to compliance with existing international obligations and procedures, are aimed at:

(a) responding to any illicit commercial practice with a view to removing the injury resulting therefrom;

(b) ensuring full exercise of the Community's rights with regard to the commercial practices of third countries.

ARTICLE 2 – DEFINITIONS

1. For the purposes of this Regulation, illicit commercial practices shall be any international trade practices attributable to third countries which are incompatible with international law or with the generally accepted rules.

2. For the purposes of this Regulation, the Community's rights shall be those international trade rights of which it may avail itself either under international law or under generally accepted rules.

3. For the purposes of this Regulation, injury shall be any material injury caused or threatened to Community industry.

The dimension behind these rules is illustrated by reference to one of the conflicts between the EC and the United States, the Commission Decision 87/251 of March 12, 1987, on the *Initiation of an International Consultation and Dispute Settlement Procedure against the United States Measure excluding Imports of Certain Aramid Fibers into the United States of America*, OJ L 117, 5th May 1987, 18 *et seq.*

H. TRADE SANCTIONS FOR POLITICAL REASONS

One of the most debated issues in external relations law is to what extent it is possible and feasible to use trade sanctions for political reasons. The EC has imposed sanctions on Rhodesia in the 1960s and 1970s, on Iran in an effort to get Iran to release the hostages taken at the US embassy in Tehran in the 1980s, on the Soviet Union to protest against its invasion of Afghanistan and its intervention in Poland, on Argentina during the Falkland crisis in 1982, on Iraq during the war with Kuwait in 1990 and, last but not least on Yugoslavia to try to force negotiations in order to stop the war in 1991.

1. Legal basis

Until the adoption of the Maastricht Treaty there had not been a specific legal basis. Article 224 came into play which required Member States to:

> consult each other with a view toward taking together the steps needed to prevent the functioning of the Common Market being affected by measures which a Member State may be called upon to take .. in the event of war, serious international tension constituting a threat of war, or in order to carry out obligations it has accepted for the purpose of maintaining peace and international security.

The Community has used Article 224 for a basis of action against Rhodesia and Iran and Article 113 for a basis of action against the Soviet Union, Argentina and Yugoslavia, sometimes with reference to Article 224 (Argentina). The conflict has come to an end since the insertion of Article 228a in the Maastricht Treaty:

Article 228a

> Where it is provided, in a common position or in a joint action adopted according to the provisions of the Treaty on European Union relating to the common foreign and security policy, for an action by the Community to interrupt or to reduce, in part or completely, economic relations with one or more third countries, the Council shall take the necessary urgent measures. The Council shall act by a qualified majority on a proposal from the Commission.

It is amazing that the Treaty has been amended to provide for an adequate legal basis for trade sanctions. The debate on the use and usefulness of such sanctions is not over.

2. A Case-study – Sanctions against Argentina

The Argentina case demonstrates the difficulties for the European Community in coming to a joint approach, the wrangle over the legal grounding and the lawfulness of trade sanctions under international law.

COMMUNITY SANCTIONS AGAINST ARGENTINA: LAWFULNESS UNDER COMMUNITY AND INTERNATIONAL LAW*

Pieter Jan Kuyper

1. INTRODUCTION

On 16 April 1982 the Council of the European Communities adopted Regulation (EEC) No. 877/82 suspending for a month's duration imports of all products originating in Argentina.[1] This Regulation was based on Article 113 of the EEC Treaty. It was accompanied by a Decision of the Representatives of the Governments of the Member States of the ECSC, meeting within the Council, which suspended imports of all products covered by the ECSC Treaty and originating in Argentina.[2]

There was no doubt this time that these measures of trade policy were taken for high-political reasons. There was a considerable contrast with the measures taken a month before in order to 'punish' the Soviet Union for its behaviour in the Polish crisis, which were virtually hidden in an unprepossessing and highly technical Council Regulation (also based on Article 113) for the amendment of the import regime for certain products originating in the USSR, of which the last but one preambular paragraph merely noted that the interests of the Community required that imports from the USSR be reduced.[3]

---

* First published in David O'Keefe and Henry G. Schermers (eds), *Essays in European Law and Integration*, Deventer, 1982, pp. 141 *et seq.*; reprinted by permission of Kluwer Law and Taxation Publishers, Deventer. The opinions expressed in this articles are purely personal. This article has benefited from discussion with Professors Allott, Evrigenis, Gaja, Manin and Schermers and with Messrs. C.D. Ehlermann and J.F. Lamoureux of the Commission's Legal Service. Thanks also due to Chris de Cooker for critical remarks and for providing me with recent ILC materials.

[1] O.J. 1982, L 102/1 of 16 April 1982.

[2] Ibid., p. 3. This decision was necessary, because the Council is of the opinion that the governments have retained their powers in the field of commercial policy of ECSC products, see Article 71 ECSC Treaty. For a contrary opinion based on Article 232 of the EEC Treaty, see R.C. Fischer, 'Der Umfang der Befugnis der Europäischen Gemeinschaft zum Abschluss von Handels- und Assoziierungsabkommen' in: *Die Aussenbeziehungen der Europäischen Gemeinschaft*. Kölner Schriften zum Europarecht, Band 25, 1–27, at 9–10.

[3] Reg. (EEC) No. 596/82, O.J. 1982, L 72/15 of 15 March 1982. For a first comment of these measures, see Klaus Friedrich, 'Die Verordnung (EWG) Nr. 596/82 des Rates über Einfuhrregelungen für sowjetischen Waren', RIW 1982/5, pp. 333–6.

The import ban against Argentina also contained a similar preambular paragraph noting that 'the interests of the Community and the Member States [my italics] demand the temporary suspension of imports of all products originating in Argentina', but this was preceded by a number of other and very interesting considerations. First of all it was considered that 'the serious situation resulting from the invasion of the Falkland Islands by Argentina' had given rise to discussion in the context of European political co-operation. These discussions in turn had led to the decision that economic measures should be taken with regard to Argentina in accordance with the relevant provisions of the Community Treaties. Consultations under Article 224 of the EEC Treaty had led to the same conclusion, according to other preambular paragraphs.

These considerations were *followed* by the visa mentioning Article 113 as the legal basis and the proposal of the Commission, whereas these visa in traditional fashion had preceded the other preambular paragraphs in the Regular concerning the reduction of imports from the USSR.

The Argentina case is not the first one where the EEC as such has taken trade sanctions for political ends. We have just mentioned the case of the USSR, and one could also point to the measures taken against the same country on the occasion of the invasion of Afghanistan. The Argentine case is, however, the first one in which the nature of measures can be openly gauged from the terms of the Regulation. This can be characterized without any doubt as an important milestone in the development of the Communities. It must be admitted that the subsequent developments have been rather curious. The sanctions were extended, first for a week and later indefinitely, but two Member States (Ireland and Italy) declared that they would not obey this Community Regulation, invoking, if necessary, Article 224, and one Member State (Denmark) declared that it would maintain sanctions, but base them on national legislation.[4]

Nevertheless the measures against Argentina as they were taken on 16 April 1982 remain important and are well worth some further analysis.

In the first place, the preambular paragraphs and their curious arrangement give rise to a number of questions of Community Law, principally concerning Articles 113 and 224 of the EEC Treaty.

In the second place, and in spite of the clear references to the Argentine occupation of the Falkland Islands, the Regulation itself gives virtually no hint what the

---

[4] See Regs. (EEC) No. 1176/82, O.J. 18 May 1982, L 136/1, and No. 8254/82, O.J. 1982, L 146/1 of 25 May 1982, both accompanied by Decisions of the Representatives of the Governments of the Member States of the E.S.S.C. meeting within the Council. For the declaration of the Member States, see *Agence Europe* of 20 May 1982 (No.3375), p. 8 and *Europa van Morgen*, 19 May 1982, p. 290.

justification for these measures might be under international law.[5] Are they lawful economic coercion administered as retorsion for 'unfriendly' Argentinian acts, are they reprisals in reply to unlawful Argentinian acts, or do they perhaps constitute an exercise of the inherent right of collective self-defence under Article 51 of the UN Charter?

Both legal aspects – communitarian and international – will concern us in this article. [...]

Argentina

[...] It appears first of all that the United Kingdom took some economic measures against Argentina with effect from 7 April.[6] Following these measures, the Member States consulted one another in the framework of Article 224 of the EEC Treaty. As the third preambular paragraph puts it, in the context of these consultations it had proved important to take urgent and uniform measures and the Member States had therefore decided to adopt a Council Regulation pursuant to the Treaty. As was already briefly described above, it was also considered that in these circumstances the interests of the Community *and the Member States* demanded temporary suspension of imports of all products originating in Argentina. The visa of Article 113 was then placed at the end of the preamble.

All this serves to make it clear to the reader of the Regulation that one can have recourse to Article 113 for the implementation of trade sanctions only after a decision in the framework either of political co-operation or of consultation under Article 224 to use that article.[7] In fact the compromise solution which was advanced in the Iranian case by some Member States has now been used. It is not the Community which implements sanctions; It is the Member States which use the Community to implement sanctions.

It seems that, if trade sanctions are imposed for political ends, Article 224 does not constitute the exception to Article 113, but Article 113 finds itself, as it were, inside Article 224, as one of the possible options for the implementation of these sanctions.

---

[5]   It is interesting to speculate whether or not the Court of Justice under the terms of Article 164 of the EEC Treaty could have reviewed such international legal motivation of the Regulation.

[6]   These British measures were effected through an amendment to the Open General Import Licence under the Import of Goods Control Order.

[7]   Consultations in the framework of political co-operation and in the framework of Article 224 could be simultaneous. It seems that any meeting between Member States may serve the purposes of consultation of Article 224.

This may seem odd, but it is not absolutely excluded by the terms of the Article concerned, in particular Article 224.[8] If, during the consultations under that Article, all Member States come to the conclusion that the best way 'to tak[e] together the steps needed to prevent the functioning of the common market being affected by measures which a Member State [in this case; originally all the Member States] may be called upon to take in the event of ... war or serious international tension constituting a threat of war ...' is the making of a Regulation based on Article 113, they can do so.

If this is the construction which must be put on Regulation 877/82 of 16 April 1982, can it also explain what happened afterwards, when this regulation was extended by Regulation No. 1176/82 of 18 May and No. 1254/82 of 24 May 1982. both of them accompanied by decisions of the Representatives of the ECSC Member States meeting within the Council?[9] As is well known, Italy and Ireland declared on that occasion that they would no longer apply suspension of imports from Argentina, but would invoke Article 224. They promised to adopt appropriate provisions to avoid deflection of trade. Denmark stated that it would enact national measures analogous to the EEC measures (and did indeed enact such measures).[10] How can such declaration and actions be reconciled with the fact that a 'regulation shall be binding in its entirety and directly applicable in all Member States'?[11]

It is not immediately clear if it can be reconciled, but once again the approach which regards Article 113 as one of the possibilities which may be utilized within the framework of Article 224, if it concerns economic sanctions, seems the most plausible. According to that approach it might be possible to argue that Member States are free to take the measures they feel 'called upon' to take (in the case of Italy and Ireland, only a weapons embargo) under Article 224, but may not wish or may not be able to block the decision-making procedure which leads to the adoption of a Regulation based on Article 113.[12] Their application of their own meas-

---

8   Most commentaries on Article 224 do not mention this interpretation; see among others Groeben-Boeckh-Thiesing, *Kommentar zum EWG Vertrag* 2. Aufl., (Baden-Baden, 1974) p. 667 (Daig); Smit & Herzog, *The Law of the EEC. A Commentary on the EEC Treaty*, New York, pp. 6–183, Quadri *et al.*, *Commentario CEE*, Milano 1965, p. 1633 (Gori).

9   See note 4.

10 Declarations made in the P.V. of the Council according to *Agence Europe*, Nos. 3375, p. 8 and 3376, p. 7.

11 This phrase from Article 189 of the EEC Treaty is traditionally repeated at the end of each Regulation.

12 This impression created by the prorogation of sanctions is that the qualified majority rule of Article 113 would have been applied, if necessary. On the other hand Member States might well argue that the decision to use Article 113 within the framework of political co-operation or Article 224 can only be taken by unanimity. This would lead to the use of a different voting formula than the one provided for in Article 113.

ures short of the Article 113 measures would then not be contrary to their obligations under the EEC Treaty. However, they would have to abide by the residual
obligations inherent in Article 225, that is to say they should be ready to adjust
their measures to the Treaty rules in co-operation with the Commission if it turns
out that these measures have the effect of distorting the conditions of competition
in the common market.[13] As a matter of fact, the Commission has had meetings
with the authorities of Ireland and Italy on the issue of possible trade deflection.[14]

The position of Denmark is also rather remarkable. Denmark has declared that it
lacks a legal basis to implement these kind of sanctions[15] and that therefore it was
necessary to enact a national law implementing the sanctions against Argentina.
This implies that Denmark is of the opinion that trade sanctions for political ends
cannot be based on Article 113 of the EEC Treaty. Normally this legal basis would
be sufficient basis, if necessary, for Danish implementation decrees, since according to the Danish act of accession, Community Regulations have the force of law in
Denmark.[16] If Denmark now acts as if this is not the case, this amounts to saying
that in its opinion the sanctions Regulations are illegal. Strictly speaking, Denmark
should have brought an action under Article 173 of the Treaty. Since that would
obviously have weakened the political strength of EEC sanctions, Denmark opted
for the action it took.

It is obvious that international politics has strongly influenced the interpretation
of the law in the case of the measures against Argentina. As we believe this to be a
normal phenomenon in such cases and since the legal interpretations which can be
put on the political actions in this case do seem to be at least defensible from the
viewpoint of Community law, we will restrict ourselves here to a few remarks of an
institutional nature.

The interpretation according to which the utilization of Article 113 as the legal
basis for economic sanctions is the result of consultation within the framework of
political co-operation or of Article 224 may carry a certain risk of upsetting the
voting rules of Article 113 (qualified majority) and replacing them by unanimity.
On the other hand there are indications that on the occasion of the prorogation of

---

13   It is interesting to note that there are no equivalents to Articles 224 and 225 in the ECSC
     Treaty. Probably, the principles underlying these articles should be applied by analogy.
14   It is interesting to speculate now the other Member States could stop such trade deflec-
     tion. Article 115 would not seem to be a suitable legal basis given its wording. Perhaps
     the wording of Article 1 of Reg. 877/82 itself ('Imports of all products originating in
     Argentina *for the purpose of putting them into free circulation in the Community* are
     hereby suspended') and of Article 113 provide sufficient basis.
15   Denmark has an instrument for the implementation of mandatory Security Council
     Sanctions, see Act No. 156 of 10 May 1967, reprinted in UN Doc. A/8085.
16   See art. 3 of Law No. 447 of 11 October 1972, E.F. Karnov 1972, p. 183. Sanctions
     against Argentina have been implemented by law No. 215 of 25 May 1982, Lovtidende
     A 1982 – Haefte 39.

the measures against Argentina, when Italy and Ireland (and in a sense, Denmark) no longer wanted to participate, the qualified majority rule was implicitly applied so that the others could go ahead with the adoption of a Regulation based on Article 113.

In the same way, the right of initiative of the Commission laid down in Article 113 (2) might be affected by the fact that first an agreement has to be reached between the Member States to use this Article. Is the Commission once more reduced to the role of a secretariat which may write the 'proposal' after the Member States have given the green light?[17] Although the Commission should be wary of attempts to utilize this formula for anything other than sanctions, for that particular purpose it constitutes a convenient and flexible procedure. Realistically speaking, an early exchange of views between the Commission and Member States on trade sanctions for political ends in inevitable. Such decisions must be taken quickly and a long discussion in Council working groups would adversely affect the effectiveness of sanctions; therefore it is desirable that the Commission, even before presenting its formal proposal under Article 113, has some indications on what kind of proposal would meet with quick approval. Moreover, the preceding political consultation leaves some traces in the preamble, which is preferable to the completely anodyne *considérants* used in the Regulation on imports of products from the USSR.

(End of excerpt)

FURTHER READING

Th. Bruha, 'Handelsembargo gegen Argentinien durch EWG-Verordnung?', *DVBl*, 1982, p.674.

F. Castillo de la Torre, 'The EEC New Instruments of Trade Policy: Some Comments in the Light of the latest developments', *CMLRev*, **30**, 1993, p.687.

M. Cremona, 'The Completion of the Internal Market and the Incomplete Commercial Policy of the European Community', *ELRev*, **15**, 1990, p.283.

P. Gilsdorf, 'Die Grenzen der Gemeinsamen Außenhandelspolitik' in G. Ress and M.R. Will (eds), *Vorträge und Berichte aus dem Europa Institut des Saarlandes in Saarbrücken*, Nr. 125, 1988.

E. Grabitz, A.v. Bogdandy and M. Nettesheim, *Europäisches Außenwirtschaftsrecht*, München: CH Beck, 1994.

R. Lauwaars, 'Scope and Exclusiveness of the Common Commercial Policy – limits and powers of the Member States' in J. Schwarze (ed.), *Discretionary Powers in the Field of Economic Policy and their Limits under the EEC Treaty*, Baden-Baden: NOMOS, 1988.

---

[17] It should be noted that the proposals for prorogation of the Argentine measures were made by the Commission without previous political agreement between Member States.

W. Meng, 'Die Kompetenz der EWG zur Verhängung von Wirtschaftssanktionen gegen Drittländer', *ZaÖRV*, **45**, 1985, p.324.

P. Pescatore, 'External Relations in the Case-Law of the Court of Justice of the European Communities', *CMLRev*, **16**, 1979, p.615.

E. Stein in collaboration with L. Henkin, 'Towards a European Foreign Policy? The European Foreign Policy Affairs System from the Perspective of the United States Constitution', in M. Cappelletti, M. Seccombe and J. Weiler (eds), *Integration through Law, Vol. 1: Methods, Tools and Institutions*, Book 3, Berlin: De Gryuter, 1986.

C.W.A. Timmermanns, 'Common Commercial Policy Art. 113 EEC and International Trade in Services', *Liber Americorum Pierre Pescatore*, Baden-Baden: NOMOS, 1987, p.675.

P. Vogelenzang, 'Two aspects of Art. 115 Treaty: Its use to Buttress Community-set sub-quotas and the Commission's Monitoring System', *CMLR*, 1981, pp.169 *et seq.*

10 The European Community in International Relations

The European Community has constantly extended the reach of its influence. The Community legal order, the Internal Market as the focus and from there onwards the EC in International relations may best be described as a system of concentric circles. The most recently concluded agreement with the former EFTA countries on the establishment of a European Economic Area extends the reach of EC law considerably. A set of common rules apply which breathe the spirit of the EC rather than of the EFTA countries. Outside Western Europe after the collapse of the communist regimes in Central and East Europe the EC has started to formulate its relations to these countries by means of association and trade agreements. What these countries get beyond access to the Internal Market is a comprehensive set of community rules. It has been one of the objectives during the negotiations to urge the East and Central European Countries to adopt EC law.

Outside Europe the EC started relatively early in elaborating a policy on its relationship with developing or lesser developed countries. The key document here is the well-known Lomé Convention. This document has been constantly extended on most of the economic issues. Today it exists as Lomé IV and includes human rights and environmental protection as well. Last but not least, the EC has obtained an official status within GATT. Over the years and mainly after 1969, when the EC was allowed to make use of its common commercial powers, the EC gradually increased its impact on the Member States in order to be accepted as their representative within GATT. One of the key issues became the necessity of making the growing 'fortress Europe' compatible with GATT rules.

The description and analysis of the EC and International relations is much less influenced by case-law of the European Court of Justice than the Common Commercial Policy (cf. Chapter 9). True, there are landmark decisions on the compatibility of the community legal order with the convention on the European Economic Area, on the relationship between EC law and EFTA countries, on the Lomé Convention and on the relationship between EC law and the GATT. However, the importance of law in international relations should not be overemphasized. International relations are much more determined by diplomacy than by the rule of law. Nevertheless, there is a growing trend towards legalization of international relations, even within GATT. This is to be noted in the results of the Uruguay Round on the development of the dispute settlement procedure, not yet to a court but to a quasi court.

A. THE EC AND THE EFTA COUNTRIES

The foundation of the EFTA must be seen as reaction to the conclusion of the Treaty of Rome in 1957. The EFTA countries among them at that time Denmark, Portugal and the United Kingdom, were seeking a closer international co-operation but they were looking for a much looser form than the members of the European Community. EFTA is a free trade area rather than a customs union. The basic objective was to eliminate barriers to trade.

The basic rules of EFTA are similar to the EC rules. They provide for the four freedoms, guarantee fair competition and forbid state aids. There is, however, no common commercial policy and there are no provisions on social policies. The real differences lie in the institutional framework. The EFTA does not have a law-making machinery and there are no administrative bodies similar to the Commission and the Council. The EFTA secretariat which is the functional equivalent of the Commission employs a hundred people and the EFTA Council cannot be put on an equal footing with the Council of Ministers. The EFTA Council may adopt binding decisions on Member States, but voting presupposes in practice unanimity in EFTA. There is no question of a new *sui generis* legal order.

1. The EFTA concept

In a way, EFTA and the EC were competing with each other. But Austria, Finland and Sweden have become Members of the European Community. So it seems to be that the EC model has prevailed over the EFTA concept. The competition may explain why the relationship between both organizations has been difficult for a long time. It took until 1984 before the EC negotiated virtually identical free trade agreements with the EFTA members. Some of them gave rise to conflicts which reached the European Court of Justice. In Case 104/81, *Hauptzollamt Mainz* v. *C.A. Kupferberg* [1982] ECR 3641 the court examined the EC–Portugal free trade agreement which was in force prior to Portugal's accession to the Community. The case involved Article 21 of the Agreement which provided that the parties would not implement tax measures that resulted directly or indirectly in discrimination between domestic and imported products. The Court had to decide on the possible direct effects of the provision.

11   The Treaty establishing the Community has conferred upon the institutions the power not only of adopting measures applicable in the Community but also of making agreements with non-member countries and international organizations in accordance with the provisions of the Treaty. According to

Article 228 (2) these agreements are binding on the institutions of the Community and on Member States. Consequently, it is incumbent upon the Community institutions, as well as upon the Member States, to ensure compliance with the obligations arising from such agreements.

12 The measures needed to implement the provisions of an agreement concluded by the Community are to be adopted, according to the state of Community law for the time being in the areas affected by the provisions of the agreement, either by the Community institutions or by the Member States. That is particularly true of agreements such as those concerning free trade where the obligations entered into extend to many areas of a very diverse nature. [...]

14 It follows from the Community nature of such provisions that their effect in the Community may not be allowed to vary according to whether their application is in practice the responsibility of the Community institutions or of the Member States and, in the latter case, according to the effects in the internal legal order of each Member State which the law of that State assigns to international agreements concluded by it. Therefore it is for the Court, within the framework of its jurisdiction in interpreting the provisions of agreements, to ensure their uniform application throughout the Community.

15 The governments which have submitted observations to the Court do not deny the Community nature of the provisions of agreements concluded by the Community. They contend, however, that the generally recognized criteria for determining the effects of provisions of a purely Community origin may not be applied to provisions of a free-trade agreement concluded by the Community with a non-member country.

16 In that respect the governments base their arguments in particular on the distribution of powers in regard to the external relations of the Community, the principle of reciprocity governing the application of free-trade agreements, the institutional framework established by such agreements in order to settle differences between the contracting parties and safeguard clauses allowing the parties to derogate from the agreements.

17 It is true that the effects within the Community of provisions of an agreement concluded by the Community with a non-member country may not be determined without taking account of the international origin of the provisions in question. In conformity with the principles of public international law Community institutions which have power to negotiate and conclude an agreement with a non-member country are free to agree with that country what effect the provisions of the agreement are to have in the internal legal order of the contracting parties. Only if that question has not been settled by the agreement does it fall for decision by the courts having jurisdiction in the matter, and in particular by the Court of Justice within the framework of its jurisdiction under the Treaty, in the same manner as any question of interpretation relating to the application of the agreement in the Community.

18   According to the general rules of international law there must be *bona fide* performance of every agreement. Although each contracting party is responsible for executing fully the commitments which it has undertaken it is nevertheless free to determine the legal means appropriate for attaining that end in its legal system unless the agreement, interpreted in the light of its subject-matter and purpose, itself specifies those means. Subject to that reservation the fact that the courts of one of the parties consider that certain of the stipulations in the agreement are of direct application whereas the courts of the other party do not recognize such direct application is not in itself such as to constitute a lack of reciprocity in the implementation of the agreement.

19   As the governments have emphasized, the free-trade agreements provide for joint committees responsible for the administration of the agreements and for their proper implementation. To that end they may make recommendations and, in the cases expressly provided for by the agreement in question, take decisions.

20   The mere fact that the contracting parties have established a special institutional framework for consultations and negotiations *inter se* in relation to the implementation of the agreement is not in itself sufficient to exclude all judicial application of that agreement. The fact that a court of one of the parties applies to a specific case before it a provision of the agreement involving an unconditional and precise obligation and therefore not requiring any prior intervention on the part of the joint committee does not adversely affect the powers that the agreement confers on that committee. [...]

22   It follows from all the foregoing considerations that neither the nature nor the structure of the Agreement concluded with Portugal may prevent a trader from relying on the provisions of the said Agreement before a court in the Community.

23   Nevertheless the question whether such a stipulation is unconditional and sufficiently precise to have direct effect must be considered in the context of the Agreement of which it forms part. In order to reply to the question on the direct effect of the first paragraph of Article 21 of the Agreement between the Community and Portugal it is necessary to analyse the provision in the light of both the object and purpose of the Agreement and of its context.

24   The purpose of the Agreement is to create a system of free trade in which rules restricting commerce are eliminated in respect of virtually all trade in products originating in the territory of the parties, in particular by abolishing customs duties and charges having equivalent effect and eliminating quantitative restrictions and measures having equivalent effect.

25   Seen in that context the first paragraph of Article 21 of the Agreement seeks to prevent the liberalization of the trade in goods through the abolition of customs duties and charges having equivalent effect and quantitative re-

strictions and measures having equivalent effect from being rendered nugatory by fiscal practices of the Contracting Parties. That would be so if the product imported of one party were taxed more heavily than the similar domestic products which it encounters on the market of the other party.

26 It appears from the foregoing that the first paragraph of Article 21 of the Agreement imposes on the Contracting Parties an unconditional rule against discrimination in matters of taxation, which is dependent only on a finding that the products affected by a particular system of taxation are of like nature, and the limits of which are the direct consequence of the purpose of the Agreement. As such this provision may be applied by a court and thus produce direct effects throughout the Community.

The key decision of the Court of Justice is undoubtedly Case 270/80, *Polydor* v. *H. Record Shops* [1982] ECR 329 where the interpretation of Articles 14 (2) and 23 of the same Agreement was at stake. Both articles resemble to Articles 30 and 36 and the Court had to decide on whether both can be given the same meaning.

Decision

[...]

7 According to the well-established case-law of the Court, the exercise of an industrial and commercial property right by the proprietor thereof, including the commercial exploitation of a copyright, in order to prevent the importation into a Member State of a product from another Member State, in which that product has lawfully been placed on the market by the proprietor or with his consent, constitutes a measure having an effect equivalent to a quantitative restriction for the purposes of Article 30 of the Treaty, which is not justified on the ground of the protection of industrial and commercial property within the meaning of Article 36 of the Treaty.

8 The first two questions, which may be considered together, seek in substance to determine whether the same interpretation must be placed on Articles 14 (2) and 23 of the Agreement. In order to reply to those questions it is necessary to analyse the provisions in the light of both the object and purpose of the Agreement and of its wording.

9 By virtue of Article 228 of the Treaty the effect of the Agreement is to bind equally the Community and its Member States. The relevant provisions of the Agreement read as follows:

Article 14 (2). "Quantitative restrictions on imports shall be abolished on 1 January 1973 and any measures having an effect equivalent to quantitative restrictions on imports shall be abolished not later than 1 January 1975."

Article 23. "The Agreement shall not preclude prohibitions or restrictions on imports ... justified on grounds of ... the protection of industrial and commercial property ... Such prohibitions or restrictions must not, however, constitute a means of arbitrary discrimination or a disguised restriction on trade between the Contracting Parties." [...]

14   The provisions of the Agreement on the elimination of restrictions on trade between the Community and Portugal are expressed in terms which in several respects are similar to those of the EEC Treaty on the abolition of restrictions on intra-Community trade. Harlequin and Simons pointed out in particular the similarity between the terms of Articles 14 (2) and 23 of the Agreement on the one hand and those of Articles 30 and 36 of the EEC Treaty on the other.

15   However, such similarity of terms is not a sufficient reason for transposing to the provisions of the Agreement the above-mentioned case-law, which determines in the context of the Community the relationship between the protection of industrial and commercial property rights and the rules on the free movement of goods.

16   The scope of that case-law must indeed be determined in the light of the Community's objectives and activities as defined by Articles 2 and 3 of the EEC Treaty. As the Court has had occasion to emphasize in various contexts, the Treaty, by establishing a common market and progressively approximating the economic policies of the Member States, seeks to unite national markets into a single market having the characteristics of a domestic market.

17   Having regard to those objectives, the Court, *inter alia*, in its judgment of 22 June 1976 in Case 119/75 *Terrapin (Overseas) Ltd.* v. *Terranova Industrie C.A. Kapferer & Co.* (1976) ECR 1039, interpreted Articles 30 and 36 of the Treaty as meaning that the territorial protection afforded by national laws to industrial and commercial property may not have the effect of legitimizing the insulation of national markets and of leading to an artificial partitioning of the markets and that consequently the proprietor of an industrial or commercial property right protected by the law of a Member State cannot rely on that law to prevent the importation of a product which has lawfully been marketed in another Member State by the proprietor himself or with his consent.

18   The considerations which led to that interpretation of Articles 30 and 36 of the Treaty do not apply in the context of the relations between the Community and Portugal as defined by the Agreement. It is apparent from an examination of the Agreement that although it makes provision for the unconditional abolition of certain restrictions on trade between the Community and Portugal, such as quantitative restrictions and measures having equivalent effect, it does not have the same purpose as the EEC Treaty, in-

asmuch as the latter, as has been stated above, seeks to create a single market reproducing as closely as possible the conditions of a domestic market.

19 It follows that in the context of the Agreement restrictions on trade in goods may be considered to be justified on the ground of the protection of industrial and commercial property in a situation in which their justification would not be possible within the Community.

20 In the present case such a distinction is all the more necessary inasmuch as the instruments which the Community has at its disposal in order to achieve the uniform application of Community law and the progressive abolition of legislative disparities within the common market have no equivalent in the context of the relations between the Community and Portugal.

21 It follows from the foregoing that a prohibition on the importation into the Community of a product originating in Portugal based on the protection of copyright is justified in the framework of the free-trade arrangements established by the Agreement by virtue of the first sentence of Article 23. The findings of the national court do not disclose any factor which would permit the conclusion that the enforcement of copyright in a case such as the present constitutes a means of arbitrary discrimination or a disguised restriction on trade within the meaning of the second sentence of that article.

QUESTIONS

Does Article 23 differ from Article 36 and, if yes, what kind of justifications are allowed under Article 23 and what kind of justifications are allowed under Article 36?

2. The European Economic Area

The establishment of the European Economic Area must be understood as a kind of revolution in comparison to the former relationship between the EC and the EFTA countries. Again the EFTA countries found themselves in the position of defendants who felt challenged by the EC's Internal Market policy. The EFTA countries had no choice. They had to come to a closer agreement with the EC in order to maintain access to the Internal Market for their countries. In order to get out of the defensive position and to take the initiative they pursued an ambitious objective: The EFTA countries wanted to see a meta-structure for the sixteen countries established, a kind of an umbrella-structure meant to govern the EC and the EFTA countries. That effort failed completely. Step-by-step, however, the EFTA countries were urged into the framework of the Community legal order, where they were supposed to play second fiddle.

With the four freedoms and the competition rules the EEA agreement cannot hide its source. The competition rules, however, do not dramatically differ from the original EFTA agreement and Article 112 (1) allows safeguard measures, 'if serious economic, societal or environmental difficulties of a sectorial or regional nature liable to persist are arising', (cf. Case 270/80, *Polydor* [1982] ECR 329). The real innovation follows from the fact that the EFTA countries have accepted secondary Community law rules, all in all around 15,000 pages of EC law.

The political institutions of the EEA are shaped along the lines of the structure of the European Community. The EEA Council is the equivalent to the Council of Ministers. It is composed of the European Commission, the Member States and the EFTA countries. The EEA Joint Committee, where representatives of the contracting parties come together, must be seen as the counterpart to the European Commission. Last, but not least, the EEA Joint Parliamentary Committee, replaces the still non existant joint EEA/EC Parliament. The democratic deficit at the EEA level is even more important than with the EC. The EFTA institutions have to be clearly distinguished from the joint institutions. The EFTA Surveillance Authority is the guardian of the treaty. It has important powers in the field of competition law, but it cannot be compared in the scope of its powers with the European Commission.

Much more importance has gained the shaping of the judicial mechanism, but is right here where the conflict between the EFTA countries and the European Community began. Initially the agreement established an independent EEA Court and EEA Court of First Instance. The Court of First Instance was to hear appeals against decisions on competition rules by the EFTA Surveillance Body. Such appeals could be brought by the addressee of the decision or by any person for whom the decision was of direct and individual concern.

The EEA court itself was to hear appeals from the EEA Court of First Instance, disputes brought to it by the Joint Committee or by a party to the EEA agreement concerning the application of the agreement, and cases brought by the EFTA Surveillance Authority. The EEA court was to consist of five judges of the Court of Justice of the EC and three judges nominated by the EFTA states. The agreement also provided that an EFTA state court would be able to refer questions of interpretation of the EEA agreement to the Court of Justice of the EC.

3. The struggle over the EFTA Court

The concept of having a common court being competent for EFTA-EC affairs must be understood, from the point of view of the EFTA countries, as a cornerstone in the original concept of building a meta-structure for EC and EFTA together. The European Commission took another approach during the negotiations, but had to accept the political compromise on the joint court. The Commission, however, went to the Court of Justice and asked for the Court's opinion under Article 228. In one of its most outspoken and vigorous statements the Court of Justice insisted on the genuine character of the community legal order, declared it a 'constitutional charter' and rejected the concept of a joint court as incompatible with the EC Treaty, *Opinion 1/91* [1991], ECR I-6079:

III

13   Before considering the questions raised by the Commission's request for an opinion it is appropriate to compare the aims and context of the agreement, on the one hand, with those of Community law, on the other.

14   The fact that the provisions of the agreement and the corresponding Community provisions are identically worded does not mean that they must necessarily be interpreted identically. An international treaty is to be interpreted not only on the basis of its wording, but also in the light of its objectives. Article 31 of the Vienna Convention of 23 May 1969 on the law of treaties stipulates in this respect that a treaty is to be interpreted in good faith in accordance with the ordinary meaning to be given to its terms in their context and in the light of its object and purpose.

15   With regard to the comparison of the objectives of the provisions of the agreement and those of Community law, it must be observed that the agreement is concerned with the application of rules on free trade and competition in economic and commercial relations between the Contracting Parties.

16   In contrast, as far as the Community is concerned, the rules on free trade and competition, which the agreement seeks to extend to the whole territory of the Contracting Parties, have developed and form part of the Community legal order, the objectives of which go beyond that of the agreement.

17   It follows *inter alia* from Article 2, 8a and 102a of the EEC Treaty that that treaty aims to achieve economic integration leading to the establishment of an internal market and economic and monetary union. Article 1 of the Single European Act makes it clear moreover that the objective of all the Community treaties is to contribute together to making concrete progress towards European unity.

18   It follows from the foregoing that the provisions of the EEC Treaty on free movement and competition, far from being an end in themselves, are only means for attaining those objectives.

19   The context in which the objective of the agreement is situated also differs from that in which the Community aims are pursued.

20   The EEA is to be established on the basis of an international treaty which, essentially, merely creates rights and obligations as between the Contracting Parties and provides for no transfer of sovereign rights to the inter-governmental institutions which it sets up.

21   In contrast, the EEC Treaty, albeit concluded in the form of an international agreement, none the less constitutes the constitutional charter of a Community based on the rule of law. As the Court of Justice has consistently held, the Community treaties established a new legal order for the benefit of which the States have limited their sovereign rights, in ever wider fields, and the subjects of which comprise not only Member States but also their nationals (see, in particular, the judgment in Case 26/62 *Van Gend en Loos* [1963] ECR 1). The essential characteristics of the Community legal order which has thus been established are in particular its primacy over the law of the Member States and the direct effect of a whole series of provisions which are applicable to their nationals and to the Member States themselves.

22   It follows from those considerations that homogeneity of the rules of law throughout the EEA is not secured by the fact that the provisions of Community law and those of the corresponding provisions of the agreement are identical in their content or wording.

23   It must therefore be considered whether the agreement provides for other means of guaranteeing that homogeneity.

24   Article 6 of the agreement pursues that objective by stipulating that the rules of the agreement must be interpreted in conformity with the case-law of the Court of Justice on the corresponding provisions of Community law.

25   However, for two reasons that interpretation mechanism will not enable the desired legal homogeneity to be achieved.

26   First, Article 6 is concerned only with rulings of the Court of Justice given prior to the date of signature of the agreement. Since the case-law will evolve, it will be difficult to distinguish the new case-law from the old and hence the past from the future.

27   Secondly, although Article 6 of the agreement does not clearly specify whether it refers to the Court's case-law as a whole, and in particular the case-law on the direct effect and primacy of Community law, it appears from Protocol 35 to the agreement that, without recognizing the principles of direct effect and primacy which that case-law necessarily entails, the Contracting Parties undertake merely to introduce into their respective legal orders a statutory provision to the effect that EEA rules are to prevail over contrary legislative provisions.

28   It follows that compliance with the case-law of the Court of Justice, as laid down by Article 6 of the agreement, does not extend to essential elements of that case-law which are irreconcilable with the characteristics of the

agreement. Consequently, Article 6 as such cannot secure the objective of homogeneity of the law throughout the EEA, either as regards the past or for the future.

29 It follows from the foregoing considerations that the divergences which exist between the aims and context of the agreement, on the one hand, and the aims and context of Community law, on the other, stand in the way of the achievement of the objective of homogeneity in the interpretation and application of the law in the EEA.

IV

30 It is the light of the contradiction which has just been identified that it must be considered whether the proposed system of courts may undermine the autonomy of the Community legal order in pursuing its own particular objectives.

31 The interpretation of the expression 'Contracting Party' which the EEA Court will have to give in the exercise of its jurisdiction will be considered first, followed by the effect of the case-law of that court on the interpretation of Community law.

32 As far as the first point is concerned, it must be observed that the EEA Court has jurisdiction under Article 96(1)(a) of the agreement with regard to the settlement of disputes between the Contracting Parties and that, according to Article 117(1) of the agreement, the EEA Joint Committee or a Contracting Party may bring such a dispute before the EEA Court.

33 The expression 'Contracting Parties' is defined in Article 2(c) of the agreement. As far as the Community and its Member States are concerned, it covers the Community and the Member States, or the Community, or the Member States, depending on the case. Which of the three possibilities is to be chosen is to be deduced in each case from the relevant provisions of the agreement and from the respective competences of the Community and the Member States as they follow from the EEC Treaty and the ECSC Treaty.

34 This means that, when a dispute relating to the interpretation or application of one or more provisions of the agreement is brought before it, the EEA Court may be called upon to interpret the expression 'Contracting Party', within the meaning of Article 2(c) of the agreement, in order to determine whether, for the purposes of the provision at issue, the expression 'Contracting Party' means the Community, the Community and the Member States, or simply the Member States. Consequently, the EEA Court will have to rule on the respective competences of the Community and the Member States as regards the matters governed by the provisions of the agreement.

35   It follows that the jurisdiction conferred on the EEA Court under Article 2(c), Article 96(1)(a) and Article 117(1) of the agreement is likely adversely to affect the allocation of responsibilities defined in the Treaties and, hence, the autonomy of the Community legal order, respect for which must be assured by the Court of Justice pursuant to Article 164 of the EEC Treaty. This exclusive jurisdiction of the Court of Justice is confirmed by Article 219 of the EEC Treaty, under which Member States undertake not to submit a dispute concerning the interpretation or application of that treaty to any method of settlement other than those provided for in the Treaty. Article 87 of the ECSC Treaty embodies a provision to the same effect.

36   Consequently, to confer that jurisdiction on the EEA Court is incompatible with Community law.

37   As for the second point, it must be observed *in limine* that international agreements concluded by means of the procedure set out in Article 228 of the Treaty are binding on the institutions of the Community and its Member States and that, as the Court of Justice has consistently held, the provisions of such agreements and the measures adopted by institutions set up by such agreements become an integral part of the Community legal order when they enter into force.

38   In this connection, it must be pointed out that the agreement is an act of one of the institutions of the Community within the meaning of indent (b) of the first paragraph of Article 177 of the EEC Treaty and that therefore the Court has jurisdiction to give preliminary rulings on its interpretation. It also has jurisdiction to rule on the agreement in the event that Member States of the Community fail to fulfil their obligations under the agreement.

39   Where, however, an international agreement provides for its own system of courts, including a court with jurisdiction to settle disputes between the Contracting Parties to the agreement, and, as a result, to interpret its provisions, the decisions of that court will be binding on the Community institutions, including the Court of Justice. Those decisions will also be binding in the event that the Court of Justice is called upon to rule, by way of preliminary ruling or in a direct action, on the interpretation of the international agreement, in so far as that agreement is an integral part of the Community legal order.

40   An international agreement providing for such a system of courts is in principle compatible with Community law. The Community's competence in the field of international relations and its capacity to conclude international agreements necessarily entails the power to submit to the decisions of a court which is created or designated by such an agreement as regards the interpretation and application of its provisions.

41   However, the agreement at issue takes over an essential part of the rules – including the rules of secondary legislation – which govern economic and

trading relations within the Community and which constitute, for the most part, fundamental provisions of the Community legal order.

42   Consequently, the agreement has the effect of introducing into the Community legal order a large body of legal rules which is juxtaposed to a corpus of identically-worded Community rules.

43   Furthermore, in the preamble to the agreement and in Article 1, the Contracting Parties express the intention of securing the uniform application of the provisions of the agreement throughout their territory. However, the objective of uniform application and equality of conditions of competition which is pursued in this way and reflected in Article 6 and Article 104(1) of the agreement necessarily covers the interpretation both of the provisions of the agreement and of the corresponding provisions of the Community legal order.

44   Although, under Article 6 of the agreement, the EEA Court is under a duty to interpret the provisions of the agreement in the light of the relevant rulings of the Court of Justice given prior to the date of signature of the agreement, the EEA Court will no longer be subject to any such obligation in the case of decisions given by the Court of Justice after that date.

45   Consequently, the agreement's objective of ensuring homogeneity of the law throughout the EEA will determine not only the interpretation of the rules of the agreement itself but also the interpretation of the corresponding rules of Community law.

46   It follows that in so far as it conditions the future interpretation of the Community rules on free movement and competition the machinery of courts provided for in the agreement conflicts with Article 164 of the EEC Treaty and, more generally, with the very foundations of the Community. [...]

VI

54   It is necessary to examine whether the machinery provided for in Article 104(2) of the agreement for the interpretation of its provisions is compatible with Community law.

55   Article 104(2) of the agreement states that provisions allowing EFTA States to allow their courts or tribunals to ask the Court of Justice to express itself on the interpretation of the agreement are laid down in Protocol 34.

56   Under Article 1 of Protocol 34, when a question of interpretation of provisions of the agreement which are identical in substance to the provisions of the Community Treaties arises in a case pending before a court or tribunal of an EFTA State, the court or tribunal may, if it considers this necessary, ask the Court of Justice to express itself on the question.

57   Article 2 of Protocol 34 provides that an EFTA State which intends to make use of that protocol is to notify the Depositary of the agreement and the Court of Justice to what extent and according to what modalities the protocol is to apply to its courts and tribunals.

58   Accordingly, this procedure is characterized by the fact that it leaves the EFTA States free to authorize or not to authorize their courts or tribunals to refer questions to the Court of Justice and does not make such a reference obligatory in the case of courts of last instance in those States. Furthermore, there is no guarantee that the answers given by the Court of Justice in such proceedings will be binding on the courts making the reference. This procedure is fundamentally different from that provided for in Article 177 of the EEC Treaty.

59   Admittedly, there is no provision of the EEC Treaty which prevents an international agreement from conferring on the Court of Justice jurisdiction to interpret the provisions of such an agreement for the purposes of its application in non-member countries.

60   Neither can any objection on a point of principle be made to the freedom which the EFTA States are given to authorize or not to authorize their courts and tribunals to ask the Court of Justice questions or to the fact that there is no obligation on the part of certain of those courts and tribunals to make a reference to the Court of Justice.

61   In contrast, it is unacceptable that the answers which the Court of Justice gives to the courts and tribunals in the EFTA States are to be purely advisory and without any binding effects. Such a situation would change the nature of the function of the Court of Justice as it is conceived by the EEC Treaty, namely that of a court whose judgments are binding. Even in the very specific case of Article 228, the Opinion given by the Court of Justice has the binding effect stipulated in that article.

The strong defence of the EC community legal order led to a revision of the EEC–EFTA agreement. It consisted mainly in a separation of the judicial power. An EFTA court will be created to hear appeals from the EFTA surveillance authority and disputes between EFTA states. The Court would have jurisdiction only within the legal order of the EFTA countries. The European Court of Justice, in a second opinion, found the new arrangement compatible with the Treaty of Rome, Opinion 1/92 [1992] ECR I-2821, 2 C.M.L.R. 217.

III

[12] By comparison with the former version of the agreement, the new provisions on the system for the settlement of disputes differ essentially in the following respects.

[13] First, the agreement no longer sets up an EEA Court. The EFTA Court will have jurisdiction only within the framework of EFTA and will have no personal or functional links with the Court of Justice.

[14] Secondly, the agreement provides for two procedures, the first being designed to preserve the homogeneous interpretation of the agreement, the other being concerned with the settlement of disputes between Contracting Parties. In the course of that dispute-settlement procedure, the Court of Justice may be asked to give a ruling on the interpretation of the relevant rules.

[15] Thirdly, under Article 107 and Protocol 34, the EFTA States may authorise their courts to ask the Court of Justice to give a decision and not, as the former version of the agreement had it, to 'express itself' on the interpretation of a provision of the agreement.

[16] Fourthly, the agreement no longer contains any provision requiring the Court of Justice to pay due account to decisions of other courts.

IV

[17] In its Opinion of 14 December 1991 the Court held that the divergences between the aims and context of the agreement and those of Community law stood in the way of the achievement of the objective of homogeneity in the interpretation and application of the law in the EEA. It was in the light of that contradiction that the Court held that the proposed system of courts was liable to undermine the autonomy of the Community legal order in pursuing its own particular objectives.

[18] Since these divergences remain, the question is whether the new provisions of the agreement replacing those which the Court regarded as incompatible with the autonomy of the Community legal order are liable to raise similar objections.

[19] In that context, it is to be noted that the agreement no longer provides for the creation of an EEA Court, but proposes that an EFTA Court be established by a separate agreement between the EFTA States. Contrary to what was proposed in the case of the EEA Court, the EFTA Court will not hear disputes between Contracting Parties and will exercise its jurisdiction only within EFTA.

[20] It therefore remains to be considered whether the procedures provided for in Articles 105 and 111 of the agreement for the settlement of disputes are compatible with the EEC Treaty and, in particular, with **Article 164** thereof.

[21] In order to achieve the most uniform interpretation possible of the provisions of the agreement and those of Community law whose substance is incorporated in the agreement, Article 105 of the agreement empowers the Joint Committee to keep under constant review the development of the case law of the Court of Justice of the European Communities and of the EFTA Court and to act as to preserve the homogeneous interpretation of the agreement.

[22] If that Article were to be interpreted as empowering the Joint Committee to disregard the binding nature of decisions of the Court of Justice within the Community legal order, the vesting of such a power in the Joint Committee would adversely affect the autonomy of the Community legal order, respect for which must be assured by the Court pursuant to **Article 164** EEC, and would therefore be incompatible with the Treaty.

[23] However, according to the '*procès-verbal agréé ad article 105*,' decisions taken by the Joint Committee under the Article are not to affect the case law of the Court of Justice.

[24] That principle constitutes an essential safeguard which is indispensable for the autonomy of the Community legal order.

[25] Consequently, the power which Article 105 confers on the Joint Committee for the purposes of preserving the homogeneous interpretation of the agreement is compatible with the EEC Treaty only if that principle is laid down in a form binding on the Contracting Parties.

[26] Under Article 111, the Joint Committee is empowered to settle any dispute brought before it by the Community or an EFTA State on the interpretation or application of the agreement, including, pursuant to Article 105(3), disputes relating to a difference in case law which the Committee has been unable to settle under the procedure laid down in Article 105.

[27] The fact that such a power is conferred on the Joint Committee raises once again the problem mentioned in paragraph 22 of this Opinion.

[28] In that regard, however, it is to be noted that Article 105(3) establishes a link between the procedure provided for in that article and that provided for in Article 111 of the agreement, and that, because of that link, those two provisions must be interpreted systematically and consistently. Such an interpretation necessarily implies that the principle set out in the '*procès-verbal agréé ad article 105*' will also apply where the Joint Committee tries to settle a dispute in accordance with Article 111 by finding a solution acceptable to the Contracting Parties.

[29] It follows that the powers conferred on the Joint Committee by Article 111 do not call in question the binding nature of the Court's case law or the autonomy of the Community legal order, since it has been established that the principle set out in the '*procès-verbal agréé ad article 105*' is binding on the Contracting Parties.

[30] The interpretation according to which the Joint Committee is bound to comply with the aforementioned principle in the context of Article 111 is the only interpretation that is consistent with the jurisdiction to interpret the relevant rules conferred on the Court of Justice by Article 111(3).

[31] The question then arises as to whether it is compatible with the Treaty to confer that jurisdiction on the Court of Justice.

[32] The powers conferred on the Court by the [EEC] Treaty may be modified pursuant only to the procedure provided for in **Article 236** EEC. However, an international agreement concluded by the Community may confer new powers on the Court, provided that in so doing it does not change the nature of the function of the Court as conceived in the EEC Treaty.

[33] It was in that context that the Opinion of 14 December 1991 accepted that an international agreement concluded by the Community might confer on the Court jurisdiction to interpret the provisions of such an agreement, provided that the Court's decisions have binding effects. The function of the Court as conceived in the EEC Treaty is that of a court whose decisions are binding.

[34] Admittedly, the aim of requesting a ruling from the Court of Justice pursuant to Article 111(3) of the agreement is not to entrust the Court with the settlement of the dispute, which continues to be the responsibility of the Joint Committee. Nevertheless, the interpretation to be given by the Court of Justice is binding, as is clear from the very wording of the two language versions of the agreement submitted to the Court, which use the French expression '*se prononcer*' and the English 'give a ruling.'

[35] It follows that, if the Court is called upon to give a ruling pursuant to Article 111(3) of the agreement, the Contracting Parties and the Joint Committee alike will be bound by the Court's interpretation of the rules at issue. Consequently, the jurisdiction conferred on the Court by that provision for the purposes of interpreting the provisions of the agreement at the request of the Contracting Parties in dispute is compatible with the EEC Treaty.

[36] As for the arbitration procedures, it is sufficient to observe that, according to Article 111(4) of the agreement, no question of interpretation of provisions of the agreement which are identical to provisions of Community law may be dealt with by such procedures. It follows that the settlement of disputes by arbitration is not liable adversely to affect the autonomy of the Community legal order.

QUESTIONS

1   What do you think of the community legal order being a constitutional charter (no. 21)? Is there a difference between a community legal order and a community legal order as a constitution?

2   The Court of Justice has decided in its first Opinion 1/91 (no. 69–72) that certain basic principles of the Community (such as the Court system) cannot be altered or amended. What is the authority for such a position and what does it mean for the future relationship between the EC and GATT?

3   What do you think of the Court's view in Opinion 1/92 that the EEA Joint Committee has to respect the binding nature of decisions of the Court of Justice within the Community legal order?

4   Is the Court's view guided by the attempt to claim supremacy of law over politics? And what for? Why is the Court so strongly defending the independence of the Community legal order? Do you see it as a danger or as a help for the further elaboration of an international legal order under the auspices of GATT?

B. EUROPEAN COMMUNITY AND THE CENTRAL AND EAST EUROPEAN COUNTRIES

The relationship between the European Community and the Middle and Eastern European countries has long been governed by the climate of cold war. It has further been complicated by the mutual non-acceptance of the European Community and the Comecon. When Comecon made repeated efforts to commence direct negotiations for comprehensive trade agreements with the EC, the latter refused on the basis that Comecon lacked the competence to conclude trade agreements on behalf of its members. It is right here where the policy of the EC is grounded to negotiate and to conclude trade agreements, if any, country by country.

1. Stages of development

The relationship can be divided into three stages of development. After the period of hostility, the European Community concluded a trading agreement with Romania in the early 1980s. The second stage is already linked to the changing political climate in the East. Pursuant to the Romania model, the EC concluded trading and co-operation agreements with Hungary, Poland, USSR, East Germany, Bulgaria and Czechoslovakia. The third stage began with a non-Communist Poland government, speculation in Hungary on a possible application for membership and the celebration of the French revolution. At the Paris summit, the Commission was given the mandate to coordinate aid for Poland and Hungary on behalf of all countries of the OECD under the Poland/Hungary Assistance for Economic Restructuring (PHARE) programme. This was the starting point for the elaboration and the conclusion of so called association agreements with a number of Central and Eastern European countries. Whether there will be a fourth stage remains to be seen. If so, it could only be some sort of membership, whether in the EEA agreement or in the European Community.

We will analyse step by step the different stages of development. David Kennedy and David Webb, *Integration: Eastern Europe and the European Economic Communities*, provide an overview on the first stage, on the second stage and on the change which resulted from PHARE. The authors underline that the policy of the EC has been astonishingly consistent over the years, concentrating on trade (to a far lesser degree dealing with politics), guided by a country by country approach to the benefit of the Member States of the European Community.

INTEGRATION: EASTERN EUROPE AND THE EUROPEAN ECONOMIC COMMUNITIES*

David Kennedy and David Webb

[...]

II. PRIOR ECONOMIC RELATIONS BETWEEN THE EUROPEAN COMMUNITIES AND EASTERN EUROPE

The EC's current intentions toward Eastern Europe should be understood as the latest stage in an evolving history of EC–Eastern European trade relations.[1] Although the political and economic changes in 1989 and 1990 have no doubt caused the EC to accelerate its policy of improving its bilateral relations with the countries of Central and Eastern Europe, this process pre-dates recent upheavals. Indeed, the EC signed its first Eastern European trade agreement with Romania in 1980 without regard to the severe internal policies of Nicolae Ceaucescu.[2] The EC's collective and economic focus has traditionally resulted in a certain distance between the bilateral political relations Member States were willing to pursue and the common trade policies developed in Brussels. Although the common policies have been used to foster foreign policy goals – most notably in applying sanctions and in certain enlargement negotiations – they remain distinct in the minds of policymakers. The relative autonomy of technocratic economic issues when pursued in Brussels continues to affect EC–Eastern European relations.

Prior to the 1980 agreement with Romania, no formal trade links existed between the EC and either Comecon or its Eastern European member countries beyond a limited number of sectoral agreements and common membership with Romania, Poland, Hungary and Czechoslovakia in the General Agreement on Tariffs and Trade (GATT).[3] Actual trade with these countries was also limited. In

---

*   First published in *Columbia Journal of Transnational Law*, 1990, pp.633 *et seq.*; reprinted by permission of *Columbia Journal of Transnational Law* Association Ltd, New York.
[1]   For a series of articles on EC–Eastern European trade relations see *The Political and Legal Framework of Trade Relations between the European Community and Eastern Europe* (M. Maresceau ed. 1989). See also Edmund Wellenstein, The Relations of the European Communities with Eastern Europe, in *Essays in European Law and Integration*, 197, D. O'Keeffe & H.G. Schermers (eds), 1982; Susan Senior Nello, Some Recent Developments in EC–East European Economic Relations, 24 J. *World Trade L.*, 5, 1990.
[2]   Council Regulation 3338/80, 23 *O.J. Eur. Comm.* (No. B 352) 1 (1980) (EC–Romania Agreement).
[3]   The General Agreement on Tariffs and Trade, *opened for signature* Oct. 30, 1947, 61 Stat. (5), (6), T.I.A.S. No. 1700, 55 U.N.T.S. 194 [hereinafter GATT]. The GATT is reprinted in *Law and Practice under the Gatt*, K.R. Simmonds & B.H.W. Hill (eds), 1989.

1987, for example, the EC's total trade with these seven countries totalled 43.7 billion ECU while its total trade with Switzerland alone totalled 59.4 billion ECU.[4]

Following an initial period of hostility to European integration, Comecon made repeated efforts to commence direct negotiations for a comprehensive trade agreement with the EC. The EC refused on the basis that Comecon lacked the competence to conclude a trade agreement on behalf of its members.[5] Instead, the EC applied a trade regime to each of the countries of Eastern Europe which included a number of import restrictions and provided neither preferential treatment nor EC aid. It is perhaps ironic that Comecon's limited competence set in motion this country-by-country approach, in contrast to the collective approach urged upon the EFTA countries.

Romania's decision to break ranks with Comecon opened a second stage of EC–Eastern European relations. During this phase, Eastern European countries endeavored to "normalize" their trade and commercial relations with the EC through bilateral agreements independent of other Comecon members. Czechoslovakia and Hungary concluded such agreements in 1988, Poland and the Soviet Union (USSR) in 1989 and East Germany and Bulgaria in 1990.[6] The focus of these agreements has been the elimination of commercial and legal barriers to trade.

---

[4] See Commission des Communautés Européenes, *Les Relations de la Communauté Européene avec le Comecon et ses Membres de l'Europe de l'Est* 3 (Jan. 1989).

[5] In contrast to the EC, Comecon does not direct a common commercial policy on behalf of its members. Its precise competence as an international organization is a matter of considerable debate which has been considered elsewhere. See, for example, Theodor Schweisfurth, 'The Treaty-Making Capacity of the CMEA in Light of a Framework Agreement between the EEC and the CMEA', 22 *Common Mkt. L. Rev.* 615 (1985); Susan Senior Nello, *supra* note 1, at 6–7; Note. The Council for Mutual Economic Assistance and the European Community, 84 *Am. J. Int'l L.* 284, 288 (1990). For our purposes, it is sufficient to say that Comecon does not have competence to conclude trade agreements on behalf of its members. Comecon has entered into agreements with several nonmember countries which are generally intended to coordinate or facilitate trade relations between Comecon members and the third countries involved. Indeed, they generally lead to, or are simultaneous with, bilateral agreements between Comecon members and third countries. Intra-Comecon trade, while facilitated by multilateral framework agreements on how trade is to be conducted, including, in particular, the intra-Comecon currency exchange system, is governed in large part by bilateral conventions. The current system is in the process of being replaced in whole or in part by a hard currency trade regime.

[6] See Council Decision 89/215, 32 *O.J. Eur. Comm.* (No. L 88) 1 (1989) (EC–Czechoslovakia Agreement); Council Decision 88/595, 31 *O.J. Eur. Comm.* (No. L 327) 1 (1988) (EC–Hungary Agreement); Council Decision 89/593, 32 *O.J. Eur. Comm.* (No. L 68) 1 (1990) (EC–USSR Agreement). The East German and Bulgarian agreements had not been published in the Official Journal at the time of this writing nor, was a second agreement concluded between the EC and Czechoslovakia signed in 1990. See '*infra* note' 31–33 and accompanying text. The EC is expected to initial a new agreement on trade and commercial co-operation with Romania shortly.

Current EC–Eastern European relations have been built on these agreements. Indeed, despite the virtual end of communist regimes throughout Eastern Europe, so far there has been only modest progress beyond the trade agreement stage. For Poland and Hungary, "normalization" of trade relations has been virtually assured under the Poland/Hungary Assistance for Economic Restructuring (PHARE) programme and the two countries have been granted certain preferential treatment and aid. For the remaining countries, as of this writing, the process of eliminating trade restrictions is still under way with aid only now forthcoming on the basis of the EC's recent decision to extend PHARE to Czechoslovakia, East Germany, Bulgaria and Yugoslavia. [...]

A. The EC's trade regime for Eastern Europe before bilateral relations: the common commercial policy

The EC's approach to trade with Eastern Europe prior to the recent changes differed from its approach to market economies in matters of form and detail but not in structure. The differences were more technical than political and their effects were felt primarily as special restrictions and duties on particular product, the traditional substance of technical trade disputes, rather than as a more dramatic ideological rupture. The atmosphere for resolution of these disputes was often cold, but nothing in the structure of relations prevented resolution of these disputes, even absent revolutionary changes in the East.

Article 113 of the Treaty of Rome (EC Treaty),[7] pursuant to which the EC has exclusive competence to conduct a common external commercial policy on behalf of the Member States, provides the basis for its trade relations with Eastern Europe.[8] On the basis of article 113, Member States may not independently impose tariffs or quantitative restrictions on products originating in third countries. Further, they may not enter into voluntary export restraint or other trade agreements with

---

Comecon itself accepted a more modest form of parity with the EC when the two organizations signed a joint declaration establishing official relations and agreeing to "develop co-operation in areas within their respective spheres of competence" 31 *O.J.Eur. Comm.* (No. L 157) 34 (1988). Ultimately, however, enhanced ties between the EC and Eastern Europe have resulted in a weakening rather than a strengthening of Comecon integration.

[7] Treaty Establishing the European Economic Community, Mar. 25, 1957, art. 113, 298 U.N.T.S. 11 [hereinafter EC Treaty] (entered into force Jan. 1, 1958).

[8] See, for example, *Criel Donckerwolcke* v. *Procureur de la République*, Case 41/76, 1976 E. Comm. Ct. J. Rep. 1921. On the common commercial policy, see E.L.M. Völker & J. Steenbergen, *Leading Cases and Materials on the External Relations Law of the E.C.* (1985) (with emphasis on the common commercial policy); F. Burrows, *Free Movement in European Community Law* (1987).

third countries. This centralization of trade competence has led to the distance be-tween Member State political alignments and the technically constituted EC com-mercial policy.[9] The importance of the common commercial policy is strengthened by articles 30 to 36 of the EC Treaty[10] which prevent a Member State from restrict-ing the free movement of goods into its territory from other Member States even if the products are of third country origin.[11]

The EC's common commercial policy is pursued within the context of the GATT, which both permits customs unions and provides a framework for their trade relations with third countries. Within that framework, third countries are gen-erally to be treated on a "most favoured nation" (MFN)[12] basis, although some are given special "preferences" as part of the Generalized System of Preferences (GSP)[13] intended to assist developing countries. The GATT also permits deroga-tions in certain cases and provides for more restrictive treatment of state-trading countries. Non-GATT members benefit only from whatever bilateral arrangements they have negotiated. In general, the EC applies the same tariffs to imports from all third countries, including those in Eastern Europe, except those countries that have either negotiated special tariff reductions (such as Israel, Turkey and the EFTA countries) or those that participate in the GSP. [...]

B. EC–Eastern European trade agreements

The central theme of the trade agreements between the various Eastern European countries and the EC is the elimination of EC quantitative restrictions on imports from these countries. This is true regardless of whether the agreements were nego-tiated prior to or after the government changes. Prior to the EC agreements with the USSR, East Germany and Bulgaria, all parties to the agreements were GATT members and the agreements sought to resolve the problem of quantitative restric-

[9] The Member States' existing bilateral arrangements with third countries can be main-tained and renewed pursuant to a notification procedure contained in Council Decision 69/494, *O.J. Eur. Comm.* (No. L 326) 39 (1969), to the extent that they do not conflict with the EC's common commercial policy. See Edmund Wellenstein, *supra* note 1, at 205–07; Puifferat, La CEE et les Pays de l'Est, 273 *Revue Du Marche Commun* [Rev. M.C.] 25 (1984).

[10] EC Treaty, *supra* note 7, arts. 30–36.

[11] On article 30 of the EC Treaty, see P. Oliver, *Free Movement of Goods in the EEC un-der Articles 30 to 36 of the Rome Treaty* (2d ed. 1988). Article 115 of the EC Treaty also operates as an exception to the free movement of goods.

[12] GATT, *supra* note 3, art. I, para. 1.

[13] Generalized System of Preferences: GATT Decision of 25 June 1971, GATT Doc. (L/3545), reprinted in GATT, *Basic Instrument and Selected Documents* [B.I.S.D.] (18th Supp. 1972).

tions largely in the manner already provided for under GATT. The agreements with these three non-GATT members apply a similar approach.

From the EC's perspective, the trade agreements purport to assure its producers access to Eastern European markets. In fact, the key legal barriers to EC exports to Eastern Europe are the import licensing systems authorized under GATT and used by various Eastern European countries to limit their balance of payments deficits, and the Coordinating Committee (CoCom)[14] restrictions on the export of certain products to Eastern Europe. Hungary is the only Eastern European country which has significantly liberalized its import licensing system.[15] It did so as part of a general economic reform, rather than in response to obligations under its trade agreement with the EC. Similarly, the loosening of CoCom restrictions is not coming about in the context of trade negotiations. In any event, non-legal barriers to EC exports to Eastern Europe and, in particular, the lack of convertible currency in Eastern Europe, are more important than any legal barriers.

Because the EC negotiates trade matters individually with each Comecon country, relations between the EC and Eastern Europe have not been uniform. Czechoslovakia and Romania signed so-called "first generation" trade agreements which cover only industrial products and did not contain a firm commitment to eliminate all discriminatory quantitative restrictions set by these countries on exports to the EC.[16] The EC signed "second generation" trade and commercial co-operation agreements first with Hungary in 1988 and with Poland in 1989.[17] The USSR, East

---

14   CoCom is a voluntary organization composed of representatives from the NATO countries (excluding Iceland and Spain) and Japan. It was formed in 1950 to control the export of goods and technology which may contribute significantly to the country potential of Communist countries. CoCom export restrictions, which must be adopted unanimously and for which implementation is up to the members, can be incorporated into three lists; the International Atomic Energy List, the International Munitions List and the International List. See, for example, Hunt, Multilateral Cooperation in Export Controls – The Role of CoCom, 14 *Toledo L. Rev.* 1285 (1983). The International List is of most importance for export to Eastern Europe because it contains so-called "dual-use" (military and non-military) items which enables the breadth of the CoCom restrictions to be quite broad. As a result, this list has been the most controversial because it is a barrier to exports of basic technology, such as in the areas of telecommunications and electronics sectors, necessary for the economic modernization process in Eastern Europe. In June 1990, a number of CoCom restrictions were abolished. See *infra* note 25 and accompanying text.

15   See Peter Naray, The End of the Foreign Trade Monopoly – The Case of Hungary, 23 *J. World Trade L.* 85 (1989). Indeed, Hungary's reform process was well underway at the time it signed its trade agreement with the EC in 1988. See also Martonyi, La Décentralisation du Systéme de Commerce Extérieur en Hongrie, 1988 *Revue Internationale de Droit Economique* [Rev. Int. Dr. Ec.] 191; Peter Naray, Hungarian Trade Reform, 20 *J. World Trade L.* 274 (1986).

16   See supra notes 1, 2 & 6.

17   See supra note 6.

Germany, Czechoslovakia and Bulgaria signed second generation accords with the EC in 1990 and the EC and Romania have initialled a second generation accord.[18] These agreements cover all products other than textiles and European Coal and Steel Community (ECSC)[19] goods and contain a firm commitment for the abolition of quantitative restrictions by a certain date. In addition, the agreements establish joint committees to consider commercial co-operation possibilities. East Germany stands apart from this third group of countries because of its special trade relationship with West Germany, and the impending reunification of Germany. [...]

C. Initiatives after the governmental changes: PHARE

Just a few months after concluding long negotiations with Hungary and Czechoslovakia, and in the middle of negotiations with Poland over the reduction of the EC's specific quantitative restrictions, the EC was faced in July 1989 with a new non-Communist government in Poland and with widespread speculation that Hungary was preparing to apply for EC membership. President François Mitterand of France concluded that the celebration of the French Revolution and the beginning of the French Council Presidency on July 14 in Paris should be capped by a meeting of the leading industrialized nations to permit the EC to take the lead on Eastern Europe. At the summit, the EC Commission was given a mandate to coordinate aid for Poland and Hungary on behalf of all the countries of the Organization for Economic Cooperation and Development (OECD)[20] under the Poland/Hungary Assistance for Economic Restructuring (PHARE) programme.[21]

In February 1990, the OECD countries decided that the aid programmes would in principle be extended to include Czechoslovakia, East Germany, Romania, Bulgaria and Yugoslavia, subject to continued progress in economic and political reform in those countries. This wait-and-see approach primarily required each country to establish economic restructuring programmes sanctioned by the Interna-

---

18 Ibid.
19 The ECSC was created pursuant to the Treaty Establishing the European Coal and Steel Community, Apr. 18, 1951, 261 U.N.T.S. 140.
20 The member countries of OECD are Australia, Austria, Belgium, Canada, Denmark, Finland, France, the Federal Republic of Germany, Greece, Iceland, Ireland, Italy, Japan, Luxembourg, the Netherlands, New Zealand, Norway, Portugal, Spain, Sweden, Switzerland, Turkey, the United Kingdom and the United States, with Yugoslavia having special status, Convention on the Organization for Economic Cooperation and Development, Dec. 14, 1960, 12 U.S.T. 1728, T.I.A.S. No. 4891.
21 The various measures which make up the PHARE programme are described in Austin Sarat, L'Assistance de la Communauté à la Pologne et à la Hongrie, 333 *Rev. M.C.* 14 (1990). See also Horst G. Krenzler, Die Europäische Gemeinschaft und der Wandel in Mittel- und Osteuropa, 45 *Europa Archiv* 89 (1989).

tional Monetary Fund (IMF) and to undergo successfully the transition to a government selected through multi-party elections. However, it was not until the EC summit in Dublin, Ireland in June 1990 that the EC Council actually approved extension of PHARE. In a reversal of its earlier policy, the EC is also considering the possibility of aid to the USSR.[22]

The PHARE programme is significant in two respects. First, the programme unifies a variety of quite different initiatives and places Brussels at the center of relations with the East. Although the OECD countries meet regularly to discuss PHARE initiatives, the EC's aid programmes are primarily being determined and implemented independent of the OECD process, with EC procedural rules often attached as conditions. This approach recognizes the importance of the EC as a "pole of attraction" for the Eastern countries, while fixing Western initiatives within the technocratic and unification oriented political processes in Brussels.

Second, the PHARE programme offers the Eastern countries precisely the mix of trade concessions, aid and investment guarantees that were available as models from pre-existing EC negotiations with the East and with developing countries. Despite the bureaucratic and monetary costs involved, this initial programme sets relations between the East and West in Europe on a path of continuity and provides for only modest integration (excluding the case of East Germany).

The PHARE programme is a grab bag of initiatives ranging from emergency food aid to Poland to the establishment of a European Bank for Reconstruction and Development (EBRD). The most significant achievement of the PHARE programme to date is the reduction or elimination of the EC's historical barriers to, and in certain cases, the granting of special treatment in favor of, Polish and Hungarian products exported to the EC. The PHARE programme has surpassed the EC's trade agreements with Poland and Hungary by abolishing all specific quantitative restrictions imposed by the Member States on Hungarian and Polish products (excluding textiles and agricultural products as well as goods governed by the ECSC).[23] This change gives Poland and Hungary treatment equal to that accorded to most of the EC's other GATT trading partners.

---

22   In response to recent political events, the decision requires further action for extension to Romania. EC officials have been particularly hesitant about sending the PHARE programme to Romania because of concerns that the current government is not committed to a non-communist political and economic system. The EC and Romania have initialed a second generation trade agreement. Furthermore, Romania has already benefitted from EC food aid.

23   Council Regulation 3381/89, 32 *O.J. Eur. Comm.* (No. L 326) 6 (1989). The Regulation became effective January 1, 1990. Similar initiatives are now planned for the other Eastern European countries (except Romania and the USSR) in connection with the extension of PHARE.

In addition, the EC adopted a regulation suspending for 1990 the application by the Member States (other than Spain and Portugal) of non-specific quantitative restrictions on Polish and Hungarian goods.[24] This regulation puts Hungary and Poland in a better trading position than most of the EC's other GATT trading partners for exporting products for which Member States maintain quantitative restrictions, such as cars, shoes and toys. Also in the context of PHARE, the EC has extended to Poland and Hungary the GSP system of preferential tariff concessions on imports from developing countries.[25]

Outside of the trade area, much of the EC aid currently being made available is either emergency food and medical assistance or direct loans to Poland and Hungary.[26] The EC initially committed three hundred million ECUs for Poland and Hungary in 1990. A significant portion of these funds are being used to purchase agricultural products in the EC at market prices for shipment to Poland. Local proceeds from the sale of the food, which is donated by the EC, are being used to establish counterpart funds to finance the modernization of local agricultural production.[27]

The remainder of these aid funds are being divided among grants for industrial "infrastructure," training programmes and environmental projects. The Hungarian and Polish governments will identify infrastructure projects to be funded. The Hungarian and Polish joint venture laws give some indication as to which projects Hungary and Poland are likely to select. For example, the Hungarian joint venture law gives special tax benefits to joint ventures in, among others, the pharmaceuti-

---

[24] Council Regulation 3691/89, 32 *O.J. Eur. Comm.* (No. L 362) 1 (1989). Non-specific quantitative restrictions are those imposed on the EC's other trading partners.

[25] Ibid. For example, the quotas imposed by France on imports of Hungarian color televisions were abolished by this regulation even though the trade agreement may have allowed them to remain in place for several more years. Separate negotiations have yielded some results with respect to quotas for imports of Eastern European products in the agricultural, textile, coal and steel sectors.

    In another trade development not technically part of PHARE, at its June meeting, the CoCom members voted to eliminate a large number of categories of items from the restricted list altogether and eased restrictions even more for Hungary, Poland and Czechoslovakia. East Germany will be subject to very few restrictions for the period prior to political union with West Germany.

[26] The EC is implementing a US $1 billion medium term loan programme for Hungary (Council Decision 90/83, 33 *O.J.Eur. Comm.* (No. L 58) 7 (1990) and several Member States will participate in a $1 billion zloty stabilization fund for Poland.

[27] Council Regulation 3906/89, 32 *O.J. Eur. Comm.* (No. L 375) 11 (1989). Romania is also receiving emergency food assistance although not technically as part of the PHARE programme. Council Regulation 282/90, 33 *O.J. Eur. Comm.* (No. 1, 31) 01 (1990). More EC money will be committed soon in connection with the extension of PHARE to the other Eastern European countries.

cal, electronics, packaging, machine tools and waste recycling fields.[28] An *ad hoc* EC committee chaired by the Commission is responsible for awarding the aid and EC tender rules are applied to awarding the related contracts. The Commission's proposal regarding public procurement in the transportation, water, energy and telecommunications sectors, requires EC Member States to favor a bid by an EC company which is no more than three percent higher than an equivalent bid by a non-EC company. This proposal indicates that EC companies will have an inside track to obtaining these funds.[29]

The PHARE programme illustrates that the EC is prepared to relinquish trade barriers against Eastern European products, except perhaps in certain "sensitive" sectors such as agriculture, textiles, coal and steel. Outside of the trade area, however, the EC appears unable to find a coherent, programmatic expression of its view that the opportunity has arrived to reverse the post-World War II division of Europe through bold action. The PHARE initiatives contain few surprises and repeat many aspects of prior development programmes, including lengthy bureaucratic procedures for each ECU spent and a bias toward purchases of EC agricultural surpluses.

(End of excerpt)

---

[28]   Act XXIV of 1988 on the Investment of Foreigners in Hungary $ 15 [hereinafter Hungarian Foreign Investment Act] (effective as of Jan. 1, 1989), reprinted in United Nations Economic Commission for Europe, *Eastwest Joint Venture Contracts* 107 (1989) [hereinafter *East-West Joint Ventures*].

[29]   32 *O.J. Eur. Comm.* (No. C 264) 22 (1989). The EC has also agreed to guarantee one billion ECUs in loans to be made by the European Investment Bank (EC) over a three-year period. Much of these funds will be committed to major public projects in such sectors as transport, energy and telecommunications. Private companies will also have access to the funds on the basis of normal EIB rules. Smaller projects will be funded pursuant to lines of credit advanced to banks in Poland and Hungary. Joint venture and other private companies in these sectors would presumably only have access to these funds when awarded a contract through the tendering process. On a long term basis, the EC has taken the lead on the establishment of a European Bank for Reconstruction and Development (EBRD), which promises to become a major source of financing for joint ventures and development of projects in Eastern Europe. EBRD's membership includes, *inter alia*, all the OECD countries and eight Eastern European countries. The EC and its Member States would hold a slightly larger than majority share with the Commission holding 3% on behalf of the Community and EIB itself holding a 3% share. EBRD would make loans for both public and private projects with a 40% cap on public lending. A formula has been agreed upon limiting the USSR's access to EBRD funding over an initial period.

2. The association agreements

After the adoption of the PHARE programme, it became necessary to develop a position on how the relationship with the Middle and East European Countries should be developed. The Commission formulated in its 1990 communication to the Council and to the European Parliament the general outline of what the Community may expect of the so-called Europe Agreements.

ASSOCIATION AGREEMENTS WITH THE COUNTRIES OF CENTRAL AND EASTERN EUROPE: A GENERAL OUTLINE[1]

From co-operation to association

The Community's network of trade and co-operation agreements with the countries of central and eastern Europe is now virtually complete. Normal diplomatic relations have been established and the opening of the first Commission delegations in the countries concerned is already facilitating co-operation. The Community has amply demonstrated its willingness to use to the full the instruments provided by these agreements, notably to stimulate trade and to create new business opportunities.

But the dramatic changes in central and eastern Europe call for a more far-reaching response by the Community. Elections have now been held in most countries and the governments subsequently formed have expressed their interest in closer links with the Community through association. Formal requests for the opening of negotiations with a view to the conclusion of association agreements have been made by several countries. [...]

The Commission in its present Communication is providing further indications concerning the objectives and the content of association agreements which could be referred to as Europe Agreements to mark the importance of the political initiative which they represent. This will be followed by the opening of exploratory conversations with those countries giving practical evidence of their commitment to the rule of law, respect for human rights, the establishment of multi-party systems, free and fair elections and economic liberalisation with a view to introducing market economies. [...]

Objectives

Association agreements should help create a climate of confidence and stability favouring political and economic reform and allowing the development of close political relations which reflect shared values. The new consensus on these values, set out in the documents of the Bonn and Copenhagen CSCE conferences,

---

[1]   Reproduced in Europe, Europe Documents No. 1646/47, 7 September, 1990.

holds out considerable hope for the consolidation of democratic political systems and market-based economies. This process will be strengthened by political dialogue, within a regular institutional framework, which will be a key feature of association.

Secondly, association agreements should strengthen the foundations of the new European architecture. They will enable partners in central and eastern Europe to participate in the wider process of European integration, exemplified by the single European market and the new relationship to be negotiated by the Community and the European Free Trade Association. This will give tangible form to aspirations to return to the mainstream of European political and economic life and bring concrete reciprocal benefits.

A third set of objectives concern the climate for trade and investment. Economic operators, especially in the private sector, will play a key role in raising living standards and stimulating non-inflationary growth. But smaller firms, in particular, are daunted by the risks involved in the uncertain conditions of new markets. These uncertainties can be reduced by a sound long-term relationship with the Community, involving progress towards free trade and the other fundamental freedoms of the single European market. Commerce will benefit from the development, in the context of association agreements, of instruments to strengthen trade, investment and the economic environment in which business decisions are taken.

Fourthly, association agreements will enable the countries of central and eastern Europe better to manage the transition from command economies and an artificial division of labour to more rational economic structures and full participation in the international economic system. They will open up new economic prospects at a time when flows of trade and investment between CMEA members are contracting. Economic relations between these countries remain important and association should improve the conditions for trade between them. The rights and obligations attaching to association with the Community will provide experience of competitive market conditions, within a framework of support and solidarity. This will be especially valuable in coping with the social consequences of structural adjustment. Technical assistance, training and contacts between management and labour in the Community and associated countries can help facilitate the necessary redeployment in acceptable social conditions. Initiatives in these areas being developed notably through the European Training Foundation and Tempus will receive renewed impetus from the association agreements.

Fifthly, association agreements will improve the transparency and coherence of Community financial support and will enable this to adapt to new priorities identified within the consultation mechanisms of the agreements. This will provide a firm basis for the multiannual financial co-operation which the Community is developing with the countries of central and eastern Europe.

Finally, association agreements will promote a better two-way flow of information and cultural co-operation. This should reinforce joint activities in the political and economic fields by encouraging a shared sense of European identity, especially among young people.

Legal Basis

The far-reaching character of association, going considerably beyond the provisions of first generation trade and co-operation agreements, requires an appropriate legal base. This should correspond with the content of the agreements and with their political significance. These involve extensive reciprocal obligations, with the associated country adopting certain rules and practices established in the Community. As indicated in the annex, the agreements will establish association councils which will be competent, where appropriate, to take decisions on matters arising under these agreements, as well as other joint institutions. For these reasons, article 238 of the EEC Treaty is appropriate. This provides for the conclusion of agreements by the Council with the assent of Parliament.

[...]

Association agreements between the European Community and Hungary, Poland and the former CSFR (the Visegrad group) were signed on 16 December 1991. They reflect the trade-orientated approach of the European Community and demonstrate how the reach of the law of the European Community is steadily extended.

COMMUNITY RELATIONS WITH THE VISEGRAD GROUP*

Marise Cremona

[...]

THE SECOND GENERATION ASSOCIATION AGREEMENTS

The Europe Agreements are association agreements based on Article 238 EEC, and are "mixed".[1] There are six main heads to the agreements:

1 Political dialogue
2 Free movement of goods, persons, services, capital
3 Approximation of Laws
4 Economic Co-operation
5 Cultural Co-operation
6 Financial Co-operation

The Associations thus have an express political as well as a purely economic dimension, and are based, according to the Preambles, on a commitment to "pluralist democracy based on the rule of law, human rights and fundamental freedoms, a multi-party system involving free and democratic elections." There is also an express commitment to the process of the Conference on Security and Co-operation in Europe and the implementation of the Helsinki Final Act. Political dialogue, intended to lead to "close political relations",[2] "lasting links of solidarity and new forms of co-operation",[3] forms the subject of Title I and provides for consultation at political level and ministerial level through the Association Council[4] and at Parliamentary level through the Parliamentary Association Committee.[5] Exchanges of information will also take place within the framework of European Political Co-

---

* First published in *European Law Review*, 1993, pp.345 *et seq.*; reprinted by permission of Sweet & Maxwell, London.
[1] Association agreements are based on Art. 238 EEC and are designed to involve "reciprocal rights and obligations, common action and special procedures". A mixed agreement is concluded by the individual member states as well as by the EEC itself, in cases where the agreement covers matters within the reserved competence of the Member States. In this case, the element of political dialogue necessitates the mixed form.
[2] Art. 1 of both the EC–Poland and EC–Hungary Agreements.
[3] Art. 2 of both the EC–Poland and EC–Hungary Agreements.
[4] Art. 3 of both the EC–Poland and EC–Hungary Agreements. Meetings of both foreign ministers and Heads of State and Government in order to further political dialogue and co-operation have already been held, prior to the coming into force of these provisions.
[5] Art. 5 of both the EC–Poland and EC–Hungary Agreements.

operation.[6] The element of political co-operation in these agreements is seen by the Commission as part of a more general process aimed at strengthening the links between western Europe and the emergent democracies of central and eastern Europe, eventually creating what the Commission has called a "European political area".[7] It also reflects the fact that, if the Treaty on European Union comes into force, membership of the Community (the stated aim of the Association Agreements) will involve membership of the Union, with its commitment to a Common Foreign and Security Policy and a growing political dimension.

A further aim of the agreements is the expansion of trade between the parties, fostering the dynamic economic developments of the Associate states. References to the principles of a market economy echo both the proposed new formulations in the EEC Treaty as a result of the European Union Treaty[8] and the Commission's 1992 paper on the Challenge of Enlargement.[9] In addition to co-operation in a range of fields with economic impact, such as industrial co-operation, science and technology, transport, financial services, telecommunications and monetary policy,[10] the provisions on free movement of goods, persons, services and capital are designed to expand economic relations between the Community and the Associate states.

INSTITUTIONAL PROVISIONS

The institutional provisions[11] are standard within association agreements. There are three main institutions established. The Association Council consists of members of the Community Council of Ministers and Commission and the government of the respective Associated states. It will have decision-making powers and a dispute settlement role, but the decisions will need implementation by the Parties, and will be taken "by agreement between the Parties" (consensus). An Association Committee (of representatives at senior civil servant level of the Council of Ministers and Commission and the governments of the Associated states) will prepare Council meetings and exercise delegated powers. An Association Parliamentary Committee

---

[6] Art. 4 of both the EC–Poland and EC–Hungary Agreements.
[7] Commission paper of June 1992 "Europe and the Challenge of Enlargement" *Bull. E.C.* Supplement 3/92 paras. 34–36.
[8] The new Art. 3b(1) inserted by the European Union Treaty, provided for the activities of the Community to include "the adoption of an economic policy ... conducted in accordance with the principle of an open market economy with free competition".
[9] Commission paper of June 1992 "Europe and the Challenge of Enlargement" *Bull. E.C.* Supplement 3/92 paras. 8–9.
[10] Title VI of the Association Agreements includes provisions on co-operation in these and other areas.
[11] Title IX of the Association Agreements.

with representatives of the parliament of the respective Associated state and of the European Parliament will have the power to make recommendations to the Association Council but not to take binding decisions.

FREE MOVEMENT OF GOODS

As a result of the Interim Agreements these provisions are already in force.[12] They envisage the establishment of a Free Trade Area within 10 years,[13] accomplished in two five-year stages, but the transition from stage one to two will depend on economic development and the progress of reform. A Free Trade Area, unlike a customs union, does not operate within a common external customs tariff, and the free movement provisions will therefore only apply to goods originating in the European Community and the Associated states, and not to goods in free circulation.[14] Unlike other free trade agreements, for example those with the EFTA states, the Association Agreements are not fully reciprocal as regards the *speed* at which customs duties and quantitative restrictions are to be abolished, but the lack of reciprocity is not intended to be permanent. As far as imports of industrial products (apart from textiles and ECSC products) into the European Community are concerned, for most products all customs duties have been abolished from the entry into force of the Interim Agreements, for some products the reduction is phased over either a one or a four year period, and some products are subject to annually increased tariff-free quotas for five years, after which all duties will be abolished.[15] All quantitative restrictions and measures of equivalent effect on imports from the Associated states into the European Community were abolished from the entry into force of the Interim Agreement.[16] The Associated states are to abolish customs

---

12 Art. 7-36 of the Association Agreements. The Interim Agreements entered into force on March 1, 1992. In the following text the Articles referred to are from the Association Agreements with the provisions of the Interim Agreements (IA) in brackets where relevant.
13 Art. 7 [Art. 1 IA].
14 Art. 8 [Art. 2(1)IA]. The rules of origin are found in Protocol 4.
15 Art. 9 [Art. 3 IA].
16 Art. 9(4) [Art. 3(4) IA]. This builds on earlier autonomous Regulations suspending quantitative restrictions, for example Regulation 2727/90 with respect to goods from Hungary, Poland, CSFR, Bulgaria and Rumania [1990] *O.J.* L262/11, For the Associated states, Regulations imposing common rules for imports from state trading countries have now been replaced as a result of the Interim Agreements by Regs. 517-521/92 [1992] *O.J.* L56/1. Reg. 517/92 applies the standard Regulation on imports into the E.C. (Reg. 288/82 [1982] *O.J.* L35/1) and Regs. 518, 519, 520/92 give details of the procedure for the adoption of protective measures by the E.C. Reg. 521/92 opens tariff quotas for agricultural and industrial products from Hungary, Poland and the CSFR.

duties progressively over the transitional period;[17] and quantitative restrictions and measures of equivalent effect on imports immediately in most cases, though for some products the abolition will be phased over the transitional period.[18] Quantitative restrictions and measures of equivalent effect on exports are to be abolished by both the Community and the Associated states by the end of the fifth year. Textiles are covered by Protocol 1: they will be governed by textile agreements in operation between the Associated states and the Community since 1987, until completion of Uruguay Round negotiations allows for the conclusion of a new protocol. This effectively delays even the beginning of any abolition of quantitative restrictions and measures of equivalent effect until the GATT negotiations are completed. For agricultural products, free movement is also delayed: reduced-tariff and tariff-free quotas are established, with the prospect of further concessions "product by product and on an orderly and reciprocal basis".[19]

The Agreements also contain clauses (standard within Free Trade Agreements) on dumping, and action to be taken in the case of serious injury to domestic producers or serious disturbance to a sector of the economy as a result of imports.[20] In addition there are special temporary provisions allowing (only) the Associated states to take exceptional safeguard measures in the form of customs duties in order to protect infant industries, or "certain sectors undergoing restructuring or facing serious difficulties",[21] thus reflecting the non-fully reciprocal nature of the agreements.

Although the provisions on the free movement of goods are a substantial advance on the previous position, they are nevertheless quite a long away from completely opening access to the Community market for the Associated states, especially for those products which are sensitive from the Community's point of view, such as textiles and steel and agricultural products. They should perhaps be seen more as a case of "normalisation" of trading relations following from the accession of the former COMECON states to the GATT than as offering major concessions.[22]

---

17 Art. 10 [Art. 4 IA].
18 Art. 10(4) [Art. 4(4) IA]. Annex V of the EC–Poland Agreement, for example, provides for some delay for the abolition of quantitative restrictions relating to motor vehicles and petroleum products.
19 Art. 20(5) [Art. 14(5) IA].
20 Arts. 30 and 33 [Arts. 24 and 27 IA].
21 Art. 28 [Art. 22 IA]. Exceptional measures within this Article may not be taken after the end of the ten year transitional period.
22 For further discussion of this point, see Dan Horwitz, "EC–Central/East European Relations: New Principles for a New Era" (1990) 27 *C.M.L.Rev.* 259, referring to the "first generation" agreements.

MOVEMENT OF WORKERS, ESTABLISHMENT AND SUPPLY OF SERVICES

The heading "Movement of Workers" to the chapter on workers is significant: the Agreements are not designed to lead to complete freedom of movement of workers between the European Community and the Associated states, but are rather concerned with the treatment of *legally resident* workers and their families. The Agreements thus do not encroach on the competence of the Member States to determine their own immigration policies towards the Central and Eastern European states.[23]

No rights of entry into the Community or the Associated states are given. There is however a reciprocal prohibition of discrimination between Community and Associated states' nationals with respect to working conditions, remuneration, and dismissal for those legally employed in the territory of a Member State.[24] The spouse and children of the worker, if legally resident, have access to the local labour market. Co-ordination of social security systems is to be implemented by the Association Council.[25] Improvement in movement of workers and access to employment is to be achieved both by individual Member States in the context of bilateral agreements, and through Association Council recommendations (the Association Council does not have a power of decision here).[26]

Establishment is given the same scope as in the EEC Treaty itself, and the Agreements provide for equal treatment with nationals.[27] As far as the European Community is concerned, companies and nationals of the Associated states will be entitled to equal treatment from the date of entry into force of the (full) Agreement. Equal treatment is to apply at once for Community companies and nationals already established within the Associated states as well as to most industrial and construction sectors, and introduced during the transitional period for other sectors, including mining, pharmaceuticals, financial and legal services.[28] A temporary derogation from the equal treatment principle will be possible for the Associated states, but such protective measures are not to affect Community companies or nationals already established in the Associated states. Non-discriminatory host state

---

[23]　Arts. 40 and 41 of both the EC–Poland and EC–Hungary Agreements, for example.
[24]　Art. 37 of both the EC–Poland and EC–Hungary Agreements.
[25]　Art. 38 of both the EC–Poland and EC–Hungary Agreements.
[26]　Arts. 41 and 42 of both the EC–Poland and EC–Hungary Agreements.
[27]　Art. 44 of both the EC–Poland and EC–Hungary Agreements. These rights are subject to limitations which mirror those in the EEC Treaty covering public policy, public security, public health and activities connected with the exercise of official authority: Art. 53.
[28]　Art. 44 of both the EC–Poland and EC–Hungary Agreements.

control is envisaged for regulatory regimes,[29] and mutual recognition of qualifications is to be achieved through Association Council action.[30]

The obligation to liberalise provision of services is less demanding.[31] No deadline is set and the European Community clearly preferred to wait for the results of the Uruguay Round negotiations in the services sector.[32] The liberalisation is to be implemented by Association Council decision and will include the right to provide services across frontiers, and the temporary movement of the service provider or of "key personnel" employed by the service provider.

Two points are of interest within the framework of both the establishment and services provisions. First, the definition of "Community company" and Associated state company, although broadly following Article 58 EEC, includes a further provision requiring a "real and continuous link with the economy of one of the Member States" or the Associated state in cases where only the registered office (and not the central administration or principle place of business) is in the relevant territory.[33] This provision prevents a Contracting Party from being used as a stepping stone in order to gain access to the market of another Party.

Secondly, the Association Agreements include what may be termed a *"Rush Portugesa"* clause:[34] the right of establishment carries with it the right to employ "key personnel" who are nationals of the home state[35] and a similar provision exists with respect to providers of services. These provisions supplement those on the

---

[29] Arts. 45 and 47 of both the EC–Poland and EC–Hungary Agreements. The introduction of full home state control, or extending the EC single licence to the Associated states, would depend on progress with approximation of laws: see Art. 83 of both the EC–Poland and EC–Hungary Agreements.

[30] Art. 46 of both the EC–Poland and EC–Hungary Agreements.

[31] Art. 55 of both the EC–Poland and EC–Hungary Agreements. This provision is subject to the "public policy" exception found in Art. 53 (see n. 27). There is separate provision for transport services (Art. 56) which provides for "unrestricted access to the market" and a "freely competitive environment" in the field of international maritime transport and envisages the negotiation of further agreements in respect of inland and air transport.

[32] In Art. 58(2) there is a reference to the possibility of adjusting the establishment and services provisions of the Agreement following the adoption of a GATT agreement in the Uruguay Round.

[33] Art. 48 of both the EC–Poland and EC–Hungary Agreements. Joint ventures between the European Community and the Associated states are also covered.

[34] After case C-113/89 [1991] C.M.L.R. 818; [1990] ECR I-1417, in which the European court held that a Portuguese company's freedom to provide services in France entailed the right to use its own employees who were not themselves at the time covered by the free movement of workers provisions.

[35] Art. 52 of both the EC–Poland and EC–Hungary Agreements. Key personnel include senior management and those with special skills or qualifications who have been employed for at least one year in the relevant company.

movement of workers, although the rights of residence and employment remain contingent on the specific employment or provision of services.

MOVEMENT OF CAPITAL

The provisions relating to payment and capital are an essential aspect of the development of trading and economic relations between the Community and the Associated states. Traders need to ensure payment for goods and services provided. Companies investing in the Associated states via the establishment and services provisions need to rely on the ability to transfer capital into and out of those states.

"Current payments" are relatively straightforward and reflect Article 106 EEC: the Parties undertake to authorise payments in convertible currency with respect to transactions concerning movement of goods, persons, or services which have been liberalised.[36] Transactions on the capital account of companies exercising the right of establishment, direct investments in companies, and the liquidation or repatriation of investments are to be liberalised from the entry into force of the agreement.[37] No new foreign exchange restrictions are to be introduced, although the Associated states will be able to introduce temporary restrictions insofar as this is allowed by IMF rules.[38] As with services, however, no firm timetable is established for full liberalisation Council is to "examine ways of enabling the Community rules on the movement of capital to be applied in full".[39]

COMPETITION AND APPROXIMATION OF LAWS

As with other Association Agreements, provisions equivalent to Articles 85, 86 and 92 EEC are included, with explicit reference to these Articles. These are to be implemented within three years through decisions of the Association Council.[40] Prior to the adoption of the implementing rules, the provision on public aid is to be interpreted according to the relevant GATT rules, and the Associated states are for at

---

[36] Art. 59 of both the EC–Poland and EC–Hungary Agreements.

[37] Art. 60(1) of both the EC–Poland and EC–Hungary Agreements. However capital transactions with respect to the establishment of self-employed persons within the Associated states are to be liberalised by the end of the first stage (planned to take five years). For the EC, the 1988 capital directive (Directive 88/361 [1988] O.J. L178/5) already establishes a principle of liberalisation with respect to third states.

[38] Art. 60(2) and 62. Any restrictions are to be non-discriminatory, the minimum necessary, and the Association Council is to be kept informed.

[39] Art. 61 of both the EC–Poland and EC–Hungary Agreements.

[40] Art. 63 of the EC–Poland Agreement; Art. 62 of the EC–Hungary Agreement. Exclusions operate for agricultural and fisheries products and coal and steel products.

least the first five years to be regarded as areas of serious economic disadvantage, within Article 92(3)(a) EEC. The provisions based on Articles 85 and 86 are in the interim to be enforced directly by the Parties in cases where material injury is caused (after consultation with the Association Council): a standard provision in Free Trade Agreements. More detailed implementation is envisaged but it is not clear whether these implementing rules will involve an enforcement agency of a similar type to the Surveillance Authority set up for the EFTA states under the European Economic Area Agreement.

The opening up of public procurement is seen as a "desirable objective," again in the context of the GATT rules. The Associated states are to be granted access to the Community procurement market at once. Reciprocal access to the markets of the Associated states is to be achieved by the end of the transitional period (envisaged as 10 years), although those Community companies already established in the Associated states will be entitled to immediate non-discriminatory treatment.[41]

The approximation of the legislation of the Associated states in certain areas to that of the European Community is recognised to be a precondition for their economic integration into the Community. These areas include company law, banking, intellectual property, employment protection, consumer and health protection, indirect taxation, technical standards and the environment.[42] There is also a specific provision on co-operation in the formation of common rules and standards for accounting, supervision and regulation in the banking, insurance and other financial services sectors.[43]

AREAS OF CO-OPERATION

Co-operation is planned over a very wide range of economic, social and cultural activity, including industry, investment, science, technology, education & training, agriculture, energy, nuclear safety, environment, transport, telecommunications, regional development, social policy and others. Activities include exchange of experts, information and experience, training programmes, technical assistance and transfer of technology and are underpinned by "financial co-operation" – essentially financial aid via PHARE and loans from the European Investment Bank.[44] It is made clear that the Community will be acting in collaboration with the G-24, the IMF, and the European Bank for Reconstruction and Development.

---

[41] Art. 67 of the EC–Poland Agreement; Art. 66 of the EC–Hungary Agreement.
[42] Arts. 68–70 of the EC–Poland Agreement; Arts. 67–69 of the EC–Hungary Agreement.
[43] Art. 83 of both the EC–Poland and EC–Hungary Agreement.
[44] Arts. 96 and 97 of the EC–Poland Agreement; Arts. 98 and 99 of the EC–Hungary Agreement.

CONCLUSION

The Europe Agreements are seen by the Community institutions as an important stage in developing relations between the Community and the Central and Eastern European states. They expressly envisage a greater degree of integration, ultimately leading to membership for at least Hungary and Poland, and the Community intends to create a network of such agreements with the new Czech and Slovak Republics, Bulgaria and Rumania.[45] The Community also hopes that this network of agreements will help to foster regional integration and in particular the establishment of free trade areas between EFTA and the Visegrad states as well as between the latter states themselves.[46] The economic and institutional underpinning of these essentially political objectives is, however, disappointing. The Associated states have found that there are still formidable obstacles to entry into the Community market for their most competitive products, whether as a result of limitations in the agreements themselves or through the continued use of anti-dumping measures where price competition becomes too keen.

The most striking feature of the Association Agreements is the emphasis placed on the alignment of the internal laws of the Associated states to those of the Community in a very wide range of sectors. There is an emphasis on approximation of laws (which does not mean mutual adjustment, but the acceptance by the Associated states of the Community model), and even those provisions which refer to co-operation rather than approximation, focus on the adoption of Community standards and levels of protection, following acceptance of Community expertise and advice, and transfers of technology and know-how.[47] This was to be expected, given on the one hand the relative lack of existing legal infra-structure in the Associated states, together with their desire for eventual membership of the Community, and on the other hand the preparedness of even the EFTA states to accept the *acquis communautaire* as part of the European Economic Area Agreement. The European Community is clearly becoming a powerful force for the development of a "common European law" within the region. Questions were raised in the context of the EEA negotiations concerning the involvement of non-member states of the

---

[45] See for example the joint statement issued by the foreign ministers of the Visegrad countries and the E.C. after their meeting on October 5, 1992: *Bull. E.C.* 10-1992, point 2.3.1.

[46] For example Art. 71(3) of the EC–Poland Agreement provides for special attention to be devoted to measures capable of fostering economic co-operation between the central and eastern European states with a view to integrated development of the region.

[47] For example, in the EC–Poland Agreement, Art. 66 on intellectual property rights, Art. 74 on compliance with EC technical standards, Art. 80(3) on environmental standards, Art. 87(1) on health and safety of workers, Art. 91 on customs systems. Equivalent provisions exist in the EC–Hungary Agreement.

Community in the development of these increasingly influential legal norms. The rather weak institutional mechanisms established by the Association Agreements are not likely to provide an answer.

(End of excerpt)

The effects of the association agreements may be summarized under four key aspects (cf. D. Kennedy/D.E. Webb, The limits of integration: Eastern Europe and the European Communities, (1993) 30 *CMLRev* 1105), which merit closer observation:

1   One of the dominant themes of the agreements is that the various stages of integration are 'conditional' on the associate's continued progress in political and market reform. Conditionality is used as a 'carrot and a stick'; serving the twin aims of preserving the EC's flexibility and providing it with a basis to influence internal policy.

2   The trade provisions of the Association Agreements maintain significant and potentially long-term barriers to trade between the EC and the Association Countries, particularly in 'sensitive' areas (such as coal, steel, textiles and agriculture).

3   The institutional links created by the Association Agreements which are identical to the EC–Turkey agreement, are relatively weak when compared to the European Economic Area (EEA) accord negotiated with the EFTA countries or even the EC's arrangements with the 68 signatories to the Lomé Convention.

4   The Association Agreements make only a small step in the complex process of the legal and political integration required for EC membership and, equally importantly, contemplate virtually no role for the Association Countries in the elaboration of future policies.

There is a quite critical tone in Kennedy's and Webb's analysis of the EC's role in the process of integrating Central and Eastern European countries into the 'West'. Where does it result from? Could you find arguments which confirm the criticism of the authors?

The fourth stage in the development would be a decision on whether there is a way for the associated countries to become members of the European Community. After the April 1993 communication of the Commission to the Council it is clear, however, that it will be a long way from association to membership (*April 1993 Communication to the Council*).

C. THE EC AND THE DEVELOPING WORLD (LOMÉ CONVENTION)

Since the decolonization process of the 1950s and 1960s industrial countries and the developing countries have sought to develop appropriate forms of co-operation. When the EC was founded in 1957, the original Member States as well as the United Kingdom had extensive colonial holdings. It suffices to look at the Articles 131–136 a. Here the so-called 'constitutional association' is laid down. The colonies of the original Member States were formally associated to the EC. The (not always voluntary) willingness to accept the sovereignty of former colonies was accompanied on the part of the original Member States by the strong desire to maintain economic relations and to accompany their social development. A new legal basis was needed. It was found in Article 238 which served to conclude association agreements between the EC/the Member States and the now independent developing countries. All parties started relatively early to develop outside bilateral agreements a contractual framework for the economic and social integration of the new states. The first Yaoundé Convention was concluded in 1963 with 18 African States and Madagascar, the second Yaoundé Convention followed in 1969.

After the United Kingdom becoming a Member of the EC in 1973, it was possible to shape a much more comprehensive contractual network between the EC and its Member States on the one hand and the developing countries emerged out of the African colonies and the Commonwealth countries, on the other. The way was free to develop a convention with 46 ACP-Countries (Africa, the Caribbean and the Pacific), the so-called first Lomé Convention. The term 'association agreements' was now replaced by 'co-operation agreements'. The Lomé policy has been constantly developed in the last 20 years and covers in Lomé IV not only trade and industrial policy, but also environmental policy and population policy. Somewhat different from the United States, the EC does not rely on the free trade and open markets alone to integrate developing countries into the world economy, it fosters a concept under which elements of free trade are combined with elements of statutory interventionism (cf. Chapter 2).

1. A new start after Maastricht – Articles 130 u–y

The Maastricht Treaty introduced into the Treaty of Rome a new set of rules on development co-operation.

TITLE XVII[1] DEVELOPMENT COOPERATION

Article 130u

1.   Community policy in the sphere of development co-operation, which shall be complementary to the policies pursued by the Member States, shall foster:

–   the sustainable economic and social development of the developing countries, and more particularly the most disadvantaged among them;

–   the smooth and gradual integration of the developing countries into the world economy;

–   the campaign against poverty in the developing countries.

2.   Community policy in this area shall contribute to the general objective of developing and consolidating democracy and the rule of law, and to that of respecting human rights and fundamental freedoms.

3.   The Community and the Member States shall comply with the commitments and take account of the objectives they have approved in the context of the United Nations and other competent international organisations.

Article 130v

The Community shall take account of the objectives referred to in Article 130u in the policies that it implements which are likely to affect developing countries.

Article 130w

1.   Without prejudice to the other provisions of this Treaty the Council, acting in accordance with the procedure referred to in Article 189c, shall adopt the measures necessary to further the objectives referred to in Article 130u. Such measures may take the form of multiannual programmes.

2.   The European Investment Bank shall contribute, under the terms laid down in its Statute, to the implementation of the measures referred to in paragraph 1.

3.   The provisions of this Article shall not affect co-operation with the African, Caribbean and Pacific countries in the framework of the ACP-EEC Convention.

Article 130x

1.   The Community and the Member States shall coordinate their policies on development co-operation and shall consult each other on their aid programmes, including in international organisations and during international conferences.

---

[1]   As inserted by Article G(38) TEU.

They may undertake joint action. Member States shall contribute if necessary to the implementation of Community aid programmes.

2.   The Commission may take any useful initiative to promote the coordination referred to in paragraph 1.

Article 130y

Within their respective spheres of competence, the Community and the Member States shall cooperate with third countries and with the competent international organisations. The arrangements for Community co-operation may be the subject of agreements between the Community and the third parties concerned, which shall be negotiated and concluded in accordance with Article 228.

The previous paragraph shall be without prejudice to Member States' competence to negotiate in international bodies and to conclude international agreements.

The new articles seem to write down what has become the EC development policy in the last decades, the emphasis on economic and social development, the intention to integrate the development countries into the world economy, the connection of development policy with human rights policy and the fostering of democracy. Exactly this policy mix, however, has been criticized because of its interventionist character. Development countries, this is the critique, are not necessarily benefiting from an EC policy which seems to rely much more on development aid than on free trade and competition. The critique is grounded in Article 130 u which gives the Community a mandate to develop action programmes beyond the already existing conventions in order to concretize the objectives of Article 130 u. The European Parliament is taking part in the elaboration under the Article 189 c procedure. Outside Article 130 y whose reach has to be tested, Article 130 x seems to be a very important basis for future activities. So far Member States are sticking to the autonomy of their development aid policies. The independence of the differing national programmes has led in the past to a rather heterogeneous and uncoordinated attitude of the Member States towards development countries within and outside the diverse conventions. Article 130 x will put an end to these intricacies and unite the Member States in a joint approach under the auspices of the Commission.

2. The Lomé Conventions

Lomé I was followed by Lomé II signed in 1979 with 58 ACP-Countries. Lomé III signed in 1984 with 65 ACP-Countries and Lomé IV signed in 1989 with 69 ACP-Countries at present. The first three programmes had terms for five years, Lomé IV for ten years, up to 2000. The 69 ACP-Countries include all African States (except South Africa and those bordering the Mediterranean), Belize, Guyana, Surinam and over 25 island countries in the Caribbean Sea, the Indian Ocean and the South Pacific.

The starting point for the first two Lomé conventions was been a Generalised Sy‚tem of Preferences (GSP). Different from the 'most favoured nation' clause development countries have been granted unilateral custom advantages. The GSP is still applicable within the Lomé Convention, but it is not restricted to the signatory states of the Lomé Convention. The break-through from a development countries' perspective came with Lomé III and Lomé IV. These conventions merit the term 'co-operation agreements'. Trade policy stays behind development policy. The countries successfully referred to the 'third generation of human rights', mainly to their right to development. The EC and the Member States were less successful in promoting the classical human rights. The preamble contains cautious concessions to basic human rights, such as human integrity. The ACP-Countries, however, feared and still fear that the human rights rhetoric is used as a means of challenging their sovereignty. Lomé IV pushes the reference to human rights somewhat further. It remains to be seen, however, to what extent Article 130 (u) 2 may enhance the Community and the Member States' human rights policy.

The rules of the four conventions are extremely complex and far from being clear. However, emphasis is put regularly on development policy – in contrast to trade policy:

- the agricultural co-operation underlines the need to increase nutrition security with the objective to come to self-supply,
- the industrial development shall contribute to the establishment of new jobs, to foster low and medium-sized industries,
- the trade policy shall strengthen intra-regional co-operation between ACP-Countries as well as cultural-social co-operation. The means to achieve these aims are not determined. That is why the GSP remains the primary instrument to foster import into the EC,
- the STABEX-system aims at stabilizing the earnings of the ACP-Countries on exports to the EC. Essentially the STABEX-system compensates a country to the extent that its export earnings from a covered commodity (mainly foodstuffs and other raw material) fall below a reference level based on the previous six years. 1.5 billion ECU have been committed by the Community towards STABEX for the period of 1990–1995;
- the SYSMIN-system is designed to help ACP-Countries that are heavily dependent on the export of mining products. The Community has committed 480 million ECU for grants over a period of five years, 1990–1995;
- a key element of Lomé III and IV represents the financial and technical co-operation in a wide area of policies: environment, agriculture, fisheries,

commodities, industrial and enterprise development, mining, energy, development of services, tourism, telecommunication and regional co-operation. The provisions on environmental co-operation prohibit the EC to export toxic waste to ACP-Countries. Lomé IV provides 12 billion ECU for a period of five years to 1990–1995 to accomplish the envisaged technical and financial co-operation.

3. Effect of EC development policy

The effects of the EC development policy are not easy to measure. A comprehensive analysis would have to include the EC agreements with Asian and Latin American countries, where various framework agreements would have to be analysed covering trade, economic co-operation and development co-operation. It may suffice, however, to reprint here, from Ad Koekkoek, A. Kuyvenhoven and Willem Molle, *Europe 1992 and the Developing Countries*, an assessment of the possible repercussions of the EC development policy:

EUROPE 1992 AND THE DEVELOPING COUNTRIES: AN OVERVIEW*

Ad Koekkoek, A. Kuyvenhoven and Willem Molle

[...]
GENERAL TRADE POLICY ISSUES

Apart from specific issues directly related to the 1992 programme, there is a more general concern stemming from the reputation of the EC in matters of trade policy. Henderson (1989), e.g., concludes that over the past two decades the trade regime of the Community has moved on balance in a non-liberal direction. This does not augur well for the future and the question is to what extent 1992 will continue this process or possibly proved for countervailing forces.

For several reasons developing countries have to fear that their export markets may suffer from more *protectionist* trade policies of developed countries in general and the EC in particular.

1   Developing countries export mostly labour-intensive products and it is notably for these that developed countries are most inclined to protect home employment.
2   Loss of alternative measures. In the 1960s, when the import tariffs of the six Member States had to be harmonized on a level roughly equal to the average of the national tariff rates, individual countries could safeguard their interests through the application of Article 115 and industrial policy measures. To maintain after 1992 the same level of protection, an EC-wide protective measure of trade policy is likely to become the preferred route. The alternative, a national subsidy, is a less likely policy measure, given the current emphasis on adequate competition and industrial policies.[1] Given its uneven consequences within the Community, the absence of a safeguard mechanism corresponding with Article 115, and the strict supervision from Brussels regarding domestic competition and industrial policies[2] increase the risk of a relatively high level of protection when replacing national measures.

---

*   First published in *Journal of Common Market Studies*, 1990, pp.111 *et seq.* (126–128); reprinted by permission of Basil Blackwell, Oxford.
1   As the *Financial Times* (1989b) notes, the Commission is already much keener in this respect.
2   National industrial policies could be replaced by an EC-wide industrial policy. This does not seem to be much of a risk, considering the experience with national industrial policies in the seventies, costing a lot of money and not accomplishing much. In general

3   Deepening and widening. Extension of the EC may aggravate internal problems. If unemployment, as a short-term consequence of adjustment to the completion of the Internal Market, is not absorbed, e.g. through the use of expansive macroeconomic policies or through flexible supply-side reactions, then the pressure for a more defensive trade policy will increase. Moreover, the recent accession of the three Southern European countries to the EC will add to protectionist interests and pressures within the EC, especially in sectors relevant to developing countries.

4   Bargaining power. The greater economic strength of the EC and its increased external identity may induce the EC to use its external trade policy instruments in a much more active way. This will probably not take the traditional form of optimum tariffs but rather of more modern variants of 'strategic trade policy'. On the other hand, LDCs have a rather weak bargaining position in trade policy matters.

There are other considerations that point towards a possible change towards a more *liberal stance* of the Community, a creed that the EC has confirmed, time and again.

1   A successful completion process leads to a more buoyant and dynamic European economy in general, so there will be less interest in defensive trade policies. After all, the 'new protectionist' upsurge started as a consequence of economic instability and stagnation in the seventies.

2   Pressures towards a more defensive trade policy will be alleviated through the use of regional policies, because these will be directed specifically at regions and sectors in trouble as a consequence of adjustment to the process of completion.

3   The Uruguay Round[3] provides for opportunities to move the EC in a more liberal direction. It must be stressed though that this will have to be two-way traffic, also where it concerns developing countries. In this respect times have

---

the economic climate for such government actions is less favourable now. Nevertheless, although defensive industrial policies may have gone out of fashion, the same does not seem to apply to equally defensive trade policies.

3   It is often stated that the EC is in a weak bargaining position in the Uruguay Round, in the sense of not having much manoeuvring space, in agriculture because of the sluggishness of the CAP, in labour-intensive industries because of high unemployment figures, and in hi-tech industries because of lack of competitiveness, partly due to the fragmentation of the Common Market. To the extent that the position of the EC in the Uruguay Round is weak indeed, completion of the internal market changes the situation regarding industries and indirectly lessens the dependence on traditional industries. The latter would allow the Community to be less defensive in sectors of great interest to developing countries. More generally, the very fact of the Uruguay Round going on right now limits the freedom of movement of the EC in matters of trade policy.

changed as compared with the sixties and the seventies. Fortunately, this is less of a problem nowadays, as the advantages of outward orientation are more fully appreciated by most developing countries.

The developments in Eastern Europe are likely to have great consequences for the trade relations between the EC and the LDCs. The negative side for the LDCs is that the countries of Eastern Europe are likely to get a better starting position in their competition with the LDCs on the EC market; their special relation with the EC is likely to bring them from the very bottom in the trade policy hierarchy to its very top, overtaking the GSP countries and catching up with the ACP countries with a greater capacity to make good use of that position. The positive side for LDCs is that the increased income growth in these countries (due to economic re-structuring, increased market access and decreases in defence spending) will en-gender an effect on LDC exports similar in character to that engendered by the EC's 1992 programme. This effect will, however, take some time really to gain momen-tum.

OTHER AREAS

Contrary to the very elaborate EC trade policy, the EC's external policy in other economic matters is still in a rudimentary stage (Molle, 1990). The 1992 pro-gramme has had some influence on the formulation of an EC-wide policy stance in matters of movement of workers and capital movements, while other issues such as world-wide co-ordination of monetary and economic policies get increasing atten-tion. Beyond this there is a growing need for international co-ordination of such policies as pollution control, health and safety, etc. As the effects of the latter in LDCs are not very clear, we will limit ourselves here to the production factors.

In matters of external capital flows the EC will in future follow a liberal policy. That would mean that no particular effect on LDCs is to be expected apart from the possibly greater competition for EC outward and inward flows. A case in point may be Eastern Europe that will attract increasing amounts of EC funds in the coming years. Trade is likely to have more impact on investment flows than the capital 'policy'; indeed, the fear of more protectionist EC trade policies may induce the diversion of FDI flows towards the EC.

In matters of international migration the EC has virtually no policy and has left this issue largely to the competence of the Members States. These are in general very little inclined to absorb more third country immigrants on top of the several millions already present in the EC. The higher standard of living in the EC is likely to exert a growing attraction on third country nationals and thus a push of EC fron-tiers.

Without internal border controls immigrants who have entered the EC in coun-tries with a relatively open border are likely to move to other countries too. Although for that reason it is likely that some EC policy will emerge, it is difficult for us to predict what this policy will be like, as the determinants are more of a political than of an economic nature. On the basis of what we know we can, however, suppose that there is little reason for LDCs to look to the EC for easing their unemployment situation through large-scale emigration and alleviating their balance of payments difficulties by workers' remittances. The question of illegal immigrants of course will remain.

(End of excerpt)

D. THE EC AND THE GATT

The General Agreement on Tariffs and Trade entered into force on a provisional basis on the 1st January 1948. The GATT performs several functions for the world trading Community. First, the GATT supplies a set of rules to guarantee worldwide free trade and services. Second, the GATT provides for a mechanism to solve disputes between the Contracting Parties and third, the GATT functions as a forum for negotiations on international trade matters.

All members of the European Community have become Contracting Parties to the GATT before the European Community was founded in 1957. Though not being a Contracting Party, the European Community has taken over step by step to represent the interests of the EC Member States within GATT. Legally it had to be clarified whether the European Community is bound to the GATT rules. The question came up when private individuals invoked before their national courts the supremacy and the direct effect of GATT rules over EC rules Case 21-24/72 *International Fruit Company NV and other* v. *Produktschap voor groenten en fruit*, [1972] ECR 1219 *et seq*. The Court decided that the European Community has succeeded to the GATT obligations of the Member States, but denied direct effect of GATT rules. Despite their Pyrrhic victory private individuals went on testing the benefits of GATT rules. And in Case 70/87, *Fediol* v. *Commission*, [1989] ECR 1781, the Court seemed to be willing to accept at least 'indirect effects' of the GATT rules. The recent conflict about Regulation 404/93 OJ L 47/1 of 13.2.1993 (common market organization for bananas) added a new dimension to the long lasting conflict on the relationship between GATT and EC rules. The ECJ rejected Germany's complaint against the Regulation 404/93, thereby denying Member States the opportunity to invoke GATT rules against EC rules, Case C-280/93 *Germany* v. *Council* [1994] ECR I-4973. The importance of GATT seems to be slackening at a time where the successful conclusion of the Uruguay Round has revitalized the GATT with the establishment of the World Trading Organisation, the WTO.

The presentation of the court rulings will concentrate on the procedural aspects of the relationship between the EC and the GATT, on direct effect and indirect effect of the GATT rules in favour and to the detriment of private individuals and Member States. It would reach beyond the framework of a book on European Economic Law to explain the substance matter of GATT. The years to come may demonstrate, however, that there is a relationship between the deepening of the European Community through its policy to complete the Internal Market and the growing number of conflicts between the EC and GATT on the relationship between free trade and industrial policies.

1. Direct and 'indirect' effect of GATT rules

The starting point for a legal reasoning is Article 228 (2) which provides that agreements concluded under Article 228 (1) 'shall be binding on the institutions of the Community and the Member States'. Can Article 228 serve as a basis for giving direct effect to an international agreement such as GATT? The landmark decision is still Case 21-24/72 *International Fruit* [1972] ECR 1219 at 2-28. International Fruit applied for a licence to import apples into the EC. When the licence application was rejected by the Dutch authorities on the basis of certain EC regulations, the company brought an action in a Dutch court claiming, *inter alia*, that the regulation violated Article XI of the General Agreement on Tariffs and Trade.

[...]

2   The first question invites the Court to rule whether the validity of measures adopted by the institutions of the Community also refers, within the meaning of Article 177 of the EEC Treaty, to their validity under international law.

3   The second question, which is raised should the reply to the first question be in the affirmative, asks whether Regulations Nos 459/70, 565/70 and 686/70 of the Commission – which laid down, by way of protective measures, restrictions on the importation of apples from third countries – are "invalid as being contrary to Article XI of the General Agreement on Tariffs and Trade (GATT)", hereinafter called "the General Agreement".

4   According to the first paragraph of Article 177 of the EEC Treaty "The Court of Justice shall have jurisdiction to give preliminary rulings concerning . . . the validity . . . of acts of the institutions of the Community".

5   Under that formulation, the jurisdiction of the Court cannot be limited by the grounds on which the validity of those measures may be contested.

6   Since such jurisdiction extends to all grounds capable of invalidating those measures, the Court is obliged to examine whether their validity may be affected by reason of the fact that they are contrary to a rule of international law.

7   Before the incompatibility of a Community measure with a provision of international law can affect the validity of that measure, the Community must first of all be bound by that provision.

8   Before invalidity can be relied upon before a national court, that provision of international law must also be capable of conferring rights on citizens of the Community which they can invoke before the courts.

9   It is therefore necessary to examine whether the General Agreement satisfies these two conditions.

10   It is clear that at the time when they concluded the Treaty establishing the European Economic Community the Member States were bound by the obligations of the General Agreement.

11   By concluding a treaty between them they could not withdraw from their obligations to third countries.

12   On the contrary, their desire to observe the undertakings of the General Agreement follows as much from the very provisions of the EEC Treaty as from the declarations made by Member States on the presentation of the Treaty to the contracting parties of the General Agreement in accordance with the obligation under Article XXIV thereof.

13   That intention was made clear in particular by Article 110 of the EEC Treaty, which seeks the adherence of the Community to the same aims as those sought by the General Agreement, as well as by the first paragraph of Article 234 which provides that the rights and obligations arising from agreements concluded before the entry into force of the Treaty, and in particular multilateral agreements concluded with the participation of Member States, are not affected by the provisions of the Treaty.

14   The Community has assumed the functions inherent in the tariff and trade policy, progressively during the transitional period and in their entirety on the expiry of that period, by virtue of Articles 111 and 113 of the Treaty.

15   By conferring those powers on the Community, the Member States showed their wish to bind it by the obligations entered into under the General Agreement.

16   Since the entry into force of the EEC Treaty and more particularly, since the setting up of the common external tariff, the transfer of powers which has occurred in the relations between Member States and the Community has been put into concrete form in different ways within the framework of the General Agreement and has been recognized by the other contracting parties.

17 In particular, since the time, the Community, acting through its own institutions, has appeared as a partner in the tariff negotiations and as a party to the agreements of all types concluded within the framework of the General Agreement, in accordance with the provisions of Article 114 of the EEC Treaty which provides that the tariff and trade agreements "shall be concluded . . . on behalf of the Community".

18 It therefore appears that, in so far as under the EEC Treaty the Community has assumed the powers previously exercised by Member States in the area governed by the General Agreement, the provisions of that agreement have the effect of binding the Community.

19 It is also necessary to examine whether the provisions of the General Agreement confer rights on citizens of the Community on which they can rely before the courts in contesting the validity of a Community measure.

20 For this purpose, the spirit, the general scheme and the terms of the General Agreement must be considered.

21 This agreement which, according to its preamble, is based on the principle of negotiations undertaken on the basis of "reciprocal and mutually advantageous arrangements" is characterized by the great flexibility of its provisions, in particular those conferring the possibility of derogation, the measures to be taken when confronted with exceptional difficulties and the settlement of conflicts between the contracting parties.

22 Consequently, according to the first paragraph of Article XXII "Each contracting party shall accord sympathetic consideration to, and shall afford adequate opportunity for consultation regarding, such representations as may be made by any other contracting party with respect to . . . all matters affecting the operation of this Agreement".

23 According to the second paragraph of the same article, "the contracting parties" – this name designating "the contracting parties acting jointly" as is stated in the first paragraph of Article XXV – "may consult with one or more contracting parties on any question to which a satisfactory solution cannot be found through the consultations provided under paragraph (1)".

24 If any contracting party should consider "that any benefit accruing to it directly or indirectly under this Agreement is being nullified or impaired or that the attainment of any objective of the Agreement is being impeded as a result", *inter alia*, "the failure of another contracting party to carry out its obligations under this Agreement", Article XXIII lays down in detail the measures which the parties concerned, or the contracting parties acting jointly, may or must take in regard to such a situation.

25 Those measures include, for the settlement of conflicts, written recommendations or proposals which are to be "given sympathetic consideration", investigations possibly followed by recommendations, consultations between or decisions of the *contracting parties*, including that of authorizing certain

contracting parties to suspend the application to any others of any obligations or concessions under the General Agreement and, finally, in the event of such suspension, the power of the party concerned to withdraw from that agreement.

26   Finally, where by reason of an obligation assumed under the General Agreement or of a concession relating to a benefit, some producers suffer or are threatened with serious damage, Article XIX gives a contracting party power unilaterally to suspend the obligation and to withdraw or modify the concession, either after consulting the contracting parties jointly and failing agreement between the contracting parties concerned, or even, if the matter is urgent and on a temporary basis, without prior consultation.

27   Those factors are sufficient to show that, when examined in such a context, Article XI of the General Agreement is not capable of conferring on citizens of the Community rights which they can invoke before the courts.

28   Accordingly, the validity of Regulations Nos 459/70, 565/70 and 686/70 of the Commission cannot be affected by Article XI of the General Agreement.

The outcome of *International Fruit Company* is abundantly clear. There seems to be no way for private individuals to strike down EC rules which run counter to the GATT rules. From approximately 12 judgments on the possible effects of GATT as well as from the Advocate Generals' conclusions several basic objections can be deduced: The ECR emphasizes the flexibility of GATT rules and the availability of dispute settlement procedure in order. It is supported by the Advocate Generals who refer to the still provisional character of GATT. The Community organs fear that direct effect would challenge the reciprocity principle of GATT and its negotiation character. Last but not least, the ECR had to define the effect of GATT in order to prevent the Member States from taking differing attitudes, Italy and the Netherlands being already on the road to accepting direct effect of GATT.

The next chance for private individuals to test the reach of GATT came with the adoption of Regulation 2641/84, the so called new commercial policy instrument (cf. chapter 9). Regulation 2641/84 conferred on the operators the right to invoke the GATT provisions in their possible complaints against the Commission in order to establish the illicit character of the trade practice. *Fediol* Case 70/87 [1989] 1781 at 18–22 had claimed that certain practices of Argentina violated GATT rules and therefore were subject to Community action under Regulation 2641/84 as illicit commercial practices. The practices in question were (1) higher export charges on soybeans than on soybean products (which would depress soybeans exports and promote soybean processing in Argentina) and (2) quantitative restrictions on the export of soybeans.

18 The Commission further maintains that when, as in this case, its decision deals with the interpretation of GATT provisions, the complainant cannot be permitted to put forward submissions calling that interpretation in question, because the interpretation which the Commission, pursuant to Regulation No 2641/84, places on the term "illicit commercial practice" and on the rules of international law, in particular those of GATT, is subject to review by the Court only in so far as the disregard or misapplication of those rules amounts to an infringement of the provisions of Community law which vest rights in individuals, directly and specifically; however, the GATT rules themselves are not sufficiently precise to give rise to such rights on the part of individuals.

19 It should be recalled that the Court has certainly held, on several occasions, that various GATT provisions were not capable of conferring on citizens of the Community rights which they can invoke before the courts [citing *International Fruit* and other cases.] Nevertheless, it cannot be inferred from those judgments that citizens may not, in proceedings before the Court, rely on the provisions of GATT in order to obtain a ruling on whether conduct criticized in a complaint lodged under Article 3 of Regulation No 2641/84 constitutes an illicit commercial practice within the meaning of that regulation. The GATT provisions form part of the rules of international law to which Article 2(1) of that regulation refers, as is borne out by the second and fourth recitals in its preamble, read together.

20 It is also appropriate to note that the Court did indeed hold in the above-mentioned judgments, that a particular feature of GATT is the broad flexibility of its provisions, especially those concerning deviations from general rules, measures which may be taken in cases of exceptional difficulty, and the settling of differences between the contracting parties. That view does not, however, prevent the Court from interpreting and applying the rules of GATT with reference to a given case, in order to establish whether certain specific commercial practices should be considered incompatible with those rules. The GATT provisions have an independent meaning which, for the purposes of their application in specific cases, is to be determined by way of interpretation.

21 Lastly, the fact that Article XXIII of GATT provides a special procedure for the settlement of disputes between contracting parties is not such as to preclude its interpretation by the Court. As the Court held in *Kupferberg* [...], in the context of the joint committees which are set up by free-trade agreements and given responsibility for the administration and proper implementation of those agreements, the mere fact that the contracting parties have established a special institutional framework for consultations and negotiations *inter se* in relation to the implementation of the agreement is not in itself sufficient to exclude all judicial application of that agreement.

22   It follows that, since Regulation No 2641/84 entitles the economic agents concerned to rely on the GATT provisions in the complaint which they lodge with the Commission in order to establish the illicit nature of the commercial practices which they consider to have harmed them, those same economic agents are entitled to request the Court to exercise its powers of review over the legality of the Commission's decision applying those provisions.

Fediol contains two messages: The Court itself took a relative distance from earlier decisions when it stated that '..various provisions were not capable of conferring rights..' although it had underlined all the time the flexibility of the GATT. Even more important seems to be that the Court showed a tendency no longer to draw a clear borderline between direct effect and a 'GATT conform interpretation of Community law' when it said '... that it cannot be inferred from those judgements that citizens may not, in proceedings before the Court, rely on the provisions of GATT in order to obtain a ruling on whether conduct criticized in a complaint lodged under Art. 3 of Regulation 2641/84 constitutes an illicit commercial practice within the meaning of that regulation'. One may conclude from *Fediol* that private individuals may invoke a GATT conform interpretation of Community law as long as EC secondary law refers explicitly or implicitly to GATT rules. GATT conform interpretation (indirect effect) and direct effect may lead to the same result for private individuals (cf. Case C-106/89 *Marleasing SA* v. *La Comercial internacional de Alimentacion*, [1990] ECR I-4035). Such a weakening of the earlier denial of direct effects of GATT, could pave the way for the gradual recognition of direct effect even if there is no reference in secondary Community law to GATT.

2. Direct effect of GATT rules to the benefit of Member States

The question of whether Member States may invoke GATT rules in the Art. 173 procedure came up for the first time in Case C-280/93 *Germany* v. *Council* [1994] ECR I-3667 at 103–112. The Court denied Germany the right to refer to GATT and transferred the direct effect doctrine to the Member States.

Infringement of GATT rules

103 The Federal Republic of Germany submits that compliance with GATT rules is a condition of the lawfulness of Community acts, regardless of any question as to the direct effect of GATT, and that the Regulation infringes certain basic provisions of GATT.

104 The Council, supported in particular by the Commission, argues that in view of its particular nature, GATT cannot be relied on to challenge the lawfulness of a Community act, except in the special case where the Com-

munity provisions were adopted to implement obligations entered into within the framework of GATT.

105 In deciding whether the applicant can rely on certain provisions of GATT to challenge the lawfulness of the Regulation, it should be noted that the Court has held that the provisions of GATT have the effect of binding the Community. However, it has also held that in assessing the scope of GATT in the Community legal system, the spirit, the general scheme and the terms of GATT must be considered.

106 It is settled law that GATT, which according to its preamble is based on the principle of negotiations undertaken on the basis of 'reciprocal and mutually advantageous arrangements', is characterized by the great flexibility of its provision, in particular those conferring the possibility of derogation, the measures to be taken when confronted with exceptional difficulties and the settlement of conflicts between the contracting parties.

107 The Court has recognized that those measures include, for the settlement of conflicts, depending on the case, written recommendations or proposals which are to be 'given sympathetic consideration', investigations possibly followed by recommendations, consultations between or decisions of the *contracting parties*, including that of authorizing certain contracting parties to suspend the application to any others of any obligations or concessions under GATT and, finally, in the event of such suspension, the power of the party concerned to withdraw from that agreement.

108 It has noted that where, by reason of an obligation assumed under GATT or of a concession relating to a preference, some producers suffer or are threatened with serious damage, Article XIX gives a contracting party power unilaterally to suspend the obligation and to withdraw or modify the concession, either after consulting the contracting parties jointly and failing agreement between the contracting parties concerned, or even, if the matter is urgent and on a temporary basis, without prior consultation (see Joined Cases 21 to 24/72 *International Fruit Company* v. *Produktschap voor Groenten en Fruit* [1972] ECR 1219, paragraphs 21, 25 and 26; Case 9/73 *Schlüter* v. *Hauptzollamt Lörrach* [1973] ECR 1135, paragraph 29; Case 266/81 *SIOT* v. *Ministero delle Finanze* [1983] ECR 731, paragraph 28; and Joined Cases 267 to 269/91 *Amministrazione delle Finanze dello Stato* v. *SPI and SAMI* [1983] ECR 801, paragraph 23).

109 Those features of GATT, from which the Court concluded that an individual within the Community cannot invoke it in a court to challenge the lawfulness of a Community act, also preclude the Court from taking provisions of GATT into consideration to assess the lawfulness of a regulation in an action brought by a Member State under the first paragraph of Article 173 of the Treaty.

110 The special features noted above show that the GATT rules are not unconditional and that an obligation to recognize them as rules of interna-

tional law which are directly applicable in the domestic legal systems of the contracting parties cannot be based on the spirit, general scheme or terms of GATT.

111 In the absence of such an obligation following from GATT itself, it is only if the Community intended to implement a particular obligation entered into within the framework of GATT, or if the Community act expressly refers to specific provisions of GATT, that the Court can review the lawfulness of the Community act in question from the point of view of the GATT rules (see Case 70/87 *Fediol* v. *Commission* [1989] ECR 1781 and Case C-69/89 *Nakajima* v. *Council* [1991] ECR I-2069).

112 Accordingly, the Federal Republic of Germany cannot invoke the provisions of GATT to challenge the lawfulness of certain provisions of the Regulation.

QUESTIONS

1   Do you think that the jurisprudence on direct effect can be transferred to the Article 173 procedure? Member States do not only defend their rights here, they act as trustees of Community law. A requirement of direct effect might not fit into such an understanding of the Member States' role.

2   Does it help to refer to the Commission as being the legal guardian of Community law? The Commission will not challenge its 'own' regulation. The corrective action needs to be taken either by the Member States or by private individuals.

FURTHER READING

A. Bleckmann, 'Die unmittelbare Anwendbarkeit der Freihandelsabkommen mit den EFTA-Staaten im Rechtsraum der EWG', in Koppensteiner (ed), *Rechtsfragen der Freihandelsabkommen der Europäischen Gemeinschaft mit den EFTA-Staaten*, 1987, p.85.

Bourgois, 'Effects of International Agreements in European Community Law: Are the Dice Cast', *Michigan Law Review*, 1984, p.1250.

N. Burrows, 'The risks of widening without deepening', *ELRev*, **15**, 1992, p.352.

M.J. Hahn and G. Schuster, 'Zum Verstoß von gemeinschaftlichem Sekundärrecht gegen das GATT – Die gemeinsame Marktorganisation für Bananen vor dem EuGH', *EuR*, 1993, p.261.

N.A.E.M. Neuwahl, 'GATT, Direct and Indirect Effects in Community Law', in D. O'Keeffe and N. Emiliou (eds), *The Common Commercial Policy after the Uruguay Round*, to be published.

E.-U. Petersmann, 'Application of GATT by the Court of Justice of the European Communities', *CMLRev*, **20**, 1983, p.397.

11 Redress in a European Context

A. THE EUROPEANIZATION OF REMEDIES

1. Direct effect and the creation of individual rights

It is explained in Chapter 1 that European Community law creates rights which individuals may enforce before national courts and tribunals. This is the notion of 'direct effect' which was first established in Case 26/62 *Van Gend en Loos* [1963] ECR 1. However, although the notion of rights now has a well developed pedigree, the construction of a remedies system which will support these rights at national level is much less well developed.

The issue of national remedies in support of European rights is of relevance to the principal theme of this book. It is an area where the European Court and the Community's legislature began with a cautious approach which involved an emphasis on the autonomy of the national system, even where European rights were in issue. However, there has been a shift. Increasingly the responsibility of the national authorities to support the Community has been invoked as a basis for curtailing the autonomy of the national system. It is increasingly plain that national laws must be opened up to the influence of Europeanization. More specifically, there is a developing body of European law governing remedies which must be available at national level. Strikingly, this has reached the stage where even non-directly effective EC law may generate enforceable rights at national level.

2. National Procedural Autonomy

In Case 45/76 *Comet* v. *Produktschap* [1976] ECR 2043 the European Court determined that

> In application of the principle of co-operation laid down in Article 5 of the Treaty, the national courts are entrusted with ensuring the legal protection conferred on individuals by the direct effect of the provisions of Community law. .... it is for the national legal order of each Member State to designate the competent courts and to lay down the procedural rules for proceedings designed to ensure the protection of the rights which individuals acquire through the direct effect of Community law

Two qualifications only were made to this statement of 'national procedural autonomy'. First, procedures made available for the vindication of Community law rights must not be less favourable than those governing the same right of action on an internal matter. Second, it must not be impossible in practice to exercise rights which the national courts have a duty to protect.

The second qualification in *Comet*, that it should not be 'impossible in practice' to vindicate EC law rights at national level, has been recast in more positive terms to require that EC law rights be 'effectively protected' by national authorities. It is this notion of effective protection which has provided the European Court with the scope to develop a significant European content to the competence of national authorities, particularly, but not only, courts. 'Europeanization' of this nature has greatly eroded national procedural autonomy. National authorities are increasingly called on to adapt their techniques in order effectively to protect rights drawn from European sources.

3. The Court's erosion of national procedural autonomy

Case 222/86 *Union nationale des entraineurs et Cadres techniques professionnels du football (UNECTEF)* v. *George Heylens* [1987] ECR 4097.

Heylens, a Belgian national with a Belgian certificate of competence as a football trainer, was engaged for 1984–85 by Lille Olympic as trainer to the professional football team. He was told that his qualifications were not recognized by the French authorities, although reasons were not given, and he was told not to work in France. Claiming rights as a worker under Community law, he challenged that rejection. Questions were referred to the European Court by a French court concerning the procedural rights to which he was entitled.

7   The question put by the national court essentially seeks to establish whether, where in a Member State access to an occupation as an employed person is dependent upon the possession of a national diploma or a foreign diploma recognized as equivalent thereto, the principle of the free movement of workers laid down in Article 48 of the Treaty requires that it must be possible for a decision refusing to recognize the equivalence of a diploma granted to a worker who is a national of another Member State by that Member State to be made the subject of judicial proceedings, and that the decision must state the reason on which it is based.

8   In order to answer that question it must be borne in mind that Article 48 of the Treaty implements, with regard to workers, a fundamental principle contained in Article 3 (c) of the Treaty, which states that, for the purposes set out in Article 2, the activities of the Community are to include the abo-

lition, as between Member States, of obstacles to freedom of movement for persons and services (see the judgment of 7 July 1976 in Case 118/75 *Watson and Belmann* [1976] ECR 1185).

9   In application of the general principle set out in Article 7 of the Treaty under which discrimination on grounds of nationality is prohibited, Article 48 aims to eliminate in the legislation of the Member States provisions as regards employment, remuneration and other conditions of work and employment under which a worker who is a national of another Member State is subject to more severe treatment or is placed in an unfavourable situation in law or in fact as compared with the situation of a national in the same circumstances (see the judgment of 28 March 1979 in Case 175/78 *Saunders* [1979] ECR 1129).

10   In the absence of harmonization of the conditions of access to a particular occupation, the Member States are entitled to lay down the knowledge and qualifications needed in order to pursue it and to require the production of a diploma certifying that the holder has the relevant knowledge and qualifications.

11   However, as the Court held in its judgment of 28 June 1977 in Case 11/77 *Patrick* v. *Ministre des Affaires culturelles* [1977] ECR 1199, the lawful requirement, in the various Member States, relating to the possession of diplomas for admission to certain occupations constitutes a restriction on the effective exercise of the freedom of establishment guaranteed by the Treaty the abolition of which is to be made easier by directives for the mutual recognition of diplomas, certificates and other evidence of formal qualifications. As the Court also held in that judgment, the fact that such directives have not yet been issued does not entitle a Member State to deny the practical benefit of that freedom to a person subject to Community law when that freedom can be ensured in that Member State, in particular because it is possible under its laws and regulations for equivalent foreign diplomas to be recognized.

12   Since freedom of movement for workers is one of the fundamental objectives of the Treaty, the requirement to secure free movement under existing national laws and regulations stems, as the Court held in its judgment of 28 April 1977 in Case 71/76 *Thieffry* [1977] ECR 765, from Article 5 of the Treaty, under which the Member States are bound to take all appropriate measures, whether general or particular, to ensure fulfilment of the obligations arising out of the Treaty and to abstain from any measure which could jeopardize the attainment of the objectives of the Treaty.

13   Since it has to reconcile the requirement as to the qualifications necessary in order to pursue a particular occupation with the requirements of the free movement of workers, the procedure for the recognition of equivalence must enable the national authorities to assure themselves, on an objective basis, that the foreign diploma certifies that its holder has knowledge and

qualifications which are, if not identical, at least equivalent to those certified by the national diploma. That assessment of the equivalence of the foreign diploma must be effected exclusively in the light of the level of knowledge and qualifications which its holder can be assumed to possess in the light of that diploma, having regard to the nature and duration of the studies and practical training which the diploma certifies that he has carried out.

14   Since free access to employment is a fundamental right which the Treaty confers individually on each worker in the Community, the existence of a remedy of a judicial nature against any decision of a national authority refusing the benefit of that right is essential in order to secure for the individual effective protection for his right. As the Court held in its judgment of 15 May 1986 in Case 222/84 *Johnston* v. *Chief Constable of the Royal Ulster Constabulary* [1986] ECR 1651, at p. 1663, that requirement reflects a general principle of Community law which underlies the constitutional traditions common to the Member States and has been enshrined in Articles 6 and 13 of the European Convention for the Protection of Human Rights and Fundamental Freedoms.

15   Effective judicial review, which must be able to cover the legality of the reasons for the contested decision, presupposes in general that the court to which the matter is referred may require the competent authority to notify its reasons. But where, as in this case, it is more particularly a question of securing the effective protection of a fundamental right conferred by the Treaty on Community workers, the latter must also be able to defend that right under the best possible conditions and have the possibility of deciding, with a full knowledge of the relevant facts, whether there is any point in their applying to the courts. Consequently, in such circumstances the competent national authority is under a duty to inform them of the reasons on which its refusal is based, either in the decision itself or in a subsequent communication made at their request.

16   In view of their aims those requirements of Community law, that is to say, the existence of a judicial remedy and the duty to state reasons, are however limited only to final decisions refusing to recognize equivalence and do not extend to opinions and other measures occurring in the preparation and investigation stage.

17   Consequently, the answer to the question put by the tribunal de grande instance, Lille, must be that where in a Member State access to an occupation as an employed person is dependent upon the possession of a national diploma or a foreign diploma recognized as equivalent thereto, the principle of the free movement of workers laid down in Article 48 of the Treaty requires that it must be possible for a decision refusing to recognize the equivalence of a diploma granted to a worker who is a national of another Member State by that Member State to be made the subject of judicial pro-

ceedings in which its legality under Community law can be reviewed, and for the person concerned to ascertain the reasons for the decision.

The Court's reference in paragraph 15 to 'effective protection of a fundamental right' represents an especially strong insistence on the linkage between rights and remedies. This explains the Court's motivation in adding a European content to the law of national remedies. Without it, European rights themselves would be diminished.

This is a theme which can be traced through three major decisions; *Factortame*, *Zuckerfabrik Süderdithmarschen und Zuckerfabrik Soest* and *Francovich*.

Factortame, Spanish fishing interests, were challenging the compatibility of a British statute with Community law. The key point was the status of the Act *pending* the eventual ruling of the European Court. Factortame sought interim relief against its application. However the House of Lords, the highest domestic court in the UK, ruled that as a matter of English law no such order could be made by a court. Factortame then relied on Community law. In May 1989, the House of Lords referred to the European Court questions relating to the duties of national courts in such circumstances. In June 1990, the European Court responded with the following ruling, Case C-213/89 *The Queen* v. *Secretary of State for Transport ex parte Factortame Ltd and others* [1990] ECR I-2433.

[...]

13   The House of Lords, before which the matter was brought, gave its above-mentioned judgment of 18 May 1989. In its judgment it found in the first place that the claims by the appellants in the main proceedings that they would suffer irreparable damage if the interim relief which they sought were not granted and they were successful in the main proceedings were well founded. However, it held that, under national law, the English court had no power to grant interim relief in a case such as the one before it. More specifically, it held that the grant of such relief was precluded by the old common-law rule that an interim injunction may not be granted against the Crown, that is to say against the government, in conjunction with the presumption that an Act of Parliament is in conformity with Community law until such time as a decision on its compatibility with that law has been given.

14   The House of Lords then turned to the question whether, notwithstanding that rule of national law, English courts had the power, under Community law, to grant an interim injunction against the Crown.

15   Consequently, taking the view that the dispute raised an issue concerning the interpretation of Community law, the House of Lords decided, pursuant

to Article 177 of the EEC Treaty, to stay the proceedings until the Court of Justice had given a preliminary ruling on the following questions:

'(1) Where

    (i) a party before the national court claims to be entitled to rights under Community law having direct effect in national law (the "rights claimed"),

    (ii) a national measure in clear terms will, if applied, automatically deprive that party of the rights claimed,

    (iii) there are serious arguments both for and against the existence of the rights claimed and the national court has sought a preliminary ruling under Article 177 as to whether or not the rights claimed exist,

    (iv) the national law presumes the national measure in question to be compatible with Community law unless and until it is declared incompatible,

    (v) the national court has no power to give interim protection to the rights claimed by suspending the application of the national measure pending the preliminary ruling,

    (vi) if the preliminary ruling is in the event in favour of the rights claimed, the party entitled to those rights is likely to have suffered irremediable damage unless given such interim protection,

does Community law either

    (a) oblige the national court to grant such interim protection of the rights claimed; or

    (b) give the Court power to grant such interim protection of the rights claimed?

(2) If Question 1(a) is answered in the negative and Question 1(b) in the affirmative, what are the criteria to be applied in deciding whether or not to grant such interim protection of the rights claimed?'

16   Reference is made to the Report for the Hearing for a fuller account of the facts in the proceedings before the national court, the course of the procedure before and the observations submitted to the Court of Justice, which are mentioned or discussed hereinafter only in so far as is necessary for the reasoning of the Court.

17   It is clear from the information before the Court, and in particular from the judgment making the reference and, as described above, the course taken by the proceedings in the national courts before which the case came at first and second instance, that the preliminary question raised by the House of Lords seeks essentially to ascertain whether a national court which, in a case before it concerning Community law, considers that the sole obstacle which precludes it from granting interim relief is a rule of national law, must disapply that rule.

18 For the purpose of replying to that question, it is necessary to point out that in its judgment of 9 March 1978 in Case 106/77 *Amministrazione delle finanze dello Stato* v. *Simmenthal SpA* [1978] ECR 629 the Court held that directly applicable rules of Community law 'must be fully and uniformly applied in all the Member States from the date of their entry into force and for so long as they continue in force' (paragraph 14) and that 'in accordance with the principle of the precedence of Community law, the relationship between provisions of the Treaty and directly applicable measures of the institutions on the one hand and the national law of the Member States on the other is such that those provisions and measures ... by their entry into force render automatically inapplicable any conflicting provision of ... national law' (paragraph 17).

19 In accordance with the case-law of the Court, it is for the national courts, in application of the principle of co-operation laid down in Article 5 of the EEC Treaty, to ensure the legal protection which persons derive from the direct effect of provisions of Community law (see, most recently, the judgments of 10 July 1980 in Case 811/79 *Ariete SpA* v. *Amministrazione delle finanze dello Stato* [1980] ECR 2545 and Case 826/79 *Mireco* v. *Amministrazione delle finanze dello Stato* [1980] ECR 2559).

20 The Court has also held that any provision of a national legal system and any legislative, administrative or judicial practice which might impair the effectiveness of Community law by withholding from the national court having jurisdiction to apply such law the power to do everything necessary at the moment of its application to set aside national legislative provisions which might prevent, even temporarily, Community rules from having full force and effect are incompatible with those requirements, which are the very essence of Community law (judgment of 9 March 1978 in *Simmenthal*, cited above, paragraphs 22 and 23).

21 It must be added that the full effectiveness of Community law would be just as much impaired if a rule of national law could prevent a court seized of a dispute governed by Community law from granting interim relief in order to ensure the full effectiveness of the judgment to be given on the existence of the rights claimed under Community law. It follows that a court which in those circumstances would grant interim relief, if it were not for a rule of national law, is obliged to set aside that rule.

22 That interpretation is reinforced by the system established by Article 177 of the EEC Treaty whose effectiveness would be impaired if a national court, having stayed proceedings pending the reply by the Court of Justice to the question referred to it for a preliminary ruling, were not able to grant interim relief until it delivered its judgment following the reply given by the Court of Justice.

23 Consequently, the reply to the question raised should be that Community law must be interpreted as meaning that a national court which, in a case

before it concerning Community law, considers that the sole obstacle which precludes it from granting interim relief is a rule of national law must set aside that rule.

In October 1990, the House of Lords responded by granting the relief sought by Factortame ([1991] 1 All ER 70, [1990] 3 CMLR 375). Eventually, in 1991, the European Court ruled that the legislation was indeed incompatible with Community law (Case C-246/89 *Commission* v. *UK* [1991] ECR I-4585; Case C-221/89 [1991] ECR I-3905).

The *Factortame* ruling is built on the principle of effectiveness. 'Effectiveness' is a manifestation of the capacity of principles of Community law to intrude into what might initially appear to be areas of reserved national competence, in this instance national remedies law. In his Opinion in Factortame Advocate General Tesauro observed that:

> ... in harmony with the principle of collaboration enshrined in Article 5 of the Treaty, which is the real key to the interpretation of the whole system, is the fact that the methods and the machinery for protecting rights conferred on individuals by provisions of Community law are and remain, in the absence of a harmonized system of procedure, those provided for in the domestic legal system of the Member States. That principle, which recurs in the Court's case-law, is nevertheless based on a fundamental pre-condition, which is also derived from the second paragraph of Article 5, namely that the methods and national procedures must be no less favourable than those applying to like remedies for the protection of rights founded on national provisions and must also not be such as to render impossible in practice 'the exercise of rights which the national courts are obliged to protect'.

The limits of 'Europeanization' in *Factortame* should be appreciated. The European Court used the principle of effectiveness to insist on an adjustment of national law, specifically the putting aside of a bar to relief. The Court did not, however, elaborate the criteria which the national court should take into account in deciding whether to award relief.

The Court proved noticeably readier to play a more influential role when asked to rule on the availability of interim relief at national level in challenges to Community acts, as in EC Decision Cases C-143/88 and 92/89 *Zuckerfabrik Süderdithmarschen und Zuckerfabrik Soest* v. *Hauptzollamt Itzehoe und Hauptzollamt Paderborn* [1991] ECR I-415:

Suspension of enforcement of a national measure based on a Community regulation

The principle

14 The Finanzgericht Hamburg first seeks, in substance, to ascertain whether the second paragraph of Article 189 of the EEC Treaty must be interpreted as meaning that it denies to national courts the power to suspend enforcement of a national administrative measure adopted on the basis of a Community regulation.

15 In support of the existence of the power to grant such a suspension, the Finanzgericht Hamburg states that such a measure merely defers any implementation of a national decision and does not call in question the validity of the Community regulation. However, by way of explanation of the reason for its question, it points out, as a ground for denying that national courts have such jurisdiction, that the granting of interim relief, which may have far-reaching effects, may constitute an obstacle to the full effectiveness of regulations in all the Member States, in breach of the second paragraph of Article 189 of the Treaty.

16 It should first be emphasized that the provisions of the second paragraph of Article 189 of the Treaty cannot constitute an obstacle to the legal protection which Community law confers on individuals. In cases where national authorities are responsible for the administrative implementation of Community regulations, the legal protection guaranteed by Community law includes the right of individuals to challenge, as a preliminary issue, the legality of such regulations before national courts and to induce those courts to refer questions to the Court of Justice for a preliminary ruling.

17 That right would be compromised if, pending delivery of a judgment of the Court, which alone has jurisdiction to declare that a Community regulation is invalid (see judgment in Case 314/85 *Foto-Frost* v. *Hauptzollamt Lübeck-Ost* [1987] ECR 4199, at paragraph 20), individuals were not in a position, where certain conditions are satisfied, to obtain a decision granting suspension of enforcement which would make it possible for the effects of the disputed regulation to be rendered for the time being inoperative as regards them.

18 As the Court pointed out in its judgment in *Foto-Frost*, cited above, (at paragraph 16), requests for preliminary ruling which seek to ascertain the validity of a measure, like actions for annulment, constitute means for reviewing the legality of acts of the Community institutions. In the context of actions for annulment, Article 185 of the EEC Treaty enables applicants to request suspension of the enforcement of the contested act and empowers the Court to order such suspension. The coherence of the system of interim legal protection therefore requires that national courts should also be able to

order suspension of enforcement of a national administrative measure based on a Community regulation, the legality of which is contested.

19   Furthermore, in its judgment in Case C-213/89 (*The Queen* v. *Secretary of State for Transport*, ex parte *Factortame Ltd and Others* [1990] ECR I-2433), delivered in a case concerning the compatibility of national legislation with Community law, the Court, referring to the effectiveness of Article 177, took the view that the national court which had referred to it questions of interpretation for a preliminary ruling in order to enable it to decide that issue of compatibility, had to be able to grant interim relief and to suspend the application of the disputed national legislation until such time as it could deliver its judgment on the basis of the interpretation given in accordance with Article 177.

20   The interim legal protection which Community law ensures for individuals before national courts must remain the same, irrespective of whether they contest the compatibility of national legal provisions with Community law or the validity of secondary Community law, in view of the fact that the dispute in both cases is based on Community law itself.

21   It follows from the foregoing considerations that the reply to the first part of the first question must be that Article 189 of the Treaty has to be interpreted as meaning that it does not preclude the power of national courts to suspend enforcement of a national administrative measure adopted on the basis of a Community regulation.

Conditions for suspension

22   The Finanzgericht Hamburg then goes on to ask under what conditions national courts may order the suspension of enforcement of a national administrative measure based on a Community regulation, in view of the doubts which they may have as to the validity of that regulation.

23   It must first of all be noted that interim measures suspending enforcement of a contested measure may be adopted only if the factual and legal circumstances relied on by the applicants are such as to persuade the national court that serious doubts exist as to the validity of the Community regulation on which the contested administrative measure is based. Only the possibility of a finding of invalidity, a matter which is reserved to the Court, can justify the granting of suspensory measures.

24   It should next be pointed out that suspension of enforcement must retain the character of an interim measure. The national court to which the application for interim relief is made may therefore grant a suspension only until such time as the Court has delivered its ruling on the question of validity. Consequently, it is for the national court, should the question not yet have been referred to the Court of Justice, to refer that question itself, setting out the reasons for which it believes that the regulation must be held to be invalid.

25 As regards the other conditions concerning the suspension of enforcement of administrative measures, it must be observed that the rules of procedure of the courts are determined by national law and that those conditions differ according to the national law governing them, which may jeopardize the uniform application of Community law.

26 Such uniform application is a fundamental requirement of the Community legal order. It therefore follows that the suspension of enforcement of administrative measures based on a Community regulation, whilst it is governed by national procedural law, in particular as regards the making and examination of the application, must in all the Member States be subject, at the very least, to conditions which are uniform so far as the granting of such relief is concerned.

27 Since the power of national courts to grant such a suspension corresponds to the jurisdiction reserved to the Court of Justice by Article 185 in the context of actions brought under Article 173, those courts may grant such relief only on the conditions which must be satisfied for the Court of Justice to allow an application to it for interim measures.

28 In this regard, the Court has consistently held that measures suspending the operation of a contested act may be granted only in the event of urgency, in other words, if it is necessary for them to be adopted and to take effect before the decision on the substance of a case, in order to avoid serious and irreparable damage to the party seeking them.

29 With regard to the question of urgency, it should be pointed out that damage invoked by the applicant must be liable to materialize before the Court of Justice has been able to rule on the validity of the contested Community measure. With regard to the nature of the damage, purely financial damage cannot, as the Court has held on numerous occasions, be regarded in principle as irreparable. However, it is for the national court hearing the application for interim relief to examine the circumstances particular to the case before it. It must in this connection consider whether immediate enforcement of the measure which is the subject of the application for interim relief would be likely to result in irreversible damage to the applicant which could not be made good if the Community act were to be declared invalid.

30 It should also be added that a national court called upon to apply, within the limits of its jurisdiction, the provisions of Community law is under an obligation to ensure that full effect is given to Community law and, consequently, where there is doubt as to the validity of Community regulations, to take account of the interest of the Community, namely that such regulations should not be set aside without proper guarantees.

31 In order to comply with that obligation, a national court seized of an application for suspension must first examine whether the Community measure in question would be deprived of all effectiveness if not immediately implemented.

32 If suspension of enforcement is liable to involve a financial risk for the Community, the national court must also be in a position to require the applicant to provide adequate guarantees, such as the deposit of money or other security.

33 It follows from the foregoing that the reply to the second part of the first question put to the Court by the Finanzgericht Hamburg must be that suspension of enforcement of a national measure adopted in implementation of a Community regulation may be granted by a national court only:

    (i) if that court entertains serious doubts as to the validity of the Community measure and, should the question of the validity of the contested measure not already have been brought before the Court, itself refers that question to the Court;

    (ii) if there is urgency and a threat of serious and irreparable damage to the applicant;

    (iii) and if the national court takes due account of the Community's interests.

The impression that 'Europeanization' of national remedies is gathering pace is confirmed by the next case.

Cases C-6, C-9/90 *Andrea Francovich and others* v. *Italian State* [1991] ECR I-5357.

Directive 80/987 is intended to guarantee employees a minimum level of protection in the event of the insolvency of their employer. This protection includes specific guarantees of payment of unpaid wage claims. Italy failed to implement the Directive. This default was recorded by the Court in its judgment in Case 22/87 *Commission* v. *Italy* [1989] ECR 143. Italian workers, including Francovich, found themselves denied the protection envisaged by the Directive but not transposed into Italian law. Proceedings were initiated before the Italian courts and an Article 177 reference was made to the European Court. The workers claimed the unpaid guarantees from the state, but the European Court refused to find the relevant provisions of the Directive directly effective. There was insufficient unconditionality as regards the person liable to provide the guarantee. However the workers claimed in the alternative compensation for the loss caused to them by the state's failure to implement Directive 80/987.

29 The national court thus raises the issue of the existence and scope of a State's liability for loss and damage resulting from breach of its obligations under Community law.

30 That issue must be considered in the light of the general system of the Treaty and its fundamental principles.

(a) *The existence of State liability as a matter of principle*

31   It should be borne in mind at the outset that the EEC Treaty has created its own legal system, which is integrated into the legal systems of the Member States and which their courts are bound to apply. The subjects of that legal system are not only the Member States but also their nationals. Just as it imposes burdens on individuals, Community law is also intended to give rise to rights which become part of their legal patrimony. Those rights arise not only where they are expressly granted by the Treaty but also by virtue of obligations which the Treaty imposes in a clearly defined manner both on individuals and on the Member States and the Community institutions (see the judgments in Case 26/62 *Van Gend en Loos* [1963] ECR 1 and Case 6/64 *Costa* v. *ENEL* [1964] ECR 585).

32   Furthermore, it has been consistently held that the national courts whose task it is to apply the provisions of Community law in areas within their jurisdiction must ensure that those rules take full effect and must protect the rights which they confer on individuals (see in particular the judgments in Case 106/77 *Amministrazione delle Finanze dello Stato* v. *Simmenthal* [1978] ECR 629, paragraph 16, and Case C-213/89 *Factortame* [1990] ECR I-2433, paragraph 19).

33   The full effectiveness of Community rules would be impaired and the protection of the rights which they grant would be weakened if individuals were unable to obtain redress when their rights are infringed by a breach of Community law for which a Member State can be held responsible.

34   The possibility of obtaining redress from the Member State is particularly indispensable where, as in this case, the full effectiveness of Community rules is subject to prior action on the part of the State and where, consequently, in the absence of such action, individuals cannot enforce before the national courts the rights conferred upon them by Community law.

35   It follows that the principle whereby a State must be liable for loss and damage caused to individuals as a result of breaches of Community law for which the State can be held responsible is inherent in the system of the Treaty.

36   A further basis for the obligation of Member States to make good such loss and damage is to be found in Article 5 of the Treaty, under which the Member States are required to take all appropriate measures, whether general or particular, to ensure fulfilment of their obligations under Community law. Among these is the obligation to nullify the unlawful consequences of a breach of Community law (see, in relation to the analogous provision of Article 86 of the ECSC Treaty, the judgment in Case 6/60 *Humblet* v. *Belgium* [1960] ECR 559).

37   It follows from all the foregoing that it is a principle of Community law that the Member States are obliged to make good loss and damage caused to

individuals by breaches of Community law for which they can be held responsible.

(b) *The conditions for State liability*

38 Although State liability is thus required by Community law, the conditions under which that liability gives rise to a right to reparation depend on the nature of the breach of Community law giving rise to the loss and damage.

39 Where, as in this case, a Member State fails to fulfil its obligation under the third paragraph of Article 189 of the Treaty to take all the measures necessary to achieve the result prescribed by a directive, the full effectiveness of that rule of Community law requires that there should be a right to reparation provided that three conditions are fulfilled.

40 The first of those conditions is that the result prescribed by the directive should entail the grant of rights to individuals. The second condition is that it should be possible to identify the content of those rights on the basis of the provisions of the directive. Finally, the third condition is the existence of a causal link between the breach of the State's obligation and the loss and damage suffered by the injured parties.

41 Those conditions are sufficient to give rise to a right on the part of individuals to obtain reparation, a right founded directly on Community law.

42 Subject to that reservation, it is on the basis of the rules of national law on liability that the State must make reparation for the consequences of the loss and damage caused. In the absence of Community legislation, it is for the internal legal order of each Member State to designate the competent courts and lay down the detailed procedural rules for legal proceedings intended fully to safeguard the rights which individuals derive from Community law (see the judgments in Case 60/75 *Russo* v. *AIMA* [1976] ECR 45, Case 33/76 *Rewe* v. *Landwirtschaftskammer Saarland* [1976] ECR 1989 and Case 158/80 *Rewe* v. *Hauptzollamt Kiel* [1981] ECR 1805).

43 Further, the substantive and procedural conditions for reparation of loss and damage laid down by the national law of the Member States must not be less favourable than those relating to similar domestic claims and must not be so framed as to make it virtually impossible or excessively difficult to obtain reparation (see, in relation to the analogous issue of the repayment of taxes levied in breach of Community law, *inter alia* the judgment in Case 199/82 *Amministrazione delle Finanze dello Stato* v. *San Giorgio* [1983] ECR 3595).

44 In this case, the breach of Community law by a Member State by virtue of its failure to transpose Directive 80/987 within the prescribed period has been confirmed by a judgment of the Court. The result required by that directive entails the grant to employees of a right to a guarantee of payment of their unpaid wage claims. As is clear from the examination of the first

part of the first question, the content of that right can be identified on the basis of the provisions of the directive.

45 Consequently, the national court must, in accordance with the national rules on liability, uphold the right of employees to obtain reparation of loss and damage caused to them as a result of failure to transpose the directive.

46 The answer to be given to the national court must therefore be that a Member State is required to make good loss and damage caused to individuals by failure to transpose Directive 80/987.

Paragraph 33 echoes the insistence on effective redress as a key component in the protection of rights which was commented on above in relation to Case 222/86 *UNECTEF* v. *Heylens*. The point emerges all the more strongly from *Francovich*, given that the right had been held *not* to be directly effective.

Paragraph 40 shows the Court's willingness to establish European criteria for a remedy which is to be available at national level. In this sense, *Francovich* has more in common with the ruling in Cases C-143/88 and C-92/89 *Zuckerfabrik Süderdithmarschen and Zuckerfabrik Soest* than that in Case C-213/89 *Factortame*. The potential for national variation and consequent legal disunity in the response to European Court rulings acts as a spur to the Court more fully to 'Europeanize' its rulings.

The ruling in *Francovich* represents a further step in the process of establishing a European floor of national remedies. It also offers the prospect of severe penalties imposed on defaulting states. In that sense it enhances the capacity of private individuals to police the Community law system. It is a further aspect of the dual vigilance structure that direct effect not only involves the creation of rights, it also doubles the opportunities for supervision of the EC legal order.

The ruling in *Francovich* need not be limited to failure to implement Directives. The European Court will have the chance to elaborate on such matters in two Article 177 references which have been joined, *Factortame* (the sequel!) and *Firma Brasseries du Pecheur*, referred from Germany, both of which concern violation of primary Treaty articles (Joined Cases C-46 & 48/93 OJ 1993 C 94/13). Each national system must now digest the implications of *Francovich* and it is important that the European Court elaborates its intent in order to reduce disharmony in the national reaction. However, in the field of non-implementation of Directives alone, *Francovich* is likely to have a significant impact in protecting the enjoyment of rights which are intended to be conferred by Directives. The intended beneficiary of rights, thwarted by state default, has a remedy against that state. In *Dori*, discussed in Chapter 1, the Court's refusal to find the Directive to be horizontally directly effective was accompanied by a clear invitation that action under *Francovich* be taken against the defaulting state, Italy. That may seem unrealistic on the facts of that case, but at least the threat of liability ought to help to dissuade future non-implementation.

4. The evolving Community system of national remedies

The Court has energetically involved itself in the creation of a minimum level of redress which must be available in national systems where protection of European rights is in issue. This process is justified by the Court with reference to Article 5 EC and the broad objective of the 'constitutionalization' of the Treaty. The implications of this evolution of the Community system are addressed in the next two extracts.

GOVERNMENT LIABILITY AFTER FRANCOVICH*

Roberto Caranta

[...]

III. PREVIOUS COMMUNITY CASE LAW ON THE EFFECTIVENESS OF THE JUDICIAL PROTECTION OF INDIVIDUALS

The ground upon which the *Francovich* case was decided is the principle of effective protection of individuals.

The case law concerning this principle has evolved remarkably during the past ten years, the court having moved from an initial position which amounted to almost complete indifference to the remedial aspect of the rights conferred on individuals by Community law, to an ever greater involvement in questions concerning the conditions under which the protection of such rights is ensured by the judiciary of the Member States.

The initial position was the result of a widespread belief that Community law in general was only interested in substantive aspects of law, the procedural aspects having been left to the competence of the Member States. In the *Rewe*[1] and *Comet*[2] cases, for example, the court ruled that it was for each national legal system to determine the procedural aspects of actions claiming the protection of individual rights provided by Community law. There were two qualifications, namely that the domestic remedies had to be no less favourable than those established for comparable national rights, and that in any case the remedies conferred had to be effective, but the actual incidence of Community law on procedure was virtually non-existent.

The *Francovich* decision does maintain the traditional rule where by procedures to ensure the execution of Community law are left to national legal systems, but with a small, and not so innocent, change; the competence of Member States ceases to be the governing principle, and becomes the rule only in the absence of relevant Community provisions.[3]

These qualifications of the principle of the competence of Member States in procedural matters acquired relevance long before *Francovich*. In the *Simmenthal*

---

* First published in *Cambridge Law Journal*, **52**, 1993, pp.279–82; reprinted by permission of Cambridge University Press.
[1] Case 33/76, [1976], ECR 1997, cons. 5.
[2] Case 45/76, [1976] ECR 2053, cons. 12–17.
[3] But for a traditional reading of the rule see G. de Búrca. "Giving Effect to European Community Directives" (1992) 55 M.L.R. 215, at p.238.

case, notably, the principle of the effectiveness of judicial protection ceased to be a mere *obiter dictum* and began to bite. In that case another Italian judge of first instance, the *Pretore* of Susa, had asked the Court of Justice whether it was consistent with Community law for a national system of judicial review of legislation to make it the duty of every judge, before excluding the operation of a national legal provision in conflict with Community law, to request a preliminary ruling by the country's Constitutional Court. The European Court, as is well known, held that:[4]

> any provision of a national legal system and any legislative, administrative or judicial practice which might impair the effectiveness of Community law by withholding from the national court having jurisdiction to apply such law the power to do everything necessary at the moment of its application to set aside national legal provisions which might prevent Community rules from having full force and effect are incompatible with those requirements which are the very essence of Community law.

On this ground the Court held that a system of centralised judicial review such as the one existing in Italy which delayed the final decision by requiring the matter to be referred to the Constitutional Court was not compatible with the principle of the effective protection of individual rights which was based upon Community law, and for this reason had to be set aside by every judge in the Member State.

Even in *Simmenthal*, however, it could be thought that the real issue was not just the effective protection of individuals; what was actually at stake in that case was which court was to have the last word when national law conflicted with Community law. If every national law with Community law, without even consulting the Court of Justice, because the Italian Constitutional Court in practice never made a reference under article 177 of the EEC Treaty. On the other hand, if every judge was left free to decide the conflict between national and Community law on his own, he would probably resort to the European Court to have Community law interpreted and the question of compatibility assessed. It was a contest for power, the Court of Justice against the Italian Constitutional Court, and the latter finally bowed to the supremacy of Community law and of its court.[5]

More relevant to the protection of individuals were the decisions concerning the repayment of wrongly paid taxes. On references by some Italian courts, the Court of Justice in the *San Giorgio* case[6] held it to be inconsistent with Community law for a national provision to subject the right to restitution of sums paid pursuant to a national tax law contrary to Community law to proof that the charge had not been

---

[4]   Case 106/77, [1978] ECR 629, para. 22.
[5]   Corte cost. 8 giugno 1984 n. 170, in *Giurisprudenza costituzionale* 1984, I, 1098; for a commentary see J.V. Louis, "Droit communautaire et loi postérieure; un revirement de la Cour constitutionnelle italienne", in *Cah. dr. europ.* 1986, 194.
[6]   Case 199/82, [1983] ECR 3595.

transferred to the final consumer of the goods; the court thought it contrary to the principle of effective judicial protection to impose on citizens invoking their Community law rights an onus of proof which it was almost impossible to discharge.

There can be no doubt that *Factortame*[7] is the most important decision so far concerning the consequences of the principle of the effectiveness of judicial protection of individuals; its impact upon the respective roles of the Community and Member States in the creation of remedies for infringements of Community law rights seriously undermines the position according to which procedure is a matter to be left to Member States.

The facts which constitute the background to, and the legal questions involved in, the *Factortame* decision are widely known on the Continent as well as in Britain.[8] It is sufficient to recall that some Spanish owners of fishing vessels had challenged the conformity with Community law of a British statute and regulations designed to ensure that ships flying the Union Jack were owned and operated by British citizens or corporations.

Fearing that irrecoverable damage could accrue pending the judgment, the plaintiffs had asked for an interim injunction, but this was refused by the Court of Appeal[9] which held that courts had no authority under the law to suspend the application of a legal provision which had not yet been judicially determined to be in conflict with Community law. The House of Lords,[10] having come to the same conclusion on the point of English law as the Court of Appeal, thought it necessary to ask the Court of Justice for a preliminary ruling under article 177 whether, in relation to the grant of interim protection in the circumstances of the case, Community law overrode English law.[11] The Court of Justice, following the learned conclusions of Advocate General Tesauro, held that:[12]

---

[7]   *The Queen* v. *Secretary of State for Transport, ex parte Factortame Ltd. No. 2.* [1991] 1 A.C. 603; see the commentaries by D. Oliver, "Fishing on the Incoming Tide" (1991) 54 M.L.R. 442, and A.G. Toth (1990) 27 C.M.L. Rev. 574; see also H.W.R. Wade. "What has Happened to the Sovereignty of Parliament?" (1991) 107 L.Q.R. 1; ibid.. "Injunctive Relief against the Crown and Ministers" ibid., 4; N.P. Gravells. "Disapplying an Act of Parliament Pending Ruling; Constitutional Enormity or Community Law Right?" [1989] P.L. 568; A Barav. "Enforcement of Community Rights in the National Courts: The Case for Jurisdiction to Grant an Interim Relief" (1989) 26 C.M.L. Rev. 369 ff.

[8]   See R.R. Churchill, "'Quota hopping': The Common Fisheries Policy Wrongfooted?" (1990) 27 C.M.L. Rev. 209, and the commentary by the same author in (1992) 29 C.M.L.Rev. 415.

[9]   [1989] 2 C.M.L.R. 353.

[10] [1990] 2 A.C. 85.

[11] [1990] 2 A.C. 85 at 152, *per* Lord Bridge of Harwich, with whom all the other Law Lords concurred.

[12] [1991] 1 A.C. 603, 644.

Community law must be interpreted as meaning that a national court which, in a case before it concerning Community law, considers that the sole obstacle which precludes it from granting interim relief is a rule of national law must set aside that rule.

Decisive to the outcome of the *Factortame* case was, according to the Court of Justice which laid great emphasis on its previous decision in the *Simmenthal* case,[13] the consideration that:[14]

the full effectiveness of Community law would be ... much impaired if a rule of national law could prevent a court seized of a dispute governed by Community law from granting interim relief in order to ensure the full effectiveness of the judgment to be given on the existence of the rights claimed under Community law.

Just as in *Factortame* it was from the principle of the effectiveness of Community law that the Court of Justice deduced the necessity for interim protection, so in *Francovich* it distilled the necessity for an entitlement to damages when Community law is infringed.

These decisions, it is submitted, mark the definitive departure by the Court of Justice from the model, recalled above, according to which Community law was confined to the substantive aspects of law, to the definition of rights and duties, while the rules governing the actual enforcement of such rights and duties depended entirely on the possibly different legal rules in force in the various Member States.

The new approach is not limited to the case law. It is sufficient to mention two EEC directives, namely directive 89/665[15] and the more recent 92/13,[16] both designed to promote uniformity of national remedies for violation of Community rules applicable to public works and procurement contracts.[17]

From a comparative point of view it is clear that, under the mounting pressure exerted by the case law of the Court of Justice and also by the legislator, Community law has increasingly begun to "fasten upon remedies", in this way introducing at a continental level a style of legal thinking which was characteristic of common law rather than civil law systems. [...]

---

[13]   [1991] 1 A.C. 603, 643–4.
[14]   [1991] 1 A.C. 603, 644.
[15]   O.J.E.C. 1989, No. L. 395/34.
[16]   O.J.E.C. 1992, No. L. 76/14.
[17]   See M. Bronckers, "Private Enforcement of 1992: Do Trade and Industry Stand a Chance against Member States?" (1989) 26 C.M.L. Rev. 528.

VIII. CONCLUDING REMARKS; THE BIRTH OF A "JUS COMMUNE" IN THE FIELD OF JUDICIAL PROTECTION OF INDIVIDUALS AGAINST PUBLIC POWERS

The *Francovich* decision has a relevance which goes beyond the field of governmental liability. It marks the birth of a "jus commune", of a law common to all the Member States and to the Community itself, in the field of the judicial protection of individuals against public powers.[18]

In *Factortame* and to a larger degree in *Zuckerfabrik Süderdithmarschen*[19] the Court of Justice laid down the rules to be applied by domestic courts when granting interim relief in Community law cases. The rules were the same as those applied by the European Court itself in proceedings under articles 185 and 186 of the EEC Treaty, the first of which was explicitly referred to by the court.[20]

In *Francovich* the Court of Justice applied to actions of the Member States inconsistent with Community law the same rules which had been elaborated by the court itself in relation to noncontractual liability for invalid acts of Community organs – but with a qualification: it forgot that in Community law the breach has to be "sufficiently serious". But qualifications are inconsistent with a "jus commune"; they destroy its inherent condition, namely, to be common.

(End of excerpt)

---

[18] See more generally J. Schwarze, "Tendencies towards a Common Administrative Law in Europe" (1991) 16 E.L.Rev. 3; J. Rivero, "Vers un droit commun européen; nouvelles perspectives en droit administratif", in *Pages de doctrine* (Paris 1980), p.489 *et. seq.*; M.P. Chiti, "I signori del diritto communitario: la Corte di giustizia e lo sviluppo del diritto amministrativo europeo", *Rivista trimestrale di diritto pubblico* 1991, 796.

[19] Joint Cases C-143/88 and C-92/89, [1991] 1 ECR 415; the decision was considered by Lord Goff of Chieveley in *Kirkless Metropolitan Borough Council* v. *Wickes Building Supplies Ltd.* [1992] 3 W.L.R. 170, 187.

[20] See cons. 27.

LIABILITY OF EC MEMBER STATES TOWARDS INDIVIDUALS FOR VIOLATIONS OF COMMUNITY LAW*

Fernand Schockweiler

CONSEQUENCES OF THE FRANCOVICH DECISION

The most evident consequence flowing from the decision is that in each Member State the national judges will have to allow a complaint for damages against the state, if the prerequisites specified in the decision are fulfilled, independent of whether or not the national legal order provides for (or permits) the possibility of such a lawsuit against the state.

Further, national law must be ignored with respect to the points concerning which the Court of Justice has decided. Thus, for example, a national regulation which grants compensation only for negligent conduct, or which excludes it in cases of excusable misconduct, cannot be applied, at least not when (as in the *Francovich* case) failure to implement a Directive is involved. For the moment, it remains an open question whether in other cases the degree of fault issue can be a significant factor, since the European Court of Justice (ECJ) has reserved its judgment concerning liability in other factual contexts, depending on the type of violations of Community law committed.

In any case, it no longer appears – contrary to what the ECJ itself said in its decision of 7 July 1981 – so clear that the legal order of the Community neither opens any new avenues of legal recourse nor obliges national judges to apply new legal remedies within the individual Member States. However, one must clarify that – as earlier in the *Factortame* case – what is involved here is not the praetorian creation of avenues of legal recourse not provided for in the national legal order, but rather the application of already existing avenues of legal recourse to a given situation for which they were not originally intended.

In this sense, the decision is rather less radical than it may at first appear. It may instead be regarded as a further development of the idea, often expressed in judicial decisions, that to safeguard EC law in the interest of individuals, the national judge

* First published in 'Die Haftung der EG-Mitgliedstaaten gegenüber dem einzelnen bei Verletzung des Gemeinschaftsrechts', *Europarecht*, **107**, 1993 pp.120–5, reprinted by permission of Nomos Verlagsgesellschaft, Baden-Baden. Translation by John Blazek, Brussels.

must draw upon all the avenues of legal recourse and remedies offered by the national law. This is to be so understood that the judge must also apply these in cases for which they were not originally conceived, and even if such application was explicitly excluded.

Nor does the decision appear aberrant on the national level to the extent that it establishes the principle of state liability. The primacy of Community law, which is now guaranteed in each Member State either through explicit constitutional provisions or by decisions of the highest national courts, should actually suffice for a violation of Community legal provisions to be treated in every Member State as a violation of the national legal order, with the peculiarity that, in each case, the Community norm takes precedence over the national norm.

Thus, even in accordance with purely *national* law, there should already exist state liability for illegal conduct.

Treating state liability for violation of Community law as equivalent to similar cases within the national legal order would have to be based on the assumption that, in each Member State, a violation of the law *per se*, without further prerequisites, can trigger state liability, no matter what type of law–violating act is involved.

The principle of uniform, undifferentiated treatment of Community citizens throughout the entire area covered by EC law must at any rate not allow any divergent rules in different Member States. If one examines the various national legal systems, one immediately notices that the principle of liability of the public authorities for unlawful action does not apply everywhere, and the conditions for enforcing this liability are not uniform; often the conditions are structured in such a way that they virtually exclude the possibility of bringing a lawsuit.

Thus, in some states the filing of a complaint is simply not permitted, or at least is subject to strict conditions if the damage arose directly from an unlawful legislative act. In other states, mere illegality is not enough to provide a basis for liability; rather, one is also required to establish either irregular or at least negligent or inexcusable conduct. Under other legal systems, the violation of law must be unambiguous or consist in the disregard of a norm intended to protect the individual.

The main concern of the *Francovich* decision was to replace these various preconditions with uniform prerequisites which are subject to Community law. The leeway still afforded to the national laws would now appear to be limited to secondary aspects. From a practical perspective, however, these can still be of decisive importance for the injured party when it involves the question of whether damages can actually be granted to him.

Because of their differing solutions, applying national laws outside the liability principles according to Community law would necessarily mean that the compensation of Community citizens who have suffered harm due to identical violations of Community law will differ from Member State to Member State.

If we assume that Community law demands a uniform application and the equal treatment of all citizens (at any rate in its sphere of application), then we must ask ourselves whether, in cases arising through violation of Community law, all rules which lead to compensation should not be subject to Community law as well. Yet *who* would establish such a comprehensive regulation (applying throughout the geographical area of the EC), and *what* should it look like?

As to the first question, one might respond that, after the ECJ has established that the field is subject to Community law, it is up to the Council as the normative body of the Community to fully regulate the problem area after the stopgap intervention of the ECJ. As long as this does not occur, it would seem to be left up to the ECJ to decide on a case by case basis wherever it appears indispensable for preserving Community law, and if necessary to derive generally applicable rules from Community law.

The question of *how* the matter is to be exhaustively regulated is perhaps less self-evident than it may at first sight appear. It might seem logical to establish the same rules for state liability as the ECJ applies when Community liability is involved. However, in the light of the limiting conditions under which the ECJ allows the Community to be held liable, this would represent a step backwards for many national legal orders compared with what their rules already afford, and would be all the more difficult to accept in the light of the primacy attributed to the Community law in the national hierarchy of norms.

Finally, however, especially in the light of the need for legal certainty, it would be appropriate for the EC legislator to work out a coherent and detailed regulation of liability for damages in cases where the Treaty is violated. Such a regulation would be more useful for ensuring compliance with EC law than the method of imposing administrative fines which is provided by the Maastricht Treaty, and which (for the injured party, at any rate) does not represent a very satisfactory solution.

CONCLUSION

After the foregoing analysis of the *Francovich* decision, can one now conclude (as did Germany's Social Minister Blüm in late November 1992, in an essay published in the news magazine *Spiegel*) that the ECJ has 'flagrantly violated the principle of the separation of powers', since on the basis of Community law it accepted state liability for Treaty-violating behaviour on the part of the Member States? Has the ECJ exceeded the limits of its right to develop the law, a right which (in spite of everything) is acknowledged even by Mr. Blüm? Didn't national judges proceed in a similar manner when, drawing from the whole of their national legal order, they established the principles regulating liability of the state with respect to sovereign actions? I would like to briefly outline the situation regarding this in various Member States.

To start with Germany: Haven't the judicial decisions recognized an objective, specific liability of the state which is independent of the written law and independent of any fault, in cases of expropriation and similar interventions which impose a special sacrifice on the injured party? This liability obligation, which deviates from the general rules, was derived from Articles 74 and 75 of the introduction to the *Allgemeines Landrecht* (General National Law) for the Prussian States of 1794, whose content was regarded as an expression of the customary law, since these provisions were no longer applicable at the time the decision was reached.

In Belgium, after the state had until then been granted complete freedom from liability with respect to sovereign activity, the Court of Cassation in a decision dated 5 November 1920 established the principle that the state in all areas of its activity could be found liable in accordance with the rules of civil law which generally apply for citizens.

The case law in this area has developed in such a way that today stricter requirements are imposed on the state than on citizens. For example, it is assumed that where the state's damage-causing act was illegal, special fault need not be proved, since the fault already consists in the illegality itself. And the state cannot exculpate itself by arguing that the conduct of the public authority must be regarded as excusable, and that even the most careful civil servant would not have behaved differently under similar circumstances. This is all the more remarkable in that, according to the general law, liability rests on fault and negligent conduct.

In Luxembourg, judicial decisions have traced a similar development.

In France, where the state is not subjected to the general rules of the civil law, the decisions of the *Conseil d'Etat* have established both the principle and the conditions of state liability. The conditions can differ depending on the type of action of the government bodies.

In general, the obligation of the state to compensate the damage it inflicts is based on the principle of the equality of the citizens for government obligations and for shouldering the resulting burdens. Liability in cases of legislative injustice can also be based on this.

In Ireland, contrary to earlier immunity, the liability obligation of the state on the basis of the general rules was established in 1972 by a decision of the High Court of Justice.

In all these states, this development – and perhaps even creation – of the law by the highest courts of justice was regarded as falling well within their scope of responsibility, and accepted without indignation.

As for the ECJ, until now no one has objected that it derived general legal principles from the Treaty and from generally applicable legal rules. On the contrary, it has been praised precisely on account of this, especially for its efforts to declare the basic rights and general legal principles to be binding for the Community legal order and to ensure that they are observed within the Community law's sphere of application. This interpretation is in a line with the general efforts of the ECJ to attribute to individuals rights flowing from the Community legal order, rights which are also to be recognized by the national legal orders, an interpretation which finds its origin in the Van Gend en Loos and Simmenthal decisions.

Thus, taking into account the legal traditions of several Member States and the prior decisions of the ECJ, one can hardly agree that the court in its Francovich decision has exceeded the limits of its acknowledged power to develop the law and committed a 'flagrant violation' of the principle of separation of powers in a democratic structure of states (one whose outlines, moreover, are not so precisely defined). It is much more logical to conclude that the court, basing itself on its previous decisions concerning the direct applicability of EC law as well as its useful effect, has drawn the final consequences with respect to the rights of Community citizens, rights that were given to individuals by the Community legal order, which is superior to the systems of the various nation states.

(End of excerpt)

5. The legislative contribution

The Court's activism in creating a nascent 'Europeanized' system of national remedies has occurred against an almost blank legislative background. Nonetheless, in one area in particular it has proved possible to establish Community remedies at national level through legislative action. This has occurred in the field of Public Procurement.

COUNCIL DIRECTIVE

of 21 December 1989

on the coordination of the laws, regulations and administrative provisions relating to the application of review procedures to the award of public supply and public works contracts

(89/665/EEC)

THE COUNCIL OF THE EUROPEAN COMMUNITIES,

Having regard to the Treaty establishing the European Economic Community, and in particular Article 100a thereof,

Having regard to the proposal from the Commission,[1]

In co-operation with the European Parliament,[2]

Having regard to the opinion of the Economic and Social Committee,[3]

Whereas Community Directives on public procurement, in particular Council Directive 71/305/EEC of 26 July 1971 concerning the coordination of procedures for the award of public works contracts,[4] as last amended by Directive 89/440/EEC,[5] and Council Directive 77/62/EEC of 21 December 1976 coordinating procedures for the award of public supply contracts,[6] as last amended by Directive 88/295/EEC,[7] do not contain any specific provisions ensuring their effective application;

Whereas the existing arrangements at both national and Community levels for ensuring their application are not always adequate to ensure compliance with the relevant Community provisions particularly at a stage when infringements can be corrected;

Whereas the opening-up of public procurement to Community competition necessitates a substantial increase in the guarantees of transparency and non-discrimination; whereas, for it to have tangible effects, effective and rapid remedies must be available in the case of infringements of Community law in the field of public procurement or national rules implementing the law;

Whereas in certain Member States the absence of effective remedies or inadequacy of existing remedies deter Community undertakings from submitting ten-

---

[1] OJ No C 230, 28.8.1987, p.6 and OJ No C 15,19.1.1989, p.8.
[2] OJ No C 167, 27.6.1988, p.77 and OJ No C 323, 27.12.1989.
[3] OJ No C 347, 22.12.1987, p.23.
[4] OJ No L 185, 16.8.1971, p.5.
[5] OJ No L 210, 21.7.1989, p.1.
[6] OJ No L 13, 15.1.1977, p.1.
[7] OJ No L 127, 20.5.1988, p.1.

ders in the Member State in which the contracting authority is established, whereas, therefore, the Member States concerned must remedy this situation;

Whereas, since procedures for the award of public contracts are of such short duration, competent review bodies must, among other things, be authorized to take interim measures aimed at suspending such a procedure or the implementation of any decisions which may be taken by the contracting authority; whereas the short duration of the procedures means that the aforementioned infringements need to be dealt with urgently;

Whereas it is necessary to ensure that adequate procedures exist in all the Member States to permit the setting aside of decisions taken unlawfully and compensation of persons harmed by an infringement;

Whereas, when undertakings do not seek review, certain infringements may not be corrected unless a specific mechanism is put in place;

Whereas, accordingly, the Commission, when it considers that a clear and manifest infringement has been committed during a contract award procedure, should be able to bring it to the attention of the competent authorities of the Member State and of the contracting authority concerned so that appropriate steps are taken for the rapid correction of any alleged infringement;

Whereas the application in practice of the provisions of this Directive should be re-examined within a period of four years of its implementation on the basis of information to be supplied by the Member States concerning the functioning of the national review procedures,

HAD ADOPTED THIS DIRECTIVE:

Article 1

1.   The Member States shall take the measures necessary to ensure that, as regards contract award procedures falling within the scope of Directive 71/305/EEC and 77/62/EEC, decisions taken by the contracting authorities may be reviewed effectively and, in particular, as rapidly as possible in accordance with the conditions set out in the following Articles, and, in particular, Article 2(7) on the grounds that such decisions have infringed Community law in the field of public procurement or national rules implementing that law.

2.   Member States shall ensure that there is no discrimination between undertakings claiming injury in the context of a procedure for the award of a contract as a result of the distinction made by this Directive between national rules implementing Community law and other national rules.

3.   The Member States shall ensure that the review procedures are available, under detailed rules which the Member States may establish, at least to any person having or having had an interest in obtaining a particular public supply or public works contract and who has been or risks being harmed by an alleged in-

fringement. In particular, the Member States may require that the person seeking the review must have previously notified the contracting authority of the alleged infringement and of his intention to seek review.

Article 2

1.   The Member States shall ensure that the measures taken concerning the review procedures specified in Article 1 include provision for the powers to:

(a)   take, at the earliest opportunity and by way of interlocutory procedures, interim measures with the aim of correcting the alleged infringement or preventing further damage to the interests concerned, including measures to suspend or to ensure that suspension of the procedure for the award of a public contract or the implementation of any decision taken by the contracting authority;

(b)   either set aside or ensure the setting aside of decisions taken unlawfully, including the removal of discriminatory technical, economic or financial specifications in the invitation to tender, the contract documents or in any other document relating to the contract award procedure;

(c)   award damages to persons harmed by an infringement.

2.   The powers specified in paragraph 1 may be conferred on separate bodies responsible for different aspects of the review procedure.

3.   Review procedures need not in themselves have an automatic suspensive effect on the contract award procedures to which they relate.

4.   The Member States may provide that when considering whether to order interim measures the body responsible may take into account the probable consequences of the measures for all interests likely to be harmed, as well as the public interest, and may decide not to grant such measures where their negative consequences could exceed their benefits. A decision not to grant interim measures shall not prejudice any other claim of the person seeking these measures.

5.   The Member States may provide that where damages are claimed on the grounds that a decision was taken unlawfully, the contested decision must first be set aside by a body having the necessary powers.

6.   The effects of the exercise of the powers referred to in paragraph 1 on a contract concluded subsequent to its award shall be determined by national law.

Furthermore, except where a decision must be set aside prior to the award of damages, a Member State may provide that, after the conclusion of a contract following its award, the powers of the body responsible for the review procedures shall be limited to awarding damages to any person harmed by an infringement.

7.   The Member States shall ensure that decisions taken by bodies responsible for review procedures can be effectively enforced.

8.   Where bodies responsible for review procedures are not judicial in character, written reasons for their decisions shall always be given. Furthermore, in such a case, provision must be made to guarantee procedures whereby any allegedly illegal measure taken by the review body or any alleged defect in the exercise of the powers conferred on it can be the subject of judicial review or review by another body which is a court or tribunal within the meaning of Article 177 of the EEC Treaty and independent of both the contracting authority and the review body.

The members of such an independent body shall be appointed and leave office under the same conditions as members of the judiciary as regards the authority responsible for their appointment, their period of office, and their removal. At least the President of this independent body shall have the same legal and professional qualifications as members of the judiciary. The independent body shall take its decisions following a procedure in which both sides are heard, and these decisions shall, by means determined by each Member State, be legally binding.

Article 3

1.   The Commission may invoke the procedure for which this Article provides when, prior to a contract being concluded, it considers that a clear and manifest infringement of Community provisions in the field of public procurement has been committed during a contract award procedure falling within the scope of Directives 71/305/EEC and 77/62/EEC.

2.   The Commission shall notify the Member State and the contracting authority concerned of the reasons which have led it to conclude that a clear and manifest infringement has been committed and request its correction.

3.   Within 21 days of receipt of the notification referred to in paragraph 2, the Member State concerned shall communicate to the Commission:

(a) its confirmation that the infringement has been corrected; or

(b) a reasoned submission as to why no correction has been made; or

(c) a notice to the effect that the contract award procedure has been suspended either by the contracting authority on its own initiative or on the basis of the powers specified in Article 2 (1) (a).

4.   A reasoned submission in accordance with paragraph 3 (b) may rely among other matters on the fact that the alleged infringement is already the subject of judicial or other review proceedings or of a review as referred to in Article 2 (8). In such a case, the Member State shall inform the Commission of the result of those proceedings as soon as it becomes known. 5. Where notice has been given that a contract award procedure has been suspended in accordance with paragraph 3 (c), the Member State shall notify the Commission when the suspension is lifted or another contract procedure relating in whole or in part to the same subject matter is begun. That notification shall confirm that the alleged in-

fringement has been corrected or include a reasoned submission as to why no correction has been made.

Article 4

1. Not later than four years after the implementation of this Directive, the Commission, in consultation with the Advisory Committee for Public Contracts, shall review the manner in which the provisions of this Directive have been implemented and, if necessary, make proposals for amendments.

2. By 1 March each year the Member States shall communicate to the Commission information on the operation of their national review procedures during the preceding calendar year. The nature of the information shall be determined by the Commission in consultation with the Advisory Committee for Public Contracts.

Article 5

Member States shall bring into force, before 1 December 1991, the measures necessary to comply with this Directive. They shall communicate to the Commission the texts of the main national laws, regulations and administrative provisions which they adopt in the field governed by this Directive.

Article 6

This Directive is addressed to the Member States.

Done at Brussels, 21 December 1989.

For the Council

The President

É. CRESSON

Directive 92/13 OJ 1992 L76/14 applies an adjusted regime to the special sectors of water, energy, transport and telecommunications.

B. REPRESENTATIVE REDRESS

The principle of direct effect, combined with the Europeanization of national remedies, serves to empower individuals in a way that confers on them rights and permits them to contribute to a more rigorous policing of Community law obligations. Individual redress, even where it is supplemented by Community law, has limitations. It must be worth the individuals' while to pursue the matter. Frequently this will not be the case. The focus then switches to enforcement action taken on behalf of the individual.

In some Community Directives examined in this book, there is an explicit recognition of the importance of administrative enforcement. For example, in both the Directive on Misleading Advertising (Directive 84/450) and the Directive on Unfair Terms in Consumer Contracts (Directive 93/13), examined in Chapters 6 and 8 respectively, the implementation obligation imposed on Member States includes requirements to put in place administrative agencies to supervise compliance. It remains generally the case that Community law makes no explicit provision for representative actions on behalf of, for example, workers, consumers or the victims of pollution. The scope of such actions remains subject to national law constraints – qualified by the impact of Article 5 EC, the principle of effectiveness, and Article 6, the prohibition against discrimination based on nationality.

What of more general supervision of compliance with Community law? The traditional institutional perception is that this is the province of the Commission. The Commission is empowered to initiate Article 169 proceedings against defaulting Member States. Since the entry into force of the Treaty on European Union, the Treaty envisages the possibility that fines may be imposed on Member States – Article 171(2) EC. The Commission is empowered to enforce the competition rules against private parties. Regulation 17/62 equips it with the power, *inter alia*, to impose fines in the event of infringement.

Where individuals cannot effectively pursue violations of Community law, the role of the Commission, enforcing the law as representative of the Community interest, comes under the spotlight. Any person is able to complain to the Commission and to request that it investigates an alleged violation of Community law. However, the Commission lacks the resources to investigate every alleged violation of Community law. This is why the role of individual redress at national level assumes such immense importance. However, to what extent is it possible for the Commission to be required in law to respond to complaints? The European Court has never been prepared to interfere with the Commission's discretion under Article 169 of the Treaty whether to commence proceedings, where complaints against Member States are at stake (eg Case 247/87 *Star Fruit Co* v. *Commission* [1989] ECR 291). However, in the following case, arising in the field of competition policy, the Court of First Instance shows itself prepared to identify legal obligations imposed on the Commission when in receipt of a complaint, *in casu* by BEUC, a consumer representative organization. This ruling suggests a limited move towards enforceable rights of participation in Commission investigation. Redress is not simply an individual matter.

Case T-37/92 [1994] ECR II-285 *BEUC* v. *Commission* judgment of 18 May 1994

BEUC complained to the Commission about an agreement struck between the British Society of Motor Manufacturers and Traders (SMMT) and the Japan Automobile Manufacturers Association (JAMA) restricting the export of Japanese cars to the United Kingdom to agreed percentages. BEUC alleged violations of both principal Treaty provisions on competition policy, Articles 85 and 86 EC. An exchange of correspondence between BEUC and the Commission followed. In a letter of 17 March 1992 the Commission explained that it saw no Community interest in investigating the matter further. It commented that in July 1991 the Commission had agreed an arrangement on motor vehicles with the Japanese authorities. In the light of this the Commission had no reason to doubt that the SMMT/JAMA arrangement would end by the start of 1993. The Commission therefore judged there to be no Community interest in an investigation. The Court of First Instance first ruled that the letter amounted to a final rejection of BEUC's complaint and that, constitutionally, it was therefore susceptible to review. The Court of First Instance then turned to the substance of the matter. The following extract from the judgment exposes one of several errors of assessment on the part of the Commission such as to support the application for annulment.

The second plea: the first ground for rejecting the complaint is misconceived

43 In their second plea, the applicants submit that insufficient reasons are given for the contested decision, contrary to the requirements of Article 190 of the EEC Treaty. They submit that the agreement complained of, whose incompatibility with Community competition law is not explicitly disputed in the contested decision, has an adverse effect on the prices and marketing of cars and did not sufficiently explain the potential effect of the commercial consensus between the Community and Japan. The decision does not explain how that consensus will put an end to the alleged anti-competitive practices; the Commission is not in a position to specify the price details of its implementation and it is apparent from the statements of the two contracting parties that a temporary restriction on exports to the United Kingdom is to continue until 1999, restricting exported vehicles to approximately 7% of total annual sales.

44 The Commission considers that the applicants' plea is based on an incorrect premise, to the effect that it is under a duty to investigate complaints relating to presumed infringements. It maintains that it made it clear that the complaint was rejected because of insufficient Community interest and that sufficient reasons are given for that conclusion.

45   As the Court of First Instance held in Case T-24/90 *Automec* v. *Commission* [1992] ECR II-2223 (hereinafter '*Automec II*'), the Commission is not under a duty to carry out an investigation when a complaint under Article 3(2) of Regulation No 17 is submitted to it. However, the Court stated in that judgment that the Commission is under a duty to consider carefully the factual and legal issues brought to its attention by the complaint, in order to assess whether those issues indicate conduct which is liable to distort competition within the common market and affect trade between Member States. Where, as in this case, the Commission has decided to reject the complaint without holding an investigation, the purpose of judicial review by the Court of First Instance is to ensure that the challenged decision is based on a correct assessment of the facts and that it is not vitiated by any error of law, manifest error of assessment or abuse of power (*Automec II*, cited above, paragraphs 79 and 80).

46   In this case, the Court notes that the Commission does not deny that there was an 'arrangement' between SMMT and JAMA, concerning the importation into the United Kingdom of cars from Japan, but considers that there is no Community interest in investigating that 'arrangement' under competition law.

47   As the Court of First Instance has held, the Commission is entitled to determine the relative priority to be accorded to the different cases pending before it by reference to their Community interest. This possibility does not have the effect of removing such determinations from the scope of judicial review since, as a result of the requirement to state reasons, set out in Article 190 of the Treaty, the Commission may not confine itself to referring in the abstract to that interest. On the contrary, a decision by which the Commission rejects, on the ground of insufficient or no Community interest, a complaint submitted to it is required, by virtue of Article 190 of the Treaty, to set out the legal and factual considerations which led the Commission to conclude that there was no sufficient Community interest to justify an investigation. It is by reviewing the lawfulness of those reasons that the Court exercises its responsibility for judicial review of the Commission's action (*Automec II*, cited above, paragraph 85).

48   In this case, in order to deal with the second plea which, as put forward by the applicants, in fact concerns the validity of the first ground for rejecting the complaint, the Court must therefore examine the lawfulness of that ground.

49   First, the Court notes that in this case the alleged anti-competitive practice is an agreement concluded between two associations of undertakings, one of which has its headquarters in one of the Member States. Consequently, it is prima facie not impossible that that agreement, whose objective is to restrict imports from a non-member country into one of the Member States, falls within the scope of Article 85(1) or Article 86 of the Treaty.

50   In order to determine whether the first ground for rejecting the complaint is valid, the Court must accordingly consider whether, as stated in the decision, the conclusion of a commercial consensus between the Community and Japan will put an end to the agreement at issue before 1 January 1993, so that the question arises whether there is a sufficient Community interest in investigating practices which essentially relate to part events.

51   The Court notes that the statement in the decision that the agreement at issue will end before 1 January 1993 is based on the fact that the Community undertook, in the context of the commercial consensus reached with Japan, to abolish all national restrictions concerning the importation of Japanese cars, including the agreement at issue in this case, by 1 January 1993 at the latest.

52   In order to demonstrate that that statement was substantially correct, the Commission relies on two series of documents. The first precede the contested decision, while the others post-date it. With regard, in the first place, to the documents preceding the contested decision, the Commission, in answer to a written question by which the Court requested it to produce the material on which it based its statement that there was no reason to doubt that the alleged agreement would end by 1 January 1993, produced the text of a notification to the General Agreement for Tariffs and Trade (hereinafter 'GATT') made jointly by the Community and Japan and referred the Court to three documents, already lodged by the applicants, namely the two statements dated 31 July 1991 made by the Member of the Commission responsible for external relations and the Japanese Minister for International Trade and Industry respectively, concerning the results of conversations between the Community and Japan concerning cars, and an extract from the report of a House of Commons debate on 17 July 1991.

53   As regards, first, the statements made by the representatives of the Community and Japan on 31 July 1991, the Court notes that the first paragraph of the statement by the Member of the Commission, listing the measures which the Community had agreed to take in the context of the commercial consensus reached with Japan, contains nothing to indicate that that consensus in itself entails the termination of the agreement at issue, although it states that 'France, Italy, Spain and Portugal will ease the levels of quantitative restrictions (including restrictions on registration) imposed upon vehicles imported from Japan from now and totally abolish them by the end of 1992 at the latest.' To the same effect, the statement by the Japanese Minister, although it says in its first paragraph that 'the Japanese side welcomes the liberalization of motor vehicle imports from Japan in France, Italy, Spain and Portugal through elimination of all existing quantitative restrictions (including restrictions on registration) —', makes no reference to the abolition of possible restrictions on imports into the United Kingdom.

54   What is more, in its second paragraph the statement of the Japanese Minister envisages expressly, as the applicants point out, that a restriction on exports of Japanese cars to the four abovementioned Member States, and to the United Kingdom, would be provisionally maintained until 31 December 1999. The Minister stated: 'The Japanese side will monitor motor vehicle exports to the market of the Community as a whole and the markets of its specific member countries: i.e. France, Italy, Spain, Portugal and the United Kingdom. Such monitoring will be completely terminated at the end of 1999.' In the fourth paragraph of the ministerial statement it is stated that the volume of Japanese exports to the United Kingdom should reach 190.000 cars in 1999, a figure which was based on an estimated demand of 2.700 000 cars. In those circumstances, it was for the Commission to specify, in the contested decision, the extent to which the transitional regime, envisaged up to 31 December 1999 and involving, moreover, as the applicants point out, a restriction of exports to approximately 7% of the total volume of sales, would be based on anything other than the agreement which gave rise to the complaint. In the absence of any specific information on that point, it cannot be excluded that the restriction of Japanese exports to the United Kingdom, expressly permitted during the transitional period expiring on 31 December 1999, would be the result of the simple renewal and the maintenance in force of the agreement between the trade associations, as concluded before the consensus of 31 July 1991. It is therefore not impossible that the arrangements for implementing the transitional regime, applicable during the period from 1 January 1993 to 31 December 1999, are incompatible with Community competition law, particularly if it is borne in mind that the Member of the Commission expressly accepted, in his statement of the same date, that restrictions on imports which, as has just been shown, the Community-Japan consensus in itself does not bring to an immediate end are incompatible with the Community rules on competition.

55   As regards, secondly, the joint notification of the consensus made to GATT on 16 October 1991, as produced to the Court by the Commission, the Court notes that, although it envisages the abolition of 'national restrictions of any kind' on the importation of motor vehicles from Japan, it refers solely to the States in which those restrictions are the result of State measures and contains no reference to the abrogation of any agreements between economic agents or groupings of such agents. Moreover, although that document confirms the restriction on Japanese exports to, in particular, the United Kingdom during the transitional period from 1 January 1993 to 31 December 1999, it none the less, like the documents considered above, contains no information as to the arrangements for implementing that restriction.

56   As regards, finally, the Parliamentary debate to which the Commission refers, the Court considers, in the light of the statements analysed above, which were made by the high contracting parties themselves after the de-

bate in question and after the consensus had been reached, that an uncorroborated assertion made in the course of a debate before the Parliament of a Member State by a member of that Parliament cannot, taken by itself, be regarded as evidence of the precise content of a commercial consensus concluded by the Commission, on behalf of the Community, with a non-member country.

57 In the light of all the documentary evidence to which the Commission refers, the Court considers that, contrary to what is said in the contested decision, it has not been established that the commercial consensus between the Community and Japan would necessarily cause the alleged agreement, which is at the origin of these proceedings, to come to an end before 1 January 1993.

QUESTIONS

1 Has the Court blurred the constitutional separation of powers between courts and legislatures in its use of Article 5 to establish a Community system of remedies which must be adopted at national level?

2 In the light of the diversity among national legal systems, is it feasible to create a structure of Community remedies applicable at national level through the medium of judicial decisions?

3 The Commission is frequently described as the 'watchdog' of the Treaties. To what extent should its willingness to bark be subject to judicial review?

FURTHER READING

A. Barav and N. Green, 'Damages in the national courts for breach of Community law', *YEL*, **6**, 1986, p.55.

J. Bridge, 'Procedural Aspects of the Enforcement of EC Law through the Legal Systems of the Member States', *ELRev*, **9**, 1984, p.28.

G. de Burca, 'Giving Effect to European Community Directives', *MLR*, **55**, 1992, p.215.

P. Craig, 'Francovich, Remedies and the Scope of Damages Liability', *LQR*, **109**, 1993, p.595.

D. Curtin, 'The Decentralised Enforcement of Community Law Rights. Judicial Snakes and Ladders' in D. O'Keeffe and D. Curtin (eds), *Constitutional Adjudication in European Community and National Law*, 1992.

H.G. Fischer, 'Staatshaftung nach Gemeinschaftsrecht', *EuZW*, **2**, 1992, p.41.

N. Gravells, 'Effective Protection of Community Law Rights: Temporary Disapplication of an Act of Parliament', *Public Law*, 1991, p.180.

P. Oliver, 'Enforcing Community rights in English courts', *MLR*, **50**, 1987, p.881.

P. Oliver, 'Interim Measures: Some Recent Developments', *CMLRev*, **29**, 1992, p.7.

C. Plaza Martin, 'Furthering the Effectiveness of EC Directives and the Judicial Protection of Individual Rights Thereunder', *ICLQ*, **43**, 1994, p.26.

S. Prechal, 'Remedies after Marshall', *CMLRev*, **27**, 1990, p.451.

M. Ross, 'Beyond Francovich', *MLR*, **56**, 1993, p.55.

F. Schockweiler, 'La responsibilite de l'autorite nationale en cas de violation du droit communautaire', *RTDE*, **28/1**, 1992, p.27.

F. Snyder, 'The Effectiveness of European Community Law: Institutions, Processes, Tools and Techniques', *MLR*, **56**, 1993, p.19.

J. Steiner, 'From Direct Effects to Francovich', *ELRev*, **18**, 1993, p.3.

S. Weatherill, 'National Remedies and Equal Access to Public Procurement', *YEL*, **10**, 1990, p.243.

12 Human Rights and Economic Rights – The Nature of Rights in European Economic Law

A. THE RELATIONSHIP BETWEEN MARKET INTEGRATION AND MARKET REGULATION

The process of market integration is driven by the application of the substantive Community rules of free trade, such as Article 30, governing the free movement of goods, and Article 59, governing the free movement of services. These rules are enforceable not only through Commission supervision of the Member States but also through individual action before national courts based on the direct effect of the relevant provisions. The combination of the substantive law of free trade and the constitutional principles of direct effect and supremacy effectively converts EC law into a system of individual rights. Economic actors have rights to trade freely.

Many of the cases in this book exemplify this trend. They show how commercial parties may exploit the law to liberalize the market both to their own benefit and also, as a matter of economic theory, to the general benefit of the whole Community as passive consumers of market integration. Although such rights are predominantly exploited by large commercial interests, the Court has had occasion to depict the right to trade freely under primary Community law as a right which is also to be enjoyed by private citizens. So in Case C-362/88 *GB-INNO* v. *CCL*, which is examined in Chapter 6, the Court declared that 'Free movement of goods concerns not only traders but also individuals'. This means that consumers may cross borders and shop under the same conditions as the local population. And in Case 186/87 *Cowan* v. *Le Trésor Public* [1989] ECR 195 the Court found that a tourist had rights under primary Treaty law. Cowan, a British national 'mugged' in Paris, was held entitled under EC law to be treated no less favourably than a French national injured in similar circumstances.

It is possible to develop from the pattern of EC law a wider pattern of social rights. The accumulation of EC secondary legislation creates a harmonized system of law in many fields of activity. One aspect to harmonization of laws is the equalization of competitive conditions throughout the territory of the Community. This is the so-called 'level playing field.' However, this process of harmonization simultaneously involves the conferral under EC law of a range of rights throughout the Community. For example, EC social policy, developed largely through Directives, establishes rights for workers at the same time as harmonizing rules which affect employers. The *Francovich* ruling examined in Chapter 11 illustrates the Court's concern to achieve the effective protection of such individual rights by national courts and tribunals. Even within the Treaty itself, a right to equal pay between the sexes is guaranteed by Article 119, which as the Court had occasion to explain in Case 43/75 *Defrenne* v. *SABENA* [1976] ECR 455 has a 'dual aim', both to iron out competitive distortion caused by legal diversity and also to ensure social progress. Consumer policy has grown through the adoption of Directives which also involve an accretion of rights for individual consumers (Chapter 8).

Chapter 1 of this book introduced the notion that negative law is characteristic of the construction of a European market, whereas positive law contributes to the creation of regulatory structures that are associated with inchoate notions of European State-building. It should have become apparent in the course of this book that this dichotomy – between negative and positive; between Market and State – is valuable as a framework for initial inquiry, but simultaneously potentially too simplistic.

A persisting tension attaches to the identification of the constitutional basis for building regulatory frameworks at European level. The Treaty pattern of attributed powers, spread unevenly between different provisions, breeds obscurity. The more extensive the power that is potentially wielded at European level, the deeper the concern that there is no European 'State' able to exercise that power in an accountable fashion. For some, that justifies a thoroughly sceptical attitude to accretion in power above national level. The subsidiarity principle reflects some of these concerns. The constitutional sensitivity of the *Bundesverfassungsgericht*, explained in Chapter 1, also reflects this tendency to take a hard look at the scope of Community competence (and, therefore, as a corollary, at the scope of Member State competence). However, the same subject matter is capable of provoking a quite different response. The rise of the European market has disabled the Member States from exercising some of the functions normally associated with the regulatory State. As under the perspective above, this sharpens awareness of the inadequacy of the European 'State'. But that, from a competing perspective to that offered above, places an ever greater urgency on the need to devote attention to the shaping of quasi-State structures at European level. At least in the sectors where the European Market has blossomed, it is only at European level that effective and accountable supervision can be delivered.

There is an ambiguous relationship between market integration and market regulation – between the deepening liberalization of the European Market and the widening reach of the powers of the 'European State'. This tension acts as a meeting point for much of the material that is examined in this book.

Frequent reference has been made in this book to the notion of 'rights' under EC law. Whatever is meant by the 'State' in the European context, it is essential to identify with precision what contribution is made by 'rights' to the constitutional pattern of the EC.

B. SOURCES OF RIGHTS: HUMAN RIGHTS AND ECONOMIC RIGHTS

The scope for the elaboration of individual rights under EC law is a fertile field of inquiry. However, such rights do not exist in isolation. Account must be taken of other sources of individual rights in Europe. This book is built on a persistent underlying theme of Europeanization. A major aspect of this process is found in discussion of the openness of the EC system to other influences, particularly the European Convention on Human Rights, to which all the Member States of the EC and a number of other non-EC European States are party. If a quasi-federal 'European State' is coming into being, there is necessarily much more to its legal system than the EC's system alone. Economic spills into social. European Community law and the European Convention begin to overlap and accordingly to reshape the notion of rights in European law.

In many respects that is a desirable process. A state requires a constitution which covers the range of social interests in a comprehensive fashion. For all the efforts of the European Court to create out of the EC Treaty a constitution based on the rule of law, there is still an inevitable patchwork appearance to what emerges. The European Convention on Human Rights has a critically important role to play in the construction of a constitution for a 'European State'. Yet the interrelation of the Convention with the EC system is by no means fully realized. In fact there are problems here running in parallel. The 'European State' is evolving erratically; so too its Constitution.

References have been scattered throughout the book to areas where there is an overlap between the two systems, the EC and the European Convention. There is, for example, discussion in Chapter 5 of situations where the state may create monopolies or exclusive rights which will distort the competitive structure of the market and diminish the individual's freedom of action. Both the EC system and the system of the European Convention are engaged in such circumstances. Chapter 6 included discussion of the scope of commercial free speech in Europe, which is similarly a matter within the purview of both legal regimes.

It might be desirable to convene a conference and to determine that although it was understandable in 1957 that the economic and the social sphere could be thought open to being kept separate and that therefore the Convention and the E(E)C could be placed in separate compartments, that is no longer feasible. A grand constitutional conference might be capable of securing agreement on a structure for the harmonious development of economic and human rights law in Europe, including appropriate institutional supervision. But for many reasons that level of political planning is unlikely. Therefore a framework for co-existence must be developed on a largely ad hoc basis. In the European Community and more broadly within the European Union, the job of building that framework for co-existence falls on all the institutions, both political and judicial.

One can observe that from the Court's perspective there is a strong commitment to interpreting Community law in the light of the European Convention in order to avoid incompatibility. The important ruling in *ERT* v. *Dimotiki* appears in both Chapters 5 and 6 (pp.**191, 297** above). It will be recalled that in that ruling the Court commits itself to appraising national rules which fall within the scope of Community law in the light of general principles of Community law, which include those taken from the European Convention. It is furthermore clear that in the exercise of its judicial review function, the European Court tests Community acts themselves against general principles of Community law including those drawn from the European Convention. In fact the absorption into EC law of principles drawn from the European Convention represents a longstanding commitment in this direction made by the European Court. For over twenty years it has accepted the task of integrating fundamental rights into the structure of the Community legal order despite the absence of explicit commitment to respect for fundamental rights in the original Treaty of Rome itself. The following extract is from the judgment in Case 11/70 *Internationale Handelsgesellschaft mbH* v. *Einfuhr- und Vorratsstelle für Getreide und Futtermittel* [1970] ECR 1125.

The protection of fundamental rights in the Community legal system

3   Recourse to the legal rules or concepts of national law in order to judge the validity of measures adopted by the institutions of the Community would have an adverse effect on the uniformity and efficacy of Community law. The validity of such measures can only be judged in the light of Community law. In fact, the law stemming from the Treaty, an independent source of law, cannot because of its very nature be overridden by rules of national law, however framed, without being deprived of its character as Community law and without the legal basis of the Community itself being called in question. Therefore the validity of a Community measure or its effect within a Member State cannot be affected by allegations that it runs counter to either fundamental rights as formulated by the constitution of that State or the principles of a national constitutional structure.

4   However, an examination should be made as to whether or not any analogous guarantee inherent in Community law has been disregarded. In fact, respect for fundamental rights forms an integral part of the general principles of law protected by the Court of Justice. The protection of such rights, whilst inspired by the constitutional traditions common to the Member States, must be ensured within the framework of the structure and objec-

tives of the Community, It must therefore be ascertained, in the light of the doubts expressed by the Verwaltungsgericht, whether the system of deposits has infringed rights of a fundamental nature, respect for which must be ensured in the Community legal system.

The next extract comes from Case 4/73 *Nold* v. *Commission* [1974] ECR 491.

12 The applicant asserts finally that certain of its fundamental rights have been violated, in that the restrictions introduced by the new trading rules authorized by the Commission have the effect, by depriving it of direct supplies, of jeopardizing both the profitability of the undertaking and the free development of its business activity, to the point of endangering its very existence.

In this way, the Decision is said to violate, in respect of the applicant, a right akin to a proprietary right, as well as its right to the free pursuit of business activity, as protected by the Grundgesetz of the Federal Republic of Germany and by the Constitution of other Member States and various international treaties, including in particular the Convention for the Protection of Human Rights and Fundamental Freedoms of 4 November 1950 and the Protocol to that Convention of 20 March 1952.

13 As the Court has already stated, fundamental rights form an integral part of the general principles of law, the observance of which it ensures.

In safeguarding these rights, the Court is bound to draw inspiration from constitutional traditions common to the Member States, and it cannot therefore uphold measures which are incompatible with fundamental rights recognized and protected by the Constitutions of those States.

Similarly, international treaties for the protection of human rights on which the Member States have collaborated or of which they are signatories, can supply guidelines which should be followed within the framework of Community law.

Finally the judgment in Case 222/84 *Johnston* v. *Chief Constable of the Royal Ulster Constabulary* [1986] ECR 1663 includes the following:

[...]

17 It must be borne in mind first of all that Article 6 of the directive requires Member States to introduce into their internal legal systems such measures as are needed to enable all persons who consider themselves wronged by discrimination 'to pursue their claims by judicial process'. It follows from that provision that the Member States must take measures which are sufficiently effective to achieve the aim of the directive and that they must en-

sure that the rights thus conferred may be effectively relied upon before the national courts by the persons concerned.

18   The requirement of judicial control stipulated by that article reflects a general principle of law which underlies the constitutional traditions common to the Member States. That principle is also laid down in Articles 6 and 13 of the European Convention for the Protection of Human Rights and Fundamental Freedoms of 4 November 1950. As the European Parliament, Council and Commission recognized in their Joint Declaration of 5 April 1977 (Official Journal C 103, p. 1) and as the Court has recognized in its decisions, the principles on which that Convention is based must be taken into consideration in Community law.

The European Court is committed to integrating the principles of the Convention into its interpretation of the Treaty. Fundamental rights inspired by the Convention are part of the general principles of Community law. They bind the Community institutions. They bind the Member States where they act within the sphere of the Treaty, although the precise location of the outer reach of the sphere of the Treaty for these purposes remains an unresolved issue. Beyond the scope of the EC Treaty, the ECHR does not bind the States via EC law, although the Convention itself continues to be applicable.

This is fertile material for examination of the Europeanization of law. The construction of channels of communication between different sources of law in Europe permits mutual replenishment. Case 222/84 *Johnston* v. *Chief Constable of the Royal Ulster Constabulary* above involves implementation of a Directive. In referring to the Convention in its ruling, the European Court allows the Convention to infiltrate EC law which in turns travels on into the domestic legal order. Using these tools, there are clear opportunities for widening the path to legal convergence in Europe.

However, the general principles of EC law including the rules drawn from the Convention do not bind the Member States as the Convention as such and they are not applied by the institutions of the European Convention system. They are the Convention as mediated through the Community system.

The development of EC fundamental rights is in part attributable to the to and fro over the principles of supremacy. The risk that EC economic law would destroy national perceptions of fundamental rights led to some national systems being unreceptive to the doctrine of supremacy. In response it seems that the EC developed fundamental rights in part as an inducement to the Member States to accept the full implications of supremacy. The decision in *Internationale Handelsgesellschaft* in particular was part of the European Court's dialogue with the German courts. The extract above illuminates the European Court's unwillingness to permit *national* law of fundamental rights to undermine Community rules, but its acceptance that it may be appropriate to subject Community acts to fundamental rights drawn from the *Community* system. This strategy, if it is correctly analysed as a strategy, worked successfully. The European Court realized the need to fix protection of fundamental rights in EC law and gradually won the support of national constitutional courts for the hierarchical rules of supremacy. So the European Convention on Human Rights became indirectly a part of EC law.

The channels of Europeanization are not purely one-way and the European Court of Human Rights has on occasion been prepared to make reference to decisions of the European Court. In *Marckx* (Series A vol. 31, judgment of 13 June 1979) the Human Rights Court discussed the principle of legal certainty and the temporal effect of rulings with reference to *inter alia* Case 43/75 *Defrenne* v. *SABENA* [1976] ECR 455. This further enriches the process of legal cross-fertilization. However, in clear contrast to the European Court's approach to EC law in the light of the Convention, the European Court of Human Rights has in no sense committed itself to interpreting the Convention to conform to EC law.

C. THE DEVELOPING RELATIONSHIP BETWEEN HUMAN RIGHTS AND ECONOMIC RIGHTS

EC law interpreted by the European Court follows and complies with the Convention. Yet what happens in the event of a deliberate choice in the EC to take a different approach from that adopted in Human Rights law? This possibility might seem remote, but it cannot be excluded given the different policy objectives of the two systems. Social rights and economic rights are of distinct character. Decisions of the European Court are not subject to the jurisdiction of the European Court of Human Rights, nor indeed are acts of any of the institutions of the Community or the Union (although State acts which implement Community rules may be challenged as incompatible with the Convention). The EC is not party to the Convention, though all fifteen Member States are. The possibility of disharmony between EC law and the European Convention is feasible because of the distinct motivations of the two legal orders, which poses important questions about how such conflicts would be resolved. Such problems are *inevitable* as economic law spreads and they are *crucial* to the development of a real European law.

Perhaps the most instructive passages are the later parts of Chapter 6 from which it emerges that the European Convention lends more weight to freedom of expression where it has a non-commercial motivation, whereas the reverse emphasis is characteristic of the approach of the European Court. This is brought out by the fact pattern which underlies *SPUC* v. *Grogan*. In that case the European Court was able to avoid deep water by denying the commercial motivation of the Students Union, but that approach merely avoided the problems embedded within the case. It did not resolve the conundrums. Such issues seem to likely to recur in the future where they will set vital questions about whether the market yields to the (national) State or whether the market subverts national policy choices even in areas not traditionally regarded as economic. One might remember that Irish law was eventually found incompatible with the Human Rights Convention in *Open Door*. It is possible to speculate that this was far less controversial and objectionable than a ruling against Ireland by the European Court in *Grogan* would have been because of an instinctive feel that the 'right' institution was involved in making the decisions. This suggests a need to develop a more sophisticated basis for future examination of the social/economic divide than is found in the *Grogan* ruling itself.

Accordingly, it is plain that the two systems, EC and ECHR, overlap so much that there is a need for alignment, yet it is far from clear that the European Court's own commitment to conformity with the Convention will suffice. Reducing or removing the overlap could be achieved only by having the EC withdraw back to a narrow economic domain, which seems implausible. A form of coexistence needs to be developed. One objective might involve the creation of a hierarchy and an institutional mechanism for formalizing the subjection of the EC system to the European Convention on Human Rights. However, this would require some bold constitutional decision-making.

These are matters for the Community's political institutions. The political commitment to the principles of the European Convention is evidenced by the fact that all fifteen Member States are party to the European Convention. Yet the EC itself is not.

A number of political statements have been made about respect for fundamental rights in the EC. In 1977 a Joint Declaration was made by the European Parliament, the Council and the Commission on Fundamental Rights (OJ 1977 C103). This insists on 'the prime importance they attach to the protection of fundamental rights, as derived in particular from the constitutions of the member states and the [ECHR]' and promises respect for these rights 'in the exercise of their powers and in pursuance of the aims of the European Communities'. The European Court has relied on this Declaration to legitimize its own respect for fundamental rights in the EC legal order (extract from Case 222/84 *Johnston* above), although in fact the Court had already taken significant steps in this direction well before the 1977 Declaration (Cases 11/70 *Internationale Handelsgesellschaft* and 4/73 *Nold* above).

The Preamble to the Single European Act, which came into force in 1987, provides as follows: 'Determined to work together to promote democracy on the basis of the fundamental rights recognized in the constitutions and laws of the Member States, in the Convention for the Protection of Human Rights and Fundamental Freedoms and the European Social Charter.' The Treaty on European Union, which came into force in November 1993 provides in Article F(2) that: 'The Union shall respect fundamental rights, as guaranteed by the European Convention for the

Protection of Human Rights and Fundamental Freedom signed in Rome on 4 November 1950 and as they result from the constitutional traditions common to the Member States, as general principles of Community law.' This may prove to be a valuable declaration, but it seems limited by its place in the Union Treaty but not in the EC Treaty, which appears to mean that it is not within the formal jurisdiction of the European Court (Article L TEU). In any event Article G(2), as a statement of intent, is unaccompanied by formal institutional coupling of the Union to the European Convention.

The Commission has proposed that the Community should adhere to the Convention (e.g. Supplements 2/79 and 1/90, Bulletin of the European Communities). In January 1994 the Parliament, which has had a long standing concern with this area, adopted a resolution in favour of accession in response to a report in this vein prepared by its Legal Affairs and Citizens Rights Committee. Also early in 1994 the European Court was asked pursuant to Article 228(6) EC for its opinion on the compatibility with the EC Treaty of the accession of the Community to the European Convention.

The next extract provides commentary on this area. From the perspective of the theme of this book, it is notable that *inter alia* the author makes explicit linkage between the place of fundamental rights in the Community legal order and the process of State-building in Europe.

METHODS OF PROTECTION: TOWARDS A SECOND AND THIRD GENERATION OF PROTECTION*

Joseph H. H. Weiler

III. PROTECTION OF FUNDAMENTAL HUMAN RIGHTS AND THE ECHR

An immense literature has emerged dealing with this issue. It was spawned first by the principled allusion of the European Court of Justice to the Convention among the sources which it would use in its jurisprudence and then its actual use. Interest reached a peak in the wake of a Commission Memorandum in 1979 advocating the adhesion of the Community to the ECHR.

I *do not* propose to give a systematic account of this relationship. It is difficult to add much that is new to the extensive literature. Where necessary I have already made specific points elsewhere in this report. The relationship is tantalizing for the legal theorist grappling with two different and developing transnational orders. In practice the problems which are raised are more illusory than real.

There is of course a two way relationship between the two systems. Community law will have developed by the influence of the Convention. Equally, each time the Court of Justice applies – and interprets – a provision of the Convention, we have an element in the development of that regime.

Much has been written on the legal basis for the application of the Convention by the Court as a source for its jurisprudence. Indeed, the Commission and some of the Advocates General of the Court regard the Convention in its substantive provisions as binding on the Community organs; the joint declaration of the three political institutions did not go so far.[1] For some the theory of substitution (which explains Community competences in the context of the GATT) provides a basis.[2] It is difficult to accept this given the very late ratification by France and the differen-

---

*   First published in A. Cassese, A. Clapham and J.H.H. Weiler (eds), *Human Rights and the European Community*, Baden-Baden, 1991, pp.617–20; reprinted by permission of Nomos Verlagsgesellschaft, Baden-Baden.

[1]   OJ (1977) C 103/1.
[2]   See extensive discussion by Mendelson, 'The Impact of European Community Law and the Implementation of the European Convention of Human Rights', *YEL*, **3**, 1983, pp.156–60.

tiated regime of reservations and adhesions to Protocols practised by the Member States. Another basis could be the duty enshrined in Article 234 EEC that prior international duties and rights of the Member States should remain unaffected. A patently false theory is one which suggests that the Member States could not have given the Community competences to violate the Convention to which they were bound.[3]

The issue today is largely moot. The Court has indicated its intention to look to the Convention whenever an issue of human rights comes up before it. The legal basis is not critical or at least no more urgent than finding a legal basis to the entire exercise of introducing this new layer of judicial review. And although in the *Panasonic* case (Cases 136 & 137/79 [1980] ECR 2033) the Court dropped in its reference to the Convention the word 'guidelines' and assimilated it to the Constitutional traditions of the Member States, not much turns on this semanticism. In its search for criteria it was only natural that the Court would have turned to the one text on which all Member States had agreed.

The procedural issues are equally intriguing in theory. Strictly speaking the Community as such is not a member to the Convention. This would mean that an application to Strasbourg against an act of a Community organ as such (assuming exhaustion of local remedies within the *Community* legal order) must fail as the applicants in the *CFDT* case ([1979]2 CMLR 229) found out. Now that France has both ratified the Convention and accepted the right of individual petition, the view has been put forward that the Member States might be liable jointly, under the regime of the Convention, for violations by the Community. There is currently a case pending before the Strasbourg organs which implicates the Member States in just this way. If the Strasbourg organs find the Member States liable for implementation of a binding Community norm this would be unsatisfactory in that the real defendant, the Community, would not have been the respondent. If the Strasbourg organs are not willing to 'pierce the Community veil' this would also be unsatisfactory since it would mean that as a result of the creation of the Communities and the transfer of competences to it by the Member States, there is a procedural gap in the protection of the individual before the Strasbourg organs. Likewise, though of lesser import, is the fact that a Member State might in theory have to defend itself before the Commission or Court of Human Rights for actions incumbent upon it by virtue of Community membership.

---

[3] It is a well known principle of international law that a State cannot, except in manifest cases, plead constitutional incompatibility as a ground for non respect of its international obligations. It could be argued that violation of human rights would be contrary to the notion of *jus cogens* under international law and found jurisdiction in that manner.

Either way, a clean solution to this issue, raised clearly in the 1979 memorandum, could only be by accession of the Community to the ECHR. For some commentators, though no longer for the Commission itself, this is a compelling reason.

I do not subscribe to this view. I do not think that the very rare occasion of this occurrence is in itself justification for accession nor do I believe that this was the real reason for the Commission 1979 Memorandum.

In my view, behind the Commission initiative in 1979 was the international personality and status implications that would have accrued to the Community as a result of Accession. It would have enhanced the 'State' like features of the Community in a period in which European integration seemed to be stagnating. If I am right in this speculation this rationale would no longer apply. The Community, once again on an upswing, does not need that kind of boost. Indeed, more than the Community needs for its internal reasons to accede to the ECHR, the ECHR needs Community accession; for without accession there is the danger that the focal point of Human Rights jurisprudence would shift from Strasbourg to Luxembourg.

It is also fairly clear that from the substantive point of view it does not seem as if accession is a real necessity. As we saw in the analysis of the *Hauer* case the Court, if not with great meticulousness, uses the Convention as its starting point for evaluation of potential violations. It is unlikely that there would be many instances of breach of the Convention by the Community which would not be nipped by the Court.

But there is another reason which may still maintain the Commission proposal as a serious prospect. The main advantage which would accrue to the Community would be the symbolism inherent in subjecting even the European Court itself to a measure of scrutiny by an outside body.

We already noted that the European Court of Justice took a rather dismissive view to the utility in this case of the Convention. It is also true that it establishes rather convincingly that it would be difficult for any *national* constitutional tribunal to evaluate better the specific regulation in the Community context. This however does *not*, in my view, exclude the possibility or even desirability of further review by an even higher body. The European Court of Human Rights does after all review the constitutional adjudication of national constitutional courts which are very well suited to understand their own national context as much as the European Court is suited to understand the Community context.

One of the basic ideas of transnational (and federal) adjudication of human rights is its exercise by a tribunal which is at least once removed from the system in which the challenge is made. In principle this review of the adjudication of the European Court by a higher tribunal is feasible. In practice, with the lesson offered in *Hauer* it is doubtful if the European Court of Human Rights would find much to criticize in the approach of the European Court of Justice but the availability of an instance of appeal would have a symbolic value the significance of which should not be underestimated.

(End of excerpt)

QUESTIONS

1 What is the function of individual rights in Europe?
2 Where are they most effectively protected?

FURTHER READING

G. de Burca, 'Fundamental Human Rights and the Reach of EC Law', *Oxford Journal of Legal Studies*, **13**, 1993, p.283.

A. Clapham, 'A Human Rights Policy for the European Community', *Yearbook of European Law*, **10**, 1990, p.309.

J. Coppel and A. O'Neill, 'The European Court of Justice: taking rights seriously?', *Common Market Law Review*, **29**, 1992, p.227.

R.M. Dallen, 'An overview of European Community protection of human rights, with some special references to the U.K.', *Common Market Law Review*, **27**, 1990, p.761.

John Temple Lang, 'The Sphere in which Member States are obliged to comply with the general principles of law and Community fundamental rights principles', *Legal Issues of European Integration*, 1991/2, p.23.

K. Lenaerts, 'Fundamental Rights to be Included in a Community Catalogue', *European Law Review*, **16**, 1991, p.367.

H. Schermers, 'The European Communities bound by Fundamental Human Rights', *Common Market Law Review*, **27**, 1990, p.249.

P. Twomey in D. O'Keeffe and P. Twomey (eds), *Legal Issues of the Maastricht Treaty*, London: Chancery, 1994.

J.A. Usher, 'Principles derived from private law and the European Court of Justice', *European Review of Private Law*, **1**, 1993, p.109.

B. de Witte, 'Community Law and National Constitutional Values', *Legal Issues of European Integration*, 1991/2, p.1.